19e

COLLEGE
C K
KEYBOARDING

LESSONS 1-110

Keyboarding &
Word Processing

COMPLETE COURSE

Microsoft® Word 2013

+ **Susie H. VanHuss**, Ph.D., Distinguished Professor Emeritus, University of South Carolina

+ **Connie M. Forde**, Ph.D., Mississippi State University

+ **Donna L. Woo**, Cypress College, California

+ **Vicki Robertson**, Southwest Tennessee Community College

SOUTH-WESTERN
CENGAGE Learning®

Australia • Brazil • Japan • Korea • Mexico • Singapore • Spain • United Kingdom • United States

Keyboarding and Word Processing, Complete Course, Lessons 1–110, Nineteenth Edition

Susie H. VanHuss, Connie M. Forde, Donna L. Woo, Vicki Robertson

SVP Global Product Management, Research, School & Professional: Frank Menchaca

Vice President/Editor-in-Chief: Karen Schmohe

Sr. Developmental Editors: Dave Lafferty, Karen Caldwell

Consultant: Catherine Skintik

Sr. Market Development Manager: Mark Linton

Sr. Content Project Manager: Martha Conway

Marketing Coordinator: Elizabeth Murphy

Sr. Media Editor: Mike Jackson

Sr. Editorial Assistant: Debra Roark

Technical Reviewers: Gayle Statman, Amy Cole

Manufacturing Planner: Charlene Taylor

Production Service: PreMediaGlobal

Sr. Art Director: Michelle Kunkler

Cover and Internal Designer: Imbue Design

Cover and Special Page Images:
© Luis Francisco Cordero/Shutterstock;
© Jezper/Shutterstock.com;
© Joe Belanger/Shutterstock.com;
© Kostsov/Shutterstock.com;
© 3d Brained/Shutterstock.com

Rights Acquisition Director: Audrey Pettengill

Rights Acquisitions Specialist, Text and Image: Deanna Ettinger

Permissions Researcher, Image and Text: PreMediaGlobal

For product information and technology assistance, contact us at
Cengage Learning Customer & Sales Support, 1-800-354-9706

For permission to use material from this text or product,
submit all requests online at www.cengage.com/permissions
Further permissions questions can be emailed to
permissionrequest@cengage.com

Keyboarding Pro Deluxe Online Illustrations: © Cengage Learning

Key reach images: © 2011 Cengage Learning, Cengage Learning/Bill Smith Group/Sam Kolich

Keyboard images: © Cengage Learning

Microsoft Office screen captures and clip art: © Microsoft Corporation. Microsoft is a registered trademark of Microsoft Corporation in the U.S. and/or other countries.

The names of all products mentioned herein are used for identification purposes only and may be trademarks or registered trademarks of their respective owners. South-Western disclaims any affiliation, association, connection with, sponsorship, or endorsement by such owners.

ISBN-13: 978-1-133-58897-9
ISBN-10: 1-133-58897-2

South-Western
5191 Natorp Boulevard
Mason, OH 45040
USA

Cengage Learning is a leading provider of customized learning solutions with office locations around the globe, including Singapore, the United Kingdom, Australia, Mexico, Brazil, and Japan. Locate your local office at: **www.cengage.com/global**

Cengage Learning products are represented in Canada by Nelson Education, Ltd.

For your course and learning solutions, visit **www.cengage.com**

Purchase any of our products at your local college store or at our preferred online store **www.cengagebrain.com**

Printed in the United States of America
1 2 3 4 5 6 7 17 16 15 14 13

SOUTH-WESTERN
CENGAGE Learning

Contents

LEVEL 1

Developing Keyboarding Skill

Module 1: Alphabetic Keys

Module 2: Figure and Symbol Keys

LEVEL 2

Formatting and Word Processing Essentials

Module 3: Word 2013 Essentials

Module 4: Memos and Letters

Module 5: Tables

Module 6: Reports

Module 7: Graphics

Module 8: Palmetto Event Solutions, Inc.

Module 9: Web Apps

Commands by Module

See Appendix F: Command Summary, for a detailed list of commands, the path, and button for each command.

See Appendix F, Command Summary, for a detailed list of commands, the path, and button for each command.

Touch Keyboarding

Word 2013

Document Design

Communication Skills

Workplace Projects

Web Apps

Windows 8 Basics

New in Keyboarding in this Edition

Level 1 Developing Keyboarding Skill, Lessons 1–25

- Direct correlation with the web-based *Keyboarding Pro DELUXE Online (KPDO)* to build, apply, and assess skills.

- Six new keyboarding review lessons increase confidence and performance.

- Text is formatted using one space after colons and periods to conform to current business usage in all textbooks in the series.

- Many drill lines were revised and keying tips placed above them to emphasize techniques and basic skills.

- Modified and added timed writings triple-controlled at the easy level of difficulty in Module 1 and the low-average level of difficulty in Module 2 to build confidence and gradually increase skill.

- Many exercises are repositioned to align them in the same sequence as *KPDO*.

Stephen Coburn/Shutterstock.com

The Power of Keyboarding...
Starts Here!

New in this Edition

Advanced Word Processing

Level 3 Beyond the Essentials—Formatting Advanced Documents

- Basic commands taught in 1–55 are reviewed and integrated in each module in Levels 3 and 4.
- Students key model documents on the letterhead shown in the textbook and that is opened automatically by KPDO.
- Projects in the *Hess Office Park* setting are included in all modules in Levels 3 and 4.
- Communication skills with emphasis on composing documents are integrated in all modules and all projects.
- The name and setting of the project *Hess Pet Center* have been changed to *Hess Office Park* to provide a different type of work experience and different communication style.
- Model documents have been shortened to increase the number of formatting jobs and build document design skills.

Word Processing Essentials

Level 2 Formatting and Word Processing Essentials

- *Word 2013* commands necessary to use *Word* as a standalone application are introduced in Lesson 26.
- *KPDO* is introduced in Lesson 27.
- Two new MLA and APA lessons give greater emphasis to academic reports.
- Short workplace projects are added to Modules 3–7 to emphasize the relevance of what students are learning to workplace success.
- Module 8 *Palmetto Event Solutions, Inc.* is a workplace project that reviews all commands and document formats in Level 2 and uses the same company setting as previous projects.
- *Communicating Today* features in all modules of the series discuss trends and the impact of technology on communication.
- New Web Apps module provides realistic exposure to SkyDrive and cloud computing.

Level 4 Beyond the Essentials—Documents for Specialized Fields

- Levels 3 and 4 have been reorganized so that all of the documents involving specialized topics or fields are relevant for workplace success.
- *Word 2013* defaults are different than those in previous versions of *Word* and are applied throughout the text.
- The restructured employment module underscores the impact and use of resume tracking systems and social media sites.
- Assessments in Levels 2, 3, and 4 have been reorganized to provide instructors with flexibility in using projects for review or authentic assessment in addition to the tests provided on the IRCD.
- Each assessment in the textbook covers two modules to allow more time for project-based learning.
- All timed writings in Levels 2, 3, and 4 are controlled at the average difficulty level to provide a consistent level of difficult for grading purposes.

Ready, Set, Key!

The keys to success include carefully designed lessons and reliable, dependable, easy-to-use technology tools.

An abundance of crafted exercises and a variety of relevant software routines keep lessons fun and help build a strong foundation.

--Online and Better than Ever

Keyboarding Pro DELUXE Online (KPDO) is an easy-to-use web-based program designed to be used with *College Keyboarding 19e*.

- Textbook directions correlate with *KPDO*
- Relevant, engaging routines that work
- Abundance of Skill Building
- Meaningful, easy-to-use reports

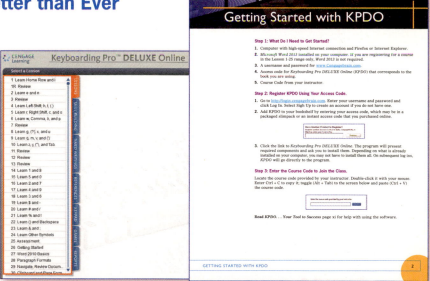

| LESSONS | SKILL BUILDING | TIMED WRITINGS | REFERENCES | KEYPAD | GAMES | REPORTS |

Accelerate Learning—Integrate Document Formatting and Word 2013

Follow the path **(Tab/Group/Command)** and illustrated step-by-step directions to make learning new commands easy.

Each new command is immediately applied within a short drill and then reinforced in **Apply It.** Data files provide immediate opportunities to practice the new command quickly.

Learn New Commands and Reinforce with Drills and Apply It

INSERT AND DELETE ROWS AND COLUMNS USING TABLE TOOLS

Rows and columns can also be inserted or deleted by using commands on the Table Tools Layout tab.

To insert rows or columns in a table:
Table Tools Layout/Rows & Columns

1. Position the insertion point where the new row or column is to be inserted, select the number of rows or columns are to be inserted.
2. In the Rows & Columns group, click the appropriate command.

To delete rows or columns in a table:
Table Tools Layout/Rows & Columns/Delete

1. Position the insertion point in the row or column that is to be deleted. If more than one row or column is to be deleted, select them first.
2. Display the Delete options and select the appropriate command.

Present concept, path, and illustrated step-by-step directions

Apply It provides reinforcement

Apply immediately. Use data file to shorten drill

DRILL 2 — INSERT ROWS AND COLUMNS

1. In the open document, insert the following rows so that the items are in correct alphabetical order.
 Toledo
 Tampa
 Lake Forest
2. Delete the row containing Hoang, Thomas.
3. Insert a column between columns B and C and key the following entries in the column.

Connors, Margaret	South	$87,560
Roberts, George	East	$97,850
Zales, Laura	West	$93,500
Office		
Wilshire		

Apply It — 40-d1

1. In the open document (39-d1), insert the following column between columns B and C.
 Division
 Commercial
 Commercial
 Military

 Insert Column/Row and Merge
2. Insert a blank row above row 1. Merge the cells in row 1. Key SAFETY AWARDS in 14-point font and apply bold.
3. Change the height of row 1 to 0.4". Use Align Center to center the text in rows 1 and 2.
4. Proofread and check, click Next Activity. (40-d1)

Ensure Success with Discover, Tips, and Quick Checks

✿ **Discover**

Enhanced ScreenTips—Position the mouse pointer over a command to display its name, a description of it, and the keyboard shortcut to apply (if available).

Justify (Ctrl+J)
Distribute your text evenly between the margins.

Justified text gives your document clean, crisp edges so it looks more polished.

Discover introduces new commands that are very simple to apply

★ **TIP**

When you key two hyphens with no spaces before or after, Word automatically converts them to an em dash.

Tip provides additional information

QUICK ✓

Compare your document to the illustration shown below.

Effective Decision Making

Quick Check shows a suggested solution

Always Relevant, Fresh, and New

The lessons are updated with an abundance of new documents and additional practice on *Microsoft Word 2013*.

Productivity tools are applied throughout: Styles, Table Styles, Themes, Quick Parts, cover pages, headers and footers, table of contents, and more.

Extra Practice Builds Confidence and Success

Skill Builders in the text, Skill Building Drills in *KPDO*, Textbook Keying, and Timed Writings provide extra practice to strengthen accuracy and techniques.

Communication Skills Integrated

Communication provides activities in the text and in *KPDO*

Communicating Today discusses trends and impact of technology on communication today

KPDO has related **Communications** activities

Document Design

Learn, Apply, and Reinforce Document Designs with Deliberate Learning Approach

Reinforce document design in authentic learning activity with unarranged copy and limited instructions

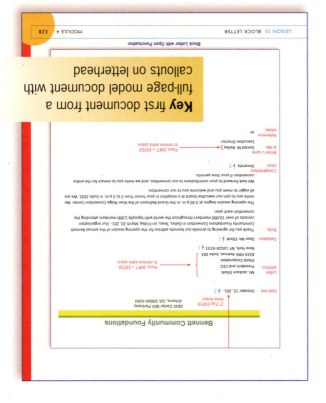

Key first document from a full-page model document with callouts on letterhead

Learn document designs with instructional narrative with illustrated examples

Short Projects at End of Modules

Workplace Success. . . Starts Here!

Realistic company setting

Realistic business documents

Standard Operating Procedures (SOPs)

Composition of realistic business document in every project

Reviews commands and document formats

Data files with logo, letterhead, memo form, and other standard documents

Timed writing in each project that can be used for assessment or "training"

Palmetto Event Solutions, Inc. is the company setting for all projects in Level 1

Hess Office Park is the company setting for all projects in Levels 2 and 3

Long Projects (Entire Module) at End of Each Level

Powerful Tools . . . Working for You

College Keyboarding 19e provides the tools students need to develop expertise in keyboarding, document formatting, and essential word processing skills using *Microsoft Word 2013*. When coupled with *Keyboarding Pro DELUXE Online (KPDO)*, students can work at home or school with ease.

TEXT/KPDO PAC BUNDLE ISBNS: 9781581759549 9781285576329 9781285576282 9781285576336

Keyboarding Pro DELUXE Online (KPDO)—Customizable

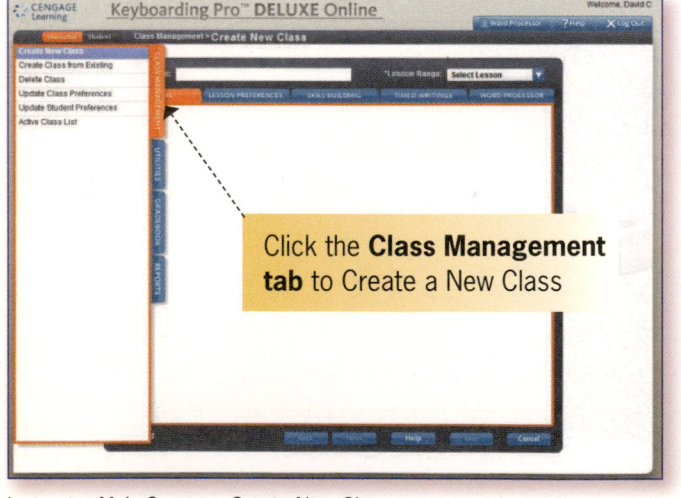

Click the **Class Management tab** to Create a New Class

Instructor Main Screen—Create New Class

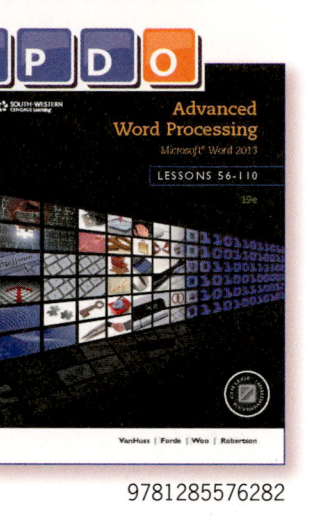

Set Class Preferences

Set Preferences for general, lessons, skill building, timed writings, and the word processor

◊ Customizable class preferences

◊ Gradebook to track progress on timed writings, daily assignments, tests, and more

◊ Quick toggle to student *Word* documents

◊ Reference tools for Communication Skills, Document Formats, and more

◊ Document checking of keystrokes with optional format checking

www.collegekeyboarding.com www.cengagebrain.com

KPDO . . . Your Tool for Success

Welcome to *Keyboarding Pro DELUXE Online (KPDO)*, a web-based, easy-to-use, tutorial software for learning the alphabetic and number keys, numeric keypad, and document processing with *Word 2013*. You are about to tap into the best digital solution available for keyboarding and word processing instruction; enjoy and learn. The essential information about *KPDO* is covered below.

WHAT DO I NEED TO GET STARTED?

- Computer with high-speed Internet connection
- Firefox or Internet Explorer browser
- *Microsoft Word 2013* installed on your computer. If you are registering for a course in the Lesson 1–25 range, *Word 2013* is not required.
- A username and password for www.cengagebrain.com.
- Access code for *KPDO* that corresponds to the book you are using. You can purchase this at cengagebrain.com or through your bookstore.
- Course Code from your instructor.

INSTALLING THE *KPDO* TOOLS

The first time you access *KPDO*, the program will check your computer for various components to make sure your computer is configured to run the software. Depending on what is already installed on your computer, you may not have to install all the components. On subsequent log ins, the student portal will display as soon as you click the link from your bookshelf.

For step-by-step help with installing the program, go to the *KPDO* student companion site.

Microsoft Visual Studio Tools for Office Version 4

Flash Player

KPDO Plug-in

KPDO Word Add In

INSTRUCTIONS FOR LOGGING INTO *KPDO*

See page 2, Getting Started with *KPDO*, steps 2 and 3.

WELCOME SCREEN

Read the Welcome screen to get a quick overview of the software. Return to the Welcome page by clicking the product name in gray. Use the **Skill Analysis** button at the bottom of the screen to test your current skill by taking the timed writing. If the Skill Analysis is required, you will not be able to go into the lessons until you take the timing. Key at a controlled pace that is comfortable and concentrate on keying accurately. Results display in the Skill Analysis report.

NAVIGATING KPDO

Left Navigation Bar

Lessons, Skill Building, Timed Writings, References, Keypad, Games, Reports—
These tabs at the left side will take you to lessons and various activities. Tabs and menus display for each option. Once you make a selection, the left navigation menu closes so that you can view your activity in a full screen.

When you select a lesson, *KPDO* opens to the first activity. The other activities associated with that lesson appear in a drop-down menu at the right. This menu collapses; simply click it when you want to navigate between activities.

Top Navigation Bar

The top navigation bar lists your name and includes access to important features.

Word Processor—A *Windows* word processor that enables you to create documents or key drills and timed writings.

Log Out—Saves your work and closes your *KPDO* session and returns you to the Cengage dashboard. Log Out of the software each time you exit the program.

Preferences—You may be able to customize some preferences, depending on whether your instructor has locked them.

Bottom Navigation Bar

Some screens have buttons at the bottom of the screen. The buttons are specific to the screen you are viewing. They will enable/disable based upon your current activity.

WORKING WITH *WORD* DOCUMENTS

Beginning in Lesson 27, you will launch *Word* directly in *KPDO* to complete all word processing documents. The Document Options box presents these options.

Begin new document—Creates a new document or **pass**.

> If you begin the document again, results will be replaced with the new pass. Some documents require opening a document from an earlier lesson. Many activities automatically open a prerecorded data file; files are identified with an icon in the textbook.

Open existing document—Opens the saved document for editing.

> Revising a document creates an **edit**. The Total Time on Document reported represents the total time of all edits of a single pass.

Print document without error report—Opens the *Word* document for printing. Errors and the header are not displayed.

Print document with error report—Displays the document in checked format.

Creating a *Word* Document in *KPDO*

1. From the Document Options dialog box, select Begin new document and select OK.
2. *Word* opens with the *KPDO* Student tab displayed; four commands are available.

 Save and Close—Saves the document and returns to the Lesson menu.

 Check Document—Checks your completed document, reports errors, and displays results. Documents must be 90% complete before the document can be checked. If it is not, you will receive a message to save the document or continue.

Document Information—Displays the activity name and page number.

Help—Provides access to global help.

3. The Insertion point is positioned in the document and ready for you to begin. To access any *Word* command, select the tab you need and the ribbon displays.
4. After creating and proofreading the document, select Check Document from the *KPDO* Student tab.

DATA FILES

Many *Word* applications utilize a data file or prerecorded file. KPDO opens this file automatically when you access the activity. Occasionally, you will be directed to **insert** a data file. In order to insert the file, you must download the data file from the student companion website or at www.collegekeyboarding.com. The files are zipped; simply download to a location on your computer and unzip the file.

REPORTS

The Report tab shown at the left displays a variety of reports for reviewing your lesson results, skill building lessons and activities, and timed writings. Many of the reports hyperlink, giving greater detail; go ahead and dig deeper into the results.

KEYPAD

The Keypad lessons and timed writings will help you build a strong foundation in 10-key skills. Extra Keypad Practice drills are in Appendix A of your textbook.

REFERENCES

The References tab includes tutorials to review Document formats, Communication Skills, videos to reinforce posture, and more.

TIMED WRITINGS

Timed Writings are keyed from the textbook. They appear in some lessons, and they are available from the Timed Writing tab. Results are reported on the Last 40 Timed Writings report. If the results meet the accuracy requirement set by your instructor, they appear on the Best Timed Writing Report. Error Diagnostics tracks the errors by row, finger, and type of reach on each timing. To improve accuracy on the type of reach you are making most frequently, see Drill Practice on the Skill Building tab. For best results when keying timed writings, focus on the words you are keying, keep calm, and concentrate.

Welcome to KPDO

- Summary Lessons 1-25
- Numeric Keypad
- Keypad Timed Writings
- Skill Analysis
- Skill Building - Accuracy
- Skill Building - Speed
- Technique Builder
- Drill Practice
- Best Timed Writings
- Last 40 Timed Writings
- Cumulative Error Diagnostics
- Summary Lessons 26-110
- WORD 2013 Documents
- Production Tests
- Lesson Report - Lessons 1-55
- Lesson Report - Accuracy
- Lesson Report - Speed
- Lesson Report - Numeric Keyp...
- Gradebook

▲ Performance Graphs

Timed Writing Settings

Select your Timed Writings in the left Navigation, then enter your settings below. Click the close button when you have completed entering your settings.

Timing Length: 1 Minute, 2 Minutes, 3 Minutes, 5 Minutes

Source: Entire Writing, Paragraph 1, Paragraph 2, Paragraph 3

Diagnostic: On, Off

General: Backspace allowed, Beep every 15 seconds, Show timer, Flash every 15 seconds

Close

Developing Keyboarding Skill

Learning Outcomes

Keyboarding

+ Key the alphabetic and numeric keys by touch.

+ Develop good keyboarding techniques.

+ Key fluently—at least 25 words per minute.

+ Develop reasonable accuracy.

Communication Skills

+ Develop proofreading skills.

+ Apply proofreaders' marks and revise text.

Mr. Patrick Hess asked you to compose a memo to **All Hess Office Park Tenants** from him. Use **Short-Term Rental Facilities** as the Subject. Use the rough notes shown below. Add other information that you think would be appropriate. Preview and edit the document carefully. Save it as *110-d3* and upload it to your SkyDrive Module 20 Solutions folder. (*110-d3*)

- Indicate that the completion of the two new buildings and the renovation of the existing short-term rental conference and office facilities have more than doubled short-term rental facilities now available.

- Thank the Short-Term Tenant Advisory Committee for working with him to survey and determine the needs of regular and occasional users. Point out that current Hess Office Park tenants represented approximately two-thirds of the past usage of these facilities.

- Tell them that next week they will receive an invitation to tour the facilities and a link to the new *Profile of Services* and detailed *Price List for Short-Term Rental Facilities*, which is currently being finalized.

Learn More

www.cengagebrain.com

Stockyimages/Shutterstock.com

! WORKPLACE SUCCESS

Employee Empowerment

Employee empowerment refers to allowing employees to participate actively in decision making relative to their jobs. Employees cannot truly be empowered unless they have the knowledge, skills, and ability to make good decisions that affect their jobs. Empowerment requires training and experience as well as a desire on the part of the individual employee to make contributions and decisions relative to the job being performed.

Step 1: What Do I Need to Get Started?

1. Computer with high-speed Internet connection and Firefox or Internet Explorer.
2. *Microsoft Word 2013* installed on your computer. If you are registering for a course in the Lesson 1-25 range only, *Word 2013* is not required.
3. A username and password for www.Cengagebrain.com.
4. Access code for *Keyboarding Pro DELUXE Online (KPDO)* that corresponds to the book you are using.
5. Course Code from your instructor.

Step 2: Register KPDO Using Your Access Code.

1. Go to http://login.cengagebrain.com. Enter your username and password and click Log In. Select Sign Up to create an account if you do not have one.
2. Add *KPDO* to your bookshelf by entering your access code, which may be in a packaged slimpack or an instant access code that you purchased online.

3. Click the link to *Keyboarding Pro DELUXE Online*. The program will present required components and ask you to install them. Depending on what is already installed on your computer, you may not have to install them all. On subsequent log ins, *KPDO* will go directly to the program.

Step 3: Enter the Course Code to Join the Class.

Locate the course code provided by your instructor. Double-click it with your mouse. Enter Ctrl + C to copy it; toggle (Alt + Tab) to the screen below and paste (Ctrl + V) the course code.

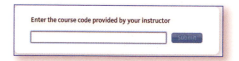

Read *KPDO. . . Your Tool to Success* page xi for help with using the software.

Profile of Services

Conference Rooms and Offices

Hess Office Park has more than doubled its short-term rental conference rooms and office suites by building new upscale facilities and renovating all of its previously existing short-term rental conference rooms and offices. All of these facilities now feature state-of-the-art technology. These changes were made based on a survey of both regular and occasional users of short-term facilities. Many of the regular users are companies of all sizes that have offices in Hess Office Park, but have short-term needs for additional facilities, such as a large boardroom, conference room, or training room. As soon as they schedule board meetings or executive staff meetings for the year, they reserve the facilities needed for each meeting during the year. A number of nonprofits also schedule all of their board meetings in our rental facilities. Some companies rent office suites for special projects, visiting executives, or investors.

All conference rooms and office suites offered on a rental basis are furnished and include all utilities and janitorial service. The upscale furnishings and services provided depend on the size, type of the facility rented, and the specific needs of the client beyond the basic package that is part of the rental fee.

Short-Term Rental Facilities

Currently, Hess Office Park has 16 short-term rental conference facilities and 24 office suites. These facilities vary in style and size to accommodate special needs of clients. The first table provides size and style information about conference facilities.

Short-Term Rental Conference Facilities at Hess Office Park			
Type of Room	Number	Capacity	Layout
Boardrooms	4	24	Fixed board style
Small conference rooms	6	12	Fixed board style
Large conference rooms	4	50	Flexible
Training rooms	2	30	Fixed classroom style

The second table provides information about the number and layout of office suites that are available for short-term rental.

Short-Term Rental Office Suites at Hess Office Park		
Office Type	Number	Number of Office Suites and Layout
Small	12	Reception, 1 office, work room, restroom
Mid-size	6	Reception, 3 offices, work room, restroom, and conference room
Large	6	Reception, 5 offices, work room, 2 restrooms, and conference room

Square footage of the conference facilities and the offices vary depending upon the building in which they are located. The new buildings have larger facilities than the original building.

Conference Rooms

Conference rooms can be rented by the day or by the week. Small rooms include a conference table, comfortable chairs with coasters, state-of-the-art projection technology including Internet access, wastebasket, a telephone, and a cabinet with countertop for food and beverage service. Larger conference rooms have flexible furnishings that can be configured in a conference table or a variety of meeting layouts. The boardrooms have elegant furnishings and accessories, including state-of-the-art technology for meetings and video conferencing. In the boardrooms located in the two new buildings, the food and beverage service area and restroom are in separate adjoining rooms.

Food and beverage service packages are available. Meeting support services available include registration, preparation and duplication of all types of meeting materials, and general secretarial services. Large restrooms are easily accessible from all conference rooms.

Office Suites

Furnished office suites can be rented by the week or by the month. Small office suites include a small reception area, a standard office, and a combined work and storage area. Larger office suites have either three or five offices plus a conference room in addition to the basic reception and work/storage area. The reception area includes a small desk and chair, four side chairs and two side tables. The work/storage area has base cabinets with counter tops and overhead storage cabinets. A work table is also provided.

Office furnishings include executive desks and chairs, credenzas, and side chairs. Desktop accessories, telephones, Internet service, and wastebaskets are also provided. Receptionist and secretarial services are available. Fee-based cards for printing, copying, and duplicating materials are also available at a reasonable cost.

Two buildings offer grill and cafeteria service for breakfast and lunch. Vending machines and break rooms are available in all office buildings. Meals are available from any of the three restaurants in the Hess Office Park Village.

110-d2

continued

Directions for Invitation

1. Format the invitation on Hess Office Park letterhead.
2. Tap ENTER twice and key the invitation shown below. Center each line; use 2.5 line spacing.
3. Apply 16-point Lucida Calligraphy font and bold to the first line.
4. Apply 14-point Lucida Calligraphy font to the remaining lines.
5. Preview and proofread carefully. (*110-d2*)

New Facilities Tour and Reception
You are cordially invited to a tour of the
Hess Office Park New Conference Facilities and
Short-Term Rental Offices on
Wednesday, May 15, 201-, at 5:15 p.m.
Tour Begins in our Headquarters Building in the
Newly Renovated Conference Center
Enjoy Refreshments at Each Facility

 Warmup

1. Open *KPDO*.
2. Click the Word Processor button in the upper-right corner.
3. Key the paragraph using wordwrap (do not tap ENTER at the end of lines). Repeat if desired.
4. Click the Close button in the upper-right corner to close the Word Processor; do not save it.

Good keyboarding skills are essential for almost all careers today. The time spent learning to key quickly and accurately is time well spent. Use good posture and good techniques to get you started on the right track. Then work diligently to achieve your speed and accuracy goals. Good keyboarding skills will save you time in preparing assignments for all of your classes. Also your work will impress your instructors.

LA ALL LETTERS

Timed Writing

1. Click the Timed Writings tab.
2. Choose Pretest.

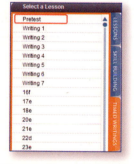

3. Choose 3' as the length; click Close.
4. Tap TAB to begin. Key from the textbook. Use wordwrap.
5. Repeat the timing for 3'.
6. Your results will be displayed in the Timed Writing Report.

Learning to key is just the first step toward developing a very meaningful career skill. The next step is to build both speed and accuracy. With basic keyboarding skills, you will be able to present information in an attractive format that is quite easy to read. You will also be able to develop your communication skills at the same time.

The next big step is to learn word processing. The software most often used in business organizations is Word, which is much more sophisticated than the basic word processor you used for your warmup. With Word you will be able to create attractive letters, memos, reports, and many other types of documents used in business.

One of the exciting things about working diligently to develop a skill is that you have the opportunity to set very specific goals and challenge yourself to meet them. Nothing is more motivating than being able to accomplish the goals that we set for ourselves. The incremental goals that you meet each day will result in major progress by the end of the course.

5. Insert a 4-column, 5-row table for the second table. Use the same format as you did for the previous table except for the row widths. For columns A and B, use 1" and for column C, use 4.5".

6. Note this table is positioned at the left margin.

Short-Term Rental Office Suites at Hess Office Park		
Office Type	Number	Number of Offices and Layout
Small	12	Reception, 1 office, work room, and restroom
Mid-size	6	Reception, 3 offices, work room, restroom, and conference room
Large	6	Reception, 5 offices, work room, 2 restrooms, and conference room

Square footage of the conference facilities and the offices vary depending upon the building in which they are located. The new buildings have larger facilities than the original building.

7. In the paragraph under the heading *Conference Rooms,* make the following edits:

 a. Replace *overhead projector and screen* with **state-of-the-art projection technology including Internet access**.

 b. At the end of the second-to-last sentence, add: **and video conferencing**. Then, add this as the last sentence: **In the boardrooms located in the two new buildings, the food and beverage service area and restroom are in separate adjoining rooms.**

8. Add this sentence at the end of the document: **Meals are available from any of the three restaurants in the Hess Office Park Village.**

9. Add a Facet Odd Page header; suppress the number on the first page.

10. Preview and proofread. Compare your solution to the Quick Check on the next page.

11. Close the file; rename it **110-d1** and copy it to your Module 20 solutions folder.

12. Copy the file (*110-d1*) to the Public folder on your SkyDrive.

13. In the Public folder, rename the file **Profile of Services.** (*110-d1*)

110-d2

Invitation

 hess letterhead

Mr. Hess has asked you to format an invitation to all employees of Hess Office Park. In the next job, you will send a memo to all employees with information about the invitation you will key in this job. Once Mr. Hess approves the final draft of the invitation, it will be uploaded to the SkyDrive and shared with the employees of Hess Office Park. The directions for formatting the invitation are shown on the next page after the Quick Check.

(continued)

Alphabetic Keys

LEARNING OUTCOMES

- Key the alphabetic keys by touch.
- Key using proper techniques.
- Key at a rate of 14 *gwam* or more.

| Lessons 1–10 | *Alphabetic and Basic Punctuation Keys* |
| Lessons 11–13 | *Review* |

Lesson 1 Home Row, Space Bar, Enter, I

Standard Plan *For Using KPDO*

1. From the Lessons tab, select the lesson (Lesson 1).
2. Follow the directions on screen. Repeat the exercise for reinforcement or continue.
3. To end a lesson, view the Lesson Report.
4. Click the Log Out button in the upper-right corner.

5. Use these directions for all lessons.

for the year, they reserve the facilities needed for each meeting during the year. A number of nonprofits also schedule all of their board meetings in our rental facilities. Some Hess Office Park companies rent office suites for special projects, visiting executives, or investors.

3. Then edit the next paragraph (first paragraph of the data file) as follows:
 a. In the second sentence, change *The furnishings* to: **The upscale furnishings**....
 b. Delete the last sentence of the paragraph.

4. Key the new material shown below after the paragraph you just edited and before the heading *Conference Rooms*. Format the first table as follows:
 a. Insert a 4-column, 6-row table. Size columns widths: A 1.8, B and C 1, and D 1.5. Increase top row height to 0.5" and all other rows to 0.4".
 b. Merge the cells in the top row and apply List Table 3 – Accent 1. Deselect First Column in the Table Style Options.
 c. Use 14-point font and apply Align Center to row 1. Apply 12-point bold font and apply Align Center to row 2.
 d. For remaining rows, apply Left Align to columns A and D and Center Align to columns B and C.
 e. Center the table.

Short-Term Rental Facilities

Currently, Hess Office Park has 16 short-term rental conference facilities and 24 office suites. These facilities vary in style and size to accommodate special needs of clients. The first table provides size and style information about conference facilities.

Short-Term Rental Conference Facilities at Hess Office Park			
Type of Room	Number	Capacity	Layout
Boardrooms	4	24	Fixed board style
Small conference rooms	6	12	Fixed board style
Large conference rooms	4	50	Flexible
Training rooms	2	30	Fixed classroom style

The second table provides information about the number and layout of office suites that are available for short-term rental.

(continued)

1. Find the new key on the illustrated keyboard. Then find it on your keyboard.
2. Watch your finger make the reach to the new key a few times. Keep other fingers curved in home position. For an upward reach, straighten the finger slightly; for a down reach, curve the finger a bit more.
3. Use these directions for learning all new keyreaches.

New Keys

1a Learn Home Row

Left Fingers **Right Fingers**

HOME-ROW POSITION

1. Drop your hands to your side. Allow your fingers to curve naturally. Maintain this curve as you key.
2. Lightly place your left fingers over the **a s d f** and the right fingers over the **j k l ;**. You will feel a raised element on the **f** and **j** keys, which will help you keep your fingers on the home-row position. You are now in home-row position.

Note the curve of your fingers when your arms are hanging loosely at your side. Maintain this same curve when you place your hands on the home row.

Lesson 110 Hess Office Park

Learning Outcomes
- Prepare, share, and edit documents on SkyDrive.
- Work independently with few specific instructions.

Project Setting

HESS OFFICE PARK

In this project, you continue to work with the management team of the Hess Office Park. Your work in this project will focus on using SkyDrive. SkyDrive was selected because it gives you the ability to work remotely with two types of tenants—small entrepreneurial businesses and short-term tenants who rent the offices and/or conference rooms on a daily, weekly, or monthly rental plan. The renovation of the initial conference rooms and rental offices has been completed, new offices and conference rooms have been brought online, and state-of-the-art technology is now available.

110-d1

Profile of Services

 services

Your first task is to update the profile of services that Hess offers to tenants on the short-term rental plan. The initial profile of services (contained in the *services* data file) was developed when the rental plan was initiated several years ago. You will update the Profile of Services using the *Word Web App* on SkyDrive. Then it will be shared with the Short-Term Tenant Advisory Committee for input and further revision if necessary.

1. Upload the *services* data file to your SkyDrive *Module 20 Web Apps* folder and open it. Note that the document format is very simple, but you will have to create and format two tables. You can insert a table and use Table Layout tools in *Word Web App*, but Table Design tools are not available. Therefore, you should select Edit in Word to edit the document.

2. You will add new material and edit some of the text in the Profile of Services document. Key Paragraph 1 shown below between the subtitle and the first paragraph in the data file.

> Hess Office Park has more than doubled its short-term rental conference rooms and office suites by building new upscale facilities and renovating all of its previously existing short-term rental conference rooms and office suites. All of these facilities now feature state-of-the-art technology. These changes were made based on a survey of both regular and occasional users of short-term facilities. Many of the regular users are companies of all sizes that have offices in Hess Office Park, but have short-term needs for additional facilities, such as a large boardroom, conference room, or training room. As soon as they schedule board meetings or executive staff meetings

(continued)

1b Learn Space Bar and ENTER

SPACE BAR AND ENTER

Tap the Space Bar, located at the bottom of the keyboard, with a down-and-in motion of the right thumb to space between words.

Enter Reach with the fourth (little) finger of the right hand to ENTER. Tap it to return the insertion point to the left margin. This action creates a **hard return**. Use a hard return at the end of all drill lines. Quickly return to home position (over ;).

```
1  j jj f ff k kk d dd l ll s ss ; ;; a aa jkl; fdsa
2  a aa ; ;; s ss l ll d dd k kk f ff j jj fdsa jkl;
```

1c Practice Home Row

```
 3  ff   jj   ff   jj   fj   fj   fj   dd   kk   dd   kk   dk   dk   dk
 4  ss   ll   ss   ll   sl   sl   sl   aa   ;;   aa   ;;   a;   a;   a;
 5  fj   fj   dk   dk   sl   sl   a;   fjdk   sla;   fjkd   ls;a
 6  fff   jjj   fjf   fff   jjj   fjf   fjf   jfj   jfj   fjf
 7  ddd   kkk   dkd   ddd   kkk   dkd   dkd   kdk   kdk   dkd
 8  sss   lll   sls   sss   lll   sls   sls   lsl   lsl   sls
 9  aaa   ;;;   a;a   aaa   ;;;   a;a   a;a   ;a;   ;a;   a;a
10  f   j   d   k   s   l   a   ;   ;   a   l   s   k   d   j   f
11  ff jj dd kk ss ll aa ;; jj ff kk dd ll ss aa ;;
12  fff   jjj   ddd   kkk   sss   lll   aaa   jjj   ;;;   fjdk   sla;
```

Keep your eyes on the textbook as you key each line.

1d Textbook Keying

1. Key each line once. Tap ENTER at the end of each line.
2. Click Stop to end the exercise.

```
13  a  a;  al  ak  aj  s  s;  sl  sk  sj  d  d;  dl  dk  dj
14  j  ja  js  jd  jf  k  ka  ks  kd  kf  l  la  ls  ld  lf
15  a;  sl  a;sl  dkfj  a;sl  dkfj  a;sl  dkfj  asdf  jk
16  a;  sl  a;sl  dk  fj  dkfj  a;sl  dkfj  fjdk  a;a
17  f  ff  j  jj  d  dd  k  kk  s  ss  l  ll  a  aa  ;  ;;  fj
18  afj;  a  s  d  f  j  k  l  ;  asdf  jkl;  fdsa  jkl;
```

7. Insert Footnote 2 as noted in blue in parentheses. Then delete the directions. Footnote 2:

 The fleet currently consists of 192 stretch limos and 450 executive cars.

8. On the third page after the Ownership paragraph, insert a basic pie SmartArt graphic (Cycle) and add two shapes after the last one. Key:

 a. **Founders 28.68%** in the exploded slice; then moving to the right:

 b. **Business Community 24.25%**

 c. **Senior Officers 16.75%**

 d. **Outside Directors 15.67%**

 e. **Employees 14.65%**.

9. Change colors to Accent 1 Gradient Range – Accent 1. (See Quick Check below.)

10. Rename the file **109-d2** and save to Module 20 Solutions. (*109-d2*)

7. Insert Footnote 1 where noted in blue in parentheses. Then delete the directions in blue. Footnote 1:

 The vehicle utilization rate in large cities is 32 percent higher than in mid-size cities.

8. Add a Grid Header to the document with **Business Plan** as the title and pick the current date. Do not show on the first page.

9. Save *109-d2* to your Module 20 Solutions. (*109-d2*)

QUICK ✔

1e i

19 i ik ik ik is is id id if if ill i ail did kid lid
20 i ik aid ail did kid lid lids kids ill aid did ilk
21 id aid aids laid said ids lid skids kiss disk dial

> *Use good posture; back and body erect; feet flat on the floor.*

1f Improve Keystroking

22 as as ask ask ad ad lad lad all all fall fall asks
23 as asks did disk ail fail sail ails jail sill silk
24 ask dad; dads said; is disk; kiss a lad; salad lid
25 fill a sail; aid a lad; is silk; if a dial; a jail
26 is a disk; dads said; did fall ill; if a lass did;

1g Build Skill

i

27 id aid ail fail sail jail ails slid dill sill fill
28 aid lads; if a kid is; a salad lid; kiss a sad dad
29 as ad all ask jak lad fad said ill kill fall disks
30 is all sad lass a lid; is silk; silk disk; dad is;

1h End the Lesson
1. View Lesson Report.
2. Log out of the software.

! WORKPLACE SUCCESS

Keyboarding: The Survival Skill

Keyboarding is a valuable and necessary skill for everyone in this technological world. It is an expected tool for effective communication throughout one's life.

Students who resort to "hunting and pecking" to key their school assignments are constantly searching for the correct letter on the keyboard. Frustration abounds for students who wish to key their research reports into the computer, but do not have the touch keyboarding skills required to accomplish the task quickly and proficiently. Students who can key by touch are much more relaxed because they can keep their eyes on the screen and concentrate on text editing and composing.

5. Click in the paragraph below the *Electrical Work* heading and edit it so that it reads as follows:

 The electrical work **requires us to add** appropriate… appliances, **move** light… places, **remove** current… lighting, **and replace** the….

6. Click Save to unlock the paragraph.

7. Delete comments in the document.

8. Rename the file **109-d1** and copy to Module 20 Solutions. (*109-d1*)

6. Click at the end of the ¶ below the *Demolition* heading and key the last sentence from your comment. Click Save to unlock the paragraph.

7. Click in the first paragraph and change the word *presents* to **confirms**. Click Save and click in one of the later paragraphs.

8. Click Save to see the edits made by Co-author 1 in the Electrical Work paragraph and review the changes.

9. Save a copy of the renamed file *109-d1* to your Module 20 Solutions. (*109-d1*)

109-d2

Business Plan

 business plan

The student who was Co-author 1 of the first document should be Co-author 2 for this document.

The student who was Co-author 2 should be Co-author 1 for this document.

Instructions for Co-author 1

1. Upload the *business plan* data file to your SkyDrive and share it with Co-author 2.

2. Open the file and scroll through the document. Note that the format is more complex than the previous document.

3. Click Edit Document and select Edit in Word.

4. Edit the second line of the first paragraph as follows:

 …has **operated as a niche** player…. and add, **Illinois** after Chicago.

5. In the first line of the second paragraph, edit as follows:

 Three **distinct** segments….

6. Add Square, Orange, Accent 1 square bullets to the three industry segments. Edit the second bulleted item as follows:

 …licenses in **virtually** every state.

Instructions for Co-author 2

1. Access the shared file on SkyDrive.

2. Open the file and scroll through the document. Note that the format is more complex than the previous document.

3. Click Edit Document and select Edit in Word.

4. Tap ENTER three times and apply the heading styles noted in blue throughout the report. After you apply each of the heading styles, delete the blue directions in parentheses.

5. Edit the second paragraph below the *Industry* heading as follows:

 …Pommery cannot **and should not try to** compete with **the major** national companies….

6. In the last sentence under the *Services* heading, edit as follows:

 Services for business and client needs….

(*continued*)

TIP

Remember to click Save after editing each paragraph to unlock the paragraph for others to edit it. Also click Save to share the edits made by others.

Lesson 1R Review

Fingers curved and upright

Left Fingers Right Fingers

```
1  ff dd ss aa ff dd ss aa jj kk ll ;; fj dk sl a; a;
2  fj dk sla; fjdk sla; a;sl dkfj fjdk sla; fjdk sla;
3  aa ss dd ff jj kk ll ;; aa ss dd ff jj kk ll ;; a;
4  if a; as is; kids did; ask a sad lad; if a lass is
```

Skill Building

1Rb Textbook Keying

1. Key each line once.
2. Click Stop to end the exercise.

> *Move fingers without moving your hands; eyes on textbook.*

```
5  f  j  fjf  jj  fj  fj  jf  dd  kk  dd  kk  dk  dk  dk
6  s  ;  s;s  ;;  s;  s;  s;  aa  ;;  aa  ;;  a;  a;  a;
7  fj  dk  sl  a;  fjdk  sla;  jfkd  lsa;  ;a  ;a  ;s
8  f  j  fjf  d  k  dkd  s  l  sls  a  ;  fj  dk  sl  a;a
9  a;  al  aka  j  s  s;  sl  sk  sj  d  d;  dl  dk  djd
10  ja  js  jd  jf  k  ka  ks  kd  kf  l  la  ls  ld  lfl
```

1Rc Improve Keystroking

```
11  f fa fad s sa sad f fa fall fall l la lad s sa sad
12  a as ask a ad add j ja jak f fa fall; ask; add jak
13  ik ki ki ik is if id il ij ia ij ik is if ji id ia
14  is il ill sill dill fill sid lid ail lid slid jail
15  if is il kid kids ill kid if kids; if a kid is ill
```

Build Skill and Game

When you finish the lesson, log out of *KPDO*.

> *Use the game to showcase your skills.*

7. Once the finished icon displays, you must click Save in order to see the changes that were made by your co-author. Clicking Save shares the changes made by the first co-author. Note that the text that was changed is now highlighted.

> Pommery Limo Service (Pommery), since it was founded as a Delaware corporation in 2008, has operated as a niche player in the limousine service industry. Headquarters for Pommery are located in Chicago, Illinois.

8. Co-authors should review any changes made in a paragraph before editing it.
9. The process is continued until all edits in the document have been made.

Apply It

109-d1

Report

 renovation final plan

To get started on this application:

1. Read the How to steps on co-authoring carefully and review them as needed when you work through this application.
2. Each student must be paired with a second student to form a co-authoring team.
3. One student must be assigned as Co-author 1 and a second student must be assigned as Co-author 2.
4. Instructions in this application are labeled as instructions for Co-author 1 and Co-author 2.
5. Establish the time that you will both work on this activity. It may be during your regular class or lab time. Both students must have each other's email address, and both should have an account that entitles them to use SkyDrive.

Instructions for Co-author 1

1. Upload the *renovation final plan* data file to your SkyDrive and share it with Co-author 2.
2. Open the file and read the document. Note that the format is the same as it was in your data files on your computer.
3. Select *flooring*, the last word in the paragraph under the heading *Demolition*. Click Comment and post the following comment to Co-author 2:

 What was the flooring quote based on?

4. Click Edit Document and select Edit in Word Web App. Note that the format has placeholders for the graphics, but they are not displayed properly. The proper format will display after you finish editing and close the document.

Instructions for Co-author 2

1. Access the shared file on SkyDrive.
2. Open the file and read the document. Note that the format is the same as it was in your data files on your computer.
3. Reply to the comment from Co-author 1:

 We need to add the following sentence to the end of that paragraph: The flooring quote is based on new flooring in that area.

4. Then mark the comment as done.
5. Click Edit Document and select Edit in Word Web App. Note that the format has placeholders for the graphics, but they are not displayed properly. The proper format will display after you finish editing and close the document.

(continued)

Lesson 2 E and N

Warmup *Lesson 2a Warmup*

```
1 ff dd ss aa ff dd ss aa jj kk ll ;; fj dk sl a; a;
2 fj dk sl a; fjdk sla; a;sl dkfj dk sl a; fjdk sla;
3 aa ss dd ff jj kk ll ;; aa ss dd ff jj kk ll ;; a;
4 if a; as is; kids did; ask a sad lad; if a lass is
```

New Keys

2b E and N

e Reach *up* with *left second* finger.

n Reach *down* with *right first* finger.

e

```
5 e  ed  ed  led  led  lea  lea  ale  ale  elf  elf  eke  eke  ed
6 e  el  el  eel  els  elk  elk  lea  leak  ale  kale  led  jell
7 e  ale  kale  lea  leak  fee  feel  lea  lead  elf  self  eke
```

n

```
8  n  nj  nj  an  an  and  and  fan  fan  and  kin  din  fin  land
9  n  an  fan  in  fin  and  land  sand  din  fans  sank  an  sin
10 n  in  ink  sink  inn  kin  skin  an  and  land  in  din  dink
```

2c All Reaches Learned

```
11 den  end  fen  ken  dean  dens  ales  fend  fens  keen  knee
12 if in need;  feel ill;  as an end;  a lad and a lass;
13 and sand;  a keen idea;  as a sail sank;  is in jail;
14 an idea;  an end;  a lake;  a nail;  a jade;  a dean is
```

Lesson 109 Co-authoring

New Commands

- Co-authoring
- Unlock a paragraph
- Save and Share

CO-AUTHORING

By definition, co-authoring is a team activity. To complete the two applications in this lesson, students should establish or be assigned to a team of two persons. Distance is not a factor since all of the work is done electronically.

The co-authoring feature on SkyDrive enables two or more co-authors to edit the same document at the same time. Using a collaborative writing and editing approach is especially beneficial for project teams that have to produce joint documents. Only one person can edit a paragraph at a time. A co-authoring session begins automatically when one person is editing a document and another person opens the same file for editing. Often co-authoring sessions are prescheduled so that authors can confer through instant comments when questions arise.

Documents can be edited using Edit in Word or Edit in Word Web App. Generally, it is easier for all co-authors to select the same option, but it is not mandatory.

To edit a document using co-authoring:

1. Upload and share the document that will be edited simultaneously; then open it. The co-authors are usually designated by their names.

2. Scroll through the document before you decide how to edit it and note if you have any initial questions or comments that you would like to send to the other author before you begin editing. Use the comment feature to accomplish this.

3. When the second person opens the document, the co-authoring session is established and the name of the co-author displays. The number of co-authors displays in the taskbar during the editing session. The co-author should scroll through the document and answer comments or send comments with questions if needed.

4. To begin editing, co-authors select Edit in Word or Edit in Word Web App.

5. When a co-author clicks in a paragraph to edit it, the paragraph is locked to other co-authors.

6. After the edits in that paragraph are made, the co-author clicks the Save button to save and unlock the paragraph to display the finished icon.

(continued)

Skill Building

2d Textbook Keying

1. Key each line once.
2. Keep your eyes on the textbook copy.

Reach with little finger; tap ENTER; return to home key.

```
15 if a lad;
16 is a sad fall
17 if a lass did ask
18 ask a lass; ask a lad
19 a;sldkfj a;sldkfj a;sldkfj
20 a; sl dk fj fj dk sl a; a;sldkfj
21 ik ik if if is is kid skid did lid aid laid said
22 ik kid ail die fie did lie ill ilk silk skill skid
```

2e Improve Keystroking

i
```
23 ik ik ik if is il ik id is if kid did lid aid ails
24 did lid aid; add a line; aid kids; ill kids; id is
```

n
```
25 nj nj nj an an and and end den ken in ink sin skin
26 jn din sand land nail sank and dank skin sans sink
```

e
```
27 el els elf elk lea lead fee feel sea seal ell jell
28 el eke ale jak lake elf els jaks kale eke els lake
```

2f Build Skill

```
29 dine in an inn; fake jade; lend fans; as sand sank
30 in nine inns; if an end; need an idea; seek a fee;
31 if a lad; a jail; is silk; is ill; a dais; did aid
32 adds a line; and safe; asks a lass; sail in a lake
```

2g Textbook Keying

Key each line once.

Keep your eyes on copy; key words at a steady pace.

```
33 send land skin faded sand kind line nine sale fail
34 dense sales lakes jaded likes jails salad kale inn
35 lad likes kale; lass likes silk; add a fee; is ill
36 kids in a lake; if in need; ask a lass; lad is ill
```

2h End the Lesson

Log out of *KPDO*.

1. In the Module 20 Web Apps folder, rename *108-drill2* to **108-drill4** and open it.

2. Click the Comment icon at the top right side of the page to view the comment from Lynn Westfield.

3. Click the Reply icon and under your name, key: **Thanks Lynn. That is a good suggestion.** Post.

4. Click on Lynn's comment and then click the Mark as Done icon to gray it out. Do the same on your comment.

5. Copy *108-drill4* to the Module 20 Solutions folder.

6. Close the document. (*108-drill4*)

Apply It

108-d1

Report

 trails

1. From your SkyDrive, click Upload on the SkyDrive toolbar and upload *trails* from your data files to Module 20 Web Apps. Rename the file **108-d1**.

2. Open the file and click scroll down until you locate the Comment icon. View the comment from Lynn Westfield on page 2.

3. Reply to Lynn by keying the following: **Lynn, I agree and will add the row at the bottom of the table.**

4. Click Edit Document and select Edit in Word Web App. Make the following changes:

 a. At the end of the first paragraph under *Healthy Heart Study*, change 55 to **65**.
 b. In the paragraph under *The Bike Trail heading*, change 125 to **100**.
 c. Go the last row of the table and click the Insert tab. Note that you cannot add a row using Edit in Word Web App. Note also that the graphics do not display correctly.
 d. Click the View tab. Select Reading View and scroll through the document. Note that the graphics and the table display properly.
 e. Click Edit in Word to open the document using *Word* on your computer.

5. Scroll to the table on page 2 and add a row on the bottom of the table. Key the following information in the new row:

 a. Column A: **Total Project**; column B: **All**; column C: **2 years**; and in column D: sum the column; then check to make sure the total is $658,500.
 b. Save and close the document to return to your SkyDrive.

6. Open the document on your SkyDrive and click Comments; mark as done and then delete the comments.

7. Click the File tab and then Exit.

8. Right-click *108-d1* and copy to Module 20 Solutions.

9. Right-click the Module 20 Solutions folder; select Sharing and share it with your instructor.

Lesson 3 Review

```
home  1  ad ads lad fad dad as ask fa la lass jak jaks alas
   n  2  an fan and land fan flan sans sand sank flank dank
   i  3  is id ill dill if aid ail fail did kid ski lid ilk
 all  4  ade alas nine else fife ken; jell ink jak inns if;
```

Skill Building

3b Textbook Keying

Key each line once.

Lines 5–8: Think and key words. Make the space part of the word.

Lines 9–12: Think and key phrases. Do not key the vertical rules separating the phrases.

easy words

```
 5  if is as an ad el and did die eel fin fan elf lens
 6  as ask and id kid and ade aid eel feel ilk skis an
 7  ail fail aid did ken ale led an flan inn inns alas
 8  eel eke nee kneel did kids kale sees lake elf fled
```

easy phrases

```
 9  el el|id id|is is|eke eke|lee lee|ale ale|jill jak
10  is if|is a|is a|a disk|a disk|did ski|did ski|is a
11  sell a|sell a|sell a sled|fall fad|fall fad|fad is
12  sees a lake|sees a lake|as a deal|sell sled|a sale
```

3c Improve Keystroking

home row: fingers curved and upright

```
13  jak lad as lass dad sad lads fad fall la ask ad as
14  asks add jaks dads a lass ads flak adds sad as lad
```

upward reaches: straighten fingers slightly; return quickly to home position

```
15  fed die led ail kea lei did ale fife silk leak lie
16  sea lid deal sine desk lie ale like life idea jail
```

double letters: stroke double letters at a steady, unhurried pace

```
17  fee jell less add inn seek fall alee lass keel all
18  dill dell see fell eel less all add kiss seen sell
```

To post a new comment in *Word Web App*:

1. Click Comments above the open document to display the Comments box with your name.

2. Select the text that applies (one word or phrase) and key the comment below your name.

To reply to a comment, mark a comment as done, or delete a comment:

1. When you open a document that contains a comment in the *Word Web App*, a Comment icon displays. Click the icon to see the comment. Note the three icons at the bottom of the comment.

2. Click the Reply icon to display your name and a box to key your reply. Key the reply and click Post.

3. When you are finished with the comment, click the Mark as Done icon or the Delete icon.

4. Click Mark as Done to gray the comment out.

5. Click Delete to remove it from the document.

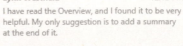

RENAME AND COPY FILES

Right-clicking a file on SkyDrive displays a number of actions that can be taken.

To rename or copy a file:

1. To rename a file, right-click it and select rename. Key the new name.

2. To copy a file, right-click it and select Copy to; select the folder and then click Copy.

DRILL 3　　　　**RENAME AND COPY FILE AND ADD A COMMENT**

1. On the SkyDrive toolbar, click Create and select New Folder. Name it **Module 20 Solutions**.

2. In the Module 20 Web Apps folder, select *108-drill1* and copy it to the Module 20 Solutions folder.

3. In the Module 20 Web Apps folder, right-click *108-drill1* and rename it **108-drill3**.

4. Open *108-drill3* and click Comments and then New Comment. Key this comment: **I renamed 108-drill1 to 108-drill3 and I will copy it to Module 20 Solutions.** Then click Post and Save the document.

5. Copy *108-drill3* to the Module 20 Solutions folder.

6. Close the document. (*108-drill3*)

3d Build Skill

19 and and land land el el elf elf self self ail nail
20 as as ask ask ad ad lad lad id id lid lid kid kids

phrases: think and key as phrases

21 if if|is is|jak jak|all all|did did|nan nan|elf elf
22 as a lad| ask dad| fed a jak| as all ask| sales fad

23 sell a lead|seal a deal|feel a leaf|if a jade sale
24 is a|is as if|a disk|aid all kids|did ski|is a silk

3e Textbook Keying

Key each line once.

© Cengage Learning

Tap Space Bar with down-and-in motion.

reach review

25 ea sea lea seas deal leaf leak lead leas flea keas
26 as ask lass ease as asks ask ask sass as alas seas

27 sa sad sane sake sail sale sans safe sad said sand
28 le sled lead flee fled ale flea lei dale kale leaf

29 jn jn nj nj in fan fin an; din ink sin and inn an;
30 de den end fen an an and and ken knee nee dean dee

3f Timed Writing

Key lines 31–34 for 1'.
If you finish before time
is up, repeat the lines.

31 el eel eld elf sell self el dell fell elk els jell
32 in fin inn inks dine sink fine fins kind line lain

33 an and fan dean elan flan land lane lean sand sane
34 sell a lead; sell a jade; seal a deal; feel a leaf

Game

Log out when you
finish the lesson.

Showcase your keyboarding skills in the game.

SHARE DOCUMENTS OR FOLDERS

SHARE

Sharing involves giving others access to documents or folders on your SkyDrive. One way of sharing is to make a folder public. Anyone with a Microsoft Live account can access any document in that folder. Access to documents can enable others to read the document or edit it if you select that option. This option should be used very sparingly and very carefully. Normally, documents and folders are shared with carefully selected individuals. A better approach is to email a link to individuals whom you want to give access to the file.

To share a document on SkyDrive:

1. Click Share above the open document to display the Share dialog box.

2. Send a link to one or more reviewers. Key the person's email address and add a message if desired. Make sure Recipients can edit box is checked.

3. Click Share.

DRILL 2　　　　**SHARE DOCUMENT**　　　　108-drill2

1. From SkyDrive, open your Module 20 Web Apps folder and click the Upload button ❋, browse and upload *108-drill2* from your data files.

2. Open the document and share it with your instructor or one of your classmates who has an Outlook email address or a Microsoft Live Account. Click Share above the open document.

3. Key the email address and the following message:
 Please review the document and give me your feedback today if possible.

4. Check the Recipients can edit box if it is not already checked.

5. Click Share. Close the document. (*108-drill2*)

COMMENTS

COMMENTS

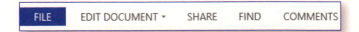

The Comments option is the last of the four options available to work on an open document on SkyDrive. In *Word*, comments are part of the Review tab and are generally thought of as an editing tool. Comments are not available when you select Edit Document and choose Edit in Word Web App.

Lesson 4 Left Shift, H, T, Period

Warmup *Lesson 4a Warmup*

home row	1	al as ads lad dad fad jak fall lass asks fads all;
e/i/n	2	ed ik jn in knee end nine line sine lien dies leis
all reaches	3	see a ski; add ink; fed a jak; is an inn; as a lad
easy	4	an dial id is an la lake did el ale fake is land a

New Keys

4b Left Shift and h

left shift Reach *down* with *left fourth* (little) finger; shift, tap, release.

h Reach to *left* with *right first* finger.

left shift

5 J Ja Ja Jan Jan Jane Jana Ken Kass Lee Len Nan Ned
6 and Ken and Lena and Jake and Lida and Nan and Ida
7 Inn is; Jill Ina is; Nels is; Jen is; Ken Lin is a

h

8 h hj hj he he she she hen aha ash had has hid shed
9 h hj ha hie his half hand hike dash head sash shad
10 aha hi hash heal hill hind lash hash hake dish ash

4c All Reaches Learned

11 Nels Kane and Jake Jenn; she asked Hi and Ina Linn
12 Lend Lana and Jed a dish; I fed Lane and Jess Kane
13 I see Jake Kish and Lash Hess; Isla and Helen hike

4d Textbook Keying
Key the drill once. Strive for good control.

14 he she held a lead; she sells jade; she has a sale
15 Ha Ja Ka La Ha Hal Ja Jake Ka Kahn La Ladd Ha Hall
16 Hal leads; Jeff led all fall; Hal has a safe lead
17 Hal Hall heads all sales; Jake Hess asks less fee;

ACCESSING AND EDITING FILES ON SKYDRIVE

If you open files from your desktop that were saved on SkyDrive from your desktop, they will open in *Word*. If you log in on SkyDrive (http://skydrive.live.com), you can choose to open the files using the *Word Web App* or to open it using *Word*.

You can do basic editing in the *Word Web App* using commands on the Home tab, but you will note that many commands on other tabs are not available. Editing is done in the *Word Web App* in the same way that it is done in *Word*.

For ease of accessing SkyDrive, bookmark it by adding it to Favorites in your browser.

To open and edit a document using *Word Web App*:

1. Log on to SkyDrive using the URL shown above. Note that the files display as tiles by default. To display a detailed list, click the List button at the top right side of the screen.

2. Click the folder to open it and then click the desired file to open it.

3. Click Edit document to display the options and select Edit in Word Web App. Note options include Share, Find, and Comments.

If you do not see the folders on SkyDrive, click Files on the left side of the screen to display them.

4. Edit the document in the same way you edit any *Word* document.

5. To find text, click Find; key text in the Search box and click the Search icon.

DRILL 1 CONTINUED EDITING IN WORD WEB APP

1. Log in on SkyDrive using the URL provided above.

2. Open *108-drill1* from your SkyDrive files.

3. Select Edit in Word Web App to edit the document.

4. Make the changes indicated at the right; then save and close the document. (*108-drill1*)

a. In the second sentence of the last paragraph on page 3, delete *Simultaneous editing* and replace with **Co-authoring**.

b. Add the following sentence as the last sentence of that paragraph: **Several authors can edit the document at the same time.**

DRILL 1 CONTINUED FIND TEXT

1. In the open document (*108-drill1*), use Find to search for *Co-authoring*.

2. Check and proofread the last sentence you added.

3. Close the document. (*108-drill1*)

4e t and . (period)

t Reach *up* with *left first* finger.

. (period) Reach *down* with *right third* finger.

t

18 t tf tf aft aft left fit fat fete tiff tie the tin
19 tf at at aft lit hit tide tilt tint sits skit this
20 hat kit let lit ate sit flat tilt thin tale tan at

Space once after a period.

. (period)

21 .1 .1 1.1 fl. fl. L. L. Neal and J. N. List hiked.
22 Hand J. H. Kass a fan. Jeff did. Hank needs ideas.
23 Jane said she has a tan dish; Jed and Lee need it.

4f Improve Keystroking

24 I did tell J. K. that Lt. Lee had left. He is ill.
25 tie tan kit sit fit hit hat; the jet left at nine.
26 I see Lila and Ilene at tea. Jane Kane ate at ten.
27 tf .1 hj ft ki de jh tf ik ed hj de ft ki 1. tf ik
28 elf eel left is sis fit till dens ink has delt ink
29 he he heed heed she she shelf shelf shed shed she
30 it is if id did lit tide tide tile tile list list

Skill Building

4g Build Skill

31 he has; he had; he led; he sleds; she fell; he is
32 it is; he hit it; he is ill; she is still; she is
33 Hal and Nel; Jade dishes; Kale has half; Jed hides
34 Hi Ken; Helen and Jen hike; Jan has a jade; Ken is

4h End the Lesson
Log out of *KPDO*.

Web Apps

Lesson 108 *Working with Files on SkyDrive*
Lesson 109 *Co-authoring*
Lesson 110 *Hess Office Park*

Lesson 108 Working with Files on SkyDrive

New Commands

- Edit in Word Web App
- Save to SkyDrive
- Create Folder
- Edit in Word
- Find
- Share
- Comments
- Upload

Review Commands

 TIP

You can also create a new folder on SkyDrive.

On the SkyDrive toolbar, click Create and select New Folder. Then key the name of the folder.

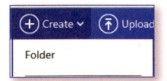

USING SKYDRIVE

In Module 20 you use *Word*, the SkyDrive, and the *Word Web App*. You will not launch nor use *KPDO* in this module. You need a Microsoft Live account and an Internet connection to complete the work in this module. You can access the SkyDrive from the URL, http://skydrive.live.com, from the *Windows 8* Start screen by clicking the SkyDrive icon or you can save documents using the File menu in *Word*. When you first accessed SkyDrive, you should have downloaded and installed the SkyDrive desktop app to keep documents on your desktop and on SkyDrive in sync.

To save a file from your computer to a new folder on SkyDrive:
File/Save As/SkyDrive/

1. With the file open, follow the path and click Browse to display the Save As dialog box.
2. Click New folder; key the name of the new folder and open it.
3. Use the current filename or key the new name in the File name box and click Save.
4. Close the file on your computer if you have finished with it.

DRILL 1 SAVE FILE ON SKYDRIVE IN NEW FOLDER overview of skydrive

1. Open *overview of skydrive* and follow the path; click Browse to display the Save As dialog box.

2. Click New folder and key the name, **Module 20 Web Apps**.

3. Click the folder to open it, key **108-drill1** in the File name box, and click Save. (*108-drill1*)

4. Close the document on your computer.

Lesson 4R Review

Warmup *Lesson 4Ra Warmup*

home row	1	sad lad hall lad sale ask jak add aka fall fad ha;
review	2	H. Le Ki J. tan tin hit at tat nat hat nit Lt. hid
all reaches	3	Jed is in sales; Kate ate fish. Hank hit his head.
easy	4	sit dial and land fit then half din hand lend disk

Skill Building

4Rb Textbook Keying

Key the drill once.

Think and key words and phrases.

words	5	slain tent Kent lent tea Jill Ned fed said laid he			
phrases	6	he fakes	she hikes	his lead is safe	she and I fish
sentences	7	Nan is ill; Ed is at the lake; Jake is at the Inn.			
sentences	8	Jed Hess did ski. Kit and I fished. Tina ate fish.			
sentences	9	Hank ate his salad. Jane has the disk in the tent.			
sentences	10	Ed said that Nate left the lake and is at the Inn.			

4Rc Build Skill

11	shelf lead jiff lead sand find dine kind fend tent
12	kale sake takes deal tended salad jaded dined left
13	if I sell it; seek a deal; find a tent; at the Inn
14	He asked Ann; I need a fan; Ed sells jade and land.
15	Linda likes to hike; Dan likes to eat at the lake.

Wordwrap: Text within a paragraph moves automatically from one line to the next; tap ENTER only to begin a new paragraph.

4Rd Timed Writing

1. Take two 1' timed writings. If you finish before time is up, begin again.
2. Use wordwrap.
3. When you are finished, log out.

 ✕ Log Out

Use wordwrap

Janet sat in the tent, and then she fished at the lake. Eddie and his dad did find the disk in the tent at the lake. Helen and the dean ate a salad at the Inn. Then she asked the dean if he had a keen idea. She said the dean did have a keen idea.

Writing 53

We are living in a wonderful period of history. This is a time when historians are recording many exciting changes in our world. The past two decades have shown that all inhabitants of this planet must learn to exist together. We no longer are able to isolate ourselves from other countries. The action of one nation has a direct effect on nearly every other nation in the world. We must quickly recognize and adjust to peaceful solutions.

Writing 54

Traffic jams, deadlines, problems at work, and squabbles at home are several ways in which tension is created. When our tension is about to reach the boiling point, what do people usually tell us? In most cases, they urge us to relax. But relaxing is not always easy to accomplish. We frequently think we cannot find the time for this important part of our daily activity.

To understand how relaxation works for us, we must realize how the stress of contemporary existence works against us. Developed for survival in a challenging world, the human body reacts to a crisis by getting ready for action. Whether we are preparing for a timed writing or for an encounter in a dark street, our muscles tighten and our blood pressure goes up. After years of this type of response, we often find it difficult to relax when needed.

Now think about the feeling which is the opposite of this turmoil. The pulse slows down, the breath comes slowly and calmly, and the tension leaves the body. This is total relaxation. And if it seems good, consider how good it must actually feel. Our bodies are already prepared to relax; it is an ability all individuals have within themselves. What we have to practice is how to use this response.

Lesson 5 R, Right Shift, C, O

Warmup *Lesson 5a Warmup*

home keys 1	a; ad add al all lad fad jak ask lass fall jak lad
t/h/i/n 2	the hit tin nit then this kith dint tine hint thin
left shift/. 3	I need ink. Li has an idea. Hank hit it. I see Kate.
all reaches 4	Jeff ate at ten; he left a salad dish in the sink.

New Keys

5b r and Right Shift

r Reach *up* with *left first* finger.

right shift Reach *down* with *right fourth* finger; shift, tap, release.

r

5 r rf rf riff riff fir fir rid ire jar air sir lair
6 rf rid ark ran rat are hare art rant tire dirt jar
7 rare dirk ajar lark rain kirk share hart rail tart

left shift

8 D D Dan Dan Dale Ti Sal Ted Ann Ed Alf Ada Sid Fan
9 and Sid and Dina and Allen and Eli and Dean and Ed
10 Ed Dana; Dee Falk; Tina Finn; Sal Alan; Anna Deeds

5c All Reaches Learned

11 Jane and Ann hiked in the sand; Asa set the tents.
12 a rake; a jar; a tree; a red fire; a fare; a rain;
13 Fred Derr and Rai Tira dined at the Tree Art Fair.

5d Textbook Keying

Key each line once.

14 ir ir ire fir first air fair fire tire rid sir
15 fir jar tar fir flit rill till list stir dirt fire
16 Renee is ill. Fred read to her. Ed Finn left here.
17 All is still as Sarah and I fish here in the rain.
18 I still see a red ash tree that fell in the field.
19 Lana said she did sail her skiff in the dark lake.

Writing 51

Educated people realize that they can find important details just through the simple act of listening. The secret, however, as is well known, is to listen with discretion. Our usual ability to hear forces us to hear many thousands of noises, while our amazing listening ability lets us select only what we think is important from what is minutiae. Often our only input is a question; and if our listening area is an exciting TV show, we are not required to reply.

Writing 52

People spend far more time listening than they spend communicating in any other way, but only a very few people have developed good listening skills. There is a big difference between hearing and listening. Hearing does not require major effort, but listening is hard work. One of the problems with listening is that we can listen about three times faster than most people speak. We are able to hear what the speaker is saying and still have extra time for our minds to wander to other things.

An active listener utilizes the difference between the listening and the speaking rates to make mental summaries of the conversation. One way to listen actively is to anticipate the next point that the individual will make. It is also important to clarify in your own mind what is being said. Generally, people try to assume too much. A good listener will let the person explain in her or his words exactly what he or she would like to say. Paraphrasing is a good way to confirm that the message is understood.

A person who has developed good listening skills will not interrupt the person who is speaking. The problem is that more people prefer to speak than to listen. Sometimes it takes a considerable amount of effort to give the person an opportunity to get the message across. Showing that you are interested in what is being said helps to put the speaker at ease. It is not enough just to listen; you also have to look like you are listening. The effective use of body language enhances listening.

5e c and o

c Reach *down* with *left second* finger.

o Reach *up* with *right third* finger.

c

20 c c cd cd cad cad can can tic ice sac cake cat sic
21 clad chic cite cheek clef sick lick kick dice rice
22 call acid hack jack lack lick cask crack clan cane

o

23 o ol ol old old of off odd ode or ore oar soar one
24 ol sol sold told dole do doe lo doll sol solo odor
25 onto door toil lotto soak fort hods foal roan load

Skill Building

5 f Improve Keystroking

o/r
26 or or for for nor nor ore ore oar oar roe roe sore
27 a rose|her or|he or|he rode|or for|a door|her doll

e/n
28 en en end end ne ne need need ken ken kneel kneels
29 lend the|lend the|at the end|at the end|need their

c/o
30 ch ch check check ck ck hack lack jack co co cones
31 the cot|the cot|a dock|a dock|a jack|a jack|a cone

32 Carlo Rand can call Rocco; Cole can call Doc Cost.
all reaches 33 Trina can ask Dina if Nick Corl has left; Joe did.
34 Case sent Carole a nice skirt; it fits Lorna Rich.

5 g Build Skill

i/t
35 is is tis tis it it fit fit tie tie this this lits
36 it is|it is|it is this|it is this|it sits|tie fits

37 Jack and Rona did frost nine of the cakes at last.
all reaches 38 Jo can ice her drink if Tess can find her a flask.
39 Ask Jean to call Fisk at noon; he needs her notes.

Skill Building *Technique Builder*

DRILL 27

Number Review

Key each line once at a comfortable rate; practice difficult lines.

1 On June 11 and July 11, 11 men and 11 women worked 11 hours each.
2 Al received Invoice 22RC22 on May 22 and paid $225.22 on June 22.
3 The 33 boys visited 3 girls at 3:30 p.m. on May 3 at 33 Oak Road.
4 The 44 men found 44 sections of 4' pipe required before 4:44 p.m.
5 On June 15, 55 women ran over 25 miles in 2 hours and 55 minutes.
6 The 66 players shot 6,666 free throws in 66 minutes and made 666.
7 The 7 rooms were 17' 7" wide and 7' 7" long with 17' 7" ceilings.
8 Those 8 coaches made 88 trips averaging 88 miles each in 88 days.
9 The 9 boys packed 9 boxes weighing 99 pounds in 9 hours on May 9.
10 Was the value listed at $10,000,000 or $20,000,000 on October 20?

Timed Writings

Writing 50

The kinds of leisure activities you choose constitute your life style and, to a great extent, reflect your personality. For example, if your daily activities are people oriented, you may balance this by spending your free time alone. On the other hand, if you would rather be with people most of the time, your socialization needs may be very high. At the other end of the scale are people who are engaged in machine-oriented work and also enjoy spending leisure time alone. These people tend to be rather quiet and reserved.

Every individual needs a certain amount of relaxation to remain physically and mentally alert. However, what one person finds relaxing may be just the opposite for another person. For example, one person may like to read a good book; another may find that reading causes nervousness and fatigue. The same holds true for the person who enjoys sports. Studies have shown that jogging may be quite good for a person who enjoys it but may be detrimental to another person who does not enjoy it.

Experts have noted that the proper balance of leisure, relaxation, and recreation is almost essential for individuals who live and work in a highly automated world. This balance is necessary if each person is to be productive in handling the everyday pressure and stress of life. Because every person has unique needs that are met in a variety of ways, one must properly assess all of the day's activities if the maximum benefit is to be gained from each day of life.

Lesson 5R Review

r/c/o/right shift 1 circle order record Frank Sarah Tonia Henri candor

r/c/o 2 effort trick scroll control clone donor salon corn

right shift 3 Sandra Forde Addie Crone Stan Jackson Rhonda Caine

all reaches 4 Jeff drank his cold tea and ate cookies in a tent.

Skill Building

Think and key words and phrases as units.

5Rb Textbook Keying

1. Key each line once.
2. Keep your eyes on the copy.

words 5 choice rejoice north crank drank cross craft order

6 creaked kitchen store lost frost train rained horn

phrases 7 to go north|I left at noon|reach up|he trusted her

8 Fred chose one|Connie cooked|Daniel ate fried food

sentences 9 Carl and Jack left for a short train ride at noon.

10 Lee and Jo can cook for their friends in the tent.

5Rc Build Skill

o/r 11 or cork for nor sore tore rote lore snore ore core

12 his or her|she rode|at the door|she tore her skirt

c/o 13 close choose color cork corn coal ocean cold scorn

14 close the door|choose a color|for a dock|cook corn

all reaches 15 Joan and Clark selected a nice color for the dock.

16 Dick sent Lori a nice skirt and Frank a red shirt.

5Rd Timed Writing

1. Key a 1' timing; use wordwrap—do not return at the end of the line. If you finish before time is up, begin again.
2. Key a 1' timed writing at a slower but fluent pace.

wordwrap ↓

Connie said that her son can cook for her friends at noon. He is a trained chef and likes to cook for others. He can locate and choose the food. Harold offered to do all of the dishes. I think that is also a nice offer.

Skill Building *Technique Builder*

TIP

Use top speed for easy words and phrases and phrases and lower speed for words that are more difficult to key. Key phrases marked with a line as a unit.

1 it to the us me you so go now we my he two in can her by of do no

2 it is | it is the | is it | is it you | he can | can he | he can go | can he go

3 who is | who is it | is it you | you can go | can you go | you can go to it

4 car mail two you may just can lake ask sail sign his form her who

5 who can sail | you can sail | you may sign | can you sign | sign his form

6 sign the form | mail the form | sign and mail | sign and mail that form

7 it was | was it so | if she can go to | can he go to the | can she go to the

8 she can | she may not | she may not go | can you go to the | so we may go

9 sign the | sign the form | they may sign that | they may sign that form

Timed Writings

Writing 49

An essential part of analyzing a career option is to determine the type and extent of education that are required for a selected career. A main factor to consider about an education is how long it will take to get the skills that are needed to compete successfully for a job. This factor includes any other training that may be essential at the outset of employment. Because jobs change, also assess how an educational program is structured to meet work changes.

Many people choose a career without considering how well they may be suited for it. For example, a person who is outgoing and enjoys being around people probably should not select a career that requires spending long hours working alone. A job that requires quick, forceful action to be taken probably should not be pursued by a person who is shy and contemplative. Just because one has an aptitude for a specific job does not mean he or she will be successful in that job. Thus, be sure to consider individual personality traits before making a final career choice.

Money and inner satisfaction are the two leading reasons why most people work. For most persons, the need for money translates into food, shelter, and clothing. Once the basic needs of a person are met, satisfaction is the greatest motivator for working. To the average person, a job is satisfying if he or she enjoys the work, likes the people associated with the work, and feels a sense of pride in a job well done. Because you may not be the average person, analyze yourself to discover what will provide job satisfaction.

Lesson 6 W, Comma, B, P

Warmup *Lesson 6a Warmup*

home row	1	ask a lad; a fall fad; had a salad; ask a sad jak;
o/t	2	to do it; to toil; as a tot; do a lot; he told her
c/r	3	cots are; has rocks; roll cot; is rich; has an arc
all reaches	4	Holt can see Dane at ten; Jill sees Frank at nine.

New Keys

6b w and , (comma)

w Reach *up* with *left third* finger.

, (comma) Reach *down* with *right second* finger.

6c All Reaches Learned

6d Textbook Keying
Key each line once.

w

5 w ws ws was was wan wit low win jaw wilt wink wolf
6 sw sw w sow ow now now row row own own wow wow owe
7 to sew; to own; was rich; was in; is how; will now

, (comma)

8 k, k, k, irk, ilk, ask, oak, ark, lark, jak, rock,
9 skis, a dock, a fork, a lock, a fee, a tie, a fan,
10 Joe, Ed, and I saw Nan, Ann, and Wes in a new car.
11 Win, Lew, Drew, and Walt will walk to West Willow.
12 Ask Ho, Al, and Jared to read the code; it is new.
13 The window, we think, was closed; we felt no wind.

Good posture builds an attitude of preciseness.

14 walk wide sown wild town went jowl wait white down
15 a dock, a kit, a wick, a lock, a row, a cow, a fee
16 Joe lost to Ron; Fiji lost to Cara; Don lost to Al
17 Kane will win; Nan will win; Rio will win; Di wins
18 Walter is in Reno; Tia is in Tahoe; then to Hawaii

DRILL 25

Direct Reach Combinations

Key each line once.

TIP

Key fluently, without rushing.

br/rb
1 break barb brawn orbit brain carbon brakes barbecue brazen barber
2 Barbara Brady brought us a new brand of barbecue to eat at break.

ce/ec
3 cease decide cent collect cell direct cedar check center peck ice
4 Cecil recently received a check for his special barbecue recipes.

mu/um
5 mull dumb must human mud lumber mulch lump mumps slump music fume
6 Bum Muse must have dumped too much muddy mulch on the bumpy lawn.

nu/un
7 nut sun fun nurse gun sinus number punch nuzzle pound lunch until
8 Uncle Gunta, a nurse, was uneasy about numerous units unionizing.

gr/rg
9 grade merge grand purge great large grab organ green margins gray
10 Margo, our great grandmother, regrets merging those large groups.

ny/yn
11 Wayne any shyness many agony balcony Jayne lynx penny larynx myna
12 Wayne and Jayne fed many skinny myna birds on that sunny balcony.

Timed Writings

Writing 48

The job market today is quite different than it was a few years ago. The fast track to management no longer exists. Entry-level managers find that it is much more difficult to obtain a promotion to a higher-level position in management than it was just a few years ago. People who are in the market for new jobs find very few management positions available. In fact, many managers at all levels have a difficult time keeping their current management positions. Two factors seem to contribute heavily to the problem. The first factor is the trend toward self-managed teams. The second factor is that as companies downsize they often remove entire layers of management or an entire division.

Layoffs are not new; but, what is new is that layoffs are affecting white-collar workers as well as blue-collar workers. Coping with job loss is a new and frustrating experience for many managers. A person who has just lost a job will have concerns about personal security and welfare, and the concerns are compounded when families are involved. The problem, however, is more than just an economic one. Job loss often damages an individual's sense of self-worth. An individual who does not have a good self-concept will have a very hard time selling himself or herself to a potential employer.

6e b and p

b Reach *down* with *left first* finger.

p Reach *up* with *right fourth* (little) finger.

b

19 bf bf bf biff fib fib bib bib boa boa fib fibs rob
20 bf bf bf ban ban bon bon bow bow be be rib rib sob
21 a dob, a cob, a crib, a lab, a slab, a bid, a bath

p

22 p; p; pa pa; pal pal pan pan pad par pen pep paper
23 pa pa; lap lap; nap nap; hep ape spa asp leap clap
24 a park, a pan, a pal, a pad, apt to pop, a pair of

Skill Building

6f Improve Keystroking

all reaches learned
25 Barb and Bob wrapped a pepper in paper and ribbon.
26 Rip, Joann, and Dick were all closer to the flash.
27 Bo will be pleased to see Japan; he works in Oslo.

reach review
28 ki kid did aid lie hj has has had sw saw wits will
29 de dell led sled jn an en end ant hand k, end, kin

s/w
30 ws ws lows now we shown win cow wow wire jowl when
31 Wes saw an owl in the willow tree in the old lane.

b/p
32 bf bf fib rob bid ;p p; pal pen pot nap hop cap bp
33 Rob has both pans in a bin at the back of the pen.

6g Build Skill

34 to do|can do|to bow|ask her|to nap|to work|is born
35 for this|if she|is now|did all|to see|or not|or if

all reaches
36 Dick owns a dock at this lake; he paid Ken for it.
37 Jane also kept a pair of owls, a hen, and a snake.

38 Blair soaks a bit of the corn, as he did in Japan.
39 I blend the cocoa in the bowl when I work for Leo.

DRILL 24

Specific Rows

Key each line once; DS between groups.

 TIP

Reach to the first and third rows with a minimum of hand movement; keep hands quiet; don't bounce on the keys.

Rows 3, 2, 1

1 you we quip try pot peer your wire put quit wet trip power toy to
2 salad fad glad lass lag has gall lash gas lad had shall flag half
3 comb zone exam man carve bun oxen bank came next vent zoo van cab

4 we try to; you were; put up your; put it there; you quit; wipe it
5 Gail asked Sissy; what was said; had Jake left; Dana sold a flag
6 Zam came back; can Max fix my van? a brave man, Ben came in a cab

7 Peter or I will try to wire our popular reports to Porter or you.
8 Ada Glass said she is glad she had half a kale salad with Dallas.
9 Zack drove a van to minimize expenses; Ben and Max came in a cab.

 Timed Writings

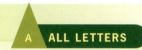

Take two 3' or one 5' writing; key with fluency and control.

Writing 47

Sports are very big business today; that is, those sports competitions in which men participate are very big business. What about sports for women? At the professional level, women have made real progress in golf and tennis; they, as well as their sponsors, can make big money in both of these events. The other sports for women still are not considered to be major revenue sports. The future may be much better, however, because sports for women at all levels are gaining in popularity. Programs that are designed to help young girls develop their athletic skills and interest are having an impact. The result is that girls now expect to play for organized clubs as well as in school programs just as boys do. Club sports often will lead to varsity teams.

Many people question how much impact the current emphasis on gender equity will have on sports at the college level. Most people agree that this new emphasis is very positive for women. Some people feel, though, that it either has had or could have a negative impact on sports for men. They believe that resources that would have been spent on sports such as football, basketball, and baseball for men are now being spent on the Olympic sports for women. Overall, most people believe that both men and women who have the ability to excel in an athletic event as well as in the classroom should have the opportunity and should be encouraged to do so. Success for both women and men is better than success for either.

Lesson 7 Review

all	1	We often can take the older jet to Paris and back.
home	2	a; sl dk fj a;sl dkfj ad as all ask fads adds asks
1st row	3	Ann Bascan and Cabal Naban nabbed a cab in Canada.
3rd row	4	Rip went to a water show with either Pippa or Pia.

7b Improve Keystroking

5 ad la as in if it lo no of oh he or so ok pi be we
6 an ace ads ale aha a fit oil a jak nor a bit a pew
7 ice ades born is fake to jail than it and the cows
8 Ask Jed. Dr. Hand left at ten; Dr. Crowe, at nine.

Skill Building

7c Textbook Keying
Key each line once.

Keep your eyes on the textbook copy as you key.

9 ws ws was was wan wan wit wit pew paw nap pop bawl
10 bf bf fb fb fob fob rib rib be be job job bat back
11 p; p; asp asp pan pan ap ap ca cap pa nap pop prow
12 Barb and Bret took an old black robe and the boot.
13 Walt saw a wisp of white water renew ripe peppers.
14 Pat picked a black pepper for the picnic at Parks.

7d Build Skill

15 Jake held a bit of cocoa and an apricot for Diane.
16 Dick and I fish for cod on the docks at Fish Lake.
17 Kent still held the dish and the cork in his hand.
18 Ask far as I know, he did not read all of the book.

DRILL 23

Specific Fingers

Key each line once;
DS between groups.

1st
1 fun gray vent guy hunt brunt buy brunch much gun huge humor vying
2 buy them brunch; a hunting gun; Guy hunts for fun; try it for fun

2nd
3 cite decide kick cider creed kidded keen keep kit idea ice icicle
4 keen idea; kick it back; ice breaker; decide the issue; sip cider

3rd
5 low slow lax solo wax sold swell swollen wood wool load logs doll
6 wooden dolls; wax the floor; a slow boat; saw logs; pull the wool

4th
7 quip zap Zane zip pepper pay quiz zipper quizzes pad map nap jazz
8 zip the zipper; jazz at the plaza; Zane quipped; La Paz jazz band

 Timed Writings

1. Take three 1' writings on each paragraph.
2. Take one 5' or two 3' writings.

Writing 46

How much power is needed? Is more power always better than less power? People often raise the question in many different instances. Regardless of the situation, most people seem to seek more power. In jobs, power is often related to rank in an organization, to the number of people reporting to a person, and to the ability to spend money without having to ask someone with more power. Most experts indicate that the power a person has should closely match the responsibilities (not just duties and tasks) for which he or she can be held accountable.

Questions about power are not limited to jobs and people. Many people ask the question in reference to the amount of power or speed a computer should have. Again, the response usually implies that more is better. A better approach is to analyze how the computer is to be used and then try to match power needs to the types of applications. Most people are surprised to learn that home computer buyers tend to buy more power than buyers in offices. The primary reason is that the computers are used to play games with extensive graphics, sound, and other media applications. Matching the needs of the software is the key.

7e Textbook Keying

Key each line once.

words 19 a an pan so sot la lap ah own do doe el elf to tot

phrases 20 if it│to do│it is│do so│for the│he works│if he bid

sentences 21 Jess ate all of the peas in the salad in the bowl.

words 22 bow bowl pin pint for fork forks hen hens jak jaks

phrases 23 is for│did it│is the│we did a│and so│to see│or not

sentences 24 I hid the ace in a jar as a joke; I do not see it.

words 25 chap chaps flak flake flakes prow prowl work works

phrases 26 as for the│as for the│and to the│to see it│and did

sentences 27 As far as I know, he did not read all of the book.

7f Timed Writing

1. Take two 1' timed writings. If you finish before time is up, begin again.
2. Use wordwrap; do not tap ENTER at the ends of the lines.
3. End the lesson.

Goal: 12 *gwam*

wordwrap ↓

gwam 1'

It is hard to fake a confident spirit. We will do 10

better work if we approach and finish a job and 19

know that we will do the best work we can and then 29

not fret. 31

| 1 | 2 | 3 | 4 | 5 | 6 | 7 | 8 | 9 | 10 |

7g Word Processor Timer

Word Processor

1. Review the Standard Plan for Using the Word Processor Timer.
2. Key the timed writing from the textbook in 7f following the directions in the textbook.

STANDARD PLAN for Using the Word Processor Timer

You can check your speed in the Word Processor using the Timer.

1. In the Word Processor, click the Timer button on the status bar.
2. The Timer begins once you start to key and stops automatically.
3. To save the timing, click the File menu and Save As. Use your initals (*xx*), the exercise number, and number of the timing as the filename. Example: *xx-7f-t1* (your initials, exercise 7f, timing1).
4. Click the Timer button again to start a new timing.
5. Each new timing must be saved with its own name.

7h Word Processor

1. In the Word Processor, key each line once for fluency.
2. Set the Timer for 30". Take two 30" writings on each line. Do not save the timings.

Goal: Reach the end of the line before time is up.

28 Dan took her to the show.

29 Jan lent the bowl to the pros.

30 Hold the wrists low for this drill.

31 Jessie fit the black panel to the shelf.

32 Patrick cooked breakfast for Jill and her friends.

DRILL 20

Adjacent Keys

Key each line once; repeat entire drill. DS between groups.

Goal: To eliminate persistent errors on side-by-side keys.

as/sa
1 has sale fast salt was saw vast essay easy say past vast mast sap
2 We saw Sam; Sal was sad; Susan has a cast; as Sam said; as I said

er/re
3 were there tree deer great three other her free red here pert are
4 we were there; here we are; there were three; here are three deer

io/oi
5 point axiom prior choir lion boil toil billion soil action adjoin
6 join a choir; prior to that action; millions in a nation rejoiced

op/po
7 polo drop loop post hope pole port rope slope power top pony stop
8 rope the pony; drop the pole; power at the top; hope for the poor

rt/tr
9 trail alert train hurt tree shirt trap smart trim start tray dirt
10 trim the tree; start the train; dirt on the shirt; alert the trio

ew/we
11 few we stew were pew went dew web sew wept crew wear brew wet new
12 we were weak; few were weeping; the crew went west; we knew a few

gh/ui
13 sight quit laugh suit might ruin ghost guide ghastly guilt ghetto
14 a ghastly suit; quit laughing; recruit the ghost; might be guilty

DRILL 21

Outside Reaches

Key each line once. DS between groups.

Goal: To key with a maximum of one error per line. (Letters are often omitted in outside reaches—concentrate.)

a/p
1 tapioca actual against casual areas facial equally aware parallel
2 impower purpose people opposed compute pimple papyrus pope puppet
3 Perhaps part of the chapter page openers can appear on red paper.

s/w
4 class sash steps essential skills business discuss desks insisted
5 wow wayworn away awkward wrong awaits wildwood waterworks wayward
6 The snow white swan swayed as the waves swept the swelling shore.

z/l
7 hazard zip zero zeolite freezer zoom zealous z-axis zodiac sizing
8 likely indelibly, laurel finally leaflet regularly eloquently lily
9 A New Zealand zoologist was amazed as a zebra guzzled the zinnias.

x/?
10 fax oxford exert excite examples xylan exercise oxygen exact taxi
11 When? Where? Which? For her? How much? What color? To whom?
12 After examining the x-rays, why did Dr. Ax exempt an exploratory?

DRILL 22

Alphabetic Sentences

Key each line once with good rhythm. Keep fingers curved and upright over the keys. DS between groups.

1 Judge McQuoy will have prizes for their next big track meet.
2 Jack may provide some extra quiz problems for the new group.
3 Gary Quazet mended six copies of books and journals we have.
4 Jack quibbled with a garrulous expert on Zoave family names.
5 Jake will study sixty chapters on vitamins for the big quiz.
6 Max asked Quin to provide a jewel box for the glossy zircon.
7 This judge may quiz the Iowa clerks about extensive profits.
8 Meg Keys packed and flew to Venezia to acquire her next job.

Lesson 8 G, Question Mark, X, U

Warmup *Lesson 8a Warmup*

all 1 Dick will see Job at nine if Rach sees Pat at one.
w/b 2 As the wind blew, Bob Webber saw the window break.
p/, 3 Pat, Pippa, or Cap has prepared the proper papers.
all 4 Bo, Jose, and Will fed Lin; Jack had not paid her.

New Keys

8b g and ? (question mark)

g Reach to *right* with *left first* finger.

? Left SHIFT; reach *down* with *right fourth* finger.

Question mark: The question mark is followed by one space.

g

5 g g gf gaff gag grog fog frog drag cog dig fig gig
6 gf go gall flag gels slag gala gale glad glee gals
7 golf flog gorge glen high logs gore ogle page grow

? (question mark)

8 ? ?; ?; ? ? Who? When? Where? Who is? Who was she?
9 Who is here? Was it she? Was it he? Did Pablos go?
10 Did Geena? Did he? What is that? Was Joe here too?

8c All Reaches Learned

11 Has Ginger lost her job? Were her June bills here?
12 Phil did not want the boats to get here this soon.
13 Loris Shin has been ill; Frank, a doctor, saw her.

8d Textbook Keying

1. Key each line once.
2. Keep your eyes on the textbook copy.

reach review
14 ws ws hj hj tf tf ol ol rf rf ed ed cd cd bf bf p;
15 wed bid has old hold rid heed heed car bed pot pot

g
16 gf gf gin gin rig ring go gone no nog sign got dog
17 to go|to go|go on|go in|go in|to go in|in the sign

?
18 ?; ?;? who? when? where? how? what? who? It is he?
19 Is she? Is he? Did I lose Paul? Is Gabe all right?

Writing 43: 85 *gwam*

Business letters can be defined by their goals; for example, a letter of inquiry, a reply letter, a promotion letter, a credit letter, or other specialized letter. While you learn to compose these letters, just keep each letter's individual goals always in front of you. If you fix in your mind a theme, a pattern, an idea for your writing, composing good business letters may emerge as one of the best tricks in your bag.

Competent business writers know what they want to say—and they say it with simplicity and clarity. Words are the utensils they use to convey ideas or to convince others to accomplish some action. The simple word and the short sentence usually are more effective than the big word and the involved sentence. But don't be afraid of the long or unusual word if it means exactly what you intend to say in your business letter.

Writing 44: 90 *gwam*

Although many of us are basically comfortable with sameness and appear to dislike change, we actually prize variation. We believe that we are each unique individuals, yet we know that we are really only a little different; and we struggle to find "sense of self" in how we think and act. Our cars, too, built on assembly lines are basically identical; yet when we purchase one, we choose the model, color, size, and style which suits us individually.

Also many people expect to create security by buying things that are in keeping with society's "image" and "status." But what we think of as "status" always changes. The wise buyer will buy those items that give most in utility, comfort, and satisfaction. Status should just be a thing we create in ourselves, not a thing created for us. Common sense should guide us in making good decisions—and if our "status" is increased thereby, well, why not?

Writing 45: 95 *gwam*

Normally, customers just do not abandon a firm because of a mistake. All firms will make mistakes at one time or another. The way aproblem is resolved is far more crucial than the fact that a problem existed. More customers leave a firm and take their business to a competitor because they get upset with an employee than for any other reason. The key qualifications for a customer service employee are superb human relations skills and product and service knowledge.

New Keys

8e x and u

© Cengage Learning

x Reach *down* with *left third* finger.

© Cengage Learning

u Reach *up* with *right first* finger.

Concentrate on correct reaches.

x

20 x x xs xs ox ox lox sox fox box ex hex lax hex fax
21 sx six sax sox ax fix cox wax hex box pox sex text
22 flax next flex axel pixel exit oxen taxi axis next

u

23 u uj uj jug jut just dust dud due sue use due duel
24 uj us cud but bun out sun nut gun hut hue put fuel
25 dual laud dusk suds fuss full tuna tutus duds full

Skill Building

8f Improve Keystroking

Think and key phrases.

26 Paige Power liked the book; Josh can read it next.
27 Next we picked a bag for Jan; then she, Jan, left.
28 Is her June account due? Has Jo ruined her credit?
29 nut cue hut sun rug us six cut dug axe rag fox run
30 out of the sun|cut the action|a fox den|fun at six
31 That car is not junk; it can run in the next race.

wordwrap ↓

8g Timed Writing

1. Take two 1' timed writings. If you finish before time is up, begin again. (The dot above various words equals 2 *gwam*; each number is another 4 *gwam*.)

2. Use wordwrap; do not tap ENTER at the end of lines.

3. Log out of *KPDO*.

Goal: 14 *gwam*

```
        •           4           •           8           •
How a finished job will look often depends on how
    12              •           16          •           20
we feel about our work as we do it. Attitude has
        •           24          •           28          •
a definite effect on the end result of work we do.
```
Tap ENTER once
```
        •           4           •           8           •
When we are eager to begin a job, we relax and do
    12              •           16          •           20
better work than if we start the job with an idea
        •           24          •           28          •
that there is just nothing we can do to escape it.
```

Writing 40: 70 gwam

Foreign study and travel take extra time and effort, but these two activities quickly help us to understand people. Much can be learned from other cultures. Today, business must think globally. Learning about the culture of others is not a luxury. Even the owner of a very small business realizes that he or she cannot just focus on the domestic scene.

Many examples can be used to show how a local business may be influenced by global competition. A hair stylist may be required to learn European styles because customers may want to try a style just like they saw on their travels. Or salons may want to offer additional services such as facials that people have tried while they were traveling abroad.

Writing 41: 75 gwam

Getting a job interview is certainly a triumph for a job seeker. Yet anxiety quickly sets in as the applicant becomes aware of the competition. The same attention to details that you used in writing the successful resume should be used for the interview. Experts often say that the first four or five minutes are the most important in making a strong impact on the interviewers.

First, people focus on what they see. Posture, eye contact, facial expression, and gestures make up over half of the message. Next, people focus on what they hear; enthusiasm, delivery, pace, volume, and clarity are as vital as what is said. Finally, people get to the actual words that are said. You can make a good impression. But, realize, you may have just four minutes.

Writing 42: 80 gwam

Would a pitcher go to the mound without warming up? Would a speaker go to the podium without practice? Of course not! These experts have spent many long hours striving to do their best. Similarly, the performance of business employees is rated. The manager's evaluation will include a record of actual performance and a list of new goals. A good mark in any of these areas will demand much hard work.

Many work factors can be practiced to help one succeed on the job. Class attendance and punctuality can be perfected by students. Because work is expected to be correct, managers do not assign zeros. Thus, students must learn to proofread their own work. A project must also be completed quickly. Students can learn to organize work and time well and to find ways to do their work smarter and faster.

Lesson 8R Review

Warmup *Lesson 8Ra Warmup*

reach review 1	Jack is glad about the response to the fundraiser.
p 2	The local paper printed their public opinion poll.
b 3	Four babies babbled as big bears rode brown bikes.
easy 4	The newest prices were not given to her and to me.

Skill Building

8Rb Textbook Keying

1. Key each line once.
2. Keep your eyes on the copy.

> **Move fingers up and down without moving your hands.**

home row	5 add hash shall slash salads flags alfalfa fall ask
	6 A fresh salad dish was added for staff and guests.
third row	7 tire wrote rewrite ripe proper papers trip picture
	8 A reporter edited the newspaper stories with ease.
1st/2nd fingers	9 returned guest changes kicked tonight flight drink
	10 Ed kept doing kind deeds for the children in need.

8Rc Timed Writing

1. Take two 1' timed writings. If you finish before time is up, begin again.
2. Use wordwrap; do not tap ENTER at the ends of the lines.

gwam 1'

Luck comes to those who are prepared for it. Think	10
about what is needed to be where one should be in a	21
decade. What will it take? Will it take additional	31
education or perhaps just other experience? One sets	41
a large goal and then works through a series of other	52
lesser goals to get there. One needs to be able to	62
know what success looks like as one finishes one of	73
the goals to get to the next one. If one does it	83
well, people will think it was all luck.	91

| 1 | 2 | 3 | 4 | 5 | 6 | 7 | 8 | 9 | 10 |

8Rd Enrichment

1. In the Word Processor, key two 30" timings on each line. Try to increase your speed the second time.
2. Log out of *KPDO*.

We use the web and work online.
We shop online and use social networks.
The web helps us as we work and share data.
While working online, we need to keep our data safe.

Writing 37: 55 *gwam*

A crucial life skill is being able to put things in proper perspective. Individuals often fail to realize that many things are just not worth fighting about. An effective way to learn quickly whether an issue is worth fighting for is to view it from a long-term perspective.

If you will care five or six years from now that you defended an issue, it is a principle worth defending. However, if you will not remember, the situation does not justify the effort required for defending it. Consider your odds of winning. Why fight a losing battle?

Writing 38: 60 *gwam*

Why do we remember some things and forget others? Often, we associate loss of memory with aging or an illness such as Alzheimer's disease. However, the crux of the matter is that we all forget various things that we prefer to remember. We tend to remember things that mean something special to us.

For many people, recalling dates is a difficult task; yet they manage to remember dates of special occasions, such as birthdays. Processing information requires one not only to hear but to ponder and to understand what you heard. We recall things that we say and do longer than things we hear and see.

Writing 39: 65 *gwam*

Humor is very important in our professional and our personal lives. Fortunately, we realize that many things can and do go wrong. If we can learn to laugh at ourselves and with other people, we will get through the terrible times. Adding a little extra laughter can help put the situation in proper perspective much quicker.

Maintaining our sense of humor lets us enjoy our positions to a greater degree. No one is perfect, and we cannot expect perfection from ourselves. However, the quality of our performance is greater when we do the things we like. We realize our prime time is devoted to work. Thus, enjoying the time at work is very important.

Lesson 9 Q, M, V, Apostrophe

all letters	1	Lex gripes about cold weather; Fred is not joking.
space bar	2	Is it Di, Jo, or Al? Ask Lt. Coe, Bill; She knows.
easy	3	We did rush a bushel of cut corn to the six ducks.
easy	4	He is to go to the Tudor Isle of England on a bus.

New Keys

9b q and m

q Reach *up* with *left fourth* finger.

m Reach *down* with *right first* finger.

q

5 q qa qa quad quad quaff quant queen quo quit quick
6 qa qu qa quo quit quod quid quip quads quote quiet
7 quite quilts quart quill quakes quail quack quaint

m

8 m mj mj jam man malt mar max maw me mew men hem me
9 m mj ma am make male mane melt meat mist amen lame
10 malt meld hemp mimic tomb foam rams mama mire mind

9c All Reaches Learned

11 Quin had some quiet qualms about taming a macaque.
12 Jake Coxe had questions about a new floor program.
13 Max was quick to join the big reception for Lidia.

9d Textbook Keying

1. Key each line once; keep your elbows at your side.
2. Keep your eyes on the textbook copy.

m/x
14 me men ma am jam am lax, mix jam; the hem, six men
15 Emma Max expressed an aim to make a mammoth model.

q/u
16 qa qu aqua aqua quit quit quip quite pro quo squad
17 Did Quin make a quick request to take the Qu exam?

g/n
18 fg gn gun gun dig dig nag snag snag sign grab grab
19 Georgia hung a sign in front of the union for Gib.

Skill Builder 5

1. Key a 1' writing on each paragraph.
2. Practice each ¶ in a set until you can complete it in 1' with no more than one error.
3. Take a 3' writing; strive to maintain your 1' rate.
4. Move onto the next set. Notice that each set progresses by 5 words.

Writing 34: 40 *gwam*

"An ounce of prevention is worth a pound of cure" is really based on fact; still, many people comprehend this statement more for its quality as literature than on a practical, common-sense philosophy.

Just take health, for example. We agonize over stiff costs we pay to recover from illnesses; but, on the other hand, we give little or no attention to health requirements for diet, exercise, and sleep.

Writing 35: 45 *gwam*

Problems with our environment show an odd lack of foresight. We just expect that whatever we may need to support life will be available. We rarely question our comforts, even though they may abuse our earth, water, and air.

Optimism is an excellent virtue. It is comforting to think that, eventually, everything can be fixed. So why should we worry? A better idea, certainly, is to realize that we don't have to fix anything we have not yet broken.

Writing 36: 50 *gwam*

Recently, a friend of mine grumbled about how quickly papers accumulated on her desk; she never seemed able to reduce them to zero. She said some law seemed to be working that expanded the stack today by precisely the amount she reduced it yesterday.

She should organize her papers and tend to them daily. Any paper that needs a look, a decision, and speedy, final action gets just that; any that needs closer attention is subject to a fixed completion schedule. Self-discipline is the key to order.

9e v and ' (apostrophe)

v Reach *down* with *left first* finger.

' Reach to the *right* with the *right fourth* finger.

Apostrophe: The apostrophe shows (1) omission (as Rob't for Robert or it's for it is) or (2) possession when used with nouns (as Joe's hat).

v

20 v vf vf vie vie via via vim vat vow vile vale vote

21 vf vf ave vet ova eve vie dive five live have lave

22 cove dove over aver vivas hive volt five java jive

' (apostrophe)

23 '; '; it's it's Rod's; it's Bo's hat; we'll do it.

24 We don't know if it's Lee's pen or Norma's pencil.

25 It's ten o'clock; I won't tell him that he's late.

Skill Building

9f Improve Keystroking

26 It's Viv's turn to drive Iva's van to Ava's house.

v/? 27 Qua, not Vi, took the jet; so did Owen. Didn't he?

28 Wasn't Vada Baxter a judge at the post garden show?

29 Viola said she has moved six times in five months.

30 Does Dave live on Vines Avenue? Must he leave now?

q/? 31 Did Viv vote? Can Paque move it? Did Valerie quit?

32 Didn't Raquel quit Carl Quent after their quarrel?

9g Timed Writing

1. Take a 1' timing on each paragraph. If you finish before time is up, start the paragraph again. The dots equal 2 words. Use wordwrap.

2. Finish the lesson; log out of *KPDO*.

wordwrap↓

The questions of time use are vital ones; we miss
so much just because we don't plan. If we structure
our week, we save time for those extra premium
things we long to do.
List the tasks to be done for the week and then
place importance on each one. Complete the tasks in
order of importance.

a. *Sadie*: Size 1.8" high; flip the image horizontally; apply a Bevel Rectangle picture style.

b. *Lizzie 2*: Size 1.5" high; apply a Metal Rounded Rectangle picture style.

c. *Andy couch*: Size 2" high; adjust Corrections: Brightness: +20% Contrast: +40%; apply a Drop Shadow Rectangle picture style.

d. *Henry and Choo*: Size 1.9" high; adjust Corrections: Brightness: +40% Contrast: 0% (Normal); apply a Bevel Perspective Left, White picture style.

e. *Molly 2*: Size 2" high; adjust Corrections: Brightness: +40% Contrast: +20%; apply a Snip Diagonal Corner, White picture style.

f. *Coco 2*: Size 2.3" high; apply a Bevel Rectangle picture style.

9. Insert the Integral footer; show the footer on both pages. Key the address in the left placeholder rather than the author's name: **186 Hess Boulevard, Austin, TX 78712-2149**

10. Preview the document. Check to see that it is a two-page document and that the pictures are placed and sized appropriately.

11. Proofread and check the document; click Exit *Word*. (19-d11)

12. Click Log out to exit *KPDO*.

© Golden Pixels LLC/Shutterstock.com

! WORKPLACE SUCCESS

Influencing Others

Effective leaders can influence others to do things even though they have no authority over them. The ability to influence others is a valuable career skill for upward job mobility.

There is no one right or wrong way to go about influencing others. However, effective leaders tend to use techniques that have common characteristics. Some examples are:

- They approach the situation from the perspective of the other person rather than from their own. They have learned how to use empathy effectively.

- They make the effort to show the benefits to the other person.

- They try to get agreement on the big concepts before getting into the details that bog people down.

- They use good human relations skills and make it easy for the other person to grant requests.

Participating in meetings with individuals from different departments provides an excellent opportunity to learn how to influence other people. A good way to get started is to observe leaders who are able to bring a group to a consensus even though the discussion might have begun with very diverse positions. Meetings provide an opportunity to demonstrate good communication skills, leadership skills, and good time management and organization skills as well as good negotiation skills.

Lesson 9R Review

all reaches	1	Quij produces both fine work and excellent volume.
g/?	2	Did he go? Where is Gianna? Did George go golfing?
b/p	3	Paul has pictures of bears, bats, pigs, and bison.
easy	4	Paige is to go in a taxi to the address we stated.

Skill Building

> **Work for smoothness, not speed.**

9Rb Textbook Keying

1. Key each line once.
2. Keep your eyes on the copy.

Apostrophe	5	I'll she'll o'clock we're didn't she's isn't don't
	6	one's job; Donnel's, gov't, it's time; p's and q's
	7	Spell out it's, doesn't, can't, gov't, and she'll.
q	8	netiquette queue quench quad FAQ quotes quit quest
	9	Quen asked a question; eat a quince; make it quick
	10	Quotes on quotas of useful equipment are required.
v	11	voice invert evoke vital prove event vacuum valid
	12	improve best speed; strive high; have clear vision
	13	Dev found five favorite websites for French class.

9Rc Timed Writing

1. Take two 1' timings on paragraph 1. If you finish before time is up, begin again.
2. Take a 2' timing on both paragraphs.
3 Log out of *KPDO* when you are finished.

Goal: 13 *gwam*

wordwrap *gwam* 1' 2'

	1'	2'
Drill practice is a good thing to do to help with	10	5
speed and control. To get the most out of practice,	20	10
use the drills that help with the most common	30	15
problems. Finger and row drills are often used. Work	40	20
is often needed with the first, second, third, and	50	25
fourth fingers and rows. Work on the use of the shift	61	31
for capital letters as needed.	67	34
Work with double letters and letters next to each	10	39
other, as these letters often cause problems in	20	43
words. Spacing can also be a major concern, so	29	48
practice in the use of the space bar will help. Be	39	53
sure to review the required drills, and work on what	50	59
seems to help the most.	54	61

```
1' |  1  |  2  |  3  |  4  |  5  |  6  |  7  |  8  |  9  |  10  |
2' |     1     |     2     |     3     |     4     |     5     |
```

Hess Pet Center News and Views

Hess Pet Center now provides full-service, luxury pet care. Our services are now offered to owners of both dogs and cats. Our survey to all of our current clients strongly endorsed broadening our services to include cats.

Grand Opening—Huge Success

Thanks to all of you who turned out for the Grand Opening ceremony. The attendance far exceeded our expectations and was a fun event for both owners and pets. Many clients enjoyed the tour of the new cat facility and meeting the new veterinarian who specializes in medical services for cats. Sadie was the first to use these new facilities.

Picture-Taking Sessions

We encourage all clients to have pictures taken of their pets. The schedule is posted in the main office and on our website. Your written permission is required to feature the pets in our publications and on the website. The form is provided at the picture taking sessions. Lizzie was the first to have her picture taken.

Suites

Andy laid first claim to reservations in one of the luxury suites and tried out the new leather

couch that arrived this week. Three levels of luxury suites are available in addition to the standard units. Luxury suites feature all of the comforts of home—couches, comfortable beds, rugs, toys, windows, climate control, premium food, a play yard, and a homey atmosphere.

Multiple Pets Per Unit

Standard units can accommodate two or three small or medium-size dogs or cats. All three levels of luxury suites are large enough to accommodate any size pet. Henry and Choo were happy that they can stay together in one of the luxury suites with comfortable furniture and a climbing tree.

186 HESS BOULEVARD, AUSTIN, TX 78712-2149 1

Grooming and Spa

Professional groomers pamper your pet with all natural products at the grooming salon and spa. Standard grooming services include:

 Bathing
 Trimming
 Scissor finishing
 Nail trimming
 Ear cleaning
 Teeth brushing

Molly particularly likes the sumptuous spa treatments including whirlpool and massage therapy. Massage therapy increases circulation, relaxes muscles, and stimulates the skin. Grooming and spa services are available by special appointment, while your pet is boarding, or in Doggy Day Camp.

Hess Pet Center Boutique

The Boutique provides one-stop shopping to meet all of your cat or dog's needs.

 Scientifically prepared food
 Treats
 Beds
 Carriers
 Bowls and dishes
 Collars, harnesses, and leashes
 Natural grooming products
 Coats, raincoats, and sweaters
 Toys
 Pet staircases
 Grooming tools

Doggie Day Camp

Day camp is a wonderful experience for daytime pet accommodations. Day camp includes supervised play, games, exercises, treats, and socialization with other pets. Coco does not like to be left behind when the family

goes on trips, but she is a regular at day camp and particularly enjoys playing with other campers in the outdoor play area. A 500-square-foot indoor pet romping room is available during inclement weather. Coco prefers the outdoor area, but enjoys the indoor facilities too. Both facilities are supervised by trained staff.

Total Professional Care

Board-certified veterinarians and highly trained technicians provide the highest level of pet care using state-of-the-art technology. Medical services for both dogs and cats include:

 Comprehensive physical exams
 Immunizations
 Preventive medicine
 Microchip database
 All areas of internal medicine
 Surgical services
 Radiology
 Dental care
 Nutritional specialists
 Pharmacy
 Pain management
 Hospice service

186 HESS BOULEVARD, AUSTIN, TX 78712-2149 2

1. In a new document, apply Narrow margins.

2. Tap ENTER once and insert the *hpc logo* data file; apply Tight Text Wrapping.

3. Key **HPC News and Views**; tap ENTER twice. Select the text and apply 28-point, Dark Red, Accent 1 font and bold to the title. Insert 18-point space before the title.

4. Move your insertion point down one space (do not tap ENTER again). The font should be Normal, 11-point, Automatic color. With the Insertion point at the first ¶ marker below the title, insert a Continuous section break.

5. On the line below the section break, insert the *hpc newsletter* data file. With the insertion point at the beginning of the inserted text, format into two columns.

6. Format all headings using Intense Emphasis and apply bold. Make sure headings stay with the text that follows. Insert column breaks or use Keep lines together, if necessary.

7. Change the bullets by using the bullet (◈) from the Wingdings 2 font. Use Decrease Indent to position the bullets at the left edge of the column.

8. Insert the pet pictures from the data files in the order indicated and apply the formats specified for each photo. Crop each picture close to the image of the pet, as shown in the illustration above. Compress all pictures and apply Tight Text Wrapping.

(continued)

Lesson 10 Z, Y, Quotation Mark, Tab

 Warmup *Lesson 10a Warmup*

all letters	1	Quill owed those back taxes after moving to Japan.
spacing	2	Didn't Vi, Max, and Quaid go? Someone did; I know.
q/v/m	3	Marv was quite quick to remove that mauve lacquer.
easy	4	Lana is a neighbor; she owns a lake and an island.

New Keys

10b Learn z and y

z Reach *down* with *left fourth* finger.

y Reach *up* with *right first* finger.

Curve the little finger tightly to reach down and in for the z key.

z

5 za za zap zap zing zig zag zoo zed zip zap zig zed
6 doze zeal zero haze jazz zone zinc zing size ozone
7 ooze maze doze zoom zarf zebus daze gaze faze adze

y

8 y yj yj jay jay hay hay lay nay say days eyes ayes
9 yj ye yet yen yes cry dry you rye sty your fry wry
10 ye yen bye yea coy yew dye yaw lye yap yak yon any

10c All Reaches Learned

11 Did you say Liz saw any yaks or zebus at your zoo?
12 Relax; Jake wouldn't acquire any favorable rights.
13 Has Zack departed? Alex, Joy, and I will go alone.

10d Textbook Keying
Key each line once.

14 Cecilia brings my jumbo umbrella to every concert.

direct reach 15 John and Kim recently brought us an old art piece.

16 I built a gray brick border around my herb garden.

17 sa ui hj gf mn vc ew uy re io as lk rt jk df op yu

Adjacent reach 18 In Ms. Lopez' opinion, the opera was really great.

19 Polly and I were joining Walker at the open house.

19-d10

Itinerary

itinerary form

To use the Quick Parts itinerary created in *19-d9* do the following:

1. In a blank document screen, change to Narrow margins and the Ion theme.
2. Insert the HPC Itinerary Quick Part and prepare an itinerary for Mr. Schmidt using the information below.

(**Note:** If you are using another computer, use the itinerary form data file.)

3. Preview and check; click Next Activity. (*19-d10*)

Trip: Chicago, Illinois Tuesday, March 12 - Thursday, March 14, 201-

Destination/Purpose: Meet in Chicago with potential suppliers of upscale merchandise for the Pet Boutique

Departure: March 12; Midtown Airlines; depart on Flight 2846 at 5:45 p.m.

Flight connections: One stop in Atlanta; same aircraft; arrive 7:45 p.m.

Ground transportation: Picked up by Executive Cars; Confirmation #OH493802; 312.555.0121

Hotel: Chicago Levernoir, 725 N. Michigan Avenue; Confirmation #87B0376519

Return: March 14; Midtown Airlines; Flight 8937 at 7:45 a.m.

Flight connections: Direct, nonstop flight; arrives 9:43 a.m.

Wednesday, March 13 Breakfast: 7:15 | Hotel Lobby
8:30 | Roger Demus, Elegant Puppy Mart, 312.555.0136 | 34 E. Division Street

10:30 | Mark Lane, Chicago Pet Spa Supplies, 312.555.0196 | 17 E. Scott Street

Lunch: 12:15 | Lynn Marcus, Marcus Pet Boutique Supplies, 312.555.0137 | Hotel Levernoir Bistro

2:00 | Martin Walker, Anna Metz, and Leslie Walker, Walker Furniture, 312.555.0186 | 2408 S. State Street

4:00 | Leon Ranson and Jan Anders, Pet Boutique Specialties, 312.555.0147 | Meet in hotel lobby; drive to Pet Boutique Specialties

Dinner: 8:30 | Elaine Beswick, President, and Rae LaFevre, Design Director, Pet Boutique Specialties | Charlie Truluck Restaurant

Comments: Reservations for lunch and dinner are in your name.

19-d11

Newsletter

hpc logo
hpc newsletter
sadie
lizzie 2
andy couch
henry and choo
molly 2
coco 2

Hess Pet Center will use the newsletter you design as the standard style for all newsletters in the future. The body of the newsletter has already been keyed; you will insert the text and format it. Before you begin, review the illustrations on the next page. Pay particular attention to the following items:

- Placement of logo and text for the banner heading.
- Placement of the pictures of pets that are featured throughout the newsletter.
- Type and position of the bullets used.
- Format of the headings.

New Keys

10e Learn " (quotation mark) and TAB

" Shift; then reach to the *right* with the *right fourth* finger.

© Cengage Learning

TAB Reach *up* with *left fourth* finger.

© Cengage Learning

" (quotation mark)

20 ";"; " " "web" "media" "videos" I like "texting."
21 "I am not," she said, "going." I just said, "Why?"

TAB key

22　　The tab key is used for indenting paragraphs and aligning columns.
23　　Tabs that are set by the software are called default tabs, which are usually a half inch.

Skill Building

10f Textbook Keying

Key each line once. Tap TAB to indent each paragraph. Use wordwrap, tapping ENTER only at the end of each paragraph.

24　　The expression "I give you my word," or put another
25 way, "Take my word for it," is just a way I can say, "I
26 prize my name; it clearly stands in back of my words."
27 I offer "honor" as collateral.
tab 28　　Tap the tab key and begin the line without a pause to maintain fluency.
29　　She said that this is the lot to be sent; I agreed with her.
30　　Tap Tab before starting to key a timed writing so that the first line is indented.

10g Timed Writing

1. Take two 1' timed writings. If you finish before time is up, begin again.
2. End the lesson and log out of *KPDO*.

Goal: 15 *gwam*

E　**ALL LETTERS**

　　　　　　　　　　　　　　　　　　　　wordwrap　*gwam*　1'

Tab → All of us work for progress, but it is not　9
always easy to analyze "progress." We work hard for　19
it; but, in spite of some really good efforts, we may　29
fail to get just exactly the response we want.　39

Tab → When this happens, as it does to all of us, it　9
is time to cease whatever we are doing, have a quiet　20
talk with ourselves, and face up to the questions　29
about our limited progress. How can we do better?　39

| 1 | 2 | 3 | 4 | 5 | 6 | 7 | 8 | 9 | 10 |

Mr. Schmidt travels frequently to visit with suppliers for Hess Pet Center. Create a form using a table for these types of trips. You will use this form to prepare an itinerary for Mr. Schmidt's trip.

1. Use Narrow margins. Tap ENTER once and insert a 2-column, 18-row table: apply List Table 3 – Accent 3 style. Place brackets around the variable information that will be selected and replaced.

2. Merge and format the first row as follows: change cell height to 1.2"; apply 20-point font to the first line and 16-point font to the next three lines. Apply Align Center to text.

3. Format the remaining rows 0.4" high and apply Align Center Left to all text.

4. Key the table as shown below. Adjust column widths as indicated.

5. After completing the travel information section, merge the cells in row 9 and leave it blank.

6. Split each of the columns in the remaining rows and format them as shown.

7. Apply Bold to the headings in row 10. Make sure all items in column A are still bold.

8. In the last row (*Other Activities or Comments*), merge cells B, C, and D.

9. Use Select All and save as a Quick Part with the name and description: **HPC Itinerary**. Select the option Insert content in its own page.

10. Proofread and check; click Next Activity. (*19-d9*)

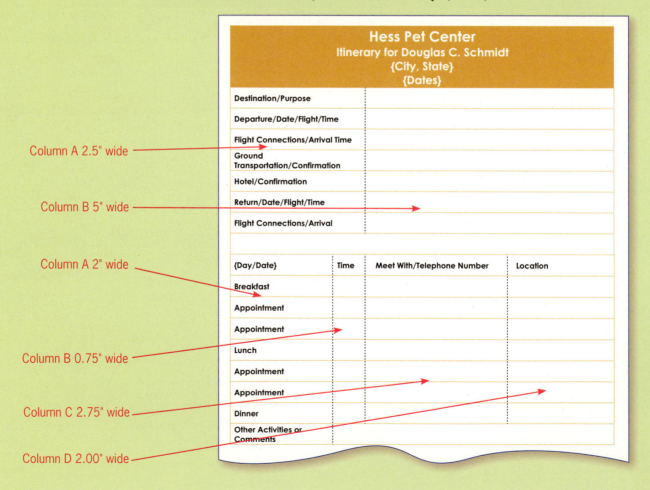

Column A 2.5" wide

Column B 5" wide

Column A 2" wide

Column B 0.75" wide

Column C 2.75" wide

Column D 2.00" wide

Lesson 11 Review

alphabet 1 Zeb had Jewel quickly give him five or six points.
" (quote) 2 Can you spell "chaos," "bias," "bye," and "their"?
y 3 Ty Clay may envy you for any zany plays you write.
easy 4 Did he bid on the bicycle, or did he bid on a map?

Skill Building

11b Improve Keystroking

Work for smoothness, not speed.

5 za za zap az az maze zoo zip razz zed zax zoa zone
6 Liz Zahl saw Zoe feed the zebra in an Arizona zoo.

7 yj yj jy jy joy lay yaw say yes any yet my try you
8 Why do you say that today, Thursday, is my payday?

9 xs xs sax ox box fix hex ax lax fox taxi lox sixes
10 Roxy, you may ask Jay to fix any tax sets for you.

11 qa qa aqua quail quit quake quid equal quiet quart
12 Did Enrique quietly but quickly quell the quarrel?

13 fv fv five lives vow ova van eve avid vex vim void
14 Has Vivi, Vada, or Eva visited Vista Valley Farms?

11c Build Skill

Key balanced-hand words quickly and as phrases to increase speed.

15 is to for do an may work so it but an with them am
16 am yam map aid zig yams ivy via vie quay cob amend

17 to do is for an may work so it but am an with them
18 for it|for it|to the|to the|do they|do they|do it

19 Pamela may go to the farm with Jan and a neighbor.
20 Rod and Ty may go by the lake if they go downtown.

The hpc Wellness Plan (Title style)

For Healthy and Happy Pets (Subtitle style)

Many families that own pets think of those pets as part of their family. Today, families express more concern about wellness for their families than was the case some years ago. And, not surprisingly, that concern also applies to the wellness of their pets. Many clients have asked hpc to provide them with sound information in a non-technical manner about wellness for pets. This report is designed to address issues of wellness for pets and to announce the new hpc Wellness Plan.

Wellness for Pets (Heading 1 style)

When you ask people what they think should be included in a successful wellness program for their families, most people will provide a list of items such as the one that follows.

- Good nutrition
- Exercise to improve fitness
- Drink a substantial amount of water
- Weight control
- Preventive health care
- Preventive dental care
- Effective medical care when needed
- Avoidance of bad habits
- Effective social interaction
- Safety awareness—avoiding hazardous situations

Interestingly, the list provided was developed by a leading authority on preventive health care for pets, Dr. Monica C. Bradford. While many differences exist in the health-care needs of pets compared to the needs of their owners, many similarities also exist. Dr. Bradford says that common sense is the key to wellness for pets.

hpc Wellness Plan (Heading 1 style)

In response to the many requests from clients, eaf interviewed a young veterinarian (Guidice), who is a former student of Dr. Bradford's, and whose research focuses on the components of effective pet wellness programs. As a result of that interview, Dr. Guidice was hired to develop the hpc Wellness Program. Dr. Guidice currently serves as the director of the program. In addition to the standard components listed above, the program utilizes highly trained technicians to monitor pet health and wellness.

(Insert *wellness report* data file here.)

11d Textbook Keying

Key each line once.

Key smoothly without looking at fingers.

```
        21  Make the return snappily
        22  and with assurance; keep
enter   23  your eyes on your source
        24  data; maintain a smooth,
        25  constant pace as you key.
```

© Cengage Learning

When spacing, use a down-and-in motion.

```
space bar  26  us me it of he an by do go to us if or so am ah el
           27  To enter the website, key "Guest" as the password.
```

Press Caps Lock key to toggle on or off.

```
caps lock  28  Use ALL CAPS for items such as TO, FROM, or SUBJECT.
           29  Did Kristin mean Kansas City, MISSOURI, or KANSAS?
```

11e Timed Writing

1. Take two 1' timed writings. If you finish before time is up, begin again. The dot above words represents 2 *gwam*.
2. End the lesson.

Goal: 16 *gwam*

```
                                    wordwrap      gwam 1'  2'
              •              4              •              8
      Have  we  thought  of  communication  as  a  kind    8 | 4
       •           12          •              16
 of war that we wage through each day?                     16 | 8
              •              4              •              8
      When  we  think  of  it  that  way,  good  language  24 | 12
       •           12          •              16
 would seem to become our major line of attack.            34 | 17
              •              4              •              8
      Words  become  muscle;  in a  normal  exchange or in 43 | 22
   •           12          •              16         •           20
 a quarrel, we do well to realize the power of words.      53 | 27
```

11f Game

Use the game to showcase your skills.

11g Enrichment

1. Click the Skill Building tab from the main menu and choose Technique Builder; select Drill 1a.

2. Key Drill 1a from page 37. Key each line once, striving for good accuracy.

3. The results will be listed on the Skill Building Report.

Maggie Coco Molly Andy Lizzie

Join your friends and their families
for the
Grand Opening of the expanded facilities
located in Hess Office Park
Refreshments, tours, and seminars
Sunday, April 14, 3:30 p.m.
at the
Hess Pet Center
186 Hess Boulevard
Austin

Join your friends and their families

for the

Grand Opening of the expanded facilities

located in Hess Office Park

Refreshments, tours, and seminars

Sunday, April 14, 3:30 p.m.

at the

Hess Pet Center

186 Hess Boulevard

Austin

19-d8

Unbound Report

wellness report
hpc cover page

★ TIP

Remember to break the link between the sections for both the header and the footer. Set the number on the first page of the report to 1. The pages should be in the following order: cover page, table of contents, page 1 of report, page 2 of report (which should be the only page with a page number).

The veterinary staff has drafted the information for a report to distribute to clients. They have asked you to prepare the report.

1. Key the report on the next page as an unbound report.

2. Apply custom dog bullets for the items that are bulleted.

3. Insert the *wellness report* data file where noted. Apply the formats noted in the comments; then delete all comments.

4. Insert a Next Page break at the beginning of the document and insert the *hpc cover page* data file. Fill in the placeholder information and add a ½-pt Dark Red, Accent 1 Box border to the cover page only.

5. Number the pages using Rounded Rectangle 3 at the top of the page. Do not show the page number on the cover page or first page of the report.

6. Insert another Next Page break on the first page of the report and generate a table of contents using Automatic Table 2 style.

7. Preview to ensure that the format is correct and that pages are numbered correctly. If necessary, update the table of contents.

8. Proofread and check; click Next Activity. (*19-d8*)

Lesson 12 Review

alphabet 1 Jack won five quiz games; Brad will play him next.
q 2 Quin Racq quickly and quietly quelled the quarrel.
z 3 Zaret zipped along sizzling, zigzag Arizona roads.
easy 4 Did he hang the sign by the big bush at the lake?

Skill Building

12b Improve Keystroking

b/f 5 bf bf fab fab ball bib rf rf rib rib fibs bums bee
6 Did Buffy remember that he is a brass band member?

z/y 7 za za zag zig zip yj yj jay eye day lazy hazy zest
8 Liz amazed us with the zesty pizza on a lazy trip.

q/u 9 qa qa quo qt. quit quay quad quarm que uj jug quay
10 Where is Quito? Qatar? Boqueirao? Quebec? Quilmes?

v/m 11 vf vf valve five value mj mj ham mad mull mass vim
12 Vito, enter the words vim, vivace, and avar; save.

all 13 I faced defeat; only reserves saved my best crews.
14 In my opinion, I need to rest in my reserved seat.

all 15 Holly created a red poppy and deserves art awards.
16 My pump averages a faster rate; we get better oil.

Keep fingers curved and body aligned properly.

12c Textbook Keying
Key each line once.

de/ed 17 ed fed led deed dell dead deal sled desk need seed
18 Dell dealt with the deed before the dire deadline.

ol/lo 19 old tolls doll solo look sole lost love cold stole
20 Old Ole looked for the long lost olive oil lotion.

op/po 21 pop top post rope pout port stop opal opera report
22 Stop to read the top opera opinion report to Opal.

we/ew 23 we few wet were went wears weather skews stew blew
24 Working women wear sweaters when weather dictates.

Ann Taylor	Technician, Internal Medicine
David P. Guidice, DVM	Director, Wellness Program
Lynn West	Technician, Wellness Program
Retail and Service Operations	
dcs	Managing Partner
Student's Name	Office Manager
Jan Cotter	Intern
Lynn Babcock	Manager, Grooming and Spa
Mark Jones	Assistant Manager, Grooming and Spa
Aaron Barr	Manager, Boutique
JoAnn Jameson	Assistant Manager, Boutique
Lisa Owens	Manager, Boarding and Pet Care
Jan Marcus	Assistant Manager, Boarding and Pet Care

19-d7

Invitation

maggie
coco
molly
andy
lizzie

1. In a new document, change the top margin to 0.5" and apply a ½-point Dark Red, Accent 1 Box border to the page. Use the Page Color Fill Effects and apply the Parchment texture.

2. Insert the five pictures from the data files in the order listed. Crop the pictures close to each dog, as shown in the illustration on the next page; apply Square Text Wrapping. Size each picture 2" high. Position the pictures against the top border and within the side borders. Make the following picture corrections:

 a. *Maggie*: Sharpen: 25%; Brightness: 0% Contrast: +20%.

 b. *Coco*: Sharpen: 25%; Brightness: +20% Contrast: +20%.

 c. *Molly*: Sharpen: 25%; Brightness: +20% Contrast: +20%.

 d. *Andy*: Sharpen: 25%; Brightness: +20% Contrast: +20%.

 e. *Lizzie*: Sharpen: 25%; Brightness: +40% Contrast: +20%. Flip the picture horizontally.

3. Draw a text box directly below the pictures; size it 0.3" high and extend it from side border to side border.

 a. Apply Dark Red, Accent 1 Shape Outline.

 b. Click in the text box and apply Shape Fill, No Fill.

 c. Set left-align tabs at 0.25", 2", 3.5", 5.25", and 6.75".

 d. Key the names of the dogs in the order shown above at each of the tab stops; apply Dark Red, Accent 1 font color and bold italic.

4. Tap ENTER five times after the text box and key the text for the invitation; center the text. Apply Lucida Calligraphy, 18-point, Dark Red, Accent 1 font.

5. Proofread and check; click Next Activity. (*19-d7*)

(continued)

12d Textbook Keying

Key each line once.

```
25  a for we you is that be this will be a to and well
26  as our with I or a to by your form which all would
27  new year no order they so new but now year who may

28  This is Lyn's only date to visit their great city.
29  I can send it to your office at any time you wish.
30  She kept the fox, owls, and fowl down by the lake.

31  Harriette will cook dinner for the swimming teams.
32  Annette will call at noon to give us her comments.
33  Johnny was good at running and passing a football.
```

12e Timed Writing

1. Take a 2' timed writing. If you finish before time is up, begin again.
2. Use wordwrap.
3. End the lesson.

Goal: 16 *gwam*

E ALL LETTERS

Copy Difficulty

What factors determine whether copy is difficult or easy? Research shows that difficulty is influenced by syllables per word, characters per word, and percent of familiar words. Carefully controlling these three factors ensures that speed and accuracy scores are reliable—that is, increased scores reflect increased skill.

In Level 1, all timings are easy. Note "E" inside the triangle at left of the timing. Easy timings contain an average of 1.2 syllables per word, 5.1 characters per word, and 90 percent familiar words. Easy copy is suitable for the beginner who is mastering the keyboard.

	gwam	2'
There should be no questions, no doubt, about	5	35
the value of being able to key; it's just a matter	10	40
of common sense that today a pencil is much too slow.	15	45
Let me explain. Work is done on a keyboard	19	49
three to six times faster than other writing and	24	54
with a product that is a prize to read. Don't you	29	59
agree?	29	60

```
2' |    1    |    2    |    3    |    4    |    5    |
```

12f Enrichment

1. Click the Skill Building tab, and choose Technique Builder; select Drill 1b.
2. Key Drill 1b from page 37. Key each line once, striving for good accuracy.
3. The results will be listed on the Skill Building Report.
4. Log out of *KPDO*.

Hess Pet Center

Contact Information
Address: 186 Hess Boulevard, Austin, TX 78712-2149
Telephone: 512.555.PETS (7387) | Fax: 512.555.7378
Website: www.hesspetcenter.com

Email address for all employees: firstname.lastname@hesspetcenter.com

Key Contacts

Veterinary Operations	
Erin A. Faulk, DVM	Managing Partner
Student's Name	Office Manager
Jan Cotter	Intern
Kathryn Moreau, DVM	Director, Surgical Services
Charles Lee	Technician, Surgical Services
Timothy T. Juk, DVM	Director, Internal Medicine
Ann Taylor	Technician, Internal Medicine
David P. Guidice, DVM	Director, Wellness Program
Lynn West	Technician, Wellness Program
Retail and Service Operations	
Douglas C. Schmidt	Managing Partner
Student's Name	Office Manager
Jan Cotter	Intern
Lynn Babcock	Manager, Grooming and Spa
Mark Jones	Assistant Manager, Grooming and Spa
Aaron Barr	Manager, Boutique
JoAnn Jameson	Assistant Manager, Boutique
Lisa Owens	Manager Boarding and Pet Care
Jan Marcus	Assistant Manager, Boarding and Pet Care

Address: 186 Hess Boulevard, Austin, TX 78712-2149

Telephone: 512.555.PETS (7387) | Fax: 512.555.7378

Website: www.hesspetcenter.com

Email address for all employees:
firstname.lastname@hesspetcenter.com

 TIP

Remember to replace *Student's Name* with your name in both the *Veterinary* and the *Retail and Service Operations* sections.

6. Insert a 2-column, 20-row table; key the table below and format as follows:

 a. Apply Grid Table 2 – Accent 1 style. Size all rows 0.27" high; apply Align Center Left text alignment.

 b. Adjust the width of the first column to 2.7" and the second column to 3.5".

 c. Merge the cells in both the *Veterinary Operations* and the *Retail and Service Operations* rows. Format both rows as follows: change the Shading to Dark Red, Accent 1; change the font color to white and the font size to 12 point.

7. Use Select All and save as a Quick Part with the name and description: **HPC Contact List**. Select the option Insert content in its own page.

8. Proofread and check; click Next Activity. (*19-d6*)

Veterinary Operations	
eaf	Managing Partner
Student's Name	Office Manager
Jan Cotter	Intern
Kathryn Moreau, DVM	Director, Surgical Services
Charles Lee	Technician, Surgical Services
Timothy T. Juk, DVM	Director, Internal Medicine

(continued)

Lesson 13 Review

Warmup *Lesson 13a Warmup*

alphabet	1	Bev quickly hid two Japanese frogs in Mitzi's box.
shift	2	Jay Nadler, a Rotary Club member, wrote Mr. Coles.
, (comma)	3	Jay, Ed, and I paid for plates, knives, and forks.
easy	4	Did the amendment name a city auditor to the firm?

Skill Building

13b Textbook Keying

Key each line once.

Key short, familiar words as units.

5 is to for do an may work so it but an with them am
6 Did they mend the torn right half of their ensign?
7 Hand me the ivory tusk on the mantle by the bugle.

Key more difficult words by letter.

8 only state jolly zest oil verve join rate mop card
9 After defeat, look up; gaze in joy at a few stars.
10 We gazed at a plump beaver as it waded in my pool.

Use variable speed; your fingers will feel the difference.

11 it up so at for you may was but him work were they
12 It is up to you to get the best rate; do it right.
13 Sami greeted reporters as stars got ready at home.

13c Improve Keystroking

14 Pat appears happy to pay for any supper I prepare.
15 Knox can relax; Alex gets a box of flax next week.
16 Vi, Ava, and Viv move ivy vines, leaves, or stems.
17 It's a question of whether they can't or won't go.
18 Did Jane go? Did she see Sofia? Who paid? Did she?
19 Ms. E. K. Nu and Lt. B. A. Walz had the a.m. duty.
20 "Who are you?" he asked. "I am," I said, "Jayden."
21 Find a car; try it; like it; work a price; buy it.

Overview (Heading 1)

(*Your Name*) reported that Mr. Schmidt and Dr. Faulk requested that the team plan an event to mark the completion of the hpc facilities expansion. hpc has been so successful in the Hess Office Park location that expansion was needed. The new facilities will give us twice the space to expand our veterinary and boarding services. All work has been completed, and the furnishings will be in place in approximately two to three weeks.

Date and Time (Heading 1)

The team discussed the advantages and disadvantages of a weekday event versus a weekend event, and an afternoon versus an evening event. The group agreed that a Sunday afternoon would probably attract the largest crowd and selected April 14 at 3:30 p.m. as the date and time.

Type of Function (Heading 1)

Mark reported that the management team wanted the function to appeal to families and to be pet friendly. JoAnn and Jan agreed to work with Mark on appropriate food and beverages to serve. Pet treats will be provided as well. The team agreed that small group tours should be hosted by a staff member in each area to showcase the state-of-the-art facilities and equipment. The veterinary staff should conduct a brief seminar on the latest trends in pet medical care.

(Insert *minutes* data file here.)

19-d6

Contact List

 hpc logo

Mr. Schmidt has asked you to prepare a company contact sheet that could be handed out or emailed to clients and potential clients.

1. Insert the *hpc logo* and apply Square Text Wrapping; position as shown in the illustration on the next page.
2. Key **Hess Pet Center** on the first line in bold, 24-point font. Apply Dark Red, Accent 1, Darker 25% font color; add 18-point spacing before the title. Tap ENTER and apply Normal style to remove formats.
3. Tap ENTER and key **Contact Information**; apply Heading 1 style.
4. Key the contact information shown on the next page. Remove the space after each paragraph except the last one. Apply Dark Red, Accent 1, Darker 25% font color to the vertical bar in the telephone line.
5. Key: **Key Contacts**; apply Heading 1 style.

(continued)

13d Textbook Keying

Key each line once.

© Cengage Learning

```
 t 22  at fat hat sat to tip the that they fast last slat
 r 23  or red try ran run air era fair rid ride trip trap
t/r 24  A trainer sprained an arm trying to tame the bear.

 m 25  am me my mine jam man more most dome month minimum
 n 26  no an now nine once net knee name ninth know never
m/n 27  Many men and women are important company managers.

 o 28  on or to not now one oil toil over only solo today
 i 29  it is in tie did fix his sit like with insist will
o/i 30  Joni will consider obtaining options to buy coins.

 a 31  at an as art has and any case data haze tart smart
 s 32  us as so say sat slap lass class just sassy simple
a/s 33  Disaster was averted as the steamer sailed to sea.

 e 34  we he ear the key her hear chef desire where there
 i 35  it is in tie did fix his sit like with insist will
e/i 36  An expression of gratitude for service is desired.
```

13e Timed Writing

1. Take two 2' timed writings. If you finish before time is up, begin again.
2. End the lesson; log out of *KPDO*.

Goal: 16 *gwam*

E ALL LETTERS

wordwrap *gwam* 2'

```
    Some people think that the first impression made     5
in the first few seconds is the best method to find      10
out what a person is like. Think of meeting friends      15
for the first time. Was this true of them? In some       20
cases, one might be correct in judging a person in a     26
few seconds. However, in most cases, one will find       31
that it takes more than the first meeting to know        36
what a person is like. But the first time meeting a      41
person could give some idea, often if a person does      46
not show good qualities. For example, one might see      51
poor speaking skills, improper dress, and poor           56
personal traits when meeting a person for the first      61
time.                                                    62
```

2' | | 1 | 2 | 3 | 4 | 5 |

19-d4

Agenda

The expansion of the facility and the new construction has been completed. Your next task is to prepare an agenda for a meeting of the Grand Opening Planning Team.

1. Use a 2" top margin and key the agenda below. Apply Title style to the title, Heading 1 style to the meeting title, and Subtitle style to the location, time, and date information; center all three lines. Tap ENTER twice after the subtitle.

2. Before keying the body of the agenda, set tabs as follows: set a left tab at 1" and a right dot leader tab at 6.5".

3. Tap ENTER twice after keying the agenda and add this note: **Note: Bring Facilities Master Plan to the meeting.**

4. Add a Draft 1 watermark to the document. Participants will be given an opportunity to make additions to the agenda.

5. Proofread and check; click Next Activity. (*19-d4*)

Agenda

Grand Opening Planning Session

Vet Conference Room		10:30 a.m.	March 5, 201-
10:30	Overview		Your Name
10:35	Date and Time of Opening		Team
10:40	Type of Function		Mark Jones
10:50	Invitation List		Lynn Babcock
11:00	Promotion Options		Aaron Barr
11:15	Budget		Your Name
11:30	Wrap Up		Your Name

19-d5

Minutes

 minutes

Prepare minutes from the the grand opening planning session.

1. Key the minutes shown below. Insert the data file *minutes* at the end of the keyed document. Use Show/Hide to remove extra spaces that are not needed.

2. Format as suggested in the comments; then remove the comments. Remove the highlight reminding you to add your name. Key your name each time it is indicated; do not include parentheses.

3. Insert Top of Page, Plain Number 3 page number. Do not show the page number on the first page.

4. Proofread and check; click Next Activity. (*19-d5*)

Grand Opening Planning Session (Title style)

Minutes—March 5, 201- (Subtitle style)

The Grand Opening Planning Team met on March 5, 201- at 10:30 a.m. in the Vet Conference Room. Team members present were Lynn Babcock, Aaron Barr, Mark Jones, JoAnn Jameson, Jan Marcus, Mary Todd, and (*Your Name*).

(continued)

Skill Builder 1

Skill Building *Technique Builder*

From the Skill Building tab, select Technique Builder and then the drill. Key each line once at a comfortable rate. Tap ENTER at the end of each line. Single-space the drill. Concentrate and key accurately. Repeat if desired.

DRILL 1

Goal: reinforce key locations

Key each line once at a comfortable, constant rate.

★ TECHNIQUE TIP

Keep
- your eyes on source copy
- your fingers curved, upright
- your wrists low but not touching
- your elbows hanging loosely
- your feet flat on the floor

Drill 1a

A We saw that Alan had an alabaster vase in Alabama.
B My rubber boat bobbed about in the bubbling brook.
C Ceci gave cups of cold cocoa to Rebecca and Rocco.
D Don's dad added a second deck to his old building.
E Even as Ellen edited her document, she ate dinner.
F Our firm in Buffalo has a staff of forty or fifty.
G Ginger is giving Greg the eggs she got from Helga.
H Hugh has eighty high, harsh lights he might flash.

Drill 1b

I Irik's lack of initiative is irritating his coach.
J Judge J. J. Jore rejected Jeane and Jack's jargon.
K As a lark, Kirk kicked back a rock at Kim's kayak.
L Lucille is silly; she still likes lemon lollipops.
M Milt Mumm hammered a homer in the Miami home game.
N Ken Linn has gone hunting; Stan can begin canning.
O Jon Soto rode off to Otsego in an old Morgan auto.
P Philip helped pay the prize as my puppy hopped up.
Q Quiet Raquel quit quoting at an exquisite marquee.

Drill 1c

R As Mrs. Kerr's motor roared, her red horse reared.
S Sissie lives in Mississippi; Lissa lives in Tulsa.
T Nat told Betty not to tattle on her little sister.
U Ula has a unique but prudish idea on unused units.
V Eva visited every vivid event for twelve evenings.
W We watched as wayworn wasps swarmed by the willow.
X Tex Cox waxed the next box for Xenia and Rex Knox.
Y Ty says you may stay with Fay for only sixty days.
Z Hazel is puzzled about the azure haze; Zack dozes.

19-d2

Memo

hpc memo form

1. In the open document, key the memo shown below to **All Employees** from **Doug Schmidt** (use *dcs* and AutoCorrect will spell it out).
2. List the attachment as: **Attachment: HPC #1 Document Processing Standards.**
3. Do not spell out HPC where shown in uppercase.
4. Proofread and check; click Next Activity. (*19-d2*)

SUBJECT: Standard Operating Procedures

Our management team has worked with most of you to develop standard operating procedures for all phases of our operations. Procedures will be reviewed and revised on a continual basis. All employees are encouraged to review procedures and suggest ways to improve hpc operations.

The office manager has been designated as the person responsible for keeping all procedures up-to-date. The procedures will be stored on the shared drive. Please note that the attached procedure is labeled HPC #1 Document Processing Standards. The HPC #1 label indicates that the procedures outlined in this document apply to all hpc documents that are prepared for internal and external use. Procedures that apply only to the Veterinary Operations are labeled HPC-VO, and those that apply only to the Retail and Service Operations are labeled HPC-RSO.

19-d3

Letter

hpc letterhead

TIP

Do not include your initials since this letter has your signature. To enhance your productivity, save your closing lines as a Quick Part.

1. Prepare the following letter for your own signature. Be sure to include your full name and your new title on a separate line.
2. Send Mr. Schmidt a copy of the letter; use his name and title: **dcs, Managing Partner | Retail and Service Operations**
3. Proofread and check; click Next Activity. (*19-d3*)

Mr. Mark Anderson | Placement Director | Austin Technical College | 2044 55th Street | Austin, TX 78710-8711

Last year you assisted me in obtaining an internship at hpc. The internship was a very valuable experience for me. My internship not only gave me an opportunity to apply the knowledge and skills I acquired in the business program at Austin Technical College, it also was a great learning experience that led to a permanent position.

I have recently been named the office manager of hpc. As you might remember, hpc is a thriving new business that resulted from a joint venture between Dr. eaf and Mr. dcs, an entrepreneur. The new business integrates a veterinary clinic with a full-service luxury pet boarding, grooming, and boutique center.

We would like to hire an intern who is academically successful, has leadership skills, and can work without close supervision. A job description listing the specific skills required is enclosed. Would you please recommend some of your outstanding junior or senior students for this position?

DRILL 2

Goal: strengthen up and down reaches

Keep hands and wrists quiet; fingers well curved in home position; stretch fingers up from home or pull them palmward as needed.

home position

1 Hall left for Dallas; he is glad Jake fed his dog.
2 Ada had a glass flask; Jake had a sad jello salad.
3 Lana Hask had a sale; Gala shall add half a glass.

down reaches

4 Did my banker, Mr. Mavann, analyze my tax account?
5 Do they, Mr. Zack, expect a number of brave women?
6 Zach, check the menu; next, beckon the lazy valet.

up reaches

7 Prue truly lost the quote we wrote for our report.
8 Teresa quietly put her whole heart into her words.
9 There were two hilarious jokes in your quiet talk.

DRILL 3

Goal: strengthen individual finger reaches

1st finger

1 Bob Mugho hunted for five minutes for your number.
2 Juan hit the bright green turf with his five iron.
3 The frigates and gunboats fought mightily in Java.

2nd finger

4 Dick said the ice on the creek had surely cracked.
5 Even as we picnicked, I decided we needed to diet.
6 Kim, not Mickey, had rice with chicken for dinner.

3rd/4th finger

7 Pam saw Roz wax an aqua auto as Lex sipped a cola.
8 Wally will quickly spell Zeus, Apollo, and Xerxes.
9 Who saw Polly? Pax Zais saw her; she is quiet now.

DRILL 4

Goal: strengthen special reaches

Emphasize smooth stroking. Avoid pauses, but do not reach for speed.

adjacent reaches

1 Falk knew well that her opinions of art were good.
2 Theresa answered her question; order was restored.
3 We join there and walk north to the western point.

direct reaches

4 Barb Nunn must hunt for my checks; she is in debt.
5 In June and December, Irvin hunts in Bryce Canyon.
6 We decided to carve a number of funny human faces.

double letters

7 Anne stopped off at school to see Bill Wiggs cook.
8 Edd has planned a small cookout for all the troop.
9 Keep adding to my assets all fees that will apply.

| 1 | 2 | 3 | 4 | 5 | 6 | 7 | 8 | 9 | 10 |

19-d1

Procedures

 TIP

Remember to proofread and preview each document as an SOP. You will not be reminded to do this.

Mr. Schmidt reviewed with you the standard operating procedures shown above. He and Dr. Faulk asked you to work with them to standardize a format for the procedures that have been developed for all areas of Hess Pet Center. The procedures will be stored electronically. Each procedure will begin with an explanatory paragraph followed by bulleted or numbered procedural steps.

1. Key the procedures shown below.
2. Apply the Ion theme and Casual document formatting.
3. Tap ENTER three times and key the title **Standard Operating Procedures** and subtitle **HPC #1: Document Processing Standards**; apply Title and Subtitle styles as appropriate. Do not spell out HPC in the subtitle.
4. Apply square bullets to the list of procedures that follow the introductory paragraph.
5. Add a Blank footer and key: **Last revised on (Current date).**
6. Proofread and check; click Next Activity. (*19-d1*)

hpc has developed standard operating procedures for all phases of its operation. Document processing standards apply to all employees in both the veterinary and the retail operations. Documents are a key part of our image and branding. Therefore, the logo, colors, fonts, and document styles must be used consistently throughout hpc. Accurate documents are critical; errors not only create a bad impression, but they could also create medical problems and liability issues.

Proofread and preview each document you prepare.

Use the standardized guide for naming and saving all files. Save a copy of each document on the shared drive if it will be accessed by others.

Use the Ion theme for each document you prepare.

Use Casual Document Formatting for reports and other documents with titles.

Create a Quick Parts building block based on the hpc letterhead so that you can insert it in documents when needed.

Spell out hpc in all documents; do not abbreviate the name unless instructed to do so.

Prepare all letters using the hpc letterhead.

Prepare all memos using the hpc memo form.

Use complete names in the closing lines of letters you prepare for the managing partners; they will sign first names on letters to individuals they know well.

Apply a draft watermark on documents that are still in draft form.

Use software features to automate as many processes as possible.

Share tips with other employees to enhance productivity.

DRILL 5

Goal: improve troublesome pairs

Use a controlled rate without pauses.

```
         1  ad add did does dish down body dear dread dabs bad
     d/k  2  kid ok kiss tuck wick risk rocks kayaks corks buck
         3  Dirk asked Dick to kid Drake about the baked duck.

         4  deed deal den led heed made needs delay he she her
     e/i  5  kit kiss kiln kiwi kick kilt kind six ribs kill it
         6  Abie had neither ice cream nor fried rice in Erie.

         7  fib fob fab rib beg bug rob bad bar bed born table
     b/v  8  vat vet gave five ever envy never visit weave ever
         9  Vic and Bev gave five very big baby beds to a vet.

        10  aft after lift gift sit tot the them tax tutu tyro
     t/r 11  for far ere era risk rich rock rosy work were roof
        12  In Toronto, Ruth told the truth about her artwork.

        13  jug just jury judge juice unit hunt bonus quiz bug
     u/y 14  jay joy lay you your only envy quay oily whey body
        15  Willy usually does not buy your Yukon art in July.
```

DRILL 6

Goal: fluency

```
     1  Dian may make cocoa for the girls when they visit.
     2  Focus the lens for the right angle; fix the prism.
     3  She may suspend work when she signs the torn form.
     4  Augment their auto fuel in the keg by the autobus.
     5  As usual, their robot did half turns to the right.
     6  Pamela laughs as she signals to the big hairy dog.
     7  Pay Vivian to fix the island for the eighty ducks.
```

DRILL 7

Goal: eyes on the copy

 Word Processor

Option: In the Word Processor, set the Timer for Variable and then either 20" or 30". Choose a *gwam* goal that is two to three words higher than your best rate. Try to reach your goal.

	words	30"	20"
1 Did she make this turkey dish? **ENTER**		12	18
2 Blake and Laurie may go to Dubuque.		14	21
3 Signal for the oak sleigh to turn right.		16	24
4 I blame Susie; did she quench the only flame?		18	27
5 She turns the panel dials to make this robot work.		20	30

HESS PET CENTER

Hess Pet Center
186 Hess Boulevard, Austin, TX 78712-2149
Telephone 512.555.PETS (7387) | Fax 512.555.7378 | www.hesspetcenter.com

In Hess Pet Center I, you worked as an intern with Dr. Erin A. Faulk and Mr. Douglas C. Schmidt at Hess Pet Center, a veterinary clinic and luxury pet spa. Hess Pet Center is located in Hess Office Park, which is managed by Hess Property Enterprises, and has become a very successful business. Because of your excellent work as an intern, you have been hired as the office manager.

Hess Pet Center has recently made changes to enhance its corporate image and to develop a strong brand. Your focus in Hess Pet Center II is to ensure that all documents enhance that image and that productivity tools are used effectively to improve your efficiency.

Prepare all documents using the Ion document theme and Casual document formatting. Letterhead and memo forms are provided in the data files, but you will need the theme for reports, newsletters, and other documents that you prepare.

 TIP

Remember to add other AutoCorrect Options for names or phrases that you key repeatedly to be more efficient.

PRODUCTIVITY TOOLS

To create AutoCorrect entries:
File/Options/Proofing/AutoCorrect Options

hpc	Replace with: **Hess Pet Center**
eaf	Replace with: **Erin A. Faulk, DVM**
dcs	Replace with: **Douglas C. Schmidt**

 TIP

It is acceptable to use *hpc* in themes, file names, and similar applications.

To reverse an AutoCorrect action such as retaining HPC as initials, press CTRL + Z or click the AutoCorrect down arrow, and select the desired option.

STANDARD OPERATING PROCEDURES (SOPs)

1. Proofread and preview each document you prepare.
2. Use the Ion theme for all documents.
3. Use the Hess Pet Center letterhead and memo data files for letters and memos.
4. Spell out *hpc* as Hess Pet Center, *eaf* as Erin A. Faulk, DVM, and *dcs* as Douglas C. Schmidt each time they appear in documents using AutoCorrect.
5. Use block letter style with open punctuation for all letters.
6. Use *Dear* + the title and last name as the salutation on all letters unless directed to use the individual's first name.
7. Add enclosure or attachment notations and copy notations when they are referenced in a letter or memo.
8. Use the current date on all documents unless directed otherwise. Use standard formatting for reports and meeting documents. (Apply Title style and position title at 2".)
9. Use the standard cover page with the logo for multiple-page reports.

Any timed writing in the book can be completed using the Timed Writing feature.

TO USE THE TIMED WRITING FEATURE:

1. From the Timed Writings tab, select the timed writing.
2. Select the source and the timing length. For example,
 - Select Paragraph 1 and 1'. Key paragraph 1; if you finish before time is up, repeat the same paragraph. Always use wordwrap when keying timed writings.
 - Select Paragraph 2 and 1'. Key paragraph 2; repeat the same paragraph if you finish before time is up.
 - Select Entire Writing and 2'. Try to maintain your 1' rate. If you finish before time is up, start over, beginning with paragraph 1.
3. Timings save automatically.
4. The Timed Writing Report displays the results of the last 40 timed writings and the best 3 timings at each timing length (1', 2', 3').

wordwrap

E ALL LETTERS

Goal: build staying power
1. Key each paragraph as a 1' timing. Use wordwrap.
2. Key a 2' timing on both paragraphs. Use wordwrap.

Writing 1: 18 *gwam*

gwam 2'

 Why spend weeks with some problem when just a few quiet 6
minutes can help us to resolve it. 9
 If we don't take time to think through a problem, it will 15
swiftly begin to expand in size. 18

Writing 2: 20 *gwam*

 We push very hard in our quest for growth, and we all think 6
that only excellent growth will pay off. 10
 Believe it or not, one can actually work much too hard, 16
be much too zealous, and just miss the mark. 20

Writing 3: 22 *gwam*

 A business friend once explained to me why he was often 6
quite eager to be given some new project to work with. 11
 My friend said that each new project means he has to 16
organize and use the best of his knowledge and his skill. 22

Writing 4: 24 *gwam*

 Just don't let new words get away from you. Learn how to spell 6
and pronounce new words and when and how to use them with skill. 13
 A new word is a friend, but frequently more. New words 19
must be used lavishly to extend the size of your word power. 25

2' | 1 | 2 | 3 | 4 | 5 | 6 |

Hess Pet Center II

LEARNING OUTCOMES

Lessons 105–107 *Hess Pet Center II*

- Apply keying, formatting, and word processing skills.
- Create a variety of documents.
- Follow standard operating procedures.
- Work independently and with few specific instructions.

 Warmup *Lesson 105a Warmup*

 ALL LETTERS

Skill Building

105b Timed Writing

1. Key one 3' timed writing on each paragraph; key at your control rate.
2. Key one 5' timed writing; key at your control rate.

Most people find it amazing that mobile telephones can create a number of etiquette and safety problems. The use of hand-held mobile telephones has increased dramatically in the past few years. Just because a mobile telephone can be taken almost anywhere does not mean that it is appropriate to use it in any place that it can be carried. Common sense and good manners seem to have been forgotten when it comes to using a mobile telephone.

The major safety hazard of using a hand-held telephone results from its use in moving automobiles. A significant percentage of all accidents is the result of drivers being distracted. Of all the distractions reported, the most frequent are those that occur while a driver is holding a telephone in one hand and trying to drive at the same time. A hands-free telephone is not as dangerous, but it can still cause a driver to be distracted.

The etiquette problem is the result of a person speaking on a telephone in a place that disturbs another person. Either the individual doing this just does not care or does not realize how rude he or she is being to another individual. It is not unusual to see signs that prohibit the use of a mobile telephone in meeting rooms, restaurants, movie theaters, concert halls, and a number of other places. What is most shocking is that these signs are necessary. Except in rare cases, a telephone should not be used in these places. What has happened to basic courtesy?

Writing 5: 26 *gwam*

gwam 2'

We usually get the best results when we know where 5

we are going. Just setting a few goals will help us quietly 12

see what we can do. 13

Goals can help measure whether we are moving at a good 19

rate or dozing along. You can expect a goal to help you find 25

good results. 26

Writing 6: 28 *gwam*

To win whatever prizes we want from life, we must plan to 6

move carefully from this goal to the next to get the maximum 12

result from our work. 14

If we really want to become skilled in keying, we must 19

come to see that this desire will require of us just a little 26

patience and hard work. 28

Writing 7: 30 *gwam*

Am I an individual person? I'm sure I am; still, in a 5

much, much bigger sense, other people have a strong voice in 12

thoughts I think and actions I take. 15

Although we are each a unique person, we work and 21

play in organized groups of people who just do not expect us to 26

dismiss their rules of law and order. 30

2' | 1 | 2 | 3 | 4 | 5 | 6 |

State of Tennessee

County of (Bookmark:COUNTY)

On (Bookmark:DATE), before me, (Bookmark:NOTARY), personally appeared (Bookmark:CLIENT), proven to me on the basis of satisfactory evidence to be the person whose name is subscribed to the within instrument and acknowledged to me that she executed the same in her authorized capacity and that by her signature on the instrument the person, or the entity upon behalf of which the person acted, executed the instrument.

WITNESS my hand and official seal.

Signature _____ (Seal)

104-d4 and 105-d5

Complete Notary Forms

1. In the open document (104-d3), key the information for each bookmark for Document 104-d4.
2. Proofread and continue to the next document. (104-d4)
3. Repeat the steps, inserting the information for Document 104-d5.
4. Proofread and check the test. Click Log out to exit *KPDO*.

Bookmark	Document 104-d4	Document 104-d5
COUNTY	Shelby	Tipton
DATE	May 2, 201-	May 20, 201-
NOTARY	Patrick Plunk, Vice President, Orion Federal Credit Union	Susan Pickens, Notary, Bank of Bartlett
CLIENT	Janice Marie Bennett	Dennis Lee Morris

Figure and Symbol Keys

LEARNING OUTCOMES

Lessons 14–18 *Figure Keys*
Lessons 19–24 *Symbol Keys*
Lesson 25 *Assessment*

- Key the numeric keys by touch.
- Use symbol keys correctly.
- Build keying speed and accuracy.
- Apply correct number expression.
- Apply proofreaders' marks.

Lesson 14 | 1 and 8

Warmup *Lesson 14a Warmup*

New Keys

14b 1 and 8

© Cengage Learning

1 Reach *up* with *left fourth* finger.

© Cengage Learning

8 Reach *up* with *right second* finger.

14c All Figures Learned

Abbreviations: Do not space after a period within an abbreviation, as in Ph.D., U.S., C.O.D., a.m.

The digit "1" and the letter "l" have separate values; do not interchange.

1

1 1 1a a1 1 1; 1 and a 1; 1 add 1; 1 aunt; 1 ace; 1 arm; 1 aye
2 1 and 11 and 111; 11 eggs; 11 vats; Set 11A; May 11; Item 11
3 The 11 aces of the 111th Corps each rated a salute at 1 p.m.

8

4 8 8k k8 8 8; 8 kits; ask 8; 8 kites; kick 8; 8 keys; spark 8
5 OK 88; 8 bags; 8 or 88; the 88th; 88 kegs; ask 88; order 888
6 Eight of the 88 cars score 8 or better on our Form 8 rating.
7 She did live at 818 Park, not 181 Park; or was it 181 Clark?
8 Put 1 with 8 to form 18; put 8 with 1 to write 81. Use 1881.
9 On May 1 at 8 a.m., 18 men and 18 women left Gate 8 for Rio.

PLEASE TAKE FURTHER NOTICE that the Defendant Susan Reckless is to vacate the premises within five (5) days of this written notice. Failure to do so will result in a default judgment for the Plaintiff Donald Hurt. As stipulated in the rental agreement, all past due rent and monetary fees and court costs incurred by Plaintiff Donald Hurt will be due from the Defendant Susan Reckless.

Dated this 19th of June, 201-

JAMES W. LEE
Attorney for Plaintiff

104-d2

SOAP Note

 SOAP notes

1. In the open document, use the information below to complete the SOAP note form.
2. Fill in the form with the following information:

Lucas, Steve

Patient No. **22653**; Age: **42**

Allergies: **None known**

Meds: **Esomeprazole Magnesium**

T: **99.0**; P: **80**; R: **15**; B/P: **118/76**

C/O: **Pain in left elbow**; Date: **4-10-201-**

S	Patient complains of pain in his left elbow. Patient fell yesterday.
O	Elbow is tender to the touch. No inflammation. X-ray shows a hairline fracture.
A	Hairline fracture in medial epicondyle.
P	Arm in cast. Recheck in two weeks. 500 mg of Ibuprofen taken every 4 hours as needed for pain.

3. Center the text vertically in the cells.
4. Proofread and continue. (*104-d2*)

104-d3

Notary Form

1. Key the notary form using default margins. Replace the text in parentheses with bookmarks.
2. Tap ENTER twice to the signature. Set a right underline tab at 3.5" to create the signature line; tap TAB to key **(SEAL)**.
3. Proofread and continue to the next document. (*104-d3*)

(continued)

Skill Building

14d Textbook Keying

Key each line once.

10 a an it been copy for his this more no office please service
11 our service than the they up was work all any many thank had
12 business from I know made more not me new of some to program
13 such these two with your about and have like department year
14 by at on but do had in letter most now one please you should
15 their order like also appreciate that there gentlemen letter
16 be can each had information letter may make now only so that
17 them time use which am other been send to enclosed have will
18 Please thank the department staff for the excellent program.
19 Therefore, send the information as they are very interested.
20 She sent a receipt and an invoice for the payment due today.
21 Our board and president are happy about the new tax service.
22 We appreciate the excellent help received from every office.
23 Please return the attached form prior to the second meeting.

14e Improve Keystroking

figures

24 Our 188 trucks moved 1881 tons on August 18 and December 18.
25 Send Mary 181 No. 188 panes for her home at 8118 Oak Street.
26 The 188 men in 8 boats left Docks 1 and 18 at 1 p.m., May 1.
27 pop was lap pass slaw wool solo swap Apollo wasp load plaque
28 Was Polly acquainted with the skillful jazz player in Texas?
29 The computer is a useful tool; it helps you to perform well.

14f Enrichment

1. Key these lines in the game.
2. Log out of *KPDO* when completed.

30 Did their form entitle them to the land?
31 Did the men in the field signal for us to go?
32 I may pay for the antique bowls when I go to town.
33 The auditor did the work right, so he risks no penalty.
34 The man by the big bush did signal us to turn down the lane.

Apply It

104-d1

Notice of Eviction

legal pleadings
28 lines

1. In the open document, key the eviction notice. Click the bracketed text (Placeholders) and key the new text. Align your text with the line numbers shown at the left. (Option: See 100-d1, pages 485–487.) Use uppercase as shown. Use the fonts of the template.

2. Proofread and click Next Activity. (*104-d1*)

LEE & DURAND, LLP
ATTORNEYS AT LAW
James W. Lee, Esquire
State Bar Number 202256
8578 Main Street, Suite 202
Huntington Beach, CA 92646-1801

Telephone: 714.555.0174

Attorneys for Plaintiffs

SUPERIOR COURT OF THE STATE OF CALIFORNIA
FOR THE COUNTY OF ORANGE

DONALD HURT, et. al., Case No.: 01 CC05144

 Plaintiff NOTICE OF EVICTION

vs.

SUSAN RECKLESS, et. al.,

 Defendant

TO: ALL PARTIES AND THEIR ATTORNEYS OF RECORD

PLEASE TAKE NOTICE that the Plaintiff has submitted a notice to vacate the premises located at 3500 Civic Center Drive, Suite 250, Santa Ana, CA 92701-3821. The Defendant Susan Reckless has violated the rental agreement. The breach of lease is based on the nonpayment of rent on the part of the Defendant for the past sixty (60) days.

(continued)

Lesson 15 5 and 0

New Keys

15b 5 and 0

5 Reach *up* with *left first* finger.

0 Reach *up* with *right fourth* finger.

5

1 5 5f f5 5 5; 5 fans; 5 feet; 5 figs; 5 fobs; 5 frus; 5 flaws
2 5 o'clock; 5 a.m.; 5 p.m.; is 55 or less; buy 55; 5 and 5 is
3 Call Line 555 if 5 fans or 5 bins arrive at Pier 5 by 5 p.m.

0

4 0 0; ;0 0 0; skip 0; plan 0; left 0; is below 0; I scored 0;
5 0 degrees; key 0 and 0; write 00 here; the total is 0 or 00;
6 She laughed at their 0 to 0 score; but ours was 0 to 0 also.

15c All Figures Learned

7 I keyed 550 pages for Invoice 05, or 50 more than we needed.
8 Pages 15 and 18 of the program listed 150, not 180, members.
9 On May 10, Rick drove 500 miles to New Mexico in car No. 08.

Skill Building

15d Textbook Keying

Key each line once.

> **Watch the copy, not the hands.**

10 Read pages 5 and 8; duplicate page 18; omit pages 50 and 51.
11 We have Model 80 with 10 meters or Model 180 with 15 meters.
12 After May 18, French 050 meets in room 15 at 10 a.m. daily.

13 Barb Abver saw a vibrant version of her brave venture on TV.
14 Call a woman or a man who will manage Minerva Manor in Nome.
15 We were quick to squirt a quantity of water at Quin and West.

Indent paragraph ——→ **IN TESTIMONY WHEREOF**, the above named Lessor and the above named Lessee have executed this instrument the _____ day of _____, 201-. ↓4

Lessee ↓4

Lessor

103-d3 and 103-d4

Complete Commercial Lease Agreement

1. In the open document (*103-d2*), key the information for each bookmark for Document 103-d3. In the paragraph beginning *TO HAVE AND TO HOLD*, insert the current year and then the subsequent year for 201-.
2. Proofread and check; click Next Activity. (*103-d3*)
3. Repeat the steps, inserting the information for Document 103-d4.
4. Proofread and check; click Next Activity. (*103-d4*)

Bookmark	Document 103-d3	Document 103-d4
LESSEE	Hutcherson Home Builders	Tune Accounting Services
BEGIN_DAY	1st	15th
BEGIN_MONTH	November	December
END_DAY	31st	14th
END_MONTH	October	November
SUM	$36,000.00	$33,000.00
MONTHLY	$600.00	$550.00

103-d5

Compose

 hess memo

1. In the open document, compose a memo to Mr. William Wright from you.
2. Inform him you have created the two lease agreements for him to review. Verify that the amounts and dates are correct for each company. Find out if he wants you to email the lease agreements.
3. Attach the lease agreements. Edit and proofread; Click Exit Word. (*103-d5*)
4. Click Log out to exit *KPDO*.

Learn More

www.cengagebrain.com

15e Textbook Keying

Key each line once.

pu/nv

16 pumps impulse campus invoices convey envy puck public canvas

17 Computer's input on environmental canvass confirms decision.

mb ey rk

18 embarked number climb eye obeying park remark thumb attorney

19 Ambitious people gambled money on unusual pieces of artwork.

tl ru pt

20 subtle apt capture excerpt adult abrupt brittle forums drug

21 Ruth opts to be greatly optimistic about seven new recruits.

ob rg un

22 objective lobster organize urge bounce tribunal global surge

23 Marge's hunger for mobile action targets frequent traveling.

15f Timed Writing

1. Take two 1' timed writings. If you finish before time is up, begin again.
2. Use wordwrap; do not tap ENTER at the end of lines.
3. End the lesson.

LA ALL LETTERS

wordwrap ↓

	gwam	1'

I thought about Harry and how he worked for me in my 11

family insurance business for 10 years; how daily at 8 he 23

parked his old car in the company lot; then, he left exactly 35

at 5. Every day was almost identical for him. 44

In a quiet way, he did an outstanding job, requesting 56

little attention. So I never recognized his thirst for travel. 68

I didn't expect to find all those travel brochures near his 80

workplace. 82

1' | 1 | 2 | 3 | 4 | 5 | 6 | 7 | 8 | 9 | 10 | 11 | 12 |

Communication

15g Enrichment

Word Processor

1. Go to the Word Processor.
2. Compose one paragraph that describes travel that you have done or perhaps that you wish to take. Include at least two attractions you visited or hope to visit while on this trip. Use proper grammatical structure. Do not worry about keying errors at this time.
3. Save the document as *xx-travel*. (Replace *xx* with your initials.)
4. Log out of *KPDO*.

Delivery at End of Lease:

And on the expiration of the term of this lease to deliver unto the Lessor the possession of said building, lot and premises, cleared of all persons, goods not properly belonging to the same, and in good condition as the same were received, destruction or damages by fire, storm or other casualty and ordinary wear and tear excepted;

Attorney Fees:

Lessee agrees to pay all costs of collection, including reasonable attorney fees, if all or any of the rent or utility charges reserved herein is collected after maturity with the aid of an attorney; also to pay reasonable attorney fees in the event it becomes necessary for the Lessor to employ an attorney to force the Lessee to comply with any of the covenants, obligations, or conditions imposed by this lease;

Indemnification:

Lessor not be liable to Lessee's employee's agents, invitees, licensees or visitors, or to any other person, for any injury to person or damage to property on or about the leased premises, whether caused by the negligence or misconduct of Lessee, its agents, servants or employees, or of any person entering upon the leased premises under express or implied invitation of Lessee, or caused by the Project and improvements located thereon becoming out of repair, or caused by leakage of gas, oil, water or steam or by electricity emanating from the leased premises. Lessee agrees to indemnify and hold harmless Lessor from any loss, attorney's fees, expenses or claims arising out of such damage or injury, such indemnification to survive the termination of this lease. Any liability insurance which may be carried by Lessor with respect to the Project shall be for Lessor's sole benefit and under its sole control.

Lessee further agrees to indemnify and hold Hess Office Park harmless from any liability which may be imposed upon Lessor and costs including attorney fees incurred as a result of any claim made against Lessor from injury arising out of machinery, caused or contributed by Lessee's or user's failure to provide safety equipment, instructions, and/or warnings necessary to operate this machinery safely. Lessee further agrees to indemnify and hold harmless Hess Office Park for any liability which may be imposed upon Lessor and any costs, including attorney fees, incurred as a result of any claim made against seller for injury arising out of use of this machinery, caused or contributed to by any actions or inactions of Lessee;

(continued)

Lesson 16 2 and 7

New Keys

16b 2 and 7

2 Reach *up* with *left third* finger.

7 Reach *up* with *right first* finger.

2

1 2 2s s2 2 2; has 2 sons; is 2 sizes; was 2 sites; has 2 skis
2 add 2 and 2; 2 sets of 2; catch 22; as 2 of the 22; 222 Main
3 Exactly at 2 on April 22, the 22nd Company left from Pier 2.

7

4 7 7j j7 7 7; 7 jets; 7 jeans; 7 jays; 7 jobs; 7 jars; 7 jaws
5 ask for 7; buy 7; 77 years; June 7; take any 7; deny 77 boys
6 From May 7 on, all 77 men will live at 777 East 77th Street.

16c All Figures Learned

7 I read 2 of the 72 books, Ellis read 7, and Han read all 72.
8 Tract 27 cites the date as 1850; Tract 170 says it was 1852.
9 You can take Flight 850 on January 12; I'll take Flight 705.

Skill Building

16d Textbook Keying

Key each line once. Keep fingers curved and relaxed; wrists low.

3rd/4th
10 pop was lap pass slaw wool solo swap apollo wasp load plaque
11 Al's quote was, "I was dazzled by the jazz, pizza, and pool."

1st/2nd
12 bad fun nut kick dried night brick civic thick hutch believe
13 Kim may visit her friends in Germany if I give her a ticket.

3rd/1st
14 cry tube wine quit very curb exit crime ebony mention excite
15 To be invited, petition the six executive committee members.

fixtures, and all other fixtures erected or put in place upon the premises by or through the Lessee or other occupants for the payment of rent and also for the satisfaction of any causes of action which may accrue to the Lessor by the Provisions of this instrument;

Lawful & Moral Uses:
That the premises and all buildings and improvements thereon shall, during the term of this lease, be used exclusively for lawful and moral purposes, and no part of the premises or improvements shall be used for any purpose in violation of the laws of the United States, the State of Texas, or the ordinances and laws of the City of Austin that are enforced;

Protection from Violations:
To save and hold the Lessor harmless from violations of the laws of the United States, of the State of Texas, and the ordinances and laws of the City of Austin;

Invalidation of Insurance:
Not to suffer anything to be or remain upon the premises which will invalidate any policy of insurance which Lessor may now or hereafter have upon said building;

Alterations:
Not to make any changes, alterations, or additions about the said building or premises without first obtaining the written consent of the Lessor and in no event to do anything that shall weaken the building or structure now on or that may hereafter be erected on the premises;

Damages, Accidents, Etc.:
To hold Lessor harmless against all damages, accidents, and injuries to persons or property caused by or in connection with any power plant, machinery, elevator, elevator shaft, stairway, signs, awnings, glass, brick, or other building material, hatch, coal chute or other openings, flag pole, and other parts of said premises in or pertaining to or upon the premises during the term of this lease or while the Lessee is occupying the premises;

Insolvency, Etc. of Lessee:
That in the event of the insolvency or bankruptcy of the Lessee, or the filing of any petition under the bankruptcy statute voluntarily or involuntarily and whether or not resulting in an adjudication in bankruptcy, or in the event of a partial or general assignment for the benefit of a creditor, the Lessor shall have the right to terminate this lease upon giving written notice thirty days in advance;

(continued)

16e Improve Keystroking

16 line 8; Book 1; No. 88; Seat 11; June 18; Cart 81; date 1881

17 take 2; July 7; buy 22; sell 77; mark 27; adds 72; Memo 2772

18 feed 5; bats 0; age 50; Ext. 55; File 50; 55 bags; band 5005

19 I work 18 visual signs with 20 turns of the 57 lenses to 70.

20 Did 17 boys fix the gears for 50 bicycles in 28 racks or 10?

16f Textbook Keying

Key each line once.

> **Think and key the words and phrases as units rather than letter by letter.**

words: *think, say, and key words*

21 is do am lay cut pen dub may fob ale rap cot hay pay hem box

22 box wit man sir fish also hair giant rigor civic virus ivory

23 laugh sight flame audit formal social turkey bicycle problem

phrases: *think, say, and key phrases*

24 is it|is it|if it is|if it is|or by|or by|or me|or me|for us

25 and all|for pay|pay dues and|the pen|the pen box|the pen box

26 such forms|held both|work form|then wish|sign name|with them

easy sentences

27 The man is to do the work right; he then pays the neighbors.

28 Sign the forms to pay the eight men for the turkey and hams.

29 The antique ivory bicycle is a social problem for the chair.

16g Timed Writing

1. Take two 2' timed writings. If you finish before time is up, begin again. Use wordwrap.

2. End the lesson; log out of *KPDO*.

Goal: 16 *gwam*

	gwam	2'	3'

When choosing a password, do not select one you have 6 | 4
already used. Create a new one quite often, perhaps every 11 | 8
three to four weeks. Be sure to use a combination of both 17 | 11
letters and numbers. 19 | 13

Know your password; do not record it on paper. If you 25 | 17
must write it down, be sure the password is not recognized. 31 | 21
Don't let anyone watch you key. Just position yourself away 37 | 24
from the person or key a few extra strokes. 41 | 27

2' | 1 2 3 4 5 6
3' | 1 2 3 4

1. Use default margins. Key the title and tap ENTER twice; apply Title Style, Underline, and Center. Single-space the text and remove spacing after paragraphs. Bold and capitalize as indicated.

2. Insert the bookmark command where indicated. Name the bookmarks in ALL CAPS. For example, the first bookmark will be for LESSEE. If you make a mistake on the location of the bookmark, delete the bookmark and re-enter it. Check spacing.

3. For the date lines in the last paragraph, key 10 underlines.

4. Tap ENTER four times before each signature line; set a right underline tab at 3.0".

5. Proofread and check; click Next Activity. *(103-d2)*

LEASE

 2

Parties:

THIS LEASE between, Hess Office Park party of the first part hereby called Lessor, and (Bookmark:LESSEE), party of the second part, hereinafter called Lessee,

Consideration:

WITNESSETH: That each of the aforesaid parties acknowledges the receipt of a valuable consideration from the other, and they and each of them act in further consideration of the engagements of the other as herein stated.

Premises:

That Lessor has and does hereby grant, demise, and lease unto Lessee the following described premises situated in the City of Austin, State of Texas; namely, a portion of the building located at 100 Hess Boulevard.

Term:

TO HAVE AND TO HOLD the above described premises unto the Lessee for the period of five (5) years commencing on the (Bookmark:BEGIN_DAY) day of (Bookmark:BEGIN_MONTH), 201- and ending on the (Bookmark:END_DAY) day of (Bookmark:END_MONTH) 201-.

Insert the current year and then the subsequent year for 201-

Rental:

Lessee hereby covenants and agrees to pay Lessor as rent for the aforesaid premises the sum of (Bookmark:SUM) payable in advance in monthly installments as follows: (Bookmark:MONTHLY) due on the first of each and every month until paid in full.

Lien on Leasehold, Etc.:

A first lien is hereby expressly reserved by the Lessor and granted by the Lessee upon the terms of this lease and upon all interest of the Lessee in this leasehold for the payment of rent and for the satisfaction of any cause of action which may accrue to the Lessor by the provisions of this instrument. A first lien is also expressly reserved by the Lessor and granted by the Lessee upon all buildings, improvements, store fixtures, water fixtures, and gas

(continued)

Lesson 17 4 and 9

New Keys

17b 4 and 9

4 Reach *up* with *left first* finger.

9 Reach *up* with *right third* finger.

4

1 4 4f f4 f f f; if 4 furs; off 4 floors; gaff 4 fish; 4 flags
2 44th floor; half of 44; 4 walked 44 flights; 4 girls; 4 boys
3 I order exactly 44 bagels, 4 cakes, and 4 pies before 4 a.m.

9

4 9 9l l9 9 9 9; fill 9 lugs; call 9 lads; Bill 9 lost; dial 9
5 also 9 oaks; roll 9 loaves; 9.9 degrees; sell 9 oaks; Hall 9
6 Just 9 couples, 9 men and 9 women, left at 9 on our Tour 99.

17c All Figures Learned

7 4 feet; 4 inches; 44 gallons, 444 quarts, 4 folders, 44 fads
8 Lucky 99; 999 leaves; 9 lottery tickets; 9 losers; 9 winners
9 Memo 94 says 9 pads, 4 pens, and 4 ribbons were sent July 9.
10 Study Item 17 and Item 28 on page 40 and Item 59 on page 49.
11 Within 17 months he drove 85 miles, walked 29, and flew 490.

Skill Building

Keep hands quiet as you reach to the top row; do not bounce.

17d Textbook Keying

Key each line once.

12 My staff of *18* worked *11* hours a day from May *27* to June *12*.
13 There were *5* items tested by Inspector *7* at *4* p.m. on May *8*.
14 Please send her File *10* today at *8*; her access number is *97*.
15 Car *947* had its trial run. The qualifying speed was *198* mph.
16 The estimated total score? *485*. Actual? *390*. Difference? *95*.

Mail Merge Letter

 hess letterhead

 NOTE

Non-KPDO users: Save the data file and main document with the filenames shown above in parentheses.

1. In the open document, prepare two letters for Mr. Wright.

2. Create the data source using the field names in the table (*103-d1data*).

3. Merge the data source and the main document (*103-d1main*).

4. Remove the extra spacing between the lines of the letter address. Refer to Lesson 76 for help with mail merge if necessary.

5. Remove the hyperlink to the URL and the email address. Add closing lines, your initials, and closing notations.

6. Proofread and check; click Next Activity. (*103-d1*)

	Letter 1	Letter 2
Title	Mr.	Mrs.
First Name	Nolen	Michelle
Last Name	Hutcherson	Tune
Company Name	Hutcherson Home Builders	Tune Accounting Services
Address	1500 Broad Street	3250 Walker Avenue
City	San Antonio	Austin
State	TX	TX
ZIP Code	78260	78724

Insert Date

«AddressBlock»

«GreetingLine»

We are pleased that «Company_Name» is considering leasing office space in Hess Office Park. Our offices have a prestigious business address for your client meetings, mail, business cards, and website.

A variety of office layouts and amenities are available to accommodate your needs. You will have 24/7 access to fully furnished executive office suites, conference rooms, as well as other shared office space.

Please review the enclosed brochure that outlines the services, prices, and other a la carte amenities that we provide. You may obtain additional information and take a virtual tour by going to our website at www.hesspropertyenterprises.com.

Once you have reviewed the enclosed brochure, please let me know if you have any questions. My direct telephone number is 512.555.0130 or my email address is william.wright@hessofficepark.com.

I look forward to assisting you with your office needs.

17e Improve Keystroking

first finger

17 buy them gray vent guy brunt buy brunch much give huge vying

18 Hagen, after her July triumph at tennis, may try volleyball.

19 Verna urges us to buy yet another of her beautiful rag rugs.

second finger

20 keen idea; kick it back; ice breaker; decide the issue; cite

21 Did Dick ask Cecelia, his sister, if she decided to like me?

22 Suddenly, Micki's bike skidded on the Cedar Street ice rink.

third/fourth finger

23 low slow lax solo wax zip zap quips quiz zipper prior icicle

24 Paula has always allowed us to relax at La Paz and at Quito.

25 Please ask Zale to explain who explores most aquatic slopes.

17f Timed Writing

Take a 2' timing on all the paragraphs. Repeat the timing. Use wordwrap.

	gwam	2'	3'

Many experts believe stress affects the mind as well as the body. However, they are not quite sure just how much damage can be caused. This may be because people deal with stress in several different ways. Some learn to either shrug it off or else put little thought to it.

 6 | 4
11 | 8
17 | 12
23 | 16
27 | 19

Coping with stress is difficult but if one is willing to make an effort, it can be handled easily. One way to deal with stress is having a good diet as well as regular exercise. Another way is to become involved with enjoyable activities such as writing, painting, or running. Last, but certainly not least, have a positive thought process, a great zest for life, and a big cheerful smile.

34 | 23
39 | 27
46 | 31
52 | 35
58 | 39
64 | 43
67 | 45

2' 1 2 3 4 5 6
3' 1 2 3 4

LA ALL LETTERS

17g Enrichment

1. From the Skill Building tab, choose Technique Builder; Drill 2.
2. Key Drill 2 from page 38. Key each line once, striving for good acuracy.
3. The results will be listed on the Skill Building Report.
4. Log out of *KPDO*.

Lesson 103 Hess Office Park

Skill Building

103b Timed Writing

Key a 3' timing on both paragraphs; work at your control rate.

Today, a huge number of white-collar workers use computers in their daily work. Most of these workers also have access to the Internet. Using the Internet for work purposes is becoming more and more common and, most of the time, is quite effective. Some organizations are finding, though, that a number of their workers do abuse the Internet. The abuse tends to occur in two forms.

The first type of abuse they find is that a large number of employees visit sites that are not related in any way to their work. Some of the sites that workers visit contain material that is very offensive to others. The problem becomes more serious when offensive emails or materials from websites are sent to other employees. In some cases, the courts have found that these materials create a hostile work environment. The second type of abuse is the waste of work time. Employees who spend excessive amounts of time surfing the Internet simply are not doing the work they are paid to do.

A number of large companies are trying to deal with this problem by buying software that they use to track the sites that workers access from their computers. These companies warn all of their employees that visiting offensive sites at work can have major consequences and might even result in job loss. They tend to be a little more lenient on the time abuse issue and often treat the Internet the same way that they deal with the telephone. Limited personal use of the Internet or email is not a major problem. If the usage becomes excessive, then action is taken.

Project Setting

HESS OFFICE PARK

In this project you will be preparing documents for William Wright, the attorney, who serves as the executive director of the legal department at Hess Office Park. As you work through each job, make sure you do the following:

- Use Hess Office Park letterhead and memo forms to create all letters and memos, use the current date, and the block letter style with open punctuation.
- Format the signature lines for Mr. Wright's letters as follows:
 Sincerely | William Wright, Executive Director | Hess Office Park Legal Department

Lesson 18 3 and 6

 Warmup Lesson 18a Warmup

New Keys

18b 3 and 6

3 Reach *up* with *left second* finger.

6 Reach *up* with *right first* finger.

Note: Ergonomic keyboard users will use *left first* finger to key 6.

3

1 3 3d d3 3 3; had 3 days; did 3 dives; led 3 dogs; add 3 dips
2 we 3 ride 3 cars; take 33 dials; read 3 copies; save 33 days
3 On July 3, 33 lights lit 33 stands holding 33 prize winners.

6

4 6 6j 6j 6 6; 6 jays; 6 jams; 6 jigs; 6 jibs; 6 jots; 6 jokes
5 only 6 high; on 66 units; reach 66 numbers; 6 yams or 6 jams
6 On May 6, Car 66 delivered 66 tons of No. 6 shale to Pier 6.

18c All Figures Learned

7 At 6 p.m., Channel 3 reported the August 6 score was 6 to 3.
8 Jean, do Items 28 and 6; Mika, 59 and 10; Kyle, 3, 4, and 7.
9 Cars 56 and 34 used Aisle 9; Cars 2 and 87 can use Aisle 10.

18d Textbook Keying

Key each line once.

word response: *think* and *key* words

10 he el id is go us it an me of he of to if ah or bye do so am
11 Did she enamel emblems on a big panel for the downtown sign?

stroke response: *think* and *key* each stroke

12 kin are hip read lymph was pop saw ink art oil gas up as mop
13 Barbara started the union wage earners tax in Texas in July.

combination response: *vary speed but maintain rhythm*

14 upon than eve lion when burley with they only them loin were
15 It was the opinion of my neighbor that we may work as usual.

102-d4

Email

 NOTE

This activity is not completed in KPDO.

1. Compose an email message to Mark Thompson at **mthompson@abc.com**. Inform this tenant that the lease is attached and needs both signatures.
2. Attach the Lease Agreement created in *102-d3* to the email.
3. Add the following privacy statement at the bottom of the message.
4. Send a blind copy or print screen to your instructor.

CONFIDENTIALITY STATEMENT: The documents accompanying this transmission may contain confidential information that is legally privileged. The information is intended only for the use of the individual or entity named above. The authorized recipient of this information is prohibited from disclosing this information to any other party unless required to do so by law or regulation and is required to destroy the information after its stated need has been fulfilled. If you are not the intended recipient, you are hereby notified that any disclosure, copying, distribution, or action in reliance on the contents of these documents is strictly prohibited. If you have received this information in error, please notify the sender immediately and arrange for the return or destruction of these documents.

Communicating Today ▶

Law Offices, Technology, and Web 2.0 Apps

Law offices have changed drastically with the use of technology. The time spent in law libraries researching information has declined. Attorneys utilize the Internet to obtain information about witnesses, opposing parties, and clients. Social networks, blogs, podcasts, and other Web 2.0 applications allow lawyers to keep up with current law, collaborate with colleagues, and communicate with clients and prospective clients.

Law offices utilize videoconferencing, Voice over IP, scanners, and other technologies to improve efficiency, saving time and money. As law offices embrace today's technology, they must not forget their responsibility to comply with confidentiality and privacy rules.

18e Improve Keystroking

long reaches

16 ce cede cedar wreck nu nu nut punt nuisance my my amy mystic
17 ny ny any many company mu mu mull lumber mulch br br furbish
18 Cecil received a large brown umbrella from Bunny and Hunter.

number review

19 set 0; push 4; Car 00; score 44; jot 04; age 40; Billet 4004
20 April 5; lock 5; set 66; fill 55; hit 65; pick 56; adds 5665
21 Her grades are 93, 87, and 100; his included 82, 96, and 54.

18f Timed Writing

Key two 3' writings. Use wordwrap.

Jim West/Alamy

gwam 3'

I am something quite precious. Though millions of people 4
in other countries might not have me, you likely do. I am very 8
powerful. I choose the new president every four years. I 12
decide if a tax should be levied or repealed. I even decide 16
questions of war and peace. I was acquired with great expense; 20
however, I am free to all citizens. But sadly enough, I am 24
often ignored; or, still worse, I am just taken for granted. I 28
can be lost, and in certain circumstances I can even be taken 33
away. What am I? I am your right to vote. Don't take me 36
lightly. Exercise your right to vote at every election; 40
consider it an opportunity and a privilege. 43

3' | 1 | 2 | 3 | 4 |

Communication

18g Composition

1. Go to the Word Processor. Compose two paragraphs, each having about three sentences, in which you introduce yourself to your instructor. Use proper grammatical structure. Disregard keying errors at this time.

2. Save the document as *xx-profile*; replace *xx* with your initials. You will edit this document later.

102-d2

Rental Property Table

1. Format the title in Heading 1 style and align at center. Tap ENTER twice.
2. Format *Assessment Key* in Heading 2 style.
3. Create a table with 5 columns and 19 rows. Use the column headings and rows below:

 Column headings: **Property Contents | Begin Lease | End of Lease | Location | Comments**

 Rows: **Doors, Windows and frames, Blinds & curtains, Floor, Carpeting, Walls, Lights and switches, Outlets, Stove, Refrigerator, Dishwasher, Garbage disposal, Sink, Cabinets and counter, Tub and shower, Toilet, Garbage & recycling containers, Other**

4. Center the column headings. Change the width of the first column to 1.65" and the last column to 2". Select columns 2–4 and change the column width to 1".
5. Apply the Grid Table 5 Dark – Accent 1.
6. Proofread and check; close the document and exit *Word*. (*102-d2*)
7. Log out of *KPDO* and complete 102-d3 in *Word*.

ASSESSMENT OF RENTAL PROPERTY

Use the table below to evaluate the condition of the property at the beginning of your lease. Complete the column "Begin Lease" using the Assessment Key below. Please keep a copy for your files and provide one for your Landlord. When your lease is terminated, complete the column "End of Lease." Your Landlord will corroborate your assessment. This information will be used to determine if your security deposit will be refunded.

Assessment Key:
- G = Good Condition
- M = Missing
- D = Damaged
- R = Repairs Needed

102-d3

Lease Form

 lease form

This activity is not completed in KPDO.

Some documents use "fill-in fields" rather than blank lines to enter variable data.

1. Launch *Word 2013* as a separate application. Open the data file *lease form*. The document will open in Read Mode. Change the mode to Print Layout.
2. Click in each Placeholder to insert the information below in each of the fill-in fields.
3. Save the document as *102-d3*. You will use this in *102-d4*.

Landlord	Wayne Marshall
Tenant	Mark and Mary Thompson
Address	534 Oak Street
City, State, ZIP Code	Memphis, TN 38111
Occupancy	From: January 1, 201- To: December 31, 201-
Monthly Installments	850 (use again for first month's rental)
Security Deposit	1,000
Dated	Select the current date

Lesson 18R Review

Skill Building

18Rb Textbook Keying

Key each line once; work for fluency.

1 Jake may pay the sixty men for eighty bushels of blue forks.
2 We used software versions 1.01, 2.6, 7.2, 8.3, 8.5, and 9.4.
3 The big box by the lake held fish, duck, apricot, and a map.
4 Adding 123 and 345 and 567 and 80 and 62 and 5 totals 1,182.
5 Lana and Jay and Ken paid to sit by the lake to fish at six.
6 We can see you at 6:30, 7:30, 8:45, 9:00, or 12:15 tomorrow.

18Rc Timed Writing

Key a 3' timing on all paragraphs. Repeat.

	gwam 3'
You want to be known as a person of good character. If	4
someone says that you have character, it usually means that	8
you are honest, have integrity, and are reliable and	12
responsible. On the other hand, if you lie, cheat, or steal,	16
or are lazy, you will be known as a person with poor	19
character. If others say that you are quite a character, it	23
usually means that you have good character.	26
You will be judged by your actions and expressions. What	30
you say and do to others affects how others will respond to	34
you. You need to be considerate of others and conscientious in	38
your work. Others will respect and trust you and want you	42
involved in their activities.	44

3' | 1 | 2 | 3 | 4 |

Communication

18Rd Number Expression

1. From the Reference tab, click Communication Skills; select Number Expression.
2. Complete the pretest; click Report to review your results.

18Re Enrichment

Word Processor

1. In the Word Processor, take a 30" timing on the first line; repeat the line as many times as possible.
2. Take a 30" timing on the second line. Try to maintain the same speed as the first line.

7 Come work with us on this new job next month.
8 Jo will be 44 years 2 months and 24 days old.
9 I see you need some help with the new assignments.
10 I will be 44 years 2 months and 24 days old today.
11 Sixteen of us can come and help you today and tomorrow.
12 Order 99 cookies; at least have 33 sugar and 39 ginger.
13 Tell us how you want the work done; we will finish it today.
14 We must deliver order 6688 for 88 chairs and 66 tables by 6.

Tenant shall take good care of the premises and all appliances, fixtures, appurtenances or equipment therein and make all repairs needed as a result of the Tenant's misuse or negligence.

Tenant shall not, without written consent from the Landlord, paint, mark, deface in any way, or make alterations or improvements in or to the premises, or any part thereof inside or out.

Tenant is responsible for insuring personal property. The Landlord shall not be liable for damage to or loss of any property by fire, theft, or otherwise.

Landlord shall have the right to enter the premises at a reasonable time for the purpose of inspecting or making any repairs that the Tenant may see fit to be made.

If the Tenant should fail to pay any installment of rent when it becomes due or fail to perform or observe any other such term or condition of this agreement, then in any such event, the Landlord may re-enter and repossess the premises without prior notice or demand, using such force as may be necessary, charge for any and all locks in the premises, all without being guilty of forcible entry or detainer, trespass, or other tort, and declare this agreement to be terminated without prejudice to the Landlord's rights to recover unpaid rent and damages.

At the end of the first year, this lease shall be automatically renewed for successive periods of one month at 125% of the monthly installment stated for the first year. Either party may terminate this lease after the first year at any time upon 30 days written notice to the other party.

It is agreed that at the termination of this lease, the Tenant shall return the premises in the same condition received; or if not so returned in the same condition, the Landlord shall be entitled to deduct the cost of restoring said property to said condition from the Tenant's security deposit. ↓2

Remove 3.5" left tab.⟶ DATED THIS _____ day of _____ 201-. ↓2

TENANT:

LANDLORD:

Lesson 19 $ and – (hyphen), Number Expression

19b Learn $ and -

$ Shift; then reach *up* with *left first* finger.

- (hyphen) Reach *up* with *right fourth* finger.

- = hyphen
- - = dash
Do not space before or after a hyphen or a dash.

$

1 $ $f f$ $ $; if $4; half $4; off $4; of $4; $4 fur; $4 flats

2 for $8; cost $9; log $3; grab $10; give Rolf $2; give Viv $4

3 Since she paid $45 for the item priced at $54, she saved $9.

- (hyphen)

4 - - -; ;- - - -; up-to-date; co-op; father-in-law; four-square

5 pop-up foul; big-time job; snap-on bit; one- or two-hour ski

6 You need 6 signatures--half of the members--on the petition.

19c All Symbols Learned

7 I paid $10 for the low-cost disk; high-priced ones cost $40.

8 Le-An spent $20 for travel, $95 for books, and $38 for food.

9 Mr. Loft-Smit sold his boat for $467; he bought it for $176.

Skill Building

19d Improve Keystroking

10 Edie discreetly decided to deduct expenses in making a deal.

11 Working women wear warm wool sweaters when weather dictates.

12 We heard very rude remarks regarding her recent termination.

13 Daily sudden mishaps destroyed several dozens of sand dunes.

14 Beverley voted by giving a bold beverage to every brave boy.

Lesson 102 Preparing Lease Agreements

Document Design

102b

LEASE AGREEMENTS

A real estate lease is a contractual agreement between the tenant or lessee to pay the landlord or lessor for use of property (also called premises). Many times this is also referred to as a rental agreement. A lease states the rights and responsibilities of each party. The terms of a lease agreement will vary depending upon the parties involved and the type of property. A "residential" lease refers to real estate used as the place a tenant lives, while a "commercial" lease applies to business property. A written lease should be prepared and signed whenever property is rented to reduce the likelihood of misunderstandings between the tenant and the landlord regarding the rental arrangement.

Apply It

102-d1

Residential Lease Agreement

1. Use default margins. Tap ENTER twice after the title; apply Title Style and center-align.

2. At the first blank, set these tabs: right underline at 3", left at 3.5", and a right underline at 5.5". Remove the left tab at 3.5" for the dateline near the bottom. For the blanks with dollar amounts, key 10 underlines.

3. Tap ENTER twice above and below the date line.

4. Proofread and check; click Next Activity. (*102-d1*)

Rental Agreement and Lease

This lease agreement is made between:

> *Set tabs: right underline at 3", left at 3.5".*

_____ (Landlord) and
_____ (Tenant)

For the property on:

_____ (Address)
_____ (City, State and ZIP code)

> *Set right underline at 5.5".*

Occupancy From: _____ To: _____

> *Use 10 underlines.*

Tenant agrees to pay in consecutive monthly installments of $_____ each month, payable on the first of each month. Receipt is hereby acknowledged of the sum of $_____ for the first month's rental, and further sum of $_____ as security deposit.

Tenant agrees to use the premises for residential purposes only and not for illegal, immoral, or hazardous purposes. Only persons who have signed this agreement and their minor children, if any, may occupy the premises.

Tenant is responsible for the electric, gas, water, and telephone service, and all other utility services used in the property during the rental period.

(continued)

19e Textbook Keying

1. Key each line once.
2. When keying easy words and phrases:
 - Think and key words and phrases rather than letter by letter.
 - Make the space part of the word.

easy words

15 am it go bus dye jam irk six sod tic yam ugh spa vow aid dug
16 he or by air big elf dog end fit and lay sue toe wit own got
17 six foe pen firm also body auto form down city kept make fog

easy phrases

18 it is | if the | and also | to me | the end | to us | if it | it is | to the
19 if it is | to the end | do you wish | to go to | for the end | to make
20 lay down | he or she | make me | by air | end of | by me | kept it | of me

easy sentences

21 Did the chap work to mend the torn right half of the ensign?
22 Blame me for their penchant for the antique chair and panel.
23 She bid by proxy for eighty bushels of a corn and rye blend.

19f Textbook Keying

1. Review the Number Expression Guidelines 1–4 in the Reference Guide. Then key sentences 24–29.
2. Key lines 30–35. Decide whether the circled numbers should be keyed as figures or as words and make needed changes.

> **Key numbers without watching your fingers.**

24 **Six** or **seven** older players were cut from the **37**-member team.
25 I have **2** of **14** coins I need to start my set. Christen has **9**.
26 Of **nine 24**-ton engines ordered, we shipped **six** last Tuesday.
27 Shelly has read just **one-half** of about **forty-five** documents.
28 The **six** boys sent well over **two hundred** printed invitations.
29 **One** or **two** of us will be on duty from **two** until **six** o'clock.

30 Jan will come by at ④ o'clock to pick up the ③ girls.
31 Lauren and Paul invited ⑳⓪⓪ guests to the reception.
32 We have ③ more days to finish ②/③ of the plan.
33 Tish sent ⑦ ㉔-pound boxes and ⑩ ③-ounce envelopes.
34 I deposited ⑮ quarters, ⑩ dimes, and ④ nickels in the ATM.
35 A quorum was established; ⑦ of the ⑫ members voted.

19g Enrichment

1. From the Timed Writings tab, choose Writing 2.
2. Set the timing length for 1'.
3. Locate Writing 2 on page 40 and key it twice. Strive to increase speed by 2 gwam the second time.
4. Log out of *KPDO*.

101-d5 and 101-d6 In the open document (*101-d4*), key the information for each bookmark in Document 101-d5. Check; click Next Activity. (*101-d5*) Repeat with the information for the next document. (*101-d6*). Log out of *KPDO*.

Bookmark	Document 101-d5	Document 101-d6
DAY	25	18
MONTH	May	June
FIRST_PARTY	Jeremy Jackson	Michael Parker
SECOND_PARTY	Ryan Ray	Dennis Davis

! WORKPLACE SUCCESS

NOTE

On the Insert tab, in the Apps group, you may add an app into your document and use the Web to enhance your work.

APPS for Office

Apps for Office · Apps

Insert/Apps for Office

As you can insert apps on your smart phone or tablet, Office has this feature allowing you to add apps from the Office Store. Free apps are available, and you may build your own apps. Apps for Office has two options—My Apps and Featured Apps. Search *Apps for Office* for *legal forms*. This will take you to Microsoft Office on the web where you will see the link to download the free Legal Forms.

Once you click on *legalzoom* click Add to download the Free Legal Forms to My Apps in Word.

After downloading the app to My Apps, click Free Legal Forms to access the various forms available. You will be prompted to agree to the terms and privacy policy. **Note:** A Legal Form Guide may be downloaded to assist with completing these forms.

My Apps

Lesson 20 # and /

New Keys

20b Learn # and /

Shift; then reach *up* with *left second* finger.

/ Reach *down* with *right fourth* finger.

= number sign, pounds
/ = diagonal, slash

#

1 # #e e# # # #; had #3 dial; did #3 drop; set #3 down; Bid #3
2 leave #82; sold #20; Lyric #16; bale #34; load #53; Optic #7
3 Notice #333 says to load Car #33 with 33# of #3 grade shale.

/

4 / /; ;/ / / /; 1/2; 1/3; Mr./Mrs.; 1/4/12; 22 11/12; and/or;
5 to/from; /s/ William Smit; 2/10, n/30; his/her towels; 6 1/2
6 The numerals 1 5/8, 3 1/4, and 60 7/9 are "mixed fractions."

20c All Symbols Learned

7 Invoice #737 cites 15 2/3# of rye was shipped C.O.D. 4/6/14.
8 B-O-A Company's Check #50/5 for $87 paid for 15# of #3 wire.
9 Our Co-op List #20 states $40 for 16 1/2 crates of tomatoes.

Skill Building

20d Build Skill

Strive to maintain your speed on the second line in the pair.

10 She did the key work at the height of the problem.
11 Form #726 is the title to the island; she owns it.

12 The rock is a form of fuel; he did enrich it with coal.
13 The corn-and-turkey dish is a blend of turkey and corn.

14 It is right to work to end the social problems of the world.
15 If I sign it on 3/19, the form can aid us to pay the 40 men.

16 Profit problems at the firm may cause it to take many risks.
17 Dale discovered that Invoice #238 for $128.83 is dated 8/15.

101-d2 and 101-d3

Complete Notary Form

1. In the open document (*101-d1*), key the information for each bookmark in Document 101-d2.
2. Proofread and check; click Next Activity. (*101-d2*)
3. Repeat the same steps but insert the information for Document 101-d3.
4. Proofread and check; click Next Activity. (*101-d3*)

Bookmark	Document 101-d2	Document 101-d3
COUNTY	Orange	Los Angeles
DATE	April 12, 201-	April 15, 201-
NOTARY	Robert Bayer, Vice President, Bank of Commerce	Andrew Park, Notary, Quicken Escrow Company
CLIENT	Louise Ann Kruger	Mary Lou Chan

101-d4

Land Trust

A **land trust** is an agreement whereby one party (the trustee) agrees to hold ownership of a piece of real property for the benefit of another party (the beneficiary).

1. Set line spacing at 1.5. Center and underline the heading. Key text in uppercase as shown. Insert a blank line before and after WITNESSETH. Key **WITNESSETH** in uppercase with a space between each letter.
2. Insert bookmarks for the items in parentheses.
3. Proofread and check; click Next Activity. (*101-d4*)

<u>LAND TRUST</u>

THIS AGREEMENT, made and entered into this (Bookmark: DAY) day of (Bookmark:MONTH), 201- by and between (Bookmark:FIRST_PARTY), hereinafter referred to as "First Party" and (Bookmark:SECOND_PARTY) individual resident of Shelby County, Tennessee, hereinafter referred to as "Second Party"; ↓2

W I T N E S S E T H ↓2

WHEREAS, First Party has heretofore conveyed or caused to be conveyed to Second Party as Trustee, the parcel or parcels of real estate located in Shelby County, Tennessee, and more specifically described on Exhibit "A" attached hereto and made a part hereof; and

WHEREAS, the parties do desire to evidence in writing certain of their agreements;

NOW, THEREFORE, and in consideration of One Dollar ($1.00) cash in hand paid this date, and other valuable considerations, each of which is hereby acknowledged, the parties do agree as included in the attachment.

20e Textbook Keying

Key each line once. Notice the difference in the rhythm of your keying.

one hand
18 lip ere him bat lion date pink face pump rear only brag fact
19 at my; oh no; add debt; extra milk; union agreed; act faster

balanced hand
20 so it is | now is the | do so when | sign the forms | is it downtown
21 He may wish to go to town with Pamela to sign the amendment.

combination
22 was for | in the case of | they were | to down | pink bowls | wet rugs
23 They were to be down in the fastest sleigh if you are right.

20f Timed Writing

1. Key a 1' timing on each paragraph; work to increase speed.
2. Key a 3' timing on all paragraphs.

gwam 1' | 3'

Most people want to be socially acceptable. In some 11 | 4
cases, the need for attention can lead to difficulties. Some 23 | 8
of us think that the best way to get attention is to try a new 36 | 12
style, or to look quixotic, or to be different somehow. 47 | 16
Perhaps we are looking for nothing much more than acceptance 59 | 20
from others of ourselves just the way we now are. 68 | 23

There is no question about it; we all want to look our 12 | 27
best to impress other people. How this is achieved may mean 24 | 31
that we try something new, or perform things differently. 35 | 34
Regardless, our basic objective is to continue to build 46 | 38
character with zeal from our raw materials, you and me. 57 | 42

LA ALL LETTERS

1'	1	2	3	4	5	6	7	8	9	10	11	12
3'		1			2			3			4	

Communication

20g Number Expression

Word Processor

1. Review Number Expression in the Reference Guide.
2. In the Word Processor, key sentences 24–27 below. Do not use bold.
3. Key sentences 28 and 29, applying the rules correctly.

24 Ask **Group 2** to read **Chapter 7** of **Book 11** (**Shelf 19, Room 5**).
25 All **six** of us live at **One Bay Lane**, not at **142--59th Street**.
26 At **8 a.m.** the owners decided to close from **12 noon** to **1 p.m.**
27 Ms. Han leaves **June 3**; she returns the **14th or 15th of July**.
28 The 16 percent discount saves $123.50. The tax was 75 cents.
29 Jim poured 3 six-liter jars of oil into the 9 gallon barrel.

DRILL 1 CREATE BOOKMARKS

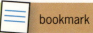 bookmark

Insert/Links/Bookmark

1. Turn on Show/Hide.

2. Delete the text #1 *bookmark*. Create a bookmark named **NAME**.

3. Replace #2 *bookmark* with a bookmark named **NAME_AGAIN**. Key the underscore between words. Be careful not to delete the comma; check spacing.

4. Replace #3 *bookmark* with the bookmark **ADDRESS**.

5. Replace #4 *bookmark* with the bookmark **HUSBAND_NAME**.

6. Replace #5 *bookmark* with the bookmark **HUSBAND_AGAIN**.

7. Replace the text #6 *bookmark* with a bookmark named **EXECUTOR**.

8. Proofread and check; click Next Activity. (*101-drill1*)

DRILL 2 USE BOOKMARK TO INSERT TEXT

Home/Editing/Find/Go To

1. In the open document (*101-drill1*), go to each bookmark, and key the text shown at the right. Key the variable information in uppercase.

2. Proofread and check; click Next Activity. (*101-drill2*)

Go To the bookmark	Key the following text
NAME	REBECCA PEREZ
NAME_AGAIN	REBECCA PEREZ
ADDRESS	One Main Street, Irvine, CA 96203-4865
HUSBAND_NAME	MATEO PEREZ
HUSBAND_AGAIN	MATEO PEREZ
EXECUTOR	GREGORY LEON

Apply It

101-d1

Notary Form

1. Key the notary form using default margins. Replace text in parentheses with bookmarks.

2. Tap ENTER twice, then key **Signature**. Set a right underline tab at 3.5" to create the signature line; tap TAB, then key **(SEAL)**.

3. Proofread and check; click Next Activity. (*101-d1*)

State of California

County of (Bookmark:COUNTY)

On (Bookmark:DATE), before me, (Bookmark:NOTARY), personally appeared (Bookmark:CLIENT), proven to me on the basis of satisfactory evidence to be the person whose name is subscribed to the within instrument and acknowledged to me that she executed the same in her authorized capacity and that by her signature on the instrument the person, or the entity upon behalf of which the person acted, executed the instrument.

WITNESS my hand and official seal.

Signature _____ (Seal)

Lesson 21 % and !

Warmup *Lesson 21a Warmup*

New Keys

21b % and !

% Shift; then reach *up* with *left first* finger.

⭐ **TIP**

- Do not space between a figure and the % or $ sign.
- Do not space before or after the dash.

% = **percent sign:**
Use % with business forms or where space is restricted; otherwise use the word "percent."
Space once after the exclamation point!

© Cengage Learning

%

1 % %f f% % %; off 5%; if 5%; of 5% fund; half 5%; taxes of 5%

2 7% rent; 3% tariff; 9% F.O.B.; 15% greater; 28% base; up 46%

3 Give discounts of 5% on rods, 50% on lures, and 75% on line.

! reach up with the left 4th finger

4 ! !a a! ! ! !; Eureka! Ha! No! Pull 10! Extra! America! Yea!

5 Attention! Now! Ready! On your mark! Get set! Go! Good show!

6 We need it now, not next week! I am sure to lose 50% or $19.

21c All Symbols Learned

7 The ad offers a 10% discount, but this notice says 15% less!

8 He got the job! With Loehman's Supermarket! Please call Mom!

9 Bill #92-44 arrived very late from Zyclone; it was paid 7/4.

21d Improve Keystroking

all symbols

10 As of 6/28, Jeri owes $31 for dinner and $27 for cab fare.

11 Invoice #20--it was dated 3/4--billed $17 less 15% discount.

12 He deducted 2% instead of 6%, a clear saving of 6% vs. 7%.

combination response

13 Look at my dismal grade in English; but I guess I earned it.

14 Kris started to blend a cocoa beverage for a shaken cowhand.

15 Jan may make a big profit if she owns the title to the land.

Lesson 101 Preparing Legal Documents

New Command • Bookmark

New Command

101b

BOOKMARK

A bookmark identifies a specific location within a document so that you can move the insertion point quickly to this location. If a document has more than one bookmark, each must have a unique name. A bookmark name may include letters, numbers, and the underscore character; do not use spaces.

In this lesson, you will use the bookmark to fill in variable information. You will use the Go To feature to move the insertion point to the specific bookmark. **Note:** As a reminder to yourself, you may want to key a bookmark name in uppercase if the replacement text will also be keyed in uppercase.

To insert a bookmark:
Insert/Links/Bookmark

1. Click the insertion point where the bookmark is to be inserted. Click Bookmark to display the Bookmark dialog box.

2. Key the name of the bookmark in the Bookmark name box. ❶ Click the Add button.
 Repeat steps 1–2 for each bookmark.

To use the bookmark:
Home/Editing/Find/Go To

1. In the Go to what pane, select Bookmark.

2. Click in Enter bookmark name box and select the name of the bookmark. Click the Go To button. Click Close.

3. The insertion point displays at the position of the bookmark. Key the information.

21e Textbook Keying

Key each line once.

1st finger

16 by bar get fun van for inn art from gray hymn July true verb

17 brag human bring unfold hominy mighty report verify puny joy

18 You are brave to try bringing home the van in the bad storm.

2nd finger

19 ace ink did cad keyed deep seed kind Dick died kink like kid

20 cease decease decades kick secret check decide kidney evaded

21 Dedre likes the idea of ending dinner with cake for dessert.

3rd finger

22 oil sow six vex wax axe low old lox pool west loss wool slow

23 swallow swamp saw sew wood sax sexes loom stew excess school

24 Wes waxes floors and washes windows at low costs to schools.

4th finger

25 zap zip craze pop pup pan daze quote queen quiz pizza puzzle

26 zoo graze zipper panzer zebra quip partizan patronize appear

27 Czar Zane appears to be dazzled by the apple pizza and jazz.

21f Timed Writing

1. Key a 1' timing on each paragraph.
2. Key a 3' timing on both paragraphs.

	gwam	1'	3'
Teams are the basic unit of performance for a firm. They		12	4
are not the solution to all the problems and needs of the		24	8
organization. However, they can perform at a higher rate		35	12
compared to other groups. Their support has great impact on		47	16
changes that are crucial to a firm.		54	18
Teams are not established just by joining people together		13	22
in a group. Team members should have a clear purpose and they		25	26
should also work with each other to reach a common goal. In		37	30
order to make a quality working plan, the team must maximize		49	38
their time and their abilities. They need to learn how to help		62	39
one another and make an effort to coordinate the tasks.		73	42

```
1' | 1  | 2  | 3  | 4  | 5  | 6  | 7  | 8  | 9  | 10 | 11 | 12 |
3' |     1      |      2      |      3      |      4      |
```

21g Enrichment

Word Processor

Take two 1' writings; the last number you key is your approximate *gwam*.

Reach for numbers with a minimum of hand movement.

1 and 2 and 3 and 4 and 5 and 6 and 7 and 8 and 9 and 10 and 11 and 12 and 13 and 14 and 15 and 16 and 17 and 18 and 19 and 20 and 21 and 22 and 23 and 24 and 25 and 26 and 27 and

1 1. Any and all documents which substantiate the claim for property damage.

2 2. Any and all documents which substantiate the claim for loss of earnings.

3 3. All photographs which in any way relate to the subject matter of this action.

4

5

6 Dated this 1st of June, 201-.

7

8 BARBARA M. JOHNSON
 NEWTON & JOHNSON
9 Attorney for Defendants
 JONATHAN MOVERS and
10 LAUREL DELIVERIES

11

12

13

14

15

16

17

18

19

20

21

22

23

24

25

26

27

28

NOTICE OF DEPOSITION AND REQUEST FOR PRODUCTION OF DOCUMENTS AT DEPOSITION - 2

Notice of Deposition and Request for Production of Documents at Deposition

Lesson 22 (and) and Backspace Key

New Keys

22b (and)

(Shift; then reach *up* with the *right third* finger.

) Shift; then reach *up* with the *right fourth* finger.

() = parentheses
Parentheses indicate off-hand, aside, or explanatory messages.

1 ((l l((; (; Reach from l for the left parenthesis; as, ((.
2)); ;))); Reach from ; for the right parenthesis; as,)).

()

3 Learn to use parentheses (plural) or parenthesis (singular).
4 The red (No. 34) and blue (No. 78) cars both won here (Rio).
5 We (Galen and I) dined (bagels) in our penthouse (the dorm).

22c All Symbols Learned

6 The jacket was $35 (thirty-five dollars)--the tie was extra.
7 Starting 10/29, you can sell Model #49 at a discount of 25%.
8 My size 8 1/2 shoe--a blue pump--was soiled (but not badly).

Skill Building

22d Textbook Keying

Key each line once.

Build confidence—trust yourself to make the correct reach.

9 Jana has one hard-to-get copy of her hot-off-the-press book.
10 An invoice said that "We give discounts of 10%, 5%, and 3%."
11 The company paid bill 8/07 on 5/2/14 and bill 4/9 on 3/6/14.
12 The catalog lists as out of stock Items #230, #710, and #13.
13 Ellyn had $8; Sean, $9; and Cal, $7. The cash total was $24.
14 A representative from the 16th District (Tom Law) will come.
15 The oldest family member (May Gray) will attend the reunion.

1 NEWTON & JOHNSON
 15 Civic Center Drive, Suite 200
2 Santa Ana, CA 92701-3821

3 Telephone: 714.55.0134

4 Attorneys for Defendants

5

6

7

8 SUPERIOR COURT OF THE STATE OF CALLIFORNIA

 FOR THE COUNTY OF ORANGE
9

10

11 HENRY HURT, et al., Case No.: SO C 87321

12 Plaintiff,

13 vs. NOTICE OF DEPOSITION AND REQUEST FOR
 PRODUCTION OF DOCUMENTS AT DEPOSITION
14 JONATHAN MOVERS, et. al.,

 Defendant
15

16

17

18
 TO: ALL PARTIES AND THEIR ATTORNEYS OF RECORD
19

20
 PLEASE TAKE NOTICE that defendants will take the deposition of plaintiff Henry Hurt on July
21
7, 201-, at 2:00 p.m., at the offices of Newton & Johnson, 15 Civic Center Drive, Suite 200, Santa Ana, CA 92701-
22
3821, before a notary public authorized to administer oaths in the State of California. The deposition will continue
23
from day to day, excluding Saturdays, Sundays, and holidays, until completed.
24
 PLEASE TAKE FURTHER NOTICE that plaintiff Henry Hurt is required to bring with him to the
25
deposition the following records, documents, and things:
26
 ///
27
 ///
28

NOTICE OF DEPOSITION AND REQUEST FOR PRODUCTION OF DOCUMENTS AT DEPOSITION - 1

Notice of Deposition and Request for Production of Documents at Deposition

22e Timed Writing

1. Take two 3' timings on both paragraphs.
2. End the lesson.
3. Go to the Word Processor and complete 22f.

It is our obligation to preserve the planet and hand it 4
down to our children and grandchildren in a better condition 8
than when we first found it. We must take extra steps just to 12
make the quality of living better. Unless we change our ways 16
and stop damaging the environment, the world will not be a 20
good place to live. 22

To help save our ozone layer, we should not use any 25
products that may have harmful gas in them. There are many 29
simple and easy ways to clean the air such as planting more 33
trees and reusing materials. Also as important is the proper 37
disposal of our garbage in order to stop our water from 41
getting more and more polluted. 43

3' | 1 | 2 | 3 | 4 |

22f Backspace Key

Word Processor

1. Key sentences 16–21 in the Word Processor; use the BACKSPACE key to correct errors.
2. Key the numbers correctly in sentences 22–26. Refer to the Number Expression section in the Reference Guide.
3. Proofread and correct errors.
4. Save as *xx-22f* (your initials–22f). Print and close the document.

Use the Backspace key effectively.

16 You should be interested in the special items on sale today.
17 If she is going with us, why don't we plan to leave now?
18 Do you desire to continue working on the memo in the future?
19 Did the firm or their neighbors own the autos with problems?
20 Juni, Vec, and Zeb had perfect grades on weekly query exams.
21 Jewel quickly explained to me the big fire hazards involved.

22 All 7 contracts must be signed before 3 o'clock p.m.
23 Purchase 2 16-gigabyte USB flash drives; they are on sale.
24 Jim poured 3 six-liter jars of oil into the 9 gallon barrel.
25 My last computer project is approximately 1/2 complete.
26 The 16 percent discount saves $123.50. The tax was 75 cents.

Communication

22g Proofreading

1. From the Reference tab, click Communication Skills; select Proofreading.
2. Complete the pretest; click Report to review your results. Review the rules and complete the exercises and posttest.

LEGAL DOCUMENTS

100c

Legal documents that are presented for filing in court must follow specific guidelines and be keyed on pleading paper. Most documents today are keyed on standard 8.5" × 11" paper; some lawyers may still use legal size paper (8.5" × 14"). Legal documents contain a double ruling, from top to bottom, at the left margin; a single ruling displays at the right margin. Legal pleading forms contain line numbers in the left margin. The pleading form contains 25, 26, 28, or 32 lines per page.

Each pleading begins with a caption to identify the action. The styles of captions vary, depending on the state; however, all captions include the jurisdiction—the name of the court that has authority to rule with reference to specific persons or subject matter. The name of the county and the state in which the court is located are usually included with the jurisdiction 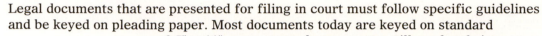.

The pleading also contains a box, which is formed with symbols. The box shows the names of the individuals or corporations involved in the lawsuit ❷. The title of the pleading is located to the right of the box ❸.

The name, address, and telephone number of the attorney originating the paper precedes the caption ❹. In some states, this information is placed at the end of the pleading.

Apply It

100-d1

Notice of Deposition and Request for Production of Documents at Deposition

 legal pleadings 28 lines

A **deposition** is a testimony of a witness taken under oath in question-and-answer form. A deposition has the same legal effect as open court testimony.

1. In the open document, key the deposition on the next two pages. Click on the bracketed text (*Placeholders*) and key the new text. Align your text with the line numbers shown in the illustration. Text shown in uppercase should be keyed in uppercase. Use the fonts of the template.

2. Center and key the placeholder for the court name.

3. Key **/ / /** on lines 27 and 28 to show that the lines were left blank by the writer.

4. To key the second page, place the insertion point on the ¶ at the end of line 28. Tap ENTER to move the insertion point to line 1 on the second page.

5. Proofread and check; close the document. (*100-d1*)

6. Click Exit Word; click Log out to exit *KPDO*.

Lesson 23 & and : (colon), Proofreaders' Marks

New Keys

23b & and : (Colon)

© Cengage Learning

& Shift; then reach *up* with *right first* finger.

© Cengage Learning

: (colon) Left shift; then tap key with *right fourth* finger.

& = ampersand: The ampersand is used only as part of company names.

Colon: Space once after a colon except when used within a number for time.

& (ampersand)

1 & &j j& & & &; J & J; Haraj & Jay; Moroj & Jax; Torj & Jones
2 Nehru & Unger; Mumm & Just; Mann & Hart; Arch & Jones; M & J
3 Rhye & Knox represent us; Steb & Doy, Firm A; R & J, Firm B.

: (colon)

4 : :; ;: : : :; as: for example: notice: Dear Sir: Gentlemen:
5 In stock: 10:30; 7:45; Age: Address: Read: Cell: Attachment:
6 Space once after a colon, thus: Telephone: Home Address: To:

23c All Symbols Learned

7 Consider these companies: J & R, Brand & Kay, Upper & Davis.
8 Memo #88-829 reads as follows: "Deduct 15% of $300, or $45."
9 Bill 32(5)--it got here quite late--from M & N was paid 7/3.

Skill Building

23d Textbook Keying

Key each line once.

10 Jane may work with an auditing firm if she is paid to do so.
11 Pam and eight girls may go to the lake to work with the dog.
12 Clancy and Claudia did all the work to fix the sign problem.
13 Did Lea visit the Orlando land of enchantment or a neighbor?
14 Ana and Blanche made a map for a neighbor to go to the city.
15 Sidney may go to the lake to fish with worms from the docks.
16 Did the firm or the neighbors own the auto with the problem?

Lesson 100 Legal Pleadings

Review Commands

100b

Pleadings will open automatically as a data file. You will not download it.

TEMPLATES

Templates are preformatted files that contain the fonts, placeholders, or locations where information is inserted each time. Legal pleading templates are available for download from Office.com. The pleading forms are preformatted to include vertical rulings, line numbers, and boxed areas.

To download the legal pleading template:
File/New

1. In the Search online templates box, key **pleadings**; tap ENTER.

2. Choose Pleading form with 28 lines.

3. Double-click on the Pleadings template to open it or click once and then click Create.

4. Once you download the template, it will be available in the template list the next time you go to File/New. In a classroom, however, you may need to save it to a flash drive or another location.

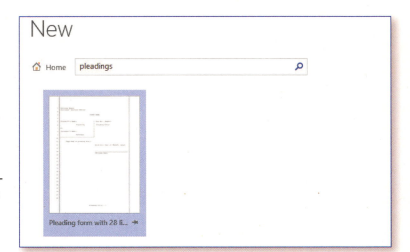

DRILL 1 — DOWNLOAD LEGAL PLEADING TEMPLATE

File/New

KPDO users: Skip this drill.

1. Search for *Pleadings* at www.Office.com.

2. Download the Pleading form with 28 lines.

3. Scroll through the document; then close it without saving it.

4. Open the Pleadings template (see Use the Legal Pleadings template).

5. To save the template to a flash drive, open the template. It will appear in *Word*'s opening screen.

6. Browse to your flash drive and save as a template file with a .dotx extension, which is assigned automatically.

23e Improve Keystroking

double letters

17 Do Bennett was puzzled by drivers exceeding the speed limit.
18 Bill needs the office address; he will cut the grass at ten.
19 Todd saw the green car veer off the street near a tall tree.

figures and symbols

20 Invoice #84 for $672.90, plus $4.38 tax, was due February 3.
21 Do read Section 4, pages 60–74 and Section 9, pages 198–225.
22 Enter as follows: (a) name, (b) address, and (c) cell phone.

23f Timed Writing

Take two 3' timings. Use wordwrap.

gwam 3'

Is how you judge my work important? Does your honest 4
opinion or feedback really matter? It does, of course; I hope 8
you appreciate the effort and recognize some basic merit in 12
it. We all expect to get credit for the hard work we put forth 16
and the good work we conclude. After all, we are all working 20
together to accomplish the goals of the company. 23

As a human being, I want approval for the ideas 27
presented, things written, and tasks completed. I always look 31
forward to your evaluations so I can learn more and continue 35
to grow. My work does not define me, but it shows my abilities 39
and skills. Through my work, I am my very own unique self. 43

3' | 1 | 2 | 3 | 4 |

Communication

23g Edit Text

Word Processor

1. In the Word Processor, key your name, class, and **23g** at the left margin. Then key lines 23–28, making the revisions as you key. Use the BACKSPACE key to correct errors.

2. Proofread and correct errors.

3. Save as xx-23g.

Symbol	Meaning	Symbol	Meaning
——	Italic	sp	Spell out
~~~	Bold	¶	Paragraph
Cap or ≡	Capitalize	#	Add horizontal space
∧	Insert	/ or lc	Lowercase
✐	Delete	⌒	Close up space
⊏	Move to left	∼	Transpose
⊐	Move to right	stet	Leave as originally written

23 We miss 50% in life's rewards by refusing to new try things.

24 do it now--today--then tomorrow's load will be 100%% lighter.

25 Satisfying work- whether it pays $40 or $400-is the pay off.

26 Avoid mistakes: confusing a #3 for a #5 has cost thousands.

27 Pleased most with a first-rate job is the person who did it.

28 My wife and/or me mother will except the certificate for me.

Enclosed you will find an envelope for returning the Certificate of Reservation of «Name» and a check for $750 to cover the processing fee.

Thank you for your attention to this matter.

Sincerely | Armando J. Reynoza | Attorney | xx | Enclosures

---

**99-d3**

**Create Resolution to Dissolve Corporation**

1. Beginning at about 2", center and underline the title. Tap ENTER five times.
2. Key the document using uppercase and bold where shown. Remove space after all paragraphs. Tap ENTER between paragraphs and between parts of the document as marked.
3. Indent the last two paragraphs 0.5" from the left margin.
4. For the signature line, set a left tab at 3" and a right underline tab at 6.5". Drag the left tab to 3.5" before keying **NAME**.
5. Proofread and check; close the document. (*99-d3*)
6. Click Exit Word.
7. Click Log out to exit *KPDO*.

<u>RESOLUTION SETTING FORTH PLAN TO</u>
<u>DISSOLVE FAIREY FOOD SHOPS</u>

 5

**WHEREAS,** the Board of Directors wishes to dissolve the Corporation, authorized by the Corporations' Articles of Dissolution date June 30, 201-, and

**WHEREAS,** the Board of Directors also deems it desirable that the Corporation dissolve its corporate form and its corporate charter in Memphis, Shelby County, Tennessee, and

**WHEREAS,** the Corporation is a Tennessee Corporation as that term is used and defined in the General Corporation Act of Tennessee;

 3

**NOW, THEREFORE, BE IT RESOLVED**

That pursuant to this resolution, the shareholders and incorporators of record hereby authorize and direct that the Corporation's Articles of Dissolution be accepted and the corporation shall be dissolved.

 6

<span style="color:red">Left tab 3"; Right underline tab 6.5"</span> ⟶ _____

<span style="color:red">Drag tab to 3.5"</span> ⟶  NAME

# Lesson 24 Other Symbols

## New Keys

**24b  Textbook Keying**

@  *  +  =

> **Be confident—watch the copy, not the hands.**

@	at
*	asterisk
+	plus sign (use a hyphen for minus and x for "times")
=	equals

**@  shift; reach *up* with *left third* finger to @**

1  @ @s s@ a a; 24 @ .15; 22 @ .35; sold 2 @ .87; were 12 @ .95

2  You may contact Calvin @: CEP@rpx.com or fax @ 602.555.0101.

3  E-mail Al ajj@crewl.com and Matt mrw10@scxs.com by 9:30 p.m.

***  shift; reach *up* with *right second* finger to ***

4  * *k k8* * *; aurelis*; May 7*; both sides*; 250 km.**; aka*

5  Note each *; one * refers to page 29; ** refers to page 307.

6  Use *.* to scarch for files; the * looks for all characters.

**+  shift; reach *up* with *right fourth* finger to +**

7  + ;+ +; + + +; 2 + 2; A+ or B+; 70+ F. degrees; +xy over +y;

8  The question was 8 + 7 + 51; it should have been 8 + 7 + 15.

9  My grades on the tests and final exam are B+, C+, B+, and A.

**=  reach *up* with *right fourth* finger to =**

10  = =; = = =; = 4; If 14x = 28, x = 2; if 8x = 16, then x = 2.

11  Change this solution (where it says "= by") to = bx or = BX.

12  Key the formula =(a2+b2)*d5/4 in the formula bar; tap Enter.

Set tabs ——→ Name: «Name»

Street Address: «Street_Address»

City: «City»        California        ZIP Code: «ZIP_Code»

V

The corporation is authorized to issue only one class of stock; and the total number of shares, which the corporation is authorized to issue is «Amount».

↓2

Left tab 3"; Right underline tab 6.5" ——————→
Move left tab to 3.5" ————————→

_____

David M. Smith, Incorporator

---

## 99-d2

**Mail Merge Letter**

1. In the open document, create the data source using the field names in the table below. (*99-d2data*)

	Letter 1	Letter 2
**Name**	LO-CARB MEALS, INC.	NEW IMAGE SURGERY CENTER
**First**	LO-CARB MEALS ARE US, INC.	A-1 PROFESSIONAL SURGERY CENTER
**Second**	LO-CARB DIETS, INC.	IDEAL SURGERY CENTER
**Third**	LO-CARB PASTA, INC.	A-1 LASER SURGERY CENTER

2. Key the letter (*99-d2main*) in block style with open punctuation. Center «Name». Set left tabs at 0.5" and 1.5" before inserting the merge fields in paragraph 2.

3. Merge the data source and the main document.

4. Proofread and check; click Next Activity. (*99-d2*)

---

Current date  |  Secretary of State  |  State of California  |  P. O. Box 12345  |  Sacramento, CA 96814-2591  |  Dear Secretary

Please reserve the following name to be used by a California corporation proposed to be formed in the near future:

«Name»

If the name is not available for corporate use, the following names are listed as alternatives:

Set tabs ——→ Alternative 1:          «First»

Alternative 2:          «Second»

Alternative 3:          «Third»

*(continued)*

# Skill Building

## 24c  Improve Keystroking

double letters
13 feel pass mill good miss seem moons cliffs pools green spell

14 Assets are being offered in a stuffy room to two associates.

balanced hand
15 is if of to it go do to is do so if to the to sign it vie to

16 Pamela or Jen may also go to town with Blanche if she works.

## 24d  Timed Writing

Take two 3' timings.
Use wordwrap.

	gwam 3'
Why do we resist change so much? Do you think perhaps it	4
is because it requires more time and effort learning new	8
things and making difficult decisions? Is it also because we	12
are set in our ways, afraid to take chances and dislike being	16
told what to do? Besides, what is the point of trying to	20
improve something that works just fine?	22
We know change can and does extend new areas of	26
enjoyment, areas we might never have known existed. If we stay	30
away from all change, we could curtail our quality of life.	34
People who are open to change are more zealous and more	38
productive than those who aren't. They are also better at	42
coping with the hardships and challenges that life often	46
brings.	46

3' | 1 | 2 | 3 | 4 |

# Communication

## 24e  Composition

1. In the Word Processor, open the file *xx-profile* that you created in Lesson 18.
2. Position the insertion point at the end of the last paragraph. Tap ENTER twice.
3. Key an additional paragraph that begins with the following sentence:

   **Thank you for allowing me to introduce myself.**
4. Finish the paragraph by adding two or more sentences that describe your progress and satisfaction with keyboarding.
5. Correct any mistakes you have made. Click Save to resave the document. Print.
6. Mark any mistakes you missed with proofreaders' marks. Revise the document and save. Submit to your instructor.

## 24f  Edit Copy

1. In the Word Processor, key your name, class, and date at the left margin on separate lines.
2. Key each line, making the corrections marked with proofreaders' marks.
3. Proofread and correct errors using the BACKSPACE key.
4. Save as *xx-24f*.

17 Ask Group 1 to read Chater 6 of Book 11 (Shelf 19, Room 5).

18 All 6 of us live at One Bay road, not at 126-56th Street.

19 AT 9 a.m. the owners decided to close form 12 noon to 1 p.m.

20 Ms. Vik leaves June 9; she returns the 14 or 15 of July.

21 The 16 percent discount saves 115.  A stamp costs 44 cents.

22 Elin gave $300,000,000; our gift was only 75 cents.

1. Use the Mail Merge Wizard to create the Articles of Incorporation (*99-d1main*). Begin by creating the data source. Use the fields and data shown in the table. (*99-d1data*)

Field Name	Entry 1	Entry 2
Corporate Name	Quality Care Medical Center	Gourmet Food Shops
Profession	providing medical care	providing retail sales
Name	Andrew Wainscott	Jeannette Smith
Street Address	5561 Golden Lantern Drive	1521 Mack Avenue
City	Laguna Niguel	Orange
ZIP Code	92677-1234	92865-2214
Amount	Ten Thousand (10,000)	Five Thousand (5,000)

2. Tap ENTER five times at the top margin of the main document for the Secretary of State to place the filing stamp. Apply Heading 1 style to the title and center-align.

3. Key the Articles of Incorporation, inserting the fields shown. In paragraph 4, set left tabs at 0.5", 2", and 3.5".

4. Tap ENTER twice before keying the signature. Clear the tabs and set a left tab at 3" and a right underline tab at 6.5". Remove spacing after the line before keying the name. Drag the left tab to 3.5" then key the name.

5. Merge the data source and the main document. Click Next Activity. (*99-d1*)

Articles of Incorporation 2

I

The name of this corporation is «Corporate_Name»

II

The purpose of the corporation is to engage in the profession of «Profession» and any other lawful activities (other than the banking or trust company business) not prohibited to a corporation engaging in such profession by applicable laws and regulations.

III

The corporation is a professional corporation within the meaning of Part 4, Division 3, Title I, California Corporation Code.

IV

The name and address in the State of California of this corporation's initial agent for service of process are:

*(continued)*

# Lesson 24R Review

## Skill Building

### 24Rb  Textbook Keying

Key each line once; work for fluency.

1 E-mail invoice #397 to gmeathe@skd.org; the $7 will be paid.
2 Jane and Ken may go to town to handle the pale and sick dog.
3 The answers to pop quiz #12 are: (1) a, (2) c, (3) b, (4) c.
4 Uncle Jeff rented a burgundy minivan for three days a month.
5 Check #42 was sent on 6/15 for the amount of $89 as payment.
6 Zale played amazing pop jazz on a saxophone and a xylophone.
7 L & D Bank pays 7% interest on savings accounts, 10% on CDs.

### 24Rc  Timed Writing

1. Key a 1' timing on each paragraph; work to increase speed.
2. Key a 3' timing on all paragraphs.

	gwam	1'	3'
Do you find yourself forgetting the names of people that		12	4
you have known for quite some time? Did you put something down		25	8
and a few minutes later were not able to find it again? Memory		37	12
lapses like these are normal, and there are things you can do		50	17
to prevent them from happening as often. Just a few simple		62	21
lifestyle changes can easily help improve your emory.		72	24
Everyone can take steps to better their memory; it will		12	28
take both time and practice. It is important to get enough		24	32
sleep and to eat properly. Exercise both the mind and the		36	36
body. Read, write, and do puzzles each day to help develop		47	44
your memory. Make time for family and friends and have a good		60	48
time with them.		63	49

```
1' |  1  |  2  |  3  |  4  |  5  |  6  |  7  |  8  |  9  | 10  | 11  | 12  |
3' |     1     |     2     |     3     |     4     |
```

### 24Rd  Enrichment

**Word Processor**

1. Key the paragraphs in the Word Processor, making revisions as you key.
2. Key your name and 24Rd below the paragraph.
3. Save as *xx-24Rd*.

Any one who expects someday to find an excellent job should learn
the value of accuracy. To be worth any thing, completed work must be
correct, accurate, without any question. Of course, we realize that the aspect of the
work equation raises always the chance of errors; we should know that
those same mistakes can be found and fixed. Every job completed should
carry at least 1 stamp; the stamp of approval in work that is outstanding.

## Document Design

**99c  Legal Documents**

In this module you will work with a variety of legal documents, including court, corporate, and personal legal instruments. Legal document formats vary from state to state, but they share many commonalities. Most law firms still use 12-point Times New Roman to format legal documents. Court documents format the title in uppercase, and some states underline the title. Legal files are downloadable from various courts within the state.

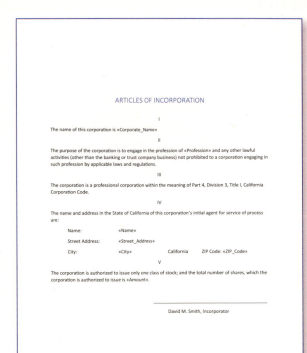

ARTICLES OF INCORPORATION

I

The name of this corporation is «Corporate_Name»

II

The purpose of the corporation is to engage in the profession of «Profession» and any other lawful activities (other than the banking or trust company business) not prohibited to a corporation engaging in such profession by applicable laws and regulations.

III

The corporation is a professional corporation within the meaning of Part 4, Division 3, Title I, California Corporation Code.

IV

The name and address in the State of California of this corporation's initial agent for service of process are:

Name:  «Name»

Street Address:  «Street_Address»

City:  «City»  California  ZIP Code: «ZIP_Code»

V

The corporation is authorized to issue only one class of stock; and the total number of shares, which the corporation is authorized to issue is «Amount».

_____

David M. Smith, Incorporator

The Articles of Incorporation at the left contains information about the name, address, purpose of the company, and share structure. Articles of Incorporation differ for medical, nonprofit, professional, and municipal corporations. The documents in this module represent various formats, such as merge documents, fill-in forms, and templates. Follow these guidelines for keying legal documents.

- **Theme:** Use default Calibri 11-point font.
- **Margins:** Use 1" default margins unless specified.
- **Spacing:** Use default single spacing (1.08).
- **Signature lines:** Set tabs as instructed to format.
- **Main headings:** Specified in the directions.

---

**DRILL 1**  REVIEW MAIL MERGE   power of attorney

*Mailings/Start Mail Merge/Step by Step Mail Merge Wizard*

Use the Mail Merge Wizard to create the main document (*99-drill1main*) and the data source (*99-drill1data*). Customize the fields and complete the merge. For further review of mail merge, see Lesson 76.

**Step 1**:  Select Letters.

**Step 2**:  Select Use the current document.

**Step 3**:  Select Type a new list; click Create.

- When the New Address List appears, click Custom Columns.
- Select each field and delete it; then click the Add button and key the three field names below. Key the data for each field from the table. Click Next.

Field Name	Recipient 1	Recipient 2
County	Orange	San Diego
Name	Rod Rodriguez	Tom Thompson
Date	June 6, 201-	June 15, 201-

**Step 4**:  Select Write your letter. Since your document is already keyed and on screen, click More items.

- To insert the first merge code, select (Field: County) and the parentheses, click Insert, and Close.
- Repeat this process for the next two fields.

**Step 5**:  Choose Next: Complete the Merge.

**Step 6**:  Select Edit individual letters.

- Preview and check for correctness.
- When the Merge to New Document displays, click OK.

**Step 7**:  Proofread and check. Click Next Activity (*99-drill1*).

---

***Non-KPDO users:*** Open the data file *power of attorney*. Then begin the Mail Merge Wizard. Save the data file as *99-drill1data*, the main document as *99-drill1main,* and the completed merge as *99-drill1*.

# Lesson 25 Assessment

## Skill Building

### 25b Improve Keystroking

n/y
1 deny many canny tiny nymph puny any puny zany penny pony yen
2 Jenny Nyles saw many, many tiny nymphs flying near her pony.

b/r
3 bran barb brim curb brat garb bray verb brag garb bribe herb
4 Barb Barber can bring a bit of bran and herbs for her bread.

c/e
5 cede neck nice deck dice heck rice peck vice erect mice echo
6 Can Cedric erect a decent cedar deck? He erects nice condos.

n/u
7 nun gnu bun nut pun numb sun nude tuna nub fun null unit gun
8 Eunice had enough ground nuts at lunch; Uncle Launce is fun.

### 25c Textbook Keying

Key each line once.

9 is if he do rub ant go and am pan do rut us aid ox ape by is
10 it is|an end|it may|to pay|and so|aid us|he got|or own|to go
11 Did the girl make the ornament with fur, duck down, or hair?

12 us owl rug box bob to man so bit or big pen of jay me age it
13 it|it is|time to go|show them how|plan to go|one of the aims
14 It is a shame they use the autobus for a visit to the field.

### 25d Timed Writing

Key two 3' writings. Strive for accuracy. Use wordwrap.

**Goal:** 3', 19–27 *gwam*.

**Build confidence—trust your reach instincts.**

gwam 3'

The term career can mean many different things to different people. As you know, a career is more than just an occupation. It includes the jobs an individual has over time. It also involves how the work life affects the other parts of our life. There are as many types of careers as there are people.

Almost every person has a career of some kind. A career can help us attain unique goals, such as having a stable livelihood or a rewarding vocation. The kind of career you have will affect your life in many ways. For example, it can determine where you live, the money you make, and how you feel about yourself. A good choice can thus help you realize the life you want.

4
8
12
16
20
20
24
28
32
36
40
44
45

3' | 1 | 2 | 3 | 4 |

# Legal Documents

## LEARNING OUTCOMES

- Format legal documents.
- Format legal business documents.
- Format personal legal documents.
- Use templates to create legal documents.
- Build keyboarding skills.

## Lesson 99 Corporate Legal Documents

**Warmup**    *Lesson 99a Warmup*      A   **ALL LETTERS**

## Skill Building

### 99b   Timed Writing

Key a 3' timing on all paragraphs.

Forms provide both a productive and an effective way to collect data. Designing an effective form often does not happen quickly, but the time spent can be justified quite easily. The time spent creating a form is productive because once the form has been finished, it can be used multiple times.

Forms provide an effective way of collecting data because they add structure. Forms can be set up so that the data is organized in exactly the way the designer wants to collect it. Analyzing data can be simplified by the way in which the form is structured. Information is also much easier to tabulate from data on a well-designed form.

When you complete information online, you are using a form. If you make a purchase, you fill in a form with your name, address, payment method and other needed information. When you create your own forms, you may link to your form or embed your form in a web page. Make sure you design your form so it is easy for the user to complete and provides the results you need.

## 25e  Figure Check

**Word Processor**

In the Word Processor, key two 3' writings at a controlled rate. Save the timings as xx-25e-t1 and xx-25e-t2. Use wordwrap.

**Goal:** 3', 14–16 *gwam*.

Do people read the stock market pages in the news? Yes; | 4
at approximately 9 or 10 a.m. each morning, I know lots of | 8
excited people who do that. Some people still like to have the | 12
paper delivered to their home each morning. Others like the | 16
convenience of reading the news on their computer or their | 20
cell phone. Nevertheless, we can't wait to obtain the first | 24
stock report each day. | 26

Some people take the stock market very seriously. They | 30
watch their stocks carefully and note the rise and fall of | 34
each stock. Most investors like to be able to "buy at 52 and | 38
sell at 60." Some would like to receive a dividend of 7 or 8 | 42
percent on their stocks. Regardless, each morning we zip | 45
immediately to the stock report to see how the market is | 49
doing. When the stock is down, we quickly purchase more shares | 53
and keep them until they increase in value. The stock market | 58
is an important and vital part of our life. | 60

3' | 1 | 2 | 3 | 4 |

# Communication

## 25f  Edit Copy

1. In the Word Processor, key your name, class, and date at the left margin.
2. Key the paragraphs and make the corrections marked with proofreaders' marks. Use the BACK-SPACE key to correct errors.
3. Check number expressions.
4. Save as *xx-25f*.

Last week the healthy heart foundation released the findings of a study that showed exercise diet and if individuals don't smoke are the major controllable factors that led to a healthy heart. Factors such as heredity can not be controlled. The study included 25 to 65 year old males as well as females. The study also showed that just taking a walk benefits our health. Those who walked an average of 2 to 3 hours a week were more then 30 percent less likely to have problems than those who did no exercise.

## 25g  Proofread and Edit

**Learn More:**

www.cengagebrain.com

1. In the Word Processor, open *xx-24Rd*.
2. Turn to page 70 and proofread your document with Writing 11.
3. Make corrections as needed. Save as *xx-25g*. Print.

## ACKNOWLEDGMENTS

Joseph Green, Mayor

Linda Rodriguez, City Council Member

Robert Smith, State Assemblyman

Accurate Results Laboratory

Arondale University Nursing Students

Austin Medical Staffing

Balfour Pharmaceuticals, Inc.

Better Meds Pharmacy

Dr. Daniel Brown, Cardiothoracic Surgeon

Crossroads Memorial Hospital

Exceptional Medical Supplies

Dr. Oscar Moore, Dermatologist

Reliance National Bank

## Community Health Fair

### Saturday, October 11, 201-

Sponsored by Arondale Medical Center and Hess Office Park

---

## Seminars

Free informational seminars are offered throughout the day in the Gold Conference Room in Building B.

### Cardiac Robotic Surgery          10:30 a.m.

This advanced procedure is performed through a few tiny openings instead of the foot-long incision to open the chest. This revolutionary procedure means fewer complications, less discomfort, and faster recoveries. Dr. Daniel Brown, Cardiothoracic Surgeon at Grace Trinity Hospital, is the seminar speaker.

### Skin Cancer          1:30 p.m.

Dr. Oscar Moore, a leading Dermatologist in the area, will discuss the dangers of sun exposure and the risk for being diagnosed with skin cancer. A variety of topics centered on skin cancer, including how skin color and type impacts your risk, why Vitamin D is important for your skin, and the various types of skin cancer.

### Weight Loss Surgery          3:30 p.m.

This seminar will cover surgical procedures, expectations, recovery, and follow-up. A board-certified bariatric surgeon and bariatric nurse coordinator will share information and answer questions.

### Building A: Drive-thru Flu Clinic

A drive-thru flu clinic will be administered on the north side of Reliance National Bank. This is convenient for those who do not want to park and walk to the clinic.

### Building B: Seminars

Seminars will be held in the Gold Conference Room. See seminar schedule for topics and times.

### Building C: Arondale Medical Center

Free health screenings and flu shots will be administered in the Arondale Medical Center.

# Skill Builder 2

Select the Skill Building tab from the Main menu and then Technique Builder. Select the drill and follow the directions in the book.

## DRILL 8

### Opposite Hand Reaches

Key each line once and DS between groups of lines. Key at a controlled rate; concentrate on the reaches.

i/e

1 ik is fit it sit laid site like insist still wise coil light
2 ed he ear the fed egg led elf lake jade heat feet hear where
3 lie kite item five aide either quite linear imagine brighter
4 Imagine the aide eating the pears before the grieving tiger.

w/o

5 ws we way was few went wit law with weed were week gnaw when
6 ol on go hot old lot joy odd comb open tool upon money union
7 bow owl word wood worm worse tower brown toward wrote weapon
8 The workers lowered the brown swords toward the wood weapon.

## DRILL 9

### Proofreaders' Marks

Key each line once and DS after each sentence. Correct the sentence as edited, making all handwritten corrections. Do not key the numbers.

= Capitalize
/ Change letter
c Close up space
ɟ Delete
∧ Insert
lc Lowercase
# Space
∽ Transpose

1. When a writer create the preliminary version of a document, they are concentrating on conveying the intended ideas.
2. This ver sion of a preliminary document is called a rough.
3. After the draft is created the Writer edits/refines the copy.
4. Sometimes proofreader's marks are used to edit the draft.
5. The changes will them be make to the original. editing again
6. After the changes have been made, then the Writer reads the copy.
7. Edit ing and proofreading requires alot of time and effort.
8. An attitude of excellance is required to produce error free message.

## DRILL 10

### Proofreading

Compare your sentences in Drill 9 with Drill 10. How did you do? Now key the paragraph for fluency. Concentrate on keying as accurately as possible.

When a writer creates the preliminary version of a document, he or she is concentrating on conveying ideas. This preliminary version is called a rough draft. After the draft is created, the writer edits or refines the copy. Proofreaders' marks are used to edit the rough draft. The editing changes will be made to the original. Then the writer reads the copy again. Editing requires a lot of time and effort. An attitude of excellence is required to produce an error-free message.

Page 2, Column 1

Seminars

Free informational seminars are offered throughout the day in the Gold Conference Room in Building B.

Cardiac Robotic Surgery      10:30 a.m.

This advanced procedure is performed through a few tiny openings instead of the foot-long incision to open the chest. This revolutionary procedure means fewer complications, less discomfort, and faster recoveries.
Dr. Daniel Brown, Cardiothoracic Surgeon at Grace Trinity Hospital, is the seminar speaker.

Skin Cancer                1:30 p.m.

Dr. Oscar Moore, a leading dermatologist in the area, will discuss the dangers of sun exposure and the risk for being diagnosed with skin cancer. A variety of topics centered on skin cancer, including how skin color and type impacts your risk, why Vitamin D is important for your skin, and the various types of skin cancer.

Weight Loss Surgery           3:30 p.m.

This seminar will cover surgical procedures, expectations, recovery, and follow-up. A board-certified bariatric surgeon and bariatric nurse coordinator will share information and answer questions.

Page 2, Column 2

(Insert site plan.tif)

**Building A: Drive-thru Flu Clinic**

A drive-thru flu clinic will be administered on the north side of Reliance National Bank. This is convenient for those who do not want to park and walk to the clinic.

**Building B: Seminars**

Seminars will be held in the Gold Conference Room. See seminar schedule for topics and times.

**Building C: Arondale Medical Center**

Free health screenings and flu shots will be administered in the Arondale Medical Center.

## Assess Skill Growth:

1. Select the Timed Writings tab from the Main menu.
2. Select the writing number such as Writing 8.
3. Select 3' as the length of the writing. Use wordwrap.
4. Repeat the timing if desired.

## Word Processor Option:

1. Key 1' writings on each paragraph of a timing. Note that paragraphs within a timing increase by two words.
   **Goal:** to complete each paragraph
2. Key a 3' timing on the entire writing.

## Writing 8

	1'	3'
Any of us whose target is to have success in our professional	12	4
work will understand that we must learn how to work in harmony	25	8
with others whose paths may cross ours daily.	34	11
We will, unquestionably, work for, with, and beside people, just	13	15
as they will work for, with, and beside us. We will judge them,	25	20
as most certainly they are going to be judging us.	35	23
A lot of people realize the need for solid working relations and	13	27
have a rule that treats others as they, themselves, expect to be	26	32
treated. This seems to be a sound, practical idea for them.	37	35

## Writing 9

	1'	3'
I spoke with one company visitor recently; and she was very much	13	4
impressed, she said, with the large amount of work she had noted	26	9
being finished by one of our front office workers.	36	12
I told her how we had just last week recognized this very person	13	16
for what he had done, for output, naturally, but also because of	26	21
its excellence. We know this person has that "magic touch."	38	25
This "magic touch" is the ability to do a fair amount of work in	13	29
a fair amount of time. It involves a desire to become ever more	26	34
efficient without losing quality--the "touch" all workers should	39	38
have.	40	38

## Writing 10

	1'	3'
Isn't it great just to untangle and relax after you have keyed a	13	4
completed document? Complete, or just done? No document is	25	8
quite complete until it has left you and passed to the next step.	38	13
There are desirable things that must happen to a document before	13	17
you surrender it. It must be read carefully, first of all, for	26	22
meaning to find words that look right but aren't. Read word for	39	26
word.	40	26
Check all figures and exact data, like a date or time, with your	13	31
principal copy. Make sure format details are right. Only then,	26	35
print or remove the work and scrutinize to see how it might look	39	39
to a recipient.	42	40

1' | 1 | 2 | 3 | 4 | 5 | 6 | 7 | 8 | 9 | 10 | 11 | 12 | 13 |
3' | 1 | | 2 | | 3 | | 4 |

    **f.** Search for the "blood pressure cuff" in Clip Art. Change the Wrap Text style to Behind Text. Change the height to 1.33" and the width to 1.06".

    **g.** Search for "blood test" in Clip Art. Change the Wrap Text style to Behind Text. Change the height and width to 1.04".

    **h.** Center the text in Britannic Bold, 11-point font at the bottom of the page.

**5.** Format page 2, column 1:

    **a.** Tap ENTER twice; then center **Seminars** in Britannic Bold, 18-point font.

    **b.** Apply Heading 1 style to the seminar names and times. Align the times by setting a right-align tab at 4.25.

    **c.** Search for a "microscope" in Clip Art. Change the height of the microscope to 7" high, if necessary. Change the color to Washout (Picture Tools Format/Adjust/Color/Washout). Change the Wrap Text style to Behind Text.

**6.** Format page 2, column 2:

    **a.** Tap ENTER; then insert the *site plan* picture from your data files.

    **b.** Key the text below the picture. Apply Heading 1 style to the headings.

**7.** Proofread and check; click Exit *Word* and Log out to exit *KPDO*. (98-d2)

Page 1, Column 1 (left column)

### ACKNOWLEDGMENTS

Joseph Green, Mayor

Linda Rodriguez, City Council Member

Robert Smith, State Assemblyman

Accurate Results Laboratory

Arondale University Nursing Students

Austin Medical Staffing

Balfour Pharmaceuticals, Inc.

Better Meds Pharmacy

Dr. Daniel Brown, Cardiothoracic Surgeon

Crossroads Memorial Hospital

Exceptional Medical Supplies

Dr. Oscar Moore, Dermatologist

Reliance National Bank

Page 1, Column 2

Community Health Fair

Saturday, October 11, 201-

(insert pictures)

Sponsored by Arondale Medical Center and Hess Office Park.

*(continued)*

## Writing 11

Anyone who expects some day to find a great job should    4
begin now to learn the value of accuracy. To be worth anything,    8
final work must be correct, without question. Of course, we    12
realize that the human aspect of the work equation always raises    16
the chance of errors; but we should understand that those same    20
errors can be found and fixed. Every completed job should carry    24
at least one stamp; the stamp of true pride in work that is exemplary.    29

## Writing 12

No question about it: Many of the personal problems we face    4
today arise from the fact that we have never been very wise    8
consumers. We have not used our natural resources well; as a result,    13
we have jeopardized much of our environment. We excused our    17
actions because we thought that our stock of most resources had no    21
limit at all. So, at last, we are beginning to realize just how indiscreet    26
we were; and we are taking steps to rebuild our world.    30

## Writing 13

When I see people in top jobs, I know I am seeing people who    4
sell. I am not just referring to employees who work in a retail outlet; I    9
mean all people who put extra effort into convincing others to    13
recognize their best qualities. They, themselves, are what they sell;    18
and the major tools they use are their appearance, their language, and    22
their personality. They look great, they talk and write well; and, with    27
much self-confidence, they meet you eye to eye.    30

3' | 1 | 2 | 3 | 4 |

Address Line 1	3401 Madison Avenue	501 Harbor Avenue	17 Superior Road
City	Austin	Austin	Austin
State	TX	TX	TX
ZIP Code	73301-9076	73344-1789	78701-0192

**Body of Letter:**

Dear *«Title» «Last Name»*

A Community Health Fair will be held in the main concourse at Hess Office Park on Saturday, October 11, 201-, from 10:30 a.m. to 4:00 p.m. The Community Health Fair will promote health education and wellness living to the tenants at Hess Office Park, their family and friends, as well as to the local community. City and state officials will also be in attendance.

*«Company Name»* has been selected to participate as a vendor at this important community event. The event will be highly promoted and publicized by Arondale Medical Center and Hess Office Park management. Your presence is welcomed; this will provide an opportunity for prominent visibility for your organization.

We would like to thank you for your interest in taking an active part in the health fair. If you would like to reserve your booth, please complete the enclosed form and return it by September 8, 201-. Please call me if you have questions or if I can be of assistance.

## 98-d2

**Health Fair Program**

hess photo
arondale logo
site plan

Insert a column break (Page Layout/Breaks/Column) to move insertion point to the next column.

1. Prepare a two-page brochure that will be printed from front and back and folded in half. Use the illustration on page 478 as a page layout guide.
2. Use landscape orientation; change the left and right margin to 0.5". Format the document in two columns, each with 4.5" width and 1" space between columns.
3. Format page 1, column 1 (left column):
   a. Key **ACKNOWLEDGMENTS** using Britannic Bold, 18-point font.
   b. Center the names.
   c. Search for "handshake" in Clip Art. Change the height and width to 1.5". Change the Wrap Text style to Square.
4. Format page 1, column 2:
   a. Use WordArt style Fill – Black, Text 1, Outline – Background 1, Hard Shadow – Accent 1 style, 26-point font to key the title. Change the text color to Dark Red.
   b. Key the dateline using Britannic Bold font; apply Heading 1 style. Center the text.
   c. Insert the picture *hess photo* from your data files. Center and size the picture accordingly. Use Square Text Wrapping.
   d. Insert the *arondale logo* from your data files; change the Wrap Text style to In Front of Text. Size and place as shown in the illustration.
   e. Search for the "stethoscope" in Clip Art. Change the Wrap Text style to In Front of Text. Change the height and width to 1.8".

## Writing 14

gwam
1' | 3'

What do you expect when you have the opportunity to travel    12 | 4
to a foreign country? Quite a few people realize that one of the real    26 | 9
joys of traveling is to get a brief, but revealing glimpse of how    39 | 13
foreigners think, work, and live.    45 | 15

The best way to enjoy a different culture is to learn as much    12 | 19
about the country being visited and its culture as you can before you    26 | 24
leave home. Then you can concentrate on being an informed guest    39 | 28
rather than trying to find local people who can meet your needs.    52 | 32

## Writing 15

gwam
1' | 3'

What do you enjoy doing in your free time? Health experts tell us    13 | 4
that far too many people choose to be lazy rather than to be    25 | 8
active. The unpleasant result of that misguided decision shows up in    39 | 13
our weight.    41 | 14

Working to control what we weigh is difficult, and seldom can    12 | 18
it be accomplished quickly. However, it is extremely important if our    26 | 22
weight exceeds what it should be. Part of the problem results from    39 | 27
the amount and type of food we eat.    46 | 29

If we desire to appear fit, we should include exercise as a    12 | 33
substantial component of our weight loss program. Walking at least    25 | 37
thirty minutes each day at a very fast rate can make a major    37 | 41
difference in our appearance and in the way we feel.    48 | 45

## Writing 16

gwam
1' | 3'

Doing what we enjoy doing is quite important; however,    11 | 4
enjoying what we have to do is equally important. As you ponder    23 | 8
both of these concepts, you may feel that they are the same, but they    37 | 12
are quite different.    41 | 14

If we could do only those things that we prefer to do, the    12 | 18
chances are that we would do them exceptionally well. Generally, we will    26 | 22
take more pride in doing those things we thoroughly enjoy    37 | 26
doing, and we will not stop until we get them done correctly.    50 | 30

We realize, though, that we cannot restrict the tasks and    11 | 34
responsibilities that we must do just to those that we prefer to do.    25 | 39
Therefore, we need to build an interest in and an appreciation of all    39 | 43
the tasks that we must do in our positions.    48 | 46

| 1' | 1 | 2 | 3 | 4 | 5 | 6 | 7 | 8 | 9 | 10 | 11 | 12 |
| 3' | | 1 | | 2 | | 3 | | 4 | |

# Lesson 98 Hess Office Park

**Warmup** *Lesson 98a Warmup*

**A | ALL LETTERS**

## Skill Building

### 98b  Timed Writing

1. Key a 1' timing on each paragraph; work for speed.
2. Key a 3' timing on all paragraphs; work for control.

Reports are one of the best means by which busy executives at any level of a business can keep well informed. The pertinent data in reports can be used to solve a wide variety of problems that often arise, make any changes that may be required, analyze results, and make precise, timely decisions.

The quality of the plans and decisions made on the basis of the information found in reports depends in large measure on how well the reports are written and produced. A good report is a thorough and objective summary of all pertinent facts and figures. If reports are not well produced, the firm or organization will surely suffer.

## Project Setting

### PREPARING FOR A HEALTH FAIR

Arondale Medical Center will be hosting a health fair for the community on Saturday, October 11, 201-, from 10:30 a.m. to 4:00 p.m. The fair will be held in the main concourse of Hess Office Park. Medical suppliers, pharmaceutical companies, hospitals, schools, and clinics will be invited to participate as vendors and presenters. Arondale University nursing students will be providing free flu shots and health screenings. Vendors and presenters will provide information tables and wellness seminars.

You will assist in the planning and preparation of the health fair by sending documents to vendors and presenters and designing the program for the event.

### 98-d1

**Mail Merge Letter**

arondale letterhead

1. In the open document (*98-d1main*), key the letter as a mail merge main document. Use the Mail Merge Wizard. Set up the letter using the current document.
2. Key a new list of recipients using the names and addresses below. (*98-d1data*)
3. Key the letter in block style with open punctuation. Supply all necessary letter parts. The letter is from **John Navarro | Community Relations Coordinator**.
4. Merge the documents.
5. Preview, check, and click Next Activity. (*98-d1*)

**Recipients:**

Field Name	Recipient 1	Recipient 2	Recipient 3
Title	Mr.	Ms.	Mrs.
First Name	Leon	Hillary	Lauren
Last Name	Thompson	Jens	Park
Company Name	Exceptional Medical Supplies	Balfour Pharmaceuticals, Inc.	Crossroads Memorial Hospital

*(continued)*

## Writing 17

gwam 1' | 3'

Many people like to say just how lucky or fortunate a person | 13 | 4
is when he or she succeeds in doing something extremely well. Does | 26 | 9
luck play a significant part in success? In some cases, it might have a | 40 | 13
small effect. | 43 | 14

Being in the right place at the right time may help, but hard | 13 | 19
work may produce far greater results than luck. Those who simply | 26 | 23
wait for luck should not expect immediate or quick results and | 39 | 27
should realize luck may never come. | 46 | 30

```
1' |  1  |  2  |  3  |  4  |  5  |  6  |  7  |  8  |  9  |  10  |  11  |  12 |
3' |     1     |        2        |        3        |        4        |
```

## Writing 18

gwam 1' | 3'

New golfers must learn to zero in on several social rules. Do | 12 | 4
not engage in conversation, stand close, or move around when | 24 | 8
another person is hitting. Be prepared to play when it is your turn. | 38 | 13

Always take practice swings in an area away from other | 11 | 16
people. Do not rest on your club on the green when waiting your turn. | 25 | 21
Proper etiquette requires you to let the group behind you play through | 39 | 25
if your group is slow. | 43 | 27

Set your other clubs down off the green. Leave the green | 11 | 31
quickly when you have finished; update your card on the next tee. | 24 | 35
Always leave the course in good condition for others to enjoy. | 37 | 39
Good sportsmanship is just as important as having a good time. | 49 | 43

```
1' |  1  |  2  |  3  |  4  |  5  |  6  |  7  |  8  |  9  |  10  |  11  |  12 |
3' |     1     |        2        |        3        |        4        |
```

## Writing 19

gwam 1' | 3'

Do you know how to utilize time wisely? If you do, then its | 12 | 4
appropriate use can help you organize and run a business better. If | 25 | 8
you find that your daily problems tend to keep you from planning | 38 | 13
properly, then perhaps you are not utilizing time well. You may find | 52 | 17
that you spend too much time on tasks that are not important. Plan | 65 | 22
your work to save valuable time. | 71 | 24

A firm that does not plan is liable to experience trouble. A | 12 | 28
small firm may have difficulty planning. It is important to know just | 26 | 32
where the firm is headed. A firm may have a fear of learning things it | 40 | 37
would rather not know. To say that planning is easy would be absurd. | 54 | 42
It requires a significant amount of thinking and planning to meet the | 67 | 46
expectations of the firm. | 72 | 48

```
1' |  1  |  2  |  3  |  4  |  5  |  6  |  7  |  8  |  9  |  10  |  11  |  12 |
3' |     1     |        2        |        3        |        4        |
```

Start new paragraph ——→ Christopher does not experience an internal source of control for his actions. He expects others to control him or to punish him after the fact. He may take responsibility for aggressive episodes. He may tend to see these as "not me" and therefore minimize them. At times these events may be repressed or dissociated.

**Summary and Recommendations**

Personality testing suggests the use of repression and dissociation that prevent him from having to remember or relive past painful experiences. Repressed feelings of frustration may return to be acted out behaviorally. Christopher may tend to not take responsibility for his actions or may minimize them.

It may be important for the staff to assess, in an ongoing fashion, indications of the degree of personality fragmentation that Christopher experiences. Some exploration of whether or not he remembers past events that have been reported by other family members may assist with this.

Christopher needs to learn techniques of anger management. He should be taught to become aware of when he is beginning to become angry so that he can voluntarily learn to control his behavior. Christopher may have much difficulty learning to access the signs that he is beginning to become upset. He may need to practice a variety of techniques in order to control his behavior and then later resolve the problem verbally.

An additional focus should be on his relational skills. Assisting him in becoming sensitive to reading cues and the teaching of some empathy and conscious awareness would also help improve his functioning level.

## Writing 20

If asked, most people will agree that some people have far more creative skills than others, and they will also say that these skills are in great demand by most organizations. A follow-up question is in order. Are you born with creative skills or can you develop them? There is no easy answer to that question, but it is worth spending a good bit of time pondering.

If creative skills can be developed, then the next issue is how can you develop these skills. One way is to approach each task with a determination to solve the problem and a refusal to accept failure. If the normal way of doing a job does not work, just keep trying things never tried before until you reach a good solution. This is called thinking outside the box.

1'	3'
13	4
25	8
38	13
52	17
64	21
74	25
13	29
25	33
38	37
50	41
63	46
73	49

```
1' | 1 | 2 | 3 | 4 | 5 | 6 | 7 | 8 | 9 | 10 | 11 | 12 | 13 |
3' |     1     |     2     |     3     |     4     |
```

## Writing 21

Figures are not as easy to key as many of the words we use. Balanced-hand figures such as 16, 27, 38, 49, and 50, although fairly easy, are slower to key because each one requires longer reaches and uses more time per stroke.

Figures such as 12, 45, 67, and 90 are even more difficult because they are next to one another and each uses just a single hand to key. Because of their size, bigger numbers such as 178, 349, and 1,220 create extra speed losses.

1'	3'
12	4
24	8
37	12
44	15
12	19
24	23
37	27
45	30

```
1' | 1 | 2 | 3 | 4 | 5 | 6 | 7 | 8 | 9 | 10 | 11 | 12 | 13 |
3' |     1     |     2     |     3     |     4     |
```

**Skill Transfer**

1. Set the Timer for 2'. Take a 2' writing on paragraph 1.

2. Set the Timer for 2'. Take a 2' writing on paragraph 2.

3. Take 2 or more 2' writings on the slower paragraph.

## Writing 22

Few people are able to attain financial success without some kind of planning. People who realize the value of wise spending and saving are those who set up a budget. A budget will help them to determine just how much they can spend and how much they can save so that they will not squander their money recklessly.

Keeping records is a ~~crucial~~ *vital* part of ~~a~~ budget. ~~Complete~~ *A detailed* records of *all* income and expens~~es~~ *ditures* over a period of ~~a number of~~ *several* months ~~can~~ *will* help t~~o~~ determine what bills, ~~as water~~ *like utilities* or rent, are *fixed* ~~static~~ and which are flexible. To get the most out of your income, *focus* ~~pay attention~~ *on* ~~to~~ the items that yo~~u~~ can ~~modify~~ *be changed*.

1'	2'
13	7
25	13
38	19
49	25
62	31
11	37
23	42
35	49
47	54
58	60

```
1' | 1 | 2 | 3 | 4 | 5 | 6 | 7 | 8 | 9 | 10 | 11 | 12 |
2' |    1    |    2    |    3    |    4    |    5    |    6    |
```

1. Follow the steps in *97-d2* to create a Psychological Testing report for Christopher Smith.
2. Proofread and check; click Exit *Word*. (*97-d3*)
3. Click Log out to exit *KPDO*.

---

**Patient Name:** Smith, Christopher     **Age:** 9     **Date of Testing:** 6/28/201-

### Reason for Referral

Christopher Smith was referred for psychological testing by his inpatient psychiatrist, Linda Murillo, M.D. Description of personality dynamics with projective tests was requested.

### Tests Administered

The Rorschach Technique

Roberts Apperception Test

### Testing Behavior

Christopher Smith was tested while he was an inpatient at the Children's Unit at Oak Ridge Hospital. He is a friendly boy with short blond hair who is moderately overweight. He related to the examiner in a friendly and cooperative way. Eye contact was good. His speech and mannerisms were normal. The patient expressed himself well and had a good vocabulary. He appeared to enjoy the testing tasks and studied each stimuli card before responding. He described his responses well. His stories were fairly lengthy and had well-developed themes.

### Testing Results

Personality testing suggests that mentally Christopher is very active, but his emotions are suppressed. There are indications of underlying depression and anger. Dissociation is also a probable defensive structure. He keeps experiences or memories dissociated so that he does not have to face or deal with them. They are potentially too overwhelming for him.

Christopher cannot keep memories and feelings detached all of the time; they occasionally break through and are likely to be acted out behaviorally. There may be periods of anger or aggressive outbursts or periods of despair or depression. The problems that Christopher experiences with anger may be apparent. His depression may be less frequently seen because he withdraws to wait it out or uses fantasy to escape from it. His feelings of depression may also be translated into anger.

*(continued)*

# Skill Builder 3

## LESSON A

### Skill Building *Accuracy Emphasis*

1. Select the Skill Building tab, Accuracy Emphasis, and then Assessment 1.

2. Key the timing from the screen for 3'; work for control.
3. Complete Lesson A or the first lesson you have not completed in either Speed Emphasis or Accuracy Emphasis as suggested by the software.
4. Your results will be summarized in the Skill Building Report.

### Timed Writings

#### Writing 23

1. Key a 1' writing on each paragraph. (Remember to change the source in the Timed Writing Settings dialog box.) Compare your *gwam* on the two paragraphs.
2. Key additional 1' writings on the slower paragraph.

	*gwam*	1'	3'
The most valuable employees stand a greater chance of		11	4
maintaining their job in hard economic times. There are many		23	8
qualities which distinguish an excellent employee from other workers.		37	12
In the first place, they remain focused and keep their minds on the		51	17
tasks at hand. Good employees think about the work they perform and		64	21
how it relates to the total success of the project. They act as team		78	26
leaders and guide the project to completion.		87	29
Second, good workers have the ability to work consistently and		14	33
fully realize every goal. Many people in the workplace perform just		27	38
bits and pieces of a job. They begin one thing, but allow themselves		41	42
to be quickly distracted from the work at hand. Many people are good		55	47
starters, but fewer are also good finishers.		64	50

1'	1	2	3	4	5	6	7	8	9	10	11	12	13
3'		1			2			3			4		

**3.** Preview, check, and click Next Activity. (*97-d2*)

**Patient Name:** Perez, Maria   **Age:** 16   **Date of Testing:** 6/25/201-

### Reason for Referral

Maria Perez was referred for psychological testing by her inpatient psychiatrist, Douglas Martin, M.D. Description of personality dynamics was requested.

### Tests Administered

Minnesota Multiphasic Personality Inventory (scored with adolescent norms)

### Testing Behavior

Not observed

### Testing Results

Test report is based solely on testing data. Profile configuration indicates a defensive attitude. This is likely to be a very ingrained defensiveness. Part of it may be an angry reaction to being in the hospital, but there is also a long-standing lack of self-awareness. She is likely to exhibit little psychological insight into herself.

She is denying feelings of depression or any kinds of physical problems. She sees herself as healthy and active. She denies problems with anger, anxiety, or depression. She may present herself as having no reason for being in the hospital or as in no need of help.

Others are likely to perceive her as defensive and very concrete and rigid in her thinking. She may be active, even hyperactive at times. She may appear easily irritable and react angrily to minor problems.

### Summary and Recommendations

At the time Maria Perez took the test she appeared to be defensive and minimizing problems. On an ongoing basis, she may have a lack of insight into her difficulties. Further testing may help describe her problems in more detail. She may lower her defensiveness so that she is more open to acknowledging and working on areas of difficulty as she adapts to the Unit and begins to feel more comfortable in the environment.

# LESSON B

## Skill Building *Accuracy Emphasis*

1. Select the Skill Building tab and choose either Speed Emphasis or Accuracy Emphasis as recommended in Assessment 1. Complete Lesson B.
2. Your results will be summarized in the Skill Building Report.

## Skill Building *Technique Builder*

### DRILL 11

**Balanced-Hand**

Key each line once, working for fluency.

1 to today stocks into ti times sitting until ur urges further tour
2 en entire trend dozen or order support editor nd and mandate land
3 he healthy check ache th these brother both an annual change plan
4 nt into continue want of office softer roof is issue poison basis

5 Did Pamela sign the title to the big lake mansion by Lamb Island?
6 Rick is to pay the eight men and women if they do the work right.
7 My time for a land bus tour will not change until further notice.
8 I am to blame for the big problem with the maid; I can handle it.

## Timed Writings

1. Key a 1' writing on each paragraph. Compare your *gwam*.
2. Key additional 1' writings on the slower paragraph.

### Writing 24

*gwam* 1' | 3'

Most of us have, at some time or another, recognized an annoying | 14 | 5
problem and had valid reasons to complain. The complaint may have | 27 | 9
been because of a defective product, poor customer services, or | 40 | 13
perhaps growing tired of talking to voice mail. However, many of us | 54 | 18
feel that complaining to a business firm is an exercise in futility | 67 | 22
so we do not bother. Instead, we just remain quiet, write it off as a | 81 | 27
bad experience and continue to be taken advantage of. | 92 | 31

Today, more than at anytime in the past consumers are taking some | 13 | 35
steps to let their feelings be known—and with a great amount of | 26 | 39
success. As a result, firms are becoming more responsive to | 38 | 43
the needs of the consumer. complaints from customers alert firms | 51 | 48
to produce or service defect and there by cause action to be taken | 64 | 52
for their benefit. | 68 | 53

1' | 1 | 2 | 3 | 4 | 5 | 6 | 7 | 8 | 9 | 10 | 11 | 12 | 13 |
3' | | 1 | | 2 | | 3 | | 4 |

# Lesson 97 Preparing Medical Reports

## Document Design

### 97b

### MEDICAL REPORT FORMS

Formats may vary slightly at different medical facilities; however, all medical reports contain similar sections: the heading, body, and conclusion. The **heading** contains pertinent information necessary to identify the patient. The heading is keyed at the top of the report. Some headings are quite lengthy and can take up to one-third of the first page. The **body** of the report contains the observations, test results, and/or findings. The **conclusion** includes the diagnosis and recommendations.

## Apply It

### 97–d1

**Medical Report Form**

 arondale logo and name

1. In the open document, center the heading **Psychological Testing** at approximately 2"; apply Title style. Tap ENTER twice.

2. Key the side headings at the left margin and apply Heading 1 style to each. Tap ENTER twice after each heading.

   **Patient Name:**

   **Age:**

   **Date of Testing:**

   **Reason for Referral**

   **Tests Administered**

   **Testing Behavior**

   **Testing Results**

   **Summary and Recommendations**

3. After keying the last heading, tap ENTER four times. Set a left underline tab at 3" for the physician's signature. Key the physician's name and title below the line. Apply the Strong style to the physician's name and title. Remove space after paragraph.

   **Laura Sanchez, Psy.D.**

   **Licensed Psychologist**

4. Preview, check, and click Next Activity. (*97-d1*)

### 97–d2

**Psychological Testing Report**

1. In the open document (*97-d1*), key the psychological testing report for Maria Perez. **Patient Name, Age,** and **Date of Testing** should be keyed on the same line as the heading. The rest of the report is keyed under the respective side heading; click the ¶ below the heading and key the text.

2. Insert a header at the top of the second page that consists of the patient's name, the page number, and the date of the testing. Format as follows:

   a. Click Insert tab/Header and Footer/Header/Blank. Key **Perez, Maria**.

   b. Tap ENTER. Key the word **Page** followed by a space.

   c. Click Insert tab/Header & Footer/Page Number. From the Page Number drop list, choose Current Position and then Plain Number.

   d. Tap ENTER and key the date of the testing. Tap ENTER and choose Different First Page.

# LESSON C

## Skill Building *Accuracy Emphasis*

Select the Skill Building tab, the appropriate emphasis, and then Lesson C. Your results will be summarized in the Skill Building Report.

## Skill Building *Technique Builder*

### DRILL 12

**Balanced-Hand**

Key each line once for fluency.

1 an anyone brand spans th their father eighth he head sheets niche
2 en enters depends been nd end handle fund or original sport color
3 ur urban turns assure to took factory photo ti titles satin still
4 ic ice bicycle chic it item position profit ng angle danger doing

5 I want the info in the file on the profits from the chic bicycle.
6 Hang the sign by the lake not by an island by six or eight today.
7 Did Vivian, the widow, pay for eight flair pens, and eight gowns?
8 When did Viviana go to the firm to sign the title to the emblems?

## Timed Writings

1. Take a 1' writing on each paragraph.
2. Take a 3' writing on both paragraphs.

### Writing 25

	gwam	1'	3'

Practicing basic health rules will result in good body condition. | 14 | 5

Proper diet is a way to achieve good health. Eat a variety of foods each | 29 | 10

day, including some fruit, vegetables, cereal products, and foods rich | 43 | 14

in protein, to be sure that you keep a balance. Another part of a good | 57 | 19

health plan is physical activity, such as running. | 67 | 22

Running has become quite popular in this country. Some people | 13 | 27

run for the joy of running, others run because they want to maximize | 27 | 31

the benefits that can be gained by running on a regular basis. Some | 41 | 36

of the benefits include weight loss, improved heart health, improved | 55 | 41

bone health, and improved mood. Running is one of the most effective | 68 | 45

forms of exercise that will help achieve ideal body weight. | 80 | 49

```
1' |  1  |  2  |  3  |  4  |  5  |  6  |  7  |  8  |  9  | 10 | 11 | 12 | 13 |
3' |        1        |        2        |        3        |        4        |
```

## Disclosure Statement and Consent to Treatment

Confirmation of arrangements for the orthodontic management of:

Patient: _____

Parent responsible party: _____

Address: _____

### Responsible Party Authorization

❏ All information displayed on the computer screen is accurate.

❏ I authorize Arondale Medical Center to send all information, not limited to orthodontic treatment and finances, to the provided email address. I also take responsibility for providing updates on my email address and mailing address.

❏ I authorize the staff at Arondale Medical Center to perform any necessary services during the diagnosis and treatment.

❏ I authorize Arondale Medical Center to release any information required to process insurance claims.

### Financial Arrangements

The undersigned hereby agrees to the following financial arrangements:

PROFESSIONAL FEE	
Limited Treatment	$5,220.00
Phase I	$875.00
Phase II	$500.00
Full Treatment (Single Phase)	
Retainer Fee	
Retainer Visit Fee	
Finance Charge	
Total	

A service charge of 15% per month will be made on all past due balances. If it becomes necessary to send your account to collection, the undersigned agrees to pay all costs and expenses including the attorney's fee.

I hereby certify that I discussed the content of this contract with the physician and I give INFORMED CONSENT for all necessary orthodontic treatment and related services.

Patient/Responsible Party Signature: _____

# LESSON D

## Skill Building *Accuracy Emphasis*

Select the Skill Building tab; choose the appropriate emphasis and then Lesson D.

## Skill Building *Technique Builder*

### DRILL 13

**Adjacent Key Review**

Key each line once; strive for accuracy.

1 nm many enmity solemn kl inkling weekly pickle oi oil invoice join
2 iu stadium medium genius lk milk talk walks uy buy buyer soliloquy
3 mn alumni hymn number column sd Thursday wisdom df mindful handful
4 me mention comment same fo found perform info le letter flew files

5 The buyer sent his weekly invoices for oil to the group on Thursday.
6 Mindful of the alumni, the choirs sang a hymn prior to my soliloquy.
7 An inmate, a fogger, and a genius joined the weekly talks on Monday.
8 They were to join in the talk shows to assess regions of the Yukon.

## Timed Writings

1. Take a 1' writing on each paragraph.
2. Take a 3' writing on both paragraphs.

### Writing 26

	gwam	1'	3'

All people, in spite of their eating habits, have two major needs  |13|4
that must be met by their food. They need food that provides a  |26|9
source of energy, and they need food that will fill the skeletal and  |40|13
operating needs of their bodies. Carbohydrates, fats, and protein  |53|18
form a major portion of the diet. Vitamins and minerals are also  |66|22
necessary for excellent health.  |72|24

Carbohydrates make up a major source of our energy needs.  |12|28
Fats also serve as a source of energy and act as defense against  |25|32
cold and trauma. Proteins are changed to amino acids, which are  |38|37
the building units of the body. These, in turn, are utilized to make  |52|41
most body tissue. Minerals are required to control many body  |64|45
functions, and vitamins are used for normal growth and aid against  |77|50
disease.  |84|52

1' | 1 | 2 | 3 | 4 | 5 | 6 | 7 | 8 | 9 | 10 | 11 | 12 | 13 |
3' |   1   |   2   |   3   |   4   |

## DOCUMENT 2 SOAP NOTE BODY

**S**	Pt complains of cough and head congestion for the past 48 hours, shortness of breath, lethargy, and low appetite.
**O**	Pt coughing up green sputum. Lungs clear, ears clear. Lymph nodes enlarged bilateral neck. Bilateral tonsils enlarged. CXR-WNL, PPD negative. CBC—elevated white count.
**A**	Acute upper respiratory infection.
**P**	Pt is to take Azithromycin, 250 mg. Take two tablets immediately, then take one tablet every day for the next four days. Increase fluids, increase rest. Pt is to stay home for three days. Recheck in one week or sooner, if needed.

## DOCUMENT 3 SOAP NOTE BODY

**S**	Pt complains of pain in right knee; tripped and fell 6/17/201-.
**O**	Inflammation/hematoma on right anterior medial patella; decreased ROM right knee, with flexion, extension.
**A**	Diagnosis: Pre-patella bursitis. Treatment: R.I.C.E. on right patella anterior medial with ice pack twice a day for 4-6 weeks. Stay off right leg. ADL: rest knee; ice right anterior knee morn/night; elevate.
**P**	Stay off right leg. Rest; ice morn/night; elevate. Week 1: decrease pain; week 2: increase ROM.

## 96-d4

**Disclosure and Consent to Treat Form**

 arondale letterhead

1. In the open document, change the bottom margin to 0.7". Key the document on the next page. Apply Heading 1 style to the title and Center; make sure a blank space is included below the title. Apply Heading 2 style to the side headings.

2. Use right underline tabs set at 6.5" for the underlines.

3. Apply Grid Table 4 – Accent 6 style to the table. Use the SUM formula to obtain the total; display the total with a dollar sign and two decimal places. Use a decimal tab to align the numbers. Key the table title in all caps, center, and bold. Center the table horizontally on the page.

4. Key a signature line below the last paragraph for **Patient/Responsible Party Signature:** and insert a line for the date below it.

5. Proofread and check; click Exit *Word*. (96-d4)

6. Click Log out to exit *KPDO*.

# LESSON E

## Skill Building *Accuracy Emphasis*

Select the Skill Building tab; choose the appropriate emphasis and then Lesson E.

## Skill Building *Technique Builder*

### DRILL 14

**Word Beginnings**

Key each line once, working for accuracy.

br
1 bright brown bramble bread breath breezes brought brother broiler
2 In February my brother brought brown bread and beans from Boston.

exe
3 exercises exert executives exemplify exemption executed exemplary
4 They exert extreme effort executing exercises in exemplary style.

bt
5 doubt subtle obtains obtrusion subtracts indebtedness undoubtedly
6 Extreme debt will cause more than subtle doubt among my creditors.

ny
7 tiny funny company nymph penny nylon many anyone phony any brainy
8 Anyone as brainy and funny as Penny is an asset to their company.

## Timed Writings

1. Take a 1' writing on each paragraph.
2. Take a 3' writing on both paragraphs.

### Writing 27

	*gwam*	1'	3'

Many people believe that an ounce of prevention is worth a pound    14   5
of cure. Care of your heart can help you prevent serious physical    27   9
problems. The human heart is the most important pump ever    39   13
developed. It constantly pushes blood through the body tissues. But    52   17
the layers of muscle that make up the heart must be kept in proper    66   22
working order. Exercise can help this muscle to remain in good    78   26
condition.    80   27

Another important way to maintain a healthy heart is just by    13   31
avoiding habits which are considered to be greatly detrimental to the    27   36
body. Food that is high in cholesterol is not a good choice. Also,    41   40
use of tobacco has quite a negative effect on the function of the    54   49
heart. You can minimize your chances of heart problems by avoiding    67   54
these bad health habits.    72   55

1'	1	2	3	4	5	6	7	8	9	10	11	12	13
3'		1		2			3			4			

## Apply It

**96-d1**

**Create SOAP Note Form**

 arondale letterhead

1. In the open document, create a table at approximately 2" for the patient's vital signs. Bold the text and change the row height to 0.4"; Align Center Left all text.

Last Name:			First Name:	
Patient No.	Age:		Allergies:	Meds:
T:	P:		R:	B/P:
C/O:			Date:	

2. Tap ENTER; then create a table for the SOAP notes. Make the letters *SOAP* 26 point and bold. Make each row height 1.25". Align Center the letters. Drag the border between columns A and B to make column A approximately 0.5" wide.

3. Select column B and change the alignment to Align Center Left; text will be centered vertically in the box when the note is keyed.

4. Modify the footer to make the tab at 3.25" a center underline tab. Place the physician's signature line in the footer.

5. Preview the document and adjust vertical placement as needed.

6. Proofread and check; click Next Activity. (*96-d1*)

---

**96-d2 and 96-d3**

**Create SOAP Notes**

1. In the open document (*96-d1*), fill in the form with the information for Document 2. **Note:** *Pt* is the abbreviation for *patient*; spell it out when keying the notes.

2. Proofread and check; click Next Activity. (*96-d2*)

3. Repeat the above steps for Document 3. (*96-d3*)

4. Proofread and check; click Next Activity.

Field Names	Document 2	Document 3
Last Name	Jones	Pham
First Name	Sarah	Lisa
Patient No.	10680	31048
Age	20	27
Allergies	None	Bee stings
Meds	None	None
T	99.5	98.5
P	84	62
R	20	15
B/P	130/87	112/72
C/O	Cough	Pain in right knee
Date	6/9/201-	6/21/201-

*(continued)*

# Formatting and Word Processing Essentials

## Learning Outcomes

### Keyboarding

+ Key fluently using good keying techniques.

+ Key about 40 words a minute with good accuracy.

### Document Design Skills

+ Format memos, letters, tables, and reports appropriately.

+ Apply basic design skills to announcements, invitations, and newsletters.

+ Enhance documents with basic graphics.

### Word Processing Skills

+ Learn essential word processing commands.

+ Apply word processing commands to create, edit, and format documents effectively.

### Communication Skills

+ Review and improve basic communication skills.

+ Compose simple documents.

+ Use proofing tools effectively.

+ Proofread and edit text effectively.

# *Lesson 96* SOAP Notes and Medical Forms

## Document Design

### SOAP NOTES

**96b**

All medical offices keep recorded notes of the patient's office visit, which are commonly called SOAP notes. SOAP notes contain the patient's complaints, the physician's findings, and the physician's assessment and plan for treatment. The letters *S O A P* stand for Subjective, Objective, Assessment, and Plan.

S—SUBJECTIVE (what the patient tells the physician)

O—OBJECTIVE (the physician's findings as a result of a physical exam or evaluation)

A—ASSESSMENT (the physician's diagnosis or impression of the problem)

P—PLAN (the planned treatment for the patient)

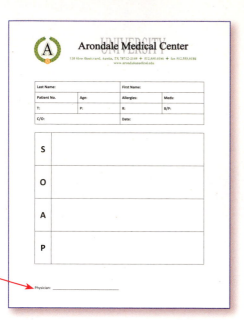

Physician's signature line in footer

## Command Review

### SET UNDERLINE TAB

**96c**

Leader tabs can be used to create the underlines for signatures, addresses, phone numbers, etc. Using underline tabs allows the underlines to align evenly.

To set an underline tab:
Home/Paragraph/Indents and Spacing/Tabs

1. Key the tab position in the Tab stop position box. Select the desired alignment.

2. Under Leader, select option 4. Click the Set button to display the tab setting in the Tab stop position box.

## DRILL 1    SET UNDERLINE TAB

1. Set a left, underline tab at 2.75". Set a left tab, with no leaders at 3.0". Set a right, underline tab at 6.5".

2. Turn on Show/Hide. Key **Name**, tap the Space Bar, and then tap TAB twice.

3. Key **Address** and tap the Space Bar; then tap TAB. Tap ENTER.

4. Key **Work Phone** and **Cell Phone** with an underscore following each.

5. Proofread and check; click Next Activity. (*96-drill1*)

# Word 2013 Essentials

## LEARNING OUTCOMES

- Learn and apply essential *Word 2013* commands.
- Create, save, and print documents.
- Apply text, paragraph, and page formats.
- Navigate, review, and edit documents.
- Build keyboarding skills.

## Lesson 26 Getting Started with Word

**New Commands**

- Launch Word
- Blank Document
- New Folder
- Save As
- Close
- Open
- New
- Print
- Exit

**New Commands**

**26a Getting Started with *Word***

### LEARNING THE BASICS

All activities in this lesson will be completed using *Word 2013* software. **Do not access *Keyboarding Pro DELUXE Online* (KPDO).** In this lesson, you will learn to use *Word* to create, format, and print documents in the same way that you will use it in your other classes, in a part-time job, or in your personal business activities. You will also learn to manage your own files.

In all other lessons, *KPDO* will perform these activities and will manage your files.

### LAUNCH WORD

*Word* can be launched in several different ways. The first time you launch *Word*, you will probably have to click the *Word* icon on the Start screen or on the taskbar at the bottom of your desktop screen. The illustration on the next page shows you how to launch *Word* using *Windows 8* as the operating system.

If your computer is using *Windows 7*, your screen may look slightly different. Your instructor will provide information on how to launch *Word* with *Windows 7*.

## Heart-Healthy Checklist

DIET
✓ Limit intake of foods that are high in saturated fats, trans fatty acids, and cholesterol. Meat, dairy products, and eggs are the biggest culprits.
✓ Eat mostly fruits, a wide variety of vegetables, and whole grains.
✓ Limit eating sugar and processed carbohydrates, such as white bread, pasta, cookies, and cake.
✓ Limit salt intake.
✓ Eat a limited amount of "good" fats, such as nuts, fish, and olive oil.

EXERCISE
✓ If you live a sedentary lifestyle, you are at risk.
✓ If you are overweight, you are at risk.
✓ Exercise 60 minutes per day.
✓ Choose an exercise program that you enjoy.

LIFESTYLE
✓ Don't smoke.
✓ Do not drink more than two alcoholic beverages a day.
✓ Enjoy life, laugh, and have fun.

## Take Care of Your Heart

#1

*Make living a heart-healthy lifestyle a top priority!*

According to the U. S. Department of Health and Human Services, heart disease is the leading cause of death in the United States. Death from heart attack, stroke, and other cardiovascular diseases claims one American life every 34 seconds.

The heart, like any other muscle in the body, requires preventative care in order to provide top performance. Some people are born with a congenital heart disease, but the majority of the people develop heart disease as they move through life. Lifestyle changes can lessen or eliminate many heart problems.

### CONTRIBUTORS TO HEART DISEASE

- Smoking. The risk of heart disease for smokers is more than twice that of non-smokers.

- High cholesterol diet. Change your diet to eating foods made without saturated fats.

- High blood pressure. A healthy diet, losing weight, exercising regularly, and restricting sodium will help lower blood pressure.

- Diabetes. Many people who are overweight are at risk for type 2 diabetes.

- Physical inactivity. The Institute of Medicine recommends 60 minutes of moderately intense physical activity each day.

- Obesity. Change your diet to include more heart-healthy ingredients and increase your physical activity to control your weight.

- Stress. Try some stress relievers such as exercise, meditation, spending time with friends, or taking up a hobby.

*MyPlate* is the current nutrition guide published by the United States Department of Agriculture. The plate is divided into four sections with a glass on the side. Each of the sections and the glass represent the five food groups.

**Fruits.** Any fruit or 100% fruit juice counts as part of the Fruit group.

**Vegetables.** Any vegetable or 100% vegetable juice counts as a member of the Vegetable group.

**Grains.** Any food made from wheat, rice, oats, cornmeal, barley or another cereal grain is a grain product.

**Protein.** All foods made from meat, poultry, seafood, beans and peas, eggs, processed soy products, nuts, and seeds are considered part of the Protein group.

**Dairy.** All fluid milk products and many foods made from milk are considered part of the Dairy group.

### Desktop

When you start your computer, your desktop will look like the illustration shown at the right with the daisies if the defaults were used when *Windows 8* was installed. The other part of the illustration shows the default colors.

Windows Default Themes

#### To launch *Word* from taskbar:

1. Check the Taskbar at the bottom of the desktop screen to locate the *Word* icon shown at the right.

2. Click the icon to launch *Word*.

If the *Word* icon is not on the taskbar, then check the Start screen.

### Start Screen

The Start screen consists of a number of tiles that enable you to access applications from your computer and from the Internet. If you are connected to the Internet, the tiles are dynamic—that is, the information may change. The *Word* icon and icons of other *Office* apps may have been added to the Start screen during the installation.

#### To launch *Word* from the Start screen:

1. Hover your mouse in the lower-left corner of the desktop screen to display the Start screen.

2. Check to see if applications are listed on the right side of your Start screen. If so, click the *Word* icon to launch it.

**✳ Discover**

Once *Word* is open, the *Word* icon displays on the taskbar. Pin it to the taskbar so that it will remain on the taskbar when *Word* is closed.

To pin *Word* to the taskbar:

1. Right-click the icon.

2. Click Pin this program to taskbar.

> **W** Word 2013
> 📌 Pin this program to taskbar
> ✕ Close all windows

3. If the icon is not on the Start screen, right-click on the Start screen to display the All apps icon on the bottom right side of the screen. Click the icon.

4. Scroll to locate the *Office 2013 Apps,* and click *Word.*

The heart, like any other muscle in the body, requires preventative care in order to provide top performance. Some people are born with a congenital heart disease, but the majority of the people develop heart disease as they move through life. Lifestyle changes can lessen or eliminate many heart problems.

CONTRIBUTORS TO HEART DISEASE

- Smoking. The risk of heart disease for smokers is more than twice that of non-smokers.
- High cholesterol diet. Change your diet to eating foods made without saturated fats.
- High blood pressure. A healthy diet, losing weight, exercising regularly, and restricting sodium will help lower blood pressure.
- Diabetes. Many people who are overweight are at risk for type 2 diabetes.
- Physical inactivity. The Institute of Medicine recommends 60 minutes of moderately intense physical activity each day.
- Obesity. Change your diet to include more heart-healthy ingredients and increase your physical activity to control your weight.
- Stress. Try some stress relievers such as exercise, meditation, spending time with friends, or taking up a hobby.

Page 2, column 2

*MyPlate* is the current nutrition guide published by the United States Department of Agriculture. The plate is divided into four sections with a glass on the side. Each of the sections and the glass represent the five food groups.

(Use SmartArt and Shapes to insert illustration of plate)

**Fruits.** Any fruit or 100% fruit juice counts as part of the Fruit group.

**Vegetables.** Any vegetable or 100% vegetable juice counts as a member of the Vegetable group.

**Grains**. Any food made from wheat, rice, oats, cornmeal, barley, or another cereal grain is a grain product.

**Protein.** All foods made from meat, poultry, seafood, beans and peas, eggs, processed soy products, nuts, and seeds are considered part of the Protein group.

**Dairy.** All fluid milk products and many foods made from milk are considered part of the Dairy group.

## OPENING WORD SCREEN

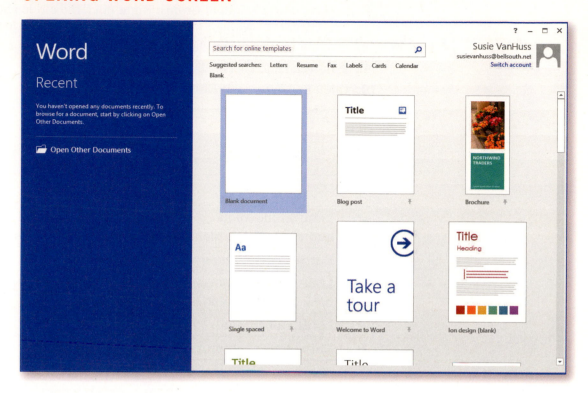

Note the following parts of the screen:

**Left pane**—contains a list of recently created documents and an option to open other documents that you may have created.

**Main pane**—provides the option to create a new blank document or create a document using one of the templates. At the top right side of this pane, your name will appear with either a picture or blank icon. If your Windows Live account has a picture, it will automatically appear at the top of your documents. Click the Blank document icon to begin working in *Word*.

**Status bar**—appears at the bottom of the screen. On the left side, the Start icons for any open applications display. The right side provides the time, date, and information about your system.

## BLANK DOCUMENT

The opening screen displays when you launch *Word*. To display the document screen, click the Blank document icon in the main pane. This screen is also referred to as the New Document screen because you use it to create new documents.

**d.** Click the Insert tab and choose Shapes. Select the oval shape and draw a circle to the right of *Grains*. Right-click the circle and choose Add Text. Key **Dairy**. If necessary, adjust the font size or the circle to accommodate the text.

8. Key the description of the food groups; bold the name of each food group as shown.

9. Proofread and check; click Exit *Word*. (95-d2)

10. Click Log out to exit *KPDO*.

<span style="color:red">Page 1, column 1</span>

### Heart-Healthy Checklist

**DIET**	
✔	Limit intake of foods that are high in saturated fats, trans fatty acids, and cholesterol. Meat, dairy products, and eggs are the biggest culprits.
✔	Eat mostly fruits, a wide variety of vegetables, and whole grains.
✔	Limit eating sugar and processed carbohydrates, such as white bread, pasta, cookies, and cake.
✔	Limit salt intake.
✔	Eat a limited amount of "good" fats, such as nuts, fish, and olive oil.
**EXERCISE**	
✔	If you live a sedentary lifestyle, you are at risk.
✔	If you are overweight, you are at risk.
✔	Exercise 60 minutes per day.
✔	Choose an exercise program that you enjoy.
**LIFESTYLE**	
✔	Don't smoke.
✔	Do not drink more than two alcoholic beverages a day.
✔	Enjoy life, laugh, and have fun.

<span style="color:red">Page 1, column 2</span>

**Take Care of Your Heart**

(Insert picture from ClipArt and add #1 using WordArt)

**Make living a heart-healthy lifestyle a top priority!**

<span style="color:red">Page 2, column 1</span>

According to the U.S. Department of Health and Human Services, heart disease is the leading cause of death in the United States. Death from heart attack, stroke, and other cardiovascular diseases claims one American life every 34 seconds.

*(continued)*

# BLANK DOCUMENT SCREEN

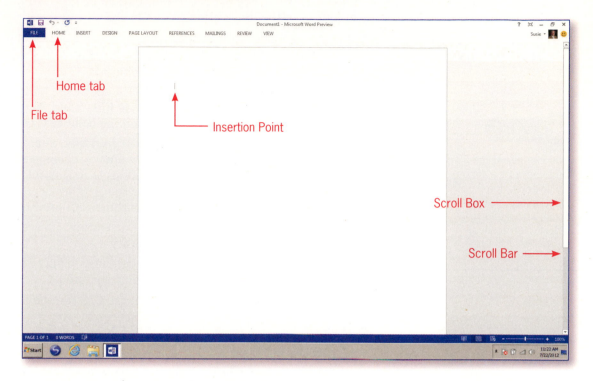

1. The document title, Document1, displays at the top center. When you save the document, you will give it a new name.

2. The Minimize or Maximize buttons appear in the top right corner of the screen. If your *Word* screen does not open large enough to fill the computer screen, enlarge it by clicking the Maximize button.

   Minimize    Maximize    Close

3. A row of tabs displays beginning in the upper-left corner with File tab and then Home tab. These tabs are part of the Ribbon.

4. The center portion is the document screen on which you will key your documents. It resembles a blank sheet of paper. The insertion point indicates the position at which you will begin to key.

5. The status bar appears at the bottom of the page. The page number and the word count are listed on the left side. The right side provides different ways to view the document on the screen.

6. The scroll bar on the right side of the screen provides options for moving through a document.

**95-d2**

**Brochure**

★ **TIP**

You can adjust the brightness of a picture by selecting the picture and clicking Picture Tools Format/ Adjust/Corrections/ Brightness/Contrast.

1. Prepare a two-page brochure that will be printed from front and back and folded in half. Use the illustrations on page 465 as a guide for page layout.

2. Use landscape orientation; change the left and right margins to 0.6". Format the document in two columns each with 4.4" width and 1" space between columns.

3. Format for page 1, column 1 (left column):

   a. Turn on Show/Hide; then tap ENTER six times. Move the insertion point to the first ¶ marker. Select WordArt style Fill – Gold, Accent 4, Soft Bevel for the title. Change the font size to 26 point and the color to Orange, Accent 2, Darker 25%.

   b. Click on a ¶ marker below the WordArt box. Search for "check mark" using Online ClipArt to find the picture shown. Change the height and width of the picture to 1.8". Change Wrap Text style to Behind Text. Position the picture as shown in the illustration. Change the Brightness to +40% and the Contrast to +20% (row 4, column 5 under Brightness/Contrast).

4. Click the insertion point below the illustration. Insert a 2-column, 15-row table. Apply Grid Table 5 Dark – Accent 2 style.

   a. Change the rows containing the headings (*Diet, Exercise, Lifestyle*) to 0.3" high. Place the headings in 14 point and bold.

   b. Insert a ✓ symbol in the left column. Change the size of the ✓ to 16 points and apply bold.

   c. Place a copy of the ✓ in each row. Center the ✓ and the text vertically in the rows as necessary.

   d. Insert a column break below the table to move the insertion point to the top of the right column.

5. Format for page 1, column 2 (front of brochure):

   a. Use 36-point, bold, Monotype Corsiva font and Red color to key the title. Center all text on the front of the brochure.

   b. Insert the picture of the heart from ClipArt. Use WordArt to place **#1** as shown; use In Front of Text Wrap Text style; change the font color to white. Change the picture to 4.54" high by 4.25" wide.

   c. Key the text in 16-point font below the picture; font style and color should match the title.

6. Format for page 2, column 1:

   a. Key text using default font.

   b. Apply Heading 1 style to heading; change color to red.

   c. Key bulleted text; then select the text and remove the check mark from the "Don't add space between paragraphs of the same style" box (Home/ Paragraph/Indents and Spacing tab/Spacing After).

   d. Select the bulleted text and click Decrease Indent to move it to the left margin.

7. Format for page 2, column 2:

   a. Insert SmartArt. Choose the Basic Pie diagram in the Relationship group. Add a shape to the diagram.

   b. ✳ Click the upper-right quarter of the pie and drag it inward to form a round plate.

   c. Key the text in each shape. To insert text in the shape you just added, right-click the shape and choose Edit text. Change the color of each shape by right-clicking the shape and choosing Fill. Select the stated color.

   **Fruits** (red);         **Grains** (orange);
   **Vegetables** (green);   **Protein** (blue)

✳ **Discover**

Insert/Illustrations/Shapes displays a gallery of shapes. Select the shape, then click in document and drag to draw the shape. To add text, right-click and choose Add Text.

*(continued)*

## FILE MANAGEMENT

File management refers to saving documents in an organized manner so that they can be easily located and used again.

**Using *KPDO*—***KPDO* manages all of your files for this class. You must manage your own files if you do not use *KPDO*.

**Not using *KPDO*—**create and name a separate folder for each module, such as Module 3. (Do the same for your classes or projects—English 101b or Scholarship Fundraising Event.) Name files logically so that you will be able to find them easily, such as *business plan*. Use the file name in parenthesis at the end of each drill (*26-drill1*) or document in the Apply It section (*28-d1*).

---

## FILE TAB

File/command

The File tab located in the upper-left corner of the document screen provides you with all of the commands that you need to work with files. When you click the File tab, the options for things you can do to a document, such as open, close, save, or print it display.

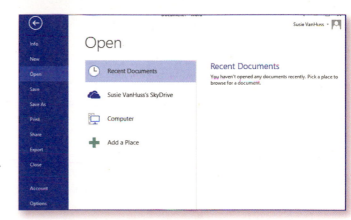

- Commands are on the left pane. The left arrow in the circle at the top takes you back to your open document.
- Places for storing documents are shown in the middle pane.
- Recent documents are shown in the right pane.
- Click the File tab any time you want to use a command to work with files.

---

**TIP**

The default in *Word 2013* with *Windows 8* is to save documents to your SkyDrive. Therefore, select the appropriate place on your computer or your flash drive when you save folders or documents.

## SAVE AND CREATE NEW FOLDER

The Save and Save As commands on the File menu preserve documents for future use.

- Save is used to save a document with the same name.
- Save As is used to save a document with a name for the first time, with a different name, or to a different place.

New folders can be created from the Save As dialog box.

9. Format the second page:

   a. Click the insertion point at the beginning of the left column on the second page. Insert a column break (you will need to do this two times); a column break code is inserted in the left column and the text moves to the right column.

   b. Click at the beginning of the column break; if needed, change the font to Calibri 11 point and tap ENTER 26 times. This inserts the line between columns on the page.

   c. Copy the logo from the banner and position it in the first column; apply In Front of Text Wrapping. Click on a ¶ marker below the logo and key **Arondale Medical Center News**. Click on the following ¶ marker and key **Page 2**. Bold the text, apply 12-point Automatic color, and Center.

10. Format the table as follows:

    a. Adjust column widths. Use a decimal tab to align numbers.

    b. Change the height of all the rows to 0.3".

    c. Apply Grid Table 5 Dark – Accent 6 style. Bold and center all column heads. Center all text vertically in cells.

11. Tap ENTER following the table and key a byline right-aligned using your name.

12. Proofread and check; click Next Activity. (*95-d1*)

 QUICK ✓

Check your document against the illustration below.

## To save a document in a new folder:

File/Save or Save As

1. Click File and then Save As. A shortcut known as a path (File/Save or Save As) lists the File tab and the command to select for this activity.

2. Click the place to store the document, such as Computer, to display the Save As dialog box.

3. Click the New Folder button to create a new folder in which to store the document. The New Folder Name box displays in blue.

4. Click in the New Folder Name box and key the name, such as Module 3.

5. Click open or double-click the new folder (Module 3) to open it.

**✳ Discover**

To save a document to a flash drive, use the same steps shown in this activity except for step 2.

In step 2, scroll down and click the name of your flash drive (or removable disk if the specific name is not listed). Note the Kingston flash drive listed below.

New folder button

New folder name box

File name box

Open folder

6. In the File name box, select Doc1 and key the name of the file, such as *26-drill1*.

7. Click Save.

---

**DRILL 1**      **SAVE DOCUMENT IN NEW FOLDER**

1. Launch *Word* and open a blank document.

2. In the new document, key your name; then tap ENTER, and key the text below.

3. Save the document on your ✳ flash drive or computer in a folder named Module 3; name the document **26-drill1**.

4. Leave the document open.

An effective way to manage files is to create folders to store related documents. Always name folders and files logically. Typically, folder names are formatted using initial caps and filenames using lowercase.

65 with chronic medical conditions who have not had this vaccine should also get this shot. The pneumonia vaccine prevents the most common cause of bacterial pneumonia that can result in hospitalization or death.

**Disease Surveillance Update**

The table below contains a summary of the surveillance data obtained from county health departments in 2013. No incidences of Congenital Rubella Syndrome or Rubella were reported in the state during the 2013 year.

Disease	Age Groups		
	**0-4 Years**	**5-17 Years**	**18+ Years**
Hepatitis A	123	305	534
Hepatitis B	83	215	350
Measles	25	47	13
Pertussis	305	278	153
Tetanus	17	31	43

**3.** Set up the columns in the newsletter:
   **a.** Select all the text below the Section Break (Continuous).
   **b.** Click Page Layout/Page Setup/Columns and choose More Columns.
   **c.** In the Columns dialog box, choose 2 columns. Deselect the box for Equal column width.
   **d.** Key 1.25" for the width of column 1. Click in the Width box for column 2; it automatically changes to 4.75".
   **e.** Place a check mark in the Line between box. Click OK.

**4.** Click the insertion point at the top of the left column; insert a column break.

**5.** Click the insertion point to the left of the column break code in the left column; tap ENTER. Click on the ¶ marker above the column break.

**6.** Insert a Simple Text Box and key **Protect Yourself Now!**

**7.** Format the text box as follows:
   **a.** Select the text box and change the text direction to Rotate all text 270° (Drawing Tools Format/Text Direction).
   **b.** Change the text to 48-point font. Increase the height of the text box until the text fits on one line. Change the Wrap Text to Square, if needed.
   **c.** Change the zoom to One Page. Move the text box so that it is attractively placed in the column.
   **d.** Change the color of the text to Orange, Accent 2, Darker 25%. Click Text Outline and apply the same color.
   **e.** Remove the outline of the text box (Drawing Tools Format/Shape Styles/Shape Outline/No Outline).

**8.** Insert a clip art of a clock in the second paragraph; change the Wrap Text format to Square. Size the picture appropriately.

*(continued)*

**TIP**

Use the Quick Check on page 461 as a guide for page layout.

## CLOSE DOCUMENT

 If you have only one document open and you click the Close button at the upper-right side of the screen, you will close the document and exit *Word*. If you have more than one document open, only that document will close.

 Clicking the Close command on the File menu, closes the document and keeps *Word* open.

To close a document and leave *Word* open:

File/Close

1. Click the File tab.
2. Click the Close command on the File menu.

---

## OPEN EXISTING DOCUMENT

 Existing documents can be opened in two ways. When you launch *Word*, recent documents will display in the left pane of the opening screen.

If you are working in *Word*, you can open existing documents not listed as recent documents by using the Open command on the File menu.

To open an existing document:

File/Open

1. Click File, Open, and then Computer.
2. Click the Browse icon, and select the folder in which you have stored the document.
3. Double-click the document name, or select it and click Open.

---

| DRILL 2 | OPEN AND CLOSE |

1. Close the open document. (*26-drill1*)

2. Open *26-drill1* and on the line below your name, key **26-drill2**.
   (**Note:** Text to be keyed is set off in bold; do not apply bold.)

3. Save as **26-drill2** and close. (*26-drill2*)

# Lesson 95 Health Promotions Documents

**Apply It**

**95–d1**

**Newsletter**

 arondale banner

1. In the open document, turn on Show/Hide.
2. Place the insertion point on the ¶ marker below the section break. Key the text below; apply Heading 1 style to side headings.

This special edition of the newsletter is published due to the rising concern among the general public of the increasing number of cases of influenza, pneumonia, and other vaccine-preventable diseases. The latest updates regarding immunization and vaccines and their availability are available at your county health department. If you have further questions on immunizations, please contact the Public Immunization Coordinator at the local health department.

**Still Some Time Left**

Influenza will be transmitted through the winter and into the spring. You can get your vaccination through January and still be protected. Despite the overall vaccine shortage, supplies are available for persons of high risk. Plenty of doses of preservative-free 0.25 ml doses, suitable for children 6 months through 3 years old, are on hand at local health departments.

**Nasal *SprayAway* Available**

Federal restrictions on the use of the nasal spray flu vaccine, *SprayAway*, have been lifted. Individuals between the ages of 5 and 49 with no chronic medical conditions and who are not pregnant can be administered *SprayAway*. It is highly recommended that individuals in the following groups get the *SprayAway* vaccine.

Insert round bullets

All health-care workers
Adults caring for children younger than 6 months of age
School-aged children
Those who come in contact with large numbers of people

**Influenza Vaccine Promotion**

Flyers promoting influenza vaccination are available in English, Spanish, Chinese, Japanese, Tagalog, and Vietnamese. These flyers can be downloaded from the Immunization Organization website at www.vaccinateyou.org.

**Pneumonia Vaccine Recommended**

A pneumonia shot is highly recommended for all adults 65 years of age and older who have not had this vaccine. Individuals between the ages of 2 and

*(continued)*

## NEW DOCUMENT

You have already opened a new blank document when you launched *Word*. If you are already working in *Word*, you can create a new document by using the New command.

### To create a new **Word** document:

File/New

1. Follow the path to display the New Document options.
2. Click the Blank document icon to open a new document.

## PRINT

Print displays the printing options next to the File menu and provides a preview of the document on the right side of the screen.

### To print a document:

File/Print

1. Follow the path to display the Print options. Note the settings that are available.
2. Preview the document.
3. Select the printing options desired.
4. Click Print.

---

**DRILL 3**          PRINT AND CREATE A NEW DOCUMENT

1. Open *26-drill2*.

2. Preview and print one copy of the document.

3. Close the document.

4. Open a new document.

5. Key your name on the first line and **26-drill3** on the line below it.

6. Save, close the document, and exit *Word*. (*26-drill3*)

---

## Apply It

**26-d1**

**Create, Save, and Print Document**

1. In a new document, key your name on the first line, and then key **26-d1** on the next line. (**Note:** Text to be keyed is set off in bold; do not apply bold.)

2. Save the document as **26-d1** in a new folder named **Applications**.

3. Preview and print the document.

4. Close the document and exit *Word*. (*26-d1*)

---

Coughing	A hacking, mucus-producing cough is often present with a cold.	A dry cough (non-mucus-producing) is often present with the flu.
Stuffy Nose	A stuffy nose is commonly present with a cold.	Flu victims do not commonly have a stuffy nose.

Stop by and see me in the medical center if I can be of further assistance or call me at extension 5378 if you have questions.

## 94-d3

**Sort Table**

1. In the open document (*94-d2*), select the table.
2. Sort the table by Symptoms in Ascending order (Table Tools Layout/Data/Sort). Remember to indicate that your list has a header row.
3. Proofread and check; click Exit *Word*. (*94-d3*)
4. Click Log out to exit *KPDO*.

Blend Images/ERproductions Ltd/Getty Images

## ! WORKPLACE SUCCESS

### Confidentiality

Information contained in a patient's record is confidential and should not be revealed without the patient's consent unless required by law. Confidentiality must be protected in order for patients to feel comfortable about revealing personal information. Health professionals are obligated to report findings of the following nature:

- A patient has threatened another person, and there is reason to believe that the threat may be carried out.
- Knife and gunshot wounds and injuries that may indicate child abuse must be reported.
- Communicable diseases, such as AIDS, hepatitis, and sexually transmitted diseases, must be reported.

# Lesson 27 Getting Started with KPDO

**New Commands**
- Font Group commands
- Mini toolbar

## Skill Building

### 27b Timed Writing

1. Key a 1' timed writing on each paragraph; work to increase speed. Use wordwrap.
2. Key a 3' timed writing on all paragraphs.

Many students and young professionals find it quite difficult to juggle the things they prefer to do with the things they ought to do. Too often the most tempting and desirable things are just distractions from doing the things that should be given priority.

The key is to set priorities and stick with them. Individuals who organize their work effectively and do the most critical things first not only accomplish more, they are the most likely to have sufficient time to do those things they enjoy doing as well.

Choosing friends wisely can help you to stay on target. Individuals who have similar expectations help each other to meet their goals. They know how important goals are to success, and they value their time and try to use it appropriately.

## New Commands

### 27c Getting Started with *KPDO*

### WORD IN KPDO

*Word 2013* enables you to create and format professional-looking documents that are easy to read. In Lesson 26, you learned the basic commands for using *Word* by itself. Going forward, you will launch *Word* directly in *KPDO*. When you select a *Word* activity, the Document Options box presents various options.

**Begin new document**: Creates a new document—a new pass.

**Open existing document**: Opens the existing (saved) document for editing.

**Print document without error report**: Displays the *Word* document as keyed.

**Print document with error report**: Displays the *Word* document in checked format.

TO: All Employees | FROM: Paula Jens, RN, MSN | Medical Center Coordinator | SUBJECT: Flu-like Illness

The local health board is anticipating that the number of people contracting influenza will reach record highs this winter. The medical center, in cooperation with the nursing students from Arondale University, will be offering free flu shots next week. Please call extension 5378 for an appointment.

As a safety precaution, we are asking employees with flu-like symptoms to practice self-isolation. This means staying away from work and limiting interactions with other people for at least 24 hours after fever symptoms have subsided.

We encourage hand hygiene and respiratory etiquette of people who are well and also those that have any flu-like symptoms. Wash your hands frequently with soap and water. Cover your nose and mouth with tissue when coughing or sneezing. If no tissue is available, use a shirt sleeve or elbow. Small bottles of hand sanitizer are available in the medical center free of charge.

Below is a chart describing how symptoms are manifested in a cold or flu virus.

Symptom	Cold Symptoms	Flu Symptoms
Chills	It is unusual for a patient to have chills with a cold.	Over 60% of flu cases include chills. Unexplained chills and shivering are often a sign of the flu.
Fever	A fever is rare with a cold.	A fever is present in approximately 80% of all flu cases. A flu victim usually has a fever of 100° F or higher for several days.
Aches	Mild body aches and pains are often associated with a cold.	Aches and pains are more severe with the flu.
Headache	Most people with colds do not have headaches.	Headaches are present in about 80% of all flu cases.
Sore Throat	A sore throat is often present with a cold.	Flu victims do not commonly complain of having a sore throat.
Sneezing	Sneezing is common with a cold.	Sneezing is not common with the flu.

*(continued)*

## CREATE WORD DOCUMENT

After you complete the Skill Building activities, *KPDO* automatically opens the Document Options dialog box for the first *Word* activity. If you skip the preliminary Skill Building activities, choose the exercise directly from the Lesson menu.

### To create a document in *KPDO*:

1. From the Document Options dialog box, select Begin new document and click OK.
2. *Word* opens with the KPDO Student tab displayed; four commands are available.

**Save and Close**: Saves the document without checking it.

**Check Document**: Checks completed document, reports errors, and displays results.

**Document Information**: Displays the activity name and page number.

**Help**: Provides access to global help.

3. The insertion point is positioned in the document and ready for you to begin. To access any *Word* command, select the tab you need and the ribbon for that tab displays.
4. After creating and proofreading the document, select Check Document.

## REVIEW CHECKED WORD DOCUMENT

After *KPDO* checks a document, a checked version displays on the screen. The KPDO Student ribbon changes and new functionality is available.

**Exit *Word***: Closes *Word* and returns to the Lesson menu.

**Document Information**: Identifies the document.

**Error Report**: Lists the reason for each error.

**94-d1**

**Modified Block Letter**

 arondale letterhead

1. In the open document, key the letter below in modified block style with open punctuation. Supply all necessary letter parts. Key the date on line 2.3".
2. Center the address lines for Good Samaritan Medical Center and press SHIFT + ENTER for correct spacing between the address lines.
3. The letter is from **David Dostourian, M.D., | President**.
4. Proofread and check; click Next Activity. (*94-d1*)

---

Dr. Sabrina Rodriguez, M.D. | Immunization Coordinator | Quality Care Medical Center | 5252 Lamar Boulevard | Austin, TX 78704-3088

Arondale Medical Center has an agreement with the Travis County Health Department which enables us to obtain vaccinations and supplies at no cost. These include Hepatitis A and B, influenza, and pneumococcal vaccines. This agreement requires that we keep detailed and accurate paperwork pertaining to the storage and administration of the vaccine.

The vaccine is currently being stored at:

> Good Samaritan Medical Center
> c/o Dr. Abrahim Jordan
> 1560 Broadway Avenue
> Austin, TX 78704-1234

The refrigerator containing the vaccine is in the infusion room. The temperature is to be measured twice a day and recorded on the form; use the thermometer in the door of the refrigerator for measuring. It is the duty of the clinic coordinator to ensure that this log is kept current. Under no circumstances should false values be added to the chart.

This agreement with Travis County Health Department provides us with an excellent opportunity to directly help the medically underserved population in the area. I am confident that you will maintain a strong relationship with the health department.

---

**94-d2**

**Two-page Memorandum with Table**

 arondale memorandum

1. Key the two-page memo shown on the next two pages. Supply all necessary memo parts.
2. Insert a table after the fourth paragraph; the table will continue on the second page. Change the width of column A to 1.6" and column B to 2". Change the height of row 1 to 0.5".
3. Apply Grid Table 5 Dark – Accent 2 style. Align Center column heads. Center the table horizontally on the page.
4. Select row 1 and click Repeat Header Rows.
5. Insert the second-page header.
6. Proofread and check; click Next Activity. (*94-d2*)

# REVIEW CHECKED WORD DOCUMENT, CONTINUED

**Previous Activity**: Opens the *Word* activity within the lesson. The Document Options dialog box gives you the option to begin a new pass or open an existing document and edit it.

**Next Activity**: Moves to the next *Word* activity in the lesson. *Word* stays open.

**Help**: Provides access to global help.

Mistakes are highlighted in the document, and errors are counted sequentially above each paragraph. If format is being checked, format errors are identified with a blue box. If the format error applies to an entire paragraph, the first word in the paragraph is highlighted in blue. To confirm the reason why an error is being charged, select Error Report.

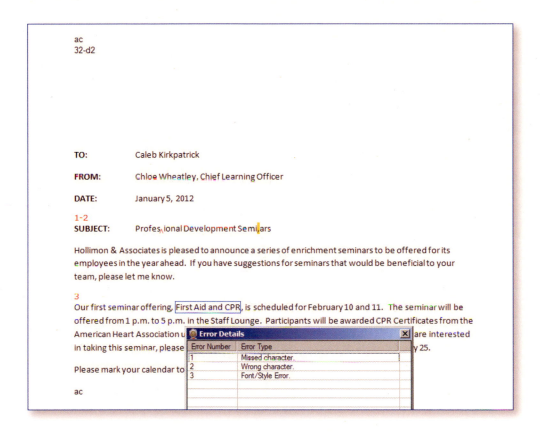

# OPEN AN EXISTING DOCUMENT

Open an existing *Word* document to complete or edit it. *KPDO* considers the first completed document as Edit 1 of Pass 1. When you open a checked document, make changes, and then check it again. *KPDO* refers to the second version as Edit 2.

# Health and Medical Documents

## LEARNING OUTCOMES

- Key and format medical correspondence.
- Key and format medical newsletters and brochures.
- Key and format SOAP notes.
- Key and format medical forms.
- Key and format medical reports.

## Lesson 94 Medical Correspondence

**Warmup** *Lesson 94a Warmup*

A ALL LETTERS

### Skill Building

**94b Timed Writing**

1. Key a 3' timing on each paragraph; work to increase speed.
2. Key a 3' timing on all paragraphs; work for control.

Something that you can never escape is your attitude. It will be with you forever. However, you decide whether your attitude is an asset or a liability for you. Your attitude reflects the way you feel about the world you abide in and everything that is a part of that world. It reflects the way you feel about yourself, about your environment, and about other people who are part of your environment. Oftentimes, people with a positive attitude are people who are extremely successful.

At times we all have experiences that cause us to be negative. The difference between a positive and a negative person is that the positive person rebounds very quickly from a bad experience; the negative person does not. The positive person is a person who usually looks on the bright side of things and recognizes the world as a place of promise, hope, joy, excitement, and purpose. A negative person generally has just the opposite view of the world. Remember, others want to be around those who are positive but tend to avoid those who are negative.

### Document Design

**MEDICAL CORRESPONDENCE**

**94c**

You will be keying medical correspondence for Arondale Medical Center. The medical center is affiliated with the Arondale University College of Medicine. The center is operated by private medical practitioners and university staff. You will be keying letters and reports to patients, other medical firms, government, and regulatory agencies. Arondale Medical Center sends informational newsletters and brochures to community members promoting health awareness and disease prevention.

To open an existing document:

1. Select the document from the Lesson menu at the far right of the screen.

2. Select Open existing document from the Document Options box and OK. You will receive a message that Word is opening.

3. Close the Document Information screen.

4. Edit the document and check it.

---

**DRILL 1**    CREATE DOCUMENT IN KPDO

1. The Document Options box displays after you have completed the timed writing. Select OK to accept the option Begin new document.

2. Close the Document Information screen.

3. At the insertion point, key the text shown below.

4. Select Check Document from the *KPDO* Student tab.

5. Mistakes are identified and counted. Select Error Report for a description of your errors. Tap the Page Down key to see your results. If you need to print the checked document, from the File tab select Print.

6. Select Close Word. You will return to the Lesson menu. (*27-drill1*)

KPDO will track my progress on all exercises that I key. My word processing documents will be checked for accuracy, which may help me become a better proofreader.

---

**DRILL 2**    OPEN EXISTING DOCUMENT

1. From the Lesson menu, select 27-Drill 1.

2. Choose Open existing document from the Document Options box.

3. After the last sentence, key the sentence below.

4. From the KPDO Student tab, select Check Document. Review your results.

5. From KPDO Student tab, select Next Activity. Notice that *Word* does not close, and you are ready to begin Drill 3.

I look forward to learning to use Word 2013 in this class.

---

## FORMAT TEXT WITH FONT COMMANDS

Text must be selected in order to format it using font commands. To access the text you wish to select, move the insertion point with the mouse or the arrow keys on the keyboard.

1. Key the following report. Use default theme, Title style, and Heading 1 style for headings. Tap ENTER twice after the title.
2. Preview and proofread; check and log out of *KPDO*. (93-d4)

## Guides for Selecting References

Deciding who to select as references is a very important strategic decision. Give careful thought to the individuals you select as references.

### Criteria for Selection

The key is to select individuals who know you well, will provide a strong, positive recommendation, and who can support your ability to do the job for which you are applying. Employers and former employers can attest to your job performance as well as colleagues and team members. Instructors can also provide valuable insight into academic ability and share workplace attributes, such as attendance, punctuality, and ability to work with others. Friends, relatives, neighbors, or others who might be viewed as biased in your favor by the prospective employer should not be selected as references unless they are employees of the company considering you for a position.

The references selected for one position may not be as strong for a different position. Banking professors may be a better choice for a position in a bank, whereas marketing professors may be a better choice for a similar position in a public relations firm. Use references who can legitimately give you a good recommendation and who also would have credibility with the company.

### Permission to Use References

Not only is it good manners to request permission to list a person as a reference; it is strategically important to do so. If a person hesitates, do not select that person as a reference. Hesitation is a sign that the person may not give you as strong a recommendation as you would like to have. Requesting permission gives you an opportunity to refresh the person's memory about you and to update him or her on recent accomplishments. You should also confirm position titles and contact information to ensure that you provide the employer with accurate information. Thank your references and update them after the job search process has been completed.

Be extremely careful about posting reference information to your website. Many references object to having their information posted on the Internet and will not serve as a reference if you post it. Posting information to an applicant tracking system on a secure company website usually is acceptable.

**Learn More:**

www.cengagebrain.com

To select text:

- Move the I-beam pointer to the beginning of the text you wish to select, and click the left mouse button.
- Drag the mouse over the text to highlight it. The selected text is highlighted in blue.

HOME

To format text, you will use commands on the Home tab of the Ribbon. Note that when you click the Home tab, the Ribbon displays with a number of commands clustered in groups.

Tab

Group     Command

**Tabs**—located at the top of the Ribbon. The Home tab is selected as shown by the blue text color. The other tabs also have commands that display as a ribbon when the tab is selected.

---

**Groups**—contain a number of related commands. Logical names are positioned at the bottom of the Ribbon below each group of commands. See the Font group.

---

**Commands**—the icons, the boxes for entering information, and the drop-list menus that provide a variety of options. The Font Color command identified changes the color of text—in this case to red. The small drop-list arrow next to the Font Color command displays the colors available.

---

To keep the Ribbon open with the commands displayed, click the Pin icon at the far right side of the Ribbon. Click the Unpin icon to display only the Tabs.

Pin                            Unpin

9:30	Call to Order	John Bennett
9:35	Open Issues	
	Conflict of Interest Policy	Roger Lettsworth
10:05	New Business	
	Investment Policy	Jeffery Harsh
	Portfolio Performance Review	Jeffery Harsh
	Investment Manager Performance	Jeffery Harsh
11:00	Adjournment	

**93–d2**

**Agenda**

  changes to draft

★ **TIP**

Check to see that your name is listed in the User name box on your computer.

1. In the open document, make the following changes to finalize the agenda:
   a. Delete the word *Draft* from the Agenda title.
   b. Make the change requested by John Bennett.
   c. Move *Investment Policy* to the position indicated by Kevin Vickers and change to his name as requested.
   d. Adjust line spacing if necessary. Then delete comments.
2. Preview and proofread; click Next Activity. (*93-d2*)

**93–d3**

**Interview Checklist**

1. Use default theme and tap ENTER three times; key **Prepare for Success** and apply Title style; then key **Develop an Interview Checklist** and apply Subtitle style.
2. Key the checklist shown below; use the customized bullet from Wingdings.
3. Proofread, preview, and click Next Activity. (*93-d3*)

Preparation is an important key to success in job interviewing. Use this simple checklist as you prepare for a job interview. Seek the advice of experts and continue to add items to this checklist.

☑ Am I comfortable with my knowledge about the company?
☑ Am I prepared to dress professionally for the interview?
☑ How long will it take me to get to the interview at least 15 minutes early?
☑ What materials should I take to the interview?
☑ Am I prepared for questions that might be asked of me, and what are the best answers to these questions?
☑ Do I know the interviewer's name, and can I pronounce it correctly?
☑ How do I handle the handshake?
☑ When should I be seated?
☑ How important is eye contact?
☑ What does my body language tell the interviewer?
☑ What questions can I ask the interviewer?
☑ Am I comfortable with my answers to the previous questions?
☑ If not, I need to do more preparation for the interview.

## FONT COMMANDS

Home tab/Font group/Font commands

Note that the path shown above (Home tab/Font group/Font commands) guides you in the location of commands. To follow the path: Click on the tab (Home); then look for the group label (Font) at the bottom of the Ribbon, and finally select the desired command (such as Font Size or Bold). The path will be provided for most commands throughout this textbook to assist you in locating commands quickly and easily. In this lesson, you will apply the format commands from the Font group to text that you have selected.

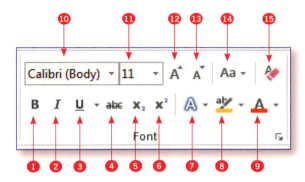

❶ Bold ❷ Italic ❸ Underline ❹ Strikethrough ❺ Subscript ❻ Superscript

❼ Text Effects and Typography ❽ Text Highlight Color ❾ Font Color

❿ Font ⓫ Font Size ⓬ Increase Font Size ⓭ Decrease Font Size

⓮ Change Case ⓯ Clear Formatting

---

### DRILL 3 — FORMAT TEXT WITH FONT COMMANDS

1. In a new document, click the Home tab and move the mouse pointer over each of the 15 commands (9 in bottom row; 6 in top row) in the Font group to identify the commands and note the short description of each.

2. Note that some of the commands such as Font and Underline have drop-list arrows on the side of the command. Click the drop-list arrow to see the gallery of options that can be selected.

3. Key the names of the 15 commands in sequential order; tap ENTER after each command. Do not key the numbers.

4. Select each of the first four commands you keyed and apply the format to the name of the command.

5. Key the number **1** at the end of *Subscript* and **2** at the end of *Superscript*; apply the format to the numbers.

6. Select Text Effects and Typography and apply Fill – Gold, Accent 4, Soft Bevel text effect (last icon in first row).

7. Select Text Highlight Color and apply yellow highlight.

8. Select Font Color and change the color to Blue from the Standard Colors palette.

9. Select Font and change to Cambria; select Font Size and change to 14 point.

10. Select Increase Font Size and click the Increase Font Size command twice.

11. Select Decrease Font Size and click the Decrease Font Size command once.

12. Select Change Case and change case to UPPERCASE.

13. Select Clear Formatting and apply Bold and Italic. Click the Underline drop-list arrow; select a double underline.

14. With Clear Formatting selected, click the Clear Formatting command to clear the formatting.

15. From the *KPDO* Student tab, select Check Document.

16. Click Next Activity command to begin Drill 4. (*27-drill3*)

---

**Note:** If you are not using *KPDO*, save the file with the name in parentheses. (*27-drill3*)

A **ALL LETTERS**

## Skill Building

### 93b  Timed Writing

Key two 3" timed writings; work on the control level.

What do you think about when you hear individuals being called student-athletes? Many people think only of the very visible football or basketball players who attract a lot of attention and often get special treatment on campus. Few people think about the large numbers of young men and women who put in long hours working and training to be the very best they can be in a wide variety of sports. These students may never receive any type of recognition in the news media, and they do not attract large crowds to watch them perform. They frequently excel in both academic and athletic performance.

What does a student-athlete in one of the less visible sports with very little opportunity to become a professional athlete gain from the significant investment of time and effort in a sport? To be successful in a sport, a student must be organized, be an effective time manager, and have self-confidence. An athlete learns that teamwork, ethical conduct, and hard work are a major part of success in any type of endeavor. The skills do not apply just to sports; they also apply to your job and your life. Most important of all, these individuals are doing what they really enjoy doing.

## Apply It

**93-d1**

**Draft Agenda**

1. Apply Metropolitan theme with default formatting style. Tap ENTER three times.
2. Key the heading **Draft Agenda | Investment Committee | Board Room | January 9, 201-, 9:30 a.m.** and format as follows:
   a. Apply Title style to first line of heading.
   b. Apply Heading 1 style to second line of heading.
   c. Apply Heading 2 style to third and fourth lines. Center all lines.
3. Tap ENTER twice; set a 1" left tab and a 6.5" right-aligned leader tab and key the body of the agenda shown on the next page.
4. Preview and proofread; click Next Activity. (*93-d1*)

*(continued)*

## MINI TOOLBAR

The Mini toolbar simplifies editing text by positioning frequently used commands at the point they are needed. It appears when you select text.

### To use the Mini toolbar:

1. Select text to which you want to apply a commonly used format.

2. Move the mouse pointer toward the Mini toolbar when it appears in a faded view.

3. Click the command(s) that you want to apply when the Mini toolbar darkens.

---

## DRILL 4     EDIT USING MINI TOOLBAR

1. Activity 27-drill4 should be open because you clicked Next Activity when you completed 27-drill3. If it is not open, select 27-drill4 from the Lesson menu.

2. Key the document name **27-drill4** at the top of the document, and tap ENTER. (**Note:** Text to be keyed is set off in bold; do not apply bold.)

3. Key the following sentence:

   **This is a new document I have created.**

4. Select the document name; use the Mini toolbar to change the font to Calibri Light and the font size to 14 point.

5. Select *new document* in the sentence you keyed, and use the Mini toolbar to highlight both words in Bright Green.

6. Proofread and ensure that you followed directions carefully.

7. Check your document and then click Next Activity on the *KPDO* Student tab to continue. (*27-drill4*)

---

## STANDARD OPERATING PROCEDURES

1. Key and format documents as directed in the textbook.

2. Proofread for keying or formatting errors. Check your document against the directions in the textbook.

3. Check the document when you are totally satisified that it is correct.

4. Review the checked document for mistakes; select Error Report to see the reasons for mistakes. See page 90 for an example.

5. Scroll to the end of the document to view the report of errors, *gwam*, etc.

6. Use the commands on the KPDO Student tab to move to the previous or next document without closing *Word*, or choose Exit Word to return to the Lesson menu.

7. Log out of *KPDO* when you are ready to end the session.

## 92-d2

**Job Posting**

 hess letterhead

1. In the open letterhead, key the abbreviated job description. Position title at 2" and apply Title style. Apply Heading 1 style to the two headings.
2. Preview, proofread, and check; click Next Activity. (92-d2)

Administrative Associate Position Available

Hess Property Enterprises is seeking a talented administrative professional to join the administrative support team in Hess Office Park. The candidate will provide support services for the executive staff and for tenants. Must have excellent customer service, communication, and Microsoft Office skills. The salary is commensurate with education and experience.

Key Duties and Responsibilities

- Serve as receptionist managing telephone calls professionally.
- Prepare correspondence and reports as requested.
- Work with tenants to ensure that their needs are met effectively.
- Schedule and maintain calendars for executive team.

Qualifications

- AS degree in office or business administration or equivalent required.
- Two years of office experience preferred.
- Knowledge of Word, Excel, and PowerPoint.
- Excellent customer service and communication skills.

A complete job description is available on the Hess Property Enterprises website along with information about submitting applications.

## 92-d3

**Compose Memo**

 hess memo form

1. Compose a memo from Mr. Hess to tenants in Hess Office Park sending them the job posting and asking them to refer qualified applicants. He will offer them a $200 gift certificate to be used at any business in Hess Office Park for each referral they provide who submits a resume for the position. Add appropriate information that you think recipients would like to have.
2. Preview, proofread, and check; log out of *KPDO*. (92-d3)

**27-d1**

**Create a New Document**

1. In a new document, key **27-d1** on the first line.

2. Key the following sentences. Do not key the letters used to identify the sentences. Tap ENTER after each sentence.

   a. The default for Heading 1 is Calibri Light 16-point font.

   b. I use red font color, yellow highlighting, or orange text effects for emphasis.

   c. This sentence illustrates bold text, italic text, and underline format.

   d. He said, "Revert back to the previous form."

   e. Use text formats to emphasize text in documents, but do not overuse them.

3. In sentence a, apply Calibri Light 16-point font size to Heading 1.

4. In sentence b, apply Red font color to the word *red*, Yellow highlight to the word *yellow*, and Fill – Orange, Accent 2, Outline – Accent 2 text effect (the third icon in the first row of the gallery) to the word *orange*.

5. In sentence c, apply bold format to the word *bold*, italic format to the word *italic*, and underline format to the word *underline*.

6. In sentence d, apply strikethrough to the word *back*.

7. In sentence e, apply bold, italic, and Red font color to the words *emphasize text*.

8. In sentence e, use clear formatting to remove all formats from the words *emphasize text*.

9. Proofread and check. Click Exit Word from the *KPDO* Student tab to close the document. (*27-d1*)

10. Click Log out to exit *KPDO*.

## ! WORKPLACE SUCCESS

### Social Networks

Pixellover RM 7 / Alamy

Social networks are websites designed to foster social interaction among a group of people with common interests. *Facebook* and *MySpace* popularized the idea of social networks and initially appealed to teenagers and college students. Today, many other networks and social media tools have been created and the profiles of those who use them have changed significantly. Millions of adults of all ages are active users of *Facebook*, *LinkedIn*, *Twitter*, *YouTube*, *Flickr*, and a host of other social media tools. Businesses as well as nonprofit organizations active use social media tools to promote their organizations and enhance their businesses. Although using social media is extremely popular and offers many advantages, care needs to be taken to protect against the abuse of the media that is also rampant.

situation might be that you can recommend only one person for an award trip, and the selection basis you use when two people have equal qualifications.

Often interviews focus on soft skills because they are important on the job, and they are difficult to measure and document. An example might be: Who on your team, other than you, had the very best client or customer service skills? Describe three personal attributes that made that individual so successful in working with clients and customers. How would you rank yourself on those three attributes with one being your greatest strength, two being the next, and three being the lowest?

Observations

An important reason to schedule a face-to-face interview is to be able to observe the applicant's body language and other soft skills. Examples to observe include:

Professional appearance.

Handshake.

Punctuality.

Manners, mannerisms, gum chewing, or unprofessional behavior.

Way the applicant interacted with people encountered other than the interviewer.

Table manners if a meal is provided.

Respect for others.

Way the person makes judgments.

Compare the format of your document to the one shown below.

# Lesson 28 Paragraph Formats

## New Commands

- Alignment
- Show/Hide
- Line Spacing
- Quick Access Toolbar

## Skill Building

### 28b  Textbook Keying

1. Key each line once, concentrating on using good keying techniques.
2. Repeat the drill if time permits.

one-hand
1 A few treats were served as reserve seats were set up on a stage.
2 In my opinion, a few trees on a hilly acre created a vast estate.

balanced hand
3 Pam and Jake did go to visit the big island and may fish for cod.
4 Ken and six men may go to visit an island with an ancient chapel.

1st/2nd fingers
5 Kimberly tried to grab the bar, but she missed and hurt her hand.
6 My name is Frankie, but I prefer to be called Fran by my friends.

3rd/4th fingers
7 Zola and Polly saw us play polo at Maxwell Plaza; we won a prize.
8 Zack quickly swam past all six boys at a zoo pool on Saxony Land.

## New Commands

### 28c

 **TIP**

From this point forward, *KPDO* will launch *Word* for all activities unless you are specifically directed otherwise.

## PARAGRAPH FORMATS

Home/Paragraph/Command

Some paragraph commands are positioned together in subgroups separated from one another by divider bars. The following overview presents the commands by the subgroups.

❶ **Alignment commands**—Align Left, Center, Align Right, and Justify—specify how text lines up.

❷ **Line and Paragraph Spacing**—determines the amount of space between lines of text and before and after paragraphs.

❸ **Shading**—applies color as a background for text and paragraphs.

❹ **Borders**—apply and remove inside and outside borders and horizontal lines.

❺ **Bullets, Numbering, and Multilevel List**—apply formats to lists of information. Bullets and Numbering present information on one level, whereas Multilevel List presents information in a hierarchy.

❻ **Decrease and Increase Indent**—move all lines of a paragraph to the right or left.

❼ **Sort**—alphabetizes selected text or arranges numerical data in ascending or descending order.

❽ **Show/Hide**—displays paragraph markings and other nonprinting characters.

1. Key the notes shown below at the end of the open document.
2. Apply Heading 1 style to *Interviews* and Heading 2 style to all other side headings. Add bullets to the list of thing to observe. Number pages at the top using Rounded Rectangle 3; do not show number on first page.
3. Preview, proofread, and check; click Next Activity. (*92-d1*)

Interviews

Effective interviews are based on the assumption that applicants are carefully screened to ensure that they have the qualifications required to be successful on the job. However, employers often indicate that the person they envisioned from reading application documents is not the same as the person they actually talk with about the job. This explains why virtually all employers insist on interviewing an individual before hiring that individual. Thus, it is important to make sure the interview meets legal requirements and produces reliable and valid information.

Types of Interviews

Different types of interviews can be used. Examples include:

**Face-to-Face Interviews:** Most employers believe that in-person interviews are more effective than telephone, video, or virtual interviews. However, face-to-face interviews are more expensive. If face-to-face interviews are not used for the first interview, the final applicants are generally invited for a second in-person interview.

**Structured Interviews:** Most employers prepare carefully for interviews. One way to structure an interview is to develop a list of questions to be asked in the interview and to ensure that all applicants answer the same questions. Many employers like to follow up on questions, and they do not limit themselves to just the list of required questions.

**Panel Interviews:** Several people interview the same applicant at the same time. They may use predetermined questions, or they may vary questions.

Interview Questions

Most interviews start with easy questions that give the applicant an opportunity to talk about themselves, their interest in this particular job, and the value they think they can bring to the job. These questions serve as a warm-up and enable the applicant to get comfortable and develop confidence. These types of questions also give the interviewer an opportunity to observe the applicant and assess verbal and nonverbal skills.

Some of the most effective questions are behavioral questions. Examples are: What was the most difficult decision you made in your last job? How did you go about making it? Behavioral questions should include both positive and negative aspects of a job. On one extreme, a question might focus on how you handle conflict situations, and on the other extreme, the

*(continued)*

# ALIGNMENT

❶ **Align Left**—all lines begin at left margin.

❷ **Center**—all lines are centered.

❸ **Align Right**—all lines are aligned at the right margin.

❹ **Justify**—all lines are aligned at both the left and right margins.

To apply alignment formats:

Home/Paragraph/Align Left, Center, Align Right, or Justify

1. Click in a single paragraph or select multiple paragraphs to which a format is to be applied.

2. Click the format to be applied.

<div style="text-align:right">Right-aligned text</div>

<div style="text-align:center">Centered Text</div>

Left-aligned text is the most frequently used alignment. All lines begin at the left margin. The right margin is uneven when text is aligned at the left side.

Justify aligns text at both the left and the right margins. All lines are even on both sides except that the last line of a paragraph may be shorter and will not end at the right margin. The system allocates additional space as needed to force the right margin to align evenly.

---

## DRILL 1     ALIGNMENT

1. In a new document, move the mouse pointer over each command to view the Enhanced ScreenTips for the format paragraph commands. Click the drop-list arrow on those commands that have a drop-list arrow to view the options.

2. Key the document shown above; do not format as you key.

3. Apply the alignment formats shown above.

4. Proofread and check; click Next to continue. (*28-drill1*)

# Lesson 92 Hess Office Park

**Learning Outcomes**
- Apply keying, formatting, and word processing skills.
- Prepare effective employment documents.
- Work independently with few specific instructions.

## Skill Building

**92b Timed Writing**

Key two 3' timed writings.

Dining etiquette is necessary as good impressions are made on both important business clients and friends. Table manners tell so much about a professional. Just notice as the well-orchestrated and zealous expert makes sure that the guest has the best place at the table and gives excellent advice on the best food items. Finally, the napkin is placed on his or her lap to signal the beginning of the meal.

To understand a seemingly difficult table setting more easily, think of a line down the middle of the serving plate. Then always remember liquids are placed on the right of the line and solids are placed on the left. Notice very carefully that glassware, cup and saucer, knives, and spoons are positioned on the right side of the line. Notice also that the bread and butter plate, salad plate, napkin, and forks are positioned on the left side. Returning these items to the same specific position after using each one will keep the table looking very good.

Never begin eating until the host unfolds his or her napkin. Upon this important signal, open your napkin and position it carefully on your lap. Should you need to leave the table momentarily, position your napkin on your chair. Remember, never move your plate away from you when completed. Wait until the host has placed his or her napkin on the table; then you may position yours to the right of the dinner plate.

## Project Setting

### HESS OFFICE PARK

The Human Resources staff of Hess Property Enterprises does seminars packaged in two-hour sessions, which are available to tenants of Hess Office Park at a very minimum cost. They are designed primarily for the small entrepreneurial businesses that do not have human resources staff. Parker Bradley has asked you to key the participant notes shown on the next page as a handout for the third segment of the HR seminar, which focuses on interviewing. Participant notes typically include a highlight summary of the other two segments provided by the seminar leaders and more comprehensive notes for the current session.

## SHOW/HIDE

Home/Paragraph/Show/Hide

Paragraph formats apply to an entire paragraph. Each time you tap ENTER, *Word* inserts a paragraph mark and starts a new paragraph. Thus, a paragraph may consist of a partial line or of several lines. You must be able to see where paragraphs begin and end to format them. Turning on the Show/Hide button displays all nonprinting characters such as paragraph markers (¶) or spaces (..). The Show/Hide button appears highlighted when it is active. Nonprinting characters can be turned off by clicking the Show/Hide button again.

---

### DRILL 2       SHOW/HIDE

1. In a new document, turn on Show/Hide. Tap ENTER three times.

2. Key the text shown below; then apply both the text formats and the alignment formats listed in the following steps.

3. Apply bold format to *My Personal Assistant*; right-align it.

4. Apply Cambria 14-point font and bold to the centered text.

5. Add italic to *KPDO* and in the last line to *personal assistant*.

6. Proofread and check; click Next Activity. (*28-drill2*)

<div align="right">

**My Personal Assistant**

</div>

<div align="center">

### Why Use Show/Hide?

</div>

Using Show/Hide will help you format your documents correctly. It can also help you earn better scores on your work as it will display symbols to indicate spacing and other errors before the checker in *KPDO* finds them.

Think of Show/Hide as a personal assistant when you key documents!

---

## LINE AND PARAGRAPH SPACING

Line and paragraph spacing enable you to choose the amount of space between lines and between paragraphs. The illustration at the right shows the options that display when you click the drop-list arrow. To view the default line and paragraph spacing, click Line Spacing Options.

The 1.08 line spacing and 8 points after paragraph defaults are shown in the illustration below.

**Maria J. Rex**
2104 Adger Road, Columbia, SC 29204-3253
803.555.0194 | Maria.Rex@wcc.edu | http://www.linkedin.com/in/rex

Current date

Mr. Miguel Mendoza
President and CEO
Blackmon Development Corporation
548 Poplar Street
Macon, GA 31201-2752

Dear Mr. Mendoza

*Begin with a buffer or neutral statement.* →
Yesterday, I received your offer for a position as a management trainee at Blackmon Development Corporation. Your offer is very interesting and very competitive. I also received an offer yesterday for a position as the office manager for a consulting alliance.

*Present reasons for declining tactfully.* →
Although the position you offered is a very desirable one and I have considered it very carefully, it does not give me an opportunity to apply my office management knowledge and experience immediately. Therefore, I have accepted the other position because it is more directly related to my long-term career goals.

*Thank the employer for considering you; end on a friendly note.* →
I do appreciate Blackmon Development Corporation offering me a position and the many courtesies that were extended to me during my interview and visit to Macon. Blackmon Development Corporation is an excellent company, and I wish you much success in finding the right person for the position you have available.

Sincerely

Maria J. Rex

**Job Refusal Letter**

To change line spacing:

Home/Paragraph/Line and Paragraph Spacing

1. Position the insertion point in the paragraph whose spacing you wish to change.
2. Click the Line and Paragraph Spacing button and select the desired spacing.

Default (1.08) spacing → **Paragraph 1** is keyed using the *Word 2013* default line spacing of 1.08 with 8 point spacing after the paragraph.

Single (1.0) spacing → **Paragraph 2** is keyed in traditional single spacing (1.0). Note below the paragraph that selecting the single spacing option did not change the 8 points of space after the paragraph.

Word 2010 default (1.15) spacing → **Paragraph 3** is keyed using the 1.15 *Word 2010* line spacing default. Again, choosing this option does not affect the amount of space after the paragraph.

Double (2.0) spacing → **Paragraph 4** is keyed using double spacing (2.0). Note that when double spacing is used, paragraphs are indented.

## DRILL 3    LINE SPACING

1. In a new document, key the four paragraphs above; then apply the formatting shown in each paragraph. Remember to apply bold and italics.

2. Note the differences between 1.08 spacing, 1.15 spacing, 1.0 spacing, and 2.0 spacing shown above.

3. Proofread and check; click Next Activity. (*28-drill3*)

**Note:** The amount of space (8 points) between paragraphs does not change when you change the line spacing. It is 8 points after each paragraph.

The Quick Access Toolbar is available from all tabs on the Ribbon.

## QUICK ACCESS TOOLBAR

The Quick Access Toolbar is located in the upper-left corner of the screen above the File and Home tabs. It contains icons for three frequently used commands: Save, Undo, and Redo. The Quick Access Toolbar provides a shortcut or one-click option for these frequently used commands. *KPDO* saves documents for you, but the Save command will be useful when you are not using *KPDO*.

## Apply It

91-d1

**Social Media Profile**

### ★ OPTIONAL

This document is listed as optional because many educational institutions block access to social media sites. It is recommended that anyone searching for a job take advantage of having an appropriate profile on a social media site. However, it may best be accomplished outside of class.

1. Determine which social media site you wish to use and make your profile public.
2. Ensure that other sites do not have unfavorable materials on it that are publically accessible.
3. Add a professional photo and then use the space below your name for your profile.
4. Transfer appropriate parts of your resume; add any additional information that may be useful.
5. Add three references who know you professionally and are willing to provide the reference.
6. Proofread and edit your site carefully. Ensure that it is free of grammar, punctuation, spelling, and word usage errors.

---

**91-d2**

**Application Letter**

 rex letterhead

1. In the open document, key the application letter to the hiring manager shown on the previous page.
2. Pay particular attention to the content of the letter and the callouts explaining the strategy used.
3. Preview, proofread, and check; click Next Activity. (*91-d2*)

---

**91-d3**

**My Application Letter**

1. Create your own letterhead for the application letter you will prepare and save it as a Quick Part.
2. Compose an application letter to accompany your resume. Use the contact information from the job description that you printed and used to design your resume.
3. Edit it carefully.
4. Preview, proofread, and check; click Next Activity. (*91-d3*)

---

**91-d4**

**Job Refusal Letter**

 rex letterhead

1. In the open document, key the letter shown on the next page.
2. Pay particular attention to the content of the letter and the callouts explaining the strategy used.
3. Preview, proofread, and check; click Next Activity. (*91-d4*)

---

**91-d5**

**Compose Job Acceptance Letter**

1. Use the letterhead you created for *91-d3* and compose an acceptance letter for the job you applied for in *91-d3*.
2. Confirm a starting salary that you think appropriate for the position and a starting date of one month from today.
3. Indicate your excitement about the position and how much you look forward to working with the team at your new company.
4. Edit your letter carefully.
5. Preview, proofread, and check; log out of *KPDO*. (*91-d5*)

## QUICK ACCESS TOOLBAR, CONTINUED

 **Save** preserves the current version of a document or displays the Save As dialog box to save a new document.

 **Undo** reverses the most recent action you have taken (such as inserting or deleting text or removing formats). The drop-list arrow displays a list of the commands that you can undo. Selecting an item on the list will undo all items above it on the list.

**Redo** reverses the last undo; it can be used several times to redo the past several actions. You can also select new text and click Redo to repeat the last redo.

---

**DRILL 4**  **QUICK ACCESS TOOLBAR**

1. Key the four sentences below.

2. In sentence 1, apply bold and underline to *Undo/Redo*.

3. Undo the underline in sentence 1.

4. Apply bold to Undo in sentence 2 and to Redo in sentence 3. Then apply italic to both.

5. Remove italic in both sentences 2 and 3.

6. In sentence 4, apply bold to *use*.

7. Select *You can* and then click Redo to repeat the bold command.

8. Key Quick Access Toolbar below the last sentence, and then right-align it. Notice that double-spacing is carried forward from the previous paragraph.

9. Use Undo to remove the right-align; then use Redo to go back to right-align.

10. Proofread and check; click Next Activity. (*28-drill4*)

Keying and formatting changes can be reversed easily by using the Undo/Redo commands.

If you make a change, one click of the Undo command can reverse the change.

If you undo a change and decide that you want to keep the change as it was originally made, you can go back to the original change by clicking the Redo command.

You can use the Redo command as a Repeat command.

**Maria J. Rex**
2104 Adger Road, Columbia, SC 29204-3253
803.555.0194 | Maria.Rex@wcc.edu | http://www.linkedin.com/in/rex

Current date

Mr. Eric Todd, President and CEO
CunCo Consulting Alliance
416 West Bay Street
Savannah, GA 31401-1115

Dear Mr. Todd

Establish a point of contact and state the job you are applying for. → Ben Sullivan, your manager of Business Development, sent me a copy of the job description posted for the office manager position open at CunCo and suggested that I contact you. My qualifications match the requirements for the office manager you are seeking. Please consider me as an applicant for that position.

Convey key qualifications → My education and my two years of experience managing the four-hour evening shift of two teams of trainers and one of nutrition counselors enabled me to develop the team management and the operational management skills that you require. Our teamwork resulted in a significant revenue increase and expense reduction.

State how the employer will benefit from your qualifications → My internship in the President's Office of Wexford Community College enabled me to refine my organizational, problem-solving, and soft skills. Both my experience at Pat's Fitness and Wellness Center and in the President's office required extensive Word, Excel, and PowerPoint use and excellent communication skills. I delivered high-quality products and met very tight deadlines consistently. I understand how those skills can be of value to CunCo.

Request an interview → After you have had an opportunity to review the enclosed resume as well as my LinkedIn Profile, I look forward to meeting with you to discuss how my qualifications and my office management career aspirations can be applied to your position at CunCo Consulting Alliance.

Sincerely

Maria J. Rex

Enclosure

**Application Letter**

1. In a new document, key all paragraphs below using default font, size, and spacing. Turn on Show/Hide.

2. Position the insertion point at the beginning of the title, *Standard Operating Procedures*, and tap ENTER three times; apply bold, 16-point Arial font to the title, and center it.

3. Apply bold and 14-point Arial font to the three side headings.

4. Proofread and check; click Next Activity. (*28-d1*)

Standard Operating Procedures

Many companies develop standard operating procedures (SOPs) for virtually every phase of their business. When standard operating procedures are mentioned, most people think of a manufacturing or service business and are surprised to learn that standard operating procedures apply to management and office administration as well. Most companies have SOPs for producing documents in their offices for several reasons.

Quality Control

SOPs ensure that company image is consistent throughout the organization. Guides are presented for using and protecting the company logo, standard colors may be specified, and document formats are standardized.

Training Tools

New and experienced employees both want to do a good job. SOPs provide an excellent training tool to ensure that all employees do their work accurately and meet company expectations consistently. Most employees do not like to be told repeatedly what to do. Having a set of guides to follow enables them to work independently and still meet quality standards.

Productivity Enhancement and Cost Reduction

Documents are very expensive to produce. SOPs are designed to be efficient, and efficiency translates to cost savings.

### 28-d2

**Apply Font and Paragraph Formats**

1. Open *28-d1*; turn on Show/Hide. Select the entire title; use the Mini toolbar to decrease the font size to 14 point.

2. Click in the paragraph below the centered title and change the line spacing to double spacing. Tap TAB to indent the first line of the paragraph. Select the entire paragraph and change the font to Times New Roman 11 point.

3. Click in the paragraph below each side heading, and change the line spacing to double spacing. Then tap TAB to indent the first line of the paragraphs. Triple-click to select the entire paragraph and change the font to Times New Roman 11 point.

4. Turn off Show/Hide.

5. Proofread and check; click Exit Word to close. (*28-d2*)

6. Click Log out to exit *KPDO*.

## Strategy for Application Letter

The purpose of an application letter, which serves as the cover letter for a resume, is to obtain an interview—not to get a job. Some recruiters suggest that cover letters are not necessary, and often are not read. However, most experts disagree with these recruiters. Hiring managers eventually get the cover letters and read them carefully. No downside exists for including a well-written letter, and it is a risk not to include a cover letter. These documents are used to determine that the applicant is qualified for the job. Virtually, all organizations require an interview before hiring an individual. Generally, the interview is granted only to qualified applicants, and it is used to determine how the applicant would fit in with the organization and its current employees. The best strategy for an application letter is to focus on showing how your qualifications match the requirements of the available job. Your empasis should be on demonstrating that you are qualified and can add value to the company.

### To write an effective application letter:

1. Establish a point of contact specifying how you learned about the company having a position available.
2. Specify the specific position you are seeking.
3. Convey your key qualificiations for that job.
4. Interpret your major qualifications in terms of how they benefit the employer.
5. Request an interview.

## Strategy for Job Acceptance or Refusal Letters

Most organizations require a written acceptance for a job offer and expect a written refusal if you do not accept the offer presented. Obviously, it is much easier to write the acceptance letter than the refusal letter. Always decline a position graciously. In the future, the company may have a position you would like to accept or may even become a customer or client.

### To write an effective acceptance letter:

1. Express your delight in accepting the position.
2. Confirm specific details, such as salary and starting date.
3. End on a friendly, optimistic note about your future with the company.

### To write an effective refusal letter:

1. Begin with a buffer or neutral statement to cushion the bad news.
2. Present the reasons tactfully and let them lead to the decline.
3. End on a friendly note thanking the employer for considering you.

# Lesson 29 Format Paragraphs/Navigate Documents

**New Commands**

- Bullets and Numbering
- Scroll bars
- Slider Zoom

- View
- Spelling and Grammar
- Thesaurus

- Define
- Word Count

 **Warmup** *Lesson 29a Warmup*

## Skill Building

### 29b Textbook Keying

Key each line once, concentrating on using good keying techniques.

balanced-hand words, phrases, and sentences

1 if me to so he is us do go or sod fir for pen may big dig got fix

2 dog jam sit men lap pay cut nap tug lake worn make torn turn dock

3 he is | it is | of it | is it | go to | to go | is he | he is it | for it | she can

4 did he | pay them | she may | is it torn | it is worn | he may go | the lake

5 He may also go with them to the dock or down to the lake with us.

6 Did she go with Keith to the lake, or can she go to town with us?

### 29c Timed Writing

1. Key a 1' timed writing on each paragraph; work to increase speed. Use wordwrap.
2. Key a 3' timed writing on all paragraphs.

Learning new software applications can be exciting, but it often requires much hard work. However, if you are willing to work hard and to work smart, in a relatively short period of time you can learn very important skills.

If you accept change easily and willingly, you are more likely to learn new things quickly. A person who avoids change has just about the same chance of learning new software applications as a lazy person.

Working smart might be just as important as working hard. Help is easy to use if you will take the time to explore the resources that are provided in your software. Valuable information is also available on the provider's website.

2. Decide which social media site you would like potential employers to access during your job search.

    a. LinkedIn is considered to be a professional network. Make your profile on the network you selected public so employers can access it easily.

    b. Use other sites such as Twitter and Facebook for networking. Make them private. Notify your contacts that you are in the job market, have updated your LinkedIn or other profile, and provide the link.

    c. Search all of the networks for companies of interest that might have job postings. Look for contacts that you might know. A job referral from a company employee or close professional associate of the employer is one of the best ways to get the job, provided you are qualified for it.

**TIP**

Note that the default for a Facebook profile is public. You have to change the default to make it private.

## DESIGN AN EFFECTIVE PROFILE

Develop or enhance your profile on the network you select to use for the job search.

1. Include a picture.
2. Use the space directly below your name for your Professional Profile.
3. Copy and paste appropriate sections of your resume to the profile.
4. Include all of employment experience—full-time, part-time, internships, volunteer work, and projects.
5. List all educational experiences, including special training you might have had. Pages are not limited on profiles.
6. Highlight computer skills, foreign languages, and other special skills.
7. Secure at least three recommendations from people who know you professionally and will provide a good recommendation.
8. Share updates periodically. Employers may see these and check your profile.

## EMPLOYMENT LETTERS

Three types of employment letters are covered specifically in this lesson: application or cover letter, job acceptance letter, and job refusal letter. Other letters are important to send during the employment process, including a thank-you letter after an interview, a request for a reference, and a thank-you letter after a reference has been provided. Good writing skills are all that you need to write these types of letters.

Design an attractive personal letterhead for your employment letter. Market yourself. Never use a company's letterhead in the search for a job. Use the same theme, colors, and style that you use for your resume. Use block letter format with open punctuation.

## BULLETS AND NUMBERING

Bullets are used for lists of unordered items, whereas numbering is used for items that are in a sequence. Bullets can be converted to numbers, and numbers can be converted to bullets. The drop-list arrow on bullets and numbering displays a library of styles for each command. If you have recently used bullets or numbering, the style used will display at the top of the library. Bullets and numbering are easier to apply after text has been keyed.

To apply Bullets and Numbering:

Home/Paragraph/Bullets or Numbering

1. Key the list.
2. Select the list and click either the Bullets or the Numbering command.

To select a different format for Bullets and Numbering:

1. Click the drop-list arrow on either the Bullets or the Numbering button to display the library of styles.
2. Select the desired style.

**Note:** The gallery that displays on your computer may have different bullet styles than the one shown at the right.

---

## DRILL 1     BULLETS AND NUMBERING

1. In a new document, key the two lists below.

2. Bold the headings. Apply bullets to the first list below the heading *Procedures for Completing an Activity.*

3. Apply numbering to the second list, *Things to Do This Weekend.*

4. Convert the first list with bullets to numbering using the number format with right parentheses (Left alignment).

5. Convert the second list with numbering to square bullets.

6. Proofread and check; click Next Activity. (*29-drill1*)

**Procedures for Completing an Activity**

Preview and proofread the document.

Print the document.

Save document with appropriate name and close it.

**Things to Do This Weekend**

Complete library research.

Pick up office supplies.

Install new software.

# Lesson 91 Social Media and Employment Letters

## Document Design

**91b**

> 1. Review the internal and external recruiting strategies on pages 1–2 in the Employment Strategies white paper (*89-d1*) you printed in Lesson 89, on page 432.
> 2. Review the *Job Sources* section on page 4 of that document.

## SOCIAL MEDIA

The *Employment Strategies* document emphasized how broadly organizations advertise positions available. Note that many sources companies use are online media. Also note in the *Job Sources* section for job seekers that companies usually post job openings internally first—that is a major part of the hidden job market and often a great source for the best jobs. Think about your contacts on social media who may be aware of job openings in their company. Companies promote themselves widely; social media gives you a free opportunity to promote yourself widely. While social media profiles are not likely to replace resumes in the near future, they can be a valuable promotion tool for a person in the job market.

Perhaps the most important thing to remember in using social media during a job search is that it often results in screening the applicant out. Both recruiters and hiring managers frequently use a search engine, such as Google, to gain information about job applicants. The search results generally include your Facebook, Twitter, LinkedIn, and other social networks. Often potential employers find offensive or unprofessional material that works against you in the job search.

## GUIDELINES FOR USING SOCIAL MEDIA

The following guides are designed for individuals who are in the midst of a job search and either already have social media accounts or plan to use social media while they are searching for a job.

1. Review your social media networks from the perspective of an employer.
   a. Would it be to your advantage for a prospective employer to read the information on this network?

   Examples of a few things to look for include:

   - offensive language
   - unprofessional pictures
   - political statements
   - strong religious statements
   - poorly written communications
   - personal or intimate information
   - drug and alcohol references
   - bad reputation of contacts

   b. If not, either remove any unfavorable information from each network or make it private so that it cannot be accessed by a potential employer. Keep in mind that neither of these options is foolproof.

*(continued)*

## NAVIGATE AND VIEW A DOCUMENT

The document window displays only a portion of a page at one time. The keyboard, mouse, and scroll bars can be used to move quickly through a document to view it.

**Keyboard options**—press CTRL + HOME to go to the beginning of a document and CTRL + END to move to the end of the document. The Page Up and Page Down keys can also be used to move through a document.

**Mouse and scroll bar**—use the scroll bar located on the right side of the screen to move through the document. Scrolling does not change the position of the insertion point; it only changes your view of the document. You must click in the text to change the position of the insertion point.

**Zoom**—enables users to view the document with enlarged or reduced text. Zoom is located on the status bar and the View menu.

**View tab**—provides additional options for viewing documents.

## SCROLL BAR

The scroll bar on the right side of the screen provides options to move through the document. The scroll bar at the bottom of the screen allows you to move to the left or right to see the entire line of writing.

To move through a document:

- Click the up and down arrows.  -or-
- Click above or below the scroll box.  -or-
- Click the scroll box and drag it to the desired position.

Note the position displays when you drag the scroll box.

## ZOOM OR SLIDER

Zoom, located on the status bar at the lower right-side of the *Word* window, controls the magnification of your document. Zoom is positioned in the center of the slider bar, which displays text at 100% of its actual size. It is sometimes called the Slider because Zoom slides to the right or left to increase or decrease text size.

Zoom

Clicking the plus or minus sign on the Slider changes the settings in increments of 10 percent.

Honors and Activities

Participated in numerous volunteer and community service projects. Received awards and served as a leader in honorary and professional organizations:

- Named a Dean's Scholar.
- Received the Outstanding Business Student Award.
- Member of Student Advisory Council.
- President of the Wexford Honor Society.
- President of the Office Management Club.

**90-d4**

**My Resume for ATS Screening**

1. Review the job description you printed and the *resume worksheet* you prepared in Lesson 89.
2. Customize the resume you prepared in *90-d2* to enhance it for ATS screening.
3. Proofread and check; click Next Activity. (*90-d4*)

## Communication

**90e**

 word usage

References/Communication Skills/ Word Usage

1. Check the list carefully to make sure that you know how the words on the list should be used.
2. If you are not sure how all of the words should be used, take one of the following actions:
   a. Go to the References in *KPDO*; in the Communication Skills section, click Word Usage and review the rules for each set of words.
   b. Look up the words in a traditional or online dictionary.
3. In the open document, key the correct option in the first column for each sentence.
4. Check and close. (*90e*)

The following list contains sets of words that are often confused and misused.

1. accept/except
2. affect/effect
3. bad/badly
4. complement/compliment
5. ensure/insure
6. farther/further

7. good/well
8. it's/its
9. principal/principle
10. their/there/they're
11. to/too/two
12. who's/whose

**To view smaller or larger versions of text:**

1. To view a larger version of a segment of text, move Zoom toward the right or positive (+) side. The text will be larger, but you see a smaller segment of it.

2. To see more of the document, move Zoom toward the left or the negative (–) side. To view two full pages, move the Zoom to about 50 percent. Clicking the plus or minus signs increases or decreases size in increments of 10 percent.

---

## VIEW

Document views display a document in different formats. The view that is selected when you save and close a document will be the view that displays when that document is opened again.

Document views can be accessed by clicking the view on the status bar or the View tab. With Outline view, the Close option must be clicked to exit it.

**To access document views from the status bar:**

1. Click the desired view. Print Layout is the default view.

2. To close the view, click Print Layout.

Read Mode | Print Layout | Web Layout

**To view documents using Views:**

View/Views/Read Mode or other views

1. Click the desired view.

   Hover the mouse over each view and review the Enhanced ScreenTip that describes the view and when it is best used. Two additional views—Outline and Draft—are added to those on the status bar.

**Welcome back!**

Pick up where you left off:

**Page 18**

VI. MANUFACTURING INFORMATION

4 minutes ago

2. Click the Close Outline view button to exit that view.

The Read Mode has additional tools designed to enhance reading. When you close a document and later return to finish reading it, the bookmark shown at the right brings you back to the page you were reading.

Note the differences in the resume you keyed for the hiring manager and the one illustrated on the previous page for ATS matching:

- The Ion theme was changed to the default Office theme because it has a smaller, but still acceptable font size.
- A bulleted list of no more than 10 core competencies (also called core strengths or keywords) is included.
  - Core competencies should be worded slightly different than the competencies included in the profile, but they are the same key requirements from the job description.
  - Different terms may be used for the heading—*Core Competencies*, *Core Strengths*, or *Keywords* are often used.
  - The list should be positioned in the middle of the resume after the major area of strength—for college students, Education.
  - Adding a bulleted list will often extend the resume to a second page. The resume should be no more than two pages.
- In the first resume you keyed, the *Honors and Activities* section was minimized to keep the resume to one page. Note that in this resume, the *Honors and Activities* section was reworded and formatted with bullets to emphasize the leadership aspect and to make it more readable.

## Apply It

### 90-d3

**Resume for ATS Screening**

In the open document (*90-d1*), customize the resume as follows:

1. Change the theme from Ion to the default Office theme.
2. Tap ENTER after the *Education* section and key **Core Competencies**. Use the same format for this heading as the other headings.
3. Then key and format the core competencies as follows:
   a. Apply bullets and position them at the left margin.
   b. After all competencies are keyed, select them and apply two equal-sized column format.
4. Revise the Honors and Activities as shown on the next page; then number the pages; do not show number on the first page.
5. Proofread, check; click Next Activity. (*90-d3*)

- AS degree; strong business knowledge.
- Two years' relevant part-time experience.
- Excellent Microsoft Office skills.
- Excellent communication, interpersonal, social, and customer service skills.
- Effective team leader and team player.
- High level of integrity and strong work ethic.
- Motivated self-starter; work independently.
- Organized; productivity focused--manage time and office effectively.
- Strong problem-solving skills.
- Records and project management experience.

*(continued)*

To view documents using Zoom options:

View/Zoom/Zoom or Page Options

1. To view smaller or larger portions of text, click Zoom and select percentage.

2. To view a full page, two pages, or page width, click the appropriate alternative.

## DRILL 2 — NAVIGATION AND VIEW

1. In the open document (*28-d2*), move to the end of the document (Ctrl + End). Tap ENTER and key **29-drill2**; right-align the document name.

2. Use the keyboard to move up and down through the document. Press CTRL + HOME to go to the beginning of the document, then CTRL + END to move to the end.

3. Use the mouse, the scroll box, and the up and down arrows to move in the document.

4. Move the Zoom to the left to 50% and view the document; then move it to 200% and view the document.

5. Move the Zoom back to the center at 100%.

6. Use the View tab to change the document view to Page Width.

7. From the View tab, hover the mouse over each document view to display the ScreenTip.

8. Click each view on the View tab. To exit Read Mode, click Print Layout view on the status bar. To exit Outline view, click the Close Outline View button.

9. Return to Print Layout view from the status bar.

10. Click Check Document and then Next Activity. (*29-drill2*)

## Proofing Tools: Technology Assisted Communication

*Communicating Today* ▶

Many errors made while you key are corrected automatically by a feature called AutoCorrect. In addition, *Word 2013* provides four enhanced proofing tools that are designed to help you compose, edit, and proofread documents.

**Spelling and Grammar.** In addition to marking errors, this feature provides the correct alternative and explains the rule that applies.

**Define.** A Dictionary application can be downloaded and is available for looking up the definition of words that you do not know.

**Thesaurus.** An online thesaurus helps you select the best word to express a particular thought and provides synonyms for words that you tend to overuse.

**Word Count.** In many situations, documents such as articles and resumes are limited to a specific number of pages or words. Document statistics are readily available.

Language tools are also available to help you if you are working with a second language. The **Translate** feature provides the translation for words to many different languages and helps you select the proper word to use.

In the first section, you keyed and formatted a traditional resume (see Rex resume on page 437) and then you created your own resume and formatted it as a traditional resume. In this section, you will key and format a customized version of the Rex resume for ATS screening. Then you will customize your own resume and format it for ATS screening.

When you seek a job in a medium-to-large-size organization or when the job description or posting indicates that the resume should be sent to the Human Resources Department, you should assume that your resume will first be screened by an ATS. The resume you keyed in *90-d1* has been customized for an ATS screening and is shown below. Note that the previous resume already has keywords in the Qualifications Profile.

---

Maria J. Rex
2104 Adger Road, Columbia, SC 29204-3253
803.555.0194 | Maria.Rex@wcc.edu | http://www.linkedin.com/in/rex

**Qualifications Profile for Office Manager**

Highly effective, results-oriented, administrative office professional with AS degree and two years of relevant part-time work experience, including demonstrated effective supervisory, customer service, records management, time management, and project management skills. Create professional documents that enhance company image and productivity using Word, Excel, and PowerPoint. Strong written, oral, and electronic communication skills. Excellent interpersonal skills. Honest, ethical, and possess strong work ethic.

**Education**

AS degree in Business Administration with majors in Office Administration and Office Management from Wexford Community College, Columbia, SC, May 2012, 3.65 GPA.

High school diploma with career emphasis in English and Business, Maxwell High School, Charleston, SC, August, 2010, 3.85 GPA.

**Core Competencies**

- AS degree; strong business knowledge.
- Two years' relevant part-time experience.
- Excellent Microsoft Office skills.
- Excellent communication, interpersonal, social, and customer service skills.
- Effective team leader and team player.
- High level of integrity and strong work ethic.
- Motivated self-starter; work independently.
- Organized; productivity focused—manage time and office effectively.
- Strong problem-solving skills.
- Records and project management experience.

**Experience**

Wexford Community College, President's Office, Columbia, SC, internship, summer 2012.

- Prepared correspondence, reports, and presentations for senior administrators.
- Scheduled and coordinated special events with high-level constituents.
- Received outstanding evaluation commending my professionalism, social skills, creativity, reliability, problem-solving skills, and the excellent quality of all work.

Pat's Fitness and Wellness Center, supervisor and promoted to office manager for the 3:30 to 7:30 shift (20-25 hours per week) from June 2010 through May 2012.

- Managed two teams of trainers and one team of nutrition counselors; resolved conflicts for clients. Responsible for correspondence with referring physician, vendors, and clients.
- Managed facility, records, billing, equipment, and supplies; developed procedures.
- Increased client participation and revenue from my shift over 20 percent and reduced expenses by 12 percent.

---

2

**Honors and Activities**

Participated in a numerous volunteer and community service projects. Received awards and served as a leader in honorary and professional organizations:

- Named a Dean's Scholar.
- Received the Outstanding Business Student Award.
- Member of Student Advisory Council.
- President of the Wexford Honor Society.
- President of the Office Management Club.

---

## SPELLING AND GRAMMAR

Review/Proofing/Spelling & Grammar

Errors that are not corrected automatically are marked in the text as you key. Although this feature is helpful, it is not totally accurate. Careful proofreading is still required. Errors are detected in three ways.

1. Color-coded squiggly lines appear in your text as you key.

   • Red indicates spelling or keying errors.

   • Blue indicates grammar or contextual errors. Right-click the errors while you are keying. An option box displays and provides the correct version as shown below. Click Grammar to display the Grammar pane which provides the rule and examples.

2. The error detection button with an X displays in the status bar when an error is detected. Click the button to display the Grammar or Spelling pane and correct the error. When the document is error free, the button displays a check (✓).

3. The Spelling & Grammar command in the proofing group is generally used to check the entire document at once. Click the command and the Spelling or Grammar pane displays to correct each error. Even if you have corrected errors as they were marked, it is important to run the Spelling & Grammar check after you have completed the document.

DRILL 3	SPELLING AND GRAMMAR

1. Key the paragraph on the right exactly as shown.

2. Correct the three errors.

3. Proofread and check; click Next Activity. (29-drill3)

Spelling errors are ofen corrected automatically. If an error are not detected by the software, you should proofread and correct it. To often writers skip the proofreading step.

**Resume**

⭐ **TIP**

Heading styles were not used in case the resume is scanned into a Human Resources management system. Using the same Dark Red color on side headings would be acceptable.

1. Key the model resume on the previous page. Use the Ion theme; this theme was selected because the Century Gothic font is a very readable one.

2. Use the following formats:

   a. Apply Moderate margins.

   b. Use Century Gothic bold 14-point heading font and apply Dark Red, Accent 1, 25% Darker font color to the name. Apply 12-point heading font for all side headings.

   c. Use the 11-point body font for all other text.

   d. Apply Dark Red, Accent 1, 25% Darker font color to the vertical lines and the two hyperlinks in the address.

3. Preview and proofread the document several times; remember an error in a resume can be disastrous. Note that the resume is aligned with the sample resume worksheet prepared in *89-d2*.

4. Check and click Next Activity. (*90-d1*)

**Compose Your Resume**

⭐ **TIP**

Using the same color as the name on side headings would be acceptable.

1. Review the *Creating or Updating a Job Description, Recruiting New Employees*, and the *Summary* of the *Employment Strategies (89-d1)* documents that you prepared in the previous lesson. Keep in mind what employers are seeking and how they go about it.

2. Review the *resume worksheet (89-d2)* and the description of your desired job that you printed in the previous lesson. Update it if you think it is necessary.

3. Then prepare the resume that you would use to apply for that job assuming that the resume would be sent directly to the hiring manager. Use the following guides:

   a. Do not use a separate keyword or core competency list in this resume.

   b. Use the format of the resume you just keyed or select a style of your preference.

   c. Ensure that the format is attractive, consistent, and looks professional.

   d. Use an appropriate theme and font.

   e. Use black and white or no more than one color in your resume. Some experts recommend finding the company's website and using the predominant color in your resume.

   f. Your qualifications profile or summary should be a minimum of four lines and a maximum of six.

   g. Limit your resume to one or at most two pages.

4. Edit your document carefully; then preview it.

5. Proofread the resume carefully and print it; proofread your printed copy.

6. Check and log out of *KPDO*. (*90-d2*)

## TIP

Define uses a dictionary app to provide the definitions requested. When you use it for the first time, you may have to download the app when requested to do so.

## DEFINE

The Define command displays the Dictionary pane, which provides the definition of a word.

### To find the definition of a word:

Review/Proofing/Define

1. Click in the word you wish to define.
2. Click the Close (X) button at the top of the pane.

## THESAURUS

The Thesaurus command displays the Thesaurus pane, which provides synonyms and in some cases antonyms.

### To find the synonym of a word:

Review/Proofing/Thesaurus

1. Click in the word for which you want to locate a synonym.
2. Select the appropriate synonym.
3. Click the Close (X) button at the top of the pane.

## WORD COUNT

The word count displays by default in the status bar. However, additional statistics can be accessed with the Word Count command.

### To find document statistics:

Review/Proofing/Word Count

1. Click Word Count to display the Word Count statistics.
2. Click Close (X) at the bottom of the dialog box.

## DRILL 4 — DEFINE AND THESAURUS

1. Key the sentence shown at the bottom right. Look up the definition and synonyms of the last three words.

2. On the next line, key a new sentence substituting the following synonyms:
   a. mind-boggling—second under *unbelievable*.
   b. albeit—first option.
   c. extravagant—fourth under *exaggerated*.

3. Determine the number of characters with spaces in the two sentences. Key the answer on the next line.

4. Proofread and check; click Next to continue. (*29-drill4*)

**My Smart TV is mind-boggling, albeit extravagant.**

## Maria J. Rex

2104 Adger Road, Columbia, SC 29204-3253 ←——Shift + ENTER
803.555.0194 | Maria.Rex@wcc.edu | http://www.linkedin.com/in/rex

### Qualifications Profile for Office Manager

Highly effective, results-oriented, administrative office professional with AS degree and two years of relevant part-time work experience, including demonstrated effective supervisory, customer service, records management, time management, and project management skills. Create professional documents that enhance company image and productivity using Word, Excel, and PowerPoint. Strong written, oral, and electronic communication skills. Excellent interpersonal skills. Honest, ethical, and possess strong work ethic.

### Education

AS degree in Business Administration with majors in Office Administration and Office Management from Wexford Community College, Columbia, SC, May 2012, 3.65 GPA.

High school diploma with career emphasis in English and Business, Maxwell High School, Charleston, SC, August, 2010, 3.85 GPA.

### Experience

Wexford Community College, President's Office, Columbia, SC, internship, summer 2012.

- Prepared correspondence, reports, and presentations for senior administrators.
- Scheduled and coordinated special events with high-level constituents.
- Received outstanding evaluation, commending my professionalism, social skills, creativity, reliability, problem-solving skills, and the excellent quality of all work.

Pat's Fitness and Wellness Center, supervisor and promoted to office manager for the 3:30 to 7:30 shift (20-25 hours per week) from June 2010 through May 2012.

- Managed two teams of trainers and one team of nutrition counselors; resolved conflicts for clients. Responsible for correspondence with referring physicians, vendors, and clients.
- Managed facility, records, billing, equipment, and supplies; developed procedures.
- Increased client participation and revenue from my shift over 20 percent while reducing expenses by 12 percent.

### Honors and Activities

Named a Dean's Scholar; received the Outstanding Business Student Award. Member of Student Advisory Council, president of the Wexford Honor Society, and president of the Office Management Club.

**Resume**

1. In a new document, key the 10 sentences; tap ENTER after each sentence.
2. Proofread and correct errors.
3. Use proofing tools as needed.
4. Proofread and check; click Next Activity. (*29-d1*)

**★ TIP**

Review proofreaders' marks in Lesson 23, page 62.

Do you assess you~~r~~ writing skills as ⟨average,⟩ ⟨great,⟩ or mediocre?

You sh~~c~~ould also ask your instructor *to assess* ~~about~~ your writing skills.

Your instructor ~~will know~~ *may teach you* how to ~~greatly~~ improve your writing skills.

Do you ~~always~~ *take the time to* edit and proofread carefully things that you write?

few people who d*#*onot bother to edit the*i*r*e* work are good writers.

Learning to edit effective*ly* may be just as important as writing well.

Another question to ~~ask~~ *answer* is: how important are writing skills?

~~G~~*r*ood writing skills are needed to be successful in ~~most~~ *many* careers.

You can improve your writing skills *;* ~~by~~ making it a priorit*y*. *to do so*

Judge your writing *after* ~~only if~~ you have proofread and edited your work.

**❋ Discover**

**Insert/Delete**—To insert text, click in the document at the point you wish to insert text and key the text.

To delete text, select the text and tap DELETE.

**29-d2**

**Compose and Edit**

1. In a new document, compose a document by filling in the information indicated. Use the information in 29-d1 to help you with your composition. Use Undo and Redo as well as proofing tools as you compose and edit.
2. Edit and proofread your document carefully.
3. Recheck the document using proofing tools.
4. Proofread and check. Click Exit Word to close. (*29-d2*)
5. Log out of *KPDO*.

Improving my writing skills during my career preparation is important to me because (*complete the sentence*). Proofreading and editing skills are especially important because (*complete the sentence*).

(*In a new paragraph, complete the following introductory sentence using three numbered sentences.*) Three things that I can do to improve my writing skills are:

# RESUME DESIGN

The resume on this page illustrates side headings, common terminology, and one way of formatting a resume. Another alternative is to use a 2-column table with the headings in the first narrow (1.5") column. Use of one color is acceptable. The font should be standard and very readable (minimum 11 point). The overall appearance should be that of a professionally designed document. List items with dates in reverse chronological order. Present strengths first—usually education for recent graduates. Use formats consistently. Ensure that the document is error free and information is factual.

---

### Maria J. Rex
2104 Adger Road, Columbia, SC 29204-3253
803.555.0194 | Maria.Rex@wcc.edu | http://www.linkedin.com/in/rex

**Qualifications Profile for Office Manager**

Highly effective, results-oriented, administrative office professional with AS degree and two years of relevant part-time work experience, including demonstrated effective supervisory, customer service, records management, time management, and project management skills. Create professional documents that enhance company image and productivity using Word, Excel, and PowerPoint. Strong written, oral, and electronic communication skills. Excellent interpersonal skills. Honest, ethical, and possess strong work ethic.

**Education**

AS degree in Business Administration with majors in Office Administration and Office Management from Wexford Community College, Columbia, SC, May 2012, 3.65 GPA.

High school diploma with career emphasis in English and Business, Maxwell High School, Charleston, SC, August, 2010, 3.85 GPA.

**Experience**

Wexford Community College, President's Office, Columbia, SC, internship, summer 2012.

- Prepared correspondence, reports, and presentations for senior administrators.
- Scheduled and coordinated special events with high-level constituents.
- Received outstanding evaluation, commending my professionalism, social skills, creativity, reliability, problem-solving skills, and the excellent quality of all work.

Pat's Fitness and Wellness Center, supervisor and promoted to office manager for the 3:30 to 7:30 shift (20-25 hours per week) from June 2010 through May 2012.

- Managed two teams of trainers and one team of nutrition counselors; resolved conflicts for clients. Responsible for correspondence with referring physicians, vendors, and clients.
- Managed facility, records, billing, equipment, and supplies; developed procedures.
- Increased client participation and revenue from my shift over 20 percent while reducing expenses by 12 percent.

**Honors and Activities**

Named a Dean's Scholar; received the Outstanding Business Student Award. Member of Student Advisory Council, president of the Wexford Honor Society, and president of the Office Management Club.

---

**Identification:** Include your name, address, telephone number, email, and a LinkedIn, other social network URL, or your website if desired.

**Qualifications Profile or Professional Profile:** Experienced applicants tend to use *professional*; less experienced use *qualifications*. Focus on your greatest strengths and results. Make sure the things you include match the qualifications listed in the job description.

**Education:** List the degree, major, educational institution, location, and date of degree. If it is to your advantage, list your GPA (generally 3.0 or higher). If you have not yet received the degree, indicate the expected or completion date. Listing high school is optional for experienced applicants—usually better for college students to emphasize educational strengths. You may want to emphasize computer skills more than shown in this illustration.

**Experience:** List all work experience unless you have many years of it; then list for past few years and summarize other experience. Use active verbs and focus on results not just activities. Show that your experience prepared you for the qualifications listed in the job description. Include internships and volunteer work if you have limited experience.

**Honors and Activities:** Select specific examples of leadership potential and commitment.

Print the resume on high-quality white or cream paper if you are mailing it. Consider sending the same resume in both printed and electronic versions to prospective employers. The resume can be sent as a *Word* document attached to an email with a cover letter.

# Lesson 30 Clipboard Commands and Center Page

## New Commands
- Clipboard
- Cut
- Paste
- Format Painter
- Center Page

**Warmup** *Lesson 30a Warmup*

## Skill Building

**30b  Textbook Keying**

1. Key each line once; concentrate on using good keying techniques.
2. Repeat the drill if time permits.

direct reach words, phrases, and sentences

1  hung deck jump cent slope decide hunt serve polo brave cedar pump

2  no way | in tune | many times | jump in | funny times | gold plated | in sync

3  June and Cecil browsed in craft shops and found many funny gifts.

adjacent reach words, phrases, and sentences

4  were pop safe sad quick column tree drew opinion excite guy point

5  we are | boil over | are we | few rewards | short trek | where are we going

6  Bert said he tries to shop where we can buy gas, oil, and treats.

## Communicating Today ▶

### Clipboard Commands: Editing Reminder

Cut, copy, and paste are excellent editing tools that make it easy to add new text, to delete unwanted text, or to move text to a new location. However, these tools also create special editing challenges. Once the changes have been made, it is very important to determine if the addition or deletion of text had any effect on surrounding paragraphs or on the whole document. Follow these steps:

- Read the entire document to ensure that all necessary information is included.
- Check the flow of information when paragraphs have been deleted or added. Often the transition from one paragraph to another is not smooth when changes have been made.
- Check to see if newly added material duplicates or conflicts with any of the existing document content.

Remember that careful editing can mean the difference between composing excellent documents and mediocre ones.

# Lesson 90 Resumes

**Warmup** *Lesson 90a Warmup*

## Skill Building

### 90b Textbook Keying

Key each line once, concentrating on using good keying techniques.

*direct reaches*

1 red much brief hunt bred zany check jump decrease music many brat
2 polo excel munch brake junk swim wreck lunch curve kick dazed bed
3 Cec and Kim enjoy a great hunting trip in June after school ends.

*adjacent reaches*

4 were guy sad junior tree trio fast point rest joint walk gas join
5 opt crew going port backlog poster web suit few folder buy porter
6 Porter saw two important guys after we walked past Union Station.

*double letters*

7 bell look deed glass upper inn odd committee cabbage effect inner
8 add spell pool happy jazz mass scurry connect office fall setting
9 Debbie Desselle called a committee meeting at noon at the office.

## Document Design

### 90c

**Traditional Resume**

### RESUME

The resume is an employment document designed to introduce you to an organization that has a position available for which you would like to be hired. Your resume should be designed to entice the potential employer to offer you an interview. It is your opportunity to showcase your qualifications (knowledge, skills, and personal attributes) for that specific position and convince the employer that you are qualified and that you would likely be successful in the position. Always focus on the value you can provide to the company. Never post your social security number on a resume.

This lesson is divided into two sections. In the first section, you prepare resumes designed to go directly to the department and person (often called the supervisor or hiring manager) to whom you would report if you were hired. In the second section, you prepare resumes that will be screened by an ATS system.

Different formatting styles, terminology, and categories are used on resumes. Design your resume to present your qualifications in the best light possible. Many experts believe that the best way to begin your resume is to provide a qualifications or professional profile or a summary of your most important qualifications—not a job objective as was recommended in previous years.

## CLIPBOARD GROUP

The commands in the Clipboard group, located on the Home tab, enable you to store text or graphics temporarily until you need them.

**Cut**—removes the selected text from its current location and saves it on the Clipboard.

**Paste**—positions text that was cut or copied in another location.

**Copy**—makes a copy of the selected text.

**Format Painter**—copies formatting from one place to another.

**Clipboard pane**—displays up to 24 items cut or copied to the Clipboard. The Clipboard pane is opened by clicking the Dialog Box Launcher (the small arrow in the lower-right corner of the Clipboard group).

## CUT, COPY, AND PASTE

Home/Clipboard/Cut, Copy, or Paste

1. Select the text or graphics to be cut or copied.

2. To remove the text or graphics, click Cut; to copy the text or graphics, click Copy.

3. To paste the text or graphics, position the insertion point in the desired location and click Paste.

**TIP**

To use the following Clipboard shortcuts, select the text and then apply the shortcut:

Cut:	CTRL + X
Copy:	CTRL + C
Paste:	CTRL + V

**89-d2**

**Job Search Plan**

resume worksheet

★ **TIP**

The resume worksheet that you complete is essential for the resumes you will prepare in the next lesson. If you do a good, thorough job on it, you will be able to produce better resumes in much less time.

You will need the job descriptions and company information that you printed in Drill 1 before you begin with the *resume worksheet* that is open. Add or delete rows if needed.

1. The heading for a resume should contain:

   a. Your full name, address, telephone number, and cmail address. Some instructors recommend including both your current and permanent address if you are a student. A better approach might be to send an address change two weeks before it takes effect. Consider it an opportunity to communicate again and affirm your interest in the job.

   b. If desired, include the URL for additional information, such as the URL for a LinkedIn public profile or a website.

2. Complete your SWOT Analysis.

   a. List your key strengths (competencies, knowledge, and personal attributes) that are relevant to the job you want to obtain.

   b. List your key weaknesses—things that are important for the type of job, but that you have not developed.

   c. List opportunities—weaknesses that can be turned into strengths. For example, a degree (associate or bachelor's) is required, but you have not finished the program yet; or in-depth knowledge of *Excel*, but you are enrolled in an *Excel* course.

   d. List threats—weaknesses that in all likelihood you cannot turn into strengths in a reasonable amount of time. For example, two years of work experience is required, but you have none; threats put you at a disadvantage in getting the job.

3. Identify and list the keywords and key phrases in the job description for the desired job.

   a. Educational requirements.

   b. Experience requirements.

   c. Specific job qualifications.

   d. Personal attributes.

4. Identify a list of core competencies:

   a. Strengths relevant to the job that match keywords in the job description.

   b. Opportunities that you feel certain that you can convert to strengths prior to obtaining the job or very shortly after and that match the keywords.

5. Check and print this document for later use. Log out of *KPDO*. (89-d2)

## Using Keywords Effectively

*Communicating Today* ▶

★ **TIP**

ATS stands for Applicant Tracking System.

Keywords are used by **ATS software** to match qualified applicants to the requirements specified in a job description. Actual phrases, sometimes called **search strings**, are used by the software. Action verbs are often part of the keyword phrase the system seeks. Unfortunately, the ATS search screens out many qualified applicants—some experts suggest that they screen out far more qualified applicants than they screen in and transfer to a hiring manager.

To get an idea of what employers want, read a variety of job descriptions in your field and review the terminology they use for the type of job you seek. Analyze the description for the specific job you are applying for thoroughly to determine the keywords. Prepare a customized resume using the company-desired keywords several times worded in a slightly different manner. Listing core competencies is one effective way to get an additional repetition of keywords.

## Paste Options

Paste options determine how the text will look once it is inserted at the target location. Paste options are accessed in two ways: the drop-list arrow at the bottom of the Paste button or the Paste Options button that displays when text is pasted.

### To apply options from the Paste button:

1. Click the drop-list arrow on the Paste button to display the paste options.

**①** Use Destination Theme
**②** Keep Source Formatting
**③** Merge Formatting
**④** Keep Text Only

2. Click the desired option.

### To apply options from the Paste Options button:

1. When the Paste command is clicked to paste text, the Paste Options button displays at the end of the pasted text.

2. Click the drop-list arrow to display the options, and select the desired option.

Note that the results occur whether you use the Paste button drop list options or those from the Paste Options button.

**★ TIP**

The Keep Text Only option does not display when a graphic or object is pasted.

---

## DRILL 1          CUT, COPY, AND PASTE

1. In a new document, key only the first two sentences below.

2. Select *carefully* in the first sentence, cut it, and paste it after *packing*. Use the Merge Formatting option.

3. Select *enclosed* in the second sentence; cut and paste it before *diagram*. Use the Keep Text Only option.

4. Copy the second sentence. Paste it below the second sentence and then key the additional text shown in the third sentence below. Use the Keep Source Formatting option.

5. Use Show/Hide and delete paragraph symbols at the end of the document if any exist.

6. Proofread and check; click Next to continue. (*30-drill1*)

Please try to carefully remove the packing before taking the computer out of the box.

The diagram enclosed provides step-by-step instructions for assembling the computer.

The enclosed diagram provides step-by-step instructions for assembling the computer. A Help number to call for assistance is provided on the diagram.

The next step for applicants is to prepare a customized resume and cover letter to apply for each specific job they have located. The type of resume prepared is determined by the size and type of company and the information listed in each job posting. Resumes prepared for recruiters must contain keywords that match the job description, or they will be rejected and not granted an interview. Recruiters typically do not focus on cover letters. They send the applicants screened in by the ATS to the hiring managers to interview, evaluate, and select appropriate applicants. Hiring managers in small companies typically evaluate both resumes and cover letters carefully to determine which applicants match the company needs most closely. Then they interview selected applicants and begin the selection process. Always bring your resume and reference list to the interview.

**QUICK ✓**

Did you locate the unmarked errors? Check below to see if you corrected these errors.

1. On page 1, in the second to last paragraph, replace *personel* with *personal*.
2. On page 2, in the second full paragraph, replace *frequent* with *frequently*.
3. On page 3, in the second full paragraph, replace *includes* with *include*.
4. On page 4, in the last full paragraph, replace *there* with *their*.
5. On page 5, in the first full paragraph, replace *applicant* with *applicants*.

If you did not locate all of the errors, remember that on a resume or cover letter, errors such as these could cause your application to be rejected.

Blaj Gabriel/Shutterstock.com

**! WORKPLACE SUCCESS**

## Applicant Tracking Systems

Understanding how companies track resumes is very important to a successful job search. Many, if not most, medium- and large-size companies manage their job recruitment process by using an applicant tracking system. They request electronic resumes or scan paper-based resumes into their system. Once a resume has become a part of an applicant tracking system, the software then determines from all resumes received which ones will be reviewed by the potential employer. Keywords are used to match the resume to the job description. The best way to format a resume depends on the software used by the company that receives it. To get the best results, check the company's website for information about submitting a resume.

## FORMAT PAINTER

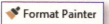 Format Painter copies a format from one paragraph to another or to multiple paragraphs

To copy a paragraph format to a single paragraph:
Home/Clipboard/Format Painter

1. Click in the paragraph that has the desired format.
2. Click the Format Painter.
3. Drag Format Painter across the paragraph to copy the desired format.

To copy a paragraph format to multiple paragraphs:

1. Click in the paragraph that has the desired format.
2. Double-click the Format Painter to keep it turned on.
3. Drag Format Painter across the paragraphs to copy the desired format.
4. Click Format Painter to turn it off or tap ESC.

**TIP**

1. To copy both text and paragraph formats, select the paragraph including the paragraph marker.
2. Apply to the text you want to format.

---

### DRILL 2    FORMAT PAINTER

Home/Paragraph/Show/Hide

1. In a new document, turn on Show/Hide, tap ENTER three times, and key the document below. Be sure to read the tip below.

2. Apply 14-point Arial font and bold to the title, **HOW MUCH IS TOO MUCH?**, and center it.

3. Use the Format Painter to copy the title format to the subtitle directly below the title.

4. Format the paragraph below the subtitle using 12-point Times New Roman font, and justify.

5. Double-click Format Painter to copy the same format to the last two paragraphs.

6. Proofread and check; click Next Activity. (30-drill2)

**TIP**

When you key two hyphens with no spaces before or after, *Word* automatically converts them to an em dash.

**HOW MUCH IS TOO MUCH?**

Executive Compensation—A Hot Topic!

Many people question the huge salaries paid to top executives. Employees earning less than $50,000 a year do not understand how their company can pay one person millions of dollars each year. The gap between executive pay and employee pay creates problems.

Shareholders clearly want to reward and retain executives who increase shareholder value, but they expect pay to be linked to performance. In many cases, executive compensation has increased at the same time that performance has decreased significantly.

Media coverage about mega-bonuses has caused an outrage among investors. In response, the SEC now requires public companies to disclose the amount and source of all compensation paid to their top executives. This information is readily available to the public and to employees.

## Apply It

### 89-d1

**White Paper**

 employment process

⭐ **TIP**

Ensuring that employment documents are error free is critical. Errors in an employment document often result in a rejection of the application.

1. In the open document, locate and correct the five unmarked errors in it.
2. Format the document.
   a. Use the Office theme with the default formatting style; use standard unbound report style.
   b. Format the headings using the directions in parentheses for heading styles: (Title), (Subtitle), (H1), and (H2); then delete the directions shown in parentheses after each heading.
3. Key the summary at the bottom of the report.
4. Number the report pages using the Facet (odd page) header; do not show the header on the first page.
5. Proofread the entire document carefully and print it. Save the printed copy; you will use it as a reference throughout Module 16.
6. Check and click Next Activity. (89-d1)

Summary (H1)

Employers begin the job process by developing a job description; then posting and advertising the position described in numerous outlets. In large organizations, recruiters began to search actively for job applicants using all of the search resources available including social networks, other online media, print media, employment agencies, placement offices, and personal contacts. They typically manage the search using an applicant tracking system (ATS), which screens resumes provided by applicants and refers applicants passing the screen to the hiring manager, who is responsible for the interviews, evaluation, and selection of employees. In small organizations, supervisors or hiring managers are typically responsible for searching for appropriate applicants, evaluating them, and selecting the best applicants that meet the needs of the organization.

Applicants begin the job process by analyzing their strengths and weaknesses to determine the types of jobs in which they could be successful. Then effective applicants begin a broad-based search using all of the resources that employers use to post and advertise positions to locate available positions and job descriptions for which they believe they are qualified. Networking is one of the most effective search tools. Some applicants prepare a generic resume and send it to numerous companies listing their strengths and the type of job they are seeking. This approach is generally not very productive. A targeted search identifying available positions that match the applicants' qualifications is a more productive approach.

*(continued)*

## CENTER PAGE

The Center Page command centers a document vertically on the page. Should extra hard returns (¶) appear at the beginning or end of a document, these blank lines are also considered to be part of the document. Therefore, it is important to turn on Show/Hide and delete extra hard returns at the beginning and end of the document before centering a page.

Page Setup — Dialog Box Launcher

Layout tab

Vertical alignment

### To center a page vertically:

Page Layout/Page Setup/Dialog Box Launcher

1. Position the insertion point on the page to be centered.
2. Turn on Show/Hide and remove any extra hard returns.
3. Display the Page Setup dialog box.
4. Click the Layout tab.
5. Click the Vertical alignment drop-list arrow and select Center.

---

## DRILL 3          CENTER PAGE

1. Open *30-drill2* and remove the three hard returns at the top of the page.
2. After the last line, key **30-drill3** and right-align it.

3. Center the page.
4. Proofread and check; click Next Activity. (*30-drill3*)

---

## Communication

### PROOFREADING

**30d**

References/Communication Skills/Proofreading

1. Complete the proofreading exercise in *KPDO*.
2. Proofread each sentence on the right and then key the sentence correcting the error in it. Do not key the number.
3. Proofread and check; click Next to continue. (*30d*)

1. The only way to proofread numbers effectively is too compare the keyed copy to the original source.
2. Concentration is an important proofreading skill, especially it you proofread on screen.
3. May people skip over the small words when they proofread; yet the small words often contain errors.
4. They sole 15 baskets at $30 each for a total of $450. Always check the math when you proofread.
5. Names are often spelled in different ways; there fore, you must verify the spelling to ensure that you use the correct version.
6. Reading copy on a word-bye-word basis is necessary to locate all errors.
7. Checking for words that my have been left out is also important.
8. Of course, you should also check to make sure the content in correct.

---

Before you can design effective documents to be used in search for a job, you need to understand how an organization goes about determining that it needs a new employee, specifying what it wants the employee to do, determining the skills and personal attributes needed to be effective in the job, and how it selects the best person to hire.

This lesson includes a drill and two activities:

1. Key the summary and format a white paper (specialized report) designed to help you understand the employment process.

2. Create a plan for writing your resume and a cover letter for a specific job that prepares you to do the remaining jobs in this module and to plan and execute a successful search for a job.

### To create a job search plan:

1. Think seriously about:
   a. Your educational and work experiences, if any.
   b. Your personal attributes and soft skills that would enhance your job success.
   c. The type of job that you would like to obtain.
   d. Your preference in company size and type.
   e. The geographic area in which you would like to work.

2. Select the broad job title—such as administrative assistant, office manager, customer service representative, accounting associate, marketing associate, events coordinator, or graphics designer, etc.—for the job you want to obtain.

3. Obtain one or more job descriptions for the position.
   a. Use the keywords, *most popular job websites*, to locate job sites online and search at least two of them, such as Indeed, CareerBuilder, Monster, or any other sites listed.
   b. To search the site, provide the job title you selected and the city and/or state in which you would like to work.
   c. Find the option for full job descriptions. Most sites provide this option.
   d. Note the companies that provided the description. Most job websites provide the option to learn more about the company. If not, search the Internet for information using the company name. Note the size, the presence or absence of a Human Resources Department, and the location of the company.

## DRILL 1          RESUME WRITING PLAN INFORMATION

1. Search a job website to find information about the job you would like to have.

2. Read several job descriptions. Print one of two that appeal to you most.

3. Access information about the company that provided the job description and make notes or print it.

4. Keep the information from this drill to use in *89-d2* and to write resumes in Lesson 90.

**NOTE:** This drill is not completed in KPDO.

1. In a new document, key the text shown below. Apply Lucida Calligraphy 14-point font. Center all lines except the last one, which should be left-aligned. Decrease the font size on the last line to 11 point. Replace 201- with the current year.

2. Apply 3.0 line spacing.

3. Center the page. Verify the page is centered.

4. Proofread and check; click Next Activity. (*30-d1*)

<div align="center">

You are cordially invited to attend a reception
Honoring Dr. Fritz H. Schmohe
Honorary Degree Recipient
September 28, 201- at 7:30 in the evening
Koger International Center
Black Tie Optional

</div>

RSVP by September 20, 803-555-0174

### 30-d2

**Heading, Indent, Format Painter**

1. In a new document, tap ENTER three times, and then key the document below.

2. Apply Verdana 16-point font and bold to the title, *Weekly Report*, and center it.

3. Use the Format Painter to copy the title format to the date shown below the title.

4. In the first sentence, cut *with reporters* and paste it after *spoke*. The sentence should read: *The head football coach spoke with reporters at his weekly news conference.*

5. Apply Verdana 12-point font to the first paragraph below the date. Justify the text.

6. Use Format Painter to copy the first paragraph's format to the last two paragraphs.

7. Proofread, check, and close. (*30-d2*)

8. Click Log out to exit *KPDO*.

## WEEKLY REPORT

June 20, 201-

The head football coach spoke at his weekly news conference with reporters. He was asked about the summer workout program and seemed to be very frustrated with some of his student-athletes.

The coach pointed out that summer workouts are voluntary programs, and it is against the rules to require student-athletes to participate. However, the workouts are a good way to judge the commitment level of your players. He indicated that some of our players are very committed and are very likely to get playing time. Others are lazy, and it is doubtful they will be ready to play when the season begins.

In response to a reporter's question, he indicated only about a dozen of the 95 scholarship players did not show up regularly. The goal of the program is to improve conditioning and lessen the likelihood of injuries.

# Employment Documents

## LEARNING OUTCOMES

- Develop a plan for a successful employment search.
- Prepare traditional and specialized resumes.
- Compose and format employment documents.
- Build keyboarding skills.

## *Lesson 89* Job Search Strategies

**Warmup**   *Lesson 89a Warmup*

A   **ALL LETTERS**

## Skill Building

### 89b   Timed Writing

1. Key a 1' timed writing on each paragraph; work to increase speed.
2. Key a 3' timed writing on both paragraphs.

An effective job search requires very careful planning and a lot of hard work. Major decisions must be made about the type of job, the size and the type of business, and the geographic area. Once all of these basic decisions have been made, then the complex task of locating the ideal job can begin. Some jobs are listed in what is known as the open job market. These positions are listed with placement offices of schools, placement agencies, and they are advertised in newspapers or journals.

The open market is not the only source of jobs, however. Some experts believe that almost two-thirds of all jobs are in what is sometimes called the hidden job market. Networking is the primary way to learn about jobs in the hidden job market. Employees of a company, instructors, and members of professional associations are some of the best contacts to tap the hidden job market. Much time and effort are required to tap these sources. But the hidden market often produces the best results.

# Lesson 31 Palmetto Event Solutions, Inc.

## Learning Outcomes

- Apply keying, formatting, and word processing skills.
- Work independently with few specific instructions.

**Warmup**  *Lesson 31a Warmup*

## Skill Building

### 31b  Timed Writing

Key two 3' timed writings.

Click fraud concerns small business owners who want to place an advertisement on a website and be charged for it based on the number of hits on it. They frequently believe they are getting the most for their advertising dollars because they only pay for those who actually read their advertisement. The problem, however, is that someone may be paid to click on the advertisement many times just to increase the revenue from it.

While business owners are working hard to maximize the impact of their businesses, frequently they are losing money because some individuals are trying to scam them. Many people try to do the right thing, but many others just are not honest. Often it is difficult to determine if you are working with an honest person or not when you use the Internet.

This problem is not a very easy one to resolve, but a few things can be done to minimize the risk. Research shows that late-night advertisements and advertisements in certain countries are the most likely to be targeted. By choosing not to run advertisements at those times and in those locations, you can lower your risk. In addition, a number of very sophisticated and very effective technical tools can be used to help detect click fraud.

## Project Setting

### ★ TIP

Palmetto Event Solutions prefers to use periods rather than hyphens and parentheses to separate units in telephone numbers, which is the current trend in industry.

## PALMETTO EVENT SOLUTIONS, INC.

At the end of each module in this book, you will work as an assistant preparing documents for various executives of Palmetto Event Solutions, a national company that specializes in managing corporate events for businesses and organizations. You will apply the formatting and word processing skills that you have developed in the module. The logo and contact information for the headquarters office are shown below.

 *Palmetto Event Solutions, Inc.*
24 Palmetto Bay Road, Hilton Head, SC 29928-3220 | 864.555.0124
www.palmettoeventsolutions.com

Row 5: 10:05 a.m.	Depart (DFW) at 10:05 a.m. on Executive West Flight 1357 and arrive at Oklahoma City Will Rogers Airport (OKC) at 11:15 a.m. Taxi to Oakie Inn, 3 Park Avenue; Confirmation #384930C.
Row 6: 2:00 p.m.	Meet with Elizabeth Glenn and various staff members at GameDay Wi-Fi Inc., 401 Couch Drive. Return to hotel at 5:30.
Row 7: 7:30 p.m.	Picked up by Connor Bass for dinner at the Southwest Country Club.
Row 9: Wednesday, January 29	Oklahoma City to Austin
Row 10: 8:15 a.m.	Depart OKC at 8:15 a.m. on Executive West Flight 1459 and arrive at DFW at 9:10 a.m.
Row 11: 10:25 a.m.	Depart DFW at 10:25 on Executive West Flight 1234 and arrive at AUS at 11:35.

## 88-d6

**Compose**

hess news release form

⭐ **TIP**

Hess Office Park uses the same style for news releases as the one illustrated on page 424.

**Learn More:**

www.cengagebrain.com

Compose a one- or two-paragraph news release for Hess Office Park to announce that Elizabeth Glenn signed a 10-year contract to move her rapidly growing high-tech company, GameDay Wi-Fi Inc., to the Technology Quad of our office park.

She told Daniel and Patrick that our office park matched the type of environment she wanted for her company perfectly. She said that she already has numerous contracts with both collegiate and professional organizations in Texas to enhance the GameDay experience for their fans. She works with all types of sports—football, baseball, hockey, soccer, basketball, and others.

When asked why she picked Texas, she said Texas and Austin in particular had excellent educational institutions, a passion for sports, and a reputation for embracing technology—all of which are critical for the success of her company. She has 125 employees now and expects to expand the operations soon.

1. Edit, proofread, and check; exit *Word*. (88-d6)
2. Click Log out to exit *KPDO*.

## 31-d1

**Standard Operating Procedures**

Your first assignment is to work with Ellen Miller, the Executive Assistant to the President and CEO of Palmetto Event Solutions, Inc. Ellen has been working on revising the standard operating procedures (SOPs) that are used in the main office and the four regional offices. This document will be sent to the regional offices for review and will continually be updated.

Pay particular attention to the SOPs and the documents you prepare in this lesson because they will provide you with information that you will use each time you work with Palmetto Event Solutions. You will be directed to review these procedures periodically.

1. Tap ENTER three times, and key the document below; apply the following formats.
2. Center the heading, and apply Calibri Light 14-point heading bold font to both lines.
3. Change the bullets to numbering using Number Alignment Left style and periods.
4. Add **Procedures revised** and today's date using 00/00/0000 format after the last numbered item and apply Align Right format.
5. Use proofing tools, proofread, and correct all errors. Click Next Activity. (*31-d1*)

Standard Operating Procedures

For Document Formatting

These procedures are designed to enhance our image and to ensure that our brand is used consistently and appropriately.

- Use the letterhead and memo form provided digitally for all letters and memos. Letterhead is provided with addresses for each of the five office locations. Use block-letter format with open punctuation.
- Ensure that all documents are error-free. Use proofing tools and then edit, proofread, and correct errors. Verify dates and all numerical data against the source copy.
- Use email for brief communications, which do not contain information needed to work with clients or as a delivery vehicle. Any information that will become a part of our records should be prepared in memo, letter, table, or report format and attached to the email for distribution.
- Additional procedures may be provided by each of the regional offices.

2. Continue to offer the discounted rate for short-term office and conference room use to nonprofit organizations. Make sure our staff realizes that these organizations provide valuable support to our community and that we want to work closely with them. These organizations are more than willing to use the conference rooms with movable tables configured appropriately to meet their needs.

3. Add six new conference rooms to our current building plans. Building 4 still has an entire floor unallocated. It could easily handle a quad layout with four conference rooms, an open lobby area with registration space, and a food service setup area. Restrooms are already provided on each floor. Two of the conference rooms on this floor would have the large fixed conference table, and the other two would have movable tables that could be configured to meet different needs. Two conference rooms could be added to the Conference Center. The space on the second floor that was previously used by Wexford QCT Trainers has been vacated. Both of these rooms would have fixed furniture with seating for 36. All of the support services are already in place on that floor of the Conference Center.

## 88-d5

**Itinerary**

Daniel Forde asked Patrick Hess if he would make a quick development trip with him to Oklahoma City. An executive in a high-tech company is considering moving her company headquarters from Oklahoma City to Austin. Her company, GameDay Wi-Fi Inc., specializes in installing Wi-Fi systems around college and professional stadiums and other venues to enhance the game day experience. Prepare the itinerary for Patrick and Daniel.

1. Tap ENTER three times and insert a 2-column, 11-row table. Apply List Table 4 – Accent 1 table style.

2. Adjust the first column to 2" width. Apply 0.4" row height to the first row and 0.3" to the other rows. Apply Orange, Accent 1 theme color, bold, and Align Center Left to the rows listing the dates and locations. Increase the font size in the first row to 14 points.

3. Add space before paragraph for each entry with text in the second column to make it easier to read. Leave a blank line between the entries for the two dates.

4. Key the information shown below for the itinerary.

5. Check and click Next Activity. (88-d5)

Row 1: Itinerary for Patrick Hess and Daniel Forde

Row 2: Austin to Oklahoma City      January 28-29, 201- (right align date)

Row 3: Tuesday, January 28      Austin to Oklahoma City

Row 4: 8:04 a.m.      Depart Austin Bergstrom International Airport (AUS) on Executive West Flight 1202 at 8:04 a.m. and arrive at Dallas/Ft. Worth (DFW) at 8:58 a.m.

*(continued)*

## 31-d2

**About Us**

Read the information below about Palmetto Event Solutions carefully. This information will become the first webpage of the About Us section of the company website. It will help you understand the type of company you will work for in each module.

1. Tap ENTER three times and key the document as shown.
2. Change the case of the title to uppercase, apply 18-point bold Verdana font, and center.
3. Select paragraph 1; apply double-spacing (2.0), Verdana 12 point. Indent the first line of the first paragraph as recommended by the web developer for draft copy.
4. Then use Format Painter to copy the formats to the remaining paragraphs.
5. Proofread as prescribed in the SOPs. Click Next Activity. (*31-d2*)

### About Us

Palmetto Event Solutions was founded by Mrs. Roberta Russell in 1992 in Hilton Head, South Carolina. The initial emphasis was on catered dinners, weddings, and other social events. Many corporate executives attended impressive functions managed by Mrs. Russell and requested her services for corporate events. By 2000, corporate events represented more than 75 percent of the business. Mrs. Russell retired, and her son Garrett Russell became president and CEO.

Many events we managed were corporate reward trips, trade shows, and professional meetings in various sections of the country. Our management team determined that clients could be served better if we focused on corporate events and established offices in other regions of the country. In 2002, four regional offices were established in the Midwest, Northwest, Northeast, and Southwest to complement the Hilton Head office.

Today, our company has more than quadrupled its size and has established key partnerships with service providers in all regions who can provide full services for virtually any type of corporate event requested.

## 31-d3

**Compose and Format an Invitation**

1. Ellen Miller asked you to compose, edit, and format a draft of an invitation. Review the instructions for 30-d1 on page 115. Use this same style and format for this invitation.
2. Use the notes below to compose the invitation. (Do not key these notes.) Remember to format the phone number with periods.
   - Ask clients to please join us for a tour of our new reception center, followed by a client appreciation reception.
   - The event will be on Friday, September 10, at 5:30 p.m. in the Palmetto Event Solutions Reception Center. Include an RSVP by September 6 and our telephone number. Tip: The number is contained in the contact information on page 116.
   - The attire for the event is business attire.
3. Proofread and check. (*31-d3*)
4. Click Log out to exit *KPDO*.

## 88-d2

**Compose Memo**

hess memo form

Hess Office Park has recently established a Director's Extranet. All Board Meeting documents and supplementary materials should be posted on the extranet once they have been finalized. Draft documents should be distributed by email after Mr. Hess reviews them.

1. Send a memo to Board members and meeting participants from you dated January 9.
2. Remind them of the meeting date, time, and location; ask them to confirm their attendance at the meeting.
3. Ask everyone to review the Agenda for the Board meeting and send you any recommended changes or additions to the agenda. Remind them that supplementary meeting materials should be posted on the Director's Extranet at least one week prior to the meeting.
4. Edit and proofread your memo carefully.
5. Check and click Next Activity. (88-d2)

## 88-d3

**Final Agenda**

agenda with changes

Mr. Hess asked you to finalize the agenda so that it could be posted to the Director's Extranet.

1. Check to see that Track Changes are turned on and All Markup displays the changes.
2. Mr. Hess indicated that all of the changes recommended were appropriate and asked you to implement them.
3. Make the required changes and finalize the document (by deleting the comments).
4. Check spacing and formatting carefully to ensure that no errors exist.
5. Proofread, check, and click Next Activity. (88-d3)

## 88-d4

**Minutes**

minutes_1_21_201-

Please use the instructions and information below to finalize the minutes of the January 21 meeting of the Hess Office Park Board.

1. Make sure your name and initials are in the User and Initials boxes.
2. Add a second-page header using Blank (three columns). Insert the Board name in the first column, the page number using Current Position in the second column, and the meeting date in the third column.
3. Review carefully the changes and the comments from each reviewer; then make the following changes:
   a. Add the information in Marcia and Mike's comments to the document.
   b. Accept the insertions and deletions indicated in the document.
   c. Key the recommendations for Hess Property Enterprises Board shown below.
4. Finalize the document; check to ensure that you have followed the SOPs.
5. Proofread and check; click Next Activity.

> The Hess Office Park Board approved the following recommendations to be presented to the Hess Property Enterprises Board:
>
> 1. Approve the budget changes required to increase the energy efficiency rating of the buildings, including the pet center, identified by the Energy Efficiency Evaluation Team. The detailed plan and cost analysis is posted on the Director's Extranet.

*(continued)*

# Memos and Letters

## LEARNING OUTCOMES

- Format memo.
- Format block and modified block business letters.
- Create envelopes.
- Edit letters.
- Build keyboarding skills.

## Lesson 32 Memos and Email

**New Commands**

- Date/Time
- Vertical Page Position

**Warmup** Lesson 32a Warmup

A  ALL LETTERS

## Skill Building

### 32b  Timed Writing

1. Key a 1' timing on each paragraph; work to increase speed.
2. Key a 3' timing on all paragraphs.

Congratulations, you have just learned to key with very little visual help and are moving quickly from one key to the next. As you continue to build speed and become productive, it is always important to continue keying with proper techniques. Because it is easy to become lazy, take a quick check of correct techniques.

Sit up straight with both feet on the floor with back against the chair. Drop hands to your side and allow your fingers to curve naturally; maintain this curve as you key. If hands are in correct position, you can balance a penny on your wrists. Keep your eyes on the copy or screen, and key continuously without any breaks. An excellent method to monitor progress is to record yourself for several minutes. Evaluate your techniques carefully, and make needed changes.

## Standard operating procedures for the project:

1. Use the Hess memo and news release forms provided in the data files. Note that they have the Retrospect theme already applied. Follow the SOPs you applied in Module 10, page 282.

2. Apply Retrospect theme and default style set to each document you prepare.

3. Use the same heading and format for all meeting, travel, and news documents that you prepare for Patrick Hess, manager of Hess Office Park. Just change the name of the document such as *Agenda* or *Minutes*. See the illustration below. To create the heading, apply Title style to the document name and Heading 2 to the Board name, location, date, and time lines. Insert an en dash with space before and after between the times in the last line. Update the information as appropriate. Save it as a Quick Part to simplify document preparation.

### Agenda

Hess Office Park Board
Board Room
January 21, 201-, 9:30 – 12:00

4. On Agendas, Patrick prefers to list the beginning and ending time of meetings and not list the time allocated for each item on the agenda.

5. Draft documents are sent to appropriate individuals for review. Mr. Hess reviews the recommended changes and comments and provides instructions on how to handle the changes. After making the recommended changes on documents, be sure to delete all comments. Note that first names are used frequently in these internal documents.

6. Hess Office Park uses action-style minutes. Include all action taken and a brief summary of the discussion of key items.

---

### 88-d1

**Draft Agenda**

1. Prepare the draft agenda for the January 21 Quarterly Board meeting.
2. Use the standard heading and set a dot leader tab at the right margin.
3. Key the items shown below.
4. Proofread and check; click Next Activity. (88-d1)

Welcome and Call to Order	Patrick Hess
Quarterly Financial Report	Carolyn Hess
Report on Energy Efficiency Evaluation	Inga Kock
Large Conference Rooms Needs Assessment	Mike Burge
Recommendations for Hess Property Enterprises Board	Patrick Hess
Review of Hess Office Park Facilities	Michael White
Business Development Update	Daniel Forde
Executive Session	Patrick Hess
Adjournment	

## DATE AND TIME

**Date & Time** The Date and Time command allows the selection of the desired format. Often the month/day/year format is used for letters, and the numerical format (00/00/0000) for memos and documents with statistics.

**To insert the date and/or time:**

Insert/Text/Date and Time

1. Click at the point the date is to be inserted.

2. Select the desired date format ❶ (July 22, 2012) or time format ❷ (17:37).

3. Leave Update automatically ❸ blank unless you want the date/time to update each time the document is opened. Click OK.

### ✳ Discover

**Automatic Current Date**

Key the first four characters of the current month and tap ENTER to accept the date. Tap Space Bar to display the remainder of the current date.

## VERTICAL PAGE POSITION

Although the default top margin is 1", not all documents are attractive beginning at the top of the page. To move the insertion point lower on the page, simply tap ENTER.

The status line is located at the bottom left of the screen and displays important information about the page, including the vertical page position when turned on.

**To display the vertical page position on the status line:**

1. Right-click on the status line located at the bottom of the screen.

2. Click Vertical Page Position. The vertical page position now displays at the bottom left of the status line, showing the default top margin at 1".

`PAGE 1 OF 1   AT: 1"`

### ★ TIP

Remember to proofread and preview each document as standard operating procedure (SOP). You will not be reminded to do this.

---

### DRILL 1     DATE AND TIME

1. In a new document, display the vertical page position on the status line.

2. Tap ENTER three times to position the insertion point at about 2". Key the first four characters of the current date, e.g., Octo for October. Tap ENTER and then the Space Bar to display the current day. Tap ENTER to begin a new line.

3. Insert the date and time in the numerical format 7/15/2012 3:35 PM, and tap ENTER.

4. Print. Verify that the date prints approximately 2" from the top of the page.

5. Proofread and check; click Next Activity. (*32-drill1*)

# Lesson 88 Hess Office Park

**Learning Outcomes**
- Apply keying, formatting, and word processing skills.
- Prepare documents with columns and graphics.
- Work independently with few specific instructions.

A  **ALL LETTERS**

## Skill Building

### 88b  Timed Writing

Key two 3' timed writings.

Employees who work together as a team are more effective than those who work solo. This concept is known as synergy. Synergy simply means that the joint action exceeds the sum of individual actions. The results are not just in the quantity of work; major increases in quality result when people work together as a team. Teamwork is critical for success.

What characterizes an excellent team member? An excellent team member understands the goals of the team and will place team values above her or his individual objectives. An excellent team member helps to determine the most effective way to reach the goals that were set by the group and will help to make each decision that affects the group. Above all, an excellent team member will support a decision made by the team. Each member must understand his or her role and respect the roles of others. Every member of a team must share in both victory and defeat.

## Project Setting

### HESS PROPERTY ENTERPRISES

In this project, you continue to work for Hess Property Enterprises and the management team of the Hess Office Park. Your work in this project focuses on helping Patrick J. Hess, manager of Hess Office Park, prepare documents related to the upcoming quarterly Board meeting of the Hess Office Park. This Board is a subset of the Hess Property Enterprises Board and deals strictly with Hess Office Park needs and issues. You will draft documents for Board review and then incorporate recommended changes and finalize documents. You will also assist Mr. Hess with the preparation of other documents.

Review the standard operating procedures (SOPs) on the next page. Use them as a check list when you proofread each document and again after you have completed all documents.

**32d**

## ELECTRONIC MAIL AND MEMOS

Informal communication shared among individuals in a company are prepared as emails, instant messages, text messages, or memos. In a business setting, correct grammar, spelling, capitalization, and professional tone are required in all messages to portray professionalism and to gain/maintain respect among supervisors and peers.

The memo is the most formal type of informal message and may be preferred when a somewhat formal communication with company employees is demanded, such as the announcement of a new policy or participation in a mandatory training program. Often this formal memo is attached to an email as a method of distribution to all employees. *Word*'s Share option allows the user to email the memo as a *Word* attachment or a PDF without even opening the email system.

An email is commonly used to convey casual internal messages that do not demand a more formal tone and presentation. Examples would include an email transmitting a memo or letter, providing the location and time of a meeting, or requesting routine information.

### To format a memo:

1. Tap ENTER three times to position the first line of the heading at about 2".
2. Key the memo headings and format them in bold and uppercase. Tap TAB once or twice after each heading to align the information. Generally, courtesy titles (Mr., Ms., etc.) are not used; however, the receiver's name may include a title depending on rank in the company.
3. Single-space (1.08 default spacing) the body of the memo. Tap ENTER once after each paragraph.
4. Add reference initials one line below the body if the memo is keyed by someone other than the sender. Do not include initials when keying your own memo.
5. Items clipped or stapled to the hard-copy memo and electronic files attached to an email are noted as attachments. Items included in an envelope with a memo are noted as enclosures.

Key enclosure or attachment notations one line below the reference initials.

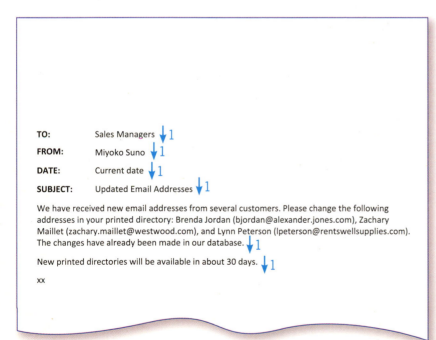

**TO:**        Sales Managers ↓1

**FROM:**    Miyoko Suno ↓1

**DATE:**     Current date ↓1

**SUBJECT:**  Updated Email Addresses ↓1

We have received new email addresses from several customers. Please change the following addresses in your printed directory: Brenda Jordan (bjordan@alexander.jones.com), Zachary Maillet (zachary.maillet@westwood.com), and Lynn Peterson (lpeterson@rentswellsupplies.com). The changes have already been made in our database. ↓1

New printed directories will be available in about 30 days. ↓1

xx

# Sun Property and Casualty Insurance Company

### 1592 S. Plaza Way | Flagstaff, AZ 86011-7155

### Phone: 928.555.0174 | Solana.Rodriquez@apic.com | Fax: 928.555.0136

**NEWS RELEASE**                                    Contact Person: Solana Rodriquez

Current date

For Release: Immediately

SUN RECEIVES NATIONAL AWARD

FLAGSTAFF, AZ—The Sun Property and Casualty Insurance Company announced today that it received the *American Family-Friendly Work Environment Award* presented by the American Council on Insurance. Only one award is given each year to an insurance company for a unique contribution to improving the work environment for families.

Sun was cited for the unique partnership it established with Century Medical University and Sunbelt Child Development Centers to create a state-of-the-art Sun Child Development and Research Center. The center is in its first year of operation. The first floor of the center provides facilities for approximately two hundred children, and the second floor research center focuses on health and development issues impacting preschool children. Children receive medical screenings, and special isolated facilities are available for sick children at the center. Sun provides partial scholarships to employees and to low-income families.

Sun is the only insurance company to ever receive this prestigious award more than once. Five years ago, Sun received the award for its creative *Surrogate Grandparents Mentoring Program* in partnership with Central Academy to mentor children from low-income families after school. That program is still in effect today and is very successful. More than forty "grandparents" mentor over a hundred students each year.

Sun has offices throughout the Southwest and has 1,274 employees—430 of whom are in the Flagstaff area.

###

**News Release**

## To prepare an email:

1. Prepare the email header:

   *To:* Key the email address of the receiver accurately.

   *Cc:* Key the email address of individuals who are to receive a copy of the message.

   *Bcc:* Key the email address of individuals designated to receive a blind copy (meaning the recipient is not aware of the message being sent to the blind recipient/s).

   *Subject:* Key a specific subject line that is helpful to the busy recipient sorting through important email to read and act upon.

   *Attachment:* Follow the steps to attach any electronic files referred to in the body of the memo.

2. Prepare the email body:

   **a.** Single-space (SS) the body of an email and tap ENTER twice between paragraphs. Do not indent paragraphs.

   **b.** Do not add bold or italic or vary the fonts. Do not use uppercase letters for emphasis. Avoid using emoticons or email abbreviations in business email (e.g., ;- for wink or BTW for by the way).

   **c.** Write a clear, concise message about one topic. State the purpose in the first paragraph, and then provide the needed details. End with a courteous closing that states the required action, if any.

Recipients who receive a copy of the email

Unique and clear subject line for each email message

TO: <null-address@vanforderesort.com>	CC: <lnylin@vanforderesort.com>
FROM: Sophia Bennett <sbennett@vanforderesort.com>	BCC: <jbrown@vanforderesort.com>
SUBJECT: Listing of Upcoming Safety Seminars	Names of blind copy recipients are not displayed in the recipient's email
ATTACHMENT: seminars.docx	

The Human Resources Department is pleased to announce a series of safety seminars required for all employees. Please see the details on the attached memo and a listing of seminar dates and topics.

If you have questions, please contact Leigh Nylin at ext. 702.

Sophia Bennett, Chief Learning Officer
Van Forde Resort
662.555.0123, FAX 662.555.0167
sbennett@vanforderesort.com

Signature block generated by email system

# Lesson 87 News Release

**Document Design**

**87b**

## NEWS RELEASE

A news release provides information that an organization wishes to publish. Typically, it is sent to reporters and news professionals at newspapers, radio and television stations, and other media outlets. The news often gets published if the release is newsworthy, well written, and easy to publish. Always design the release with the important information first because many outlets will publish only a portion of it.

Note in the illustration on the next page that a heading is included in addition to the letterhead. It typically includes the release date, the contact person, and a title that could serve as a news headline. Usually, ### or *-30-* is used to indicate the end of the article. If the news release goes to a second page, the word *more* is centered in a footer. The second page should have a short heading (often called a slug line) and the page number.

Many experts agree that traditional news releases do not work well on social media, especially media such as Facebook. If you are going to post a release on a professional network, such as LinkedIn, make it shorter, more visual, and conversational. A better alternative is to use a blog, but again keep it more visual and conversational.

## Apply It

### 87-d1

**News Release**

 sun news release

1. In the open document, key the news release shown on the next page. Pay particular attention to the heading information and the way it is formatted. Key an em dash (two dashes) after the state in paragraph 1.
2. Proofread and check; click Next Activity. (*87-d2*)

### 87-d2

**News Release**

 sun news release
sun ceo

1. Insert the current date. The news will be released immediately. Key the first paragraph shown below.
2. Insert the data file *sun ceo* after the first paragraph.
3. Then key the following closing paragraph: **Ledbetter is married to Kirk T. Parham, a nationally known pediatrician. They have two teenage children—a son, Joseph, and a daughter, Caitlyn.**
4. Proofread and check; click Log out to exit *KPDO*.

SUN NAMES NEW PRESIDENT AND CHIEF EXECUTIVE OFFICER

FLAGSTAFF, AZ—The Sun Property and Casualty Insurance Company announced today that its Board of Directors unanimously approved Amy T. Ledbetter as its new chief executive officer. Ledbetter replaces Mark R. Daff, who served as chief executive officer for the past eight years.

**Sterling**

**1195 Singing Cactus Avenue**
**Tucson, AZ 85701-0947**

<span style="color:red">About 2" (Tap ENTER three times)</span>

**TO:**　　　　All Employees ↓1

**FROM:**　　　Sophia Bennett, Human Resources Director ↓1

**DATE:**　　　Current date ↓1

**SUBJECT:**　Safety Seminars Offered for Certification ↓1

The Human Resource Department is pleased to announce a series of safety seminars for all employees. The purpose of the seminars is to provide safety knowledge and procedures included in the certification examination administered at the end of the seminar. ↓1

The seminars are offered in two formats to meet the needs of all employees. Face-to-face seminars are scheduled in room 310 on Wednesday afternoons from 1 to 5 p.m. and Thursday mornings from 8 a.m. until noon. Online seminars are also available which can be completed at times that meet your specific schedule.

Please meet with your supervisor to determine the seminars needed for your position. Thank you for your participation in these important seminars. ↓1

xx ← <span style="color:red">Student's first and last initials</span>

**Memo**

1. Tap ENTER and key the itinerary using a 2-column table with default theme and margins. Insert an en dash between the dates in the heading and add a space before and after the en dash. Adjust the width of the first column to 2".

2. Apply List Table 4 – Accent 5. Deselect First Column in the Table Style Options.

3. Use 1" row height for the first row; apply 16-point Calibri Light and Align Center to the title.

4. Bold the information in the three rows with the dates. Adjust row height to 0.4" and apply Align Center Left to those rows. Add a blank row before days 2 and 3.

5. Compare the Heading style of this itinerary to the previous one you keyed.

6. Proofread and check; click Log out to exit *KPDO*. (*86-d3*)

## Itinerary for Laurie Hammer
## July 14 – 16, 201-

**Wednesday, July 14**	**Columbia to Cincinnati**
4:40 p.m.	Leave Columbia on non-stop Cincola Flight 5173 and arrive in Cincinnati at 5:55 p.m.; Metro Rental Car (Confirmation #67540912); Riverside Hotel (Confirmation #34898732)
8:15 p.m.	Picked up at hotel by Dave Calhoun and Jack Shaut; dinner at Royal Mason
**Thursday, July 15**	**Cincinnati**
8:00 a.m.	Leave for Natorp Publishing Center; 6319 Natorp Boulevard, Mason, Ohio
9:00 a.m.	Meet with President and Editor-in-Chief; President's office, Suite 600
9:45 a.m.	Meet with the Editorial Team, Fifth Floor Conference Room
11:45 a.m.	Break
12:00 noon	Working lunch, Fifth Floor Conference Room
2:00 p.m.	Meet with book designers, Fifth Floor Conference Room
2:30 p.m.	Break
3:00 p.m.	Meet with the Production Team, Fifth Floor Conference Room
5:30 p.m.	Return to hotel
7:30 p.m.	Meet Project Team for dinner; Chez Ruby; 644 Walnut Street; map in Travel folder
**Friday, July 16**	**Cincinnati to Columbia**
7:45 a.m.	Return rental car; Cincola Flight 6754 departs at 9:20 a.m. and arrives in Columbia at 10:40 a.m.

## 32-d1

**Memo**

↩ Undo Automatic Capitalization
Stop Auto-capitalizing First Letter of Sentences
🖅 Control AutoCorrect Options...

1. Tap ENTER three times and key the memo illustrated on page 123. Do not key the memo letterhead. *Hint:* Select *TO:* and then apply bold; bold the colon. Remember to turn off bold and uppercase. Repeat for remaining heading items. Be sure to insert the date.

❄ 2. If the first letter of your reference initials is automatically capitalized, point to the initial until the AutoCorrect Options button appears. Click the button; then choose Undo Automatic Capitalization.

3. Proofread and check; click Next Activity. (*32-d1*)

---

## 32-d2

**Memo**

⭐ **TIP**

**Numbering**

Home/Paragraph/
Numbering

1. Key the memo below.

2. Proofread and check; click Next Activity. (*32-d2*)

TO:	Emily Welch, Brian McKenzie, Olivia von Staden
**FROM:**	Michael Holcomb
**DATE:**	July 18, 201-
**SUBJECT:**	Video Conference Call Scheduled Friday, July 26, 201-

The final video conference call to select the contractor for the Keystone Community Project will be held on Friday, July 26, 201-, from 3:30 to 5:00 p.m. EST. To join the video conference, follow these steps:

1. Call 601.555.0168 and enter the passcode 8103622 when prompted.

2. Go to www.conferences.com/holcomb/PDS/ and join the meeting.

Please review the proposals carefully and be prepared to make a recommendation at the meeting. If you have questions about the proposals, please call me at 601.555.0193 or email me at mholcomb@svdco.com.

xx

---

## 32-d3

**Compose Email**

1. Compose an email to your instructor from you. Key **Email Etiquette** as the subject of the email. Send a copy to one of your classmates.

2. In the body of the email, share three specific email etiquette rules that are important but often abused. Number the three items. Refer to the discussion on email on page 122.

3. Proofread and check; close the document. (*32-d3*)

4. Click Exit *Word*.

5. Click Log out to exit *KPDO*.

## Itinerary for Landon Winn

Chicago to Atlanta	October 9-11, 201-
**Wednesday, October 9**	**Chicago to Atlanta**
8:45 a.m.	Leave Chicago Midway Airport (MDW) on Southern Express Flight 1387 and arrive at Atlanta Hartsfield (ATL) at 11:20 a.m.; take MARTA to Buckhead Station (N-7). Taxi to Buckhead Inn (Confirmation #204857) 260 Pharr Road, NE. (45 minutes)
2:30 p.m.	Meeting with Rhett Brown, Joyce Downy, and Hudson Davis in Conference Room A of the Buckhead Inn. Refreshments ordered.
**Thursday, October 10**	**Atlanta**
9:45 a.m.	Picked up at the hotel by Michael Jones; drive to Dunwoody Conference Center. Full-day meeting with Pearce Sports Equipment Company.
7:15 p.m.	Dinner with Michael Jones, Kevin Pearce, and Trinity Jenkins. Restaurant to be determined by hosts. Return to hotel by 10:15 p.m.
**Friday, October 11**	**Atlanta to Chicago**
8:30 a.m.	Breakfast at hotel with Trey Meyer, Travis Smoak, and Drew Dyson.
9:45 a.m.	Leave for Atlanta Airport (ATL) with Trey Meyer. Southern Express Flight 1436 departs at 11:35 a.m. and arrives at Chicago (MDW) at 1:10 p.m.

**Itinerary**

# Lesson 33 Block Letter

**New Commands**
- Remove Space after Paragraph

## New Commands

### 33b

### REMOVE SPACE AFTER PARAGRAPH

*Word* automatically adds extra white space after ENTER is tapped to make text easier to read and to save the user time in only tapping ENTER once between paragraphs.

To remove space after a paragraph when the extra space is not needed, press SHIFT + ENTER to begin a new line.

## DRILL 1 — REMOVE SPACE

1. Key the following letter address; press SHIFT + ENTER at the end of each line.

2. Proofread and check; click Next Activity. (*33-drill1*)

**Mr. Grayson T. Winston**
**Winston & Smith Law Firm, LLC**
**389 Main Street**
**San Antonio, TX 78229-0389**

## Communication

### 33c

References/Communication Skills/Spelling

1. Complete the Spelling exercise in *KPDO*.
2. Proofread each statement at the right, and then key the statement correctly using the numbering feature.
3. Proofread and check; click Next Activity. (*33c*)

### SPELLING

1. Turkeyes are in the meat department.

2. The locker room for gentlemens is being remodeled.

3. Companys with more than 50 employees have different requirements.

4. Managers are asked to investigate reoccuring tardiness.

5. Only cash or checkes are accepted at the ice cream store.

6. Do you beleive the time is right for you to invest in higher risk investments?

7. Mr. Jones closes his letters with Yours truley or Sincerely yours.

8. The theives were apprehended, and the stolen property was returned.

9. Give the reciept to the accounting manager.

10. Are you refering to Purchase Order #2051?

An itinerary is a detailed plan for a trip. Itineraries for work-related trips provide details about the business activities and the travel information. Typically, an itinerary includes the following information.

- Heading with name and dates of trip.
- Transportation information—maps and route information for driving trips; or airline flight numbers and times, ticket information, passport or other identification, visa requirements, rental car or ground transportation for air travel.
- Hotel information—name and address, confirmation number, special requests made.
- Restaurant information—name and address, reservation information, participants.
- Meetings or appointments—individual and company names, times, addresses, and transportation information if needed.
- Leisure-time information.

Generally, itineraries are prepared using a table. Review the document shown on the next page; pay particular attention to the way the content is presented. Also review the format.

## Apply It

### 86-d1

**Itinerary**

1. Tap ENTER three times and apply Retrospect theme.
2. Insert a table with 2 columns and 13 rows. Change the design to Grid Table 1 Light – Accent 1. In the Table Style Options group, deselect the check mark for First Column.
3. Key the table shown on the next page. Leave a blank row between days of the trip.
4. Merge cells in row 1, and apply Heading 1 style and Align Center.
5. In row 2, apply Heading 2 style and Bold; apply Align Center Left to column A and Align Center Right to column B.
6. Apply Heading 3 style and Bold to the rows containing the day and date.
7. Change the height of the remaining rows to 0.3". Adjust the width of the columns to utilize the space well.
8. Apply Add Space Before Paragraph to each row without a heading to enhance reading.
9. Proofread and check; click Next Activity. (*86-d1*)

### 86-d2

**Modified Itinerary**

1. Open *86-d1* and turn Track Changes on. Make sure your name is in the User name box.
2. Make the following changes in the itinerary:
   a. On Wednesday, October 9, add:

      **7:00 p.m. | Dinner at Pat's Buckhead Café with Rhett Brown, Joyce Downy, and Hudson Davis.**

   b. Change the time on the return flight to Chicago to **11:40 a.m.** with arrival at **1:15 p.m.**
   c. Click at the end of the entry and insert the comment: **Southern Express Airlines called with the flight schedule change.**
3. Review in All Markup and Simple Markup views.
4. Proofread and check; click Next Activity. (*86-d2*)

## BUSINESS LETTERS

Business letters are used to communicate with persons outside of the business. Business letters carry two messages: the first is the tone and content; the second is the appearance of the document. Appearance is important because it creates the critical first impression. Stationery, use of standard letter parts, and placement should convey that the writer is intelligent, informed, and detail minded.

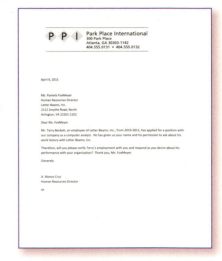

### Stationery

Letters should be printed on high-quality (about 24-pound) letterhead stationery. Standard size for letterhead is 8½" × 11". Envelopes should match the letterhead in quality and color.

## SALUTATIONS AND COMPLIMENTARY CLOSINGS

The salutation, or greeting, consists of the individual's personal title (*Mr., Ms.,* or *Mrs.*) or professional title (*Dr., Professor, Senator, Honorable*), and his or her last name. Do not use a first name unless you have a personal relationship. The salutation should agree in number with the addressee. If the letter is addressed to more than one person, the salutation is plural.

	Receiver	Salutation
To individuals	Dr. Alexander Gray	Dear Dr. Gray
	Dr. and Mrs. Thompson	Dear Dr. and Mrs. Thompson
To organizations	TMP Electronics, Inc.	Ladies and Gentlemen
Name unknown	Advertising Manager	Dear Advertising Manager

Choose a complimentary closing that reflects the relationship with the receiver. Use *Sincerely* to show a neutral relationship, *Cordially* for a friendly relationship, and *Respectfully* when requesting approval.

## PROOFREAD AND FINALIZE A DOCUMENT

Apply these procedures when processing all documents:

1. Use Spelling and Grammar to check spelling when you have completed the document.
2. Proofread the document on screen to be sure that it makes sense.
3. Preview the document, and check the overall appearance.
4. Save the document and compare it to the source copy (textbook).
5. Revise, save, and print if necessary.

**Review/Tracking/Track Changes/Change User Name**

1. Turn on Track Changes; check to see that you are listed in the User name box; if not, change to your name and initials. *Nursing Partnerships* should remain in Title style.

2. Change all side headings in the document to Heading 1 style; then make the changes in Section 1.

3. Lynn West asked you to make the changes Section 2 for her. Change the name and initials in the User name box from your name to **Lynn West** and **lw**. Check the box: Always use these values regardless of sign in to Office, which is located below the Initials box.

4. Make the changes in Section 2 starting with the paragraph after the heading, *Hospitals*, to the end of the document.

5. Proofread and check; click Next Activity. (*86-drill1*)

---

Nursing Partnerships

~~Demand for Nurses Exceeds Supply~~

**Section 1—Make changes in this section with your name in the User box.**

~~As we all know,~~ the demand for nurses far exceeds the supply of nurses in ~~this~~ the entire
central
~~region~~ of the state.  Local ~~colleges~~ educational institutions are unable to prepare an adequate supply of nurses to meet this growing demand. *The result is that healthcare facilities are unable to meet workforce demand.*

**Partnership Proposed**

The ~~four~~ five local hospitals, the ~~local~~ technical college, and the ~~local~~ university in
central        have
the region ~~has~~ developed a ~~strong comprehensive and~~ viable plan to increase
over the next
the supply of both licensed practical nurses and registered nurses, ten years

**Hospitals**

**Section 2—Make changes in this section with Lynn West's name in the User box.**

Five
~~Four~~ area hospitals will contribute $1,000,000 each to the Nursing Partnership this year.  Of the $4,000,000 [5], the university will be allocated $3,000,000 [4], and the technical college will be allocated $1,000,000.  In addition, the hospitals each pledged to invest $50,000 a year in the Nursing Partnership for the next five years.  These annual funds will be split ~~50/50~~ equally between the technical college and the university.

The attached table summarizes the five-year funding plan for the hospitals and the five-year spending plan for the educational institutions.

**Program Implementation**

The agreement will be finalized and signed within three weeks, and the funds will be made available within three months. Other potential partners are being contacted to determine their willingness to participate in the program.

# LETTER PARTS AND BLOCK LETTER STYLE

Businesspeople expect to see standard letter parts arranged in the proper sequence. ___tters consist of three main parts: the opening lines to the receiver (letter address and salutation), the body or message, and the writer's closing lines. Standard letter parts and the required spacing using the defaults of *Word* are explained below and illustrated on the following page.

Block letter style is a typical business letter format in which all letter parts are keyed at the left margin. For most letters, use open punctuation, which requires no punctuation after the salutation or the complimentary closing.

**Letterhead:** Preprinted stationery that includes the company name, logo, address, and other optional information such as telephone number and fax number.

**Dateline:** Date the letter is prepared. Position at about 2" (tap ENTER three times). Be sure to begin at least 0.5" below the letterhead.

**Letter address**: Complete address of the letter recipient. Begin two lines below the date (tap ENTER twice).

Generally includes receiver's name, company name, street address, city, state (one space after state), and ZIP Code. Include a personal title, e.g., Mr., Ms., Dr. Press SHIFT + ENTER after each line of the letter address to remove the added space.

**Salutation (or greeting):** Begin one line below the letter address (tap ENTER once). Include courtesy title with person's name, e.g., Dear Mr. Smith.

**Body:** Begin one line below the salutation.

Use the default line spacing; tap ENTER once between paragraphs. Use *Ladies and Gentlemen* when addressing a company.

**Complimentary closing:** Begin one line below the body. Capitalize only the first letter of the closing.

**Writer's name and title:** Begin two lines below the complimentary closing (tap ENTER twice). Include a personal title to designate gender only when the writer's name is not gender specific, such as Pat or Chris, or when initials are used, such as J. A. Moe.

Key the name and title on either one or two lines, whichever gives better balance. Use a comma to separate name and title if on one line. If two lines are used, press SHIFT + ENTER to remove the added space between the two lines.

**Reference initials:** Begin one line below the writer's name and title. Key reference initials, e.g., **xx** in lowercase. Replace *xx* with your initials.

## TRACKING OPTIONS

Track Changes Options provide a convenient way to change the user name, and they also provide advanced options to display the default Track Changes Options or to change the tracking options. The Track Changes Options defaults meet the needs of most users, and they do not change them. View the options so that you will be aware of the way changes made in a document with Track Changes display.

**To change the user name and initials:**

Review/Tracking/Dialog Box Launcher

1. Display the Track Changes Options dialog box and click Change User Name.
2. Key the appropriate name and initials and click OK.

**To view the Track Changes Options dialog box:**

1. Click Advanced Options and note:

   a. How insertions, deletions, and comments display.

   b. How changes in repositioned text (moves) display.

   c. How color is used to show cells inserted, deleted, merged, or split.

   d. How track formatting controls whether or not formatting is tracked and how options are displayed.

   e. Size and position of balloons and how the way they display can be changed.

2. Click OK without changing the defaults.

# Bennett Community Foundations

**3840 Cedar Mill Parkway**
**Athens, GA 30606-4384**

**2" (Tap ENTER three times)**

**Date line**   October 15, 201- ↓ 2

**Letter address**
Mr. Jackson Elliott
President and CEO
Elliott Corporation
8333 Fifth Avenue, Suite 203
New York, NY 10028-8333 ↓ 1

*Press SHIFT + ENTER to remove extra space*

**Salutation**   Dear Mr. Elliott ↓ 1

**Body**   Thank you for agreeing to provide our keynote address for the opening session of the annual Bennett Community Foundations Convention in Dallas, Texas, on Friday, March 20, 201-. Our organization consists of over 10,000 members throughout the world with typically 2,000 members attending the convention each year.

The opening session begins at 3:30 p.m. in the Grand Ballroom of the River Ridge Convention Center. We invite you to join our executive board at a reception in your honor from 2 to 3 p.m. in Suite 2035. We are all eager to meet you and welcome you to our convention.

We look forward to your contributions to our convention, and we invite you to remain for the entire convention if your time permits.

**Complimentary close**   Sincerely ↓ 2

**Writer's name & title**
Gerald M. Bailey
Executive Director

*Press SHIFT + ENTER to remove extra space*

**Reference initials**   xx

**Block Letter with Open Punctuation**

**New Commands**
- Change User Name
- View Track Change Options

 **Warmup** *Lesson 86a Warmup*

## Skill Building

**86b** Textbook Keying

Key each line once, concentrating on using good keying techniques.

1st row
1 Zack and Max became exercise advocates, but they ate many pizzas.
2 Max Mizel verbalized his excessive love for throwing curve balls.

home row
3 Ada Hall's class was at a lake in Dallas; Kala Klass had a salad.
4 Sally's glass flask was full of salt; Sal also saw a glass flask.

3rd row
5 Terry or Peter saw Perry at the polo tryout; you were there, too.
6 Trey, a poet, wrote the quote for Peter; we were there with Trey.

4th row
7  10487 24680 31579 90642 35179 86210 38764 21430 79538 24680 97315
8  63829 87321 90543 28645 80902 21354 87654 23890 27480 46572 89340

balanced hand
9 pens turn fur slam pay rifle worn pan duck ham lap slap burn girl
10 Andy Clancy, a neighbor, may visit at the lake and at the island.

one hand
11 read ploy create kiln crate plum were pony cats jump severe hump
12 Phillip, as you are aware, was a reader on deferred estate cases.

combination
13 did you we spent pony street busy jump held severe pant exert due
14 Were profits better when we were on Main Street than Duck Street?

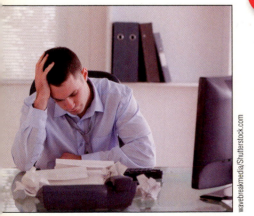
wavebreakmedia/Shutterstock.com

## ! WORKPLACE SUCCESS

### Fear of Failure

Many employees—particularly young employees—limit their success because they have an unfounded fear of failure. They often confuse failing with being a failure. If they take on a project and it fails, they think of themselves as failures and avoid taking on similar projects. This type of behavior is often referred to as a self-fulfilling prophecy. If you think you can do something, you are likely to, but if you do not think you can do something, you are not likely to do it. The attitude that leads to success is to view failed projects as something that did not work, to try to learn why, and to move to something that might work. The owner and chef of a great restaurant had a total failure with his first restaurant, then took a job as a chef and was fired; his next venture was a resounding success—arguably the leading restaurant in the country. Baseball home-run kings often also have high strikeout numbers. Successful people are persistent—when something does not work, they try alternatives and learn from each trial until they reach success.

**33-d1**

**Block Letter**

1. Tap ENTER three times to position the date at about 2". Key the model block letter on page 128. Do not key the letterhead.

2. Press SHIFT + ENTER to remove the added space in the letter address and between the writer's name and title.

3. Replace the reference initials *xx* with your initials. Be sure to undo automatic capitalization of the first letter of your initials.

4. Follow the proofreading procedures outlined on page 126. Use Show/Hide ¶ to view paragraph markers to confirm that you have correct spacing between letter parts. Use Print Preview to check the placement.

5. Proofread and check; click Next Activity. (*33-d1*)

**33-d2**

**Block Letter**

1. Key the letter below in block format with open punctuation. Insert the current date. Add your reference initials in lowercase letters. Remove added space in the letter address and the writer's name and title.

2. Proofread and check; click Next Activity. (*33-d2*)

Current date

Ms. Ramona Vilella
Wicker Hotel and Resort
89 Airport Road
Omaha, NE 68105-0089

Dear Ms. Vilella

Certainly having a web presence is essential, but have you updated your hotel's website recently? Advances in technology and the increased sophistication of your clients are both good reasons for you to meet with our designers at Internet Solutions to discuss advanced hotel web design that will improve your marketing efforts.

Our online reservation system is designed for today's clients; it is easy to navigate and provides many extras such as 360-degree panoramic pictures of the hotel lobby, guest rooms, restaurants, spa, and pool, as well as maps to your beautiful hotel. Two-way communication is also important today as clients are eager to provide review rating and valuable comments to others desiring a pleasant hotel experience. Our design offers seamless means of valuable dialog between you and your clients.

Call today for a consultation with one of our designers and discuss our many innovative website marketing strategies. Give your clients the best when they are shopping for hotel reservations.

Sincerely

Daniel Jankoski
Marketing Manager
xx

### Terms

Bentley Burns presented the changes reflecting the additional $1,000,000 committed by the fifth area hospital. The hospital also committed to the $50,000 annual contribution. The Board decided to use the same distribution formula for the funds contributed by the other hospitals. Mary Freeman was asked to revise the final agreement to reflect the additional funds, and she agreed to finalize all documents within one week.

### Hospital Perspective
Tyler Walker presented the attached funding plan submitted by the hospitals. The Board approved the plan.

### Technical College Perspective
Jane Metze presented the attached fund usage plan submitted by the technical college. The Board approved the plan.

### University Perspective
Lester Caldwell presented the attached fund usage plan submitted by the university. The Board approved the plan.

### Approval
After considerable discussion of how plans would be implemented, the Board approved the entire project.

### Adjournment
The meeting adjourned at 12:05 p.m.

---

### 85-d2

**Document with Graphics**

 draft minutes

1. Turn Track Changes on and select All Markup view. Check that your name and initials are in the User name and Initials boxes. (File/Options/General)

2. Delete the first sentence in paragraph 1.

3. Add a second-page header using Blank (three columns). In the first column, key **Minutes—Nursing Partnership Board**; in the second column, insert the page number using Current Position, and key the meeting date **January 15, 201-**.

4. Insert a new heading, **Next Meeting**, before *Adjournment* and key: **The Chair reminded the group that the next Nursing Partnership Board Meeting is scheduled for February 8 at 10:30 in the Hospital Atrium.** Apply Heading 2 style to the heading.

5. Review the summary in the Reviewing Pane. Then review changes by each reviewer separately. Remember to check the reviewer's name that you wish to review and deselect the other reviewers. Accept all changes shown for each reviewer.

6. View your changes and accept all changes in the document.

7. Preview, proofread, check, and close. (85-d2)

1. Key the following letter in block style with open punctuation. Begin the date at about 2". Remember to remove the extra space by using SHIFT + ENTER.
2. Proofread and check. (*33-d3*) Click Exit Word.
3. Click Log out to exit *KPDO*.

April 4, 201- | Ms. Rose Shikamuru | 55 Lawrence Street | Topeka, KS 66607-6657 | Dear Ms. Shikamuru

Thank you for your recent inquiry about employment opportunities with our company. We are happy to inform you that Mr. Edward Ybarra, our recruiting representative, will be on your campus on April 23–25 to interview students who are interested in our company.

We suggest that you talk soon with your student placement office, as all appointments with Mr. Ybarra will be made through that office. Please bring with you the application questionnaire the office provides.

You will want to visit our website at www.skylermotors.com to find facts about our company mission and accomplishments as well as learn about the beautiful community in which we are located. We believe a close study of this information will convince you, as it has many others, that our company builds futures as well as small motors.

If there is any way we can help you, please email me at mbragg@skylermotors.com.

Sincerely | Margaret K. Bragg | Human Services Director | xx

## ⚠️ WORKPLACE SUCCESS

### Organizational Skills

StockLite/Shutterstock.com

Well-organized employees accomplish daily tasks in a timely manner, avoid stress, and impress their employers and coworkers. Following simple daily time management practices reaps benefits and often even a promotion. How would you rate yourself on the following time management practices?

1. Prioritize tasks to be done each day and the amount of time needed to complete each task. Assign tasks to a specific time on the calendar.
2. Set designated times to answer email and return phone calls.
3. Place calendar/planner on desk in location for easy access to add notes and see priority items.
4. Record notes, phone numbers, addresses in calendar and not on post-it notes.
5. Place phone, notepad, and pen on desk for easy reach.
6. Keep reference books in a designated location—not on the desk.
7. File any materials for which you no longer need immediate access.
8. Prepare folders for pending items, projects, and reading, and file those materials away instead of keeping them piled on the desktop.

# Minutes

## Nursing Partnership Board
### Hospital Atrium
### January 15, 201-, 10:30 a.m.

The Nursing Partnership Board met on January 15, 201- at 10:30 a.m. in the Hospital Atrium. Board members present were Lester Caldwell, chair; Mary Freeman, meeting facilitator; Jane Metze, technical college representative; Wanda Stewart, project coordinator; Bentley Burns, project assistant; and Tyler Walker, hospital representative.

## Proposal
Mary Freeman presented the agreement with the markup showing all changes in it. She pointed out that these changes were made in the last meeting. The Board agreed that the revised version reflected the discussion of the previous meeting. Mary Freeman was asked to revise the final agreement with the changes noted.

## Terms
Bentley Burns presented the changes reflecting the additional $1,000,000 committed by the fifth area hospital. The hospital also committed to the $50,000 annual contribution. The Board decided to use the same distribution formula for the funds contributed by the other hospitals. Mary Freeman was asked to revise the final agreement to reflect the additional funds, and she agreed to finalize all documents within one week.

## Hospital Perspective
Tyler Walker presented the attached funding plan submitted by the hospitals. The Board approved the plan.

## Technical College Perspective
Jane Metze presented the attached fund usage plan submitted by the technical college. The Board approved the plan.

## University Perspective
Lester Caldwell presented the attached fund usage plan submitted by the university. The Board approved the plan.

## Approval
After considerable discussion of how plans would be implemented, the Board approved the entire project.

## Adjournment
The meeting adjourned at 12:05 p.m.

**New Commands** • Envelopes

 **Warmup** *Lesson 34a Warmup*

**A  ALL LETTERS**

## Skill Building

### 34b  Timed Writing

1. Key a 1' timing on each paragraph; work to increase speed.
2. Key a 3' timing on all paragraphs.

Many people are sometimes quite surprised to learn that either lunch or dinner is included as part of a job interview. Most of them think of this component of the interview as a friendly gesture from the organization.

The meal is not provided to be thoughtful to the person interviewing. The organization expects to use that function to observe the social skills of the person and to determine if he or she might be effective doing business in that type of setting.

What does this mean as you prepare for a job interview? Spend time reading and practicing social etiquette just as you would on how to answer questions or about what to wear. The time committed to reading about and learning to apply excellent social skills pays off during the interview and also after you accept the job.

### 34c  Textbook Keying

1. Key each drill, concentrating on using good keying techniques.
2. Repeat the drill if time permits.

*adjacent reach*

1 The people were sad as the poor relish was opened and poured out.

2 Sophia moved west with her new silk dress and poor walking shoes.

*direct reach*

3 Freddy stated that hurricanes are much greater in number in June.

4 Many juniors decide to work free to add experience to the resume.

*balanced hand*

5 The eight ducks lay down at the end of right field for cozy naps.

6 Kala is to go to the formal town social with Henry and the girls.

## Document Design

**85d**

 **TIP**

For minutes that are more than one page long, include an appropriate header on all pages except the first one. Generally, the header would include the meeting name and the page number.

## MINUTES

Minutes provide a record of what occurred in a meeting. Typically, minutes are prepared relatively soon after a meeting and distributed to all participants. Minutes may vary significantly depending on the type of meeting. In some cases, only a brief summary of the action taken is recorded. In other cases, a verbatim transcript of everything said in a meeting is recorded. Most organizations prefer to record only the essential or very important information that needs to be preserved for future reference. These minutes are usually called *action minutes* because they capture the decisions that are made and the actions that take place. Some minutes are very formal; others are very informal using first names and a casual writing style.

Typically, minutes contain the following information:

1. Heading information—*Minutes*, meeting name, date, time, and location.
2. Name of presiding officer or meeting leader and names of attendees.
3. Introduction of topics or outcomes expected.
4. Summary of decisions and actions.
5. Handouts and meeting materials may be attached to be part of the record.

## Apply It

**85-d1**

**Draft Minutes**

1. Apply Organic theme with Word 2013 Document Formatting style to a new document. Tap ENTER three times and insert the *NPB Agenda Heading* from the Quick Part Gallery (created in *84-d1*). Select *Agenda* and replace it with **Minutes**. Save the selection as a Quick Part. Use the *NPB Minutes Heading* for the name and description.

2. Review the Draft Minutes model document on the next page. Then key the minutes shown below and on page 416, using normal margins.

3. Apply Heading 2 to all headings.

4. Preview, proofread, check, and click Next Activity. (*85-d1*)

The Nursing Partnership Board met on January 15, 201- at 10:30 a.m. in the Hospital Atrium. Board members present were Lester Caldwell, chair; Mary Freeman, meeting facilitator; Jane Metze, technical college representative; Wanda Stewart, project coordinator; Bentley Burns, project assistant; and Tyler Walker, hospital representative.

Proposal

Mary Freeman presented the agreement with the markup showing all changes in it. She pointed out that these changes were made in the last meeting. The Board agreed that the revised version reflected the discussion of the previous meeting. Mary Freeman was asked to revise the final agreement with the changes noted.

*(continued on page 416)*

## ENVELOPES

The Envelopes command can insert the delivery address automatically if a letter is displayed. The default is a size 10 envelope (4⅛" by 9½"); other sizes are available by clicking the Options button on the Envelopes tab.

**To generate an envelope:**

Mailings/Create/Envelopes

1. Select the letter address and click Envelopes; the mailing address automatically displays in the Delivery address box.

2. Click the Return address Omit box if using business envelopes with a preprinted return address (assume you are).

   To include a return address, do not check the Omit box; click in the Return address box and key the return address.

3. Click Print to print the envelope or click Add to Document to add the envelope to the top of the document containing the letter.

Delivery address box

---

### DRILL 1    CREATE ENVELOPE

1. In the open document (*33-d1*), select the letter address. Create an envelope. Omit the return address.

2. Add the envelope to the document.

3. Proofread and check; click Next Activity. (*34-drill1*)

**Note:** Your instructor may have you print envelopes on plain paper.

---

### DRILL 2    CREATE ENVELOPE

1. In a new document, go to the Envelopes and Labels dialog box without keying a letter address.

2. Key the following letter address in the Delivery address box.

   **Mr. Andrew Callais**
   **993 North Carpenter Lane**
   **Shreveport, LA 71106-0993**

3. Add the envelope to the document.

4. Proofread and check; click Next Activity. (*34-drill2*)

---

Review/Tracking/Reviewing Pane   Review/Changes

1. In the open document (*85-drill1*), display the Reviewing Pane vertically.

2. Accept each change in sequence until you get to the comment. Select the text in the comment, and copy and paste it before the last sentence in the document; then delete the comment.

3. Click All Changes in Document to accept the remainder of the changes.

4. Check and click Next Activity. (*85-drill3*)

## Communication

### 85c

References/Communication
Skills/Pronoun Agreement

 pronoun agreement

1. Review the guides at the right and those in *KPDO*.

2. In the open document, click on the View tab, then Edit Document. Follow the specific directions provided.

3. Proofread and check; click Next Activity. (*85c*)

## PRONOUN-ANTECEDENT AGREEMENT

1. The antecedent is the word in the sentence to which the pronoun refers. In the examples, the antecedent is bold and the pronoun is in italic.
   **Players** must show *their* birth certificates.
   The **boy** lost *his* wallet.

2. The antecedent must agree with the pronoun in **person** (first, second, third).
   **I** am pleased that *my* project placed first. (Both are first person.)
   **You** must stand by *your* display at the science fair. (Both are second person.)
   **He** has lost *his* watch. (Both are third person.)

3. The antecedent must agree with the pronoun in **gender** (neuter when gender of antecedent is unknown).
   **Gail** said that *she* preferred the duplex apartment.
   The adjustable **chair** sits firmly on *its* five-leg base.
   The **dog** looked for *its* master for days.

4. The antecedent must agree with the pronoun in **number**. If the antecedent of a pronoun is singular, use a singular pronoun. If the antecedent is plural, use a plural pronoun.
   All **members** of the class paid *their* dues.
   **Each** of the Girl Scouts brought **her** sleeping bag.

## Team Collaboration on Documents

*Communicating Today* ▶

Too often team members leave the final writing and editing of the reports of their team projects to one person. Team members have equal responsibility for the quality of the final reports and other documents they produce in their team projects. Comments and track changes are useful editing tools that enhance collaboration. Documents with track changes can be shared in a number of ways—through email, a company intranet, or through Web Apps. With *Web Apps 2013*, co-authoring (two or more individuals working on the same document at the same time) makes it easier for teams to work together to enhance the quality of their documents.

## ADDITIONAL LETTER PARTS

In Lesson 33, you learned the standard letter parts. Listed below are several optional letter parts.

**Enclosure notation/Attachment notation:** If an item is included with a letter, key an enclosure notation/attachment notation one blank line below the reference initials. If enclosures/attachments are itemized, tap TAB to align the enclosures at 1" using default tabs.

Left tab at 1"

Enclosures:          Certificate of Completion
                     Receipt

Enclosures:     2

**Copy notation:** A copy notation (c) indicates that a copy of the document has been sent to the person(s) listed. Key the copy notation one line below the reference initials or enclosure notation (if used). Tap TAB to align the names. If necessary, click Undo Automatic Capitalization after keying the copy notation to lowercase the letter c.

Left tab at 0.5"

c          Francine Milam
           Janet Bevill

When two lines are keyed for either the enclosure notation or the copy notation, press SHIFT + ENTER to remove the extra space after the paragraph.

xx

Enclosures:      Certificate of Completion
                 Receipt

c        Francine Milam
         Janet Bevill

## Communicating Today ▶

### Business Letters: Then and Now

The delivery of business letters has changed dramatically since the origin of the U.S. Post Office in 1775 and the Internet Protocol Suite (TCP/IP) introduced in 1982. Documents that once took two to three days or longer to deliver are now delivered instantaneously with a reply supplied in the same speed.

Reading a business letter on the computer screen has become the new normal. Default fonts designed for online reading and increased spacing in word processing software address these new approaches to accomplishing our work. Reading online also makes accessing links seamless. When the letter is read and action taken, the recipient can easily store the letter electronically, which also supports today's focus to protect the environment. However, the increased focus on speed of delivery can lead to challenges.

Do remember that sending letters quickly does not change the need for factual accuracy, completeness, appropriate format, correct spelling, proper grammar, and precise punctuation. Write clearly and proofread all documents carefully before sending them by any means of distribution. Your reputation is on the line.

Review/Tracking/Track Changes

1. In the open document, turn Track Changes on and make the changes shown below.

2. Review the document by checking All Markup, then Simple Markup, and No Markup.

3. Proofread and check; click next activity. (*85-drill2*)

The first on site meeting is scheduled for November 10. We plan to meet at the main entrance at 10:30 o'clock *a.m.* to tour the property and review the procedures that NatureLink plans to use in redesigning the trails close to *near* the Red-cockaded Woodpecker (RCW) habitat. Since the RCW is an endangered species, we want to balance the wishes of ecotourists to observe these birds and the need to preserve *protect* them.

---

## REVIEWING PANE

The Reviewing Pane provides a summary of the tracked changes and comments in a document. The Vertical pane displays at the left side, and the Horizontal pane displays at the bottom of the screen.

**To view a summary of tracked changes and comments:**
Review/Tracking/Reviewing Pane

- Click Reviewing Pane and select either Reviewing Pane Vertical or Reviewing Pane Horizontal.

---

## REVIEW CHANGES AND COMMENTS

Changes and comments can be reviewed in sequence, and each change can be accepted or rejected. Comments should be marked done or deleted after they have been read and action has been taken. Changes can also be accepted or rejected at once.

**To accept or reject changes:**
Review/Changes/Previous or Next

1. Click Previous or Next to move to a change.
2. To accept a change, click Accept and Move to Next; to reject a change, click Reject and move to Next.
3. To accept all changes at once, click Accept All Changes. To reject all changes at once, click Reject All Changes.

## 34-d1
**Block Letter**

1. Key the letter below in block style with open punctuation. Tap ENTER three times to begin the date at about 2". Press SHIFT + ENTER to remove the extra space in the letter address, signature line, and enclosures.
2. Add an envelope to the letter.
3. Proofread and check; click Next Activity. (34-d1)

---

May 19, 201- | Ms. Coralia Lopez | Chief Financial Officer | Midland Corporation | 1001 North Tenth Avenue | Chicago, IL 60290-1001 | Dear Ms. Lopez

Thank you for your continuing business with Henderson, Blakney, Hardin, Mayfield CPA Firm. We appreciate the long-term partnership between our organizations.

The audit for Midland Corporation is scheduled for September 1-5, 201-. Ken Smith and Jill Matthews, the on-site auditors, will arrive at 9 a.m. on September 1. They will meet with you for approximately one hour before beginning the audit. Please review the enclosed audit questionnaire prior to this meeting. Also, to ensure security of sensitive financial records, they will require a private office with Internet access.

Ms. Lopez, if you have questions concerning the audit, please call me at 312.555.0138.

Sincerely | John D. Henderson, Partner | xx | Enclosure |
c Ms. Lynda Maxwell, President

---

## 34-d2
**Edit Letter**

1. In the open document (34-d1), make the following edits.
2. Change the ZIP Code to 60291-1001; update the envelope.
3. Change the dates of the audit to October 1-5; auditors will arrive on October 1.
4. Ken Smith will not be assigned to this audit. Change to Rory Jones.
5. Move the third sentence of the second paragraph to the end of the paragraph.
6. Send a copy also to Mr. Wendell Havard, Controller. Remember to press SHIFT + ENTER to remove the extra space between the names; tap TAB and key Mr. Havard's name.
7. Proofread and check; click Next Activity. (34-d2)

---

## 34-d3
**Envelope**

1. Key an envelope to the following address and add to the document.
2. Proofread and check. (34-d3) Click Exit *Word*.
3. Click Log out to exit *KPDO*.

---

Mr. Jacob Gillespie
1783 West Rockhill Road
Bartlett, TN 38133-1783

## DISPLAY FOR REVIEW

Documents with tracked changes can be viewed from four different perspectives.

**❶ Simple Markup:** Shows comments and the document as it would look if all changes are accepted. Lines on left indicate corrections.

**❷ All Markup:** Shows the document with all proposed changes included.

**❸ No Markup:** Shows the document as it would look with all changes accepted.

**❹ Original:** Shows the document before changes were made.

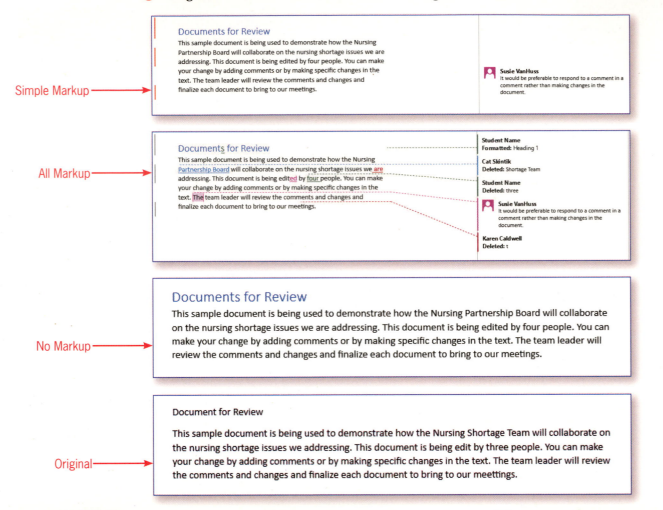

Simple Markup →

**Documents for Review**
This sample document is being used to demonstrate how the Nursing Partnership Board will collaborate on the nursing shortage issues we are addressing. This document is being edited by four people. You can make your change by adding comments or by making specific changes in the text. The team leader will review the comments and changes and finalize each document to bring to our meetings.

**Susie VanHuss**
It would be preferable to respond to a comment in a comment rather than making changes in the document.

All Markup →

**Documents for Review**
This sample document is being used to demonstrate how the Nursing Partnership Board will collaborate on the nursing shortage issues we are addressing. This document is being edited by four people. You can make your change by adding comments or by making specific changes in the text. The team leader will review the comments and changes and finalize each document to bring to our meetings.

**Student Name**
Formatted: Heading 1

**Cat Skíntik**
Deleted: Shortage Team

**Student Name**
Deleted: three

**Susie VanHuss**
It would be preferable to respond to a comment in a comment rather than making changes in the document.

**Karen Caldwell**
Deleted: t

No Markup →

**Documents for Review**

This sample document is being used to demonstrate how the Nursing Partnership Board will collaborate on the nursing shortage issues we are addressing. This document is being edited by four people. You can make your change by adding comments or by making specific changes in the text. The team leader will review the comments and changes and finalize each document to bring to our meetings.

Original →

**Document for Review**

This sample document is being used to demonstrate how the Nursing Shortage Team will collaborate on the nursing shortage issues we addressing. This document is being edit by three people. You can make your change by adding comments or by making specific changes in the text. The team leader will review the comments and changes and finalize each document to bring to our meettings.

---

## DRILL 1     DISPLAY FOR REVIEW

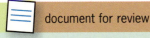

document for review

**Review/Tracking/Show Markup**

1. Note that the open document is in Simple Markup view. Click the line on the left and hover the mouse above each change and review the information provided.

2. Insert an **s** after document in the title, and then apply Heading 1 format to the title.

3. View the document in each of the four options for review.

4. Check to see that your name is listed as a reviewer in All Markup. Then turn Track Changes off.

5. Proofread and check; click next activity. (*85-drill1*)

# Lesson 35 Modified Block Letter

New Commands • Tabs

## New Commands

### TABS

**35b**

Tabs are used to indent paragraphs and to align text vertically. The default tab stops are set every half inch. *Hint:* If the ruler is not displayed, go to View/Show and click Ruler.

**To set a left tab:**

1. Check the tab selector to be sure the left tab is selected.
2. Click the Horizontal Ruler where you want to set the left tab.

When a new tab stop has been set, all default tabs to the left of the newly set tab are automatically cleared. Therefore, if other tabs are needed, simply choose the desired tab alignment, and then click the Horizontal Ruler where the desired tab is to be set.

**To move a tab:**

Select all of the text that will be affected, and drag the tab to be moved to the new desired location. *Note:* If you do not select all of the text, only the tab that your cursor is on will be moved.

**To clear a tab:**

Select all of the text that will be affected and drag the tab off the Horizontal Ruler bar.

---

## DRILL 1  SET TABS

1. Set a left tab at 3.25". Insert the current date at 3.25", and tap ENTER twice.

2. Set a left tab at 1". Key the following lines and tap ENTER once. Press SHIFT + ENTER to remove the added space between the items.

   **Enclosures:  Promissory Note**
   **Amortization Schedule**

3. Set a left tab at 0.5". Key the following lines. Press SHIFT + ENTER to remove the added space between the lines. Be sure to undo automatic capitalization so the c in copy notation is not capitalized.

   **c  Ashley Nobles**
   **Ethan Vilella**

4. Proofread and check; click Next Activity. (*35-drill1*)

# Lesson 85 Minutes with Track Changes

**New Commands**
- Track Changes
- Show Markup
- Review Changes
- Reviewing Pane
- Accept/Reject Changes

## New Commands

**85b**

## TRACK CHANGES

**Off**    **On**

Track changes show suggested revisions or changes in a document in the form of insertions, deletions, and formats without the document itself changing. Each change can be viewed and accepted or rejected. Once changes are accepted, the document actually changes. Comments differ from tracked changes in that suggestions are offered, but they cannot be accepted and made a part of the document. Comment text must be copied or keyed to be integrated in the text.

> **TIP**
>
> Use Show/Hide with Track Changes.

**To turn Track Changes on or off:**
Review/Tracking/Track Changes

1. Click Track Changes to turn tracking on; the button turns blue.
2. To turn tracking off, click the blue Track Changes button.

## MARKUP

Markup provides options for viewing changes that have been tracked. Some reviewers prefer to focus on insertions and deletions and deal with other revisions separately. Others prefer to review the suggestions of one reviewer at a time.

**❶ Display for Review:** Choose how to review proposed changes in the document.

**❷ Show Markup:** Choose the type of markup to show in the document.

**❸ Reviewing Pane:** Show revisions in a vertical or horizontal pane.

> **TIP**
>
> Colors will vary on different computers. However, each author should have a different color.

**To show markup:**
Review/Tracking/Show Markup

1. Display the markup options.
2. Check options that you wish to display and deselect options that you do not wish to display.

# MODIFIED BLOCK LETTER

35c

References/Document
Formats/Modified Block Letter

In the modified block format, the date line and the closing lines (complimentary close and writer's name and title) begin at the center point of the page. All other guidelines for the block letter style are applied to the modified block letter. Remember to remove the extra spacing between the letter address and other short lines. Review the model modified block letter on the next page.

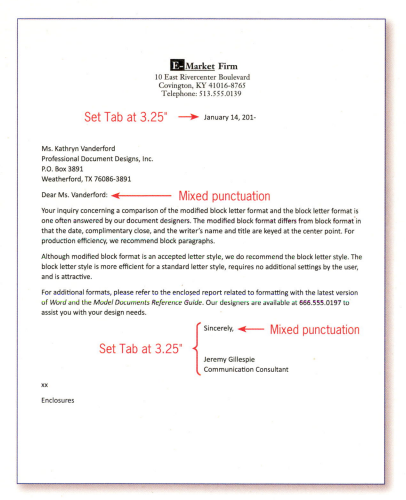

**Dateline:**

- Position at about 2".

- Begin at least 0.5" below the letterhead.

- Set a left tab at 3.25". Determine the position of the tab by subtracting the side margin from the center of the paper.

> 4.25" Center of the paper
> −1.00" Margin
> 3.25" Tab setting

**Complimentary closing:** Begin keying at 3.25".

**Writer's name and title:** Begin keying at 3.25".

## MIXED PUNCTUATION

Although most letters are formatted with open punctuation, some businesses prefer mixed punctuation. To format a letter using mixed punctuation, key a colon after the salutation and a comma after the complimentary close.

Dear Mr. Hathorn:

Sincerely,

**84-d1**

**Agenda with Comments**

1. Prepare the agenda illustrated on the previous page, formatting it as indicated below.
2. Tap ENTER three times and apply Organic theme with *Word 2013* Document Formatting styles.
3. Key the heading and apply the following styles: line 1 Title; line 2 Heading 1, and lines 3 and 4 Heading 2. Then center all four lines.
4. Set a left tab at 1" and a right-aligned dot leader tab at the right margin (6.5).
5. Add and edit the following comments to the agenda:
   a. Select *Call to Order* and add Comment 1: **Please confirm your attendance.**
   b. Select *Proposal* and add Comment 2: **Copies will be delivered at least three days prior to the meeting.**
   c. Select *Approval* and add Comment 3: **If the Board is not ready to finalize the decision, another meeting will be scheduled.**
   d. Edit Comment 1 as follows: **Please confirm your attendance and indicate any additional agenda items desired.**
6. Select the heading and save it for future use as a Quick Part with the name and description **NPB Agenda Heading**.
7. Preview and proofread the document carefully.
8. Check and click Next Activity. (*84-d1*)

**84-d2**

**Revised Agenda**

1. In the open document (*84-d1*), make the following revisions to the preliminary agenda.
2. **Approval of Minutes** needs to be added. Mary Freeman does not require additional time for that item. Position after Call to Order and do not list a time.
3. The three speakers giving their perspective on the proposal indicated that 10 minutes would be adequate for their comments. Reduce their times to 10 minutes each and add the 15 minutes saved to the discussion time.
4. Delete all comments.
5. Check and click Next Activity. (*84-d2*)

**84-d3**

**Agenda Formatted in Table**

 training agenda

1. In the open document, select the date and replace it with **5/14/201-**.
2. Key the response to Comment 2 made by Karen Jones: **I agree. The Bradford, Eastman, and McAlexander proposals should be reviewed separately.**
3. Select *Discussion* and add a new comment: **I think we should allow 10 minutes for each proposal and 20 minutes for discussion.**
4. Check and click Next Activity. (*84-d3*)

**84-d4**

**Revised Agenda**

1. In the open document (*84-d3*), make the following revisions to the agenda.
2. Add two rows below row 4 (2:50 time slot). Add the following information:
   Row 5:    **3:00**    **Review of Eastman Proposal**        **Carolyn Mayes**
   Row 6:    **3:10**    **Review of McAlexander Proposal**    **Student's Name**
3. In row 4, modify the text in column B to **Review of Bradford Proposal** and then mark the Tapp, Jones, and Turnquist comments as done.
4. Change times: Discussion **3:20**; Recommendations **3:40**; and Adjournment **4:00**.
5. Delete all comments.
6. Check and close. (*84-d4*)

**E–Market Firm**
10 East Rivercenter Boulevard
Covington, KY 41016-8765
Telephone: 513.555.0139

<span style="color:red">About 2"</span>

<span style="color:red">Set tab at 3.25"</span> → January 14, 201-

Ms. Kathryn Vanderford
Professional Document Designs, Inc.
P.O. Box 3891
Weatherford, TX 76086-3891

<span style="color:red">Press SHIFT + ENTER to remove extra space</span>

Dear Ms. Vanderford: ← <span style="color:red">Mixed punctuation</span>

Your inquiry concerning a comparison of the modified block letter format and the block letter format is one often answered by our document designers. The modified block format differs from block format in that the date, complimentary close, and the writer's name and title are keyed at the center point. For production efficiency, we recommend block paragraphs.

Although modified block format is an accepted letter style, we do recommend the block letter style. The block letter style is more efficient for a standard letter style, requires no additional settings by the user, and is attractive.

For additional formats, please refer to the enclosed report related to formatting with the latest version of *Word* and the *Model Documents Reference Guide*. Our designers are available at 666.555.0197 to assist you with your design needs.

Sincerely, ← <span style="color:red">Mixed punctuation</span>

Jeremy Gillespie } <span style="color:red">Press SHIFT + ENTER</span>
Communication Consultant ↓ 2

xx

Enclosures

**Modified Block Letter with Mixed Punctuation**

**84d**

An agenda is a plan for conducting a meeting. Prior to the meeting, participants are asked to review the agenda and respond with additional items. Then the final agenda is distributed to participants prior to the meeting so that they can prepare appropriately for it. Agendas normally contain five types of information:

1. A heading with the general topic of the meeting, the date, the time, and the location.

2. A list of specific topics to be discussed in the meeting.

3. The individual or group responsible for leading the discussion on each topic.

4. Time allocated for the discussion of each topic, -or- the beginning and ending time of the meeting. Time allocation depends on company philosophy.

5. Attachments that provide information about some of the discussion topics. In some cases, this information is distributed separately from the agenda.

Agendas may be prepared using a traditional format, a template, a table, or building blocks. The heading format varies widely among companies. The theme and style set often determine the most appropriate way to design the document. Meeting documents generally follow report format guides. Unless the meeting is very long, agendas typically fit on one page even if the margin spacing at the top of the first page has to be reduced.

# Agenda

### Nursing Partnership Board
### Hospital Atrium
### January 15, 201-, 10:30 a.m. ↓2

10:30	Call to Order	Mary Freeman
10:35	Proposal	Mary Freeman
10:45	Terms of the Agreement	Student's Name
11:00	Hospital Perspective	Tyler Walker
11:15	Technical College Perspective	Jane Metze
11:30	University Perspective	Lester Caldwell
11:45	Discussion and Approval	All
12:00	Adjournment	

**35-d1**

**Modified Block Letter**

1. Key the model letter on page 137 in modified block format with mixed punctuation.
2. Set a left tab at 3.25". Tap ENTER three times to position the date at about 2". Do not key the letterhead.
3. Press SHIFT + ENTER to remove the added space in the letter address and between the writer's name and title. Use Show/Hide to view paragraph markers to confirm correct spacing between letter parts.
4. Add an envelope to the letter. Omit a return address.
5. Proofread and check; click Next Activity. (*35-d1*)

**35-d2**

**Modified Block Letter**

1. Key the following letter in modified block letter style with mixed punctuation. Add all required letter parts. ❋ Remove the hyperlink in the second paragraph. **Note:** Remove the hyperlink if the document is not read on screen.
2. Add an envelope to the letter.
3. Proofread and check; click Next Activity. (*35-d2*)

### ❋ Discover

**Remove Hyperlink**

Insert/Links/Hyperlink

Click the hyperlink and follow the path above. Then click Remove Link.

*Shortcut:* Right-click and click Remove Hyperlink.

Current date | Mr. Ricardo Delgado | Wildwood Sports Goods | 1525 South Ash Street | Gainesville, FL 32601-1525 | Dear Mr. Delgado:

Thank you for your generous donation of 100 golf caps for the players in our upcoming Carter Alverston Scholarship Golf Tournament. Your kind contribution will allow us to attract more players, thereby increasing funding for our scholarship program. Last year's tournament raised over $10,000 to assist our students in pursuing distant internships. This year's goal is to attract 100 players and 20 sponsors.

As one of our key sponsors, you are invited to participate with a team in the tournament. All participant fees are waived for sponsors. We also ask you to encourage your business colleagues and personal contacts to join us either as sponsors or players. Sponsor and player forms can be downloaded at www.sw-de.edu/tournament.pdf.

Once again, thank you for your generous support of this important scholarship program.

Sincerely, | Leslie Gregory | Director of Public Relations | xx

**35-d3**

**Edit Letter**

 **REVIEW**

**Clear Tabs**

Home/Paragraph/Line and Page Breaks Tab/Tabs/Clear All

1. Open *35-d2* and edit to change to a block letter style with open punctuation. *Hint:* Select the entire letter (CTRL + A) and remove the tabs. If necessary, tap Backspace to return date and closing lines to the left margin.
2. In the company name in the letter address, change *Sports* to **Sporting**. Change the house address to **323 Second Street**.
3. Select the letter address, and create a new envelope. Click Change Document to accept the change on the previously created envelope.
4. Proofread and check. (*35-d3*) Click Exit *Word*.
5. Click Log out to exit *KPDO*.

## COMMENTS

**84c**

Comments enable multiple reviewers to critique a document and insert remarks or annotations. Comments are generally displayed in balloons positioned in the right margin.

To insert/edit a comment:
Review/Comments/New Comment

1. Select the text or click at the end of the text on which you wish to comment, and click New Comment to display the Comment balloon.

2. Key the comment you wish to make.

3. To edit a comment, click in the balloon of the comment you want to edit and key the changes you want to make.

---

**★ TIP**

Before you enter comments, check to see that your name and initials are in the User name and Initials boxes on your computer.
File/Options/General

---

To reply to a comment:

1. Click Reply in the top right corner of the balloon ❶.

2. Key your response below your name in the balloon that displays.

---

**❋ Discover**

To navigate from one comment to another, click Next to jump to the next comment or Previous to jump back to a comment.

---

To mark a comment done:

1. Right-click the balloon containing the comment you want to mark done.

2. Click Mark Comment Done. The comment is dimmed.

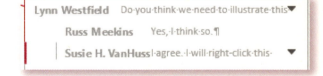

To delete a comment:
Review/Comments/Delete

1. Click in the balloon containing the comment you want to delete.

2. Click Delete. -or-

1. Right-click the balloon containing the comment you want to delete.

2. Click Delete Comment.

---

DRILL 1	COMMENTS	comments

1. Read the open document and review each comment that is attached to text in the document.

2. Select *Comments* in the first line of the document and add the new comment: **Adding a new comment is very easy to do.**

3. Click the Reply icon in the first Susie H. VanHuss comment and key the following response: **Will most people include pictures?**

4. Click in the comment attached to Delete Comments and read it; then delete it.

❋ 5. Use the Previous command to navigate to the comment you added at the beginning of the document. Mark the comment done.

6. Preview and check; click next activity. (*84-drill1*)

# Lesson 36 Palmetto Event Solutions, Inc.

## Skill Building

### 36b Timed Writing

1. Key a 1' timing on each paragraph; work to increase speed.
2. Key a 3' timing on all paragraphs.

Have simple things such as saying please, may I help you, and thank you gone out of style? We begin to wonder when we observe front-line workers interact with customers today. Frequently their careless attitudes indicate that the customer is a bother and not important. But we realize there would be no business without the customer. So what can be done to prove to consumers that they really are king?

First, require that all workers train in good customer service. They must recognize that their jobs exist for the customer. Also, explain why they should talk to their supervisors about any problem. You do not want workers to talk about lack of breaks or schedules in front of customers. Remember customers must always feel that they are king and should never be ignored.

## Project Setting

### ★ TIP

Read the *About Us* section on page 118 to review information about Palmetto Event Solutions. Read the Standard Operating Procedures for the project carefully. You will not be reminded to do these steps. Refer to them as needed during the project.

In this project, you are assigned to the regional office of Palmetto Event Solutions, Inc., located in Portland, Oregon. You report to Jennifer Anderson, Senior Account Executive, who is charged with planning the City Center Centennial Gala, a major fundraising event sponsored by the Tri-City Partnership.

**Standard operating procedures for the project:**

1. Use block letter style with open punctuation and the Palmetto letterhead from the data files. Use appropriate opening and closing lines. Use the Date command to add the current date and begin the date at approximately 2".
2. Create envelopes for letters only when directed, as many letters are attached to an email.
3. The data files also contain a Palmetto memo form. Use appropriate subject lines if a subject line is not provided.
4. Add your reference initials, enclosure notations, and copy notations as appropriate.
5. Proofread and check; when you are satisfied with the document, click Next Activity.

### DATA FILES

Data files are extra documents you will need to complete an assignment. When a data file is required, an icon and filename are listed after the drill name or document name.

- In *KPDO (Keyboarding Pro DELUXE Online)*, the data file opens automatically when you select the activity. For example, in *36-d1* below, the file *palmetto memo* will open automatically.
- Non-*KPDO* users: Download the data files from www.cengagebrain.com; go to the student companion resources site. Save the data files to your hard drive or flash drive. The files are organized by module.

# Meeting, Travel, and News Documents

## LEARNING OUTCOMES

- View, insert, respond, mark done, and delete comments.
- Track changes, show markup, review changes, and accept or reject changes.
- Design and format meeting, travel, and news documents.
- Enhance communication skills.
- Build keyboarding skills.

## Lesson 84 Agenda with Comments

**New Commands**

- New Comment
- Delete Comment
- Previous Comment
- Next Comment
- Respond to Comment
- Mark Comment Done

**Warmup**  *Lesson 84a Warmup*

A ALL LETTERS

### Skill Building

**84b  Timed Writing**

1. Key a 1' timed writing on each paragraph; work to increase speed.
2. Key a 3' timed writing on all paragraphs.

Americans tend to have a different view of vacation than citizens of many other countries. In this country, companies usually provide employees with a maximum of two or three weeks of vacation each year. Many companies wait to award the second week of vacation until employees have five years of tenure with them. Those who earn more than three weeks of vacation typically do so by staying with the same company for many years.

In many other countries, the case is quite different. Employees typically receive four to six weeks of vacation each year. It is also awarded much earlier in their tenure with the company. Vacation is thought of as just another benefit that has value to the company as well as to the employee. Employees often spend a whole month on holiday as they call vacation time.

While some individuals think how wonderful and luxurious it would be to have extra days or weeks of vacation, the fact is that a large percentage of Americans do not take the vacation time they are allotted by their companies. The American culture is such that many employees feel they cannot be away from their positions for more than two weeks at one time.

## 36-d1

**Memo**

 palmetto memo

1. Prepare the following memo to Susan Walker, Executive Chef. Key the subject line **Menu for City Center Centennial Gala Due Tomorrow**.
2. Proofread and check; click Next Activity. (36-d1)

Please send the menu for the City Center Centennial Gala by close of day tomorrow. As always, include all details required for caterers submitting bids.

Bids to the top ten caterers that you recommended will be mailed on Monday with a response required in ten days. You will be called upon to evaluate the bids.

Thank you for your excellent work on the catering needs of this project.

## 36-d2

**Letter**

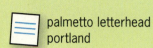 palmetto letterhead
portland

1. Key the letter below. Create an envelope and add to the letter.
2. Key the writer's name and title on separate lines.
3. Proofread and check; click Next Activity. (36-d2)

Current date | Mr. Neil Ferguson | Ferguson Catering | 4535 Lakeview Street | Portland, OR 97204-4535 | Dear Mr. Ferguson

Congratulations! I am pleased to inform you that Ferguson Catering was selected as the caterer for the City Center Centennial Gala. Your bid for $20,000 was well within the budget set by our client, Tri-City Partnership. Your creative menu complements perfectly the farm-to-table philosophy of our organizers.

A contract outlining your responsibilities is enclosed for your review and signature. Please sign both copies and return to me by the end of next week.

I have tentatively scheduled our initial meeting for Thursday, September 23, at 10 a.m. at the convention center offices. Other participants include Jacob Burch of the Tri-City Partnership, Jean Blake, convention center manager, and Tyler Crockett, one of our event planners.

Please contact me if you have any questions about the contract or if we need to plan a different date and time for the meeting.

# Documents for Specialized Fields

## Learning Outcomes

### Document Design Skills

+ Apply effective designs to a variety of complex documents.

+ Organize content effectively with graphics.

+ Improve document quality using review and collaboration tools.

+ Design documents in administrative and specialized areas, including meeting, travel, news, employment, legal, and medical documents.

### Word Processing Skills

+ Learn and apply word processing commands to create and format specialized documents.

### Communication Skills

+ Review and improve basic communication skills.

+ Produce error-free documents and apply language arts skills.

### Keyboarding

+ Improve keyboarding speed and accuracy.

## 36-d3

**Letter**

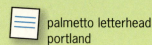
palmetto letterhead
portland

1. Key the letter below in 11-point Calibri font; do not create an envelope as it will be attached to an email.
2. Send a copy to Garrett Russell, President (of Palmetto Event Solutions, Inc.).
3. Proofread and check; click Next Activity. (36-d3)

---

Mr. Jacob Burch | Tri-City Partnership | 760 Rockdale Street | Portland, OR 97204-0760 | Dear Mr. Burch

We are pleased to have been chosen as your event planner for the upcoming City Center Centennial Gala. Planning for this event is progressing as projected, and listed below are major activities at this point:

- Neil Ferguson with Ferguson Caterers has agreed to cater the food for the event. Ten caterers submitted bids, and five finalists were interviewed. Ferguson Caterers was selected based on five criteria deemed essential for this prestigious event. His creative menu complementing the farm-to-table philosophy and his budget projection were very impressive in the final decision.
- Bids have been solicited from 12 local florists. We are expecting to make this selection in two weeks.
- The entertainment committee is busy scouting available talent and will report their top three choices to me on Friday.

An initial meeting with Neil Ferguson of Ferguson Caterers, Jean Blake, convention center manager, and Tyler Crockett, account associate, is scheduled for September 23, 201-, at 10 a.m. at the convention center offices. You are invited to attend this meeting to meet these key players and to tour the venue. Please let me know if your schedule permits you to attend.

---

## 36-d4

**Compose Email**

1. Compose an email to your instructor, who is posing as Jennifer Anderson. You have been asked to draft an email that Ms. Anderson will send to the nine caterers who were not selected for the event. Key **Draft of Email to Caterers Not Selected for the City Center Centennial Gala** as the subject line.
2. The first paragraph should tell Ms. Anderson that the draft of the email to the nine caterers not selected for the event follows in the email.
3. The remaining paragraphs should be the draft email to the nine caterers. First, thank the caterers for submitting a bid and let them know that the submissions were very competitive. Using a kind tone, state that the bid was not chosen. In a new paragraph, build goodwill by sharing that other events are scheduled in the coming months and encourage the caterer to submit future bids. End with how important excellent caterers are to the success of Palmetto Event Solutions.
4. Proofread and check. (36-d4) Click Exit *Word*.
5. Click Log out to exit *KPDO*.

Compare your report to the one shown below.

---

**Page 1 (Title page):**

2014

# Hess Pet Center Business Plan

PRELIMINARY DATA

SUSIE H. VANHUSS

---

**Page 2 (Table of Contents):**

## Table of Contents

ii

---

**Page 3 (Body text):**

## Hess Pet Center Business Plan

Preliminary Data

The Hess Pet Center is a new venture that integrates an existing successful veterinary clinic, Faulk Pet Care, with a full-service luxury pet boarding, grooming, day camp, and boutique center and moves to a new location—Hess Office Park. The joint venture has been branded as Hess Pet Center to capitalize on the popularity of its new location.

### Revenue Projections

The purpose of this study is to analyze the revenue-generating potential of each segment of the center and project the contribution each segment can be expected to make during the first year of operation. Accurate revenue projections are needed to complete the business plan.

### Historical and Market Data

Hess Pet Center has historical data only for Faulk Pet Care, the veterinary clinic, which has been operated by Dr. Erin Faulk for more than five years. Sources of data for the luxury boarding segment, the day camp, the grooming and spa facility, and the boutique are based on surveys of clients of the veterinary clinic, industry data, and on market research in the Austin area. Focus groups were held with representatives of the companies located in Hess Office Park and surrounding upscale neighborhoods.

### Revenue Potential Analyzed

Both qualitative and quantitative data were analyzed to determine the revenue potential for each market segment. A conservative approach was used in the analysis because the negative consequences of projections on the high side were much more significant than projections on the low side.

### Veterinary Clinic

The new clinic, formerly known as Faulk Pet Care, is located near a very high-income residential and office park area. Most clients are owned by affluent families. The clinic also has a relationship with the managers of the Hess Office Park. Because of lack of space, boarding has been limited to pets with medical conditions being treated at the clinic and to selected clients.

Growth of the veterinary business has been flat for the past two years because the facilities were fully utilized. Very few new clients were accepted because the center was operating at full capacity. Growth for the first year has been projected at 20

---

**Page 4 (Body text, page 2):**

2

percent. New board-certified veterinarians and trained technicians are being phased in during the year. Completion of the new surgical facilities including the installation of the new technology and reorganization of the operations is scheduled within three months. Major growth is expected in the second year of operation when all facilities are fully utilized. The revenue projection for this segment is $1,860,300.

### Luxury Suite Boarding

Both standard units and luxury suites are included in this segment. A number of kennels and boarding facilities operate in the Austin area. Several are upscale facilities, but they do not offer true luxury suites for discriminating clientele who want their pets pampered. Even the Hess Pet Center standard units are more upscale than the typical "luxury" suites at other facilities. Industry data show that luxury suites are in high demand in high-income residential and in upscale office parks.

Clients bringing pets in for medical treatment were surveyed to determine how frequently they would use boarding facilities and the type of facilities desired. Clients clearly indicated a strong preference both for using the Hess Pet Center and for luxury accommodations for their pets. Local market data showed that upscale facilities were more profitable than moderately priced facilities. The revenue projection for this segment is $675,480.

### Doggie Day Camp

Historically, this segment of the industry accounted for a very small part of the market. However, during the past three years, this area has grown dramatically. Information we collected shows that growth in the use of Doggie Day Camp facilities has grown more than 40 percent nationally. Day camp facilities in the Austin area appear to be in high demand with local residents who do not have full-time help at home and with employees who can drop off pets at the beginning of the workday and pick them up after work. Focus groups with managers of Hess Office Park companies confirmed the need for day camp facilities. Projected revenue for this segment is $480,840.

### Pet Grooming and Spa

The primary source of data for this segment was the surveys of clients who brought their pets in for medical treatment. A major requisite for success in this area is one-stop shopping. Clients indicated in the interviews that they want to have grooming and spa treatments done while pets are receiving other services such as medical attention or are being kept in day camp or in the overnight boarding facility. Both national industry data and local market data were analyzed. The revenue projected for this segment is $360,720.

### Boutique

Success of the retail operation is more difficult to predict than other segments of the business. The one-stop shopping phenomenon is critical in this area. Having an attractive display of items that appeal to pet owners promotes impulse shopping, which is important in a high-income area. Having premium pet food in the boutique that is generally not available in other outlets is also important. The pharmacy can be

---

**Page 5 (Body text, page 3):**

3

operated out of either the veterinary clinic or the boutique. Current plans are to locate the pharmacy in the boutique to increase the traffic flowing through the retail area. It was very difficult to obtain reliable data in this area, but the analysis team believes that the projections will be met because they are so conservative. Revenue projections for the first year are $240,480.

### Total Revenue Projections

Revenue projections for all of the segments are provided on a monthly and an annual basis. The monthly revenue figures are averages. Averages were used because data were not available to determine the seasonal impact. Figure 1 summarizes the revenue projections for the first year of operation.

Hess Pet Center	Monthly Revenue	Annual Revenue	Percentage
Veterinary Clinic	$155,025	$1,860,300	51
Pet Boarding	56,290	675,480	19
Doggie Day Camp	40,070	480,840	13
Grooming and Spa	30,060	360,720	10
Boutique	20,040	240,480	7
Total Revenue	$301,485	$3,617,820	100

The projections for revenues for the first year of operation are significantly higher than originally anticipated.

Figure 2 shows the percentage of revenue contributed by each of the five segments of Hess Pet Center.

---

**Page 6 (Body text, page 4):**

4

Note from Figure 2 that the veterinary clinic and the pet boarding segments are projected to produce more than two-thirds of the total revenue for the first year of operation.

### Comparison to Pro Formas

The initial pro formas, prepared when the joint venture was formed, projected revenue for the first year of operation to be $3,017,820. The initial pro formas assumed that the new surgical facilities would not be completed during the first year of operation and only the standard units would be available. Completion of both the surgical facilities and the luxury suites is scheduled within three months and can be fully utilized within six months. Therefore, the current revenue projections are $600,000 higher than the initial projections. These projections are conservative and are based on solid data.

### Hess Pet Center Profitability

The expense projections need to be updated to reflect the additional variable costs that result from the availability of the surgical facilities and the luxury suites during the last six months of the first year of operation. Virtually all of the fixed costs have already been accounted for; therefore, most of the additional revenue projected will go directly to the bottom line. Profitability for the first year of operation has been enhanced significantly.

---

Learn More:

www.cengagebrain.com

# *Lesson 37* Assessment Modules 3 and 4

**Warmup** *Lesson 37a Warmup*

## Apply It

### 37-d1

**Announcement**

1. In a new document, key the title centered; apply Calibri Light 72-point font; and apply Fill - Black, Text 1, Shadow text effect.
2. Key the remainder of the text. Apply Calibri Light 36-point font and bold.
3. Center the page vertically.
4. Preview, check with proofing tools, then proofread, correct errors, and continue to the next document. (*37-d1*)

### ▶▶ REVIEW

**Center Page**
Page Layout/Page Setup dialog box launcher/Layout tab, Vertical alignment

Room Change Notice

All classes and laboratories held in Room 250 of Westbrook Hall have been moved to Room 102 of Eastbrook Hall. This change will be in effect from October 10 until October 25.

### 37-d2

**Block Letter**

1. Key the letter below in the block letter style with open punctuation. Add an appropriate salutation. Send a copy of the letter to **Olivia Cavenaugh.**
2. Add an envelope to the document.
3. Continue to the next document. (*37-d2*)

Current date | Mr. John Long, Manager | Durrington Electronics Store | 9822 Trevor Avenue | Anaheim, CA 92805-5885

With your letter came our turn to be perplexed, and we apologize. When we had our refund coupons printed, we had just completed a total redesign program for our product boxes. We had detachable logos put on the outside of the boxes, which could be peeled off and placed on a coupon.

We had not anticipated that our distributors would use back inventories with our promotion. The e-book readers you sold were not packaged in our new boxes; therefore, there were no logos on them.

We are sorry you or your customers were inconvenienced. In the future, simply ask your customers to send us their sales slips, and we will honor them with refunds until your supply of older e-book readers is depleted.

Sincerely | Cynthia Wertz | Sales and Promotions Department | xx

## 14-d10

**Business Plan**

 business plan

Dr. Faulk and Mr. Schmidt asked you to work with a small team of analysts to put together the preliminary data needed to update and complete the Hess Pet Center Business Plan. You will prepare a professional unbound report that will be distributed electronically.

1. In the open document (*business plan*), apply Title and Subtitle styles. Select all text below the subtitle and apply Justify.

2. Apply Heading 1 style to all headings except for the five market segment headings after the *Revenue Potential Analyzed* heading; apply Heading 2 style to those five headings.

3. Format the table as follows:

   a. Apply Grid Table 4 – Accent 1.

   b. Apply 0.3" row height to all rows.

   c. Apply Align Center to all headings in row 1 and Align Center Left to the remainder of the table.

   d. Set a decimal tab at the center of each column with numerical data.

   e. Use the *Annual Revenue* column to sort the data in descending order.

   f. Sum the columns with numerical data. Apply Number format #,##0; add a dollar sign ($) in the bottom row of columns B and C.

4. Change the design of the SmartArt from a Radial Cycle to a Radial Cluster. Select the Doggie Day Camp shape and click Move Up so that the percentages will be in descending order to match the table.

**❄ Discover**

When a document is created from scratch, your name should appear automatically as the Author Name from the User box on your computer.

5. Insert the Ion (Light) cover page. Select the Year and key the title and subtitle of the report. ❄ Key your name as the Author Name. Add a blank page after the cover page for the table of contents.

6. Position the insertion point at the top of the blank page after the cover page and create a table of contents. Apply Automatic Table 2 style.

7. Format page numbers as follows:

   a. Insert a Continuous section break at the top of the first page of the report. Go to the header of Section 2 and click Link to Previous to break the link between the sections. Do the same for the footer.

   b. Go to the Footer on the second page of Section 1 and insert a Plain Number 2 and format it in lowercase roman numerals. Check Different First Page.

   c. Go to the Header of the first page of the report (Section 2), and click Format Page Numbers and Start at page 1.

   d. Go to the second page of Section 2 and insert the Facet (Odd Page) header. Make sure Different First Page is checked. Select the page number at the bottom of the page and delete it.

8. Add a 1-point Dark Red, Accent 1, Darker 25% page border to the whole document.

9. Preview the document to ensure that the preliminary pages and the body of the report are numbered and formatted correctly. Compare your report to the Quick Check shown on the next page.

10. Check and log out of *KPDO*. (*14-d10*)

## 37-d3

**Modified Block Letter**

1. Key the following letter in the modified block format with mixed punctuation. Insert the current date. Remove extra spacing as necessary.
2. Supply the correct salutation, a complimentary closing, your reference initials, and an enclosure notation.
3. Create an envelope and add it to the letter.
4. Preview for letter placement, and continue to the next document. (*37-d3*)

Ms. Mukta Bhakta
9845 Buckingham Road
Annapolis, MD 21403-0314

Thank you for your recent inquiry about our wireless pet fence. The Hilton Pet Fence was developed to assist many pet owners like you who desire the safety of their pets without the barrier of a traditional fence.

Hilton Pet Fence also provides a customer support service to assist you in training your pet and a technical support team for providing technical assistance. For additional information, please call:

<div align="center">

Customer and Technical Support
Telephone: 410.555.0112
9:00 a.m.-5:30 p.m. EST, Monday-Friday

</div>

Please look over the enclosed brochure. I will call you within the next two weeks to discuss any additional questions you may have.

Alexander Zampich | Marketing Manager

## 37-d4

**Memo**

1. Key the following memo in correct format.
2. Check the test and close. (*37-d4*) Click Exit *Word*.
3. Click Log out to exit *KPDO*.

TO:         All Sunwood Employees

FROM:       Julie Patel, Human Resources Director

DATE:       Current date

SUBJECT:    Eric Kershaw Hospitalized

We were notified by Eric Kershaw's family that he was admitted into the hospital this past weekend. They expect that he will be hospitalized for another ten days. Visits and phone calls are limited, but cards and notes are welcome.

A plant is being sent to Eric from the Sunwood staff. Stop by my office before Wednesday if you wish to sign the card. If you would like to send your own "Get Well Wishes" to Eric, send them to Eric Kershaw, County General Hospital, Room 401, P.O. Box 13947, Atlanta, GA 38209-4751.

**Learn More:**

www.cengagebrain.com

This newsletter summarizes all of our services that are currently available for both dogs and cats. The veterinary clinic is more than 50 percent larger than our previous clinic and offers the highest level of pet care available. The new facility has state-of-the-art technology. The number of luxury units available for boarding has been increased and the boutique features many more items.

We look forward to seeing you at the *hpc* soon.

 **QUICK ✓**

Check your documents against the illustrations below.

**14-d9**

**Labels**

1. Use the Mail Merge Wizard to create address labels for the recipients of the form letter prepared in *14-d8*.
2. Use Avery US Letter 5162 labels. (*14-d9*)

*Communicating Today* ▶

## Business Plan—Effective Communication Tool

A business plan is not only an excellent tool for managing a business; it is also a key tool for communicating with potential and current investors, bankers, suppliers, and clients. Individuals and organizations that invest in a company want to have enough reliable information about a company to be able to make a good decision before risking the investment. A business plan provides information about the strategic direction of the company and how it plans to reach its goals. It shows that the company understands the market and competition and has access to the financial resources needed to make the business successful.

# Tables

## LEARNING OUTCOMES

- Create tables.
- Change table structure.
- Format tables.
- Create tables within documents.
- Build keying speed and accuracy.

## *Lesson 38* Create Tables

**New Commands**

- Table Grid
- Insert Table

**Warmup**    *Lesson 38a Warmup*

A   **ALL LETTERS**

## Skill Building

### 38b   Timed Writing

Key two 3' timings on all paragraphs; work for control.

Your perception of yourself has a strong impact on how others perceive you. The more confidence you have, the more likely it is you will succeed. Having confidence in yourself and your abilities helps you when you are making a difficult decision or adapting to a new situation. A great number of factors that affect self-confidence are beyond your control, but there are many things that you can do to build confidence.

People with confidence are just full of energy and have established goals; they have places to go, people to see, and important work to do. Confident people make a positive impression on others and empower others. They stand up straight, walk quickly, hold their head up high, and make eye contact. They present themselves well by having a good personal appearance and are cognizant of the new styles.

Educating yourself and being prepared are some of the keys to being a confident person. If you are asked to give a speech, for example, research the topic ahead of time. Use the research as supporting evidence in your speech. Finally, practice your speech over and over to make it a polished presentation. So prepare and you will feel more comfortable and confident.

**Mail Merge**

molly and lizzie
andy and bentley
fred

Prepare a form letter that will be sent to the owners of pets that will be featured in the next newsletter.

1. In the open document (*14-d8 main*), insert the current date at 2.2"; check update automatically.

2. Create the data source using the records shown in the table below. Customize the field names to include those shown in the first column. (*14-d8data*)

Field Names	Record 1	Record 2	Record 3
Title	Mr. and Mrs.	Mr. and Mrs.	Mr. and Mrs.
First Name	Tommy	Pat	John
Last Name	Suggs	VanHuss	Forde
Address Line 1	823 Harris Avenue	3106 Duval Street	4105 Avenue G
City	Austin	Austin	Austin
State	TX	TX	TX
ZIP Code	78705-2540	78705-3089	78751-4707
Pets	Molly and Lizzie are	Andy and Bentley are	Fred is

3. Key the main document shown below and insert the merge fields in it.

4. For the closing lines, use your name and title (**Intern**).
   Tap ENTER twice and insert the three pictures across the bottom of the page. Size them 1.5" high. Position Molly and Lizzie at left margin, Andy and Bentley at the center, and Fred at the right margin.

5. Sort by ZIP Code in ascending order. Preview and proofread the document.

6. Merge the data source and the main document.

7. Compare your letter to the Quick Check on the next page.

8. Check; click Next Activity. (*14-d8*)

**TIP**

Remember to remove the space after paragraph in the address block and between the name and title in the closing lines when you preview and check the letters.

«AddressBlock»

«GreetingLine»

We are currently preparing a new newsletter that will be sent to all of our current clients and the employees of Hess Office Park. When you receive the newsletter, you will note that «Pets» featured in it. The pictures of all pets in the newsletter are shown at the bottom of this letter. We hope you enjoy reading it.

*(continued)*

## TABLE OVERVIEW

The Table commands make it easy to present data and graphics in a *Word* document. A table helps you easily align columns and rows of text and numbers.

**Table:** Columns and rows of data—either alphabetic, numeric, or both.

**Column:** Vertical list of information labeled alphabetically from left to right.

**Row:** Horizontal list of information labeled numerically from top to bottom.

**Cell:** An intersection of a column and a row. Each cell has its own address consisting of the column letter and the row number (cell A1).

The table displays with end-of-cell and end-of-row markers. These markers are useful when editing tables. Place the mouse pointer on the table to see the Table Move handle in the upper-left corner of the table. Drag the Table Move handle to move the table to a different location in the document. Use the Sizing handle at the lower-right corner of the table to make the table larger or smaller.

## USE THE TABLE GRID

Tables are inserted into existing documents or new documents. Begin creating a table by locating the Tables group on the Insert tab. The Table button contains options for creating various types of tables; you will use two of the options in this module.

Tables are created by using the grid or the Insert Table command. Click the Table button to display the Insert Table menu, which provides several methods for creating tables. The Table grid ❶ is often used to create tables with a few columns and rows. Larger tables can be created by using the Insert Table command ❷.

Hess Pet Center now provides full-service luxury pet care to dog owners. Recently, we have been inundated with requests from current clients and from employees in Hess Office Park to expand our services to cat owners. Providing services to cat owners has always been part of our long-range business plan; therefore, we decided to survey all of our clients and Hess Office Park employees.

Survey Results

First, we asked our current clients if they had any objections to adding cats to the facilities. We are happy to report that there were no objections. More than 20 percent of our current clients have both dogs and cats. Approximately 25 percent of Hess Office Park employees indicated that they needed services for cats.

What was even more surprising were responses from clients who only have dogs, but who suggested many of their friends would like to use our services for their cats. Several sent pictures of their friends' cats. They all indicated we could publish their names and pictures in our newsletter. Sadie, shown above, is one that would likely be a frequent boarder at Hess Pet Center.

Some of our clients even sent pictures of their dogs with cats that belonged to their friends who want to use our services. Andy is pictured below with his friend Choo.

Action Plan

We will begin immediately with a pilot project that will include three types of services for cats:

- Total professional care provided by board-certified veterinarians and highly trained technicians.
- Luxury boarding.
- Boutique that provides one-stop shopping to meet your cat's needs and desires.

The architects and construction team met and agreed that we could finish an expansion area of the new addition and have a nice area to meet the demand for accommodating cats. This expansion will not impact the construction completion dates. Space in the veterinary clinic and the boutique is already available.

To create a table using the Table grid:

Insert/Tables/Table

1. Click the insertion point at the position where the table is to be inserted. Follow the path to display the Insert Table menu.

2. Drag on the grid to select the number of columns and rows needed for the table.

3. Click the left mouse button to display the table in the document.

4. Click in the first cell (A1); key your text. The cell widens as you key to accommodate the length of your text. Tap TAB to move to the next cell, and then key the text. Continue to tap TAB and key until all text has been keyed.

## MOVE WITHIN A TABLE

The insertion point displays in cell A1 when a table is created. Tap TAB to move to the next cell, or simply use the mouse to click in a cell. Refer to the table below as you learn to key text in a table.

Press or Tap	Movement
TAB	To move to the next cell. If the insertion point is in the last cell, tapping TAB will add a new row.
SHIFT + TAB	To move to the previous cell.
ENTER	To increase the height of the row. If you tap ENTER by mistake, tap BACKSPACE to delete the line.

### DRILL 1    CREATE TABLE USING THE TABLE GRID

1. Create a 3-column, 4-row table using the Table grid. Turn on Show/Hide.

2. The insertion point is in cell A1. Tap TAB to move to cell B1. Tap TAB to move to cell C1.

3. Tap ENTER. Notice the increase in the row height. Delete the ¶ symbol by tapping the BACKSPACE key.

4. Position the mouse pointer on the table to display the Table Move handle and the Sizing handle. Notice the markers at the end of each cell and each row.

5. Drag the Table Move handle down the page. This moves the table. Drag the handle back to the original position.

6. Click in the last cell (C4). Tap TAB to insert an additional row at the bottom of the table.

7. Click Check Document and then Next Activity. (38-drill1)

**14-d7**

**Newsletter**

sadie
andy and choo

## ✷ Discover

**Rotate**

Picture Tools Format/
Arrange/Rotate Objects

1. Click the drop-list arrow on Rotate Objects to display rotate options.

2. Click Flip Horizontal.

1. In a new document, apply Moderate margins and tap ENTER twice.

2. Key the information shown on the next page. Apply Heading 1 style to both headings.

3. Apply Dark Red, Accent 1, Darker 25% square bullets and position at the left edge of the column.

4. Select the text and apply two-column layout with equal-width format.

5. Insert the picture *sadie* from the data files and position it after the first line of the paragraph in which she is mentioned. Format it as follows:

   a. Crop the picture so that only the cat is shown. Size the picture 2.3" high.

   b. ✷ Rotate the picture horizontally and compress it.

   c. Apply Square Text Wrapping and position the picture at the left side of the column.

6. Insert the picture *andy and choo* immediately below the paragraph in which they are mentioned. Size the picture 2.4" high and compress it.

7. In the space at the top of the page above the Section Break (Continuous) line, key **Hess Pet Center News and Views** and format as follows:

   a. Apply 26-point font and Fill – Black 1, Text 1, Outline – Background 1, Hard Shadow – Background 1 Text Effects.

   b. Dark Red, Accent 1, Darker 25% theme color and center the text horizontally.

   c. Add a 1-point, Dark Red, Accent 1, Darker 25% page border.

8. See the illustration on the next page.

9. Proofread and check; click Next Activity. (*14-d7*)

## USE THE INSERT TABLE COMMAND

The Insert Table dialog box lets you specify the number of columns and rows for the table. This option can be easier to use than dragging over the Table grid if you need a large number of rows or columns.

To create a table using the Insert Table command:
Insert/Tables/Table

1. Click the insertion point where the table is to be inserted.

2. Display the Insert Table menu.

3. Click Insert Table ❶ to display the Insert Table dialog box.

4. Insert the number of columns by keying the number or using the spin arrows ❷.

5. Insert the number of rows by keying the number or using the spin arrows ❸.

*Word* automatically creates a table with fixed column widths. You can adjust the column widths in the Insert Table dialog box, or choose an AutoFit option to fit column widths to the longest line or to the current window size.

---

**DRILL 2**     **CREATE AND FORMAT TABLE**

1. Use the Insert Table command to create a 2-column, 4-row table.

2. Key **Name** in cell A1 and **Position** in cell B1. Row 1 contains the column heads and is often called the header row. Key the rest of the table below (your columns will be wider).

3. Place the insertion point in the last cell and tap TAB to add a row at the bottom of the table.

4. Key the following text in cell A4.

   **Ms. Clara Lynn Ramirez**

5. Key the following text in cell B4.

   **Vice Chairman and President**

6. Proofread and check; click Next Activity. (*38-drill2*)

Name	Position
Mr. Jason Thomas Carmichael	Chairman of the Board
Ms. Man Jin Callentonni	Chief Executive Officer
Mr. Alexander Paul Fairtlough	Chief Financial Officer

← Header row

Unit Type and Pet Size	Daily Cost	Weekly Cost	Doggie Day Camp
Standard Units			20
Luxury suites	75	325	NA
Junior suites	70	300	NA
Luxury units	60	275	30
Small: <35 pounds	35	175	
Medium: 35-75 pounds	40	200	
Large: >75 pounds	45	225	

**QUICK** ✓

Compare your table to the one shown below.

Hess Pet Center

**PET BOARDING FEES**

Unit Type and Pet Size	Daily Cost	Multiple Pets in Same Unit		Weekly Cost	Multiple Pets in Same Unit	
		Two	Three		Two	Three
Standard Units						
Small: <35 pounds	35	45	50	175	225	250
Medium: 35–75 pounds	40	50	55	200	250	275
Large: >75 pounds	45	Not available		225	Not available	
Luxury unit	60	No extra charge		275	No extra charge	
Junior suite	70	No extra charge		300	No extra charge	
Luxury suites	75	No extra charge		325	No extra charge	

## 14-d6

**Organization Chart**

1. Prepare the organization chart for the Retail and Service Operations, shown on the next page, using the Name and Title Organization Chart from the Hierarchy category of SmartArt diagrams.
2. Use Landscape orientation and Narrow margins.
3. Add your name to the chart.
4. Size the chart 7" high and 10" wide.
5. Use the following font sizes:
   a. Use 20-point font for all names; use SHIFT + ENTER to remove space after the paragraph to key the second line.
   b. Use 16-point for the second line in each shape and for all titles.
6. Select the shape for each manager and click Add Shape/Add Shape Below to insert additional shapes. Key the names and titles of the assistant managers.
7. Proofread and check; click Next Activity. (*14-d6*)

**38-d1**

**Create Table**

★ **TIP**

Text is keyed left-aligned. Numerical amounts are right-aligned.

1. Create and key the table below. Your solution will look different than the table below.

2. Select cells C2–C5 and click Align Right (Home/Paragraph/Align Right) to right-align the numbers in column C. Select row 1 and click Center.

3. Place the insertion point in the last cell and tap TAB to add a row.

4. Key the following copy in row 6:

   **Lawrence Jose Gonzalez          East          $83,479**

5. Proofread and check; click Next Activity. (*38-d1*)

Sales Representative	Region	Amount of Sale
Stephanie Acosta	Northwest	$1,157,829
Mitzi Fujitsu	Central	$99,016
Joanna B. Breckenridge	Southwest	$6,301,625
Jack M. Harrigan	Midwest	$4,245,073

**38-d2**

**Create Table**

1. Create the 3-column, 4-row table below.

2. Key column C using wordwrap. Your columns will be wider, so your text will not wrap at the same position as shown.

3. Proofread and check; click Next Activity. (*38-d2*)

The Golden Mile	Boutique Shops	The Golden Mile is one square mile of boutique shops located between Beverly Boulevard and Pacific Coast Highway. You will find many designer-label retail outlets, high-end jewelry stores, and charming sidewalk cafes.
Birds of Paradise	Floral District	The Floral District offers exceptional values on fresh flowers, plants, and floral arrangements. Flowers and plants are locally grown.
Wellington Gardens	Mall	The Wellington Gardens Mall provides a luxury shopping experience with over 200 retail shops and 12 department stores. This mall is noted for its extraordinary boutiques, personal service, and upscale amenities.
Sew and Sew Fabrics	Textile District	Sew and Sew Fabrics houses over 150 vendors of fabrics and notions from around the world. Shoppers will find fabrics for apparel, crafts, and home décor.

## 14-d5

**Table**

hpc logo

Design a table for pet boarding fees.

1. Apply Landscape orientation. Insert the *hpc* logo at the top line and apply Square Text Wrapping. Tap TAB and key the title, *hpc*; apply Title style and Dark Red, Accent 1, Darker 25% font color.

2. Tap ENTER three times and create a 4-column, 8-row table and key the information shown in the table on the next page.

3. Change the text direction of the *Daily* and *Weekly Costs* headings to vertical; Align Bottom Center.

4. Sort the data in the *Daily Cost* column in ascending order.

5. Delete the *Doggie Day Camp* column.

6. Insert one column to the left of the *Weekly Cost* column and one to the right of it; change the text direction back to horizontal and key **Multiple Pets in Same Unit** for both column heads.

7. Adjust the width of columns A, C, and E to 2.3" and the width of columns B and D to 1".

8. In the first three rows under the *Multiple Pets in the Same Unit* headings (columns C and E), split the rows into two columns; key the following information:

   a. In the Standard Units row, key **Two** in the first split column and **Three** in the second. Do the same for the second split column.

   b. In the Small and Medium pet rows, key **45** and **50** for the daily costs for two pets and **50** and **55** for three pets.

   c. In the Small and Medium pet rows, key **225** and **250** for the weekly costs for two pets and **250** and **275** for three pets.

   d. In the *Large* row under both *Multiple Pets in Same Unit* columns, key **Not available**.

   e. In the three remaining rows under the *Multiple Pets in the Same Unit* columns, key **No extra charge**.

9. Add a row at the top of the table, merge the cells, and key **PET BOARDING FEES**.

10. Apply Grid Table 4 – Accent 1 table style. Apply Align Center and 16-point font to the heading.

11. Apply the following formats to the table:

    a. Deselect First Column in the Table Style Options group.

    b. Bold all headings in rows 2 and 3.

    c. In row 2, apply Align Center Left to the heading in column A, Align Center to columns C and E, and Align Bottom Center to columns B and D.

    d. Set row height at 0.8" for rows 1 and 2.

12. In rows 3–9, increase the row height to 0.3" and apply Align Center Left to the first column and Align Center to all other columns.

13. Compare your table to the Quick Check on the next page.

14. Proofread and check; click Next Activity (*14-d5*)

★ **TIP**

Align column heads at the left or center them in the column, whichever looks better.

1. Key the 3-column, 8-row table below. Your columns will be wider, so your text will not wrap as shown below.

2. Select cells C1–C8 and click Center. When all the items in a column are the same length, the column will look better centered.

3. Select cells A1 and B1 and click Center.

4. Proofread and check; click Log out to exit *KPDO*. (*38-d3*)

Movie Title	Time of Showing	Location
The Amazing Bionic Woman	1:15, 4:10, 7:10	Theatre 1
Global Warming: 3D	1:20, 6:25, 9:10	Theatre 2
The Hourglass	12:00, 2:30, 5:10, 7:45, 10:25	Theatre 3
The Circus Comes to Town: 3D	12:25, 2:40, 5:00, 7:40, 10:10	Theatre 4
Time Marches On	12:30, 3:30, 6:30, 9:30	Theatre 5
Humpty Dumpty's Great Fall	11:00, 1:40, 4:20, 7:10	Theatre 6
The Silver Knight: The IMAX	12:00, 3:30, 7:00, 10:30	Theatre 7

StockLite/Shutterstock.com

## ! WORKPLACE SUCCESS

### High-Tech Etiquette

In today's day and age, high-tech manners can be just as critical as dining etiquette in developing your professional image. Knowing the difference between Bluetooth and houndstooth is just as important as knowing how to host a business luncheon.

Improper or ill-timed use of new high-tech devices can destroy your professional image rather than enhance it. Using a smartphone may make you appear technically savvy; however, continually glancing at your device during a meeting is like checking your watch. It is considered rude and inappropriate behavior.

Cell phone usage should be limited during work hours. Some companies require that employees keep their cell phones in their car. If your company allows you to bring your cell phone to your desk, set it on vibrate. Do not walk around the office building talking on a cell phone; it annoys others and is not professional. If you work in a cubicle environment, be mindful that others can hear your conversation and that what you say may not be appropriate for coworkers to hear.

 Compare your announcement to the one shown below.

### Hess Pet Center
### Open House

All employees of the companies in Hess Office Park are cordially invited to join us any day Monday through Thursday, January 14–17, from 5:00 p.m. to 6:30 p.m. for refreshments and a tour of our new business in Hess Office Park. You will also have an opportunity to view our new plans to expand the veterinary clinic and to build additional boarding and day camp facilities.

Hess Pet Center offers:

- Complete veterinary services
- Hess Pet Boutique
- Pet grooming and spa
- Pet boarding
- Doggy day camp

We will custom tailor our hours to meet the needs of Hess Office Employees. In addition, all Hess Office Park employees will have an opportunity to sign up for a special Hess discount card to receive a 10 percent discount on all purchases at the Hess Pet Boutique and for all grooming, boarding, and day camp services this year.

You are welcome to bring family and friends with you to the Open House. We look forward to meeting all of our neighbors in Hess Office Park.

---

## 14-d4

**Compose Memo**

hpc memo form

Mr. Hess indicated to Mr. Schmidt and Dr. Faulk that March Walker, from his office, would be happy to email an announcement to all of the Hess Office Park employees for *hpc*. Compose the memo to her from you. The announcement will be attached.

1. Use the subject: **Please Distribute**; use **January 7, 201-** as the date.
2. Refer to the offer Mr. Hess made for March to assist with the distribution.
3. Indicate that the announcement is attached and to whom it should be distributed.
4. Show appreciation for her assistance and indicate that you hope she will attend.
5. Proofread and check; click Next Activity. (*14-d4*)

---

## ! WORKPLACE SUCCESS

Oberhaeuser/Caro/Alamy

### Click Fraud

Buyer or user beware is an appropriate term to remember anytime you use the Internet. Many companies advertise on the Internet and agree to pay the host an advertising fee based on the number of clicks or hits on their ad. To increase advertising fees and to make buyers believe the advertising is being viewed by numerous visitors, many unscrupulous hosts pay individuals to do nothing but click on the ad as quickly as they can. Some individuals are in foreign countries and some sites even have robots to click on the ads. The scam could have a very serious effect on the future of advertising on the Internet. Most buyers are willing to pay for legitimate prospects to view their ad, but not for scams.

# Lesson 39 Table Tools—Layout

**New Commands**

- Adjust Column Width
- Center Table on Page
- Change Cell Size
- Text Alignment in Cells

## Skill Building

**39b   Textbook Keying**

1. Key each line, concentrating on good keying techniques.
2. Repeat the drill if time permits.

t  1  it  cat  pat  to  top  thin  at  tilt  jolt  tuft  mitt  flat  test  tent  felt

r  2  fur  bur  try  roar  soar  ram  trap  rare  ripe  true  rear  tort  corral

t/r  3  The  track  star  was  triumphant  in  both  the  third  and  fourth  heats.

m  4  me mine memo mimic named clam month maximum mummy summer remember

n  5  no  snow  ton  none  nine  ninety  noun  mini  mind  minnow  kennel  evening

m/n  6  Men and women in management roles maximize time during commuting.

## New Commands

**39c**

### LAYOUT TAB

When you click in a table, the Table Tools tab displays with two tabs—the Design tab and the Layout tab. The Design tab contains commands for changing the appearance of the table. The Layout tab contains commands for altering the table structure.

### SELECT PORTIONS OF A TABLE

To alter the table structure, select the cells, column, or row that will be altered. Use the mouse to select the cells or the Select command on the Table Tools Layout tab to select parts of the table or the entire table.

*To use the Select command to select portions of a table:*
Table Tools Layout/Table/Select

1. Click the insertion point in a table cell; then display the Select options.

   a. Choose Select Cell to select only the cell the insertion point is in.

   b. Choose Select Column or Select Row to highlight the entire column or row that contains the cell.

   c. Choose Select Table to highlight the entire table.

also finalizing our plans for the boarding and day camp facilities to be built on the property that has now officially been annexed into Hess Office Park. As we agreed, we will move our grooming operation to that facility as soon as it is ready for occupancy. Doing so will provide a significant part of the extra space needed for the veterinary clinic. Our contractor tells us the type of facility needed can be constructed within a month.

Erin and I look forward to our meeting with you on Friday so that all of these details can be finalized. We also would like to spend some time with your marketing and business development staff to talk about ways we can promote Hess Pet Center to the many potential clients who are part of Hess Office Park.

## 14-d3

**Announcement**

 hpc logo

Drag the WordArt text box to the right of the logo and expand it to the right margin. The title will appear on two lines.

Mr. Schmidt asked you to key the Open House announcement, shown below, for all Hess Office Park employees. It will be distributed electronically.

1. Tap ENTER once and insert the *hpc* logo.
2. Insert WordArt, Fill – Black, Text 1, Outline – Background 1, Hard Shadow – Accent 1 WordArt. Apply Dark Red, Accent 1, Darker 50% font color. Position it on the right side of the logo and key the title.
3. Tap ENTER four times after the logo. Change font size to 14 point and Justify text.
4. Apply square bullets with Dark Red, Accent 1, Darker 50% font color to the five items *hpc* offers. Add a 1-point page border the same color as the bullets.
5. Review the Quick Check on the next page.
6. Proofread and check; click Next Activity. (*14-d3*)

Hess Pet Center | Open House

All employees of the companies in Hess Office Park are cordially invited to join us any day Monday through Thursday, January 14-17, from 5:00 p.m. to 6:30 p.m. for refreshments and a tour of our new business in Hess Office Park. You will also have an opportunity to view our new plans to expand the veterinary clinic and to build additional boarding and day camp facilities.

Hess Pet Center offers:

Complete veterinary services | Hess Pet Boutique | Pet grooming and spa | Pet boarding | Doggy day camp

We will custom tailor our hours to meet the needs of Hess Office Employees. In addition, all Hess Office Park employees will have an opportunity to sign up for a special Hess discount card to receive a 10 percent discount on all purchases at the Hess Pet Boutique, and for all grooming, boarding, and day camp services this year.

You are welcome to bring family and friends with you to the Open House. We look forward to meeting all of our neighbors in Hess Office Park.

*(continued)*

You can also select an entire table, a row, or a column by moving the mouse pointer to different locations on or near the table.

To select	Move the insertion point:
Entire table	Over the table and click the Table Move handle at the upper-left corner of the table. To move the table, drag the Table Move handle to a new location.
Column	To the top of the column until a solid down arrow (↓) appears; click the left mouse button.
Row	To the left area just outside the table until the pointer turns to an open diagonal arrow (↗); then click the left mouse button.

Cells can also be selected by clicking in the cell, holding down the mouse button, and dragging across or down.

## ADJUST COLUMN WIDTH

A new *Word* table extends from margin to margin when first created, with all columns the same width regardless of the width of the data in the columns. Some tables, however, would be more attractive and easier to read if the columns were narrower or adjusted to fit the data in the cells.

Use the AutoFit option on the Layout tab to adjust the width of a column to fit the widest entry in each column.

To adjust column width using AutoFit:
Table Tools Layout/Cell Size/AutoFit

1. Click a table cell.
2. Display the AutoFit options.
3. Select the desired option.

You can also change column width manually using the mouse. Using the mouse enables you to adjust the widths as you like. Columns look best when approximately 0.5" of blank space is left between the longest line and the column border.

---

**DRILL 1**     ADJUST COLUMN WIDTH USING AUTOFIT

Table Tools Layout/Cell Size/AutoFit

1. In the open document (*38-drill2*), click in the table.
2. Click AutoFit Contents. The columns adjust to fit the data.
3. Click AutoFit Window to restore the table to full size.

4. Place the insertion point in the last cell and tap TAB.
5. Key your name and **Administrative Assistant** in the last row.
6. Proofread and check; click Next Activity. (*39-drill1*)

This week I was offered and accepted an internship at the newly created Hess Pet Center, which is a joint venture between Dr. Erin Faulk, owner of Hess Pet Care, a veterinary clinic, and Mr. Douglas Schmidt, an entrepreneur. The new business integrates the veterinary clinic with a full-service luxury pet boarding, grooming, and boutique center.

This position offers me a great opportunity to work in an environment that I have learned about in my Small Business Management and Financial courses, while applying the word processing and document formatting skills I learned in your class. I will work with Dr. Faulk and Mr. Schmidt to develop standard operating procedures and to standardize the formats for letters, memos, reports, and table styles, for documents that are specifically related to the business. They both have indicated to me that they expect me to take full responsibility for my position and to expect very little direct supervision.

I have agreed to work for a minimum of six months for at least 10 hours per week, but I have the option to work as many as 25 hours a week. My plan is to average 20 hours per week. The type of position and the number of hours worked meet and exceed all of the requirements for receiving academic credit for my internship. Dr. Faulk and Mr. Schmidt have agreed to evaluate my work and complete the required forms for the internship. Therefore, I respectfully request that you approve this internship for academic credit.

Please let me know if you need additional information.

## 14-d2

**Letter**

 hpc letterhead

Mr. Schmidt asked you to prepare the following letter to **Mr. Patrick J. Hess, Manager | Hess Office Park | 100 Hess Boulevard | Austin, TX 78712-2149** with a copy to Dr. Faulk. Use only the DVM title after her name for copies.

All of the information you need to prepare the letter is contained in the SOPs. After you have completed the document, proofread and check; click Next Activity. (*14-d2*)

This letter confirms that Erin Faulk and I have finalized our joint venture, Hess Pet Center, and will begin our operations today. We especially appreciate being able to use the Hess name as part of our brand. It gives us instant credibility and name recognition, especially with all of the employees in companies located in Hess Office Park and with residents of the surrounding neighborhoods.

Signing a long-term lease provided us with the security and the incentive that we needed to invest heavily in this venture. Our architect is reviewing the plans you submitted for the expansion of the veterinary clinic. He is

*(continued)*

**To adjust column widths using the mouse:**

1. Point to the column border that needs adjusting.

2. When the pointer changes to ⊷, hold down the left mouse button and drag the border to the left to make the column narrower or to the right to make it wider.

3. Adjust the column widths appropriately. Leave approximately 0.5" to 0.75" between the longest line and the border. Use the Horizontal Ruler as a guide.

4. The widths of the columns can be displayed by pointing to the column marker on the Ruler, holding down the ALT key, and clicking the left mouse button.

Column width ⟶

Column marker ⟶

Point to the column border and hold down the left mouse button to display the dotted line ⟶

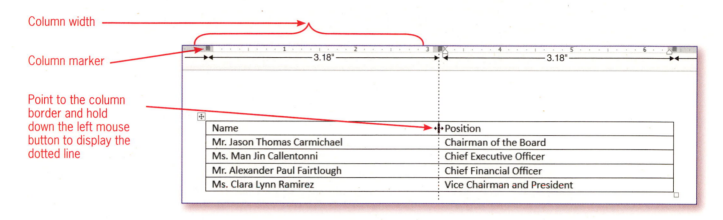

Name	Position
Mr. Jason Thomas Carmichael	Chairman of the Board
Ms. Man Jin Callentonni	Chief Executive Officer
Mr. Alexander Paul Fairtlough	Chief Financial Officer
Ms. Clara Lynn Ramirez	Vice Chairman and President

## CENTER TABLE HORIZONTALLY

Once column widths have been adjusted, a table will no longer be full-page width. Use the Table Properties dialog box to center the table horizontally on the page.

To center table horizontally on page:
Table Tools Layout/Table/Properties

1. Click in a table cell.

2. Open the Table Properties dialog box.

3. On the Table tab, select Center.

 **TIP**

Another method of centering a table horizontally is to click the Table Move handle to select the table and then click the Center button on the Home tab.

---

**DRILL 2**   ADJUST COLUMN WIDTH AND CENTER TABLE

1. In the open document (*39-drill1*), click in the table.

2. Use the mouse to adjust column borders. Leave approximately 0.5" between the longest line and the right border.

3. Center the table horizontally on the page.

4. Proofread and check; click Next Activity. (*39-drill2*)

---

The primary goals are to maintain the current clients of Faulk Pet Care and to develop new business from the numerous employees in Hess Office Park and the surrounding upscale residential neighborhoods.

Legal and financial consultants have finalized the formal documents for the new joint-venture business. Dr. Faulk and Mr. Schmidt hired you as a part-time intern to help with the office work.

## STANDARD OPERATING PROCEDURES (SOPs)

Dr. Faulk has talked with you about setting up and following standard operating procedures, which are important in creating a consistent image and establishing the corporate brand. SOPs can enhance productivity and provide employees with access to information needed to work independently.

1. Preview and proofread each document you prepare.
2. Use the Hess Pet Center letterhead and memo form from the data files for letters and memos. Do not prepare envelopes. In this office, most documents are distributed as attachments to email.
3. Apply the Ion theme with Casual document formatting style to all documents. The letterhead and memo form already have this style applied.
4. Use the current date for all documents requiring a date unless directed otherwise; position it at 2.5" or two blank lines below the letterhead.
5. Use block letter format with open punctuation as the standard style.
6. Use *Dear* + the title and last name as the salutation unless directed otherwise. The partners use first names for individuals they know well.
7. Use the following closing lines spaced appropriately:

   **Sincerely**
   **Douglas C. Schmidt, Managing Partner**
   **Retail and Service Operations**

   **Sincerely**
   **Erin A. Faulk, DVM, Manager Partner**
   **Veterinary Operations**

8. Use first names on memos you prepare for Mr. Schmidt and Dr. Faulk.
9. Save all documents as *14-d* + the document number.
10. As a shortcut, employees often use *hpc* for Hess Pet Center; always spell it out in documents.

### TIP
Use these procedures as a checklist for each document you prepare.

### TIP
Save the formatted closing lines and your reference initials as a Quick Part to save keying time and increase productivity.

## 14-d1

**Memo**

 hpc memo form

1. Prepare a memo from you to **Dr. Lynn F. Hudson**.
2. Use the subject: **Request for Internship Credit**.
3. Key the memo on the next page.
4. Proofread and check; click Next Activity. (*14-d1*)

### TIP
Do not add your initials to the memo since you are preparing it for yourself.

## CHANGE CELL SIZE

Cell Size

The Cell Size group on the Layout tab allows you to set cell height and width to exact dimensions. The height of a row is often increased to provide some blank space above and below the text to make the contents in the cell easier to read.

To change cell height or width:

Table Tools Layout/Cell Size

- Click in the cell or column and then key the dimension in the Height box or use the spin arrows to set the height dimension.
- Select the cell or row and then key the dimension in the Width box or use the spin arrows to set the width dimension.

---

## CHANGE TEXT ALIGNMENT IN CELL

Table Tools Layout/Alignment

Alignment

By default, text displays left aligned at the top of the cell. When cell height is increased, text may need to be centered vertically in the cell to make the table more attractive.

Commands in the Alignment group allow text to be aligned at the top, middle, or bottom of the cell. You can also align text at the left, middle, or right of the cell. Select the button that provides the best combination of vertical and horizontal alignment.

To change the alignment of the text in the cell, select the cell(s) and click the appropriate alignment command.

---

## DRILL 3      ADJUST CELL HEIGHT AND WIDTH

1. In the open document (*38-d1*), select column A. Change the width of the column to 2.2".

2. Select column B. Change the width of column B to 1.4".

3. Select column C. Change the width of column C 1.5".

4. Select row 1. Change the height of row 1 to 0.3".

5. Align Center the column heads in row 1.

6. Apply bold to the column heads.

7. Center the table horizontally on the page.

8. Proofread and check; click Next Activity. (*39-drill3*)

# Hess Pet Center I

Lessons 81–83   *Hess Pet Center I*

- Apply keying, formatting, and word processing skills.
- Work independently with few instructions.

**Warmup**   *Lesson 81a Warmup*

A   **ALL LETTERS**

## Skill Building

**81b   Timed Writing**

Key two 3' timed writings.
Strive for control.

You have most likely heard it said that people would rather die than speak before a group. To assist in overcoming this fear, many experts recommend preparation. Spending a large amount of time preparing will result in big dividends. Select a topic you like and research it completely, know your audience, and practice before a mirror and in front of a group of friends.

Finally, presenting with ease requires an excellent knowledge of technology. Come to the room early to open the show and to practice in the presentation room. Determine which key to press to jump to the next slide or to move to a previous position. Know how to move to an exact position in the show. Practice these success skills and prepare your next presentation with zeal and confidence.

## Project Setting

### HESS PET CENTER

**Hess Pet Center**

186 Hess Boulevard, Austin, TX 78712-2149
Telephone 512.555.PETS (7387) | Fax 512.555.7378 | www.hesspetcenter.com

Welcome to Hess Pet Center—a new joint venture between a veterinarian, Dr. Erin A. Faulk, and an entrepreneur, Mr. Douglas C. Schmidt. Dr. Faulk owns Faulk Pet Care, which offers a wide range of services to dog owners. Mr. Schmidt owns a 10-acre outparcel adjacent to Hess Office Park and is making an investment in Hess Pet Center.

The leased building has adequate facilities for the offices, boutique, grooming area, and most of the Veterinary Clinic. Mr. Schmidt has an agreement with Hess Office Park to expand the space for the Veterinary Clinic and to use the outparcel to build additional boarding and pet day camp facilities so that it will not be disruptive to other tenants of Hess Office Park.

## 39-d1

**Create Table, Adjust Cell Height and Width, and Center Horizontally**

1. Key the table below.
2. Adjust the width of column A to 1.95". Adjust the width of column B to 1.5". Adjust the width of column C to 1.15".
3. Center the table horizontally on the page.
4. Adjust the height of row 1 to 0.3". Align Center and bold the column heads.
5. Proofread and check; click Next Activity. (*39-d1*)

Award Winners	Department	Amount
Lorianna Mendez	Accounting	$2,000
William Mohammed	Marketing	$800
Cynthia Khek	Engineering	$1,500
Charles Pham	Purchasing	$1,000

## 39-d2

**Create Table, Adjust Cell Sizes**

1. Key the table; adjust column width so that the text does not wrap to a second line.
2. Center columns B and D. Right-align the values in column C.
3. Adjust Cell Size height to 0.3" for the entire table. Center the text vertically in the cells. Align Center and bold the column heads. Center the table horizontally.
4. Proofread and check. (*39-d2*)
5. Click Log out to exit *KPDO*.

Book Title	Publication	Sales	Unit Price
*Computer Crimes*	2014	$478,769.00	$69.50
*Digital Data Forensics*	2014	$91,236.00	$63.00
*Computer Criminology*	2014	$89,412.50	$75.50
*Law and Ethics in Computer Crimes*	2015	$104,511.00	$93.50
*Role of Operating Systems in Computer Forensics*	2015	$194,137.50	$83.50

Prepare the main document and data source for a form letter to participants of a summer workshop. You will need to edit your data source after you create it.

1. In the open document (*80-d2main*), create the data source as shown below (*80-d2datasource*).

Field names	Record 1	Record 2	Record 3
Title	Mr.	Ms.	Ms.
First Name	Phillip	Anele	Anna
Last Name	Lancaster	Nyiri	Skelton
Address Line 1	35 Wallace Circle	16060 Aspen Road	1355 Palomino Drive
City	Norfolk	Richmond	Richmond
State	VA	VA	VA
ZIP Code	23501-3849	27173-5721	27173-0616
Date	June 15-16	June 23-24	June 23-24
Room	204	205	205

2. Move Ms. Skelton to the June 15-16 workshop. Change Mr. Lancaster's address to **89 Castle Road**.

3. Key the main document (block style with open punctuation style) and insert the merge fields. Key the date as **May 1, 201-**. Add notations as needed. Save the changes.

4. Sort by ZIP Code in ascending order. Filter to select only the participants attending the June 15-16 workshop. For the Address Block, remove space after paragraphs when the letters are previewed.

5. Preview, proofread, and complete the merge.

6. Check the test and close. (*80-d2*)

<<AddressBlock>>

Dear <<First_Name>>:

I am delighted you will be attending the STEM Workshop on <<Date>> at Braswell Community College. Please arrive at Room <<Room>> of the Harper-Kock Union Building at 8 a.m. for registration and a brief orientation.

Directions to Hathorn Hall, the residence hall designated for summer workshop participants, are enclosed. You may check in at Hathorn from 8 a.m. to 10 p.m. Housing payment can be made at the residence hall.

<<First_Name>>, should you have any questions about the workshop, please call me at 540.555.0123. I look forward to your being a part of our workshop series.

Sincerely | Jane D. Gunter | Workshop Coordinator

# Lesson 40 Change Table Structure

**New Commands**
- Insert and Delete Columns and Rows
- Merge and Split Cells

## Skill Building

**40b  Textbook Keying**

1. Key each line concentrating on good keying techniques.
2. Repeat the drill if time permits.

d   1   do did dad sad faded daddy madder diddle deduced hydrated dredged

k   2   keys sake kicked karat kayak karate knock knuckle knick kilometer

d/k   3   The ten tired and dizzy kids thought the doorknob was the donkey.

w   4   we were who away whew snow windward waterway window webworm award

o   5   on to too onto solo oleo soil cook looked location emotion hollow

w/o   6   Those who know their own power and are committed will follow through.

b   7   be bib sub bear book bribe fiber bombard blueberry babble baboons

v   8   vet vat van viva have over avoid vapor valve seven vanish vanilla

b/v   9   Bo gave a very big beverage and seven coins to everybody bowling.

r   10   or rear rare roar saturate reassure rather northern surge quarrel

u   11   yours undue unity useful unique unusual value wound youth succumb

r/u   12   The truth of the matter is that only Ruth can run a rummage sale.

## New Commands

**40c**

### INSERT A COLUMN OR ROW

A row can be inserted in a table by placing the mouse pointer at the left edge of the table and pointing to the position where the new row is to be inserted. If you need to add a row below Lorianna Mendez, in the illustration below, place the insertion on the border between Lorianna Mendez and William Mohammed. Click the plus symbol to insert a new row. If more than one row is to be inserted, first select the number of rows, place the insertion point where the new rows will be inserted, then click the plus symbol.

Award Winners	Department	Amount
Lorianna Mendez	Accounting	$2,000
William Mohammed	Marketing	$800
Cynthia Khek	Engineering	$1,500
Charles Pham	Purchasing	$1,000

## Economic Conditions

Similar economic conditions exist in the three market regions. Leading economic indicators in all three regions support the conclusion that the economy is growing slowly and at a sustainable rate. The unemployment rate in the three areas ranges from 4.1% to 4.4%, explaining the gradual increase in wages in all three areas. Demand for temporary services remains strong. Demand may even increase as employers hesitate to fill permanent positions until the economy improves significantly. Unemployment is predicted to remain under 5% for the next six to twelve months. ← Insert footnote

## Wage Survey

The wage survey focused on the three broad categories of jobs that Marcus specializes in providing temporary workers—computer specialists, office assistants, and healthcare services. Approximately fifty separate job titles were analyzed as part of this study. Complete data for all of the specific jobs that were analyzed can be accessed from the detailed report that is available on the human resources website. The standard access restrictions apply to these data.

Careful analysis of the data is needed to determine if the rates Marcus charges employers need to be adjusted in any of the specific job categories. Virtually all of the office assistant and legal assistant positions required knowledge of word processing, spreadsheet, presentation, database, and personal information management software. The few positions that did not list this requirement had significantly lower pay rates.

## Job Growth

The predicted growth of jobs in many positions in which Marcus supplies employees is much higher than previously estimated. The current plan for hiring workers will not meet the predicted demand in any of the three market areas. Further analysis of the data collected is warranted before making any adjustments in the hiring plan. Although the data collection design matches the design used in the previous surveys, the changing market situation may require some modification in the data collection methodology to verify these high growth rates.

## Conclusions

Market conditions make it feasible to raise the hourly rates Marcus charges employers in many categories. However, it is also evident that Marcus will have to increase the wages paid to its staff of temporary workers in order to retain the quality of worker required to meet market demand.

If further analysis supports the job growth data presented, significant changes must be made in the strategic plan for all regions. The current strategic plan for Marcus is based on a much lower growth rate than this study shows.

A column can be inserted using the same process. Move the mouse pointer above the table and point to the border where the new column is to be inserted; then click the plus symbol.

Award Winners	Department	Amount
Lorianna Mendez	Accounting	$2,000
William Mohammed	Marketing	$800
Cynthia Khek	Engineering	$1,500
Charles Pham	Purchasing	$1,000

## DRILL 1     INSERT ROW AND COLUMN

1. In the open document (*38-drill2*), insert a row following Ms. Man Jin Callentonni.

2. Key **Mr. Frederick Douglas, Compliance Committee Chair** in the blank row.

3. Insert a column between columns A and B.

4. Key: **Extension | 5278 | 4902 | 2561 | 9302 | 3715.**

5. Center the text in column B.

6. Align Center the column heads in row 1.

7. Apply bold to the column heads.

8. Adjust column width and center the table horizontally on the page.

9. Proofread and check; click Next Activity. (*40-drill1*)

## INSERT AND DELETE ROWS AND COLUMNS USING TABLE TOOLS

Rows and columns can also be inserted or deleted by using commands on the Table Tools Layout tab.

To insert rows or columns in a table:

Table Tools Layout/Rows & Columns

1. Position the insertion point where the new row or column is to be inserted. If several rows or columns are to be inserted, select the number you want to insert.

2. In the Rows & Columns group, click the appropriate command.

To delete rows or columns in a table:

Table Tools Layout/Rows & Columns/Delete

1. Position the insertion point in the row or column that is to be deleted. If more than one row or column is to be deleted, select them first.

2. Display the Delete options and select the appropriate command.

# Lesson 80 Assessment Modules 12 and 13

## Apply It

### 80-d1

**Leftbound Report**

 **TIP**

Remember to proofread and preview each document for placement before you move to the next one.

1. Key the report that starts below and continues to page 390. Format the report as a leftbound report. Apply the Retrospect document theme and apply appropriate styles to the title and headings.

2. Insert the Retrospect cover page and add the following information:

   Document title: See report title below; shrink font so title fits on one line

   Subtitle: **Three Market Regions**

   Author: **Livia Baresi**

   Company: **Marcus Employment Services**

   Address: **39 East Ridgewater Nook, Destin, FL 32541-3933**

3. Insert the following content footnote at the end of the second paragraph.

   [1] **Employment statistics provided by Phil Tidwell**.

4. Insert a blank page after the cover page for the table of contents you will generate in step 10.

5. Position the insertion point at the top of the first page of the report and insert a Continuous section break.

6. Click in the footer of the second page of Section 1 and insert a page number at the bottom of the page using the Plain Number 2 page number style. Change the page number format to lowercase Roman numerals. Start number at ii.

7. Click Go to Header and click Next twice to position the insertion point in the header of Section 2. Deselect Different First Page if it is selected. Break the links between the headers for both sections. Go to the footer of Section 2. Break the link between the footers for both sections. Delete the page number in the Section 2 footer.

8. Go to header of Section 2 and number the pages of the report at the top right using the Banded header style.

9. Go to footer of Section 2 and insert the Retrospect footer style. Change the page number format to begin with page 1. Click Different First Page to suppress the header and footer on the first page of the report.

10. Position the insertion point on the blank page left for the table of contents (not in the header section). Generate the table of contents using the Automatic Table 2 style. Position the heading at approximately 2" and apply Title style. Click ENTER after the TOC title to leave a blank line.

11. Add **Prediction** to the *Job Growth* heading. Update the table of contents.

12. Continue to the next document. (*80-d1*)

Regional Employment Analysis

The Executive Committee of Marcus Employment Services requested an analysis of the labor market in three service regions. Previous studies show that these three regions are representative of the total market Marcus serves.

*(continued)*

1. In the open document, insert the following rows so that the items are in correct alphabetical order.

Connors, Margaret	South	$87,560
Roberts, George	East	$97,850
Zales, Laura	West	$93,500

2. Delete the row containing Hoang, Thomas.

3. Insert a column between columns B and C and key the following entries in the column.

**Office**
**Wilshire**

**Toledo**
**Lake Forest**
**Tampa**
**Las Vegas**
**Boston**
**Chicago**
**San Francisco**

4. Left-align cells C2–C9. Click in column C and change the column width to 1.3" so that *San Francisco* does not wrap.

5. Proofread and check; click Next Activity. (*40-drill2*)

## MERGE AND SPLIT CELLS

Merging is the process of combining two or more table cells located in the same row or column into a single cell. Cells can be joined horizontally or vertically. For example, you can merge several cells horizontally to create a table heading row that spans several columns. A cell or several selected cells can be divided into multiple cells and columns by using the Split Cells feature.

**To merge cells:**

Table Tools Layout/Merge/Merge Cells

1. Select the cells that are to be merged.
2. Click Merge Cells to merge the selected cells.

**To split cells:**

Table Tools Layout/Merge/Split Cells

1. Click in the cell that is to be divided into multiple cells. If multiple cells are to be split, select them.
2. Display Split Cells dialog box.
3. Key the number of columns or rows that the selected cells are to be split into.

## 79-d1
**continued**

We ask you to please sign the enclosed rent agreement and return it by December 15. Please let me know if you have questions concerning the new agreement. We look forward to continuing to serve you in the first-rate manner that you have come to enjoy.

## 79-d2
**Envelopes**

1. Create the envelopes for the form letters created in *79-d1*. Sort by Last Name in ascending order (*79-d2envelopes*).
2. Proofread, complete the merge, and check; click Next Activity. (*79-d2*)

## 79-d3
**Edit Form Letter**

Mr. Hess just added another person to the list of short-term renters receiving rent increases beginning January 1. You must add a new record to the data source (*79-d1datasource*) and create the form letter for this one company.

**Mr. James Garcia**

**Iotasecond, Limited**

**100 Hess Boulevard, Suite 2199**

**Austin, TX 78712-3111**

Current rent: **5,500**

New rent: **6,000**

1. In the open document (*79-d1main*), add the new record.
2. Filter the data source and merge to generate the one new letter.
3. Add an envelope to the letter generated.
4. Proofread, complete the merge, and check; click Next Activity. (*79-d3*)

## 79-d4
**Compose Memo**

 hess memo

Compose a memo to the Conference Room Reservation Staff and Hess Office Park Copy Center Director informing them of the new complimentary services being provided to the four short-term renters.

1. Explain that the Board of Directors approved the new services to the short-term renters effective January 1, 201-.
2. Include the specific services that will be complimentary to these renters. Refer to the letter in *79-d1* for details.
3. In a table, list the company name and contact person of the four short-term renters approved. List in alphabetical order by company name.
4. Proofread the document. Check and close. Click Exit *Word*. (*79-d4*)
5. Click Log out to exit *KPDO*.

*Learn More*

www.cengagebrain.com

1. Create a 2-column, 5-row table.

2. Merge the cells in row 1; key the main heading in uppercase 14-point bold font. Change the height of row 1 to 0.4".

3. Key **Course Name** in cell A2 and **Enrollment Figures** in cell B2.

4. Select cells B3–B5; split these cells into two columns and three rows. Key **Undergraduates** in cell B3 and **Graduates** in cell C3. Key the rest of the table as shown.

5. Select cells A2 and A3; merge the cells. Select all the headings and apply Align Center. Bold all column heads.

6. Right-align all numbers.

7. Adjust column width and center table horizontally.

8. Proofread and check; click Next Activity. (*40-drill3*)

FINAL SEAT COUNT		
Course Name	Enrollment Figures	
	Undergraduates	Graduates
English Reading and Composition	12,875	97
Medical Microbiology	782	1,052

## Apply It

### 40-d1

**Insert Column/Row and Merge**

1. In the open document (*39-d1*), insert the following column between columns B and C.

   **Division**
   **Commercial**
   **Space Shuttle**
   **Military**
   **Commercial**

2. Insert a blank row above row 1. Merge the cells in row 1. Key **SAFETY AWARDS** in 14-point font and apply bold.

3. Change the height of row 1 to 0.4". Use Align Center to center the text in rows 1 and 2.

4. Proofread and check; click Next Activity. (*40-d1*)

### 40-d2

**Insert and Delete Rows**

1. In the open document (*40-d1*), insert a row after Lorianna Mendez and add the following information:

   **Robert Ruiz | Research | Military | $2,250**

2. Insert a row at the end of the table and add the following information:

   **Frank Cousins | Security | Space Shuttle | $500**

3. Delete the row for William Mohammed.

4. Proofread and check; click Next Activity. (*40-d2*)

hess letterhead

The first assignment is to send a form letter to four short-term renters informing them of an increase in their rent. Send a copy to **Jayden Mason**.

1. Prepare the main document (*79-d1main*) and key the following information in the data source (*79-d1datasource*).

Field names	Record 1	Record 2	Record 3
Title	Ms.	Mr.	Ms.
First Name	Maryanne	Tim	Chan
Last Name	Fair	Drechsler	Chao
Company Name	Zisusu Company	Voxihi, LLC	Rivcu Company
Address Line 1	100 Hess Boulevard, Suite 3105	100 Hess Boulevard, Suite 2619	100 Hess Boulevard, Suite 2061
City	Austin	Austin	Austin
State	TX	TX	TX
ZIP Code	78712-2149	78712-3893	78712-8333
Current rent	3,000	4,000	6,000
New rent	3,500	4,500	6,750

2. Sort by Last Name in ascending order.

3. Proofread, complete the merge, and check; click Next Activity. (*79-d1*)

We are very appreciative of the fine short-term renters who have chosen to be a part of Hess Office Park, and our goal is to provide the best services possible to our tenants. We are very fortunate to be located in a beautiful 5,000-acre wooded area that is a perfect backdrop for our businesses. The large conference center, day care center, pet center, and copy center are nice amenities that make the office park one of the best in the region.

After careful financial analysis, our Board of Directors has determined a slight rent increase is necessary to offset increases in energy and maintenance costs of the property. Beginning January 1, it will be necessary to adjust your rent from the current rate of $<<Current rent>> to a new rate of $<<New Rent>>. However, as a way of showing our appreciation of your business, Hess Office Park is extending two new benefits as part of the new rental agreement.

First, you will have a two-day complimentary access per month to the beautiful conference room located in the Hess Office Park conference center. This room includes a large conference table that accommodates 20 people and a spacious adjoining kitchen for preparing breaks and meal functions. Reservations should be requested at least one month in advance. Second, you will receive up to 1,000 complimentary black and white copies per month at our copy center in the Hess Office Park suite.

*(continued)*

## 40-d3

**Insert and Delete Columns and Rows**

1. In the open document (*39-d2*), delete column D (*Unit Price*).

2. Insert a new column between columns A and B.

3. Key the text below in the new column. Align Center the column head and align the remainder of the column with Align Center Left.

   **Publisher**
   **Bodwin**
   **American**
   **TWSS**
   **Bodwin**
   **TWSS**

4. Insert a new row above *Law and Ethics in Computer Crimes* and add the following information:

   **Digital Data Analysis Tools | American | 2014 | $9,675.95**

5. Insert a blank row above row 1; merge the cells in the new row. Key **OXFORD LEARNING SYSTEMS** in 14-point font and apply bold. Change the row height to 0.4" and center the text vertically and horizontally in the cell.

6. Proofread, finalize, and check the document. (*40-d3*)

## Communication

### ABBREVIATIONS

**40d**

References/Communication
Skills/Abbreviations

abbreviations

1. Complete the Abbreviations exercise in *KPDO*.

2. Review the guidelines on abbreviations in the *abbreviations* data file.

3. In the *Corrected* column, key a corrected copy of the text in the *Original* column, applying the abbreviation guidelines.

4. Add a row above row 1 of the Application table and merge the cells. Key the main heading, **USING ABBREVIATIONS CORRECTLY**, in 14-point bold font. Change the height of row 1 to 0.4". Center the main heading vertically and horizontally in the row.

5. Change the height of row 2 to 0.25" and apply bold to the headings. Center the text vertically and horizontally in the row.

6. Proofread and check; click Exit *Word*. (*40-d*)

7. Click Log out to exit *KPDO*.

# Lesson 79 Hess Office Park

## Skill Building

### 79b  Timed Writing

1. Key a 1' timing on each paragraph; work to increase speed.
2. Key a 3' timing on all paragraphs.

Still a major trend in the workplace today is telecommuting. In fact, millions of workers own home-based businesses or work for a business from home. This number of workers grows each year with companies of all sizes hiring workers who will work from home offices.

Why do workers choose to telecommute? Reasons include reducing stress of rush hour traffic, being flexible to balance family and work time, and being able to work when they work best. Workers often find an increase in work done because of fewer stops to answer the telephone or talk to another person.

Working successfully from home requires new considerations. Of course, it is obvious that technology needs must be in place in the home office. Yes, the worker must have a home office, one that is separate from the rest of the house. He or she must set a daily routine and request that family respects the new freedom and knows the work performance that is expected to be achieved.

## Project Setting

### HESS OFFICE PARK

You are continuing your work as an assistant to Patrick J. Hess, the manager of Hess Office Park, the 500-acre office park managed by Hess Property Enterprises.

You will use mail merge to create a form letter and envelopes to the short-term renters of Hess Office Park. Updating the short-term renters' database is another important responsibility that you are assigned.

Use November 15, 201- as the date for all documents in this project.

**Standard operating procedures for the project:**

1. Use the Retrospect document theme for all documents.
2. Use block letter style with open punctuation and the Hess Office Park letterhead from the data files. Include an appropriate salutation and use **Sincerely** as the complimentary closing. Begin the data at approximately 2". Use **Patrick J. Hess, Manager** as the writer's name and title.
3. The data files also contain a Hess Office Park memo form. Use an appropriate subject line if a subject line is not provided.
4. Add your reference initials and other notations as appropriate.
5. Use the List Table 4 – Accent 2 table style for all tables and center tables horizontally.
6. Use mail merge to create form letters and envelopes.

# Lesson 41 Table Tools—Design

## New Commands

- Table Styles
- Memos with Tables
- Letters with Tables

A ▸ ALL LETTERS

## Skill Building

### 41b Timed Writing

Key two 3' timed writings.

I have an interesting story or two that will transport you to faraway places, to meet people you have never known, to see things you have only fantasized, to experience things that you thought would only be a figment of everyone's imagination.

I can help you master appropriate skills you desire and need. I can inspire, excite, instruct, challenge, and entertain you. I answer your questions. I work with you to realize a talent, to express a thought, and to determine who you really are and desire to become.

I am your online library. My digital format provides easy and fast access from most places in the world as long as you have a computer and an Internet connection. You can use the library any hour of the day or evening; I do not close. You will never have a problem with a book being checked out, as books in an online library are available to many users simultaneously. You can quickly search for information in my vast collection using my information retrieval software. Use any search term, such as a word, phrase, title, name, or subject, to quickly find needed information.

## New Commands

### 41c

### DESIGN TAB

After a table is created, it needs to be formatted to make it more attractive and enhance its readability. Table design features can be accessed by clicking in the table and then clicking the Design tab. The Design tab is divided into three groups: Table Style Options, Table Styles, and Borders.

### TABLE STYLES

*Microsoft Word* has preformatted table styles that you can use to make your tables more attractive. The styles contain a combination of font attributes, colors, shading, and borders to enhance the appearance of a table.

opportunity to enter your name in a drawing for a complimentary laser vision correction procedure to be presented at the close of the seminar.

Would you like to join the millions of people who have chosen laser vision correction and be free of the daily hassles of glasses and contact lenses? Get started today by completing the enclosed reservation card indicating you will attend the seminar on <<Date>> and learn for yourself the details of laser vision correction.

Sincerely | Edward S. Vickery, M.D. | xx | Enclosure

3. Sort by Last Name in ascending order and then First Name in ascending order. Merge the data source and the main document.

4. Proofread and check; click Next Activity. (78-d1)

---

## 78-d2

**Edit Data Source**

1. In the open document (78-d1main), edit the data source as follows.
   - Invite Dr. Karen Wiseman to the February 25 seminar.
   - Ms. Mary Wiseman's new address is **235 N. Fifth Street, Omak, WA 98841-3592**.

2. Add two new records for the February 25 seminar.

   **Mrs. Darlene Chism**          **Mr. James Lee**

   **830 Yorkville Street**         **332 Matilda Road**

   **Tonasket, WA 98855-1251**     **Omak, WA 98841-2028**

3. Filter to select records of patients invited to the February 25 seminar. Preview and proofread.

4. Complete the merge and check; click Next Activity. (78-d2)

---

## 78-d3

**Envelopes**

Prepare envelopes for all the patients invited to the February 25 laser vision correction seminar.

1. In the open document (78-d3envelopes), prepare envelopes for the records stored in the data source 78-d1datasource.

2. Filter appropriately and sort by Last Name and then First Name.

3. Proofread, complete the merge, and check; click Next Activity. (78-d3)

---

## 78-d4

**Name Badges**

1. In the open document (78-d4labels), prepare name badges (Avery 5095) for the records stored in the data source 78-d1datasource. Include the First Name and Last Name fields on the name badge. Sort by Last Name and First Name in ascending order. Change font to Arial 14-point and center.

2. Click Update all labels.

3. Proofread, complete the merge, and check; click Exit *Word*. (78-d4)

4. Click Log out to exit *KPDO*.

Table styles are located in the Table Styles group on the Design tab. As you move the mouse over each style, you will also see your table formatted in that style. A ToolTip also displays with the name of the style. Click the More button to display the entire list of styles.

The styles are arranged in three groups: Plain Tables display at the top, Grid Tables follow, and List Tables display at the bottom.

More button

**Table Styles**

Table styles can be modified by selecting and deselecting options in the Table Style Options group of the Table Tools Design tab. For example, if you choose a table style that places extra emphasis on the header row and you do not want the first row emphasized, you can deselect Header Row to remove the formatting.

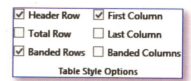

## To apply table styles:

Table Tools Design/Table Styles

1. Click in the table to display the Table Tools tabs.

2. Click the More button to display the Table Styles gallery.

3. Move the mouse pointer over each table style until you find the desired one. Use the scroll bar, if needed, to view all available styles.

List Table 4 - Accent 2

4. Click a style to apply it to the table.

5. Adjust Table Style options, if necessary.

6. Recenter the table horizontally after applying a style.

Modify Table Style...

Clear

New Table Style...

ToolTip displays style name

---

**DRILL 1**      **TABLE STYLES AND STYLE OPTIONS**       styles

1. Click in the table and display the Table Styles gallery.

2. Apply Grid Table 2 – Accent 1 style. (*Hint:* Grid table styles display as the second group.)

3. Insert a row at the end of the table. Key **Total** in cell A8. Key **$581,700** in cell C8.

4. Click the Total Row checkbox in the Table Styles Options group so that additional formatting will be applied to the total row.

5. Remove the check mark from the First Column checkbox to change the look of the first column.

6. Center the table horizontally on the page.

7. Proofread and check; click Next Activity. (*41-drill1*)

1. Follow the directions provided on the previous page to prepare address labels for the data source file *76-drill1datasource*. *Hint:* Click Remove Space Before Paragraph after inserting the Address Block.

2. Click Update all labels.

3. Proofread and check; click Next Activity. (*78-drill3*)

## Apply It

**78-d1**

**Mail Merge**

The Holland Eye Center is hosting two seminars to inform its patients about laser vision correction. Prepare the form letters for the records shown below.

1. In the open document (*78-d1main*), create the data source (*78-d1datasource*).

Field names	Record 1	Record 2	Record 3
Title	Mr.	Dr.	Ms.
First Name	Angelo	Karen	Mary
Last Name	Seay	Wiseman	Wiseman
Address Line 1	P.O. Box 88	137 Sonoma Drive	539 Swoope Avenue
City	Tonasket	Omak	Tonasket
State	WA	WA	WA
ZIP Code	98855-3918	98841-0174	98855-8096
Date	January 31	January 31	February 25

2. Key the main document and insert the merge fields in it. Use block letter style with open punctuation. Save the changes. (**Note:** The date should update automatically.)

**TIP**

When previewing letters at the end of the merge job, select the first two lines of the letter address and remove the extra spacing after paragraph.

<<AddressBlock>>

<<GreetingLine>>

Do you ever imagine being able to see the alarm clock when you wake up? Do you ever imagine no more hassles of daily contact lens maintenance? Perhaps you may have imagined playing your favorite sport with complete peripheral vision—no fogging or slipping glasses. Millions of people across the world have chosen laser vision correction as an alternative to glasses and contact lenses. They now are enjoying these freedoms that you have only imagined. The Holland Eye Center invites you to attend a special seminar sponsored for our patients who are potential candidates for laser vision correction. This seminar held at our clinic on <<Date>> at 7 p.m. will feature a panel of doctors and patients and a live laser vision correction procedure. A question/answer period will also provide an opportunity to have all your questions answered by these laser vision correction experts. You'll also have an

*(continued)*

## POSITION A TABLE IN A DOCUMENT

In previous lessons, you worked with stand-alone tables, or tables that are introduced by a simple heading and/or subheading. In the business world, however, tables are frequently inserted within documents. A table showing sales by quarter may be inserted in a memo on annual sales, for example, or a table showing items ordered may be included with a purchase confirmation.

When inserting a table into a document, care must be taken to provide the same amount of space below the table as above the table. *Word*'s default Normal style inserts an 8-point space after a paragraph and uses 1.08 line spacing. However, *Word* defaults to single spacing in a table with no spacing after a paragraph. Therefore, when a table is keyed within a document, extra spacing needs to be inserted below the table. The extra space can easily be inserted by clicking on the paragraph below the table, clicking the Line and Paragraph Spacing drop-list arrow, and choosing Add Space Before Paragraph.

1.0
1.15
1.5
2.0
2.5
3.0
Line Spacing Options...
Add Space Before Paragraph
Remove Space After Paragraph

Tables in documents may be formatted with the same design and layout options as stand-alone tables. A table that is less than the full-page width should be centered horizontally.

Default paragraph formats with 1.08 line spacing and 8 points after ¶

The items you requested on Purchase Order 7051 are in stock and will be shipped from our warehouse today.

Item Number	Description	Unit Price
531-8741	Base cabinet	$365.00
596-1285	Hutch	$765.00
542-6509	Shelf unit	$275.00

Click in this paragraph and select Add Space Before Paragraph

Please call us if we can assist you any further.

## DRILL 2  POSITION A TABLE IN A DOCUMENT

1. Key the text as shown in the illustration above.

2. Turn on Show/Hide.

3. Click the Line and Paragraph Spacing drop-list arrow and choose Add Space Before Paragraph.

4. Adjust column width and center the table horizontally on the page.

5. Center and bold column heads. Center the data in columns 1 and 3.

6. Proofread and check; click Next Activity. (*41-drill2*)

1. Prepare envelopes for the records stored in data source *76-d1datasource*. In the open document (*78-drill2envelope*), from the More items list, select the following merge fields and arrange as shown here:

**Title First Name Last Name**

**Company Name**

**Address Line 1**

**City, State ZIP Code**

2. Sort by ZIP Code in ascending order. Complete the merge.

3. Proofread and check; click Next Activity. (*78-drill2*)

## MERGE LABELS

Labels designed for printers are available in all sizes and for many purposes, including file folder labels, mailing labels, name badges, and business cards. The data source is often used for merging letters, registration forms, envelopes, and numerous types of labels. Merging labels is very similar to merging envelopes.

To create labels:

Mailings/Start Mail Merge/Step-by-Step Mail Merge Wizard

1. Open a new document and save with an appropriate file name. (For Drill 3, save it as *78-drill3labels*.)

2. Follow the path above and click Step-by-Step Merge Wizard.

3. Under Select document type, select Labels. Click Next: Starting document.

4. Under Select starting document, be sure Change document layout is selected.

5. Under Change document layout, click Label options. Choose Avery US Letter from the label vendor list and 5160 from the product number list. Click OK. Click Next: Select recipients.

6. Under Select recipients, click Use an existing list. Under Use an existing list, click Browse. From the appropriate disk drive, select *76-drill1datasource*. The Mail Merge Recipients dialog box displays the records. Click OK and Next: Arrange your labels.

7. Under Arrange your labels, click Address Block and click OK. Click Remove Space Before Paragraph to remove the extra spacing between the address lines. (Click More items to select the merge fields individually for the Address Block.)

8. Under Replicate labels, click Update all labels to replicate the Address Block merge field on each label on the page. Save the main document again. Click Next: Preview your labels.

9. From Preview your labels, click the navigation buttons if needed. (If changes in the data source are needed, click Edit recipient list.) Click Next: Complete the merge.

10. From Complete the merge, click Edit individual labels. Click All; then OK. The merged labels will appear on the screen.

11. Resave the main document.

**TIP**

**Remove Space After Paragraph**

Home/Paragraph/Line Spacing/Remove Space After Paragraph

**41-d1**

**Table with Table Style**

 **TIP**

Grid table styles are displayed in the second group.

 **TIP**

Key the text in cell C3 so that the name and address of the Surgery Center is easily readable. Adjust column width so that the ZIP Code fits on the same line as the city and state.

1. Key the table below; tap ENTER twice to double-space between paragraphs beginning in row 3.
2. Format the main heading using 14-point font, uppercase, and bold, and the secondary heading in 12-point bold, capitalizing each word. Align Center the headings in row 1.
3. Change the height of row 1 to 0.75"; change the height of row 2 to 0.3".
4. Apply Grid Table 4 – Accent 5 table style. Adjust column widths to display the information attractively.
5. Use the Quick Check on page 165 to compare your table.
6. Proofread and check; click Next Activity. (*41-d1*)

REGENTS MEMORIAL MEDICAL CENTER February Seminars		
**Seminar Title**	**Description**	**Registration**
**Surgical Weight Loss**	Methods of losing weight, including healthy diet, exercise, and medication, will be discussed in detail.  Surgical weight loss is an option for those who are motivated and willing to commit to lifestyle changes.	Classes will be held at the Outpatient Surgery Center 75 Pacific Crest Laguna Niguel, CA 92677-5773.  Call 949.555.0111 to register.
**Life in Motion with Osteoarthritis**	Osteoarthritis no longer means that you need to live with a painful disability. Modern medicine, diet, exercise, and surgery can help you enjoy life more fully.  Intricate surgical procedures including joint replacement and spinal fusion will be covered.	Register online at www.regents.org/calendar. Materials fee $10.00.
**Experts' Cancer Updates**	The cancer experts of Regents Medical Center will unveil the results of the latest cancer studies. New breakthrough treatments will be discussed.  They will explain what you should know about cancer screenings. Tips on preventing various types of cancers will be provided.	Call 949.555.0100 or register online at www.regents.org/calendar.

# Lesson 78 Merge with Envelopes and Labels

**New Commands** • Merge Envelopes • Merge Labels

**New Commands**

**78b**

## MERGE ENVELOPES

Envelopes can be merged from the data source. When printing envelopes, you will need to know the type of envelope feeder your printer uses. In this lesson, you will create #10 landscape envelopes (standard business envelope).

To create envelopes:

Mailings/Start Mail Merge/Start Mail Merge

1. Open a new document and save it with an appropriate name, e.g., *78-drill1envelope*.
2. Follow the path above and click Step-by-Step Merge Wizard to display the Mail Merge pane at the right of the screen.
3. Under Select document type, select Envelopes. Click Next: Starting document.
4. Under Select starting document, check that Change document layout is selected.
5. Under Change document layout, click Envelope options. The Envelope Options dialog box displays. The Size 10 envelope is default. Click OK; then Next: Select recipients.
6. Under Select recipients, click Use an existing list. Click Browse. From the appropriate disk drive, select *76-drill1datasource*, the data source created in Lesson 76. The Mail Merge Recipients dialog box displays the records. Click OK. Click Next: Arrange your envelopes.
7. Under Arrange your envelope, position the insertion point in the letter address area. Click Address Block to insert as a merge field. Click Next: Preview your envelopes.
8. Under Preview your envelopes, click the navigation buttons to preview envelopes. Click Edit Recipient List to edit the data source. Click Next: Complete the merge.
9. Under Complete the merge, click Edit individual envelopes and select the records to merge (all).
10. Save the main document again (for Drill 1, save it as *78-drill1envelope*).

**Non-*KPDO* Users:**

Open a new document and save it as the main document with an appropriate name, e.g., *78-drill1envelope*. Remember to resave; then the main document is complete.

---

## DRILL 1    PREPARE ENVELOPES

1. Follow the directions in 78b to prepare envelopes for the data source *76-drill1datasource*.

2. Merge the main document and the data source.

3. Proofread and check; click Next Activity. (*78-drill1*)
(**Reminder:** Resave the main document *78-drill1envelope* after you insert the merge fields but before you preview your document.)

## 41-d2

**Memo with Table**

 **REVIEW**

Remember to insert space before the paragraph that follows the table.

Home/Paragraph/Line and Paragraph Spacing/Add Space Before Paragraph

1. Key the memo below to **Roberto Perez** from **Marcia Lewis**. The subject is **Purchase Order 5122**. Insert the current date.
2. Apply the List Table 6 Colorful – Accent 1 table style. (*Hint:* List table styles are located toward the bottom of the list.) Center columns A and C. Adjust column width to remove extra space in each column; center the table horizontally.
3. Proofread and check; click Next Activity. (*41-d2*)

The items you requested on Purchase Order 5122 are in stock and will be shipped from our warehouse today. The shipment will be transported via Romulus Delivery System and is expected to arrive at your location in five days.

Item Number	Description	Unit Price
329-8741	Lordusky locking cabinet	$265.00
336-1285	Anchorage heavy duty locking cabinet	$465.00
387-6509	Lordusky locking cabinet (unassembled)	$195.00

Please call us if we can assist you any further.

## 41-d3

**Block Letter with Table**

1. Key the block letter below with open punctuation. The letter is from **Veejah Patel | Collections Manager**. Supply necessary letter parts.
2. Center the data in column A; right-align the amounts in column D. Apply the table style Grid Table 1 Light – Accent 2.
3. Adjust column width and center table horizontally on the page.
4. Proofread and check; click Exit Word. (*41-d3*) Click Log out to exit *KPDO*.

Ms. Beatrice Snow | Collections Manager | Precision Office Products | 2679 Orchard Lake Road | Farmington Hills, MI 48333-5534

Thank you for allowing International Financial Systems to assist you in managing your delinquent accounts. We provide you with the fastest interface to International Systems Collection Services. The activity report for last month is shown below.

Client Number	Last Name	First Name	Current Balance
1487	Rodriguez	Delia	$1,567.00
1679	Kim	Lisa	$954.35
1822	Batavia	Kirsten	$1,034.21
1905	Vokavich	Kramer	$832.09

Please verify the accuracy of the names transmitted by your billing office. If you find any transmission errors, please contact Joseph Kerning at 888.555.0134 immediately. | Sincerely

4. Edit the records with the following data:

Record	Representative
Quarrels	**Beth Stevens**
Bouchillon	**Kelly Cancienne**
Vang	**Patrick Konscak**
Andres	**Wade Sanford**
Seuffer	**Jennifer Fleming**

5. Edit the writer's name and title in the closing lines. Delete *Hunter Nyiri, Director* and insert the merge field *Representative*. Add the word **Representative** as the writer's title.

6. Sort by Last Name in ascending order and merge to a new document.

7. Proofread and check; click Next Activity. (*77-d1*) (**Reminder:** Save the main document, *76-d1main*.)

---

**77-d2**

**Filter Data Source**

1. In the open document (*76-d1main*), filter the data source to select records in Oktibbeha County.

2. Merge to a new document.

3. Proofread and check; click Next Activity. (*77-d2*)

---

**77-d3**

**Directory**

 77-d3datasource

1. Prepare the main document and data source for a membership directory. Choose Directory as the document type. Name the main document *77-d3directory*.

2. Use the existing data source *77-d3datasource* from the data file. Add information for three people in your personal address book.

3. Arrange the directory as follows. Set left tabs at 2.5", and 5.5". Bold Last Name.

   **Last Name**, First Name        Email Address        Cell Phone

4. Sort by Last Name and then First Name in ascending order and merge to a new document.

5. Apply the document theme Celestial with Basic (Elegant) document formatting style set.

6. Add the title **Membership Directory** at the top of document; apply the Title style and center.

7. Proofread and check; click Exit *Word*. (*77-d3*)

8. Click Log out to exit *KPDO*.

---

 Check your document format against the illustration below (solutions will vary).

## MEMBERSHIP DIRECTORY

**Forde**, Connie	cforde@ck.com	662.555.0133
**VanHuss**, Susie	svanhuss@ck.com	803.555.0145

REGENTS MEMORIAL MEDICAL CENTER February Seminars		
**Seminar Title**	**Description**	**Registration**
**Surgical Weight Loss**	Methods of losing weight, including healthy diet, exercise, and medication, will be discussed in detail.  Surgical weight loss is an option for those who are motivated and willing to commit to lifestyle changes.	Classes will be held at the Outpatient Surgery Center 75 Pacific Crest Laguna Niguel, CA 92677-5773.  Call 949.555.0111 to register.
**Life in Motion with Osteoarthritis**	Osteoarthritis no longer means that you need to live with a painful disability. Modern medicine, diet, exercise, and surgery can help you enjoy life more fully.  Intricate surgical procedures including joint replacement and spinal fusion will be covered.	Register online at www.regents.org/calendar. Materials fee $10.00.
**Experts' Cancer Updates**	The cancer experts of Regents Medical Center will unveil the results of the latest cancer studies. New breakthrough treatments will be discussed.  They will explain what you should know about cancer screenings. Tips on preventing various types of cancers will be provided.	Call 949.555.0100 or register online at www.regents.org/calendar.

**41-d4**

**Composition**

1. Key a memo to your instructor. In the first paragraph, request a meeting to discuss the agenda for the next Business Club meeting. Tell your instructor that you are available to meet at any time that you are not scheduled to be in class.

2. Key your class schedule in a table; the table will be the second paragraph.

3. In the third paragraph, ask your instructor to email you with a couple of dates and times that will be convenient to meet. Include your email address.

## Power and Versatility of Tables

*Communicating Today* ▶

Tables have traditionally been used to present data in documents. Today, the table feature is one of the most widely used tools in *Microsoft Word*. A table can be used to create a page layout, forms, newsletters, brochures, flyers, resumes, certificates, and more. Tables often provide the structure for web pages.

The Table feature is one of the most powerful and flexible features available in *Word*. You can use a table to organize a complex page layout. A table can hold text, graphics, or contain a nested table. You can remove the borders so that the table structure is not visible. If you are keying a table that contains numbers, you can perform basic calculations without having to use a calculator. *Word* also allows you to convert regular text to table format and vice versa.

You can always dress up a document by displaying text or data in a table and applying an attractive table style. The colorful table will attract the reader's attention and add some pizzazz to your document.

1. In the open document (*76-drill1main*), filter as follows:

    Field: State

    Comparison Phrase: Equal to

    Compare to: Illinois (IL)

2. Merge to a new document.

3. Proofread and check; click Next Activity. (*77-drill5*)

## DRILL 6      FILTER DATA RECORDS

1. In the open document (*76-drill1main*), clear filters used in Drill 5.

2. Filter to select records of speakers who live in Illinois and are scheduled to speak at 8:30 a.m. (*Hint*: Because both conditions must be met, select *and*; then key the requirements for the second condition.)

3. Merge to a new document.

4. Proofread and check; click Next Activity. (*77-drill6*)

## Personalize Form Letters

*Communicating Today* ▶

A personal letter is always preferred to a form letter; however, a form letter can be personalized by remembering these tips:

1. Format the letter with all the letter parts of a personal letter, such as letter address and personal salutation. Avoid using *To Whom It May Concern*.

2. Be sure the salutation is coded with the correct merge fields. A form letter is a dead giveaway if the greeting is *Dear Smith* instead of *Dear Mr. Smith*.

3. Use merge fields in the body of the letter to make it personal. Using a robust data source with complete variables for each record allows the writer to personalize each letter very specifically. A data source may be created in *Word*, but an *Excel* or *Access* database can also be used as the data source.

4. Proofread the variables carefully to ensure accuracy when the data source is merged with the main document. Proofread the spacing between the merge field and the main document text. These spacing errors can be another signal to the reader that this is a form letter.

## Apply It

**77-d1**

**Edit Data Source**

1. In the open document (*76-d1main*), edit data source as follows:

    • Mr. Bouchillon now works for **Prestage Technology Company**.

    • Ms. Vang's new address is **983 Old Cedar Place**; ZIP Code is **39704-0983**.

2. Add two new records:

**Ms. Brenda Andres**	**Mr. Juan Seuffer**
**Gifts and More**	**Kubly and Ross Associates**
**1456 W. 18th Street**	**356 Airline Road**
**Starkville, MS 39759-1456**	**West Point, MS 39773-0356**
**Oktibbeha County**	**Clay County**

3. Add **Representative** as a new field.

*(continued)*

# Lesson 42 Palmetto Event Solutions Inc.

**Learning Outcomes**
- Apply keying, formatting, and word processing skills.
- Work independently with few specific instructions.

 **Warmup** *Lesson 42a Warmup*

**A** | **ALL LETTERS**

## Skill Building

**42b**    **Timed Writing**

Key two 3' timed writings.

Whether your company can succeed depends on how well it fits into the economic system. Success rests on certain key factors that are put in line by your management team that has set goals for the company and has enough good judgment to recognize how best to reach these goals. Because of competition, only those companies that are very well organized get to the top.

A commercial enterprise is formed for a specific purpose; that purpose is usually to equip others, or consumers, with whatever they cannot equip themselves. Unless there is only one provider, a consumer will search for a company that returns the most value in terms of price; and a relationship with such a company, once set up, can endure for many years.

Thus our system assures that the businesses that manage to survive are those that have been able to combine successfully an excellent product with a low price and the best service—all in a place that is convenient for the buyers. With no intrusion from outside forces, the buyer and the seller benefit both themselves and each other.

## Project Setting

### WEALTH PROTECTION STRATEGIES SEMINAR

The Southwest office of Palmetto Event Solutions accepted a contract to promote, set up, and direct the Wealth Protection Strategies Seminar to be held in Newport Beach, California. Renowned speakers from around the country will be presenting at the seminar. The three-day seminar will be held at the Thirty-nine Palms Hotel and Resort.

You will assist Ellen Miller, the Executive Assistant to the President and CEO of Palmetto Event Solutions, Inc. with preparing promotional material, creating the agenda, and scheduling appointments for the speakers.

1. In the open document (*76-drill1main*), sort by ZIP Code in ascending order and merge to a new document.

2. Proofread and check; click Next to continue. (*77-drill2*)

3. Close *76-drill1main* without saving.

## DRILL 3     SORT IN DESCENDING ORDER

1. In the open document (*76-drill1main*), sort by ZIP Code in descending order and merge to a new document.

2. Proofread and check; click Next to continue. (*77-drill3*)

3. Close *76-drill1main* without saving.

## DRILL 4     MULTIPLE SORT

1. In the open document (*76-drill1main*), sort in ascending order first by State, then by City, and then by Last Name.

2. Merge to a new document.

3. Proofread and check; click Next to continue. (*77-drill4*)

4. Close *76-drill1main* without saving.

## FILTER RECORDS

Filtering records before merging the main document and the data source allows you to select a specific set of records to merge. For example, you can create a target mailing to individuals in a specific state or ZIP Code area.

To filter data records:

Mailings/Start Mail Merge/Edit Recipient List

1. Open the main document and display the Mail Merge Recipients dialog box.

2. From the Refine Recipient List, click Filter.

3. From the Filter and Sort dialog box, select the Filter Records tab **1**.

4. Choose the appropriate data field **2** (e.g., State); click a comparison phrase **3** (e.g., Equal to); and key the text or data you will use for the comparison **4** (e.g., IL). Click OK. (**Note:** Click the down arrow for comparison and note the comparison phrases.)

5. Note the records displaying in the Mail Merge Recipients dialog box to determine if you have filtered correctly. Click OK.

(**Reminder:** In the Filter and Sort dialog box, click the Clear All button to remove filters before using the main document again to ensure all records will merge.)

1. Create a 4-column, 12-row table. Key the table below. Merge the cells as needed for row 1 and column A.
2. Apply Grid Table 5 Dark – Accent 6 style. Adjust column widths to display the information attractively.
3. Change the height of row 1 to 0.6". Change the title to 16-point font. Align Center the title.
4. Change the height of row 2 to 0.3". Apply bold to the column heads in columns B, C, and D. Align Center the column heads in row 2.
5. Change the text in cells A3–A5 to 12-point font; change the text to Align Center.
6. Align Center Right the time of the breakout sessions in column B. Align Center Left the room names in column C.
7. Proofread and check; click Next Activity. (*42-d1*)

WEALTH PROTECTION STRATEGIES			
**Day**	**Time**	**Room**	**Breakout Session**
Monday  To Tax or Not to Tax the Estate	9:30 a.m.	Harvard	Protect your estate for the family.
	10:30 a.m.	Princeton	The why, what, and how of a Revocable Living Trust.
	1:30 p.m.	Harvard	Resolve probate and conservatorship problems.
	3:30 p.m.	Yale	Solutions to eliminate 37%–45% estate taxes.
Tuesday  Using Trust Accounts to Minimize Estate Taxes	9:30 a.m.	Princeton	Dynasty Trusts are used to protect family wealth, real estate, and business interests.
	10:30 a.m.	Duke	Use Irrevocable Life Insurance Trusts to protect life insurance from estate taxes.
	1:30 p.m.	Harvard	Wealth Accumulation Trusts and Income Savings Trusts can be used to minimize federal and state taxes.
	3:30 p.m.	Yale	Qualified Personal Residence Trusts can be used to safely transfer your home.
Wednesday  Wealth Preservation	9:30 a.m.	Duke	Protect your family, business, and assets from the risks of lawsuits.
	10:30 a.m.	Yale	Use limited partnerships and limited liability companies to hold real estate and other investments.

## SORT DATA RECORDS

Start Mail Merge · Select Recipients · Edit Recipient List

Start Mail Merge

Sorting records determines the order in which the records are merged. You might sort records in ZIP Code order, Last Name order, or City order. Occasionally, a multiple sort is needed to sort first by one field and then a second field, and so forth. For example, merged name badges or registration letters might be sorted first by state, then by city, and then by last name. Records are sorted either in ascending order (A to Z or 1, 2 …) or descending order (Z to A or 100, 99, …).

### To sort records by one field:

<span style="background-color: yellow">Mailings/Start Mail Merge/Edit Recipient List</span>

1. Open the main document and display the Mail Merge Recipients dialog box.

2. Click the column heading of the field to be sorted to display the data (such as Last Name) in ascending order ❶.

   Click again to display in descending order. Click OK.

   **Note:** You may also click the drop-list arrow by each field ❷ and select Sort Ascending or Sort Descending.

3. To merge, in the Finish group, click the Finish & Merge button. Click one of the merge options.

### To sort records by multiple fields:

<span style="background-color: yellow">Mailings/Start Mail Merge/Edit Recipient List</span>

1. Open the main document and display the Mail Merge Recipients dialog box.

2. From the Refine Recipient List, click Sort.

3. From the Filter and Sort dialog box, select the Sort Records tab ❶.

4. Click the Sort by ❷ drop-list arrow and select the first field to be sorted in the multiple sort.

5. Click the arrow for Then by ❸ and select the second field, and so forth. Click OK.

palmetto memo form

1. Key the memo to **Wealth Protection Strategies Seminar Attendees**, from **Carlos Torres, Regional Manager**. The subject is **Appointment with Seminar Speaker**.

2. Create the table. Change the width of column A to 0.3". Change the width of column B to 3.5".

3. Apply Grid Table 4 – Accent 5 table style. Center the table horizontally.

4. Change the row height to 0.4" for the entire table.

5. Change the font size in row 1 to 12-point. Align Center the text in row 1.

6. Proofread and check; click Next Activity. (42-d2)

Your seminar speakers are renowned practitioners in their respective career fields. One of the benefits your participation in the seminar provides you is the opportunity to meet in a one-on-one basis with these noted speakers.

Please indicate the speaker(s) with whom you would like to meet. If you would like to meet with more than one speaker, indicate your first, second, and third choices. We will attempt to honor all requests. Individual sessions will be scheduled for 20 minutes each.

√	Name	Indicate 1st, 2nd, or 3rd Choice

Complete the form above and return to me no later than September 1, 201-. A list of the speakers, their contact information, and the topics they will be addressing is attached.

xx

Attachment

Changes to fields are made by editing the data source. Once the change is made, all of the records are revised.

To edit fields:

Mailings/Start Mail Merge/Edit Recipient List

1. In the Edit Data Source dialog box, click the Customize Columns button.
2. Edit as follows:
   a. *Add new field:* Click the Add button; key the field name. Use the move buttons to position correctly. (**Reminder:** Be sure to update the main document by inserting the new merge field.)
   b. *Delete field:* Select the field to be deleted. Click the Delete button.
   c. *Rename field:* Select the field to be renamed. Click the Rename button. Key new name.
3. Save your main document to update your data source.

## DRILL 1    EDIT RECORDS AND FIELDS

1. In the open document (*76-drill1main*), add **Fax Number** as a new field after the ZIP Code field.

2. Update the records with the following fax numbers:

   Ms. Hershbarger **217.555.0181**

   Dr. Hodnett **414.555.0194**

   Mr. Zuber **708.555.0192**

3. Change Ms. Hershbarger's address to **206 Fourth Avenue, Springfield, IL 62701-0206**.

4. Proofread and check; click Next Activity. (*77-drill1main*)

EDHAR/Shutterstock.com

## ! WORKPLACE SUCCESS

### Multicultural Skills

What is your multicultural quotient? Companies are seeking employees who have multicultural awareness, knowledge, and skills. These valuable employees are aware that their attitudes, beliefs, assumptions, etc., do affect how they work with others who are of different cultures. These employees are very knowledgeable of the many aspects of these cultures, including history, practices, and values. They also have developed skills that are needed to interact effectively with those of different cultures. One skill might be learning the language of that culture.

Spend some time in this module increasing your own multicultural literacy. Develop an awareness, knowledge, and skills in another culture.

## 42-d3

**Table with Table Style**

1. Key the table below. Arrange the speakers in alphabetical order according to the speaker's last name.
2. Apply Grid Table 5 Dark – Accent 4 table style. Adjust column widths to display the information attractively.
3. Change the height of row 1 to 0.5". Change the font to 16-point and Align Center the text in row 1.
4. Change the height of row 2 to 0.3". Bold the column heads in columns B and C. Align Center all the columns heads in row 2.
5. Apply Align Center Left alignment to the names in cells A3–A6.
6. Apply Align Center Left alignment to the topics in cells B3–B6.
7. Proofread and check; click Next Activity. (*42-d3*)

WEALTH PROTECTION STRATEGIES SPEAKERS		
Speaker	Topic	Address
James M. Kohn	Estate Protection The Probate Process	Kohn and Crane, Attorneys at Law 325 Munras Avenue Carmel, CA 93923
Lindsey Cunningham, CPA	Estate Taxes Trust Accounts	Certified Public Accounting Services 364 Toro Parkway Lake Forest, CA 92610
William L. Nelson	Wealth Preservation	Gottrocks Financial Planners 6590 Madison Avenue New York, NY 10022
Maria C. Hernandez	Risk Management	Ortega Risk Management Consultants 100 Redwood Avenue, Suite 200 Palo Alto, CA 94304

## 42-d4

**Compose Letter**

 palmetto letterhead – las cruces

**Learn More:**

www.cengagebrain.com

1. Compose a letter to William Nelson (see address in table above) telling him that Carlos Torres would like to meet with him to discuss his speech at the opening session. Mr. Torres will be picking him up at the airport and taking him to the hotel. Request the date, time, airline, and flight number of his arriving flight to Orange County Airport so that Carlos can schedule the meeting.
2. Use your name and title (Administrative Assistant) in the closing.
3. Proofread and print. (*42-d4*)

## USE MERGE COMMANDS ON MAILINGS TAB

An alternate method for creating and editing a mail merge document is to access the merge commands on the Mailing tab.

Use the Address Block ❶, the Greeting Line ❷, and Insert Merge Field ❸ buttons to create the placeholders for the merge fields in the main document. The Edit Recipient List ❹ button is used to edit the data source, while the Finish & Merge button ❺ is used to complete the merge.

## EDIT DATA SOURCE

Sometimes you will need to edit the data source (list of variables) by changing individual records or revising the fields for all records.

### To edit records:

Mailings/Start Mail Merge/Edit Recipient List

1. In the Data Source box, click the data source, e.g., *76-drill1datasource* ❶. Click Edit.
2. Click the desired entry ❷ or click Find ❸ to locate a record quickly.
3. Make the desired changes.
4. Click New Entry to add a new record, or click Delete Entry to delete a record. Click OK.

# Reports

## LEARNING OUTCOMES

- Format two-page reports with document themes and styles.
- Insert footnotes.
- Insert file.
- Format academic reports in MLA and APA style.
- Find and replace text and formatting in a document.
- Build keyboarding skills.

## Lesson 43 Unbound Reports

**New Commands**
- Themes
- Styles
- Footnotes

**Warmup**   *Lesson 43a Warmup*

**A   ALL LETTERS**

## Skill Building

### 43b   Timed Writing

1. Key a 1' timing on each paragraph; work to increase speed.
2. Key a 3' timing on all paragraphs.

The most vital element of a business is its clientele. It is for this reason that most organizations adopt the slogan that the customer is always right. The saying should not be taken literally, but in spirit.

Patrons will continuously use your business if you provide an exceptional product and service. The product you sell must be high quality and last a long time. The product must perform just as you claim. The environment and surroundings must be safe and clean.

Customers expect you to be well groomed and neatly dressed. They expect you to know your products and services and to be dependable. When you tell a customer you will do something, you must perform. Patrons expect you to help them willingly and quickly. Add a personal touch by greeting clientele by name, but be cautious about conducting business on a first-name basis.

# Lesson 77 Edit the Data Source

## New Commands

- Edit Data Source
- Sort Data Records
- Filter Data Records

## Skill Building

### 77b Textbook Keying

Key each line once.

i	1	sit in said did dirk city did fin its lit iris wit hit ilk simmer
e	2	gem ewe men eke ever me le hen cede key led fen eye be pen leader
i/e	3	pie lei piece feign mein feint neigh lie reign die veil vein diem
i/e	4	Either Marie or Liem tried to receive eight pieces of cookie pie.
w	5	new jaw awe win we was awe away hew saw flaw law wan pew wit wavy
o	6	to onto rot job coho sox box oboe wok roe out oil dot tote oriole
w/o	7	ow wows how won worn now woe wool mow row work cow woke flows low
w/o	8	Women won't want to work now; we are worn out after woeful worry.
k	9	Keep keen keg kayak keno keepsake kerchief kennel kernel kerosene
d	10	drag mind ride made ahead drove trade proud riddle riding discuss
k/d	11	dark kind dock katydid drink awkward grandkids padlock jackknifed
k/d	12	Dozens of ducks dunked up and down in a murky pool at the bridge.

## Communication

### 77c

References/Communication Skills/Quotation Marks and Italics

1. Review the Quotation Marks and Italics exercise in *KPDO* before completing this activity.
2. Key each sentence single-spaced, correcting any quotation and italic errors as you key. Use automatic numbering.
3. Proofread and check; click Next Activity. (*77c*)

### QUOTATIONS AND ITALIC

1. Dr. Waites recommended, When you are a guest in a new country, experience the culinary differences by dining at authentic restaurants.
2. Excellent reads for an overseas trip are the book International Travel Made Easy and the magazine International Travel.
3. The lyrics for the song International Fiesta were written by a music student.
4. What is Your Cultural IQ, an article published in the International Journal, won best article for 2014.
5. The word diversity is clearly explained in the opening scene of the movie Today's World.
6. Do you know who coined the phrase bottom line that is used often by American business executives?

## DOCUMENT THEMES

Built-in document themes incorporate colors, fonts, and effects that can be applied to a *Word* document or to documents in other *Microsoft Office* applications. The default theme is Office Theme.

To apply a document theme:
Design/Document Formatting/Themes

1. Click the down arrow to display the gallery of Built-in themes. The default theme is Office.
2. Click the document theme you wish to use.

---

| **DRILL 1** | THEMES |  document themes |

1. Review the open document; read the information about the headings and Live Preview.

2. Display the Document Theme gallery and use Live Preview to view at least six of the theme options. Note changes in color and font styles.

3. Apply Facet document theme.

4. Proofread and check; click Next Activity. (43-drill1)

---

**76-d2**

**Compose Mail Merge**

1. Decide on a form letter that would be useful to you personally or to your class. Secure the names and addresses of the recipients of the form letter.
2. In the open document (*76-d2main*), create the data source (*76-d2datasource*).
3. Compose the main document and insert the merge fields in it.
4. Merge the data source and the main document.
5. Proofread and check; click Exit *Word*. (*76-d2*)
6. Click Log out to exit *KPDO*.

! **WORKPLACE SUCCESS**

## Managing Information Overload

Business employees are under siege with the volume of information that is coming at them from all sides—text messages, voice mail, email, the Internet, television, radio, fax, magazines, news feeds, and many others. Interestingly, much of the data that business employees review is not relevant to their jobs. Because managing information overload is a critical skill needed by today's business employees, please consider the following technology and behavior suggestions.

**Technology**—Use email information filters to screen messages that do not demand your attention. Use delegation features to allow an assistant to respond to email when possible. Delete participation in list servers not desired. Take advantage of RSS feeds to compile data from the Internet and to allow the review of one set of data. Locate reputable blogs in the area of your research to decrease search time on the Internet and provide views of many individuals.

**Behavior change**—Maintain responsibility in email use; do not copy to another person just in case he or she may need it. Limit the control information has on your life and set the hours you will work per week. Set limits on when you check emails and use the cell phone, including vacation time.

## STYLES

The Styles feature enables you to apply a group of formats automatically to text, which saves time and ensures a consistent and professional format. When a new document is opened, the Office theme and the Normal style are the default settings. Text keyed using these defaults is 11-point Calibri, left-aligned, 1.08 spacing, 8-point spacing after a paragraph, and no indent. Other styles available include Heading 1, Heading 2, Heading 3, Heading 4, and Title. Each style has its own specific formatting associated with it.

Styles include both character and paragraph styles. The attributes listed in the Font group on the Home ribbon and in the Font dialog box make up the character styles.

**Character styles** apply to a single character or characters that are selected. In Lesson 27 you learned how to apply character styles using the Font group.

**Paragraph styles** include both the character style and other formats that affect paragraph appearance such as line spacing, bullets, numbering, and tab stops.

To apply paragraph styles:
Home/Styles

1.  Select the text to which you wish to apply a style.

2.  Choose a desired style from the Quick Styles gallery.

3.  If the desired style does not display, click the More button ❶ to expand the Quick Styles gallery.

4.  Select the desired style from the expanded list of styles.

---

**DRILL 2**          **STYLES**           schedule

1. In the open document, apply Integral document theme.

2. Select the title on the first line. Apply Title style. Click the More button to select this style if it is not visible.

3. Select the subtitle on the second line. Apply Subtitle style.

4. Select *Monday;* apply Heading 1 style. **Hint:** Click the scroll buttons to the right of the Styles button to move in the Styles list.

5. Select *Monday* and use Format Painter to copy the Heading 1 style to the remaining days of the week and the heading *Extracurricular Activities.*

6. Proofread and check; click Next Activity. (*43-drill2*)

**76-d1**

**Mail Merge**

1. In the open document (*76-d1main*), create the data source. Customize the address list to include the fields below.

2. Key the following data for each of the three records. (*76-d1datasource*)

Field names	Record 1	Record 2	Record 3
Title	Mrs.	Mr.	Ms.
First Name	Jessica	Allen	Paje
Last Name	Quarrels	Bouchillon	Vang
Company Name	Hendrix Plastics	Magnolia Chemicals	Faulkner Florists
Address Line 1	5689 Old Vinton Road	538 Hill Street	885 N. Third Street
City	Starkville	Columbus	West Point
State	MS	MS	MS
ZIP Code	39759-5689	39701-0538	39773-0885
County	Oktibbeha	Lowndes	Clay

3. Key the main document that follows and insert the merge fields in the main document. Use open punctuation. Insert the date to update automatically. Save the changes.

4. Merge the data source and the main document.

5. Proofread and check; click Next Activity. (*76-d1*)

★ **TIP**

Press SHIFT + ENTER after each line of the letter address except the last one.

<<Title>> <<First_Name>> <<Last_Name>>

<<Company Name>>

<<Address_Line_1>>

<<City>>, <<State>> <<ZIP_Code>>

<<GreetingLine>>

Thank you for submitting your proposal for enacting a more culturally diverse employment program for city workers to the American Studies Association.

The American Studies Association continually strives to work with city governments in three area counties to provide work environments that value diversity. The goal, of course, is to employ persons who reflect differences in age, gender, and interests. Different people solve problems differently, and having diverse groups leads to better decisions.

You may be contacted, <<Title>> <<Last_Name>>, to represent <<County>> County on the special Council for Managing Diversity that is being established in our three-county region. Again, thank you for letting us know what you are doing to ensure diversity at <<Company_Name>>.

Sincerely | Hunter Nyiri, Director | xx

## FOOTNOTES

References cited in a report are often indicated within the text by a superscript number (. . . story.[1]) and a corresponding footnote with full information at the bottom of the same page where the reference is cited. Additionally, content footnotes supplement the information included in the body of the report.

*Word* automatically numbers footnotes sequentially with Arabic numerals (1, 2, 3), positions them at the left margin, and applies 10-point type.

A footnote is positioned with the same margin widths as the body of the report. Do not indent the footnotes.

### To insert and edit footnotes:

References/Footnotes/Insert Footnote

1. From Print Layout view, position the insertion point in the document where the footnote reference is to be inserted.

2. Click the Insert Footnote button. The reference number and the insertion point appear at the bottom of the page. Key the footnote ❶.

   A footnote divider line ❷ is automatically added above the first footnote on each page. Tap ENTER once to add one blank line between footnotes.

3. Click anywhere above the footnote divider line to return to the document.

4. To edit a footnote, click in the footnote at the bottom of the page and make the revision.

5. To delete a footnote, select the reference number in the text and tap DELETE.

❷ _____

❶ [1] All computers are installed with the *Windows 8* operating system and *Office 2013*.

[2] Instructors must pick up the gift certificate from Mary Katherine Morgan, Office 208.

---

### DRILL 3     FOOTNOTES      checklist

1. In the open document, insert the following content footnotes to the administration checklist. Add a blank line between footnotes.

**18 computers[1]**

    **[1] All computers are installed with the Windows 8 operating system and Office 2013.**

**Door prize—Joey's Steak House Gift Certificate[2]**

    **[2] Instructors must pick up the gift certificate from Mary Katherine Morgan, Office 208.**

2. Proofread and check; click Next Activity. (*43-drill3*)

## Step 5: Preview your letters

1. When previewing letters, select the lines of the letter address except the last one and remove the extra spacing after the paragraph. Click the navigation buttons to preview and proofread each of your letters. *Tip:* To edit variables, click Edit recipient list and make the necessary changes to the data source file.

2. Click Next: Complete the merge.

## Step 6: Complete the merge

1. Click Edit individual letters **10**. Click All; then OK. The merge letters will *not* appear on the screen. You will see the message: *Mail merge is done and document is generated. Click OK.*

2. Check. The merged letters will appear on the screen as the checked document. Click Next Activity. (*76-drill1*)

---

## EDIT MAIL MERGE DOCUMENT

Mailings/Start Mail Merge/Start Mail Merge/Step-by-Step Mail Merge Wizard

Often it is necessary to edit the main document. Perhaps the user did not finish the job before closing the document, or perhaps changes are now needed in the main document.

With the main document open, follow the path above and open the Mail Merge Wizard. Click the Next or Previous button until you locate the desired step to be edited. Make the desired changes or continue creating the main document.

## Troubleshooting Tips

1. When you open the main document, you will be prompted that data from your database will be placed in the document. Click Yes to accept the data if the desired data source is connected to the main document. If you wish to use another data source, click No and select the new data source.

2. When in the *Write your letter* step of the Wizard, the merge field codes will display; but when in the *Preview your letters* step of the Wizard, actual data from the data source will display. Click Next or Previous to move to the correct step.

**DRILL 4**   DELETE FOOTNOTES

1. In the open document (*43-drill3*), delete the second footnote.   2. Proofread and check; click Next Activity. (*43-drill4*)

## Why Styles Cannot Be Overlooked

Often it is easy to overlook time-saving word processing features because you are not familiar with them. The styles feature is a command that you cannot afford to overlook.

Styles provide consistent and attractive formatting with a quick click. The Format Painter can even be used to copy a style once it has been applied.

Most importantly, when styles are applied, the headings are listed in the navigation bar for easy movement within a large document. At the right you can see the Level 1 heading displayed at the far left. The two Level 2 headings are indented beneath that and Level 3 headings are indented again. Simply click on the heading to go to that section of the paper. No more time-consuming scrolling is needed.

Another major advantage of using styles, especially in a long report, is the ability to generate an automatic table of contents. Once the proper level of heading styles is applied, one click of the mouse creates a beautifully formatted table of contents. If changes are made in the report, one click updates the table of contents. Why would you want to overlook this time-saving feature?

- From the Mail Merge task pane (at far right), click Greeting Line. Click the down arrow to the right of the comma and select none. Click OK. Tap ENTER one time and continue keying the letter until the Speech merge code.

- Insert the merge field for Speech. Continue keying the letter shown below. Insert the merge fields for *Time* and *Room* at the appropriate places.
- When finished keying letter, click Next: Preview your letters.

Insert Merge Field ▾

April 6, 201- (ENTER 2 times)

«AddressBlock» (ENTER 1 time)

«GreetingLine» (ENTER 1 time)

Thank you for agreeing to present your paper titled «Speech» at the International Conference on Technology to be held at the Omni Hotel in San Francisco on May 12. Your presentation is scheduled for «Time» in the «Room».

You are also invited to be our special guest at the annual awards luncheon on Friday at 11:45 a.m. in the Grand Ballroom. Your conference registration materials and a luncheon ticket will be held for you at the hotel registration desk. If you need assistance when you arrive at the hotel, please call conference headquarters at ext. 7532.

«Title» «Last_Name», we look forward to your presentation and to your outstanding contribution to our program.

Sincerely (ENTER 2 times) | Jacqueline VonKohn | Program Coordinator | xx

**TIP**

Press SHIFT + ENTER after name to remove extra spacing between writer's name and title.

References/Document
Formats/Reports

# UNBOUND REPORT FORMAT

Reports prepared without binders are called unbound reports. Unbound reports may be attached with a staple or paper clip in the upper-left corner. Often reports are attached to an email. Study the illustration below to learn to format a one-page unbound report. A full-page model is shown on page 176. In this module you will generally use the default Office theme.

**Margins:** Use the default 1" top, side, and bottom margins.

**Font size:** Use the 11-point default font size.

**Spacing:** Use the default line spacing for all reports.

**Title:** ❶

- Position at about 2". (Tap ENTER three times.)
- Capitalize the first letter of all main words.
- Tap ENTER twice after the title.
- Apply Title style. If the title is long, shrink the font so the title fits on one line.

**Side heading:** ❷

- Key side headings at the left margin.
- Capitalize the first letter of all main words.
- Apply Heading 1 style.
- Tap ENTER once after heading.

**Enumerated or bulleted items:** ❸

- Use the default 0.25" indention of bulleted and numbered items.
- Tap ENTER once after each item.

---

## AUP 13.02 Email Acceptable Use Policy ❶

To encourage acceptable, consistent, and appropriate use of email, Sudduth and Associates has adopted AUP 13.02—Email Acceptable Use Policy.[1] To reap full benefit of this means of communication, follow the basic guidelines regarding message content and communication preferences.

### Message Content ❷

Although perceived as informal documents, email messages are business records and archived as a part of the official records of Sudduth and Associates. Follow these effective communication guidelines:

❸
- Write clear, concise sentences, avoiding clichés, slang, redundancies, and wordiness.
- Avoid emoticons and text message jargon or acronyms.
- Break the message into logical paragraphs, sequencing in an appropriate order. White space is important in email messages as well as printed documents, so be sure to add extra space between paragraphs.
- Limit email messages to one idea per message, and preferably limit to one screen.
- Always include a subject line that clearly defines the email message.
- Consider carefully the recipients of the email; do not waste your colleagues' valuable time by sending or copying unnecessary emails.
- Spell-check email messages carefully; verify punctuation and content accuracy.
- Check the tone of the message carefully. If angry, wait at least one hour before clicking the Send button. Review the message, modify if needed, and then send the message.

### Preferences

Although email is a common means of communication, other methods include face-to-face communication, telephone, voice mail, and instant messaging. It is important to realize that each person has preferred methods of communication, and the method will vary depending upon the message content. To accomplish tasks more effectively, be aware of individuals' preferred channels of communication and use those channels if appropriate for the business purpose.

Remember that effective communication is essential to be successful in reaching the goals of Sudduth and Associates. Apply these important email acceptable use guidelines as directed in AUP 13.02.

---
[1] Adopted 1/15/2009; revised 6/30/2014

- The Save Address List dialog box displays. Key a filename (**76-drill1datasource**) in the File name box and click Save. In the Save box, choose the appropriate folder for saving this file.

- The Mail Merge Recipients dialog box now displays and shows the variables in table format. Click OK.

- **Note:** To move within the Mail Merge Recipients dialog box, click the desired row. Use the scroll bar to navigate in the record. With a long recipient list, click Find recipient to search for the desired recipient **8**.

- Click Next: Write your letter from the Mail Merge task pane.

## Step 4: Write your letter

- Begin keying the main document at approximately 2". In this drill, key **April 6, 201-** as the date. Often the Date command is inserted with option selected to update automatically. Tap ENTER two times.

- Insert the merge fields for the letter address:

  **a.** From the right pane, click More items **9**.

  **b.** Select Title, click Insert, and then click Close. Tap Space Bar.

  **c.** Repeat step b to add First_Name and Last_Name. Press SHIFT + ENTER to remove extra spacing between lines of the letter address.

  **d.** Continue inserting the merge fields for the remaining lines of the letter address.

«Title» «First_Name» «Last_Name»  ← Press SHIFT + ENTER after each line except last line.
«Company_Name»
«Address_Line_1»
«City», «State» «ZIP_Code»  ← Tap ENTER one time.

Title → # AUP 13.02 Email Acceptable Use Policy   Title Style ↓2

To encourage acceptable, consistent, and appropriate use of email, Sudduth and Associates has adopted AUP 13.02—Email Acceptable Use Policy.[1] To reap full benefit of this means of communication, follow the basic guidelines regarding message content and communication preferences. ↓1

Side Heading → ## Message Content   Heading 1 Style                                    1"

Although perceived as informal documents, email messages are business records and archived as a part of the official records of Sudduth and Associates. Follow these effective communication guidelines: ↓1

Bulleted list →
- Write clear, concise sentences, avoiding clichés, slang, redundancies, and wordiness.
- Avoid emoticons and text message jargon or acronyms.
- Break the message into logical paragraphs, sequencing in an appropriate order. White space is important in email messages as well as printed documents, so be sure to add extra space between paragraphs.
- Limit email messages to one idea per message, and preferably limit to one screen.
- Always include a subject line that clearly defines the email message.
- Consider carefully the recipients of the email; do not waste your colleagues' valuable time by sending or copying unnecessary emails.
- Spell-check email messages carefully; verify punctuation and content accuracy.
- Check the tone of the message carefully. If angry, wait at least one hour before clicking the Send button. Review the message, modify if needed, and then send the message. ↓1

## Preferences

Although email is a common means of communication, other methods include face-to-face communication, telephone, voice mail, and instant messaging. It is important to realize that each person has preferred methods of communication, and the method will vary depending upon the message content. To accomplish tasks more effectively, be aware of individuals' preferred channels of communication and use those channels if appropriate for the business purpose.

Remember that effective communication is essential to be successful in reaching the goals of Sudduth and Associates. Apply these important email acceptable use guidelines as directed in AUP 13.02.

--------

[1] Adopted 1/15/2009; revised 6/30/2014

**Unbound Report**

- Click Customize Columns  5 to edit the default field names.

  a. To delete a field name: Select the field and click Delete 6. Click Yes to confirm the deletion. For this drill, delete Address Line 2, Country or Region, Home Phone, Work Phone, and E-mail Address.

  b. To add a field name: Select it and click Add 7. Add three fields: Speech, Room, and Time.

  c. To position the new fields correctly, select the field to be moved. Click Move Up or Move Down as appropriate. Move the field names so they are positioned as shown at the right. Click OK.

- Key the variables for Record 1 in the New Address List dialog box. Tab to the next field. Click New Entry to begin a new record, and key the variables for Record 2. Repeat for Record 3. Click OK after keying all of the records.

Field names	Record 1	Record 2	Record 3
Title	Ms.	Dr.	Mr.
First Name	Alison	Lisa	Joseph
Last Name	Hershbarger	Hodnett	Zuber
Company Name	Hershbarger & Ward Attorneys	Columbia Hospital	First Bank of Chicago
Address Line 1	844 Locksley Way	303 Park Circle Road	1106 Whispering Pines Road
City	Salt Lake City	Milwaukee	Chicago
State	UT	WI	IL
ZIP Code	84110-0844	53221-0303	60650-1106
Time	8:30 a.m.	9:30 a.m.	10:30 a.m.
Room	Colonnade Room	Diplomat Room	Laurel Suite
Speech	"Copyright Issues in the Digital Age"	"Creating Interactive Presentations"	"Using Social Media to Market Your Organization"

## 43-d1

**Unbound Report**

1. Key the model report on the previous page. Tap ENTER three times to position the title at about 2". Use default side margins. Key a dash in line two of the report after *13.02*.

2. Capitalize the first letter of all main words in the title; tap ENTER twice after the title. Then select the title and apply Title style.

3. Select the side headings and apply Heading 1 style. Tap ENTER once after the side heading.

4. Insert the footnote in the first paragraph.

5. Apply square bullets to the list.

6. Proofread and check; click Next Activity. (*43-d1*)

## 43-d2

**Edit Report**

1. In the open document (*43-d1*), apply Integral theme.

2. Change the word *appropriate* in the first paragraph to *effective*.

3. Key the word **Communication** before the word *Preferences* in the second heading.

4. In the footnote, change the revision date to 9/2/2014.

5. Delete the last paragraph and replace with the following text:

   **Contact the General Administration Office with questions.**

6. Insert a footnote after the word *Office* in the last sentence just added. Key the footnote text below:

   **Anne Holifield, Information Officer, extension 6932,**

   **AHolifield@sa.com**

7. Select the bulleted list and change to numbers. Reorder the items as shown below and make the one correction shown.

8. Proofread and check; click Exit Word. (*43-d2*)

9. Click Log out to exit *KPDO*.

4 1. Write clear, concise sentences, avoiding clichés, slang, redundancies, and wordiness.

5 2. Avoid emoticons and text message jargon or acronyms.

6 3. Break the message into logical paragraphs, sequencing in an appropriate order. ~~White space is important in email messages as well as printed documents, so be sure to add extra space between paragraphs.~~

2 4. Limit email messages to one idea per message, and preferably limit to one screen.

3 5. Always include a subject line that clearly defines the email message.

1 6. Consider carefully the recipients of the email; do not waste your colleagues' valuable time by sending or copying unnecessary emails.

7. Spell-check email messages carefully; verify punctuation and content accuracy.

8. Check the tone of the message carefully. If angry, wait at least one hour before clicking the Send button. Review the message, modify if needed, and then send the message.

## MAIL MERGE WIZARD

The Mail Merge Wizard is a straightforward way to produce a merged document such as the form letters you will create in this lesson. The Mail Merge task pane displays in the far right of the screen and is used to navigate through the six steps of the Wizard.

### To start the Mail Merge Wizard:

Mailings/Start Mail Merge Step-by-Step/Start Mail Merge Wizard

1. The main document automatically opens and is saved by *KPDO*.
2. Follow the path above to display a list of mail merge options.
3. Click Step-by-Step Mail Merge Wizard ❶.

---

## DRILL 1   MAIL MERGE WIZARD

1. The open document (*76-drill1main*) is the main document. Follow the path above to display a list of mail merge options. Click Step-by-Step Mail Merge Wizard.

2. Follow the six steps of the Mail Merge Wizard explained below and on the next few pages. To move from one step to the next, click Next located at the bottom of the pane. This drill will lead you through the steps for using the Mail Merge Wizard.

---

### Step 1: Select document type

- Choose Letters ❶.
- Click Next: Starting document to go to step 2 of the Wizard.

### Step 2: Select starting document

- Click Use the current document ❷ to create a new form letter in the active window.
- Click Next: Select recipients. (**Note:** You may click Previous: Select document type to return to the previous step.)

### Step 3: Select recipients

- Click Type a new list ❸.
- Under Type a new list, click Create ❹ to display the New Address List dialog box.

---

# Lesson 44 Leftbound Reports

## New Commands
• Margins
• Find and Replace

 **Warmup** *Lesson 44a Warmup*

## Skill Building

**44b** **Textbook Keying**

**first row**

1 Take the Paz exit; make a right turn; then the street veers left.
2 Stop by and see the amateur videos of Zoe at six o'clock tonight.
3 I made an excellent pizza with leftover bread, cheese, and beef.

**home row**

4 Dallas shall ask Sal to sell fake flash fads; Sal sells all fads.
5 A small fast salad is all Kallas had; Dallas adds a dash of salt.
6 Dallas saw all flasks fall; alas Dad adds a fast fake hall flask.

**third row**

7 We used thirty pails of yellow powder; Wesley threw the rest out.
8 I should go to the store with Paul to get eggs for the apple pie.
9 Did you see the request for Sy to take the test with your sister?

## Communication

### NUMBER EXPRESSION

**44c**

References/Communication Skills/Number Expression

1. Review the Number Expression exercise in *KPDO* before completing this activity.
2. Key the numbered list at the right single-spaced; correct any number expression errors as you key.
3. Proofread and check; click Next Activity. (*44c*)

1. Address the letter to 1 Elm Street and postmark by April 15th.
2. The retirement reception will be held on the 1st of May in Room Twelve at 5 o'clock.
3. Program participants included fifteen supervisors, five managers, and two vice presidents.
4. 12 boxes arrived damaged and about 2/3 of the contents were crushed.
5. The manager reported that 85% of the project was complete, with 9 days remaining until the March 15th due date.
6. The presiding officer called the meeting to order at two p.m. and requested that the 2 50-page reports be distributed.
7. Nearly 10 million people visited the virtual museum this year.
8. Jim lives at nine 21st Street and works on 6th Avenue.

## MAIL MERGE

Creating personal form letters, printing labels, and addressing envelopes to a large number of individuals are tasks done easily using the Mail Merge feature. Mail merge is creating a new (merged) document by combining information from two other documents—the main document and the data source.

The **main document** contains the text and graphics that remain the same for each version of the merged document. Within the main document, **merge fields** are inserted as placeholders in locations where you want to merge names, addresses, and other variable information that comes from the data source file.

The **data source** is a file that contains the names, addresses, and other variables to be merged with the main document. All the variables for one individual are called a **record**. The separate variables for each record are called **fields**.

Main document

Data source

The data source was merged with the main document to produce the final document.

## MARGINS

Margins are the distance between the edge of the paper and the text of a document. The default margins referred to as "Normal" are 1" top, bottom, right, and left. To fit more information on a page, select Narrow margins or select Wide margins to increase the white space.

### To change margin settings:

Page Layout/Page Setup/Margins

1. Click on the down arrow to display the gallery of margins options.

2. Click the desired margins option.

### To set custom margins not listed in the gallery:

3. Click Custom Margins ①. From the Margins tab, click the up or down arrows to increase or decrease the default settings ②.

4. Apply margins to the Whole document ③ unless directed otherwise. Click OK.

Last Custom Setting			
Top:	1"	Bottom:	1"
Left:	1"	Right:	1"

Normal			
Top:	1"	Bottom:	1"
Left:	1"	Right:	1"

Narrow			
Top:	0.5"	Bottom:	0.5"
Left:	0.5"	Right:	0.5"

Moderate			
Top:	1"	Bottom:	1"
Left:	0.75"	Right:	0.75"

Wide			
Top:	1"	Bottom:	1"
Left:	2"	Right:	2"

Mirrored			
Top:	1"	Bottom:	1"
Inside:	1.25"	Outside:	1"

Office 2003 Default			
Top:	1"	Bottom:	1"
Left:	1.25"	Right:	1.25"

Custom Margins...

---

 custom margins

Page Layout/Page Setup/Margins/Custom Margins

1. In the open document, apply Wide margins.

2. Apply Narrow margins.

3. Change the left, right, and top margins to 1.5". Apply margin settings to the whole document.

4. Proofread and check; click Next Activity. (44-drill1)

---

# Mail Merge

## LEARNING OUTCOMES

- Merge form letters.
- Merge envelopes and labels.
- Edit the data source.
- Sort and filter records.

## Lesson 76 Mail Merge

### New Command

- Mail Merge

**Warmup** *Lesson 76a Warmup*

A ALL LETTERS

### Skill Building

**76b** **Timed Writing**

1. Key a 1' timed writing on each paragraph. Work to increase speed.
2. Key a 3' timing on all paragraphs.

What characterizes the life of an entrepreneur? Those who have never owned their own businesses may think owning a business means being your own boss, setting your own hours, and making a lot of money. Those who have run their own businesses are quick to report that owning a business may be exciting and challenging, but it also requires hard work, long hours, and personal sacrifice. A good idea is not the only prerequisite for a successful business. A little luck even helps.

Many small businesses are operated as businesses from the initial stages. However, some small businesses that turn out to be successful are just hobbies in the early stages. The entrepreneur has a job and uses the income from it to support the hobby. When the hobby begins to require more and more time, the entrepreneur has to choose between the job and the hobby. The decision is usually based on finances. If enough money can be made from the hobby or can be obtained from another source, the hobby is turned into a business.

# FIND AND REPLACE

 Find ⌄
ab̲c Replace
⌕ Select ⌄

Editing

Locating text, headings, footnotes, graphics, page breaks, comments, formatting, and other items within a document quickly is an essential skill when working with long documents such as reports.

## To find text:
Home/Editing/Find

1. Display the Navigation pane on the left side of the screen.

2. Key the text to be located in the search box ❶. The matches display below the search box. Click each match ❷ to go to the location in the document.

## To display other find options:

Click the Magnifying Glass button ❸. Click Options. The Find Options dialog box displays. Review the various find options to determine its usefulness in a search.

## To group search results by headings:

1. Click HEADINGS below the Search document box ❹. Headings that contain text with the search results display in yellow.

2. Click the desired heading ❺ to go to that heading in the document.

Summary

The fourth quarter has shown positive growth, and preliminary data indicates additional growth for the first quarter of next year. Additional information is available on our website at www.hesspropertyenterprises.com.

**75-d4**

**Compose Memo**

 hess memo

Mr. Hess asks you to compose a memo for him to send to the **Owners and Tenants Association** informing the members of the dates the Hess Office Park office will be closed for the upcoming year.

1. In the first paragraph, explain that the Board of Directors have approved the holiday closings for Hess Office Park and indicate the list is shown in the table below.

2. After the first paragraph, insert the table saved as a Quick Part in 75-d2.

3. In the last paragraph, give the name of **Colton Blake** as the contact to call in case of emergency. Colton's number is **512.555.0100**.

4. Date the memo **November 20, 201-**. Supply an appropriate subject line.

5. Proofread the document. Check the test and close. Click Exit *Word*. (75-d4)

6. Click Log out to exit *KPDO*.

**Learn More:**

www.cengagebrain.com

## To group search results by pages:

1. Click PAGES below the Search document box ❶. Only pages that contain results will display.

2. Click the desired page ❷ to go to that heading in the document.

3. Click x ❸ to end your search and display all your pages.

**Note:** For other searches, click the Magnifying Glass button to search for Graphics, Tables, Equations, Footnotes/Endnotes, or Reviewers.

## To replace text:

<mark>Home/Editing/Replace</mark>

1. Display the Find and Replace dialog box.

2. Key the text you wish to locate in the Find what box.

3. Key the replacement text in the Replace with box.

4. Click Find Next to find the next occurrence of the text. Click Replace to replace one occurrence or Replace All to replace all occurrences of the text.

## To find text and apply a format such as highlight:

<mark>Home/Editing/Replace</mark>

1. Display the Find and Replace dialog box.

2. Key the text you wish to locate in the Find what box.

3. Click More to display additional options.

4. Click in Replace with and then click Format ❹ and select the desired format. ❺

Note the search options available when you click More, such as Match case or Find whole words only. Finding whole words only prevents you from finding letters within a word.

These changes represent an increase of 5 percent over last year's fourth quarter and a gain of 20 percent this year. This past year Patrick Hess, manager of Hess Office Park, has added the following recruitment activities:

- Joined the Chamber of Commerce and five civic organizations.
- Accepted office of vice president for one civic organization.
- Accepted leadership role in securing funding for college scholarships for area students.

These networks are producing excellent connections and resulted in one added owner and two additional tenants to Hess Office Park.

5K Scholarship Fun Run

Hess Office Park is the site for the 5K Scholarship Fun Run sponsored by the East Central Education Foundation (ECEF) to be held on April 10, 201-. Scholarship monies are awarded to freshmen students entering college in the fall semester.

Mr. Robert Kaczynski, president of ECEF, is the contact person and has signed the official agreement with our office. Hess Office Park will designate spaces in the south parking lot on Friday afternoon and all day on Saturday. Tables and chairs will be set up along the race route for volunteers to distribute drinks and snacks to the runners/walkers. Security and police assistance will be provided at the main intersection of Hess Boulevard and Elm Street. Space will also be provided for vendors near the entrance of the office park.

Staff Updates

We are pleased to welcome Dan Rivera, who joined our staff on October 1 as an accountant. Dan holds a master's degree in accounting and has worked as an auditor for seven years and three years as a forensic accountant. Dan and his wife, Marilyn, recently moved to Austin from San Antonio. They have two sons. Danny is 3 and Sam is 1. We look forward to Dan's contributions to our office.

Holiday Closings

Holiday closings are approved annually by the Board of Directors. The table below lists the six approved closings.

Insert holiday closings Quick Part created in 75-d2.

In case of emergency, tenants and owners are to contact Colton Blake at 512.555.0100.

**REVIEW**

**Insert Quick Part**

Insert/Text/Quick Parts

Select the saved Quick Part.

*(continued)*

Home/Editing/Find

1. Click the Find button to display the Navigation pane.

2. Display all occurrences of the word *speeches* and replace with **presentations**.

3. Display all occurrences of the word *objective*. Click on the last occurrence and replace with **goal**.

4. Display all occurrences of the word *confident*. Click Options and select Find whole words only. Replace the one occurrence with **assured**.

5. Find *audience* and highlight each occurrence in yellow. **Hint:** Be sure to set the Highlight button in the Font group on the Home tab to yellow.

6. Key **discussion** in the Search box. Click PAGES to browse the pages where this word occurs.

7. Click HEADINGS to display the headings where the word *discussion* occurs. Click on the second heading and then the third heading to move in the report.

8. Click the Magnifying Glass button and click Tables to go to the table in the report.

9. Proofread and check; click Next Activity. (*44-drill2*)

## Document Design

### LEFTBOUND REPORT

**44e**

References/Document Formats/Reports

Reports prepared with binders are called leftbound reports. The binding takes 0.5" of space. Study the illustration below and the full model on page 183 and note the 1.5" left margin required for leftbound reports. Review the other report formats that are the same for unbound and leftbound reports.

**Theme:** Use the default Office theme.

**Left margin:** 1.5"

**Right margin:** 1"

**Bottom margin:** Approximately 1"; last page may be deeper

**Font:** 11 point for body of report

**Title:** ❶

- Position at about 2".
- Capitalize the first letter of all main words and apply Title style. Tap ENTER two times.

**Side headings:** ❷

- Capitalize the first letter of all main words and apply Heading 1 style.

**TIP**

Follow the steps for 74-d1 if you need additional help with the steps.

Mr. Hess has drafted the fourth-quarter report he will present to the Owners and Tenants Association meeting in January. Use leftbound report format and the Retrospect theme. Shrink the title to fit on one line.

1. Use this information for the cover page. Obtain other information from the letterhead.

   Title: **Hess Office Park Fourth Quarter Activity Report**
   Subtitle: **October – December, 201-**

2. Apply styles to the title and side headings. Adjust space after each table.

3. Insert a picture of the new staff person at the beginning of the paragraph. Search for a photograph of a businessperson from the online pictures. Use square wrapping and size attractively. (Insert/Illustrations/Online Pictures)

4. Leave a blank page after the cover page for the table of contents. Number the table of contents page with small Roman numerals and the report with Arabic numbers. Remember to insert a section break at the top of the first page of the report.

5. Use the Integral header and footer style. The style will populate the content automatically. Display the page number in the footer on all pages of the report body.

6. Create a table of contents at 2" using the default template format; apply Title style.

7. Proofread and check; click Next Activity. (75-d3)

Title    Hess Office Park Fourth Quarter Activity Report

Subtitle    Quarter Ended December 31, 201-

The Hess Office Park Fourth Quarter Activity Report is prepared for the Owners and Tenants Association and is presented at the January meeting of the Association. The staff of Hess Office Park is pleased to report the following activities during the fourth quarter, ending December 31, 201-. Activities include work accomplished in the community as well as achievements in the office park.

New Owners and Tenants

One new owner and three new tenants have joined Hess Office Park in the fourth quarter. One tenant vacated space as of December 1. The table below outlines the changes in detail.

Space Changes in Fourth Quarter				
	Type of Lease			
	Owner	Tenant	Change	Suites Assigned
1		Ayesha Liem	Add	311
2		Ethan Madison	Add	323-325
3	Riley Grant		Add	410-412
4		Jackson Price	Add	422-423
5		Paula Bowen	Terminate	521-525

*(continued)*

Title ⟶ # Identify Your Audience and Purpose  Title style ↓ 2

Effective presenters realize the need to prepare for a successful presentation. Two areas of extensive preparation are the development of a thorough audience analysis and identification of a well-defined presentation purpose. ↓ 1

Side heading ⟶ ## Audience Analysis  Heading 1 style

The presenter must conduct a thorough audience analysis before developing the presentation. A listing of common audience demographics is shown in the table below. ↓ 1

Audience Profile	
Age	Gender
Education	Ethnic group
Marital status	Geographic location
Group membership	Vested interest in topic

1.5"  Given sufficient time, the presenter will research each of these areas carefully. Additionally, interviews with program planners and organization leaders will provide insight into the needs, desires, and expectations of the specific audience. ↓ 1    1"

Many successful presenters find it useful to arrive early to the presentation and greet participants as they enter the meeting room. Often presenters may begin the presentation with one or two directed questions to understand the profile and demeanor of the audience. Knowing the audience is an important first step in preparing a successful presentation. ↓ 1

## Purpose of the Presentation

After initially analyzing the audience profile well in advance, the presenter has a clear focus on the needs of the audience and then writes a well-defined purpose of the presentation. With a clear focus, the presenter confidently conducts research and organizes a presentation that is on target. The presenter remembers to state the purpose in the introduction of the presentation to assist the audience in understanding the well-defined direction of the presentation.

**Leftbound Report**

## 75-d1

**Letter**

 hess letterhead

Key a letter to **Mr. Jackson Price, President** of **Price & Price Company,** with information about the Owners and Tenants Association and an invitation to the December meeting. The mailing address is **100 Hess Boulevard, Suite 3532, Austin, TX 78712-2196.** (Include the company name in the letter address.)

1. Date the letter **November 20, 201-.**
2. Add **Enclosures** since this letter is being mailed. Create an envelope and add to the letter.
3. Proofread and check; click Next Activity. (*75-d1*)

We are pleased to welcome you as a new tenant in the Hess Office Park and invite you to the Owners and Tenants Association December meeting on Tuesday, December 2, at the offices of Schniepp Enterprises. The meeting begins at 6:30 p.m. with snacks and drinks provided by our host and offers a casual environment for meeting other owners and tenants.

The Owners and Tenants Association meets regularly on the first Monday of each month at 6:30 p.m. at the location of one of the owners and tenants. However, the December meeting was moved to Tuesday evening to accommodate the many businesses involved with the local Christmas parade. The January meeting will return to Monday evening and will be hosted by Hess Office Park at our newly renovated conference center.

To acquaint you with our association, I am enclosing the current directory and the most recent newsletters. I look forward to seeing you at the December meeting and am eager to introduce you to our fine group of owners and tenants.

## 75-d2

**Table**

 **REVIEW**

**Save Quick Part**

Insert/Text/Quick Parts down arrow/Save Selection to Quick Part Gallery

Select the text to be saved and then follow the path to save it.

Create a two-column table showing the list of holiday closings of the Hess Office Park; make the company name the first line heading and **201- Holiday Closings** the second line.

**New Year's Day: January 1; Memorial Day: May 26; Independence Day: July 4; Labor Day: September 4; Thanksgiving: November 23-24; Christmas: December 24-26**

1. Create a 2-column table using the required table style. Center the text in rows 1 and 2.
2. Adjust the column spacing attractively and center the table horizontally.
3. Select the table and save as a Quick Part named **holiday closings**.
4. Proofread and check; click Next Activity. (*75-d2*)

## Apply It

 **REVIEW**

**Add Space Before Paragraph**

Home/Paragraph/Line and Paragraph Spacing/Add Space Before Paragraph

1. Key the model leftbound report shown on the previous page. Change the left margin to 1.5". Tap ENTER three times to position the title at about 2". Tap ENTER twice.

2. Apply appropriate styles to the title and side headings.

3. Key the table and apply the Grid Table 6 Colorful – Accent 1 style. Size the columns attractively and center the table horizontally. Click in the paragraph below the table and apply Add Space Before Paragraph to adjust the spacing after the table.

4. Proofread and check; click Next Activity. (44-d1)

44-d2

**Edit Report**

 brochure

 **TIP**

**Replace Font Attribute (Italic)**

Find what:

1. Click Format and then Font.
2. Under Font style, click Italic.

Replace with:

1. Click Format and then Font.
2. Under Font style, click Not italic.

1. Format as a leftbound report. Apply the Retrospect document theme.

2. Key the paragraph shown below as the last paragraph. Apply Heading 1 style to the side heading.

3. Search for the word *photos* and replace with **photographs**.

4. Search for all occurrences of italics and replace them with no italic.

5. Search for all occurrences of bold and replace them with no bold except the side headings. **Hint:** Click the No Formatting button in the Find and Replace dialog box before you begin the new search. Click Find Next to review each replacement.

6. Click PAGES in the Navigation pane. Search for the word *readability*. Which page displays as a result of your search?

7. Click HEADINGS (*readability* is displayed in the search box). Which heading is displayed in yellow to indicate readability is discussed under that heading in the document?

8. Proofread and check; click Exit Word. (44-d2)

9. Click Log out to exit *KPDO*.

**Summary**  Apply Heading 1 style

Remember to plan your page layout with the three basic elements of effective page design. Always include sufficient white space to give an uncluttered appearance. Learn to add bold when emphasis is needed, and do consider your audience when choosing typestyles. Finally, use typestyles to add variety to your layout, but remember, no more than two typestyles in a document.

# Lesson 75 Hess Office Park

## Skill Building

### 75b  Timed Writing

1. Key a 1' timing on each paragraph; work to increase speed.

2. Key a 3' timing on all paragraphs.

You must prepare early for an international trip. If you do not have a passport, you will need to apply for a passport well in advance of the travel date. Also, you will need to attach a recent photograph that meets passport rules. Begin reading books and browsing websites that offer details on international travel to your destination. Be sure to update your immunizations and buy digestive medicines that might be needed when exploring new foods.

Frequently the time on the plane is quite long, with some international flights over ten hours in the air. Travel delays are possible, so keep a small bag with a change of clothes, toiletries, medicine, and other important items with you. Bringing your own travel pillow, a good book, and other entertainment along with that provided by the airline will make your trip an enjoyable one.

When you leave the plane, you will be given a card to be presented upon entry to the country and one to present when you exit the country. Keep those cards and your passport with you at all times. When you remember these preparation guides, you are on your way to a memorable international experience.

## Project Setting

### HESS OFFICE PARK

You are continuing your work as an assistant to Patrick J. Hess, the manager of Hess Office Park, the 500-acre office park managed by Hess Property Enterprises. Your assistance in preparing the annual report is required for this project as well as a letter to a new tenant inviting him to the Owners and Tenants Association meeting and a memo announcing the office closings for the next year.

#### Standard operating procedures for the project:

1. Use the Retrospect document theme for all documents.
2. Use block letter style with open punctuation and the Hess Office Park letterhead from the data files. Include an appropriate salutation and use *Sincerely* as the complimentary closing. Begin the data at approximately 2". **Use Patrick J. Hess, Manager** as the writer's name and title.
3. Create envelopes for letters only when directed, as many letters are attached to an email.
4. The data files also contain a Hess Office Park memo form.
5. Add your reference initials and other notations as appropriate.
6. Use the List Table 4 – Accent 2 table style for all tables and center tables horizontally.

# *Lesson 45* Multiple-Page Reports

**New Commands**

- Page Number
- Line/Page Breaks
- Insert File
- Symbols
- Special Characters

**New Commands**

**45b**

## PAGE NUMBERS

Multiple-page documents, such as reports, require page numbers. The Page Number command automatically inserts the correct page number on each page. Page numbers may be positioned in the header position (0.5" from top of page) or in the footer position (bottom of page). To prevent the number from printing on the first page, you can modify the page layout on the first page.

To insert page numbers:

Insert/Header & Footer/Page Number

1. Display a list of page number positions and formatting options.

2. Click an option such as Top of Page ❶ to display a gallery of page number styles.

3. Click the down scroll arrow to browse the various styles ❷. **Note:** To remove page numbers, click Remove Page Numbers ❸ .

Double-click in the body of the document to close the header. Double-click in the header area to open the header.

To remove the page number from the first page:

Header & Footer Tools/Design/Options/Different First Page

When the page number is inserted, the Header & Footer Tools Design conceptual tab displays. On the Design tab from the Options group, click Different First Page ❹. The page number does not display on the first page.

**Option:** Select Different First Page from the Layout tab of the Page Setup dialog box (Page Layout/Page Setup/Dialog Box Launcher).

**Edit Report**

 market report

1. In the open document, click the Table of Contents button and then Custom Table of Contents. Change to the Formal style with dot leaders. Click Yes to the prompt to replace the selected table of contents.

2. Modify the report as follows and update the table of contents. Click Update entire table.

   a. Split the window into two panes. In the first pane, position so you can see the Market Analysis section on page 1 of the report. In the second pane, position so you can see the Developers section on page 2.

   b. In the top pane, select the Marketing Analysis section, drag across the split bar, and drop just before the side heading *Developers*. The Market Analysis section is now on page 2. Remove the split pane.

   c. In the paragraph heading *Small Businesses*, change *Businesses* to lowercase.

3. Select the *Appendix* title on the last page of the report and click Add Text to add this text to the table of contents. Select Level 1. Click Update Table button to update the entire contents page.

4. Verify that the page numbers were updated, the heading was changed, and the Appendix was added to the table of contents. Apply Title style to title if needed.

5. Proofread and check; click Exit *Word*. (74-d2)

6. Click Log out to exit *KPDO*.

**QUICK ✔**

Check your table of contents against the illustration below.

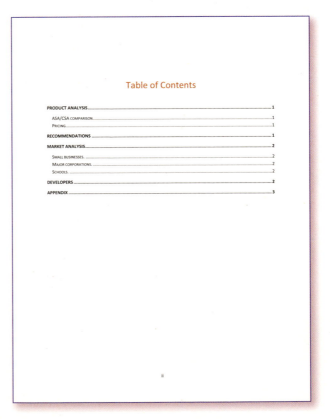

Table of Contents

PRODUCT ANALYSIS............................................................................................................................1
    ASA/CSA COMPARISON.....................................................................................................1
    PRICING.......................................................................................................................1
RECOMMENDATIONS ........................................................................................................................1
MARKET ANALYSIS.............................................................................................................................2
    SMALL BUSINESSES..........................................................................................................2
    MAJOR CORPORATIONS....................................................................................................2
    SCHOOLS......................................................................................................................2
DEVELOPERS ....................................................................................................................................2
APPENDIX .........................................................................................................................................3

ii

## LINE AND PAGE BREAKS

Pagination or breaking pages at the appropriate location can easily be controlled using two features: Widow/Orphan control and Keep with next.

**Widow/Orphan control** prevents a single line of a paragraph from printing at the bottom or top of a page. A check mark displays in this option box indicating that Widow/Orphan control is "on" (the default).

**Keep with next** prevents a page break from occurring between two paragraphs. Use this feature to keep a side heading from being left alone at the bottom of a page.

To use Keep with next:

<mark>Home/Paragraph/Dialog</mark> Box Launcher

1.  Select the side heading and at least two lines of the paragraph that follow it.
2.  Display the Paragraph dialog box.
3.  From the Line and Page Breaks tab, select Keep with next.

---

**DRILL 1**      **PAGE NUMBERS**  keep with next

Insert/Header & Footer/Page Number

1. Add page numbers positioned at the top of page at the right. Do not print a page number on the first page.

2. Select the side heading at the bottom of the page along with the entire address and the 9:00 entry. Apply Keep with next so the side heading moves to page 2.

3. Preview to verify that the page number appears on page 2 only and that the side heading appears on page 2.

4. Proofread and check; click Next Activity. (*45-drill1*)

---

**QUICK ✔**

View/Window/Split

1. In the open document, click Split to divide window into two panes. Drag the split bar and drop just before #3.

2. In the bottom pane, scroll to #9.

3. In the top pane select the second numbered item (accept, except and examples). Do not select the automatic number 2.

4. Drag the selection across the split bar. Drop to the left of the word *fewer* (Item #9). The entry for *accept/except* will now be #8. **Note:** If you did not drop the text correctly, you may have to make minor spacing and numbering adjustments.

5. Double-click the split bar to remove it.

6. Proofread and check; click Next Activity. (*74-drill2*)

---

## Apply It

### 74-d1

**Review Report**

 review

### ❊ Discover

**Document Formatting Style**
Design/Document Formatting

Select one of the document formatting styles sets. Note the change in appearance of the Title, Heading 1, and Heading 2 styles in this report using the Centered document formatting style set.

### ★ TIP

Follow the directions exactly in order shown. You must:

- Step 6: Deselect Different First Page before you break the link and insert page numbers.

- Step 7: Break the link before deleting the page number.

---

1. In the open document, change the left margin to 1.5".

❊ 2. Apply the Retrospect document theme with Centered document formatting style set. On page 1, shrink the main heading to fit on one line.

3. Insert the Retrospect cover page and shrink the title to fit on one line.
   Document title: **Marketing Analysis Report**
   Subtitle: **Administrative Skills Assessment**
   Author: **Anna Mitchell, Forms Design Consultant**
   Company: **Mitchell Productivity Design, Inc., 78 Cottondale Street, Henderson, NV 89011-0078**

4. Position the insertion point at the top of the first page of the report and insert a Continuous section break.

5. *Number preliminary pages:* In the table of contents page, insert a page number at the bottom of the page using the Plain Number 2 style. Change the page number format to lowercase Roman numerals and change page number to start at ii.

6. *Add header to report pages:*
   - Click Go to Header; click Next twice to position the insertion point in the Header – Section 2.
   - Click Different First Page (deletes checkmark); click Link to Previous to break link. Insert the Banded header.
   - Click Different First Page (adds checkmark) to suppress the header on the first page of the report.

7. *Delete number in footer and insert page number:*
   - Click Go to Footer and click Next twice to move to Footer – Section 2.
   - Click Link to Previous to break link and then select the page number in the footer and tap DELETE.
   - Insert the Retrospect footer. Change the page number format to begin with page 1.

8. On the First Page Footer – Section 2 (first page of the body of the report), insert Retrospect footer to display on page 1. The footer and page number will display. This design is attractive with the footer on all pages of the body.

9. Position the insertion point on the blank page for the table of contents (not in the header section). Generate the table of contents using the Automatic Table 2 style. Position the heading at approximately 2" and apply Title style. Tap ENTER once after the title.

10. Change the left margin in Section 1 to 1.5".

11. Proofread and check; click Next Activity. (*74-d1*)

---

## SYMBOLS AND SPECIAL CHARACTERS

Symbols and special characters that are not on your keyboard can be inserted using the Symbol command. Different types of symbols can be inserted depending on the font selected. Some symbols are scientific or mathematical and are generally located on the Symbols font. Other symbols are decorative and are generally located on the Wingdings font.

**To insert symbols:**

Insert/Symbols/Symbol

1. Click in the document where the symbol is to be inserted.

2. Display the gallery of symbols. The gallery generally contains the symbols that have been recently used on that computer. If the symbol you want to insert is not among the options, click More Symbols to display the Symbol dialog box.

3. Make sure the Symbols tab is selected and then check the Font box for the appropriate font. If Symbol (or the font you want to use) is not displayed, click the drop-list arrow and scroll to the desired font and select it.

4. Scroll down to locate the desired symbol and select it.

5. Click Insert and Close.

Special characters not located on the keyboard are located on the Special Characters tab. Examples include the em dash, nonbreaking hyphen, registered, trademark, and paragraph characters.

**To insert special characters:**

Insert/Symbols/Symbol

1. Click in the document where the special character is to be inserted.

2. Click the Special Characters tab in the Symbol dialog box.

3. Select the special character desired; click Insert and then click Close.

---

## DRILL 2    SYMBOLS AND SPECIAL CHARACTERS

1. Apply Verdana 16-point font.

2. Insert these symbols; do not key the description or the parentheses. Tap ENTER after each symbol.

   Plus or minus symbol (±) from the Symbol font

   Smiley face (☺) from the Wingdings font

   Checkbox (☑) from the Wingdings 2 font

3. Key the text below and insert the special characters; do not key the description of the character in parenthesis. Tap ENTER after each character.

   **Farbe Microfiber™** (Trademark)
   **§** (Section)
   **¶** (Paragraph)

4. Proofread and check; click Next Activity. (45-drill2)

---

## New Commands

### GO TO

The Go To command is also used to navigate within a document. A variety of document segments can be located with the Go To command, such as pages, footnotes, tables, or headings.

 **TIP**

Use the keyboard shortcut CTRL + G to bring up the Go To command.

**To use the Go To command:**
Home/Editing/Find

1. Click the drop-list arrow on the Find command; then click Go To.

2. Click on the item you wish to find, such as Page or Heading. Then key the number in the text box.

   **Option:** Click the Magnifying Glass button and click Go To.

---

**DRILL 1**          **GO TO**                                                   go to

1. In the open document, use the Go To command to go to Section 2.

2. Go to Table 1.

3. Go to Footnote 2.

4. Go to Heading 2.

5. Go to Page 3.

6. Go to Page 1. Click Next Activity. (*74-drill1*)

---

### SPLITTING PANES

To view two parts of the document at the same time, split the window into two panes. To return to a single window, double-click the split bar.

**To split panes:**
View/Window/Split

Click, hold, and drag the split bar to the desired location and release it where you want it ❶. Note that you have two panes, with each having a ruler bar and scroll bars.

## MULTIPLE-PAGE REPORT

**45c**

Because reports are often longer than one page, page numbers are required for ease in reading the report. Remember when formatting a multiple-page document, insert page numbers on all pages except the first page.

Traditionally, page numbers are positioned at the top right of the page. However, in lengthy and more formal documents such as annual reports or manuals, attractive headers and footers are designed. The applications that follow will include the Simple gallery of page number designs. Advanced headers and footers will be presented later.

Study the illustration below, noting specifically the position of page numbers. Review the callouts to reinforce your understanding of report formats.

### To format a multiple-page report with page numbers at the top right:

1. Insert page numbers at the upper-right corner in the header position (0.5").
2. Suppress the page number on the first page.
3. Protect side headings that may be separated from the related paragraph with the Keep with next command. **Note:** When styles are applied to side headings, Keep with next is automatically applied, and side headings will not display alone at the bottom of a page.

---

Report Writing and Technology

Being able to communicate effectively in a clear, concise, and logical manner continues to be one of the most demanded work skills. Employees who practice effective revision skills are far ahead of their counterparts who have had the mind-set that the first draft is the final draft. This report details excellent procedures for revising a report draft, explaining effective technology tools that make the process easier. The result is a more professional and accurate final product.

Revising the Draft

After a first draft of a report is completed, the writer is ready to refine or polish the report. The writer must be objective when revising the report draft and cultivate an attitude for improving the report by always considering the draft as a process.

First, read the draft for content. This might mean rewriting sections of the report or adding information to areas that appear weak in this review. In this evaluative review, the writer may realize that one section would fit more logically after another section.

When the writer is satisfied with the content, it is time to verify that all style rules have been followed. For example, check all headings to ensure they are "talking" headings. Do the headings describe the content of the section? Also, be sure all headings are parallel. If the writer chooses the side heading Know Your Audience, other side headings must also begin with a verb. Note that the side headings in this report are parallel, with both beginning with a gerund.

Ensuring Correct and Attractive Formats

The effective writer understands the importance of using technology to create an attractive document that adheres to correct style rules. Here are a few examples of how to use technology to create a professional final document.

- Select attractive headers and footers from the built-in design galleries to provide page numbers and other helpful information to the reader.
- Suppress headers, footers, and page numbering on the title page and on the first page of the report.
- Invoke the Widow/Orphan control feature to ensure that no lines display alone at the bottom or top of a page. Use the Keep with next command to keep side headings from appearing alone at the bottom of the page.
- Take advantage of automatic features, such as a table of contents and citations.
- Use styles to format tables and charts.

Header position, right side                2

- Be sure to use the online thesaurus, spelling, and grammar features of the word processing software.
- Bookmark widely accepted online desk references and style manuals for easy use.
- Use the Show/Hide command to show the ¶ marks and other hidden formatting symbols.

These simple steps will assist you in your goal to create well-written and attractive reports. The next step is to practice, practice, and practice.

# Lesson 74 Productivity Tools for Reports

**New Commands**
- Go To
- Splitting Panes
- Document Formatting Style Set

## Skill Building

### 74b Textbook Keying

1. Key each line, concentrating on using good techniques.
2. Repeat the drill if time permits.

b  1 bib box baboo abbey abduct babka bubbles beaux bulk bebop abdomen
r  2 rebuke roux army carry organize warrant review ajar rough explore
b/r  3 brain bridge celebrate fabric debris zebra brusque broccoli bread
b/r  4 Brett wrote rubrics for the bronze broadcast assignment at break.
n  5 nods name naive nail barn napkin conquest pound kerning neon zone
u  6 none union untie ugly ultra usher flux menu bayou justice vaguely
u/n  7 under unique unwrap nudged nuzzle nutrient account immunize nouns
u/n  8 Hunter saw a number of squirrels lug nuts to the hidden bungalow.

## Communication

### 74c

References/Communication Skills/Other Internal Punctuation

1. Review the other internal punctuation rules and examples in *KPDO* before completing this activity.
2. Key each sentence single-spaced, correcting punctuation errors related to the apostrophe, colon, parenthesis, hyphen, and dash as you key. Do not key directions shown in parentheses in blue. Key the sentences as a numbered list.
3. Proofread and check; click Next Activity. *(74c)*

1. Youre to pick up Dr. Thames gift at the registration table.
2. The three speakers credentials are included in the head coordinators information packet.
3. Concurrent sessions are scheduled for 50 while computer sessions are scheduled for 90. (Denote time in minutes.)
4. Exhibit booths measuring 10 x 20. (Denote measurements in feet.)
5. The resort amenities illustrated on the website are: two golf courses, three pools, exercise room, and activity room.
6. The layout of the condominium shows the following rooms master bedroom with bath, guest bedroom with bath, kitchen, dining room, and laundry room.
7. Registration opened at 7 30 a.m. and closed at 4 30 p.m.
8. Exhibit space includes space rental, standard pipe and drape, two chairs, wastebasket, and general security. (Denote items with parentheses.)
9. Thirty five volunteers staffed the busy convention registration area during the three day conference.
10. The officers not the committee chairs are seated at the head table.

### 45–d1

**Multiple-Page Report**

 writing

**Insert a File**

Insert/Text/Object

1. Click the arrow next to Object.
2. Click Text from File.
3. Select the desired file and click Insert.

1. Key the first paragraph of the leftbound two-page report shown on the next two pages. Apply the appropriate style for the title of the report. Tap ENTER two times after title.

✳ 2. Insert the data file *writing* below the first PARAGRAPH. **Note:** Be sure to position the insertion point where you want the text to appear before inserting the file.

3. Apply the appropriate style for the side headings.

4. In the last bulleted item, delete the word *paragraph* and insert the ¶ mark from the Special Characters tab of the Symbol dialog box.

5. Use the Page Number command to number the pages at the top right. Select the Plain Number 3 number style. Click Different First Page to suppress the page number on the first page.

6. Preview the document to verify page numbers and that side headings are not left alone at the bottom of the page.

7. Proofread and check; click Next Activity. (45-d1)

### 45–d2

**Edit Report**

1. From the open document (45-d1), change the leftbound report to an unbound report. Apply the Facet document theme.

2. Position the insertion point on page 2 of the report. Change the page number style to Accent Bar 2.

3. Key the following as the last item in the bulleted list. Insert the symbols from the Wingdings font or the Special Characters tab.

- **Use a wide array of symbols to provide a fresh and up-to-date appearance, such as ❶, ☑, ©, or ®.**

4. Proofread and check; click Exit Word. (45-d2)

5. Click Log out to exit *KPDO*.

© Jupiterimages/Photos.com

## ❗ WORKPLACE SUCCESS

### Integrity

Integrity is synonymous with the word *honesty* and is confronted by employees in the workplace daily. Think about these rather common situations where integrity is clearly a choice:

- Arriving at work ten minutes late and then drinking coffee and chatting with coworkers for ten more minutes
- Talking with relatives and friends throughout the day
- Leaving work early regularly for personal reasons
- Presenting a report to the supervisor as original work without crediting the proper individuals for thoughts and ideas in the report
- Presenting a report that was completed at the last minute and that includes facts and figures that have not been verified as accurate

In all situations, ask the question, "Am I being honest?"

**73-d1**

 forms report

1. In the open document, add the captions shown below to the two tables. Position the caption above the table and number with Arabic numbers. Choose Table as the caption.

   Table on first page: Table 1 **Form Sources from 2011 Survey**

   Table on second page: Table 2 **Form Sources from 2014 Survey**

2. Insert a blank page after the page break on the table of contents page. Remember to click Show/Hide so you can see the Page Break.

3. Create the table of figures using the default format. Key the title **Table of Figures** at approximately 2" and apply Title style.

4. Edit both table captions as follows. Update the table of figures.

   Table 1 **Sources of Company Forms (2011 Survey)**

   Table 2 **Sources of Company Forms (2014 Survey)**

5. Proofread and check; click Next Activity. (73-d1)

**73-d2**

**Edit Table of Figures**

 pictures

1. In the open document, create a new label named **May Photos**. Insert a caption for the pictures as follows:

   a. May Photo 1: **Maggie and the Bradford Pear**

   b. May Photo 2: **Our Morning Visitors at the Beach House**

   c. May Photo 3: **Giraffes Seen on Last Day of Safari**

2. Click on page 2 after the title and create a table of figures using the default format (From Template).

3. Proofread and check; click Exit *Word*. (73-d2)

4. Click Log out to exit *KPDO*.

Title $\longrightarrow$

# Report Writing and Technology ↓2

Being able to communicate effectively in a clear, concise, and logical manner continues to be one of the most demanded work skills. Employees who practice effective revision skills are far ahead of their counterparts who have had the mind-set that the first draft is the final draft. This report details excellent procedures for revising a report draft, explaining effective technology tools that make the process easier. The result is a more professional and accurate final product.

Heading 1
## Revising the Draft ↓1

After a first draft of a report is completed, the writer is ready to refine or polish the report. The writer must be objective when revising the report draft and cultivate an attitude for improving the report by always considering the draft as a process.

1.5"

First, read the draft for content. This might mean rewriting sections of the report or adding information to areas that appear weak in this review. In this evaluative review, the writer may realize that one section would fit more logically after another section.

1"

When the writer is satisfied with the content, it is time to verity that all style rules have been followed. For example, check all headings to ensure they are "talking" headings. Do the headings describe the content of the section? Also, be sure all headings are parallel. If the writer chooses the side heading Know Your Audience, other side headings must also begin with a verb. Note that the side headings in this report are parallel, with both beginning with a gerund.

## Ensuring Correct and Attractive Formats

The effective writer understands the importance of using technology to create an attractive document that adheres to correct style rules. Here are a few examples of how to use technology to create a professional final document. ↓1

- Select attractive headers and footers from the built-in design galleries to provide page numbers and other helpful information to the reader.
- Suppress headers, footers, and page numbering on the title page and on the first page of the report.
- Invoke the Widow/Orphan control feature to ensure that no lines display alone at the bottom or top of a page. Use the Keep with next command to keep side headings from appearing alone at the bottom of the page.
- Take advantage of automatic features, such as a table of contents and citations.
- Use styles to format tables and charts.

**Multiple-Page Report**

Check your table of figures from the illustration below.

## Table of Figures

# ! WORKPLACE SUCCESS

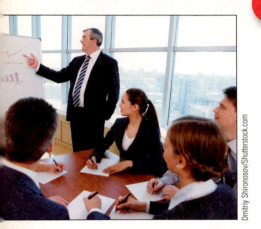

Dmitriy Shironosov/Shutterstock.com

## What Is Your Listening Grade?

Isn't it interesting that students are not required to complete a course in listening when 80 percent of our time each day is spent listening? To perform well in organizations, a keen listening skill is essential. Evaluate yourself on the following areas and start today working on a listening improvement plan in those areas. Search for excellent listening quizzes to assist you.

### BODY LANGUAGE

Do you ...  sit with your arms closed?
stand with your hand on the door as you listen to someone?
doodle while listening or play with a pen or some other object?
look at your watch while others are talking?
continue checking your email while listening to someone on the phone or someone face to face?

### MINDSET

Do you ...  think you already know what the speaker has to say?
think the speaker is wasting your time?
tune out anything boring? or too long?
disregard anything being said if you do not agree with it?
judge the speaker before he/she begins to speak?

### RESPONSES TO THE SPEAKER

Do you ...  finish the speaker's sentence because you know what he/she is going to say?
think about what you will say while the speaker is talking?
interrupt the speaker so you can start talking sooner?
look ridiculous sometimes when you respond in a manner that tells others that you were not listening?

2

- Be sure to use the online thesaurus, spelling, and grammar features of the word processing software.
- Bookmark widely accepted online desk references and style manuals for easy use.
- Use the Show/Hide command to show the ¶ marks and other hidden formatting symbols.

1.5"    These simple steps will assist you in your goal to create well-written and attractive reports. The    1"
next step is to practice, practice, and practice.

**Multiple-Page Report**

1. Position the insertion point where the table of figures is to be positioned (two lines below the Table of Figures title). Display the Table of Figures dialog box.

2. Click the down arrow beside the

   a. Tab leader box and select the leader type.

   b. Formats box and select the format.

   c. Caption label box and select the caption label, e.g., Table. Click OK.

**To update a table of figures:**

1. Change the caption as desired.

2. Click in the table of figures. From the Captions group, on the References tab, click Update Table. *Shortcut:* F9.

3. Select Update page numbers only or Update entire table. Click OK.

---

**DRILL 1**  **TABLE OF FIGURES**  guide

1. In the open document, insert captions below the figure for the first two figures in this file. Label as follows:

   Figure 1 **Caption Box**

   Figure 2 **Caption Numbering Box**

2. Create a table of figures on the first page using the Formal format and the Figure caption label. Choose the dot leaders (second option).

3. Add the word **Dialog** before the word *Box* in both figures.

4. Insert caption below the third figure and label Figure 3 as: **New Label Dialog Box**

5. Update the table of figures. Reapply the format if necessary. Compare your work to the illustrations below.

6. Proofread and check; click Next Activity. (*73-drill1*)

*Figure 1 Caption Dialog Box*

*Figure 2 Caption Numbering Dialog Box*

*Figure 3 New Label Dialog Box*

# *Lesson 46* Reports in MLA Style

New Commands

- Header
- Save As Template
- Hanging Indent

**New Commands**

## HEADER

**46b**

Header

A header contains text that is keyed in the top margin of the page. In this lesson you will create a header for an MLA report that displays on all pages.

To insert a header with text and page number:

Insert/Header & Footer/Header

1. Display the Built-in gallery of Header styles. Click the Blank style.
2. Tap the TAB key twice to place the insertion point at the far-right position. Key the desired text followed by a space.
3. From the Header & Footer group, click the Page Number drop-list arrow and choose Current Position. Choose the Plain Number style.

To edit a header:

Insert/Header & Footer/Header

To edit a header, click Edit Header. An alternate method is to double-click in the header section of the document. To move to the text of the document, double-click in the document—not the header.

To remove a header, click Remove Header.

Top of Page	▶
Bottom of Page	▶
Page Margins	▶
Current Position	▶
Format Page Numbers...	
Remove Page Numbers	

## DRILL 1    HEADER

1. Double-click in the header section. Change to 12-point Times New Roman font.

2. Click the Align Right command and key **LNAME**. Tap the Space Bar and insert the Page Number command as shown above.

3. Proofread and check; click Next Activity. (*46-drill1*)

# Lesson 73 Report Features

 **Warmup**   *Lesson 73a Warmup*

## New Commands

**73b**

### TABLE OF FIGURES

A table of figures is a list of all of the captions for tables, charts, pictures, graphics, and equations in a document. Captions can be added automatically or manually to an existing object. See the illustration below. Generally, tables are labeled above the table, and figures are labeled below the figure.

## Table of Figures

FIGURE 1 CAPTION DIALOG BOX ------------------------------------------------------------------1
FIGURE 2 CAPTION NUMBERING DIALOG BOX --------------------------------------------------1
FIGURE 3 NEW LABEL DIALOG BOX --------------------------------------------------------------1

**To insert a caption:**

References/Captions/Insert Caption

1. Select the item to be captioned. In the caption text box, space once after the number and key the caption.

2. From the Label list, click the drop-list arrow and select the desired label, e.g., Figure, Table, Equation.

3. From the Position list, click the drop-list arrow and choose Above selected item or Below selected item.

4. Click the Numbering button to choose the desired number format, e.g., 1, 2, 3. Click OK.

5. Click New Label to create a new label group, such as Sports Photos. Click OK.

**Note:** Click AutoCaption to select the objects for which you want captions created automatically, e.g., *Microsoft Word* Table.

## SAVE AS TEMPLATE

A template is a set of predefined styles for a particular type of document. The purpose of a template is to reuse a document's formatting while easily changing the content. Templates are available for numerous types of documents and others can be downloaded from the Microsoft website. However, when existing documents are unique, it is useful to save them as a template.

By default, templates are saved to the Templates folder within the program. In a classroom environment, you will want to save templates you create to a USB memory device (flash drive) or another location.

### To save a document as a template:
File/Save As

1.  Click the File tab and then Save As. Click Computer and Browse. The Save As dialog box displays.

2.  *Save to a USB memory device (flash drive):* Select Computer and browse to the flash drive.

    -or-

    *Save to a hard drive:* By default the software will save to the Templates folder or browse to the desired location.

3.  In the File name box, key an appropriate template name such as **my memo**.

4.  In the Save as type box, click the down arrow and select Word Template. Click Save. The extension *.dotx* is assigned automatically.

### To use the template:
File/New

*From a flash drive:* Click the File tab and select New. From the Available Templates pane, browse to locate the desired template. Click OK.

-or-

*From a hard drive:* Click the File tab and select New. From the Available Templates pane, choose My templates; browse to locate the desired template. Click OK.

**Update Table of Contents**

final report

1. In the open document, move the section Conversion from Paper to Electronic Forms to appear below the Existing System section. Add the word *Implementation* after the heading *Forms Inventory*.

2. On page iv, select the words *Executive Summary* and click Add Text and select Level 1 to add this preliminary section to the table of contents.

3. In the table of contents, key **Letter of Transmittal** as the first entry. Tap TAB key and then key **ii** as the page number.

4. Click Update Table to update the entire table of contents. Check that all changes were made.

5. Proofread and check; click Exit *Word*. (72-d2)

6. Click Log out to exit *KPDO*.

## Writing Matters

**Communicating Today** ▶

It seems that everyone is blogging, tweeting, messaging, and sharing on all types of social media sites. The smartphones and tablets make communication so easy, quick, and fun for billions of users every day.

When browsing these posts, one might raise the question if grammar and spelling are still important. Is proofreading something of the past? As a writer (bloggers and tweeters are writers), it is important to remember that assumptions (good or bad) can be easily made by the readers. Once released the written word (or text or tweet) is evaluated, and it showcases one's abilities. It is a known fact that employers are viewing social media websites to gain more information about prospective employees. The social media postings readily portray the individual's knowledge and use of proper English as well as other sought-after workplace skills, such as attitude and respect for others.

The growing popularity of social media also raises a need for increased awareness of plagiarism. With the ease of copying and pasting, online plagiarism is a common trap in which today's writers find themselves. Content similarity tools are available for checking one's text to ensure originality. Bloggers are aware of these tools and other precautions to protect their work.

Enjoy the ease of communicating with friends and family, but remember it always pays to use correct and appropriate writing skills.

File/Save As

1. In the open document, replace (*Student's name*) with **Sophia Johnson.**

   KPDO: Your document will be saved as a *Word* file and not as a template.

2 Proofread and check; click Next Activity. (*46-drill2 Keyboarding progress template*)

---

## HANGING INDENT

Hanging indent places the first line of a paragraph at the left margin and indents all other lines to the first tab. It is commonly used to format bibliography entries, glossaries, and lists. Hanging indent can be applied before or after text is keyed.

### To create a hanging indent:

1. From the Horizontal Ruler, click on the Hanging Indent marker ❶.
2. Drag the Hanging Indent marker ❷ to the position where the indent is to begin.
3. Key the paragraph. Note that the second and subsequent lines are indented beginning at the marker.

---

1. In the open document, select all the glossary entries and format them with a hanging indent. **Hint:** Use the shortcut CTRL + T.

2. Proofread and check; click Next Activity. (*46-drill3*)

★ **TIP**

Follow the directions exactly in order shown:

- Step 7: Deselect Different First Page before you break the link and insert page numbers.
- Step 8: Break the link before deleting the page number.

7. *Delete number in report footer:* Click Go to Footer and click Next once to go to Footer – Section 2.

 a. Click Link to Previous.

 b. Select the page number and tap DELETE. Click Close Header and Footer.

8. Position the insertion point on the blank page left for the table of contents (not in the header section). Tap ENTER 4 times to position the heading at approximately 2". Create the table of contents using the Automatic Table 2 style. Apply Title style. Tap ENTER after the title.

9. Proofread and check; click Next Activity. (*72-d1*)

Goal of the System

The goal of the system was to convert 70 to 75 percent of the forms to an electronic format within a three-year time period. During this same time frame, the company planned to upgrade computers and make the network available to all employees except warehouse and delivery personnel.

Follow-Up Study

This phase of the study was authorized to determine the effectiveness of the program that was implemented. The following table shows the progress made since the program was instituted.

Form Type	Percentage
Employee—Paper	8%
Company—Paper	5%
Vendor—Paper	3%
External—Paper	4%
Company—Electronic	48%
Employee—Electronic	32%

Results

Currently, 80 percent of all forms are in electronic format, and 20 percent are paper based. The four forms that are currently purchased from vendors are being redesigned so that they can be made available electronically. The remaining paper-based forms are used primarily by warehouse and delivery personnel. However, the Technology Committee has recommended providing these employees with handheld computers to perform their work. As soon as this recommendation is implemented, the forms they use can be converted to electronic format.

The new system has resulted in a 20 percent cost savings over the previous system. In addition, more than 80 percent of the employees indicated that the new system improved their efficiency and effectiveness.

# MLA REPORT STYLE

Study the guidelines shown below for an academic report formatted in MLA style. Refer to the full-page model on pages 197–198 and always check the *MLA Handbook for Writers of Research Papers* and your teacher's instructions.

- Use 12-point Times New Roman font.
- Use 1" margins (top, bottom, left, and right).
- DS paragraphs and indent 0.5".
- DS long quotations of 40 or more words and indent 1" from the left margin.
- Key heading information beginning at 1"; include full name, instructor's name, assignment name, and current date.
- Center the report title and capitalize all main words.
- Place page numbers at the top right of every page. Include the writer's last name and the page number (Last Name 1).
- Include a complete alphabetical listing of all references cited in the report and label it **Works Cited**; DS.

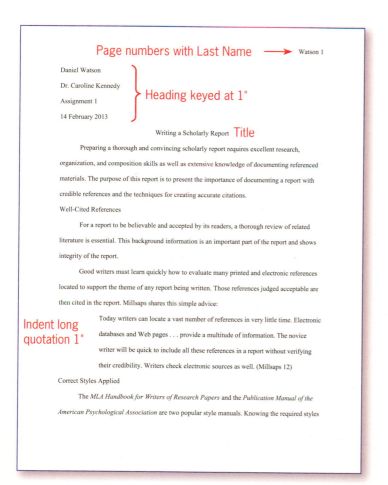

Page numbers with Last Name →  Watson 1

Daniel Watson

Dr. Caroline Kennedy

Assignment 1          Heading keyed at 1"

14 February 2013

Writing a Scholarly Report   Title

Preparing a thorough and convincing scholarly report requires excellent research, organization, and composition skills as well as extensive knowledge of documenting referenced materials. The purpose of this report is to present the importance of documenting a report with credible references and the techniques for creating accurate citations.

Well-Cited References

For a report to be believable and accepted by its readers, a thorough review of related literature is essential. This background information is an important part of the report and shows integrity of the report.

Good writers must learn quickly how to evaluate many printed and electronic references located to support the theme of any report being written. Those references judged acceptable are then cited in the report. Millsaps shares this simple advice:

Indent long quotation 1"   Today writers can locate a vast number of references in very little time. Electronic databases and Web pages . . . provide a multitude of information. The novice writer will be quick to include all these references in a report without verifying their credibility. Writers check electronic sources as well. (Millsaps 12)

Correct Styles Applied

The *MLA Handbook for Writers of Research Papers* and the *Publication Manual of the American Psychological Association* are two popular style manuals. Knowing the required styles

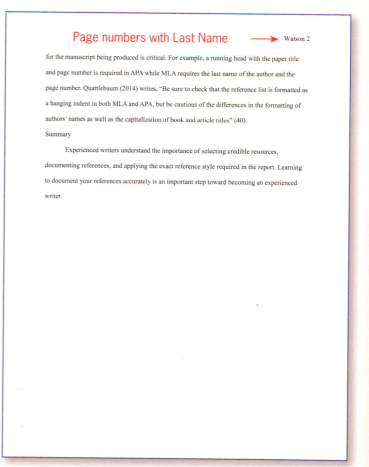

Page numbers with Last Name →  Watson 2

for the manuscript being produced is critical. For example, a running head with the paper title and page number is required in APA while MLA requires the last name of the author and the page number. Quattlebaum (2014) writes, "Be sure to check that the reference list is formatted as a hanging indent in both MLA and APA, but be cautious of the differences in the formatting of authors' names as well as the capitalization of book and article titles" (40).

Summary

Experienced writers understand the importance of selecting credible resources, documenting references, and applying the exact reference style required in the report. Learning to document your references accurately is an important step toward becoming an experienced writer.

## TABLE OF CONTENTS

A table of contents contains a list of the headings in a document, along with the page number on which each heading appears. Begin the title at about 2". Apply Title style and tap ENTER twice after the title.

About 2" (tap ENTER 3 times)

**Table of Contents**    Title style

## Apply It

**Report**

 forms

1. Position the insertion point at the end of the open document (*forms*). Then key the remainder of the report shown on the next page; apply Plain Table 1 style and center the data in column 2.

2. Apply the Integral document theme and then apply appropriate styles to the title and side headings of the report beginning after the Executive Summary.

3. Insert the Semaphore cover page and key the following:

   Date: Current date

   Document title: **Forms Design and Management**

   Subtitle: **Summary of Three-Year Implementation**

   Author: **Anna Mitchell, Forms Design Consultant**

   Company: **Mitchell Productivity Design, Inc., 78 Cottondale Street, Henderson, NV 89011-0078**

4. Position the insertion point at the top of the first page of the report (Forms Design and Management) and insert a Continuous section break.

5. *Number preliminary pages:* Position the insertion point in the second page (transmittal letter) of the Footer – Section 1. (Section 1 ends with the Executive Summary.)

   a. Insert a page number at the bottom of the page using the Plain Number 2 style.

   b. Change the page number format to lowercase Roman numerals and change page number to start at ii. **Note:** Different First Page is selected (check mark is in box).

6. *Number report pages:* Click Go to Header; click Next twice to go to Header – Section 2.

   a. Deselect Different First Page and click Link to Previous.

   b. Insert a page number at the top right using the Plain Number 3 style. Change the page number format to begin with page 1.

   c. Click Different First Page.

*(continued)*

# INTERNAL CITATIONS IN MLA STYLE

The last name of the author(s) and the page number of the cited material are shown in parentheses within the body of the report (Crawford 134). When the author's name is used in the text to introduce the quotation, only the page number appears in parentheses: *Crawford said, "Faculty are uploading podcast lectures to their distance website" (134).*

Short, direct quotations of three lines or fewer are enclosed within quotation marks. Long quotations of four lines or more are indented 1" from the left margin and DS. Tap ENTER once before and after the long quotation.

According to Estes, "Successful business executives have long known the importance of good verbal communication" (29).

**Short Quotation**

Probably no successful enterprise exists that does not rely upon the ability of its members to communicate for its success. Shaefer adds:

> Make no mistake, both written and verbal communication are the stuff upon which success is built in all types of organizations. Both forms deserve careful study by any business that wants to grow. Successful businesspeople must read, write, speak, and listen with skill. Often professional development in these areas is needed. (p. 28)

**Long Quotation**

# WORKS CITED PAGE IN MLA STYLE

References cited in the report are listed at the end of the report in alphabetical order by authors' last name. Study the guidelines and the model shown below.

1"

Watson 3

Works Cited

Millsaps, John Thomas. *Report Writing Handbook: An Essential Guide.* Columbus: Wellington Books, 2014. Print.

Quattlebaum, Sarah. "Apply Reference Styles Correctly." *The Quarterly Reference Journal* 27.1 (2014): 35-42. Print.

- Begin the references on a new page (insert manual page break at the end of the report).
- Center the title at the top of the page (1") with main words capitalized.
- Double-space the references. DS is 2.0 line spacing.
- Format references with hanging indent.
- Number the reference page at the top right of the page using same format as the report.

**References/Table of Contents/Table of Contents**

1. In the open document (*72-drill1*), go to the table of contents page. Click the Table of Contents button and change the style to Automatic Table 1.

2. Change the first subheading under Section Breaks to **Selecting Types of Section Breaks**.

3. Select the entire Section Breaks section and move after the Headers and Footers section.

4. Select the *Appendix* title on the last page of the report and click Add Text to add this text to the table of contents. Select Level 1.

5. Click the Update Table button and update the entire table.

6. Proofread and check; click Next Activity. (*72-drill2*)

---

## DRILL 3     CHANGE TOC FORMAT

1. In the open document (*72-drill2*), click Custom Table of Contents and change to the Formal style. Click Yes to the prompt to replace the selected table of contents.

2. Proofread and check; click Next Activity. (*72-drill3*)

---

## NUMBER PRELIMINARY PAGES

Preliminary pages are numbered with lowercase Roman numerals. Change the number format when inserting the page number in a report.

**To change page number format:**

Insert/Header & Footer/Page Number

1. Click Page Number Format.
2. Click the down list arrow and select the desired page number format. If necessary, set the starting page number.

---

## DRILL 4     NUMBER PAGES

1. In the open document (*72-drill3*), position the insertion point at the top of the first page of the report (page after table of contents). Insert a Continuous section break.

2. *Number preliminary pages:* Position the insertion point in the footer of Section 1 page 2 (table of contents).

   - Insert a page number at the bottom of the page using the Plain Number 2 style. Change the page number format to lowercase Roman numerals. Change Start at to ii.

3. *Number report pages:* Click Go to Header and click Next twice to go to the header of Section 2.

   - Deselect Different First Page. Click Link to Previous to break the link.

4. Insert a page number at the top right using the Plain Number 3 style. Change the format to Arabic (1, 2, 3).

   - Change Start at to 1. If your insertion point jumps, return to the same header position.
   - Click Different First Page (check mark in box).

5. *Delete number in footer:* Click Go to Footer and click Next twice to go to Footer – Section 2.

   - Click the number in the footer on page 2 section 2.
   - Click Link to Previous to break link.
   - Then delete the number in the footer of Section 2. Be sure to break link before deleting the number.

6. Update the page numbers in the table of contents.

7. Proofread and check; click Next Activity. (*72-drill4*)

Last Name + one space and
Page Number command

1"

Daniel Watson

Dr. Caroline Kennedy

Assignment 1

14 February 2013

1

Writing a Scholarly Report

1"

Preparing a thorough and convincing scholarly report requires excellent research,

1"

organization, and composition skills as well as extensive knowledge of documenting referenced

materials. The purpose of this report is to present the importance of documenting a report with

credible references and the techniques for creating accurate citations.

Well-Cited References

For a report to be believable and accepted by its readers, a thorough review of related

literature is essential. This background information is an important part of the report and shows

integrity of the report.

Good writers must learn quickly how to evaluate many printed and electronic references

located to support the theme of any report being written. Those references judged acceptable are

then cited in the report. Millsaps shares this simple advice:

Long quotation indented 1"

Today writers can locate a vast number of references in very little time. Electronic

databases and Web pages . . . provide a multitude of information. The novice

writer will be quick to include all these references in a report without verifying

their credibility. Writers check electronic sources as well. (Millsaps 12)

Correct Styles Applied

The *MLA Handbook for Writers of Research Papers* and the *Publication Manual of the*

*American Psychological Association* are two popular style manuals. Knowing the required styles

1"

**MLA Report Style**

# MODIFY TABLE OF CONTENTS

A table of contents is often modified after it has been created, because of updating changes in the headings and page numbers, choosing another format, or adding text.

## To update a table of contents:

1. At the top of the generated table of contents, click Update Table ❶. The Update Table of Contents dialog box displays.

2. Select Update page numbers only or Update entire table and click OK.

## To change the format:
References/Table of Contents/Table of Contents

1. Click the Table of Contents button ❷ and select another table of contents style.

   -or-

2. For additional styles, click Custom Table of Contents to display the Table of Contents dialog box.

   a. Accept the defaults to show page numbers, right-align page numbers, and use leaders; or click the arrow next to Format and select the desired format, such as Formal.

   b. Indicate the number of heading levels to be included in the table of contents in the Show Levels box (up to nine). Click OK.

## To add text to the table of contents:
References/Table of Contents/Add Text

1. Select the text to be added to the table of contents.

2. Click Add Text.

3. Choose the desired level of heading.

4. Click in the table of contents and click Update Table.

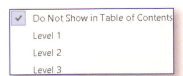

Note: You may also key text directly in a table of contents. Use the Format Painter to copy the format of the entry; then key the correct page number.

for the manuscript being produced is critical. For example, a running head with the paper title and page number is required in APA while MLA requires the last name of the author and the page number. Quattlebaum (2014) writes, "Be sure to check that the reference list is formatted as a hanging indent in both MLA and APA, but be cautious of the differences in the formatting of authors' names as well as the capitalization of book and article titles" (40).

Summary

Experienced writers understand the importance of selecting credible resources, documenting references, and applying the exact reference style required in the report. Learning to document your references accurately is an important step toward becoming an experienced writer.

**MLA Report Style**

## New Command
- Table of Contents

 **Warmup** *Lesson 72a Warmup*

**72b**

## TABLE OF CONTENTS

A table of contents (illustrated at the left) includes the side headings and often the paragraph headings within the report. If these headings have been formatted using styles (Heading 1 and Heading 2), a table of contents can be created automatically using the Table of Contents command. A table of contents can be modified after it has been created. Similar to a cover page, the table of contents is one of the preliminary pages of a report (see page 340).

In Web Layout view, the entries in the table of contents are hyperlinks. Clicking an entry moves the insertion point to the appropriate page in the document. In Print Layout view, tapping CTRL plus clicking on an entry moves the insertion point to the appropriate page in the document.

### To create a table of contents:
References/Table of Contents/Table of Contents

1. Position the insertion point where the table of contents is to be created (normally on a blank page immediately before page 1 of the report).
2. Display the Built-In gallery of table of contents styles.
3. Choose the Automatic Table 2 style. The table of contents automatically displays.
4. The title *Table of Contents* generates automatically. Tap ENTER to position it at approximately 2".

To remove a table of contents, click Remove Table of Contents.

---

## DRILL 1     TABLE OF CONTENTS

 table of contents

1. In the open document, turn on Show/Hide. Position the insertion point on the blank page after the cover page at about 2".

2. Generate a new table of contents using the Automatic Table 2 style.

3. Scroll through the document and notice if the page numbers agree with the table of contents. (You will not be able to read the body.)

4. Proofread and check; click Next Activity. (*72-drill1*)

---

## Apply It

### 46-d1
**MLA Template**

1. In a new document, click No Spacing style and change line spacing to 2.0.
2. Change to 12-point Times New Roman font.
3. Key the following heading at 1":

   **Student's Full Name**

   **Instructor's Full Name**

   **Name of Assignment**

4. Tap ENTER after *Name of Assignment and* insert the current date using the MLA-required date format (9 September 2012); click option to update automatically.
5. Double-click in the header section and change to 12-point Times New Roman font.
6. Click Align Right and key **LName**, space one time, and insert Page number command (Insert/Header & Footer/Page Number/Current Position. Click Plain Number). Close the Header & Footer.
7. Proofread and check; click Next Activity. (*46-d1*)

### 46-d2
**MLA Report**

#### ✷ Discover

**Increase Indent**

Home/Paragraph/
Increase Indent or
Decrease Indent

1. In the open document (*46-d1*), with the MLA formatting already applied, key the MLA report shown on pages 197–198.
✷ 2. Highlight the long quotation and click Increase Indent twice to indent it 1" from the left margin. Key a space after each period in the ellipsis.
3. Click Decrease Indent twice to return the insertion point back to the left margin.
4. Double-click in the header and change *LName* to **Watson**.
5. Edit the information at the top of page 1 with Watson's information.
6. Check that side headings are not alone at the bottom of the page. Use the Keep with next command if needed.
7. Proofread and check; click Next Activity. (*46-d2*)

### 46-d3
**Works Cited Page**

#### ✷ Discover

**Page Break**

Insert/Pages/Page Break

*Shortcut:* CTRL + ENTER

To remove a manual page break, position insertion point at the beginning of the page break (with Show/Hide on) and tap DELETE.

✷ 1. In the open document (*46-d2*), position the insertion point at the end of the report. Press CTRL + ENTER to begin a new page.
2. Key the works cited shown below with hanging indent formatting. Try the shortcut, CTRL + T.
3. Proofread and check; click Exit Word. (*46-d3*)
4. Click Log out to exit *KPDO*.

Works Cited

Millsaps, John Thomas. *Report Writing Handbook: An Essential Guide.*

   Columbus: Wellington Books, 2014. Print.

Quattlebaum, Sarah. "Apply Reference Styles Correctly." *The Quarterly*

   *Reference Journal* 27.1 (2014): 35-42. Print.

**71-d2**

1. In the open document (*71-d1*), change the cover page to Banded.

2. Double-click in the header on the second page of the report and change the header style to Facet (Odd Page).

3. Double-click in the footer and change the footer style to Ion (Dark).

4. Click in the footer of the first page of the report (First Page footer – Section 2). Insert the Ion (Dark) footer. **Note:** A header should not appear on page 1 of the report body.

5. Proofread and check; click Exit *Word*. (*71-d2*)

6. Click Log out to exit *KPDO*.

**QUICK ✓**

Check your document against the illustration below.

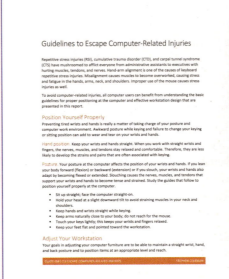

Footer displays on first page

# Lesson 47 Reports in APA Style

**Document Design**

**47b**

## APA REPORT STYLE

Study the guidelines shown below for an academic report formatted in APA style. Refer to the full-page model on pages 201–202 and always check the *Publication Manual of the American Psychological Association* and your teacher's instructions.

- Use 12-point Times New Roman font.
- Use 1" margins (top, bottom, left, and right).
- DS paragraphs and indent 0.5".
- DS long quotations of 40 or more words and indent 0.5" from the left margin.
- Key a running head in ALL CAPS at the top of each page that includes the title of paper (limited to 50 characters) at the left margin and page number aligned at the right.
- Center the report title and capitalize all main words.
- Include a complete alphabetical listing of all references cited in the report and label it **Bibliography**; DS.

**Page 1**

**Page 2**

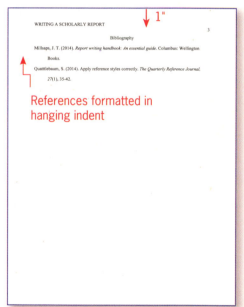

**Bibliography Page**

**71-d1**

**continued**

8. Go to the header of Section 2 and insert the Retrospect header. Select the current date.

   - Go to the footer of Section 2 and insert the Retrospect footer.
   - Change the page number format to begin with page 1. The Different First Page option should already be checked to suppress the header and footer on the first page of the report.

9. Proofread and check; click Next Activity. (*71-d1*)

Guidelines to Escape Computer-Related Injuries

Repetitive stress injuries (RSI), cumulative trauma disorder (CTD), and carpal tunnel syndrome (CTS) have mushroomed to afflict everyone from administrative assistants to executives with hurting muscles, tendons, and nerves. Hand-arm alignment is one of the causes of keyboard repetitive stress injuries. Misalignment causes muscles to become overworked, causing stress and fatigue in the hands, arms, neck, and shoulders. Improper use of the mouse causes stress injuries as well.

To avoid computer-related injuries, all computer users can benefit from understanding the basic guidelines for proper positioning at the computer and effective workstation design that are presented in this report.

Position Yourself Properly

Preventing tired wrists and hands is really a matter of taking charge of your posture and computer work environment. Awkward posture while keying and failure to change your keying or sitting position can add to wear and tear on your wrists and hands.

**REVIEW**

**Insert File**

Insert/Text/Object down list arrow/Text from File

Hand position. Keep your wrists and hands straight. When you work with straight wrists and fingers, the nerves, muscles, and tendons stay relaxed and comfortable. Therefore, they are less likely to develop the strains and pains that are often associated with keying.

Insert file injuries; format like the rest of the report.

6. Do you tilt your neck backward to see the computer screen? (No)

7. Do you take two 5-minute breaks and one 15-minute break in the morning and afternoon? (Yes)

8. Do you vary your activities to break the repetitive motion? (Yes)

9. Do you drink plenty of water to lubricate your joints? (Yes)

For each of your responses that do not match the desired response, please accept the challenge today to correct the undesired practice and avoid computer-related stress injuries.

Running head on each page with title of page and page number

1"

Writing a Scholarly Report        Title

Preparing a thorough and convincing scholarly report requires excellent research, organization, and composition skills as well as extensive knowledge of documenting referenced materials. The purpose of this report is to present the importance of documenting a report with credible references and the techniques for creating accurate citations.

Well-Cited References

1"

For a report to be believable and accepted by its readers, a thorough review of related literature is essential. The background information is an important part of the report and shows integrity of the report.

Good writers must learn quickly how to evaluate many printed and electronic references located to support the theme of any report being written. Those references judged acceptable are then cited in the report. One writer shares this simple advice:

Long quotation indented 0.5"

> Today writers can locate a vast number of references in very little time. Electronic databases and Web pages . . . provide a multitude of information. The novice writer will be quick to include all these references in a report without verifying their credibility. Writers check electronic sources as well. (Millsaps, p. 12)

Correct Styles Applied

The *MLA Handbook for Writers of Research Papers* and the *Publication Manual of the American Psychological Association* are two popular style manuals. Knowing the required styles for the manuscript being produced is critical. For example, a running head with the paper title and page number is required in APA while MLA requires the last name of the author and the page number. Quattlebaum (2014) writes, "Be sure to check that the reference list is formatted as

1"

**APA Report Style**

# REPORT WITH HEADERS AND FOOTERS

Built-in headers and footers enhance the professional design of a report. Remember a page number must display either in the header or the footer of a multiple-page document. The page number is often suppressed on the first page.

## Apply It

**Report**

 injuries

1. Key the leftbound report shown on page 345. Tap ENTER three times to position the title at about 2". Apply Title style to the main heading, Heading 1 to side headings, and Heading 2 to paragraph headings. Tap ENTER twice after the title.

2. Change the left margin to 1.5".

3. Apply the Retrospect document theme. Shrink title font to fit on one line.

4. Format the bulleted lists with square bullets.

5. Insert the Retrospect cover page. Key the following information:

   Document title: Refer to report title for *71-d1*. Shrink to fit on one line.

   Document subtitle: Click the subtitle text box; click the Subtitle control above the text box, and tap DELETE.

   Author: **Stephen Coleman**

   Company: **Galey Financial, LLC**

   Company address: **2901 Manhattan Road, San Jose, CA 95101-2901**

6. Insert a Continuous section break at the first paragraph marker on the first page of the report.

7. Position the insertion point in the header of page 2 of the body in Section 2 (Header – Section 2—not First Page – Header). The status bar reads *Section 2 page 3 of 3*.

   - Break the links between the headers for both sections.
   - Go to the footer of Section 2 (page 2). Break the link between the footers for both sections.

*(continued)*

**TIP**

Break the link for the header and footer in Section 2 before inserting the header and footer style.

a hanging indent in both MLA and APA, but be cautious of the differences in the formatting of

authors' names and book and article titles" (p. 40).

Summary

Experienced writers understand the importance of selecting credible resources,

documenting references, and applying the exact reference style required in the report. Learning

to document your references accurately is an important step toward becoming an experienced

writer.

WRITING A SCHOLARLY REPORT

3

Bibliography

Millsaps, J. T. (2014). *Report writing handbook: An essential guide*. Columbus: Wellington

Books.

Quatttlebaum, S. (2014). Apply reference styles correctly. *The Quarterly Reference Journal,*

*27*(1), 35-42.

**APA Report Style**

1. In the open document, position the insertion point at the beginning of page 2 (cover page is page 1). *Hint:* Click Show/Hide and click on the first paragraph marker at the beginning of the first word *Practice* at 1".

2. Insert a Continuous section break.

3. Check the status bar; if you do not see the section and page number, right-click the insertion point on the status bar. Select Section.

> **SECTION: 2    PAGE 2 OF 3    AT: 1"**

4. Position the insertion point in the header of page 2 of the body of Section 2 (Header – Section 2—not First Page – Header). The status bar reads *Section 2 page 3 of 3.*

   - Click Link to Previous to break the links between the headers in Sections 1 and 2. This button will not display in blue if the link is correctly broken.

   - Go to footer of Section of Section 2 (page 2). Break the link between the footers for both sections.

5. Go to the header of Section 2 and insert the ViewMaster header.

   - Click Go to Footer and insert the ViewMaster (Horizontal) footer. Click Date and select the current date.

   - Click Page Number and Format Page Numbers. Change the page number format to Start at page 1. The Different First Page option should already be checked to suppress the page number on the first page of the report.

6. Proofread and check; click Next Activity. (*71-drill3*)

---

**QUICK ✔**      Check your document against the illustration below.

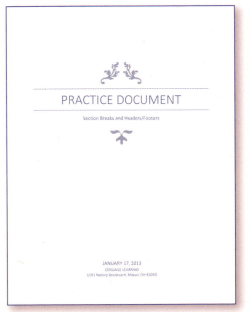

Page 1

Practice Document

This is page 1 of the report.

Page 2

Page 3

# INTERNAL CITATIONS IN APA STYLE

1. When cited information is paraphrased, the last name of the author(s) and the publication year of the paraphrased material are shown in parenthesis. Example: *Podcasts are effectively used by distance faculty (Crawford, 2014).*

2. When the author(s) names are used in the text, the publication year is keyed after the author name(s). Example: *According to Crawford (2014), podcasts are effectively used by distance faculty.*

3. When the citation is a direct quote, the page number appears in parenthesis after the quote. Example: *Crawford (2014) said, "Faculty are uploading podcast lectures"* (p. 134).

4. Long quotations of 40 words or more are indented 0.5" from the left margin and DS. Tap ENTER once before and after the long quotation. See the example below.

Probably no successful enterprise exists that does not rely upon the ability of its members to communicate for its success. Shaefer (2014) adds:

> Make no mistake, both written and verbal communication are the stuff upon which success is built in all types of organizations. Both forms deserve careful study by any business that wants to grow. Successful businesspeople must read, write, speak, and listen with skill. Often professional development in these areas is needed. (p. 28)

**Step 2: Insert page numbers in Section 2:**

4.  Click Go to Header to return to the header section where the page number is to be inserted.

5.  In the Header & Footer group, click Page Number. Click Top Right and select a page number style that displays numbers at the top right.

6.  From the Options group, click Different First Page to select the option to suppress page numbers on the first page. **Note:** If cover page is inserted already, this option is automatically selected.

☑ Different First Page
☐ Different Odd & Even Pages
☑ Show Document Text

Options

**Step 3: Start number at page 1:**

Header   Footer   Page Number

Header & Footer

7.  In the Header and Footer group, click Page Number and then Format Page Number. Click the Start at up arrow until 1 displays ❸.

8.  Check the numbers in Section 2. No number should appear on page 1, and remaining pages should be numbered at the top right.

Page Number Format

Number format:   1, 2, 3, ...

☐ Include chapter number

Chapter starts with style:   Heading 1

Use separator:   -   (hyphen)

Examples:   1-1, 1-A

Page numbering
○ Continue from previous section
◉ Start at:  1   ❸

OK          Cancel

## Troubleshooting Tips

Save the document before you paginate it. If you have trouble with the page numbers, close the document without saving and start over; the reason for not saving it first is that *Word* seems to remember what you did previously and starts doing it automatically.

**Important Points to Remember**

1.  Click Link to Previous before inserting the page number.

2.  To suppress the page number on the first page, select the Different First Page option.

**47-d1**

**APA Template**

1. In a new document, click No Spacing style and change line spacing to 2.0.
2. Change to 12-point Times New Roman font.
3. Double-click in the header section and change to 12-point Times New Roman font. Key **TITLE OF PAPER** at the left margin. Tap TAB twice and insert page number. Close the Header & Footer.
4. Key **Title of Paper** at 1" and center.
5. Proofread and check; click Next Activity. (*47-d1*)

**47-d2**

**APA Report**

1. In the open document (*47-d1*), key the APA report shown on pages 201–202 using the template with the APA formatting already applied. Do not key the Bibliography page.
2. Double click in the header and change *TITLE OF PAPER* to **WRITING A SCHOLARLY REPORT**. Close the header.
3. In the title line, replace *Title of Paper* with **Writing a Scholarly Report**.
4. Click Increase Indent once to indent the long quotation 0.5" from the left margin.
5. Check that side headings are not alone at the bottom of the page. Use the Keep with next command if needed.
6. Proofread and check; click Next Activity. (*47-d2*)

**47-d3**

**Bibliography**

1. In the open document (*47-d2*), position the insertion point at the end of the report. Press CTRL + ENTER to begin a new page.
2. Begin at 1" and key the bibliography shown below. DS and format the references in hanging indent style.
3. Proofread and check; click Exit Word. (*47-d3*)
4. Click Log out to exit KPDO.

Capitalize only the first word and proper nouns in book titles and journal titles.

<center>Bibliography</center>

Millsaps, J. T. (2014). *Report writing handbook: An essential guide.*

Columbus: Wellington Books.

Quattlebaum, S. (2014). Apply reference styles correctly. *The Quarterly*

Italicize journal name and volume number. → *Reference Journal, 27*(1), 35-42.

**REVIEW**

**Draft View**

**View/Views**

In Draft View, section breaks appear as a dotted line with the type of break indicated.

The current section number displays on the status bar. If you do not see the section number, place the insertion point on the status bar and right-click. Select Section.

SECTION: 1    PAGE 1 OF 5    AT: 3.1"

### To delete a section:

1.  In Draft View, select the section break to be deleted.
2.  Tap DELETE.

## BREAK LINK BETWEEN SECTIONS AND INSERT PAGE NUMBERS

*Word* continues to use the same format for page numbers in a new section as it did in the previous section. In order for the page number format to be different between sections, you must break the link between the sections. When the link is broken, the preliminary pages can be numbered in Roman numerals and the report body in Arabic numbers.

### Step 1: Break the links in Section 2:

1.  Scroll to the second page of the report body. Move the insertion point to the top 0.5" ❶ and double-click to position the insertion point in the header section. Header – Section 2 label displays and the Same as Previous label displays at the right.

Header & Footer Tools Design/Navigation

2.  In the Navigation group, click the Link to Previous button ❷ to break the link between the headers in Section 1 (preliminary pages) and Section 2 (body of the report). The Go to Header button is dimmed, meaning the insertion point is in the header.

3.  In the Navigation group, click Go to Footer to move to the footer of Section 2. Click the Link to Previous button to break the link between the footers in Sections 1 and 2.

**Note:** The Link to Previous button will display in blue until the link is successfully broken.

# Lesson 48 Palmetto Event Solutions, Inc.

## Skill Building

**48b** **Textbook Keying**

caps
1 James Carswell plans to visit Austin and New Orleans in December.
2 Will Peter and Betsy go with Mark when he goes to Alaska in June?
3 John Kenny wrote the book *Innovation and Timing—Keys to Success*.

double letters
4 Jeanne arranges meeting room space in Massey Hall for committees.
5 Russell will attend to the bookkeeping issues tomorrow afternoon.
6 Todd offered a free book with all assessment tools Lynette sells.

balanced hand
7 Jane, a neighbor and a proficient auditor, may amend their audit.
8 Blanche and a neighbor may make an ornament for an antique chair.
9 Claudia may visit the big island when they go to Orlando with us.

## 48c

**Timed Writing**

1. Key a 1' timing on each paragraph; work to increase speed.
2. Key a 3' timing on all paragraphs.

Whether any company can succeed depends on how well it fits into the economic system. Success rests on certain key factors that are put in line by a management team that has set goals for the company and has enough good judgment to recognize how best to reach these goals. Because of competition, only the best-organized companies get to the top.

A commercial enterprise is formed for a specific purpose: that purpose is usually to equip others, or consumers, with whatever they cannot equip themselves. Unless there is only one provider, a consumer will search for a company that returns the most value in terms of price; and a relationship with such a company, once set up, can endure for many years.

Thus our system assures that the businesses that manage to survive are those that have been able to combine successfully an excellent product with a low price and the best service—all in a place that is convenient for the buyers. With no intrusion from outside forces, the buyer and the seller benefit both themselves and each other.

# SECTION BREAKS

A section is part of a document that may have its own look. You might think of a section as a document within a document but with unique differences such as different margins, headers, or page number style. A section break divides a document into sections. Section breaks either can begin on a new page or you can choose to have the section break begin at the insertion point. Next Page and Continuous are the two types you will use most often; you will use Continuous breaks in this module.

The preliminary pages of a report are numbered at the bottom of the page with lowercase Roman numerals. The body of the report is usually numbered in the upper right with Arabic numerals. Page numbers are inserted as either headers or footers. These differences in page numbering are handled with a section break.

To use different page number formats within the same document, you insert a section break at the beginning of the report body. As a result, the title page and other preliminary pages become Section 1; the body of the report is in Section 2. *Word* continues to use the same format for page numbers in a new section until you break the link between the sections. Later in this module you will add additional preliminary pages and number the preliminary pages as well as the report page.

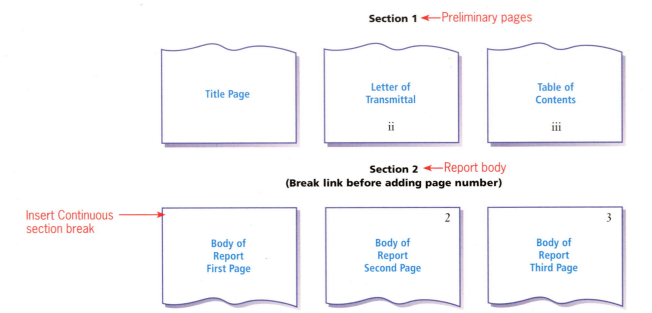

Section 1 ←—Preliminary pages

Title Page | Letter of Transmittal (ii) | Table of Contents (iii)

Section 2 ←—Report body
**(Break link before adding page number)**

Insert Continuous section break →

Body of Report First Page | Body of Report Second Page (2) | Body of Report Third Page (3)

**To enter a section break:**
Page Layout/Page Setup/Breaks

Section Breaks

**Next Page**
Insert a section break and start the new section on the next page.

**Continuous** ❶
Insert a section break and start the new section on the same page.

**Even Page**
Insert a section break and start the new section on the next even-numbered page.

**Odd Page**
Insert a section break and start the new section on the next odd-numbered page.

1. From the Section Breaks category, click the desired section break ❶, and then OK.

   **Next Page:** Begins a new page at the point the section break is entered.

   **Continuous:** Begins a new section at the insertion point on the same page.

## PALMETTO EVENT SOLUTIONS, INC.

For the project in this module, you will be preparing documents for Carlos Torres, the regional vice president in the Southwest office in Las Cruces. The Southwest office was recently contracted to coordinate events for the Southwest Culinary Association Convention to be held in San Antonio next year. You have been assigned exclusively to this project.

As you work through each job, make sure you do the following:

- Use Southwest letterhead for all letters and the block letter style with open punctuation.
- Key **Mr. Torres** as the author of all letters and format the signature line as follows: **Sincerely | Carlos Torres | Regional Vice President**. Letters are generally emailed as attachments unless otherwise directed. Items attached to the letter would be considered attachments.
- Apply the Ion theme for all documents.
- Apply the Grid Table 4 – Accent 5 table style for all tables.
- Use the Accent Bar 2 page number style for all reports.

---

### 48-d1

**Request for Proposals**

Prepare the Request for Proposals below as an unbound report.

1. Apply the Title style to the title and Heading 1 style to side headings.
2. Format the table appropriately and number the pages.
3. Proofread and check; click Next Activity. (*48-d1*)

Request for Proposals

The purpose of this Request for Proposals (RFP) is to solicit speakers for the Southwest Culinary Association Convention to be held on February 1-4, 201-, in San Antonio, Texas, at the San Antonio Hotel. Approximately 2,000 members, exhibitors, and guests are expected to attend this annual convention.

The Southwest regional office of Palmetto Event Solutions, Inc. is the official event planner of this conference and will oversee the RFP and the final selection program presenters. Send all questions to the following address before May 1:

Mr. Carlos Torres
Regional Vice President
Palmetto Event Solutions, Inc.
590 S. Solano Drive
Las Cruces, NM 88001-3290
575.555.0152

*Press SHIFT + ENTER for these short lines.*

The conference speakers will be carefully selected individuals who have expertise in the current trends and issues, use of cutting edge technology needed by today's chefs, and a showcase of best practices in the field.

*(continued)*

## COVER PAGE

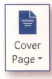

Cover Page ▾

Longer and more formal reports include a cover or title page as the first page of the report. Using the Cover Page command, the user can select from a variety of attractive cover pages.

To create a cover page:
Insert/Pages/Cover Page

1. Click the scroll arrows in the gallery to select the desired style ❶. The cover page opens as a *Word* document.

2. Select [Document title] ❷ and key the report title. Repeat for all other items located in the template. **Note:** A blank page follows the cover page for keying the report.

---

## DRILL 2     COVER PAGE

Insert/Pages/Cover Page

1. Create a cover page using the Cover Page command. Select the Whisp style in the Built-In category.

2. Click [Document title] and key **Cyberspace Security Issues**.

3. Key **Review of Company Policies** as the document subtitle.

4. Click [*Date*], select the drop-list arrow, and select the current date. Key **Jun Yoshino** as the author name.

5. Key **Mac-Donovan Industries, Inc**. as the company name. It will be shown in All Caps.

6. Proofread and check; click Next Activity. (*71-drill2*)

## Session Descriptions

Convention participants will choose from four types of convention sessions. In preparing the proposal, use the following information to select the most appropriate type of session for the proposed session content.

Type	Length	Room Setup	Audience Size
Lecture (L)	60 minutes	Tables	50
Roundtable (RT)	60 minutes (20 minutes per rotation)	Roundtables	8 per table
Hands-on Computer Workshop (W)	90 minutes	Lab with 20 laptop computers	20
Demonstrations (D)	60 minutes	Theater seating in teaching kitchen	100

## Submission Information and Deadlines

Email proposals to Carlos Torres carlos.torres@palmettoeventsolutions.com by May 15 at 5 p.m. If you have questions, please call Carlos Torres at 505.555.0152.

## Guidelines

The proposal must be no more than four single-spaced pages and must include the following information:

1. Cover Page that includes the title of presentation, type of session (Lecture, Roundtable, Hands-on Computer Workshop, or Demonstration), names of all presenters, and contact information for all presenters (company name, mailing address, email address, and telephone numbers)
2. Title of Presentation with description of presentation for program (limit to 50 words)
3. Purpose of Presentation and Justification for Acceptance
4. Topical Outline

## Notification

Authors of accepted proposals will be notified on June 15.

# Lesson 71 Report with Section Breaks

**New Commands**

- Header and Footer
- Cover Page
- Section Breaks
- Page Number Format

**Warmup** *Lesson 71a Warmup*

## New Commands

### 71b

Header Footer Page Number

Header & Footer

## HEADERS AND FOOTERS

A header appears in the top margin of a multipage report; a footer appears in the bottom margin. The built-in gallery offers a wide variety of preformatted attractive headers and footers. The Retrospect header and footer were selected in the illustration at the left.

### To insert a header or footer:

Insert/Header & Footer/Header or Footer

1. From the built-in gallery of header or footer styles, click the down arrow to browse the various styles and select the desired style.

2. If needed, click [Type the document title] and key the text for the header or select the date if included in the selected style.

3. From the Options group, click Different First Page to remove the page number from the first page if desired.

### To create a custom header or footer:

Double-click in the header or footer area. Key the header or footer; add the page number if desired. Suppress the header or footer on the first page.

### To remove a header or footer:

Follow the same path and click Remove Header or Remove Footer.

Built-in

Blank

[Type here]

Blank (Three Columns)

[Type here]        [Type here]        [Type here]

Austin

[Document title]

Banded

[DOCUMENT TITLE]

- More Headers from Office.com
- Edit Header
- Remove Header
- Save Selection to Header Gallery...

---

## DRILL 1   HEADER AND FOOTER                    benefits

Insert/Header & Footer/Header or Footer

1. In the open document, insert the Banded header. Click [DOCUMENT TITLE] in the header and key **Benefits: A Matter of Choice**. Click Go to Footer in the Navigation group.

2. From the Header and Footer group, insert the Banded footer, which includes the page number. Click Different First Page.

3. Proofread and check; click Next Activity. (*71-drill1*)

---

A speaker form will be sent to presenters of proposals that were accepted for the convention program.

1. Create the table below as a 2 × 10 table. Split the cells in rows 8 and 9 into 5 columns, then merge row 9 as shown.

2. Select the entire table and change the height of the table rows to 0.3".

3. In row 1, change the text to Align Center; for text in rows 2–10, change text to Align Center Left.

4. Proofread and check; click Next Activity. (48-d2)

SPEAKER CONTACT INFORMATION				
Name:				
Professional Credentials:				
Title:				
Company:				
Address 1:				
Address 2:				
City:		State:		ZIP Code:
Telephone:		Fax:		
Email:				

**QUICK ✓**

Check your document against the illustration below.

Speaker Contact Information				
Name:				
Professional Credentials:				
Title:				
Company:				
Address 1:				
Address 2:				
City:		State:		ZIP Code:
Telephone:		Fax:		
Email:				

1. In the open document (*70-d1*), apply the Dividend document theme.

2. Change the left margin to 1.5" to convert this unbound report to a leftbound report.

3. Select the footnote number in the text and drag it to display after the word *survey* in the second sentence of that paragraph.

4. Double-click in the header and change the page number style to Accent Bar 2.

5. Show the navigation pane. (View/Show/Navigation Pane)
   - Click Headings and then the heading *Summary* to move to that section.
   - Click Pages and click on the miniature page 1 to move to the first page.
     **Note:** Use this shortcut to move quickly in reports as you complete this module.

6. Proofread and check; click Next Activity. (*70-d2*)

1. Key an outline for the report keyed in *70-d1*. Use the multilevel list with Roman numerals (I., A., 1.). Key the title at about 2"; tap ENTER twice; apply Title style.

2. Check your document against the illustration. Click Exit *Word*. (*70-d3*)

3. Click Log out to exit *KPDO*.

**QUICK ✓**

Analysis of Listening Skills Study

I.  Communication Skills Ranked

II. Issues in Listening
    A.  Rate
    B.  Listening barriers

III. Poor Listening Habits

IV. Summary

Much communication will be necessary between Mr. Torres and Mr. Romero, the president of Southwest Culinary Association. Prepare the following letter.

1. Include all necessary letter parts. Address to **Mr. Jason Romero, President | Southwest Culinary Association | P.O. Box 3759 | Oklahoma City, OK 73101-3759**. Date the letter **January 15, 201-**.

2. Proofread and check; click Next Activity. *(48-d3)*

Our office is very pleased to be working with you on event planning for the Southwest Culinary Association Convention to be held in San Antonio on February 1-4. We distributed the Request for Proposals yesterday to the lists provided by Ms. Janet Wiseman, the treasurer of your association.

Next we are focusing our attention on sponsorships for the following major events:

1. Board dinner on March 31

2. Opening reception on February 1

3. Morning and afternoon coffee breaks on February 2 and 3

4. Wine and cheese reception on February 3

Event proposal forms are attached for each of the events listed above. Please complete the forms and return by email to me at conference201@palmettoeventsolutions.com. Your return of these forms by next Monday will be greatly appreciated. Our goal is to solicit at least two sponsors for each event, and this information is valuable to us as we plan our campaign.

Thank you for your valuable input in our event planning.

**48-d4**

Compose Letter

palmetto
letterhead - las cruces

Mr. Torres has asked you to compose a draft of the letter to be emailed to the presenters whose proposals are being accepted for the Southwest Culinary Association Convention. Date the letter May 31 and key on the Southwest letterhead. The following details are important to include.

1. Congratulate the presenter for having a proposal accepted for the convention.

2. Explain that the assignment of day, time, and room are not complete and will be emailed within the month.

3. Attach the speaker form you prepared earlier and ask the speaker to complete and return to you by June 15. Also request a brief biographical sketch to be used in the convention program and by the session facilitator who will introduce the speaker.

4. End with a gracious thank-you for their willingness to speak at the convention.

5. Proofread and check; click Exit Word. *(48-d4)* Click Log out to exit *KPDO*.

**Learn More:**

www.cengagebrain.com

The final report will include recommendations that address the components of a listening-training program. Training objectives will address the needs of the participants as determined by this study.

Issues in Listening (Heading 1 style)

Two issues in listening were considered in the observation of listening skills. Observers considered the rate that listeners can process words and common barriers to listening.

(Heading 2 style) Rate. Studies show that listeners can recognize words at a rate approximately five times faster than the rate at which speakers can talk. With the mind processing information at over 1,000 words per minute, the listener is challenged to listen actively.

(Heading 2 style) Listening barriers. Listeners are also confronted with other barriers to effective listening. These barriers might include assumptions already made about the topic, the speaker, the potential message, or the specific setting. All of these assumptions may lead the listener to tune out what the speaker is actually saying. Another barrier may simply be fatigue—the listener is too tired, too hungry, or too busy to listen. Distractions often influence the listener's ability to be an active listener. These annoyances may include loud noises near the speaker or a room that is too cold or too warm.

Poor Listening Habits (Heading 1 style)

Observers noted that poor listening habits are quite common and often unknown to listeners. The following habits were noted by the observers.

- Pretending to listen by nodding, saying yes, and looking directly at the speaker fakes the customer into believing that the customer service agent is listening.
- Not looking at the customer results in poor listening as facial expressions and gestures are not communicated.
- Recording detailed notes results in poor listening or over listening.
- Making judgments about the customer or the topic is not effective.
- Rushing the customer causes the customer to think the customer service agent's time is being wasted.
- Interrupting the customer is rude and does not enhance listening.
- Showing interest in something else and allowing distractions to obtain the customer service agent's attention result in poor listening.

Summary (Heading 1 style)

Understanding that listening is not easy is a first step in becoming a better listener. Identifying individual habits that do not enhance effective listening is the next step.

**Warmup**   *Lesson 49a Warmup*

## Apply It

**49-d1**

**Table**

1. Key the table shown below. Apply Grid Table 5 Dark – Accent 6 style to the table.

2. Insert a row at the beginning of the table. Key the title **Occupational Health and Safety Department Survey**. Merge the cells and center the title.

3. Change row height of row 1 to 0.4" and click Align Center to center the text vertically and horizontally in the row.

4. Proofread and correct any errors; click Continue. (*49-d1*)

Safety and health is a primary concern in every operation at Areorbit Corporation, and our goal is to be in compliance with the state's job safety and health laws and regulations. A summary of the annual safety report is shown below. The necessary adjustments are being made to produce a safer working environment.

Safety Standard	Madison Facility	Central Park Facility
Adequate lighting in hallways and stairwells.	Pass	Pass
Aisles and passageways are sufficiently wide for easy movement and should be kept clear at all times.	Pass	Pass
Temporary electrical cords that cross aisles are taped or anchored to the floor.	Pass	Electrical cord to coffee maker needs to be anchored in kitchen.
Adequate lighting is provided during night hours.	Two exterior lights need to be replaced in front of the building.	Pass
Floor surfaces are even; no bulges in carpet that can cause tripping hazards.	Stretch carpet in employee lounge to eliminate bulges.	Pass
Signs leading to exits are posted and are easily visible in the dark.	Pass	Light needs to be replaced in exit sign 7.

1. Key the report on pages 335–336. Use default side margins. Tap ENTER three times to position the title at about 2".

2. Apply Title style to the main heading; tap ENTER twice (one blank line below heading).

3. Apply Heading 1 style to the side headings and Heading 2 to the paragraph headings.

4. Apply the Grid Table 4 – Accent 3 style to the table. Adjust column widths. Merge the cells in the first row and center the title of the table; adjust the font size of the title so that it fits on one line. Center Align the cells with numbers. Center the table horizontally.

5. In the paragraph below the table, apply Add Space Before Paragraph to add space below the table. (Home/Paragraph/Line Spacing/Add Space Before Paragraph)

6. Insert the following content footnote marked in the report.

   [1] **Results of survey administered prior to the observation period.**

7. Use the Page Number command to number the pages at the top right. Select the Plain Number 3 number style. Click Different First Page to suppress the page number on the first page.

8. Proofread and check; click Next Activity. (70-d1)

Analysis of Listening Skills Study (Title style)

The initial phase of a communication skills study of customer service agents at Fernwell Communications has been completed. Findings of this study showed that listening is the communication task that customer service agents spend almost 50 percent of their time doing, but they clearly have had little instruction in performing this skill effectively. The purpose of this report is to highlight major barriers to effective listening and to identify poor listening habits observed in the 50 customer service agents who participated in this study.

Communication Skills Ranked (Heading 1 style)

Contrary to common belief, listening is not an easy task. Interestingly, our survey findings showed that listening is a skill that was seldom taught to the participants of this study. The table[1] below compares the rank of four communication skills in terms of amount of time used and time taught. Note that writing ranks last in time used and ranks first in amount of time taught, while listening is used the most and taught the least.

Comparison of Communication Skills		
	Rank in Time Used	Rank in Time Taught
Listening	1	4
Speaking	2	3
Reading	3	2
Writing	4	1

*(continued)*

## 49-d2

**Leftbound Report**

 study

1. Key the remainder of the report shown below and format as a leftbound report.

2. Apply the Retrospect theme. Format the title and side headings with the appropriate style. Tap ENTER twice after the title.

3. Key the table below, placing it in the report below the paragraph that describes Table 1; apply the Grid Table 6 Colorful – Accent 3. Merge the cells as shown. Center the headings as shown. Insert a right tab at the approximate center of columns B–E to align the numbers in the approximate center of the column.

4. Choose the open circle bullet for the bulleted list.

5. Insert the second content footnote as marked in the report.

6. Number the pages at the top right using the Accent Bar 2 page number style.

7. Proofread the document. Check the test and close. Click Exit Word. (49-d2)

8. Click Log out to exit *KPDO*.

Table 1

Comparison of Adherence of Dress Code Policy to Absenteeism and Tardiness

	Absenteeism		Tardiness	
	Male	Female	Male	Female
Adhered to policy	2%	2%	1%	0%
Did not adhere to policy	25%	30%	12%	10%

The findings clearly verify our review of the business literature that employees who dress more professionally are absent fewer days and are on time for work more often.

Recommendations

Although complete adherence to the dress code was not found, the findings of the study do show that the compliance to our policy (89%) is much better than companies included in the NABASW Study.[2] However, because the findings in our company show a correlation between absenteeism and tardiness, this subcommittee respectfully submits the following recommendations.

- Consider employing an image consultant to teach employees what is appropriate business casual and to plan the best business attire to project the image of our company.

- Prepare online materials that more clearly explain the areas of the dress code that appeared in the study as violations.

In summary, the current dress code is fulfilling the company philosophy to provide a comfortable work environment and to project a positive corporate image. Professional development is recommended in selected areas.

**Footnote text:**

[2] Study of 500 companies revealed that 80 percent of the companies reported a 60 percent level of compliance by employees to established company dress policy.

actually saying. Another barrier may simply be fatigue—the listener is too tired, too hungry, or too busy to listen. Distractions often influence the listener's ability to be an active listener. These annoyances may include loud noises near the speaker or a room that is too cold or too warm.

## Poor Listening Habits

Observers noted that poor listening habits are quite common and often unknown to listeners. The following habits were noted by the observers.

- Pretending to listen by nodding, saying yes, and looking directly at the speaker fakes the customer into believing that the customer service agent is listening.
- Not looking at the customer results in poor listening as facial expressions and gestures are not communicated.
- Recording detailed notes results in poor listening or over listening.
- Making judgments about the customer or the topic is not effective.
- Rushing the customer causes the customer to think the customer service agent's time is being wasted.
- Interrupting the customer is rude and does not enhance listening.
- Showing interest in something else and allowing distractions to obtain the customer service agent's attention result in poor listening.

## Summary

Understanding that listening is not easy is a first step in becoming a better listener. Identifying individual habits that do not enhance effective listening is the next step.

*Heading 1 style*

*Bulleted list*

**Unbound Report—Page 2**

# Graphics

**LEARNING OUTCOMES**

- Learn and apply essential *Word 2013* commands.
- Create documents with pictures, clip art, SmartArt, WordArt, and borders.
- Create documents with equal-width columns and graphics.
- Build keyboarding skills.

## Lesson 50 Pictures and Online Pictures

**New Commands**

- Insert Pictures
- Picture Tools Format
- Size Pictures

- Crop Pictures
- Compress Pictures
- Wrap Text

- Position Pictures
- Insert Online Pictures
- Page Borders

**Warmup**   *Lesson 50a Warmup*

A   **ALL LETTERS**

### Skill Building

**50b   Timed Writing**

1. Key a 1' timed writing on each paragraph; work to increase speed.
2. Key a 3' timed writing on both paragraphs.

Most of us know that having a good professional image can help us to create a good first impression when we meet people. The same general principle applies to the letters, memos, reports, and other documents that we prepare and send to our business associates, clients, or customers. The way that a document appears when the recipient opens it and looks at it makes either a good or a bad first impression.

The quality and the organization of the content are very important when a document is examined in detail, but they are not the factors that create the first impression. The general appearance does that. The judicious use of color and certain types of graphics can create a good visual impact, but using too much color or the wrong type of color or graphic can do just the opposite.

Title style

# Analysis of Listening Skills Study

1"

The initial phase of a communication skills study of customer service agents at Fernwell Communications has been completed. Findings of this study showed that listening is the communication task that customer service agents spend almost 50 percent of their time doing, but they clearly have had little instruction in performing this skill effectively. The purpose of this report is to highlight major barriers to effective listening and to identify poor listening habits observed in the 50 customer service agents who participated in this study.

Heading 1 style

## Communication Skills Ranked

Contrary to common belief, listening is not an easy task. Interestingly, our survey findings showed that listening is a skill that was seldom taught to the participants of this study. The table[1] below compares the rank of four communication skills in terms of amount of time used and time taught. Note that writing ranks last in time used and ranks first in amount of time taught, while listening is used the most and taught the least.

Add Space Before Paragraph to adjust spacing between table and paragraph

Comparison of Communication Skills		
	Rank in Time Used	Rank in Time Taught
**Listening**	1	4
**Speaking**	2	3
**Reading**	3	2
**Writing**	4	1

The final report will include recommendations that address the components of a listening-training program. Training objectives will address the needs of the participants as determined by this study.

## Issues in Listening

Two issues in listening were considered in the observation of listening skills. Observers considered the rate that listeners can process words and common barriers to listening.

Heading 2 style

**Rate.** Studies show that listeners can recognize words at a rate approximately five times faster than the rate at which speakers can talk. With the mind processing information at over 1,000 words per minute, the listener is challenged to listen actively.

**Listening barriers.** Listeners are also confronted with other barriers to effective listening. These barriers might include assumptions already made about the topic, the speaker, the potential message, or the specific setting. All of these assumptions may lead the listener to tune out what the speaker is

Footnote

[1] Results of survey administered prior to the observation period.

**Unbound Report—Page 1**

## LEARNING ABOUT GRAPHICS

Many different types of graphics can be used to enhance documents. Typically, graphics are used in documents such as announcements, invitations, flyers, brochures, reports, and newsletters. However, they can be used in virtually any type of document to enhance the document and to clarify or simplify concepts. For example, a picture may convey a concept that would take many words to describe adequately. It is important to use graphics strategically and not to overuse them. The overuse of graphics can be distracting to the reader.

## PICTURES

  *Word* provides two different commands to insert pictures based on the source of the picture. The Pictures button enables you to insert pictures from your computer or other computers on your network. The Online Pictures button enables you to insert pictures from Microsoft Clip Art, from web searches, your SkyDrive, or from Flickr—a photo-sharing social media site.

**To insert pictures from your computer:**

Insert/Illustrations/Pictures

1. Click at the position you wish to insert a picture and then click Pictures to display the Insert Pictures dialog box.

2. Browse through your files of digital pictures and select the one you wish to insert.

3. Double-click the picture or click the Insert button at the bottom of the dialog box to insert it.

Note that the size of the picture varies, but it is usually large.

DRILL 1	INSERT PICTURE	sand castles

1. In a new document, insert the *sand castles* picture from your data files.

2. Preview and check; click next activity. (*50-drill1*)

## FORMAT PICTURES

 Pictures are formatted using the tools on the Format tab that displays when you select a picture. These tools are used in a similar manner to the way you used Table tools in Module 5. Note that when you click the Picture Tools Format tab, the Ribbon displays with four groups of commands used to format pictures: Adjust, Picture Styles, Arrange, and Size. Remember you must select a picture before you apply any format.

**70d**

References/Document
Formats/Reports

# UNBOUND AND LEFTBOUND REPORTS

Review the formatting guides for preparing unbound and leftbound reports that you learned previously. Study the illustration of a two-page unbound report shown below and on pages 333–334. In the following lessons in this module you will learn more advanced report formatting.

**Margins:** Use the default side margins and bottom margin in an unbound report. In a leftbound report, set the left margin at 1.5", allowing ½" for the binding.

**Font size:** Use the 11-point default font size.

**Spacing:** Use the default line spacing for all reports.

**Page numbers:** ❶ Insert page numbers at the top right. Suppress the page number on the first page.

**Enumerated or bulleted items:** ❷ Use the default 0.25" indention of bulleted and numbered items. Tap ENTER once after each item.

**Content footnote:** ❸ Superscript appears in report text and reference displays at the bottom of the page where the reference was cited.

**Headings:** Headings should reflect a hierarchy of importance.

*Title:* ❹ Tap ENTER three times to position title at about 2". Apply Title style. Capitalize the first letter of all main words. Shrink the font so the title fits on one line. Tap ENTER twice after the title.

*Side heading:* ❺ Key at the left margin; apply Heading 1 style. Capitalize the first letter of all main words. Tap ENTER once after the heading.

*Paragraph heading:* ❻ Key at the left margin. Capitalize the first word and follow the heading with a period. Apply Heading 2 style.

Use the Keep with Next command if necessary to keep side headings from displaying alone at the bottom of the page. (Home/Paragraph dialog box launcher/Line and Page Breaks tab)

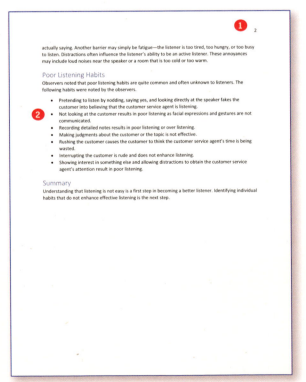

## To size pictures:

Picture Tools Format/Size/Height or Width Arrows

Pictures can be sized or cropped. Cropping removes unwanted portions of the picture. The file size of a picture can be reduced by compressing it.

1. To change the size of a picture, select it and use the height or width arrows to increase or decrease the size. -or-

2. Select the picture, position the mouse over the sizing handles; when the pointer turns to a double-headed arrow, drag to the size desired.

Sizing handles

Double-headed arrow

## To crop pictures:

Picture Tools Format/Size/Crop

1. To crop one side of a picture, click Crop and drag the cropping handle on the side inward. The cropping line will illustrate what will be cut off.

2. To crop the same amount on two sides, press CTRL while you drag the handle.

3. To finish, click off the picture.

---

## DRILL 2     SIZE PICTURE

1. Open *50-drill1*; size the picture to 2.5" high.

2. Crop the picture to focus only on the sand castles as shown above.

3. Click off the picture to finish it; then size it to 2" high.

4. Preview and check; click Next Activity. (*50-drill2*)

---

## MULTILEVEL LIST

**70c**

A multilevel list shows the list of items at different levels rather than at one level that is created when bullets and numbering commands are used.

To format items in a multilevel list:
Home/Paragraph/Multilevel List

1. Select the items to be formatted and click the Multilevel List button.
2. Use the Increase Indent button to demote items in the list or Decrease Indent button to promote in the list.

## DRILL 1 — MULTILEVEL LIST

1. Key the information shown in the left column below.

2. Select the items under Phase 1 and format them as a multilevel list, applying the numbered decimal option. Use the Increase Indent command to demote items 1.1 and 1.2. Repeat for Phase 2 items.

3. Compare your solution to the one shown in the right column. Check; click Next Activity. (*70-drill1*)

Phase 1

Identify risks

Click Increase Indent to Demote → Collect data

Analyze data

Click Decrease Indent to Promote → Review plan

Phase 2

Analyze risk

Evaluate costs

**Solution**

Phase 1

1. Identify risks
   1.1. Collect data
   1.2. Analyze data
2. Review plan

Phase 2

1. Analyze risk
2. Evaluate costs

## DRILL 2 — REVIEW COMMANDS

  progress report

1. In the open document, position the insertion point after the title *Technique Rating Sheet and Progress Report* and insert the following footnote. Italicize the book title. (References/Footnotes/Insert Footnote)

**Technique rating sheet used with permission of Cengage Learning from the keyboarding textbook *College Keyboarding: Microsoft Word 2013 Keyboarding & Word Processing*, 19th edition.**

2. Apply the Retrospect document theme. (Design/Themes)

3. Use the Page Number command to number the pages at the top right. Select the Plain Number 3 number style. Click Different First Page to suppress the page number on the first page. (Insert/Header & Footer/Page Number)

4. Proofread and check; click Next Activity. (*70-drill2*)

## To compress a picture:

Picture Tools Format/Adjust/Compress Pictures

 Compress Pictures

Compressing the picture reduces the file size; note that for email you can reduce the size even smaller.

1. Select the picture and click Compress Pictures to display the Compress Pictures dialog box.
2. Note the options that are available; then click OK to accept the defaults.

## To move a picture:

Picture Tools Format/Arrange/Position

Pictures may be moved with the Position command or by dragging them with the mouse.

1. To position a picture, select the picture and click Position to display the position options.
2. Select the desired position as shown to the right. -or-
3. To move a picture with the mouse, select it and hover over the picture until the mouse turns to a four-headed arrow. Then drag the picture to the desired position.

## To wrap text:

Picture Tools Format/Arrange/Wrap Text

★ **TIP**

Note that the default for wrapping text is In Line with Text as shown by the red arrow in the illustration.

 Wrap Text ▾

Wrap Text determines how text wraps around a selected object, such as a picture. Wrap Text can be applied by using the Layout Options button that displays when a picture is selected or by using the Wrap Text command.

1. Select the picture and then click Layout Options button or the Wrap Text drop-list arrow to display the options.
2. Select the desired option, such as Square or Tight as shown on the right.

---

**DRILL 3**  **FORMAT PICTURE**   format pictures

1. With *format pictures* data file open, read the information in the document, and then complete the five numbered steps.

2. Preview and check; click Next Activity. (*50-drill3*)

---

# Reports

## LEARNING OUTCOMES

- Format two-page reports with cover pages.
- Insert page numbers in report with preliminary pages.
- Insert multilevel list.
- Create and modify table of contents.
- Create and modify table of figures.
- Use navigation tools.
- Build keyboarding skills.

## Lesson 70  Review Reports

**New Command**
- Multilevel List

**Warmup**  *Lesson 70a Warmup*

A  **ALL LETTERS**

## Skill Building

**70b  Timed Writing**

1. Key a 1' timing on each paragraph; work to increase speed.
2. Key a 3' timing on all paragraphs.

Do you ever "goof off" for an hour or more with a television program or a visit on the telephone and realize later that you haven't actually enjoyed your leisure? Each nagging little vision of homework or chores to be completed always seems to result in taking the edge off your pleasure. And then you must hurriedly complete whatever you postponed. Why do so many people end up rushing around in a frenzy, trying to meet their deadlines?

First, do not waste time feeling guilty. Check with your friends who always seem ready for a good time but are also ready for unexpected quizzes. Learn their secrets to managing time. Knowing that there are sixty seconds in every minute and sixty minutes in each hour, you can schedule your activities into the time available. Second, learn to set priorities. You can achieve your plans and enjoy your leisure as well.

## ONLINE PICTURES

The Online Pictures command is used to access digital pictures and illustrations from sources other than your computer and your computer network. Note that some of the sources require you to set up an account if you do not already have one.

*To insert online pictures:*

Insert/Illustrations/Online Pictures

1. Click Online Pictures to display the Online Pictures options. If you have used previous versions of *Word*, you will notice that Clip Art is now an online option.

2. Key the keywords in the search box to search for the desired clip or other picture.

3. Select the desired clip and double-click it or click Insert to insert the clip.

**TIP**

The free *Microsoft Live* account for your SkyDrive gives you access to Microsoft Web Apps.

The free Flickr account from Yahoo gives you access to the photo-sharing social media site. You can also access Flickr from a Facebook account.

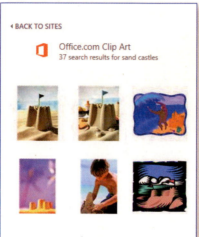

**Note:** You can format clip art and other online pictures and illustrations using the commands on the Picture Tools Format tab.

---

## DRILL 4 — INSERT AND FORMAT ONLINE PICTURES

1. In a new document, search *Office.com* clip art for *sand castles*.

2. Select the first picture shown above in the search results and insert it.

3. Size the picture 2.5" high, and apply Square Text Wrapping.

4. Move the picture to the right side of the page.

5. Crop the top of the picture to just above the flag.

6. Position the picture in the Middle Center with Square Text Wrapping.

7. Preview and check; click Next Activity. (*50-drill4*)

4. Select the paragraphs and place them in two columns; make the left column 1.7" wide and the right column 4.3" wide. The spacing between columns is 0.5". Insert a line between columns.

5. Click the insertion point at the beginning of the first column and insert a column break to move the text to the second column.

6. With Show/Hide displayed, click the insertion point at the beginning of the Column Break in the left column.

7. Change the Zoom setting to Whole Page (View/Zoom/Zoom). Use Draw Text Box to draw a text box in the left column. The text box should be 8" high by 1.9" wide. Change the Shape Fill color to match the title. Search for a picture of a courthouse and insert it at the top of the text box.

8. Key the following text so that it displays attractively in the text box; use the White, Background 1 color. Key the telephone number in 14-point bold font.

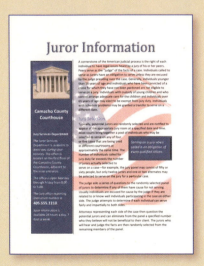

Camacho County Courthouse (Bold, center, 16-point font)
Jury Services Department

The Juror Services Department is available to assist you during your services. The office is located on the first floor of the Camacho County Courthouse, adjacent to the main entrance.

The office is open Monday through Friday from 8:00 to 5:00. The Jury office reporting instruction number is 405.555.1210. Juror information is available 24 hours a day, 7 days a week.

9. Insert a text box, 1.1" high by 2" wide, in the first paragraph below Jury Selection with Square Text Wrapping. Make the fill color and font the same as in the left column. Key: **Serving on a jury when called is an obligation of every qualified citizen.** Place the text in italic and Align Text Middle. Apply Convex Beveling to the text box.

10. Search for a clip art of the U.S. flag and insert it as a picture watermark.

11. Proofread the document. Check the test and close. Click Exit *Word*. (69-d3)

12. Click Log out to exit *KPDO*.

## PAGE BORDER

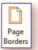

Page borders can be formatted using a variety of settings, styles, colors, and line widths. They can be applied to the whole document or to various sections of the document.

### To apply a page border:
Design/Page Background/Page Borders

1. Click Page Borders to display the Borders and Shading dialog box.
2. Make sure the Page Border tab is active.
3. Choose the desired setting, style, color, and width.
4. In the Apply to box, choose the desired option.

---

## DRILL 5     PAGE BORDERS

1. Open *50-drill4* and apply a Box page border.

2. Choose the thick-and-thin line style, 3 pt. width shown in the illustration above.

3. Choose Standard Blue color.

4. Apply to the whole document.

5. Preview and select Next Activity. (*50-drill5*)

---

## ⚠ WORKPLACE SUCCESS

### Positive Attitude

*Elena Elisseeva/Shutterstock.com*

What makes a successful employee? Employers say that "soft skills" are critical. A positive attitude is generally one of the top five soft skills required. Why? Because it enhances performance. People with positive attitudes tend to be problem solvers. They view problems as challenges with opportunities and find ways to solve them.

Self-confidence is also linked to a positive attitude. If you think you can do something, you are quite likely to do it. Workers with a poor self-image are more likely to look for faults than strengths.

Another important reason for developing a positive attitude is that other employees prefer to work with individuals who have a positive attitude. Most companies require employees to work on teams; thus, having a positive attitude enhances teamwork and contributes to the success of the team.

---

5. Insert the totals in the last row and last column. Totals should contain a comma and two decimal places. Use a decimal tab to align all numbers. Change the height of rows 2–7 to 0.25"; center text vertically in the cells.

6. Change Bennet's Disability Insurance to **55.00** and Fraser's Tax Shelter Annuity amount to **375.00**. Update the totals to reflect the changes.

7. Proofread and correct any errors; click Continue. (*69-d2*)

MONTHLY DEDUCTIONS	Employee	Tax Shelter Annuity	Health Insurance	Disability Insurance	Total Deduction
	Bennet, Susan	500.00	425.00	35.00	
	Carillo, Marlan	175.00	685.00	75.00	
	Fraser, Elisol	275.00	420.00	0.00	
	Jones, Anna	325.00	475.00	55.00	
	Tanaka, Ellen	200.00	510.00	55.00	
	Total				

## 69-d3

**Newsletter**

 69-d3 text

1. In the open document, turn on Show/Hide; then click the insertion point at the beginning of the document. Tap ENTER.

2. Move the insertion point to the ¶ marker in the first line. Key the title **Juror Information**. Apply 48-point Cambria font and Blue, Accent 1, Darker 50% color. Apply the Outer Offset Right shadow and Center.

3. Tap ENTER, change the font to Calibri 11-point, Automatic font color, remove shadow, and Align Left. Key the text shown below. Apply Heading 1 style to the side heading.

A cornerstone of the American judicial process is the right of each individual to have legal issues heard by a jury of his or her peers. Peers serve as the "judge" of the facts of a case. Individuals called to serve as jurors have an obligation to serve unless they are excused by the judge presiding over the case. Generally, individuals younger than 18 years of age and individuals who have been convicted of a crime for which they have not been pardoned are not eligible to serve on a jury. Individuals with custody of young children and who cannot arrange adequate care for the children and individuals over 65 years of age may elect to be exempt from jury duty. Individuals with schedule problems may be granted a transfer to serve on a different date.

Jury Selection

*(continued)*

**Document with Graphics**

closed for work focus
open for interaction

1. Tap ENTER three times and key the title.
2. Key the report shown below and then apply the formats listed after the report.

Open vs. Closed Office Environments

Finding the Right Balance

For several decades, the trend has been to move from the traditional closed office to an open office environment. Rather than continuing the debate on which is better, searching for a workable balance may be a better approach. Obviously, both settings have advantages and disadvantages. The right balance would maximize the advantages and minimize the disadvantages of each.

Closed Office

Employees often think of the closed office as the power or image office. Clearly, offices with walls and a door offer more privacy, fewer interruptions, and better noise control. At the same time, they are more expensive and are not as conducive to open communication and teamwork.

Open Office

Employees often call it *Cubicle Village* because of the large number of cubicles and lack of walls and doors. Defining what the open office looks like is difficult because the look varies widely. Most people think of the open office as being in a setting similar to the illustration below.

The advantages are putting more people in less space at a lower cost and making employees more accessible to each other, thereby enabling open communication and enhancing teamwork.

Blended Environment

Office furnishings are now available that enable employees to close or open doors and windows of cubicles that provide time in which the employee can focus on work without interruption and time in which the employee welcomes conversation with team members. Employees are not closed off, but at the same time have some degree of privacy and noise is reduced. See the illustrations below.

3. Apply the Slice theme.
4. Apply Title style to the title, Subtitle style to the subtitle, and Heading 1 to the three headings. Decrease the title font size to fit on one line.
5. Use the Online Pictures command and the keywords *busy cubicles* to search for clip art illustrating an office. See the Quick Check on the next page.
   a. Tap ENTER after the first paragraph under the *Open Office* heading and insert the clip that is located.

*(continued)*

 **Warmup** *Lesson 69a Warmup*

## Apply It

### 69-d1

**Block letter**

 69-d1 letterhead

1. Camacho County Courthouse letterhead should be displayed on the screen. The insertion point should be at the left margin, 2.5". Key the letter using block style and open punctuation.
2. Begin the date at approximately 2". Be sure to press SHIFT + ENTER after the short lines in the letter address and closing lines to adjust spacing.
3. Create an envelope and add to the letter.
4. Proofread and correct any errors; click Continue. (*69-d1*)

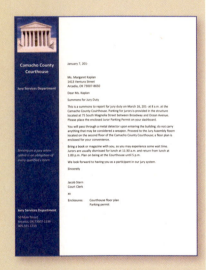

---

January 7, 201- | Ms. Margaret Kaplan | 1413 Ventura Street | Arcadia, OK 73007-8650 | Dear Ms. Kaplan

Summons for Jury Duty

This is a summons to report for jury duty on March 16, 201- at 8:00 a.m. at the Camacho County Courthouse. Parking for jurors is provided in the structure located on 75 South Magnolia Street between Broadway and Ocean Avenue. Place the enclosed Juror Parking Permit on your dashboard.

You will pass through a metal detector upon entering the building; do not carry anything that may be considered a weapon. Proceed to the Jury Assembly Room, located on the second floor of the Camacho County Courthouse; a floor plan is enclosed for your convenience.

Bring a book or magazine with you, as you may experience some wait time. Jurors are usually dismissed for lunch at 11:30 a.m. and return from lunch at 1:00 p.m. Plan on being at the Courthouse until 5:00 p.m.

We look forward to having you as a participant in our jury system.

Sincerely | Jacob Stern | Court Clerk | Enclosures: Courthouse floor plan | Parking permit

---

### 69-d2

**Table with Calculations**

1. Create the 6-column, 7-row table shown on the next page. Merge the cells in column A.
2. Key the main heading **MONTHLY DEDUCTIONS** in bold, 14-point caps. Rotate the text, Align Center, and apply White, Background 1, Darker 15% shading. Change the width of column A to 0.5".
3. Change the height of row 1 to 1". Key the column headings in bold, 12-point font, center them vertically and horizontally in the cells; rotate the headings in columns C–F.
4. Key the table; adjust column widths, and center the table horizontally.

*(continued)*

    **b.** Size the clip 2.4" high and use the Center command on the Home tab to center it.

**6.** Insert the *closed for work focus* and the *open for interaction* picture data files on the line below the last paragraph.

    **a.** Compress both pictures; accept the defaults.

    **b.** Size both pictures 2.4" high and apply Square Text Wrapping.

    **c.** Position the *closed for work focus* picture on the left and the *open for interaction* picture on the right.

**7.** Number the pages on the top of the page using Plain Number 3. Do not show the number on the first page.

**8.** Preview and proofread the document carefully. Check the position of the photos against the illustration below.

**9.** Check and select Next Activity. (*50-d1*)

---

**50-d2**

**Document with Page Border**

**1.** Open *50-d1* and apply a box page border.

**2.** Use a single line style with Dark Blue – Accent 1 theme color and 1-point line width.

**3.** Apply to the whole document.

**4.** Preview, check, and exit *Word*.

**5.** Click Log out to exit *KPDO*. (*50-d2*)

**QUICK ✓**

The illustration on the left shows *50-d1* page 1 (photo may vary); the one on the right shows *50-d2* page 2 (with the border).

Total Estimated Cost by Facility		
Venue and Facility	Facility Costs	Venue Costs
Aquatics Center		
Sailing Club	$1,375,000	
Swim Center	225,000	
Marina	165,000	
Total		
Golf Center		
Golf Course	5,350,000	
Practice Areas	250,000	
Walking Trails	195,000	
Clubhouse	1,600,000	
Total		
Olympics Center		
Courts	1,275,000	
Fields	1,325,000	
Track	890,000	
Total		
Total Costs		

The total cost is projected to be $12,650,000. Detailed costs of each facility and venue are provided in the comprehensive report. Conceptual designs are also available.

Apply Heading 1 style. Insert three text boxes to the right of the paragraphs. Key the text from the instructions on page 324.

Investment Opportunities

Qualified investors are being offered the opportunity to invest in the Crown Lake SportsPlex. Extensive pro formas have been prepared, and investment professionals will attend the March 15 seminar to explain the investment opportunities and offer professional opinions about the project. They will discuss the projected return on investment and other benefits associated with the project. In addition to the return on the investment, all levels of investment include private club membership benefits.

The reward provided with this investment opportunity is significant, but it is important to understand that the risk involved in this project is also significant.

This document contains confidential and proprietary information that is provided only to investors and potential investors of the Crown Lake SportsPlex. Do not copy, distribute, or share this information.

# Lesson 51 SmartArt and WordArt

## New Commands
- Insert SmartArt
- SmartArt Design Tools
- SmartArt Layout Tools
- Add Text to SmartArt
- Add Shapes
- Insert WordArt
- Format WordArt

 **Warmup** *Lesson 51a Warmup*

## Skill Building

### 51b Textbook Keying

1. Key each line once, concentrating on using good keying techniques.
2. Repeat the drill if time permits.

1st row	1 Max, Zam, and a local man saw an amazing cave on a long bus ride.
	2 Janna came back home six times to visit the bat caves at the zoo.
3rd row	3 We wrote Terry to try to get a quote; Perry tried to get a quote.
	4 Perry peeped at Terry's quote; were you there with Perry or Pete?
home row	5 Kala was glad Alyssa sold a glass flask at a gala sale in Dallas.
	6 Jack Hall's dad was in Dallas at a glass sale; a sad lad saw him.
one hand	7 Jimmy saw him carve a great pumpkin; John deserved better awards.
	8 Nikki saved a million as a minimum reserve on debt; Jimmy agreed.
balanced hand	9 Jamale Rodney, a neighbor, and Sydney may go to the lake by auto.
	10 Bud got the tub of big worms to go to the dock to fish with them.

## New Commands

### 51c

### SMARTART

SmartArt consists of predesigned diagrams that help to simplify complex concepts. Note in the SmartArt graphic dialog box that SmartArt layouts are grouped into eight categories. You can view all of the layouts or the layouts in one category.

To insert and add text to SmartArt:
Insert/Illustrations/SmartArt

1. Position the insertion point where you want to add the graphic, and click SmartArt to open the Choose a SmartArt Graphic dialog box shown on the next page. Categories of SmartArt are listed on the left, layouts for each category display in the center, and the preview and description of the appropriate use appear in the right pane.

*(continued)*

10. Create three text boxes.

    a. Copy the text box that you created in the *Venues* section and paste it three times in the *Investment Opportunities* section as shown in the illustration.

    b. Replace the text in the text box with the following text. (Press SHIFT + ENTER after each level of investor.)

**Level-One Investor**
**Minimum investment of $250,000 but less than $500,000.**

**Level-Two Investor**
**Investments larger than $500,000 but less than $1,000,000.**

**Level-Three Investor**
**Investments of $1,000,000 or more.**

    c. Change the alignment of the text in the third text box to Middle.

11. Proofread and check. Click Exit *Word*. (68-d2) Click Log out to exit *KPDO*.

---

The Crown Lake SportsPlex concept and conceptual drawing of the campus plan have been approved by its Board of Directors. The plan will be unveiled at a special seminar for potential investors on March 15.

*Apply Heading 1 style* →

Concepts

The SportsPlex is envisioned as a three-tiered venue. The tiers match users and type of sports offered. The tier structure is based on revenue-generating potential, with the individual and corporate users expected to produce the bulk of the revenue. Students, competitive athletes, and the general public are expected to produce the highest volume of use but the lowest level of revenue.

*Insert Pyramid List SmartArt graphic here* →

The SportsPlex will be divided into three component venues—the Aquatics Center, the Golf Center, and the Olympics Center. Supporting facilities, restaurants, pro shops, boutiques, and family-oriented activities will be provided with each of the three venues.

*Insert Converging Radial SmartArt graphic here* →

Venues

*Apply Heading 1 style; Insert the venues data file after the heading; position the text box on the right side of the first paragraph under the Venues head; copy the second sentence and place it in the text box.* →

Estimated Project Costs

Land and existing facilities, including the Crown Lake Special Events Center, have been purchased by the Crown Lake SportsPlex founders at a cost in excess of $10 million. The estimated costs of the facilities are shown in the following table.

*(continued)*

**TIP**

If desired, apply a document theme so that the SmartArt layout will use the appropriate colors of the theme.

**TIP**

The Text Pane options adjust to match each layout. If the text pane is not displayed, follow the path and click Text Pane.

SmartArt Tools Design/
Create Graphic/Text Pane

2. Click the category desired, or scroll through all layouts and click the desired layout, and OK to insert it.

3. Key text in the text pane that displays or directly in each shape. Note that the text size adjusts to fit the shape.

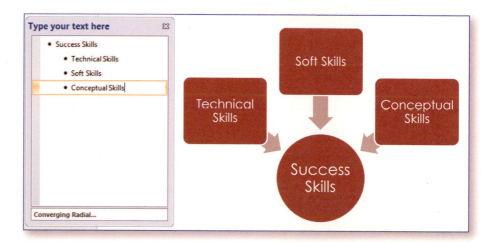

---

**DRILL 1**      SMARTART

1. In a new document, apply Ion theme and insert a SmartArt Converging Radial from the Relationship category.

2. Key the text shown at the right in the shapes using the Text pane.

3. Compare your solution to the illustration above; click Next Activity. (*51-drill1*)

Success Skills

   Technical Skills

   Soft Skills

   Conceptual Skills

5. Insert a Converting Radial SmartArt graphic (in the Relationship group) at the top of page 2. Change the SmartArt design style to Cartoon and the colors to Colorful Range – Accent Colors 4 to 5. Add text:

   a. Left shape: **Aquatics Center**

   b. Center top shape: **Golf Center**

   c. Right shape: **Olympics Center**

   d. Bottom shape: **Crown Lake SportsPlex**

6. Insert the text from the *venues* data file below the *Venues* heading. Apply Heading 2 style to all headings in the data file.

7. Insert a Simple Text Box as shown in the illustration at the left; copy the second sentence under *Venues* into the text box. Apply Standard Color Blue, Shape Fill; Shape Effects/Shadow/Inner, Inside Diagonal Top Right; Shape Effects/Bevel/Circle. Size the text box 0.9" high and 2.5" wide. Format using Align Text/Bottom. Bold the text and change the color to White, Background 1.

8. Insert the *events* picture from the data files as shown in the *Golf Center* section. Crop about 0.25" from the top and 0.5" from the bottom of the picture. Compress the picture.

   Size the picture to 4.5" high and 6.5" wide as follows:

   a. Select the picture and click the Size dialog box launcher to display the Layout dialog box. Click the Size tab.

   b. Key **4.5** in the Height box, Absolute should be selected. Key **6.5** in the width box. Deselect Lock aspect ratio and Relative to original picture size.

9. Key and format the table using Grid Table 5 Dark – Accent 6 style.

   a. Merge the cells in the top row; increase row height to 0.4"; Align Center the title using bold and 16-point font. Bold and center columns B and C headings.

   b. Set a 0.25" left tab in the first column to indent the items as shown.

   c. Select column B and set a decimal tab at 1.4" in the Tabs dialog box. Repeat this procedure for column C.

   d. Use the SUM(ABOVE) formula to total the cost of each venue and place the results in the *Total* row of the *Venue Costs* column.

      1) Place the insertion point in cell B7.

      2) Use the SUM(ABOVE) feature to obtain the total. The total should include a dollar sign and two decimal places.

      3) Select the total and drag it to cell C7.

      Repeat above steps for each venue.

   e. Obtain the total costs of the three venues and position the results in the last row of the *Venue Costs* column. In the Formula box, key **=c7+c13+c18**; no spaces, then click OK.

## ADD SHAPES

Each SmartArt diagram offers a few shapes by default. You can add more shapes by tapping ENTER after the last entry or from the SmartArt Tools Design tab.

### To add shapes to SmartArt:

SmartArt Tools Design/Create Graphic/Add Shape

1. Click in the shape before or after which you want to add another shape.

2. Follow the path to add a shape, or click the drop-list arrow and select an option from the Add Shape options.

3. Repeat the process until you have as many shapes as you need in the layout.

**TIP**

The options available on the Add Shape list depend on the type of diagram you are working with.

---

**DRILL 2**          ADD SHAPES

1. Apply Organic theme and key **Effective Decision Making**; apply Title style and tap ENTER twice.

2. Insert a Block Cycle from the SmartArt Cycle category; add a shape after the last shape.

3. Key the text in the text pane.

4. Compare to the Quick Check and click Next activity. (*51-drill2*)

Identify decision to be made
Determine options
Analyze options
Select best option
Implement option
Evaluate decision

---

**QUICK ✓**

Compare your document to the illustration shown below.

## Effective Decision Making

---

## WORDART

WordArt adds special effects to text to make it more interesting. It is typically used in announcements, flyers, newsletters, and other casual documents.

---

## 68-d1

**Block Letter**

 hess letterhead

The following letter will be sent to community members and Crown Lake investors.

1. Key the letter in block letter style with open punctuation.
2. Proofread and check; click Next Activity. (*68-d1*)

Dear Community Member

Crown Lake, Inc. invites you to attend an information session for the opportunity to discover how you can be an investment partner in the Crown Lake SportsPlex. Many of you have invested with us in past projects that have produced high-yield returns.

The community has expressed a need to develop a sports facility that will yield long-term positive results. This project will include integration of education, athletics, campus recreation, student athlete, alumni/donor, business, and local community interests.

The information session will be held on February 15, 201- at 7:00 p.m. in the Diamond Conference Room, Hess Office Park Conference Center. Our team of sports facility and recreation center business consultants will provide expert advice on this exciting opportunity. Please call (insert your name) at 800.555.1002 by February 10, 201- to reserve a seat at the information session.

Sincerely | Robert A. Callihan, President | Board of Directors

## 68-d2

**Report Summary**

 venues events

This document will be given to the attendees at the February 15th information session. It summarizes a large, comprehensive report that will be presented at a seminar for investors on March 15th. Use the illustrations in the left margin on page 324 as a guide for page layout and positioning of graphics and text boxes.

1. Tap ENTER three times to key the title **Crown Lake SportsPlex** at 1.9" and apply Title style; key the subtitle **Executive Summary** and apply Subtitle style. Center both titles and change the font color to Blue, Accent 5, Darker 25%.
2. Key the document that begins on page 325. Number pages using Plain Number 3 at the top of the page. Apply Different First Page. Follow instructions in the callouts.
3. Apply a dropped cap to the *C* in the *Concept* heading.
4. Insert a Pyramid List SmartArt graphic where indicated. Add text:
   a. Top shape: **Students and General Public**
   b. Middle shape: **Competitive Athletes**
   c. Bottom shape: **Individual and Corporate Users**

Change the SmartArt design style to Cartoon (SmartTools Design/SmartArt Styles). Change the colors to Colorful Range – Accent Colors 5 to 6.

*(continued)*

1. Click WordArt to display the WordArt gallery.

2. Preview and select the desired option.

3. Select the text in the text box that displays and replace it with your text.

4. Size and position the WordArt as desired.

WordArt can be formatted using the tools on the Drawing Tools Format tab.

- *Styles*—can be changed to any style in the gallery.

- *Text Fill*—used to add color or change the color of the interior of the letters.

- *Text Outline*—used to change the color, style, or weight of the lines of the exterior border of the letters.

- *Text Effects*—add depth or emphasis to text. See Text Effects and Transform options below.

To apply WordArt formats:

Drawing Tools Format/WordArt Styles/Text Fill, Text Outline, Text Effects, or WordArt Styles

1. To change to a new WordArt style, preview and click the desired style.

2. To change Text Fill, Text Outline, or Text Effects, select the text, click the appropriate drop-list arrow, and select the desired color, line, or effect.

## DRILL 3  WORDART

1. Display the WordArt gallery and select Fill – Black Text 1, Outline – Background 1, Hard Shadow – Background 1, and key **Happy Birthday to You!**

2. Select the text and apply Dark Red Standard Color fill.

3. Apply text effects: Art Deco Bevel (last icon) and Triangle Up Transform.

4. Size 1.5" high and 5.5" wide, and position in Top Center with Square Text Wrapping.

5. Compare your document to the Quick Check on the next page.

6. Preview and click Next Activity. (*51-drill3*)

# Lesson 68 Hess Office Park

## Skill Building

### 68b Timed Writing

1. Key one 3' timing on the entire writing.
2. Key one 5' timing on all paragraphs.

Surrogate grandparents and pet therapy might not be the types of terms that you would expect to find in a medical journal, but they are concepts that are quite popular with senior citizens. Two of the most common problems experienced by senior citizens who do not live with or near a family member are loneliness and the craving to feel needed and loved.

Senior citizens who are healthy and who are stable mentally often can have a high-quality relationship with deprived children who do not have grandparents of their own. They often have time to spare and the desire to give these needy children extra attention and help with their school work and other needs. At first, it may seem that children gain the most from being with seniors. However, it soon becomes evident that the surrogate grandparents tend to benefit as much or even more than the children.

Both assisted-living and total-care residential facilities are using pets to keep senior citizens from feeling alone. In those cases in which a single person lives in one of the housing units, the pet can help to reduce the feeling of being alone and lonely. Even patients in the total-care units who do not communicate very much become animated and will talk to a very gentle pet brought in on a regular basis to play with the patients.

## Project Setting

### CROWN LAKE INC. AT HESS OFFICE PARK

Crown Lake Inc. is an investment firm with offices located in major cities throughout the country; Hess Office Park is one of its many locations.

Crown Lake rents the large conference room at Hess Office Park to hold information sessions for prospective investors. They utilize the services of the print and copy center to prepare handouts, signs, and mailings for the information sessions. As the administrative assistant for the Hess Office Park print and copy center, you will be working with Crown Lake to prepare for the Crown Lake SportsPlex Information Session scheduled for February 15, 201-.

## Communication

### CAPITALIZATION

**51d**

References/Communication
Skills/Capitalization

1. Review the capitalization rules and examples in *KPDO*.
2. Key the sentences, correcting all capitalization errors. Use the Numbering command to number the sentences.
3. Proofread and check; click Next Activity to continue. (*51d*)

1. according to one study, the largest ethnic minority group online is hispanics.
2. the american author mark twain said, "always do right; this will gratify some people and astonish the rest."
3. the grand canyon was formed by the colorado river cutting into the high-plateau region of northwestern arizona.
4. the president of russia is elected by popular vote.
5. the hubble space telescope is a cooperative project of the european space agency and the national aeronautics and space administration.
6. the train left north station at 6:45 this morning.
7. the trademark cyberprivacy prevention act would make it illegal for individuals to purchase domains solely for resale and profit.
8. consumers spent $7 billion online between november 1 and december 31, 201-, compared to $3.1 billion for the same period in 2010.
9. new students should attend an orientation session on wednesday, august 15, at 8 a.m. in room 252 of the perry building.
10. the summer book list includes *where the red fern grows* and *the mystery of the missing baseball.*

## *Communicating Today* ▶

### Electronic Document Distribution

Electronic document distribution is a key factor leading to the increased use of color and graphics in business documents today especially in small businesses. Previously, small businesses limited the use of color and graphics because they did not have the graphic arts staff or the budget to create effective color graphics. Although the cost of color printing has declined dramatically, it still costs significantly more than black-and-white printing. When documents are distributed electronically, printing costs are eliminated.

SmartArt and color digital pictures make it easy to create effective graphics that simplify complex concepts. Color and SmartArt not only make documents more interesting; used effectively, they help make documents more understandable.

# Crown Lake News and Views

Newsletter Staff

Eric Burge
    Editor

Nancy Suggs
Christopher Hess
Anne Reynolds
    Associate Editors

Wayne Martin
    Editorial Assistant

*Crown Lake News and Views* is a weekly newsletter compiled by the staff of the Human Resources Department, and it is sent to all employees.

## New Development Project

Crown Lake won the bid to develop and construct the new multimillion-dollar Business Center adjacent to Metro Airport. Connie McClure, one of the three senior project managers, had been named as the Business Center project manager. The project is expected to take more than two years to complete.

Approximately fifty new permanent employees will be hired to work on this project. All jobs will be posted within the next two weeks. The recruiting referral program is in effect for all jobs. You can earn a $100 bonus for each individual you recommend who is hired and remains with Crown Lake for at least six months. You may pick up your recruiting referral forms in the Personnel Office.

## Blood Drive Reminder

The Crown Lake quarterly blood drive is set for next Friday in the Wellness Center. The Community Blood Bank needs all types of blood to replace the supplies sent to the islands during the recent disaster caused by Hurricane Lana. Employees in all divisions are being asked to participate this quarter because of the current supply crisis. All three donation sites will be used. Several volunteers will be needed to staff the two additional sites. The regular division rotation will resume next quarter.

## Lee Daye Honored

The Community Foundation honored Lee Daye of the Marketing Department with the Eagle Award for outstanding service this year. The Eagle Award is presented each year to three citizens who have made a significant impact on the lives of others. The Community Foundation recognized  Lee for his work with underprivileged children, the Community Relations Task Force, the Abolish Domestic Violence Center, and the Community Transitional Housing Project. Congratulations, Lee. You made a difference in the lives of many citizens in our community. Your award was richly deserved.

## New Training Program

The pilot test of the new Team Effectiveness training program was completed last month, and the results were excellent. Thanks to all of you who participated in the development and  testing of the program. Your input is vital to its success. The training schedule will be announced shortly.

## Apply It

**51-d1**

**Memo Form with Graphics**

  farbe logo

### ✳ Discover

**Recolor**

Picture Tools Format/
Adjust/Color

1. Click the drop-list arrow on Color to display the color options.
2. Click the desired color.

1. Apply Facet theme style to a new document and insert the *Farbe logo* from the data files.

2. Farbe now distributes its documents electronically and wants to recolor ✳ the logo color to Green – Accent Color1 Light.

3. Insert Fill-Green – Accent 1, Shadow WordArt to the right side of the logo; select the text and key **Farbe Enterprises**; apply Cool Slant Bevel Text Effects (last bevel on first row).

4. Size the WordArt 1" high and 4.2" wide.

5. Key the memo headings as shown in the Quick Check on the next page.

6. Preview, proofread, check, and click Next Activity. (*51-d1*)

---

**51-d2**

**Document with Graphics**

  credenza

1. Open *51-d1* and key the memo shown below, inserting the SmartArt Name and Title Organization chart where noted.

2. Click in the top shape and add another Assistant shape. Use the Text Pane to key the names in the organization chart. Click in the Title boxes to key the titles. In the second Assistant shape, use **New** as the name.

3. Use In Line with Text wrapping and size the organization chart 3.8" high by 6.5" wide.

4. Tap ENTER after the reference initials and insert the *credenza* picture from the data files. Size it 5" high and position at Top Center with Square Text Wrapping. Compress the picture, accepting the defaults.

5. Proofread and check; click Next Activity. (*51-d2*)

Marketing Employees | Mark Redman | Current date | Feedback from Executive Management Retreat

The Executive Team approved the reorganization of the Marketing Department. The new organization chart is shown below. You will be pleased to note that our three area managers have been promoted to directors.

**(Insert Name and Title Organization Chart here. Key the names and titles shown below in the chart.)**

Mark Redman Vice President | Trista Blackmon Executive Assistant | New Executive Assistant | Andrea Kelly Director | Daniel Wexford Director | Jodye Bristow Director

The Communications, Advertising, and Public Relations Teams will report to Andrea, the Marketing and Strategic Planning Teams will report to Daniel, and the Inside Sales and the Field Sales Teams will report to Jodye. A new assistant will be hired to support the three directors.

The Executive Team also approved the purchase of credenzas that we requested for all of the Marketing Department offices. Of the three styles proposed, the team selected the style that is in Pat's office in the Finance Department. See the picture on the next page.

xx

## 67-d1

**Newsletter with Unequal Columns**

 business center

1. Change the margins to Narrow. Tap ENTER once and key **Crown Lake News and Views**; apply 36-point Trebuchet MS font and Blue, Accent 5, Darker 50% font color. Center the title.

2. Tap ENTER once after the title. Change to Left Align, Calibri 11-point font size, and the font color to Automatic.

3. Tap ENTER and insert a Continuous section break. Begin keying on the line below the section break. Key the newsletter shown on the next page as a one-column document. Apply Heading 1 style to all headings. Remove the space after paragraph between the staff names and positions as illustrated on the next page. Key staff titles at the left margin; they will be indented later.

4. Select the text of the newsletter and format it using the Left Preset and three columns. Check Line between. Change the settings in the Columns dialog box as follows:

   Column 1 width: 1.5" | Spacing: 0.3"

   Columns 2 and 3 width: 2.7" | Spacing: 0.3"

5. Place the insertion point at the beginning of the heading *New Development Project* and insert a Column break.

6. Insert the *business center* picture from the data files; use Square Text Wrapping, size it 2.3" high, and position it as shown on the next page.

7. Click in the paragraph below the business center picture and select Add Space Before Paragraph (Home/Paragraph/Line and Paragraph Spacing).

8. Find the picture shown of the eagle from the Online Clip Art gallery; use Square Text Wrapping, size it 1.2" high, and position it after the Eagle Award has been mentioned.

9. Find the picture shown on team building from the Online Clip Art gallery; use Square Text Wrapping, size it 1.25" high, and position it in the paragraph below the New Training Program heading.

10. Select the text in the left column and set a left tab at 0.25". Tap TAB before each staff title.

11. Proofread and check; click Next Activity. (*67-d1*)

## 67-d2

**Position Graphic**

1. In the open document (*67-d1*), select the picture of the eagle and click Fix Position on Page in the Wrap Text drop list.

2. Select the *Lee Daye Honored* heading and the text below it (do not select *New Training Program*). Move the text before the heading *Blood Drive Reminder*. The picture of the eagle remains in the third column.

3. Proofread and check; click Exit *Word* (*67-d2*)

4. Click Log out to exit *KPDO*.

Compare your document to the illustration shown below.

## 51-d3

**Announcement with Online Picture, WordArt, and Border**

1. Turn on Show/Hide. Apply Integral theme and Landscape orientation.

2. Apply Moderate margins.

3. In Online Pictures, search for *4th of July* clip art, and select the clip (or similar) shown at the left. Crop the black border from all sides, and resize 2" high.

4. Insert WordArt Fill – White, Outline – Accent 2, Hard Shadow – Accent 2.

   a. Select text and replace with **Fourth of July Celebration**; apply Red from Standard Colors Text Fill.

   b. Size the WordArt 1.5" high and 7" wide.

   c. Apply Transform Stop Text Effects (second icon under Warp).

   d. Position in Top Right with Square Text Wrapping.

5. Tap ENTER three times below the clip and apply 36-point font size. Key the text shown below. Justify the text.

6. Apply a thick and thin page border, using Blue from the Standard Colors.

7. Proofread and check; click Exit *Word*.

8. Click Log out to exit *KPDO*. (*51-d3*)

**QUICK** ✔

Fourth of July Celebration

Pack your lawn chairs or blankets and bring the entire family to join your friends and neighbors for the annual Fourth of July celebration at City Park. Music and festivities begin at 7:30 p.m. and end with a spectacular fireworks display at 10:30.

Pack your lawn chairs or blankets and bring the entire family to join your friends and neighbors for the annual Fourth of July celebration at City Park. Music and festivities begin at 7:30 p.m. and end with a spectacular fireworks display at 10:30.

To fix the position of an image:
Picture Tools Format/Arrange/Wrap Text

1. Select the image; then display the Wrap Text drop menu.

2. Choose Fix Position on Page if you need to keep the picture at the current location. Otherwise, click More Layout Options.

3. In the Layout dialog box, click the Position tab. Key the desired horizontal and vertical positions.

4. In the Options section, deselect Move object with text. Select Lock anchor to keep the image at a particular position.

## DRILL 2 — POSITION GRAPHIC IN COLUMNS OF UNEQUAL WIDTH

 litter

1. In the open document, click the insertion point at the top of the document. Use the WordArt Fill – White, Outline – Accent 1, Shadow style and key **Are you a Litterbug?**

2. Change the width of the WordArt text box to 6". Select the title and apply Green, Accent 6, Darker, 25% Fill Color. Apply Gold, Accent 4, Lighter 60% Text Outline color.

3. Position the insertion point at the beginning of the line "Students Going Green" and insert a Continuous section break.

4. Display the Columns dialog box and select Left in the Presets box. Check to see that the number of columns is set for 2.

5. Check Line between and click OK.

6. Place the cursor at the beginning of the first paragraph ("Does the appearance . . .") and insert a Column break.

7. Search for clip art related to **litter** and insert it in the second paragraph. Crop the picture as needed; compress the picture. Adjust the width of the picture to 1.2".

8. Change the text wrapping to Square. Move the picture to the right edge of the second paragraph. In the Wrap Text menu, select Fix Position on Page.

9. Move the third paragraph before the second paragraph.

10. Preview the document to ensure that it fits properly on the page.

11. Proofread and check; click Next Activity. (67-drill2)

## Creating a Flyer in the 21st Century

**Communicating Today** ▶

Use of a QR Code (Quick Response Code) in marketing materials has become a popular trend. We see them on flyers, business cards, posters, brochures, and many other types of advertising media. Some people even put QR Codes on T-shirts. QR Codes are scanned with an app on a smartphone, which then takes the user to a website, provides the user with a coupon, or gives information about a product or promotion. These codes can even be used to send a message.

Businesses have been quite creative in how they use QR Codes, especially if they are targeting a younger market that is typically very smartphone savvy. Use a QR Code to trigger an action; marketing with a QR Code is most effective when you get a "WOW" or "COOL" reaction from its users.

# *Lesson 52* Documents with Columns

- Equal-Width Columns
- Balance Columns
- Revise Column Structure
- Line between Columns
- Format Banner

**Warmup**   *Lesson 52a Warmup*

## Skill Building

**52b  Textbook Keying**

1. Key each line once, concentrating on using good keying techniques.
2. Repeat the drill if time permits.

1st finger

1  Freddie just gave a friend that nice ring for her fifth birthday.
2  Ginger and Gretchen recently found three cute bunnies in my yard.

2nd finger

3  David decided to compete as a place kicker for the football team.
4  Cecilia and Kit decided to kill time playing on the deck at noon.

double letters

5  Jarrett cheerfully killed millions of bugs near the pool at noon.
6  All planning committees have four dinner meetings with key staff.

## New Commands

### COLUMNS OF EQUAL WIDTH

**52c**

Columns

Text formatted in multiple columns on a page is easier to read. The text flows down one column and then to the top of the next column. The heading on a document with multiple columns, called a banner or masthead, usually spans multiple columns. Newsletters, flyers, brochures, and programs are typically formatted in columns. Columns may be of equal or varying widths. Columns may be formatted before or after text is keyed, but generally, it is easier to format text in columns after it has been keyed. Columns are usually balanced or forced to end at approximately the same point on the page.

#### Productivity Enhancement Program

The Executive Committee's new Productivity Enhancement Program resulted in standardizing all computer software applications for the company in all locations. The Training and Development Team, at the request of the Executive Committee, developed a training program designed to help all employees learn how to integrate applications available in the standardized suite and to use electronic mail and the Internet.

The Productivity Enhancement Program specifies that each employee must develop in-depth skill in at least two applications, basic skill in the other applications, and be able to produce a compound document—that is, a document that includes elements from multiple software applications in the suite. Employees must also be able to use electronic mail. The Productivity Enhancement Program specifies that most internal documents will be distributed electronically.

To meet the needs of all employees, the Training and Development Team structured the Integrating Computer Applications training program in three phases.

Assessment provides employees who already have developed skill in an application to demonstrate that competence without taking the training module. Two levels of assessments—basic skill and in-depth skill—are available for each application. Each computer-administered and scored assessment contains three versions.

An employee who does not successfully complete the assessment in three tries or who elects not to take the assessment option must take the training module for that application. Assessments are also used at the conclusion of training modules.

Development follows assessment. Two options are available for developing skill in the various applications. Employees may sign up for regular training classes or may elect to use the new computer-based training programs (CBT) to develop the skill. The advantage of using the CBT program is that it can be completed at your own workstation. A combination of both instructor-led training and the CBT program may be the best alternative for most employees. An assessment must be completed at the end of each training session to demonstrate the level of skill attained on each software application.

Integration is the final phase of the program. The integration program accomplishes two objectives—teaching employees how to prepare documents that use objects from the various applications in the suite and standardizing the format for frequently used documents. Detailed information about the integration phase will be provided at least three weeks prior to the training.

1. In the open document, select the title and apply WordArt Fill – Black, Text 1, Outline – Background 1, Hard Shadow – Accent 1 style.

2. Change the width of the WordArt text box to 6".

3. Select the text, click Columns, and select Three.

4. Preview the document and then revise the column structure; select the text again and click Two columns.

5. Insert a ClipArt image of your choice in the first and last paragraphs, size them appropriately, and change the text wrapping to Square.

6. Add a Continuous section break at the end of the columns to balance them (Page Layout/Page Setup/Breaks).

7. Proofread and check; click Next Activity. (*67-drill1*)

## COLUMNS OF UNEQUAL WIDTH

When newsletters include organization information, they are often formatted with that information in a narrow first column.

To format columns of unequal width:
Page Layout/Page Setup/Columns

1. Click More Columns at the bottom of the drop-list options to display the Columns dialog box.

2. In the Presets box, choose Left; then select the number of columns desired. The width of each column and the amount of space between columns displays. The settings can be altered by using the spin arrows.

3. Click Line between if a line is desired between columns.

## POSITION GRAPHICS IN COLUMNS

Once the layout of a graphic image has been changed to any setting other than In Line with Text, the image is automatically anchored to the paragraph closest to where it was inserted. You will see an anchor symbol displayed to the left of the paragraph to which the image is anchored (the image must be selected with Show/Hide on). The image moves with the paragraph to which it is anchored.

You can keep the image at the same position regardless of where the text moves by clicking Fix Position on Page at the bottom of the Wrap Text drop list. You can place the image at a specific horizontal and/or vertical position by clicking More Layout Options and then specifying the position on the Position tab in the Layout dialog box.

## To format equal-width columns:

Page Layout/Page Setup/Columns

1. Select the text you want to format in columns; click Columns and select the desired number of columns from the options that display.
2. To balance columns on a page, click at the end of the columns and insert a Continuous section break.

---

**DRILL 1**  **COLUMNS**  productivity

1. In the open document, select the title and apply Fill – Orange, Accent 2, Outline – Accent 2 Text Effect from the Font group on the Home tab.

2. Select the text, click Columns, and select Three.

3. Preview the document and then revise the column structure; select the text again and click Two columns.

Page Layout/Page Setup/Breaks

4. Add a Continuous section break at the end of the columns to balance them.

5. Proofread and check; click Next Activity. (*52-drill1*)

---

## To add a line between columns:

Page Layout/Page Setup/Columns

1. From the number of column options, click More Columns ❶ to display the Columns dialog box.
2. Click Line between ❷ . To remove the line, remove the check from the box.

---

**DRILL 2**  **LINE BETWEEN COLUMNS**

1. Open *52-drill 1* and add a line between the columns.

2. Preview and check; click Next Activity. (*52-drill2*)

---

# Lesson 67 Documents with Columns and Graphics

A **ALL LETTERS**

## Skill Building

**67b** Timed Writing

1. Key a 3' timing on each paragraph; work to increase speed.
2. Key a 3' timing on all paragraphs; work for control.

Eating is often the solution to any and all problems for many people. Our society has been known to use food as a tranquilizer. Many times if a child expresses unhappiness, someone will try soothing the child with cookies.

Food cravings may mean that a person is hungry. But for emotional eaters, it may mean that they need something else. For some people, it may be a sign of boredom, frustration, or loneliness. It is important to understand the reason for eating and then try confronting those issues.

You can control your eating by changing the way you do things. Work on a hobby during commercials rather than going to get something to eat. Special events do not need to be centered around food. Celebrate a special occasion by going dancing rather than going out for dinner.

## New Commands

**67c**

### COLUMNS OF EQUAL WIDTH

Newsletters are usually keyed in a two- or three-column format. Text is keyed beginning at the left column. When that column is full, the text automatically flows to the top of the next column; this is called *snaking*.

Columns are created using the Columns command. The Two and Three columns options make the columns equal width.

To format equal-width columns:
Page Layout/Page Setup/Columns

1. Select the text to be formatted in columns; click Columns and select the desired number of columns from the options that display.
2. To balance columns on a page, click at the end of the columns and insert a Continuous section break.

	One
	Two
	Three
	Left
	Right
	More Columns...

1. Open *52-drill2* and remove the line between the columns.

2. Search for an appropriate clip for training from Online pictures using the keywords *business people on computers*. Size it 1.8" high and position it in the Middle Center with Square Text Wrapping.

3. Apply an Orange – Accent 2 thick and thin box page border. See Quick Check below.

4. Preview and check; click Next Activity. (*52-drill3*)

 QUICK ✓     Check your document against the illustration below. Photo may vary.

## Apply It

### 52-d1

**Newsletter**

1. Apply Organic theme and Narrow margins.

2. Tap ENTER four times; then key the newsletter as it is shown. Do not format as you key.

The architects have put the final touches on the arena plans, and the groundbreaking has been scheduled for March 18. Put the date on your calendar and plan to be a part of this exciting time. The Groundbreaking Ceremony will begin at 5:00 at the new arena site. After the ceremony, you will join the architects in the practice facility for refreshments and a thrilling video presentation of the new arena. The party ends when we all join the Western Cougars as they take on the Central Lions for the final conference game.

*(continued)*

**66-d1**

**Picture Watermark**

 river camp

1. In a new document, apply landscape orientation.
2. Change the font to Baskerville Old Face 28-point.
3. Key **River Camp Experience**. Tap ENTER twice.
4. Key the remainder of the invitation, as shown below, with text centered.
5. Use WordArt for the title; format as follows:
   a. Select *River Camp Experience* and click Insert/WordArt.
   b. Choose the WordArt style Fill – White, Outline – Accent 2, Hard Shadow – Accent 2.
   c. Change the width of the WordArt box to 9".
   d. Change the font to Rockwell.
   e. Change the Text Fill color to Orange, Accent 2, Darker 25%.
   f. Apply Text Effects Transform: Chevron Up.
6. Insert the *river camp* picture watermark.
7. Apply the Center Page command (Page Layout/Page Setup/Layout/Vertical alignment/Center).
8. Proofread and check; click Next Activity. (66-d1)

**QUICK ✔**

Check your document against the illustration below.

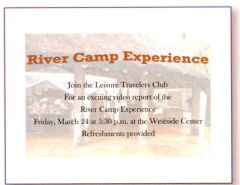

Join the Leisure Travelers Club

For an exciting video report of the

River Camp Experience

Friday, March 24 at 5:30 p.m. at the Westside Center

Refreshments provided

**66-d2**

**Financial Statement**

 financial statement

1. In the open document, use Fill Effects to add the Stationery background.
2. Add a Confidential1 watermark to the document.
3. Add a ½-point page border using the Plum, Accent 2, Darker 25% theme color.
4. Check and click Next Activity. (66-d2)

**66-d3**

**Draw Text Box**

1. In the open document (65-d1), insert a footer (Insert/Footer/Blank). Click the ¶ marker below [Type here] and draw a text box that extends from left to right margin in the footer.
2. Key: **Good Samaritan Adoption Agency ◇ 5228 Hope, Shelbyville, TN 37162-0070 ◇ 800.555.2122.** Center the text. (Insert the diamond symbol from the Wingdings group.)
3. Fill the text box with the Dark Red color (Drawing Tools Format/Shape Fill). Change the text to the gold color and apply bold. Delete [Type here] but do not delete the ¶ marker after it.
4. Proofread and check; click Exit *Word*. (66-d2)
5. Click Log out to exit *KPDO*.

**Cornerstone Club Named**

Robbie Holiday of the Cougars Club submitted the winning name for the premium seating and club area of the new arena. Thanks to all of you who submitted suggestions for naming the new club. For his suggestion, which was selected from over 300 names submitted, Robbie has won season tickets for next year and the opportunity to make his seat selection first. The Cornerstone Club name was selected because members of our premium club play a crucial role in making our new arena a reality. Without the financial support of this group, we could not lay the first cornerstone of the arena.

Cornerstone Club members have first priority in selecting their seats for both basketball and hockey. Club members also have access to the Cornerstone Club before the event, during halftime, and after the event. They also receive a parking pass for the lot immediately adjacent to the arena. If you would like more information about the Cornerstone Club and how you can become a charter member, call the Cougars Club office during regular business hours.

**What View Would You Like?**

Most of us would like to sit in our seats and try them out before we select them rather than look at a diagram of the seating in the new arena. Former Cougar players make it easy for you to select the perfect angle to watch the ball go in the basket. Mark McKay and Jeff Dunlap, using their patented Real View visualization software, make it possible for you to experience the exact view you will have from the seats you select. In fact, they encourage you to try several different views. Most of the early testers of the new seat selection software reported that they came in with their minds completely made up about the best seats in the house. However, after experiencing several different views with the Real View software, they changed their original seat location request.

3. Select the text and format it into two equal-width columns. Note that a Continuous section break is positioned above the columns.

4. Apply Heading 1 to both headings.

5. Apply a Green – Accent 1, 1½-point box border.

6. Insert Fill – Green – Accent 1, Shadow WordArt.

   a. Size WordArt 0.8" high.

   b. Key the title **Arena Update**.

   c. Position in the Top Center with Square Text Wrapping. Note that it should be between the top border and the Continuous section break.

7. Position the picture described in the following steps after the third line under the last heading.

   a. Search for clip art in Online Pictures using *stadium seats* as the keywords.

   b. Insert the clip shown on the next page; apply Top and Bottom Text Wrap.

   c. Size it 2.75" high and drag to the center of the column.

*(continued)*

**TIP**

You must have either a blank paragraph marker or an unselected title for the system to add a Continuous section break above the columns.

## TEXT BOX

Text boxes enable you to position text at any location on a page. Because they can be moved around, they are often called *floating boxes*. Two types of text boxes are used—built-in (preformatted) text boxes and text boxes that you draw and format yourself. Many of the built-in text boxes are used to format pull quotes and sidebars in newspapers, magazines, reports, brochures, or newsletters.

**To insert a Built-In text box:**
Insert/Text/Text Box

1. Display the gallery of Built-in text boxes.
2. Scroll through the thumbnails and click the text box you wish to insert.
3. Select the text in the placeholder and key your text, or copy and paste text in the placeholder.

---

**DRILL 6**        **TEXT BOXES**         text boxes

1. In the open document, read to learn about sidebars and pull quotes. Position the insertion point at the top of the page.

2. Display the Text Box gallery. Scroll down to locate and insert the Whisp Sidebar text box.

3. Click [Sidebar Title] and key **Attractive Sidebars** in the placeholder. Click the sidebar text and key the following:

> This sidebar is used to illustrate one of the many readily available preformatted text boxes that enhance the appearance of documents and make them more interesting to read.

4. Position the insertion point on the right side of the second paragraph containing the quote. Insert the Semaphore Quote text box.

5. Select the quote in the second paragraph; copy and paste it in the placeholder. Size and position the text box as shown at the right.

6. Scroll to the bottom of the page and choose Draw Text Box from the bottom of the Text Box drop list.

7. Draw a text box at the bottom of the page that begins at approximately 2.5" and extends to 6.5". Use the Ruler as a guide.

8. Key **You can draw a text box and position it any place in the document.** Center the text.

9. Change the size of the text box to 0.3" high and 4.5" wide.

10. Proofread and check; click Next Activity. (*66-drill6*)

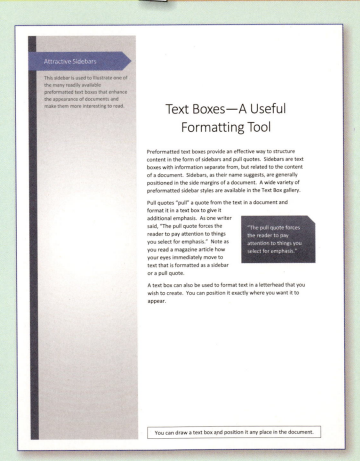

8. Insert an Alternating Flow SmartArt graphic (second icon in the second row) from the Process category.

   a. Click in the line below the Continuous section break and change the column format to one column.

   b. Size the entire graphic 2.5" high and 6.0" wide.

   c. Position it in the Bottom Center with Square Text Wrapping.

   d. Key the text shown below in the SmartArt text pane.

9. Proofread and check; click Next Activity. (*52-d1*)

---

Architectural Plans
      Contract 6/25
      Approved 3/3
Next Steps
      Groundbreaking 3/18
      Cornerstone Club 3/18
Grand Opening
      Construction contract 6/15
      Completion 12 to 15 months

---

**QUICK ✓**

Check your document against the illustration below. (Photo may vary.)

---

**52–d2**

**Composition**

cornerstone club memo form

1. Use the following information to compose a memo to Robbie Holiday from Jeff Crane inviting him to represent the Cornerstone Club at the groundbreaking ceremony. Date it March 5, 201-; add an appropriate subject line. Ask him to confirm his acceptance.

   a. Five people will participate in the ceremony; use the Arena Update for time, date, site, and other information as needed.

   b. Shovels and hardhats will be provided.

   c. Media will be present and may interview participants. Business attire is requested.

2. Edit and proofread to ensure that you used complete sentences and well-formed paragraphs.

3. Proofread and check; click Next Activity. (*52-d2*)

## PAGE COLOR

A color page background is used predominantly in Web browsers; however, the subtle use of page color, and particularly fill effects, can enhance the appearance of a document. More formal documents should be limited to page color using fill effects, such as parchment or stationery. Less formal documents may be formatted using a background with more color.

To apply page color and fill effects:
Design/Page Background/Page Color

1. To apply a color, click the desired theme or standard color. Custom colors (often used to match company brand colors) can be accessed by clicking More Colors.

2. To apply an effect, click Fill Effects to display the gallery of effects. Click the appropriate tab (Gradient, Texture, Pattern, or Picture) to display the desired effect. To display the name of the effect, click the thumbnail image.

---

| DRILL 4 | PAGE COLOR |  invitation |

1. Apply Blue-Gray, Text 2, Lighter 90% color to the document.

2. Add a 1½-point Orange, Background 2, Darker 25% page border.

3. Proofread and check; click Next Activity. (*66-drill4*)

---

| DRILL 5 | FILL EFFECTS |  roswell |

1. In the open document, display the Fill Effects dialog box.

2. Click each tab and preview the options.

3. Click the Texture tab, select Parchment (column C, row 4), and then click OK. Do not edit the body of the letter.

4. Proofread and check; click Next Activity. (*66-drill5*)

---

# Lesson 53 Palmetto Event Solutions, Inc.

**Learning Outcomes**
- Apply keying, formatting, and word processing skills.
- Prepare documents with columns and graphics.
- Work independently with few specific instructions.

 **Warmup** *Lesson 53a Warmup*

## Skill Building

**53b Timed Writing**

Key two 3' timed writings.

Most people today realize that they cannot count on their employer or on the government to provide for their retirement. They must plan for their own future. Young people who are healthy and are not concerned about retirement often do not consider the value of the benefits when they compare job offers they have. They tend to focus more on the salary they will earn.

Most companies provide some type of health benefits. The portion that the employee has to pay tends to vary widely, however. Therefore, it is wise to analyze the quality, the type of coverage provided, and the cost of the benefits to the employee. A lower salary with benefits paid by the company may produce more net income than a higher salary with high benefit costs to the employee.

To recruit bright young people who are likely to change jobs many times, companies set up portable savings plans that defer taxes on income. The company matches a certain percentage of the savings to provide incentives for the employee to contribute to the plan. Usually the plan vests in less than five years, and employees can take the entire amount with them when they leave.

## Project Setting

### PALMETTO EVENT SOLUTIONS, INC.

For the project in this module, you will be preparing documents for Willie Straton, our Northeast Regional Vice President in Newport, Rhode Island. You will use the Newport letterhead and the standard memo form. You may wish to review the SOPs for Palmetto Events Solutions and the *About Us* section on pages 117 and 118. All documents are to be reviewed by Mr. Straton before they are sent to the recipients. Do not prepare envelopes or emails to transmit the documents at this time.

As you work through each job and after all jobs are completed, make sure that you have used or done the following:

- Correct letterhead or the memo form for letters and memos.
- Block letter style for letters.
- Ion theme for all documents.
- Previewed and proofread documents carefully.

**To insert a watermark with custom text:**
Design/Page Background/Watermark

1. Display the gallery of built-in watermarks.
2. Click Custom Watermark at the bottom of the gallery to display the Printed Watermark dialog box.
3. Select Text watermark and then key the desired text in the Text box. Select font and layout.
4. Click Apply and Close.

---

DRILL 2	CUSTOM TEXT WATERMARK	team writing

1. In the open document, display the Watermark gallery. Click Custom Watermark at the bottom of the gallery.

2. Select Text watermark and then key **GREAT JOB!** in the text box. Use Arial font and Diagonal layout.

3. Click Apply and Close. Preview the watermark to ensure that it displays on both pages.

4. Proofread and check; click Next Activity. (*66-drill2*)

---

**To insert a picture watermark:**
Design/Page Background/Watermark

1. Display the gallery of built-in watermarks.
2. Click Custom Watermark at the bottom of the gallery to display the Printed Watermark dialog box.
3. Select Picture watermark and then click Select Picture to browse, select, and insert the desired picture.
4. Click Apply and Close.

---

DRILL 3	PICTURE WATERMARK	picnic, lake house

1. In the open document, remove the ASAP watermark (Design/Page Background/Watermark/Remove Watermark).

2. Insert a custom watermark, click Picture watermark, and then click Select Picture.

3. Browse the data files, select *lake house*, and then click Insert.

4. Click Apply and Close.

5. Proofread and check; click Next Activity. (*66-drill3*)

## 53-d1

**Organization Chart**

A client who is considering a proposal for a project that Mr. Straton submitted has requested an organization chart showing the Senior Management Team. Abbreviate Vice President (VP) on the chart. Note from the Quick Check that you will need to add additional shapes.

1. Insert a SmartArt Name and Title Organization chart from the Hierarchy category, and include the members of the Senior Management Team:

   a. **Garrett Russell, President and CEO**

   b. **Ellen Miller, Executive Assistant**

   c. **Jennifer Anderson, Northwest Regional VP**

   d. **Rachel Barnett, Midwest Regional VP**

   e. **Aydyn Ellison, Chief Financial Officer**

   f. **Willie Straton, Northeast Regional VP**

   g. **Carlos Torres, Southwest Regional VP**

2. Size the chart 3.5" high and 6.5" wide; position it in the Top Center with Square Text Wrapping.

3. Proofread and check; click Next Activity.

---

**QUICK ✓**

Compare your document to the one shown below.

---

## 53-d2

**Memo with Graphics**

upscale in-home event

palmetto memo form

Prepare the memo below for Mr. Straton; he will attach it to an email to the Senior Management Team.

1. Use the current date and subject line: **Senior Management Team Retreat.**

2. Tap ENTER after the last paragraph and insert the *upscale in-home event* picture from the data files. Size it 3.5" high and apply Center from the Home tab.

3. Proofread and check; click Next Activity.

The past two Senior Management Team Retreats were held in Portland and Hilton Head. Please consider letting the Northeast Region host this year's Senior Management Team Retreat on Goat Island. Goat Island, as most of you know, is a gorgeous and historic island located in the Newport Harbor.

*(continued)*

# *Lesson 66* Document Backgrounds

New Commands

- Watermarks
- Page Colors
- Text Box

 **Warmup** *Lesson 66a Warmup*

## Skill Building

**66b** **Textbook Keying**

Key each line once; concentrate on using good keying techniques.

left hand

1 crazed bass averages dessert cedar badger affect braggart detects
2 beware greatest feet effects gag faster bazaar assess drawers ads
3 grease estate carafe awarded exerted get careers agrees beads ear
4 In my opinion, today anyone can play pool or monopoly with Jimmy.
5 honk million kimono pumpkin yolk poplin oil lumpy homily hoop lip
6 pill nylon million puppy uphill yoyo ninny opinion lion polio mum

right hand

7 Jimmy minimum pupil holly imply kinky monopoly pool union you ohm
8 Their neighbor's mangy dog and lame duck slept by a box of rocks.

## New Commands

**66c**

### WATERMARKS

A watermark is text or a picture that displays behind document text in a light or washed-out version. It displays in Print Layout and Full Screen Reading views and on printed documents. Watermarks are grouped in three categories: Confidential, Disclaimers, and Urgent. The logo of a business is often displayed as a watermark.

To insert a text watermark:

Design/Page Background/Watermark

1. Display the gallery of built-in watermarks.
2. Scroll down and click the desired option, such as DO NOT COPY 1, to insert it. Note that watermarks are typically positioned either horizontally or diagonally on the page.

---

**DRILL 1** TEXT WATERMARK 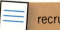 recruitment

1. In the open document, display the Watermark gallery.
2. Click DO NOT COPY 1.

3. Preview the watermark.
4. Proofread and check; click Next Activity. (*66-drill1*)

**Begin new paragraph** →

I also encourage you to add an extra day to the length of the retreat and devote it to an intensive seminar entitled Upscale Corporate Marketing. This past quarter, our marketing team worked with a marketing consultant focusing on using an upscale, in-home event for senior executives of our top ten clients. We experimented with one event that produced very interesting results that we would like to share at the retreat. The setting for the event is shown below.

## 53-d3

**Newsletter**

 isle of capri boat trip

You are working with Mason James, the senior event planning manager in the Newport office, on a reward trip for one of your major clients, Market Trust Insurance Company. This is the third time the Newport team has planned the annual reward trip. This is an all-expense paid trip for the 25 CEOs and their spouses of insurance companies that provide Market Trust the most revenue for the previous year. Your job is to prepare a one-page newsletter providing a few trip highlights that will be emailed to each attendee one week before their departure to get participants excited about the trip. They will have a complete packet of information when they arrive at the resort.

1. Apply Narrow margins. Turn Show/Hide on. Tap ENTER three times.
2. Key the newsletter shown below. Then follow directions to format the document.

One week from today you will arrive at the five-star Palazzo Ravello on the cliffs of the medieval town of Ravello for five exciting days on the Amalfi Coast of Italy! The spectacular view from your balcony high above the Mediterranean is simply breathtaking. Luxurious rooms with exquisite furnishings; impeccable service; a rooftop sun terrace; gym; spa; outdoor pool; three restaurants including a world-renowned, highly rated fine dining restaurant; and many other amenities await you.

Day One Highlights

Your first day is designed to be a relaxing one. You can have a delightful lunch on the Cliff Terrace overlooking the Mediterranean or at the Grille near the pool. A ten-minute walk will bring you to the Town Square with shops featuring hand-painted china and a variety of other art objects as well as a panoramic view of the area. The day ends with a reception and dinner so that you will have the opportunity to meet all of the President's Award Trip winners.

Day Two Highlights

Get your camera ready for a sightseeing boat trip around the Amalfi Coast and to the Isle of Capri. Bring your bathing suit if you want to swim in the Mediterranean near one of the famous grottos on the mountainous side of the island or at the Isle of Capri beach. You will have a sightseeing tour in a convertible and a delightful lunch. In the evening, transportation will be provided to some of the local dinner and entertainment places.

*(continued)*

**Table, Graphics, Sort**

1. Use WordArt to create the main heading:
   a. Turn on Show/Hide; then tap ENTER three times.
   b. Click the insertion point on the first ¶ and insert WordArt using the Fill, White, Outline – Accent 1, Shadow style. Key **Power-Packed Foods May Save Your Life**.
   c. Change the WordArt text to 26 point so that it fits on one line.
   d. Change the Text Fill to Green, Accent 6, Darker 25%. Change the Text Outline to White, Background 1.
   e. Change the shape of the WordArt by applying the Chevron Up style on the Text Effects/Transform gallery.

2. Click on the fourth ¶ marker and key the following paragraphs.

No one will dispute the fact that we must eat to stay alive. There has been much talk about whether what we eat affects how long we live and our quality of life. Some foods are packed with nutrients that, when incorporated into your diet, can help prevent future illnesses.

Check out this list of power-packed foods; including them in your diet may improve the length and quality of your life.

3. Tap ENTER twice after the last paragraph. Insert a 2-column, 5-row table. Change the width of column A to 1.55" and the width of column B to 3.75". Center the table horizontally on the page. Key the text shown below in column B; tap ENTER after each item.

4. Search for and insert appropriate clip art of each item in column A; size to fit in the row. Center the clip art horizontally in each cell.

5. Sort the table so that the items in column B display in alphabetical order. Choose to sort by column 2, using the Text Type, and Ascending.

6. Select the table and remove all borders. Center the copy vertically on the page (Page Layout/Page Setup/Layout/Vertical alignment/Center).

7. Proofread and check; Click Exit *Word*. (65-d2)

8. Click Log out to exit *KPDO*.

Use **cereal** as the keyword to search for the oat bran clip art.

---

*Carrots* are rich in beta carotene. Eating two carrots every other day will provide enough beta carotene to reduce stroke by half for men who already display symptoms of heart disease.

*Spinach* contains vitamins A and C, folic acid, and magnesium. Spinach may help control cancer, reduce heart disease and stroke risk, and may help prevent osteoporosis.

*Garlic* may lower cholesterol and blood pressure. Garlic may also contain chemicals capable of destroying cancer cells.

*Oat bran* may reduce the risk of colon cancer. Eating oat bran for breakfast will keep you from getting hungry mid-morning.

*Mangos* contain bioflavonoids that can aid the immune system. Mangos are also rich in fiber.

### Day Three Highlights

On this day, you go back in time about 2,000 years to visit the ancient city, Pompeii. It is often called the forgotten city because the volcano Mount Vesuvius erupted and buried residences, temples, artwork, and many other objects. You will have a full-day tour to visit the ruins and excavations as well as the surrounding areas.

### Day Four Highlights

On this day, you select the surrounding city or town from a number of options that you would like to tour. Our staff will provide you with information about the many alternatives and will arrange your transportation to the desired destination.

### Day Five Highlights

You can relax, swim, golf, play tennis, visit the spa, shop, or do whatever you would like as you prepare for your departure. Our final evening is a memorable banquet and gala with the award presentations followed by dancing.

#### ✿ Discover

**Remove Space Before Paragraph**

Home/Paragraph/Line and Paragraph Spacing

1. Position the insertion point in the heading.
2. Click Remove Space Before Paragraph.

3. Select the text and format it in two equal-width columns. Insert a Continuous section break at the end of the second column to balance the columns.

4. Apply Heading 1 format to each of the headings; then ✿ remove the space before each of the headings.

5. Key the title, **Amalfi Coast—Here We Come** at the second paragraph marker above the Continuous section break; apply 28-point Heading font.

6. Apply Text Effects: Fill – Dark Red, Accent 1, Shadow. Center the title.

7. Insert *the isle of capri boat trip* data file; size it 2.5" high. Position in Middle Center with Square Text Wrapping.

8. Proofread and check; click Next Activity. (53-d3)

## 53-d4

**Compose**

 palmetto memo form

Several employees have suggested that it would be nice to have an electronic employee newsletter with information supplied by each office. You talked with Mr. Sutton about it and he asked you to compose a memo to be sent to all Palmetto executive assistants.

1. Tell them about the suggestion and ask them to discuss it with their colleagues to determine the level of interest.

2. List questions that would need to be answered and ask everyone to share their thoughts on each question. The following examples are just to help you get started.

   a. What types of information would be included? Business activities and results from each office? Information about employees and their families? Company news? Tips for being more effective, etc.

   b. Who would report news from each office? Who would coordinate and distribute it?

   c. How often? How long would it be? What would it be named?

3. Edit, proofread, and check; exit *Word*. (53-d4)

4. Click Log out to exit *KPDO*.

**Learn More:**

www.cengagebrain.com

## DRILL 2 — APPLY PICTURE STYLE AND CHANGE PICTURE OPTIONS

1. Tap ENTER three times, then insert the *portrait* file. Crop the picture 0.5" on the right and 0.25" on the left; compress the picture.

2. Apply Metal Oval picture style.

3. In Picture Border, choose Orange, Accent 2, Lighter 40% color.

4. In Picture Effects, choose Bevel Convex style. Also in Picture Effects, choose Glow, then Orange, 18-point glow, Accent color 2.

5. Change the width of the picture to 6".

6. Insert WordArt and select the Fill – Gold, Accent 4, Soft Bevel style. Key **Genevieve**.

7. Select the text and change the font to Lucida Calligraphy. Change the Text Fill color to Orange, Accent 2, Lighter 40%. Change the text outline to Orange, Accent 2, Darker 25%.

8. Change the Wrap Text style to In Front of Text. Change the Zoom to One Page (View/Zoom/One Page). Move the WordArt so that it is centered attractively below the picture.

9. Proofread and check; click Next to continue. (65-drill2)

---

## Apply It

**Form with ClipArt and WordArt**

★ **TIP**

Insert the first checkbox; then key the sentence that follows. Tap ENTER to automatically insert the next checkbox.

1. In a new document, insert WordArt using the Fill – Gray-50%, Accent 3, Sharp Bevel style. Key **Adoption Agreement**. Change the width of the WordArt to 6.5". Change the Text Fill color to Orange, Accent 2, Darker 25%. Change the Text Outline color to Gold, Accent 4, Lighter 40%. Change the shape to Chevron Up (Text Effects/Transform/Chevron Up).

2. Use **dog** or **cat** as the keyword and search Clip Art for an appropriate clip. Insert the clip of your choice below the WordArt title. Change the Wrap Text to Square and size and position the picture attractively.

3. Key the paragraphs and checkbox items shown below. Apply a dropped cap to the paragraph; make the drop cap the same color as the title.

4. Select an appropriate checkbox from Wingding Symbols. Insert checkbox; then press TAB and key the text. Tap ENTER three times after keying the last checkbox item.

5. Insert a signature line by setting a Right Underline tab at 6.5" (Home/Paragraph/Tabs) and then tapping TAB. Click on the ¶ marker at the end of the line and choose Remove Space After Paragraph (Home/Paragraph/Remove Space After Paragraph).

6. Key **Signature** below the line; set a left tab at 5.0" on the Ruler, tap TAB, and key **Date**.

7. Proofread and check; click Next Activity. (65-d1)

Adoption of a pet can be extremely rewarding. However, it is important to remember that adoption is a privilege that requires the new owner to take appropriate care of the pet. Read the five items checked below that contain the specific requirements for the adoption of a pet. Your signature below the five checked items obligates you to follow all of these guides.

☑ I agree to take my new pet to the veterinarian within five days of adoption.

☑ I will provide appropriate food, fresh water, and shelter for my pet.

☑ I will exercise my pet daily.

☑ I will spay or neuter my pet within six months.

☑ I will not sell my pet.

# Palmetto Event Solutions, Inc.

**Lessons 54–55** *Palmetto Event Solutions, Inc.*

## LEARNING OUTCOMES

- Apply keying, formatting, and word processing skills.
- Work independently with few instructions.

---

**Warmup** *Lesson 54a Warmup*

**A ALL LETTERS**

## Skill Building

### 54b Timed Writing

Key two 3' timed writings. Strive for control.

Voting is a very important part of being a good citizen. However, many young people who are eligible to vote choose not to do so. When asked to explain or justify their decision, many individuals simply shrug their shoulders and reply that they have no particular reason for not voting. The explanation others frequently give is that they just did not get around to going to the polls.

A good question to consider concerns ways that we can motivate young people to be good citizens and to go to the polls and to vote. Some people approach this topic by trying to determine how satisfied people who do not vote are with the performance of their elected officials. Unfortunately, those who choose not to vote are just as satisfied with their elected officials as those who voted.

One interesting phenomenon concerning voting relates to the job market. When the job market is strong, fewer young people vote than when the job market is very bad. They also tend to be less satisfied with their elected officials. Self-interest seems to be a powerful motivator. Unfortunately, those who do not choose to vote miss the point that it is in their best interest to be a good citizen.

---

## Project Setting

### PALMETTO EVENT SOLUTIONS, INC.

In this project, you are an executive assistant in the Kansas City office. This experience gives you an opportunity to apply the document formatting and word processing skills that you learned in Modules 3–7. Review the SOPs that are summarized on the next page, and apply them to your work.

**Special instructions for non-KPDO users:**

Set up a folder named Palmetto Event Solutions. Save each document as 8-d + the document number. (*8-d1, 8-d2, 8-d3*, etc.)

---

## DROP CAP

A drop cap is a large capital letter at the beginning of a text block. The drop cap usually extends from the top of the paragraph down two or three succeeding lines with text wrapped around it.

### To create a dropped cap:
Insert/Text/Drop Cap

1. Click in the paragraph that is to begin with a dropped cap.
2. Select Drop Cap; then select Dropped or In margin.

The dropped cap can be modified by clicking on Drop Cap Options. The font style, number of lines to drop, or the distance from the text can be changed. The color of the dropped cap can be altered by selecting the dropped cap and choosing a different Font Color on the Home tab.

---

**DRILL 1** | **PAGE AND PARAGRAPH BORDERS, SHADING, AND DROP CAP** | architecture

1. In the open document, click in the first paragraph and apply an In margin drop cap.

2. Select the drop cap and change the color to Orange, Accent 2, Darker 25%.

3. Select the drop cap and change the style to Dropped.

4. Use Drop Cap Options to change the font style to Lucida Calligraphy.

5. Insert a box border around the second paragraph. Make the line color the same as the drop cap color.

6. Apply Orange, Accent 2, Lighter 80% shading to the second paragraph.

7. Create a Box page border with a single-style, ¾-point line, and Orange, Accent 2, Darker 25% color.

8. Check and click Next Activity. (65-drill1)

---

## PICTURE STYLES

The Picture Tools Format tab displays when an image is selected in your document. The Picture Styles gallery contains predesigned styles and other options in the Picture Styles group that allow you to modify a picture.

### To apply a picture style:
Picture Tools Format/Picture Styles

1. Click on the picture to be formatted to display the Picture Tools Format tab.
2. Click the More button to display all the styles in the Picture Styles gallery.
3. Click the desired style to apply it to the picture.

The color and line style of the picture border can be modified by applying options in Picture Border. Special effects, such as 3-D Rotation, Shadow, Reflection, and Bevel, can be applied by using Picture Effects.

# KANSAS CITY OFFICE

You will report to Ms. Rachel Barnett, the Midwest Regional Vice President. She follows the SOPs and often leaves directions on yellow sticky notes. Check each document to make sure you have used or done the following:

- Ion theme for all documents.
- Use the Kansas City letterhead and the standard memo form for all letters and memos. Use block letter style with open punctuation.
- Note the standard for bulleting items has been changed. Use the new square bullet style with Dark Red, Accent 1 color.
- Unless directed otherwise, use the salutation *Dear + personal title and last name*, such as Dear Ms. Miguel.
- Unless otherwise directed, use: **Sincerely | Rachel C. Barnett | Regional Vice President** for the closing lines. Position the name and title on two lines; do not use a title on any documents sent to Palmetto Event Solutions offices.
- Provide an appropriate subject line for memos and emails if one is not provided.
- Use the current date unless instructed otherwise.
- Add your reference initials, attachment notation, and copy notations as needed.
- Ensure that all documents are error-free. Use proofing tools and then edit, proofread, and correct errors. Verify dates and numerical data against the source.

## 8-d1

**Letter**

 palmetto letterhead - kansas city

1. Prepare the following letter for Ms. Barnett with all necessary letter parts.
2. Proofread and check; click Next Activity. (8-d1)

Send the letter to:

Ms. Elena T. Miguel, President

Miguel Enterprises, Inc.

One Ward Parkway

Kansas City, MO 64114-2601

Thank you for accepting our proposal to manage the grand opening and marketing of your new gift shop, Miguel Emporium. We are very pleased to have the opportunity to work with you on another new store opening.

The senior staff of Palmetto Event Solutions, Inc. would be happy to meet with you next Tuesday at 10:30 a.m. in our offices as you requested. Prior to that meeting, we will prepare a proposed plan for the grand opening event. As we discussed, we will build on the same model that we used on your previous store openings.

Please sign the attached agreement and return one copy to us. We look forward to helping you make this a memorable event.

# Lesson 65 Graphic Features

- Page Borders
- Paragraph Borders
- Drop Cap
- Picture Styles

 **Warmup** *Lesson 65a Warmup*

**New Commands**

**65b**

## PAGE AND PARAGRAPH BORDERS

Borders can be applied to an entire page, or to paragraphs or selected text. A variety of options can be applied to borders, such as line style, color, and line width.

To apply a page border:
Design/Page Background/Page Borders

1. In the Borders and Shading dialog box, click the Page Border tab.
2. Choose the desired setting, style, color, and width.
3. In the Apply to box ❶, choose the desired option.

To apply a paragraph border:
Design/Page Background/Page Border

1. Click in the paragraph in which the border is to be applied.
2. In the Borders and Shading dialog box, click the Borders tab.
3. Choose the desired Setting option; then select line style, color, and width. The Apply to box should display Paragraph.

To apply shading:
Design/Page Background/Page Border

1. Click in the paragraph in which the shading is to be applied.
2. In the Borders and Shading dialog box, click the Shading tab.
3. Choose the desired fill and pattern; then click OK.

**Memo**

 palmetto memo form

1. Prepare the following memo:
   a. Use the information provided below to complete the heading on the memo.
   b. Use Find and Replace to locate *contract* each time it is used and replace it with **agreement**.
2. Proofread and check; click Next Activity. (8-d2)

> This memo will be distributed to Haley Edwards, Jackson Moore, Lance Davis, and Cristina Kulchar with a copy to Karl Metze.
>
> RB

To: Senior Executives | Subject: Miguel Contract

Miguel Enterprises accepted the Palmetto Event Solutions proposal to manage the grand opening and marketing of the new Miguel Emporium. Elena Miguel called me today to indicate that she had signed the contract without any modifications whatsoever, and she was having it hand delivered to us today.

Ms. Miguel also requested that our senior staff, as well as the Miguel Enterprises senior account manager, meet with her next Tuesday at 10:30 a.m. in our offices. Please plan to attend this important session, which will take place in the Board Room.

Marlene Delhomme, who is no longer with us, was the account manager responsible for the last two Miguel events. Karl Metze has been assigned as the senior account manager for the Miguel account. Please work with Karl on the proposed plan that we will present at the meeting.

c   Karl Metze

**8-d3**

**Invitation**

 invitation
miguel logo

Format the invitation as follows:

1. In the open document, center each line except the *rsvp*, which should be left-aligned.
2. Apply Lucida Calligraphy 16-point font and Dark Red standard color; use 2.5 line spacing.
3. Remove the space after the paragraph on each line, and change orientation to landscape.
4. Use the Insert Picture command to insert the company logo, *miguel logo*, at the top of the page. Change the size of the logo to 1" high, and use Center alignment on the Home tab to position the logo.
5. Proofread and check; click Next Activity. (8-d3)

> Please format the draft invitation Sarah created. It is saved as *invitation* in the data files.
>
> RB

Ms. Coles is a gifted artist who created a beautiful work of art that will be cherished for many years. The fountain has substantially exceeded our expectations. All of the specifications were met, and the fountain fit perfectly into the area designed for it, as you will note from the picture below.

Ms. Coles requested that we notify you that the project has been completed to our satisfaction so that you will release the final payment for the work. We are delighted to convey this information to you, and we highly recommend Carey Coles for future projects.

2. Turn on Show/Hide and click the insertion point on the second ¶ marker. Using WordArt, add the heading **Fountain Installation and Setting** applying the Fill – White, Outline – Accent 2, Hard Shadow – Accent 2 style. Apply Dark Red Text Fill. Change the font size to 26 point. Change the width of the text box to 6".

3. Create the diagram shown below following the second paragraph. Use the Vertical Process layout; add shapes as needed. Key the following text in the shapes: **Fountain delivered | Prepare setting sketch | Obtain sketch approval | Begin planning | Install fountain and landscaping**

4. Size the diagram by clicking on the outer frame of the diagram; then in the Format tab, click Size and change the Height to 5".

5. Select the frame that borders the entire SmartArt; then in the SmartArt Tools Design tab, choose Change Colors. Under Accent 2, choose Colored Fill – Accent 2.

6. Insert the *gate fountain* picture at the end of the document; crop approximately 1" off the left side and compress the picture. Center the picture horizontally.

7. Number the pages at the top of the page using Plain Number 3 and Different First Page.

8. Proofread and check; click Exit *Word*. (64-d1) Click Log out to exit *KPDO*.

Check your document against the illustration below.

Prepare the following budget to present to Ms. Miguel for approval.

1. Tap ENTER three times, and key the table shown below; then apply the following formats.

2. Add a column between columns B and C and key the following data: **Unit Cost, $24.50, 65.75, 250.00, 4.25,** and **3.75.**

3. Insert a row above the column heads; merge all cells in the row. Set the row height at 0.5". Key the table title **Pre-Grand Opening Celebration Budget** using 16-point font.

4. Apply Grid Table 4 – Accent 1. Apply Align Center to Table title.

5. Change the row height of rows 2–8 to 0.3". Apply Align Center and bold to the column heads.

6. Align text in the columns as follows—A: Align Center Left, B: Align Center, C and D: Align Center Right.

7. Preview, proofread, and check; click Next Activity. (8-d4)

Description	Quantity/Number	Estimated Cost
Food/beverage	120	$2,940.00
Floral arrangements	4	263.00
Decorations	1	250.00
Party favors	125	531.25
Invitations/mailing	150	562.50
Total cost		$4,546.75

 QUICK ✓

Check your document against the illustration below.

Pre-Grand Opening Celebration Budget			
**Description**	**Quantity/Number**	**Unit Cost**	**Estimated Cost**
Food/beverage	120	$24.50	$2,940.00
Floral arrangements	4	65.75	263.00
Decorations	1	250.00	250.00
Party favors	125	4.25	531.25
Invitations/mailing	150	3.75	562.50
Total cost			$4,546.75

To add shapes to SmartArt:
SmartArt Tools Design/Create Graphic/Add Shape

1. Click in the shape before or after another shape that will be added.

2. Click Add Shape or click the drop-list arrow and select an option from the list that displays. Repeat as needed.

## DRILL 3    USE WORDART AND SMARTART

1. Turn on Show/Hide. Tap ENTER four times. Click the insertion point on the first ¶ marker.

2. In WordArt, choose the style Fill – Blue, Accent 1, Shadow. Key **Assessment Cycle**.

3. Click on the last ¶; then click Insert/SmartArt. In the left pane of the SmartArt Graphic box, click Cycle.

4. Select the Continuous Cycle layout in the center pane.

5. Key the text shown in the diagram.

6. Click the frame that holds the diagram. On the SmartArt Tools Format tab, click Size. Change the width to 4".

7. Click on the border of the SmartArt and position it in Middle Center.

8. Click the border of the WordArt and position it in Top Center.

9. Proofread and check; click Next Activity. (*64-drill3*)

## Apply It

### 64-d1

**Report with Graphics**

 gate fountain

1. Tap ENTER until the insertion point is at approximately 2.2"; then key the paragraphs below.

The wrought iron gate fountain that you commissioned Carey Coles to design and craft has been completed and was delivered two weeks ago. The installation was completed this week, and the fountain is now fully operable.

The process used to prepare the setting for the new fountain is shown in the diagram below.

The process worked well, and the results were very good. The fountain was delivered on time, and the draft of the setting was approved with minor modifications. Installation was completed in a timely manner with minimal disturbance of the surrounding area. The work on the landscape began immediately and was completed on schedule.

*(continued)*

## 8-d5

**Report with Table**

wexford facilities

Prepare a draft of the following report:

1. Apply the following formats in the open document:

   a. Apply Title style to the title; decrease the font size to fit on one line.

   b. Apply Heading 1 style to all headings except for the specific meeting and training rooms that follow the meeting facilities paragraph.

   c. Apply Heading 2 to the meeting and training rooms listed.

   d. Number the pages at the top of the page using Plain Number 3. Do not number the first page.

2. Key Insert #1 after the paragraph below the Guest Accommodations heading and Insert #2 after the paragraph below the Summit and Lakeview Rooms. Apply Heading 1 format to the headings in Insert #2.

> Our Northwest Regional VP requested a report on the Wexford Center for a three-day leadership seminar for one of her Portland clients. I talked with her today, and she agreed Wexford is the best choice for her client.
>
> RB

**Insert #1**

In addition to the on-site fitness center, extensive fitness and recreational facilities are available at the nearby Oak Park SportsPlex. Guests can access tennis, swimming, golf, walking trails, and a host of other activities with less than a five-minute ride on the free Wexford shuttle.

**Insert #2**

Outdoor Functions

The patios and large gazebo area provide excellent venues for receptions and picnics when the weather is appropriate for outdoor functions. Large climate-controlled tents can also be rented for special functions.

Food Service

The Wexford dining room provides full breakfast and lunch buffets for residential guests and for conference functions that do not have group meals for participants. Chef Pat receives rave reviews for the theme buffets he offers in the evening. The Wexford lounge is open daily from 5:00 p.m. until 11:00 p.m.

Meals are competitively priced. The following table shows the meal prices per person. Prices shown in ranges vary depending on the menu selection.

The chef requests that the number of participants for meal events be confirmed at least 24 hours in advance.

*(continued)*

WordArt can be formatted using the tools on the Drawing Tools Format tab in the WordArt Styles group.

- *WordArt Styles* applies another style.
- *Text Fill* allows you to change the interior color of the letters.
- *Text Outline* can be used to change the exterior border of the letters.
- *Text Effects* adds depth or emphasis to text.

## SMARTART

SmartArt consists of predesigned diagrams that help simplify complex concepts. SmartArt layouts are grouped into nine categories: List, Process, Cycle, Hierarchy, Relationship, Matrix, Pyramid, Picture, and layouts from Office.com. You can elect to view all the layouts or the layouts in one of the categories.

To insert and add text to SmartArt:
Insert/Illustrations/SmartArt

1. Position the insertion point where the SmartArt is to be inserted. Display the Choose a SmartArt Graphic dialog box. Categories of SmartArt are listed on the left, layouts for each category display in the center, and a preview and description of the appropriate use appear in the right pane.

2. Click the category desired or scroll through all layouts and click the desired layout, and then OK to insert it.

3. Key text directly in each shape. The text size will adjust to fit the shape. -or-

4. Display the text pane shown at right (SmartArt Tools Design/Create Graphic/Text Pane) and key the text there.

Each SmartArt diagram offers a few shapes by default. If you need more shapes than the diagram offers, you can add them in the diagram. If you are keying text in the text pane, tapping ENTER after your last entry adds a new shape. Or you can add a shape at a specific location in the diagram using the SmartArt Tools Design tab.

3. Key and format the following table; place it below the paragraph in which it is referenced in the report. Key a dash between price ranges.

Lunch buffet in dining room	$10.00
Lunch in a separate meeting room	$12.00–$18.50
Theme buffet in the evening	$20.00
Seated dinners in the dining room	$25.50–$75.00
Indoor and outdoor receptions	$15.50–$50.00

a. Size column A 4.5" wide and column B 2" wide.

b. Add a row above row 1 and merge the cells; increase row height to 0.4".

c. Key the table title **Meal Charges Per Person**; apply 16-point font.

d. Apply Grid Table 4 – Accent 1 table style. Apply Align Center format to the title and Align Center Left to the remaining cells.

e. Apply 0.3" row height to the rows with data.

f. In the Table Style Options group on the Design tab, remove the check from the first column.

4. Print a copy of this report; you will use it in *8-d7*.

5. Proofread, check, and click Next Activity. (*8-d5*)

---

8-d6

**Newsletter**

pen
new office

★ **TIP**

If Heading 3 is not displayed in the Styles group on the Home tab, click Heading 2. Note that Heading 3 will then display.

Format the open pen data file as follows:

1. Use the keywords *tablet computer with pen* to find an image of a tablet computer with a pen and insert it. Size it 1" high and 1" wide. Position in Top Left with Square Text Wrapping. See the illustration at the right.

2. Insert Fill – Black, Text 1, Outline – Background 1, Hard Shadow – Accent 1 WordArt (second icon in bottom row). Select the text and key **The Pen—Kansas City News**. Reduce the font size to 28 point. Position in Top Right with Square Text Wrapping.

3. Select the text and apply two-column format.

4. Apply Heading 3 format to each of the headings.

5. Insert the *new office* picture from the data files. Size it 1.5" high. Position in Bottom Right with Square Text Wrapping. Then drag it to the center of the column.

6. Proofread, check, and click Next Activity. (*8-d6*)

The Newsletter Committee has written the articles for The Pen; please format so we can send it to Hilton Head.

RB

 The Pen—Kansas City News

 When a picture is selected, a Layout Options button displays next to the picture. You can click the button to display some of the layout options, or you can click the Wrap Text drop-list arrow to obtain a more detailed list.

### To wrap text around a picture:
Picture Tools Format/Arrange/Wrap Text

1. Select the picture and click Wrap Text to display the Wrap Text options.
2. Select the desired option, such as Square or Tight. Then drag the picture to the desired position.

### To position a picture:
Picture Tools Format/Arrange/Position

1. Select the picture and click Position to display the position options.
2. Click on the desired position as shown below.

---

## DRILL 2          FORMAT CLIPART

1. In the open document (*64-drill1*), click to select the picture.

2. Click Picture Tools Format tab; then click Crop.

3. Crop to remove all images except the one in the lower right (art supplies in container).

4. Click Compress Pictures; click OK to accept the defaults.

5. Decrease the height of the picture to 0.5".

6. Change the Wrap Text to Behind Text. Change the Wrap Text to In Front of Text. Notice how the image is displayed with each setting.

7. Click the Position down arrow and choose Position in Top Center with Square Text Wrapping. Change the position to Position in Top Left with Square Text Wrapping.

8. Check and click Next Activity. (*64-drill2*)

---

## WORDART

 WordArt is graphical text that can be used for document headings to make them more visually appealing. It is typically used in announcements, flyers, newsletters, and other casual documents.

### To insert WordArt:
Insert/Text/WordArt

1. Display the WordArt gallery.
2. Preview and select the desired option.
3. Select the text in the text box that displays and replace it with your text.
4. Size and position the WordArt as desired.

## 8-d7

**Compose Memo**

 palmetto memo form

1. Compose the memo; use subject **Wexford Information Requested**.

2. Read the report you printed in 8-d5 for reference in composing this memo. The report will be attached to the email along with this memo when it is sent to Jennifer Anderson.

3. Tell her that you have obtained the information about the Wexford Conference Center that she requested, and you think Wexford is ideal for her client.

4. Things to point out include how easy Julie Anders, the director, is to work with; the great facilities; and how cost-effective it will be. Include the options, but recommend the 80 percent room guarantee with all meals at Wexford if they have a need for that many rooms.

5. Note that the A/V situation is state-of-the-art (see report).

6. Remember the notes are rough and unorganized. Organize your thoughts, write complete sentences, and edit your memo very carefully. Check to see that you included all information requested. Remember to use the report for information as needed.

7. Proofread and check; click Exit *Word*. Click Log out to exit *KPDO*. (8-d7)

> Please draft a memo for me to Jennifer Anderson in our Northwest Office. Be sure to include the recommendations we agreed on. My handwritten notes are shown below for your reference.
>
> RB

Information based on client's estimate of 75 to 90 rooms needed.

Options:

- Guarantee 70% rooms get 50% discount—A/V, media and equipment needed and use of Oak Room & computer lab. 80%—A/V free.

- 80% all rooms plus all meals for participants; entire facility limited to your group except remaining residence rooms.

- Best food deals—buffet in dining room best breakfast & lunch; combination of themed buffets and seated dinners night meals. Outdoor recpts—especially gazebo area super if weather OK.

Julie Anders will provide negotiated room rate by email tomorrow. Might get suites for senior managers at same rate as room with 80% guar. Also requested discounted rates golf and tennis for one afternoon; menus for food selection and pricing.

## FORMAT PICTURES

 Most pictures that are inserted into documents will need to be sized, cropped, and positioned in the document. The text will then need to be wrapped around the image.

### To size pictures:
Picture Tools Format/Size/Height or Width Arrows

 Pictures can be resized or cropped. Cropping removes unwanted portions of the picture. After a picture has been cropped, it should be compressed to reduce the size of the file.

1. To change the size of a picture, select it and use the Height or Width arrows to increase or decrease the size. -or-

2. Select the picture and position the mouse over the sizing handles. When the pointer changes to a double-headed arrow, drag to the desired size.

### To crop pictures:
Picture Tools Format/Size/Crop

 1. To crop one side of a picture, click Crop and drag the cropping handle on the side inward. The cropping line will illustrate what will be cut off.

2. To crop the same amount on two sides, press CTRL, while you drag the handle.

3. To finish, click off the picture.

After a picture has been cropped, it is good practice to compress it to reduce the file size.

### To compress pictures:
Picture Tools Format/Adjust/Compress Pictures

1. Select the picture and click Compress Pictures to display the Compress Pictures dialog box.

2. Note the options that are available; then click OK to accept the defaults.

### To use Wrap Text:
Picture Tools Format/Arrange/Wrap Text

 To move a picture with the mouse, you must first apply Wrap Text. The Wrap Text command coordinates the flow of text and pictures. By default, pictures are inserted with the In Line with Text wrapping style, which limits your ability to move the picture. Changing the wrap style to one of the other layout options allows you to freely move the picture.

The other layout options also determine how the text will flow around the picture. For example, *Square* wraps the text around all sides of the picture, forming a square. *Top and Bottom* wraps the text above and below the picture, but not on the sides. *Behind Text* places the picture in back of the text.

# Web Apps

Web Apps

Palmetto Event Solutions, Inc.

## New Commands

### GETTING STARTED WITH OFFICE WEB APPS

In Module 9 you use *Word*, the SkyDrive, and the *Word Web App.* You will not launch nor use *KPDO* in this module. You need to do two things to use the SkyDrive and Office Web Apps.

1. Download and install the SkyDrive software to your computer if that was not done in the *Office* installation process.
2. Establish a free Microsoft Live account. Note you will already have a Microsoft Live account if you have an Outlook.com email account, an Xbox account, or a Windows phone.

**To download the SkyDrive desktop app for Windows:**

1. Open a *Word* document and click File. If the Download button appears, click Download now and install the SkyDrive desktop app. -or-
2. If you see your name with SkyDrive such as shown at the right, you may already have the app and a Microsoft Live account.

**To get a Microsoft Live account:**

1. Click Sign up for Microsoft Live account during the installation process.

   -or-

2. Go to https://skydrive.live.com and click Sign up now.
3. Complete the short form that displays. Note you may use your current email address and password or you may get an Outlook.com address and password.

> ★ **TIP**
>
> Hotmail accounts have been replaced by the free Outlook.com email accounts. If you have a Hotmail email address, you can continue to use it, but you cannot get a new Hotmail account.

Download now

SkyDrive

Microsoft account What's this?
someone@example.com
Password
☐ Keep me signed in

Sign in

Can't access your account?
Sign in with a single-use code

Don't have a Microsoft account? Sign up now

# Lesson 64 Graphics Review

**Review**

**64b**

## GRAPHICS

Proper use of graphics can greatly enhance the appearance of a document, help illustrate a point, or convey important information.

## PICTURES AND CLIP ART

The Pictures and Online Pictures commands are used to insert pictures and Clip Art in *Word* documents. The Pictures command enables you to insert pictures from your computer or other computers on your network. The Online Pictures command is used to access Clip Art from sources other than your computer and computer network.

To insert pictures from your computer:
Insert/Illustrations/Pictures

1. Click at the position where the picture is to be inserted; then click Pictures to display the Insert Pictures dialog box.
2. Browse to locate the picture you wish to insert.
3. Double-click the picture or select it and click the Insert button at the bottom of the dialog box to insert it.

To insert clip art:
Insert/Illustrations/Online Pictures

1. Click at the position where the picture is to be inserted; then click Online Pictures to display the Online Pictures options.
2. Click the Office.com Clip Art search box, enter a search term, and then tap ENTER to find the desired clip.
3. Double-click the clip art or select the image and click the Insert button to insert it.

In most cases, the illustration will need to be formatted to appropriately fit in the document.

---

**DRILL 1**   **INSERT CLIP ART**    graphics

1. In the open document, click the insertion point at the beginning of the document.

2. Click the Online Pictures command.

3. In the Office.com Clip Art search box, key **easel** and tap ENTER.

4. Scroll to find the image at the right and insert it in the document.

5. Check and click Next Activity. (*64-drill1*)

---

## Access SkyDrive

Once you have obtained your Microsoft Live ID, you can access the SkyDrive by going to https://skydrive.live.com and sign in with your email address and password. To simplify accessing your SkyDrive from your browser after you have signed in, add it to Favorites to set a bookmark for it. You can also access the SkyDrive from the File menu on a *Word* document. Note the opening screen that displays from the browser (you may have different file folders):

On the blue bar near the top of the screen, click the down arrow on SkyDrive for access to Mail, Messaging, Calendar, and return to SkyDrive.

The Create command on the blue bar is used to create a new folder or a new *Word* document, *Excel* workbook, *PowerPoint* presentation, *OneNote* notebook, or *Excel* survey.

The Upload command is used to upload files from your desktop.

In this module, you will work with the *Word Web App*.

The left pane of the opening screen provides access to Files, Recent documents, Shared documents, Groups, and files on your laptop or desktop.	The right pane contains folder icons or detailed listings showing the names of the files, the date modified, whether they are shared, and the file size.
Note that the space available on SkyDrive is shown at the bottom left side.	

## 63-d4

**Create and Format Table**

1. Key the table below. Adjust column widths. Center columns D and E.
2. Apply Grid Table 1 Light – Accent 5 style. Center column heads and center the table horizontally.
3. Proofread and check; click Next Activity. (63-d4)

Last Name	First Name	City	State	ZIP
Louie	Melinda	Seattle	WA	98101-1075
Palms	Jacob	Minneapolis	MN	55455-8415
Straus	Patricia	Omaha	NE	68105-4398
Soey	Helen	San Francisco	CA	94107-0357
Zampich	Alex	Hayden Lake	ID	83835-2735
Le	Trinh	Oxnard	CA	93033-4890
Phan	Chinh	San Francisco	CA	94107-6592
Kumar	Sanjeet	Durham	NC	27703-5283
Williams	James	New Bern	NC	28562-7963
Toyota	Janice	Del Rio	TX	78840-3122
Carpenter	Roger	Laredo	TX	78040-2361
Garcia	Pena	Bellevue	WA	98005-9407

## 63-d5

**Sort Table and Apply Style**

1. In the open document (63-d4), sort the table in ascending order by last name. (*Hint:* Check to see that Header row is selected.)
2. Sort the table in descending order by ZIP Code. (The Sort by entry you will see is ZIP.)
3. Apply Grid Table 4 – Accent 4 style. Center the table horizontally.
4. Proofread and check; click Next Activity. (63-d5)

## 63-d6

**Multiple Sort**

1. In the open document (63-d5), sort the table in ascending order by state, then by city, and then by last name.
2. Insert a row above the table and merge the cells.
3. Key **NATIONAL TEAM LEADERS** in 14-point, bold, all caps.
4. Change the height of the row to 0.4". Align Center the text in row 1. Bold and center all column heads.
5. Proofread and check; click Exit *Word*. (63-d6)
6. Click Log out to exit *KPDO*.

## CREATING A FOLDER

You can create folders on the SkyDrive or from your computer.

### To create a folder on the SkyDrive:

1. In the opening screen, click the down arrow on Create on the blue bar at the top of the screen.

2. Click Folder from the drop-list to display the new folder.

3. Key the desired folder name.

---

**Apply It**

**Activity 1**

**Access SkyDrive and Create a New Folder**

1. Go to https://skydrive.live.com and sign in to SkyDrive. If you do not have a Microsoft Live account, click Sign up now and create one.

2. Create a new folder in your files.

3. Key the name **Module 9 Web Apps**.

4. Minimize the SkyDrive.

---

## SAVE A FILE

You can save documents on your computer to the SkyDrive.

### To save a file on the SkyDrive:

1. With the document you wish to save open, click the File menu and Save As.

2. Click your SkyDrive and then click the Browse button.

3. Locate the folder in which you want to save the document or create a new folder.

4. Key the file name and click Save.

---

**Apply It**

**Activity 2**

**Save Document to SkyDrive**

overview of skydrive

1. With *Word* open on your computer, open the data file *overview of skydrive*.

2. Read the document carefully. This document is designed to help you understand what the SkyDrive is and how you will be using it in this module.

3. Save the document in the Module 9 Web Apps folder that you set up on your SkyDrive in Activity 1. Name the file **Activity 2**. Note that you may have to click Files in the left pane if you do not see the folder. Close the document.

---

## WORKING WITH A DOCUMENT ON SKYDRIVE

Click the document that you saved on the SkyDrive to open it in the *Word Web App*. The four commands that can be used to work with a document display above the open document.

---

1. Create a 4-column, 6-row table. Key the table below; decimal-align columns B–D.

2. Add a row at the bottom of the table. Key the word **TOTAL** in cell A7. Calculate and insert the total expenses for each month. Verify the number format is the same as the other numbers in the table.

3. Add a column to the right of the table. Key **Total** in cell E1. Insert the totals for each expense in column E (change the formula to SUM(LEFT) as needed).

4. Add a row above the table. Merge the cells in row 1 and change the row height to 0.7". Key **EXPENSES FOR LAURA PEREZ** in bold, 14-point font, all caps. Tap ENTER; then key **First Quarter, 201-** in bold, 12-point font.

5. Apply Grid Table 4 – Accent 6 style. In Table Style Options, select Total row and Last Column. Adjust column widths to display the information attractively.

6. Bold and Align Center all column heads.

7. Proofread and check; click Next Activity. (*63-d1*)

Expenses	January	February	March
Rent	$1,200.00	$1,250.00	$1,250.00
Food	$275.50	$255.25	$295.00
Transportation	$260.00	$280.00	$675.00
Clothing	$395.00	$110.00	$225.00
Miscellaneous	$135.00	$170.00	$165.00

1. In the open document (*63-d1*), change the February rent to **$1,375.00** and the March rent to **$1,425.00**.

2. Recalculate the totals in cell E3, C8, and D8.

3. Proofread and check; click Next Activity. (*63-d2*)

1. In the open document (*63-d2*), insert a row between Rent and Food. Key the following information in the new row: **School | $875.00 | $460.00 | $515.00**.

2. Insert the total in cell E4. Recalculate the totals in row 9.

3. Select cells A3–A8 (*Rent – Miscellaneous*). Sort column 1 in ascending order. (Sort by Column 1; Text; Ascending.)

4. Proofread and check; click Next Activity. (*63-d3*)

### To share a document on SkyDrive:

1. Click Share above the open document.

2. Send a link by email to one or more reviewers. Key the person's email address and include a message if desired.

3. Click Share.

**Apply It**

(Activity 3)

**Share a Document on SkyDrive**

1. Share the document with your instructor or one of your classmates who has an Outlook.com email address or a Microsoft Live Account.

2. Click Share above the open document.

3. Key the person's email address in the To box.

4. Key the following message in the Message box:

   **Please review this document and give me your feedback.**

5. Click Share.

### To add a comment on SkyDrive:

1. Click Comments above the open document.

2. The Comments box with your name displays.

3. Select the text that applies and key the comment.

4. Click Post to send your comment.

**Apply It**

(Activity 4)

**Add a Comment**

1. Post a comment on the shared document. The person with whom you shared the document texted you and asked you to post the following comment on the document.

2. Click Comments above the open document.

3. Select the heading *Overview of SkyDrive* and then click New Comment.

4. Key the comment below your name in the Comments box.

   **I read the Overview, and I think it is really helpful. The only suggestion I have is to add a closing summary.**

5. Click Post.

## SORT IN TABLES

Data can be sorted in three ways:

- **Text sort.** Text is sorted alphabetically. Numbers sorted in a text sort are based only on the first digit. If the numbers 1, 7, and 100 are sorted, the resulting list will be in this order: 1, 100, 7.

- **Number sort.** Numbers are sorted numerically. For example, a list of 1, 100, 7 would be sorted as 1, 7, 100.

- **Date sort.** When dates are involved, text is sorted chronologically.

### To sort data in a table:
Table Tools Layout/Data/Sort

1. Click in the table; then display the Sort dialog box.

2. When row 1 contains column headings, it is called the *header row*. Click the appropriate button indicating whether the table contains a header row.

3. Click the drop-list arrow next to *Sort by*. (**Note:** *Sort by* tells *Word* how to arrange the information.)

4. Select Ascending to sort the list from A to Z. Descending sorts from Z to A.

5. If the first-level sort cannot establish the sort order (this will be true if several cells are identical in the first column), then you will need to establish a second-level sort in the first *Then by* section. You can also enter a third-level sort in the subsequent *Then by* section.

---

**DRILL 4**   SORT TABLE    sort

Table Tools Layout/Data/Sort

1. In the open document, sort the table by Dish in ascending order. (Sort by Dish; Ascending.)

2. Sort the table by Cost in descending order. (Sort by Cost; Number; Descending.)

3. Sort the table by Nationality in ascending order and then by Dish in descending order. (Sort by Nationality; Text; Ascending; Then by Dish; Text; Descending.)

4. Your sorted table should look like the one at the right.

5. Proofread and check; click Next Activity. (*63-drill4*)

Dish	Nationality	Cost
Hamburger	American	6.50
Sweet and Sour Pork	Chinese	8.95
Hong Kong Steak	Chinese	15.95
Veal Marsala	Italian	18.75
Shrimp Tempura	Japanese	11.50
Fish Burrito	Mexican	6.96

---

### To find text in a document on SkyDrive:

1. Click Find above the open document and key the search information.

2. Click the search icon. The results display.

## Apply It

### Activity 5

**Find Text in a Document**

1. Use Find to check and ensure that *co-authoring* was covered in the document.
2. Click Find and key **co-authoring** in the Search box. Then click the search icon.
3. Use the results that display to verify that the topic was matched.

---

### To edit a document on SkyDrive:

1. Click Edit Document.
2. Select the option you wish to use to edit the document. If the edits are easy to make, select Edit in Word Web App. If they are complex, select Edit in Word, which opens the Word application on your computer.

---

## Apply It

### Activity 6

**Compose Closing Paragraph**

In this activity, you will edit the document using the *Word Web App.*

1. Click Edit Document and then click Edit in *Word Web App.*
2. At the end of the document, key the heading **Summary** and apply Heading 1 style.
3. Use the information below and the information in the Overview to compose a summary paragraph. Save (will save as *Activity 2*).
4. Proofread and edit your paragraph carefully using the commands on the Ribbon; then share your document with your instructor.

- Begin with one or two sentences indicating that SkyDrive is a place to store documents on the Web and to work with Web-based Office applications. Name the applications.
- Point out that you can edit using the web apps or the applications on your computer.
- End with a sentence or two about the three services that complement the desktop version of the software.

To total a column or row of numbers:

Table Tools Layout/Data/Formula

1. Position the insertion point in the empty cell that is to contain the answer.

2. In the Formula dialog box, the SUM formula appears with either ABOVE or LEFT depending if you clicked below a column or at the end of a row.

3. Select the number format desired and click OK.

The SUM feature only works with adjacent cells. To add nonadjacent cells, key the formula in the Formula box (=b3 +b7+b9).

To recalculate a column or row of numbers:

1. Right-click in the cell where the new total is to appear; then click Update Field.

–or–

2. Highlight the cell where the new total is to appear and tap F9.

---

## DRILL 2        SUM FUNCTION

 sum

Table Tools Layout/Data/Formula

1. In the open document, position the insertion point in the last cell and tap TAB to add a row at the bottom.

2. Key **TOTAL** in cell A8.

3. Insert the total for column C in cell C8. Insert the total for column D in cell D8. Verify the number format is the same as the numbers in the column.

4. Insert a column at the right of the table.

5. Key **Total per Employee** in cell E1; it will wrap to a second line. Align Center the column head.

6. Add the numbers in columns C and D (=C2+D2, etc.) and place the total for each row in column E; you do not need to insert a sum for the total row. If the formula displays as SUM(ABOVE), replace the word *ABOVE* with **LEFT**. Center the numbers vertically in the cells to match the other columns.

7. Proofread and check; click Next Activity. (*63-drill2*)

---

## DRILL 3        RECALCULATE

1. In the open document (*63-drill2*), position the insertion point in cell D5 (Palombo/Software).

2. Change the number to **950,225**.

3. Click the insertion point in cell E5; then tap F9 to recalculate the total.

4. Click the insertion point in cell D8 and tap F9 to recalculate the total.

5. Change the amount in cell C7, to **85,150,000**.

6. Recalculate the totals in cells E7 and C8.

7. Proofread and check; click Next Activity. (*63-drill3*)

## CREATE A DOCUMENT USING THE WORD WEB APP

You can create a *Word* document using the *Word Web App*. Remember that you will have limited commands available. However, the commands that are available are exactly the same ones you have been using in *Word* on your computer.

### To create a document using the *Word Web App*:

1. Use your browser to access your SkyDrive.
2. Click the folder you wish to use to store your document, or create a new folder if you do not have an appropriate folder to use.
3. Click Create on the blue bar near the top of the screen and select Word document to display the New Microsoft Word document name box.
4. Key the name of the document and click Create.
5. A new document will open in the *Word Web App*.
6. Key, format, and edit the document using the available commands.

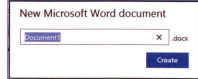

New Microsoft Word document

Document1          ×   .docx

Create

---

## Apply It

### Activity 7

**Report with Table**

1. Access SkyDrive and click Module 9 Web Apps folder.
2. Click Create on the blue bar near the top of the screen. Select Word Document.
3. Key **Activity 7** in the document name box and click Create to open a blank document.
4. Tap ENTER three times and key the following document. Then apply the formats listed below the document.

Volunteer Celebration

Our Fifth Annual Endowed Scholarship Fundraising Campaign was very successful. The model of naming the scholarship in honor of a community leader proved to be very successful once again.

Model Success Factors

Several primary factors are responsible for its success:

Many potential donors believe that providing a needy student with a scholarship is a worthy cause, and they are willing to support worthy causes.

Endowing a scholarship makes it a gift that keeps giving. The funds raised are invested in the Foundation's portfolio, and only the interest is used to fund the scholarship each year. Usually 4 to 5 percent of the total fund (principal plus interest) is used each year. Therefore, a scholarship is granted every year in perpetuity.

Friends and family of the community leader being honored often support the scholarship simply because they want to honor that particular person.

*(continued)*

## DECIMAL TABS

 Decimal tabs are used to align numbers containing decimals in a column or to right-align numbers in a column. You have already used the Align Text Right command to right-align numbers in a column. Setting a decimal tab keeps the numbers right-aligned and makes them appear centered in the column. If the tab for the column needs to be moved, select all the numbers in the column before moving the tab or the change will only occur in the cell where the insertion point is positioned.

### To set a decimal tab:

1. Key the table with the numbers left-aligned in each column. Select the column or the cells in the column where the decimal tab will be used.

2. Click the tab selector at the left edge of the Ruler until the decimal tab displays.

3. Click the Horizontal Ruler where you want to set the tab. The numbers immediately align to the decimal tab.

4. If you need to move the decimal tab, first select the column or the necessary cells before moving the tab marker on the Ruler.

> ★ **TIP**
>
> If you click the tab selector and miss the decimal tab, continue clicking the selector button until the decimal tab displays again.

Numbers with Decimals	Align Right	Decimal Tab
2.1	56	56
10.75	100	100
325.333	1,050	2,050

## DRILL 1     DECIMAL TAB AND COLUMN WIDTH

1. Create the table shown above. Apply Grid Table 4 – Accent 5. Center the column headings. Uncheck First Column in the Table Style Options group.

2. Change the width of column A to 1.9", column B to 1.2", and column C to 1.3".

3. Center the table horizontally on the page.

4. Select cells A2–A4 and set a decimal tab at 1" on the Horizontal Ruler. The numbers automatically align with the decimal tab.

5. Select cells B2–B4 and click the Align Right button.

6. Select cells C2–C4 and set a decimal tab at 3.5".

7. Select cells C2–C4; move the decimal tab on the Ruler to 4".

8. Proofread and check; click Next Activity. (*63-drill1*)

## FORMULAS

*fx* Formula    When numbers are keyed in a table, *Word* can perform basic mathematical calculations such as addition, subtraction, multiplication, and division. SUM (addition) is the default formula that appears if you click in a cell below a column of numbers or to the right of a row of numbers.

If a change is made to one of the numbers that is part of the calculation, *Word* can recalculate the answer. Fields can be updated by right-clicking in a field and then clicking Update Field or by clicking in the field and then tapping F9.

Fundraising Committee

Each year five volunteers agree to handle the fundraising for the scholarship. This year our volunteers exceeded their goals significantly. The following table provides the results.

Celebration for Volunteers

The volunteers were honored at a special dinner recognizing their outstanding work for setting a record both on the number of donors and on the total amount raised. At the request of the volunteers, Chef Pat once again prepared the four-course dinner featuring his special crown pork roast.

Fundraiser	Number of Donors	Amount Raised
Susie	78	$146,750
John	43	96,520
Peter	38	74,925
Alden	56	62,750
William	64	59,250
Total	279	$440,195

5. Apply Title style to the title and Heading 1 to the headings.

6. Format the table as follows:

   a. Center and bold the headings in row 1.

   b. Align data in column A at the left, in column B at the center, and in column C at the right.

7. Save the document using the Save command on the Quick Access Toolbar.

8. Then click Save As to download the document to your computer. Create a new folder named **Module 9 Solutions**. Close the *Web Apps* document.

---

**Activity 8**

**Edit in Word from SkyDrive**

**TIP**

To apply commands that are not part of the *Word Web App*, select Edit in Word. The *Word Web App* does not contain the commands needed for Activity 8.

1. On your computer, open *Activity 7* from the Module 9 Solutions folder and save it to the SkyDriveModule 9 Web Apps folder; name it **Activity 8**.

2. From the SkyDrive, open *Activity 8* in the Module 9 Web Apps folder and edit it. Click Edit in Word.

3. Apply Ion theme. Click in the table and apply List Table 3 – Accent 1.

4. Insert a row above the first row, merge the cells, and key **Endowed Scholarship**.

5. Increase height of rows 1 and 2 to 0.3" and apply Center Align.

6. Save the document.

# Lesson 63 Table Functions

**New Commands**
- Decimal Tabs
- Formulas
- Sort in Tables

 **Warmup** *Lesson 63a Warmup*

## Skill Building

**63b  Timed Writing**

Key two 3' timed writings.

What is a college education worth today? If you asked that question to a random sample of people, you would get a wide range of responses. Many would respond that you cannot quantify the worth of a bachelor's degree. They quickly stress that many factors other than wages enhance the quality of life. They tend to focus on the benefits of sciences and liberal arts and the appreciation they develop for things that they would never have been exposed to if they had not attended college.

Research shows, though, that you can place a value on a college education in respect to wages earned. Less than twenty years ago, a high school graduate earned only about fifty percent of what a college graduate earned. Today, that number is quite different. The difference between the wages of a college graduate and the wages of a high school graduate has more than doubled in the last twenty years.

The key factor in economic success is education. The new jobs that pay high wages require more skills and a college degree. Fortunately, many high school students do recognize the value of getting a degree. Far more high school graduates are going to college than ever before. They know that the best jobs are jobs for knowledge workers and those jobs require a high level of skill.

## Project Setting

### Activity 9

**Upload and Edit Letter**

internship completed

1. Open the *internship completed* data file on your computer and upload it to a new folder on your SkyDrive.

   a. Click Save As and select your SkyDrive as the place.

   b. Click Browse and then click New Folder in the Save As dialog box that displays. Key the folder name **Module 9 Palmetto Project**.

   c. Then save the file in the new folder; name the file **Activity 9**.

2. Open the document on your SkyDrive and edit the letter in the *Word Web App*. Include the current date, your name and address formatted properly, and your first name in the salutation.

3. Click Save on the Quick Access Toolbar to save the document.

### Activity 10

**Upload Form and Compose Memo**

palmetto memo form

1. Upload the *palmetto memo form* data file and save it to the Module 9 Palmetto Project folder; name it **Activity 10**.

2. Open it on your SkyDrive. Select Edit in Word.

3. Complete the memo heading to your instructor from you. Use the current date and the subject **Internship Completed**.

4. Compose the memo from the information shown below. Format the table attractively using a style that fits with the theme and logo of Palmetto Event Solutions.

5. Proofread and edit the memo carefully; then share the folder with your instructor.

   a. Click the Module 9 Palmetto Project folder and then click Share on the blue bar above the files pane.

   b. Key your instructor's email in the Send link to box. Add a message if desired.

   c. Click Share.

- Write a paragraph describing your experience with the Palmetto Event Solution projects and what you liked about them. Indicate that you are sharing the letter from Mr. Garrett Russell.

- Key the sentence above the table, the table, and the sentence below the table.

You requested that I summarize my experiences both quantitatively in a table and qualitatively to describe the value derived from the experience.

Office	Number of Jobs	Estimated Time
Hilton Head, South Carolina	5	8 hours
Portland, Oregon	4	5 hours
Las Cruces, New Mexico	8	11 hours
Newport, Rhode Island	4	6 hours
Kansas City, Missouri	7	9 hours

Please note that I completed two different projects in two of the cities—Las Cruces and Hilton Head.

- Add a paragraph or two about the value of this practical experience in a real job setting.

**Memo with Table**

1. Key the following memo according to memo formatting guides.
2. Insert the table after the first paragraph; adjust column widths and center the table horizontally.
3. Apply List Table 4 – Accent 2 table style.
4. Center the dollar amounts in each column.
5. Proofread and check; click Exit *Word*. (62-d2)
6. Click Log out to exit *KPDO*.

⭐ **TIP**

Insert space between table and following paragraph by clicking in the paragraph below the table and choosing Add Space Before Paragraph (Home/Paragraph/Line and Paragraph Spacing).

TO: Parents | FROM: Lynn Marshall | DATE: May 15, 201- | SUBJECT: Tuition Increase

The Board of Directors has reviewed our financial statements, the proposed budget for next year, and our current tuition plan. Although we have tried to maintain tuition at the current rate, it is not possible to do so. Our costs for utilities, food, supplies, and gasoline for the buses have increased substantially. Therefore, we have applied a 2.5% increase in tuition for next year. The following table summarizes our new weekly rates.

Age Group	Single-Child Rate	Multi-Child Rate	Half-Day Rate
Infant/Toddler	$368	$345	$195
Preschool 2	$363	$333	$185
Preschool 3	$340	$330	$175
Preschool 4	$337	$328	$173
Preschool 5	$335	$325	$173

The new rates take effect on July 1 and will be guaranteed not to change for one full year. The Children's Center will continue to accept credit cards and personal checks. Tuition may be paid weekly, monthly, or annually. If you have questions about tuition or other financial issues, please check with our business manager at the Children's Center.

We look forward to seeing all of you at the annual picnic next week.

# Beyond the Essentials— Formatting Advanced Documents

## Learning Outcomes

### Document Design Skills

+ Design and prepare attractive documents.

+ Organize content effectively in tables and graphics.

+ Enhance report formats with design elements that add structure, provide a consistent image, and increase readability.

+ Create merged documents with envelopes and labels.

### Word Processing Skills

+ Review and apply basic *Word 2013* commands.

+ Learn and apply *Word 2013* commands to create and format effective documents.

### Communication Skills

+ Review and improve basic communication skills.

+ Produce error-free documents and apply language arts skills.

### Keyboarding

+ Improve keyboarding speed and accuracy.

1. In the open document, change the page orientation to landscape.

2. Insert a column on the right side of the table.

3. Key in cell C1: **120,000 square feet of office space available for lease.**

4. Key in cell C3: **58,000 square feet on first floor available for lease.**

5. Align Center the text in columns B and C.

6. Proofread and check; click Next Activity. (*62-drill2*)

## Apply It

1. Create a 7-column, 7-row table. Key the following text in row 1.

Name of College	Bachelor's Degree	Associate's Degree	Certificate	Classroom	Online	Hybrid

2. Change the Text Direction of the column heads in columns B–G so that the text reads bottom to top.

3. Increase the height of row 1 to 1.5" so that all column heads fit on one line.

4. Change the page orientation to Landscape.

5. Add a column to the right of the table and key **Financial Aid** as the column head.

6. Change the width of column A to 3.0". Make column H narrower so that the right border of column H is at approximately 9" on the Ruler.

7. Select columns B–H and click the Distribute Columns command.

8. Apply Grid Table 4 – Accent 3 style.

9. Insert a row above row 1; merge the cells. Change the row height to 0.75".

10. Key **COLLEGE COMPARISON CHART** in row 1. Apply 16-point bold font; Align Center the title.

11. Apply bold and Align Center to all column heads.

12. Change the height of rows 3–8 to 0.4".

13. Use the Quick Check below to compare your table.

14. Proofread and check; click Next Activity. (*62-d1*)

## QUICK ✔

Check your document against the illustration below.

COLLEGE COMPARISON CHART							
Name of College	Bachelor's Degree	Associate's Degree	Certificate	Classroom	Online	Hybrid	Financial Aid

# Skill Builder 4

## DRILL 15

**Keystroking Patterns**

Key each line once for fluency; DS between groups.

**3rd row**

1 it we or us opo pop you rut rip wit pea lea wet pit were quiet
2 pew tie toe per rep hope pour quip rope your pout tore rip quirk

**Home row**

3 ha has kid lad led last wash lash gaff jade fads half sash haggle
4 as dad had add leg jug lads hall lass fast deal fall leafs dashes

**1st row**

5 ax ban man zinc clan bank calm lamb vain amaze bronze back buzzer
6 ax sax can bam zag cab mad fax vans buzz caves knack waxen banana

 **Timed Writings**

1. Take a 1' writing on each paragraph.
2. Take one 3' or one 5' writing on both paragraphs.

**Writing 28**

Who is a professional? The word can be defined in many ways. Some think of a professional as someone who is in an exempt job category in an organization. To others the word can denote something quite different; being a professional denotes an attitude that requires thinking of your position as a career, not just a job. A professional exerts influence over her or his job and takes pride in the work accomplished.

Many individuals who remain in the same positions for a long time categorize themselves as being in dead-end positions. Others who remain in the same position for a long time consider themselves to be in a profession. A profession is a career to which you are willing to devote a lifetime. How you view your profession is up to you.

## DISTRIBUTE ROWS OR COLUMNS

When a table has many columns or rows, it is difficult to set each column width or height the same dimension. The Distribute Rows and Distribute Columns commands will distribute the columns and rows evenly for you.

To distribute rows or columns:
Table Tools Layout/Cell Size/Distribute Rows or Columns

1. Select the rows or columns that are to be distributed evenly.
2. Click Distribute Rows or Distribute Columns.

⊟‡ Distribute Rows
⊞ Distribute Columns

## REPEAT HEADER ROWS

Repeat Header Rows — When a table is divided between pages, repeat the header row (column heads) at the top of each page so the reader understands the data that displays in each column. More than one header row can be repeated by first selecting the rows and then applying the command.

To repeat header row(s):
Table Tools Layout/Data/Repeat Header Rows

1. Select the row or rows that are to be repeated.
2. Click Repeat Header Rows.

---

**DRILL 1**  TEXT DIRECTION, DISTRIBUTE COLUMNS, REPEAT HEADER ROW

 text direction

1. In the open document, select cells B1–F1.

2. Click Text Direction until the text reads from bottom to top.

3. Increase the row height by clicking the Height up arrow until the column heads in columns B–D display on two lines.

4. Bold and Align Center the column heads.

5. Change the width of column A to 2.5".

6. Select columns B–F and click Distribute Columns.

7. Select rows 2–13. Click the Insert Below command three times to add more rows to the table.

8. Click the cursor in row 1. Click the Repeat Header Rows command. Scroll to verify that column heads display at the top of the next page.

9. Center the table horizontally on the page.

10. Proofread and check; click Next Activity. (*62-drill1*)

---

## PAGE ORIENTATION

 A page may be displayed in either portrait (8 ½" × 11") or landscape (11" × 8 ½") orientation. Use landscape orientation when a table is extremely wide.

To change page orientation:
Page Layout/Page Setup/Orientation/Landscape

📄 Portrait
📄 Landscape

**Skill Building** *Technique Builder*

## DRILL 16

**Keyboarding Technique**

Key each line once for fluency; DS between groups.

1st  1 Zam and six lazy men visited Cecil and Bunn at a bank convention.
     2 Zane, much to the concern of Bev and six men, visited their zone.

2nd  3 Jill said she wished that she had fed Dale's dog a lot less food.
     4 Jake Hall sold the glass flask at a Dallas "half-off" glass sale.

3rd  5 Did either Peter or Trey quip that reporters were out to get you?
     6 Either Trey or Peter tried to work with a top-quality pewter toy.

4th  7 18465 97354 12093 87541 09378 34579 74629 45834 28174 11221 27211
     8 02574 29765 39821 07623 17659 20495 39481 10374 32765 77545 22213

---

## Timed Writings

1. Take three 1' writings on each paragraph.
2. Take one 5' writing or two 3' writings. Proofread; circle errors; determine *gwam*.

**Writing 29**

Students for decades have secured part-time jobs to help pay for college expenses. Today, more students are gainfully employed while they are in college than ever before. Many of them are employed because their financial situation requires that they earn money. Earnings from jobs go to pay tuition, books, living costs, and other necessities. Some work so that they can own cars or buy luxury items; others seek jobs to gain skills or to build their vitas. These students are aware that many organizations prefer to hire a person who has had some type of work experience than one who has had none.

Students often ask if the work experience has to be in exactly the same field. Obviously, the more closely related the experience, the better it is. However, the old adage, anything beats nothing, applies. Regardless of the types of jobs students have, they can demonstrate that they get to work regularly and on time, they have good human relations skills, they are organized and can manage time effectively, and they produce good results. All of these factors are very critical to employers. The bottom line is that employers like to use what you have done in the past as a predictor of what you will do in the future.

# Lesson 62 Table Commands

## New Commands

- Text Direction
- Distribute Rows or Columns
- Repeat Header Rows
- Page Orientation

## Skill Building

### 62b Textbook Keying

Key each line once; concentrating on using good keying techniques.

<div>

az
1 Zen and Ozzie zealously played the anthem in the Aztec Jazz band.

2 Batz went to Phoenix, Arizona, to take a math quiz he had missed.

by
3 Boyd drove by the Blue Bayou to bypass the roadblocks at the Bay.

4 By daybreak, Mary will stop by to bake a birthday cake for Jayne.

cx
5 Please carry the X-ray from exit C to exit X for Cece and Xavier.

6 Carol can meet Xian at the exit doors following the movie Exodus.

dw
7 Don walked the dog at dawn when he dwelled in his downtown condo.

8 Did Dwight drive Wendy to the new drive-in or the new drive-thru?

figures
9 The 12 teams spent $3,489.00 on groceries for the 567 boy scouts.

10 Judy's 13 puzzles had 60,789 pieces, but 524 pieces were missing.

</div>

## New Commands

### 62c

### TEXT DIRECTION

Occasionally it is preferable to display text vertically in a cell, such as when a number of narrow columns are included in a table. The Text Direction button rotates text in a cell 90 degrees each time you click the button. Rotated text will be easier to read if it is centered in the table cell.

To change text direction:
Table Tools Layout/Alignment/Text Direction

1. Click in the cell where the text will be rotated.
2. Click the Text Direction button to rotate the text. Continue clicking Text Direction until the text displays in the desired direction.
3. Use Align Center to center the text in the cell.

## DRILL 17

**Number Reaches**

Key each line once at a comfortable rate; practice difficult lines.

1 My staff of 11 worked 11 hours a day from May 11 to June 11.
2 Her flight, PW 222, lands at 2:22 p.m. on Thursday, June 22.
3 We 3, part of the 333rd Corps, marched 33 miles on August 3.
4 Car 444 took Route 4 east to Route 44, then 4 miles to Aden.
5 The 55 wagons traveled 555 miles in '55; only 5 had trouble.
6 Put 6 beside 66; result 666, and add another 6 to get 6,666.
7 She sold 7,777 copies of Record 77, Schubert's 7th Symphony.
8 In '88, it took 8 men and 8 women 8 days to travel 88 miles.
9 The 9 teams, 9 girls and 9 boys, depart on Bus 999 at 9 a.m.
10 Billion has nine zeros; as 000,000,000. Ten has but one 0.

## Timed Writings

### Writing 30

Planning, organizing, and controlling are three of the functions that are familiar to all sorts of firms. Because these functions are basic to the managerial practices of a business, they form the very core of its daily operations. Good managerial procedures, of course, do not just occur by accident. They must be set into motion by people. Thus, a person who plans to enter the job market, especially in an office position, should study all of the elements of good management in order to apply those principles to her or his work.

Leadership is another very important skill for a person to develop. Leaders are needed at all levels in a business to plan, organize, and control the operations of the firm. A person who is in a key position of leadership usually is expected to initiate ideas as well as to carry out the goals of a business. Office workers who have developed the qualities of leadership are more apt to be promoted than those without such skills. While leadership may come naturally for some people, it can be learned as well as be improved with practice.

Attitude is an extremely important personality trait that is a big contributor to success in one's day-to-day activities. Usually a person with a good attitude is open-minded to the ideas of others and is able to relate with others because he or she has an interest in people. Thus, one's attitude on the job often makes a great difference in whether work gets done and done right. Because teamwork is a part of many jobs, developing a good attitude toward work, people, and life seems logical.

**Insert and Delete Columns and Rows**

**TIP**

It may be necessary to readjust column width after a table style is applied to make the table more attractive.

1. In the open document (*61-d1*), insert a column between columns B and C. Key the following information in the new column and left-align.

   **Department | Public Relations | Maintenance | Accounting | Engineering**

2. Delete the row containing *Holsonback*.

3. Insert two additional rows and key the names and accompanying information below in correct alphabetical order. Adjust column widths as necessary.

**Baxter, L.**	**K511**	**Accounting**	**44,296,101**	**971,360**
**Talbert, S.**	**P053**	**CFO**	**82,091,433**	**985,201**

4. Insert a row above row 1. Merge the cells and key **LAUREL CANYON ENTERPRISES** using 14-point font, all caps.

5. Apply List Table 4 – Accent 5 style. Bold and center all headings. Adjust column widths to make the table more attractive.

6. Proofread and check; click Next Activity. (*61-d3*)

---

## Communication

**61d**

References/Communication Skills/Semicolons

### SEMICOLONS

1. Create the table shown below. Adjust the width of column A to 2.25".

2. Review the rules in the left column and the examples in the right column. Apply the rule and key a corrected copy of the sentence labeled *Application*.

3. Insert a row above the table and merge the cells. Key **Use a Semicolon** in 16-point font and change the row height to 0.5". Change the height of row 2 to 0.3".

4. Apply Grid Table 4 – Accent 3 style. Align Center and apply bold to all headings. Center the table horizontally.

5. Proofread and check; click Exit *Word*. (*61d*) Click Log out to exit *KPDO*.

Rule	Example and Application
To separate independent clauses in a compound sentence when the conjunction is omitted.	**Example:** Please review the information; give me a report by Tuesday. **Application:** The citizens voted to recall the mayor an election will be held in November.
To separate independent clauses when they are joined by conjunctive adverbs (however, nevertheless, consequently, etc.).	**Example:** The traffic was heavy; consequently, I was late. **Application:** Mr. Smith refused to increase our travel expense budget furthermore he suggested that we decrease it by 10 percent.
To separate a series of elements that contain commas.	**Example:** The new officers are: Fran Pena, President; Harry Wong, Treasurer; and Muriel Williams, Secretary. **Application:** We will be driving this summer to Las Vegas Nevada Phoenix Arizona Austin Texas and Chicago Illinois.

## Skill Building *Technique Builder*

### DRILL 18

**Improve Response Patterns**

Key each line once; DS between 4-line groups; work at a controlled rate; repeat drill.

**direct reaches: reaches with the same finger; keep hands quiet**

1 brand much cent numb cease bright music brief jump special carved
2 create mumps zany mystic curve mummy any checks brag brunch after
3 Bradley broke his left thumb after lunch on a great hunting trip.
4 After having mumps, Cecil once saw June excel in a funny musical.

**adjacent reaches: keep fingers curved and upright**

5 were junior sad yuletide trees polo very join safe property tweed
6 tree trio trickle tripod quit excess was free easy million option
7 Gwen and Sumio are going to be quite popular at the Western Club.
8 Fred said we were going to join the guys for polo this afternoon.

**double letters: strike keys rapidly**

9 dill seem pool attic miss carry dragged kidded layoff lapped buzz
10 commend accuse inner rubber cheer commission football jazz popper
11 Tammy called to see if she can borrow my accounting book at noon.
12 Lynnette will meet with the bookseller soon to discuss the issue.

## Timed Writing

**Writing 31**

Working at home is not exactly a new phenomenon, but the concept is growing quite rapidly. For many years, people have worked at home. In most instances, they were self-employed and operated a business from their homes. Today, the people who work at home fit into a variety of categories. Some own their own businesses; others bring extra work home after the workday ends. A key change is the large group of people who are employed by huge organizations but who work out of home offices. These employees are in jobs that include sales, creative, technical, and a host of other categories.

The real change that has occurred is not so much the numbers of people who are working at home and the variety of jobs, but the complex tools that are now available for doing the job. Technology has truly made the difference. In many cases, clients and customers are not even aware that they are dealing with individuals working at home. Computers, printers, fax machines, telephone systems, and other office equipment enable the worker in the home to function in the same way as workers in a typical business office.

**61-d1**

**Create Table**

⭐ **TIP**

Text is keyed left-aligned. Numerical amounts are right-aligned.

1. Create the table below; adjust column widths and center the table horizontally.
2. Center column B; right-align columns C and D. Bold and center column heads.
3. Proofread and check; click Next Activity. (*61-d1*)

Employee	I.D.	Hardware	Software
Alexander, J.	R492	$105,134,384	$1,868,553
Courtenay, W.	R856	79,364,091	1,384,219
Holsonback, E.	C845	27,386,427	1,098,237
Rajeh, C.	M451	82,665,900	1,052,564

**61-d2**

**Merge and Split Cells**

1. Insert a 3-column, 7-row table at 2".
2. Merge rows 1 and 2 in column A; select rows 2–7 in column B and split into two columns. Do the same for column C.
3. Key the table below; right-align all numbers. Adjust column widths.
4. Insert a row above the table and merge the cells. Center **WEXMARK COLLEGE** in 14-point, all caps. Tap ENTER and key **201- Enrollments** in 12-point font.
5. Apply Grid Table 1 Light – Accent 2 style.
6. Change the height of rows 2–8 to 0.25". Center the copy vertically in the cells.
7. Change the height of row 1 to 0.6". Bold and Align Center all headings.
8. Center the table horizontally on the page.
9. Proofread and check; click Next Activity. (*61-d2*)

College	Semester		Division	
	Fall	Spring	Upper	Lower
Business Administration	1,296	677	395	1,586
Computer Science	945	322	124	1,143
Allied Health Sciences	3,925	2,650	4,500	7,125
Arts and Sciences	98	76	29	108
Engineering Technology	179	156	32	96

### Writing 32

Many small businesses fail. Surprisingly, though, many people are still willing to take a chance on starting one of their own. A person who is willing to take the risks necessary to manage a business in order to receive the potential rewards is called an entrepreneur. In a sense, such individuals are pioneers who enjoy each step on the way to achieving objectives that they have determined to be important. This type of person has had a profound impact on shaping our economy and our quality of life.

What does it take to start a business venture, and what kinds of people make it work? Obviously, the desire to make money and to be one's own boss are two basic incentives, but these alone are not enough to guarantee success. Two qualifications common to most successful entrepreneurs, whatever field they are in, are an attentiveness to detail and a knack for solving day-to-day problems without losing sight of long-range goals.

While there is a high risk in organizing any new business, the entrepreneur who is successful is seldom someone who could be considered a gambler. Most gamblers expect to have the odds against them. On the other hand, a clever businessperson sees to it that the odds are as good as possible by getting all of the facts and planning carefully before going ahead. Luck helps, to be sure, but a new business enterprise depends far more on good ideas and detailed plans.

## DESIGN TAB

The Table Styles group is located on the Table Tools Design tab. Styles contain font attributes, color, shading, and borders to enhance the appearance of a table.

Display additional styles by clicking the More button to show the entire style gallery. Three groups of table styles display: Plain, Grid, and List. Each style is given a name that indicates its group and the row in which it displays. For example, Grid Table 5 Dark – Accent 2 indicates that the style is located in the fifth row in the Grid Tables group. The table colors are labeled Accents 1 – 6 from left to right.

Move the mouse over each style to see your table formatted in that style. The name of the style will be displayed.

### To add, change, or remove a table style:
Table Tools Design/Table Styles

1. Click in the table where the style is to be applied and select the desired table style.

2. To see the entire style gallery, click the More button.

3. To change to another style, click in the table and choose a different style.

4. To remove a style, click the table and then click the More button. Below the gallery of styles, click Clear.

5. To make a change to the style, click in the table and then click the option you wish to change in the Table Style Options group.

☑ Header Row	☑ First Column
☐ Total Row	☐ Last Column
☑ Banded Rows	☐ Banded Columns
**Table Style Options**	

---

## DRILL 3 — APPLY STYLE AND TABLE STYLE OPTIONS

1. In the open document (*61-drill2*), display the entire style gallery. In the first row of the style gallery, choose Plain Table 1 style.

2. Move the mouse to the fourth row below Grid Tables; all styles in this row have the name *Grid Table 4*. The color of each table is labeled with Accent 1 – Accent 6. Move the mouse to the right to select Grid Table 4 – Accent 4 style.

3. Scroll down to display List Tables. Select List Table 6 Colorful – Accent 3 style (sixth row below List Tables).

4. Select Grid Table 5 Dark – Accent 6 style. In Table Style Options, deselect First Column. Reapply bold to the title row, if necessary.

5. Align all text vertically in the cells.

6. Center the table horizontally.

7. Proofread and check; click Next Activity. (*61-drill3*)

## Skill Building *Technique Builder*

### DRILL 19

**Opposite Hand Reaches**

Key at a controlled rate; concentrate on the reaches.

1 yj my say may yes rye yarn eye lye yap any relay young berry
y/t 2 tf at it let the vat tap item town toast right little attire
3 Yesterday a young youth typed a cat story on the typewriter.

4 bf but job fibs orb bow able bear habit boast rabbit brother
b/n 5 nj not and one now fun next pony month notice runner quicken
6 A number of neighbors banked on bunking in the brown cabins.

7 gag go gee god rig gun log gong cog gig agog gage going gang
g/h 8 huh oh hen the hex ash her hash ah hush shah hutch hand ache
9 Hush; Gregg hears rough sounds. Has Hugh laughed or coughed?

10 row or rid air rap par rye rear ark jar rip nor are right or
r/u 11 cut us auk out tutu sun husk but fun cub gun nut mud tug hug
12 Ryan is sure you should pour your food from an urn or cruet.

## Timed Writing

### Writing 33

Most people think traveling is fun because they associate travel with exciting vacations. People who have to travel as part of their jobs have a very different view of travel. They are more prone to view business travel as a hassle than a pleasure. Business travelers often have to work under less than ideal circumstances. While they are away from the office, regular work tends to pile up; and they often return to find stacks of work waiting for them. Many business travelers learn to utilize wisely the waiting time that is a part of most travel.

A successful business trip requires careful planning. The typical business traveler tends to think of a trip as a success if two conditions are met. The business goals must be achieved, and the trip must be totally free of headaches. The person making the trip has to worry about achieving the business goals, but a good travel agent can relieve the traveler of many of the worries of making travel arrangements. A good checklist can help to ensure that all the personal items as well as business items needed for the trip will be handy when they are needed.

### To adjust column width and row height:
Table Tools Layout/Cell Size

Column width can be adjusted by dragging column borders. Leave approximately 0.5" between the longest line and the border. Row height can be adjusted by dragging the row border until the row is the desired height.

For more precision, use the commands in the Cell Size group. Click in a cell, or select multiple cells, then use the spin arrows to increase or decrease column width or row height.

### To change text alignment:
Table Tools Layout/Alignment

The options in the Alignment group offer combinations of vertical and horizontal alignment that allow you to position text at the top, middle, or bottom of a table cell, as well as at the left, center, or right side of a cell.

### To change table alignment:
Table Tools Layout/Table/Properties

A table that is not full-page width is usually centered horizontally on the page. Use the Center Alignment command in the Table Properties dialog box to center the table horizontally.

The Table Properties dialog box can also be used to set table width. Place a check mark in the Preferred width checkbox and then key the desired table width in the box, or use the spin arrows to set the width.

## DRILL 2 — INSERT ROW, ADJUST COLUMN WIDTH, ROW HEIGHT, AND ALIGNMENT

1. In the open document (*61-drill1*), insert a row above row 1 and merge the cells.

2. Key **VOLARO NATIONAL PARK** in bold, 14-point font. Change the height of row 1 to 0.4". Align Center the text.

3. Change the height of rows 2–6 to 0.25". Align all text vertically in the cells.

4. Align Center all column heads.

5. Adjust column widths and center table horizontally.

6. Proofread and check; click Next Activity. (*61-drill2*)

# Advanced Business Correspondence

## LEARNING OUTCOMES

- Format memo and use templates.
- Format block and modified block business letters with special features.
- Format two-page memos and letters.
- Create envelopes with special notations.
- Improve keying speed and accuracy.

## Lesson 56 Memos and Productivity Tools

**New Commands**    • Templates    • Quick Parts

**Warmup**    *Lesson 56a Warmup*

A   ALL LETTERS

### Skill Building

#### 56b   Timed Writing

1. Key a 1' timing on each paragraph; work to increase speed.
2. Key a 3' timing on all paragraphs.

Good plans typically are required to execute most tasks successfully. If a task is worth doing, it is worth investing the time that is necessary to plan it effectively. Many people are anxious to get started on a task and just begin before they have thought about the best way to organize it. In the long run, they frequently end up wasting time that could be spent more profitably on important projects that they might prefer to tackle.

A task plan may or may not include organizational steps. The better a plan is organized, the more likely the execution of the plan will be successful. The way you plan and organize a task generally will depend on how frequently it has to be done. For tasks that are done occasionally, determine the quickest and the easiest way to complete the job. For repetitive tasks, try to automate them to save future time. The importance of the job is another factor that should be considered.

## TABLE TOOLS

Table tools are used to design and format tables. To display the Table Tools, click in the table and select either the Design or Layout tab.

### LAYOUT TAB

Commands in the Rows & Columns group and the Merge group can change the table structure and enhance its readability.

To insert and delete rows and columns:
Table Tools Layout/Rows & Columns

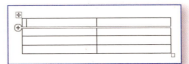

1. Click in the row or column to insert or delete.
2. Click the desired Insert option or click the Delete drop-list arrow and select the appropriate command.

   –or–

1. Position the mouse on the left edge or above the table.
2. Click the plus symbol to insert a new row or column.

To merge and split cells:
Table Tools Layout/Merge/Merge Cells or Split Cells

Merge joins cells horizontally or vertically. A common use of this command is to combine the cells in the first row for the heading of the table. Use Split Cells to create multiple columns below a single cell for a heading that spans multiple columns.

1. To merge cells, select the cells and click Merge Cells.
2. To split cells, click in the cell to be divided, or select multiple cells to divide, and then click the Split Cells command. Key the number of columns or rows into which the selected cell(s) will be divided.

## DRILL 1 — MERGE AND SPLIT CELLS

1. Create a 2-column, 5-row table.

2. Select cells B2–B5 and split into 2 columns and 4 rows. Merge cells A1 and A2.

3. Key the table below. Bold and center column heads. Align Right the cells that include pricing.

4. Proofread and check; click Next Activity. (61-drill1)

Hotel	Room Rates (per night)	
	Sunday – Thursday	Friday – Saturday
Bellflower Gardens	$139.00	$99.00
House of Five Gables	$265.00	$180.00
Ramona Beach House	$250.00	$325.00

## TEMPLATES

Templates are preformatted documents that can be used to create multiple documents with the same formats. Featured templates are placed on the hard drive during installation, and online templates are available from office.com. Suggested searches for templates include letters, resume, fax, labels, cards, calendar, and blank. After a template is opened, it can be customized with the user's specific information and saved as a custom office template.

---

## DOWNLOAD TEMPLATE AND CREATE A TEMPLATE

File/New

1. Click one of the suggested searches **1** or click in the Search for online templates box **2** and key a descriptive keyword. Click the Start searching arrow or tap ENTER.

2. Click the desired template and click Create.

3. Customize the template by adding company name, addresses, or other template elements.

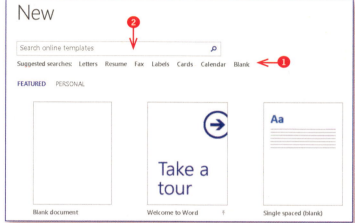

To save as a new template:

File/Save As

1. Click Computer and then Browse. Key a name such as **vanhuss memo** in the File name box. Change the Save as type to Word Template **3** and click Save. Note that the template is saved in the Custom Word Templates folder.

2. Click File, New, and then Personal. Click on the custom template you just created.

*KPDO* will open your template file as a document (*.docx*) data file. You will not download it.

# Documents with Tables and Graphics

## LEARNING OUTCOMES

- Create and format tables.
- Change table structure.
- Use table functions.
- Insert and format graphics.
- Use WordArt and SmartArt.
- Create documents with columns and graphics.
- Build keying speed and accuracy.

## Lesson 61 Table Tools

**Warmup**   *Lesson 61a Warmup*

**A   ALL LETTERS**

### Skill Building

#### 61b   Timed Writing

1. Key a 3' timing on each paragraph; work to increase speed.
2. Key a 3' timing on all paragraphs; work for control.

Beginning college students are very eager about beginning the next step in the journey after high school. Going away to college offers many opportunities and challenges to these young students. Choosing what time to attend classes, when to go to bed, when to get up, what to eat each day, and how to spend their money seems fantastic at an initial glance. But, wait, are these students adequately prepared for the hard choices that come with these freedoms?

One major area in which students need help is in making good food selections. Pizza, pasta, and macaroni and cheese do not make a wise choice even if these foods are easy to make and affordable. Be sure to have five fruits and vegetables each day and add some physical activity in the schedule. Remember nutritious meals and exercise are important to success in college.

If you saved the template to a flash drive, open the template and save as a *Word* document.

<think>The tip box content goes here</think>

## To create a new document with the template:
File/New

1. Click Personal to display the templates you have created.
2. Select the new template and click OK.
3. Key the new document and save it.

---

**DRILL 1**  |  **CREATE NEW TEMPLATE**

1. *KPDO* Users: Start with step 6. *Word* Users: In a new document, key **Memo** in the Search for online templates box.

2. Tap ENTER. Select Interoffice Memo (Professional Design) and download it.

3. Key **VanHuss & VanHuss, Inc.** in the Company Name box.

4. Delete the text below the horizontal line. Change font to Arial 10 point.

5. Save the template as **vanhuss memo**. (*Word* Users only; not for *KPDO*.)

6. In the open document (*vanhuss memo*), key the memo shown below.

7. Proofread and check; click Next Activity. (*56-drill1*)

---

To: Pat VanHuss | From: Susie VanHuss | cc: Connie Forde | Date: Current Date | Re: Customized Template for VanHuss & VanHuss

This template was downloaded from online templates by searching for memos in the Search for online templates box.

Note that the template was customized with our company name. Having our name stored with the template makes us more productive as we prepare memos. | xx

---

**QUICK ✓**

Check your document against the illustration below.

## 60-d4

**Letter**

 hess letterhead

Key a letter to **Mr. Robert Kaczynski, President | East Central Education Foundation**, with details about their fun run/walk that will be held on the Hess Office Park property. The mailing address is **30032 Johnson Street, Austin, TX 78712-0388**.

1.  Date the letter **November 14, 201-**.

2.  Use an attachment notation since this letter is being emailed to Mr. Kaczynski.

3.  Proofread and check; click Next Activity. (60-d4)

We are pleased to confirm that you will be hosting your annual 5K Scholarship Fun Run/Walk on our property Saturday, April 10, 201-. As we discussed at our initial meeting, parking will be available in the south parking lot all day Saturday. We will also have several spaces designated for you and your staff Friday beginning at noon.

We will have the entire boulevard around the office park blocked from 6 a.m. to 2 p.m. on Saturday starting at the intersection of Elm Street and Hess Boulevard. The run will start at 9 a.m. in front of the Hess Office Building and end at the same location. Tables and chairs will be set up along the race route for your volunteers to distribute drinks and snacks.

Security and police assistance will be provided at the main intersection of Hess Boulevard and Elm Street. Space will also be provided for your vendors near the entrance to the office park. Please provide all vendors with the attached traffic rules and map to our complex.

A wrap-up meeting is needed to finalize the remaining details. Please call or email me so we can schedule the meeting. We are pleased to assist you in this worthwhile event.

## 60-d5

**Compose Memo**

 hess memo

Mr. Hess has asked you to compose a memo for him to send to the **Owners and Tenants Association** informing the members of the change of date for the December meeting.

1.  In the first paragraph, explain that the December meeting was originally scheduled for Monday, December 1, at the offices of Schniepp Enterprises but has been changed to Tuesday, December 2. Explain that the reason for the change was to allow members to participate in the Christmas Parade scheduled for December 1.

2.  In the last paragraph, remind members that the January meeting will return to the first Monday of the month.

3.  Date the memo **November 15, 201-**. Supply an appropriate subject line that alerts the member to the date change.

4.  Proofread the document; then close. Click Exit *Word*. (60-d5)

5.  Click Log out to exit *KPDO*.

## BUILDING BLOCKS OVERVIEW

Quick Parts ▾

Documents can be segmented into parts called building blocks. Building blocks consist of formatted text, images, or other objects that can be saved and reused in other documents, such as a memo heading or closing lines of a letter.

## CREATE QUICK PARTS

The Quick Part Gallery is one of the galleries of building blocks. A Quick Part is created by selecting a segment of formatted text or an image and saving it in the Quick Part Gallery for reuse in other documents. The text and format can be used in new letters or memos without rekeying them. When you create the building block, save the following information about the new building block.

Name	Key a unique name that suggests the content of the building block.
Gallery	Click the down arrow to view all the galleries.
Category	General is a broad category to use, or create your own category name.
Description	Key a brief description of the building block.
Save in	Name of an open template. Typically, you will use Building Blocks.
Options	The options include: Insert content only, Insert content in its own paragraph, or Insert content in its own page.

To create a content building block that can be used in other documents:
Insert/Text/Quick Parts

1. Select the text you want to save as a building block. Make sure the text is formatted in the way you plan to use it.

2. Follow the path and click Save Selection to Quick Part Gallery ❶ to display the Create New Building Block dialog box. Note the options in the Create New Building Block dialog box that are described above.

3. Key the name of the building block (if you want to change the default name that displays) and the description. For now, use the other options that are filled in—Quick Part Gallery, General Category, Save in Building Blocks, and Insert content only. Click OK.

Hess Office Park is located at 100 Hess Boulevard and is home to 125 businesses that either own or lease offices located on 500 acres of beautiful wooded property that is conveniently located to downtown. Hess Office Park is managed by Hess Property Enterprises with a board of directors representing owners and investors of the office park. In addition to selling or leasing office space, we offer a number of other services that you may find beneficial. These services include the following:

**Insert Quick Part named *services* created in *60-d1*.**

As a tenant in Hess Office Park, you are automatically a member of the Owners and Tenants Association that meets the first Monday of each month at 7 p.m. at a hosting owner/tenant's office. In addition to the excellent programs initiated by the association, members also partner with the local community to sponsor award-winning programs that are enhancing our communities.

A map of the office park is attached with available office space highlighted including detailed space specifications. Additional brochures and fact sheets about Hess Office Park are also enclosed for your review.

I do look forward to meeting with you to discuss your leasing office space with us.

**60–d3**

Memo

 hess memo

Prepare the memo below for Mr. Hess to the **Owners and Tenants Association** informing them of the upcoming energy efficiency inspection.

1. Date the memo **November 14** and key the subject **Energy Efficiency Evaluation Scheduled for January**.
2. Proofread and check; click Next Activity. (*60-d3*)

As a result of action taken at the October meeting of the Owners and Tenants Association, I have contracted with Lehman-Bass Energy Services to complete an energy efficiency evaluation of all office space in our property. Inga Koch, senior engineer assigned to our contract, will attend our December meeting and explain the details of the energy efficiency evaluation and provide checklists for our preparation prior to the inspections.

Ms. Koch has already scheduled our inspections for January. You will be notified of your specific day and time at the December meeting.

If you have any questions, please call or email me.

**TIP**

Key the name or part of the name of the Quick Part and tap F3 to enter the Quick Part.

To add Quick Parts to a document:
Insert/Text/Quick Parts

1. Position the insertion point where you wish to insert the Quick Part in the document.
2. Follow the path and view the list of Quick Parts you have added.
3. Click the Quick Part you wish to insert. Repeat these steps for each Quick Part you want to add to the document.

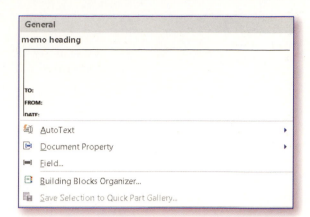

---

## DRILL 2 — CREATE QUICK PART

 heading

1. In the open document, select the entire document (CTRL + A).
2. Save the selection as a Quick Part.
3. Key the name and description **memo heading**; then click OK.
4. Proofread and check; click Next Activity.

---

## DRILL 3 — USE QUICK PART

1. Insert the building block *memo heading* that was created in Drill 2.
2. Complete the memo heading with **Julia Fortenberry** as the recipient of the memo and **Stephen Dill** as the sender.
3. Use the current date. The subject is **Memo Heading Inserted as Building Block**.
4. Proofread and check; click Next Activity. (*56-drill3*)

---

**QUICK ✔**

Check your document against the illustration below.

**TO:**	Julia Fortenberry
**FROM:**	Stephen Dill
**DATE:**	Current date
**SUBJECT:**	Memo Heading Inserted as Building Block

## 60-d1

**Quick Part**

You have worked for only one day and have observed that you are constantly keying a list of services for insertion in various office documents. To save keying time, key the bulleted list below and save as a Quick Part named **services**.

1. After keying the list, proofread carefully and save as a Quick Part. You will use the Quick Part in the next document.
2. Click Next Activity.

- A fee-based print and copy service center that is used by most of the small businesses managed by our company.

- Conference rooms that can be rented for the day or week and offices that can be rented by the month.

- A fee-based health and fitness center that is open 24 hours a day and 7 days a week. Personal trainers are available to outline the best possible fitness plan for each client.

- Three food service facilities that are managed by the company. These facilities are conveniently located and offer numerous dining options, including gluten-free and vegetarian.

- A fee-based child care center that is convenient for parents and managed by the company. The child care center opens at 6 a.m. and closes at 8 p.m.

- A fee-based pet center that offers two full-time veterinarians as well as grooming and boarding services.

## 60-d2

**Two-Page Letter**

 hess letterhead

In the open document, key the two-page letter for **Mr. Hess** to **Mr. Aiden Madison**, a prospective tenant he met at the Chamber Of Commerce meeting today. You are to add all the letter parts and format the letter. Mr. Madison's address is **1289 Maple Street, San Antonio, TX 78201-1289**.

1. Insert the Quick Part created in *60-d1* as directed in the text below.
2. Insert the second-page heading and suppress the heading on the first page.
3. Send a copy to **Jayden Mason**.
4. Create an envelope and add to the document.
5. Proofread and check; click Next Activity. (*60-d2*)

It was a pleasure meeting you today at the local Chamber of Commerce meeting. I know John Forde very well and appreciate his inviting you to our meeting and introducing you to me. I am pleased that you will be locating your business in Austin and am happy to share some information with you about the property and services available at Hess Office Park.

*(continued)*

**56d**

The memo is the most formal type of informal message and may be preferred over email when a somewhat formal communication with company employees is demanded, such as the announcement of a new policy or participation in a mandatory training program. While a memo may be printed and distributed internally, often this formal memo is attached to an email and distributed to all employees. In fact, *Word*'s Share option allows the user to email the memo as a *Word* attachment or a PDF without even opening the email system.

Study the formatting guidelines below and refer to the full model on the next page.

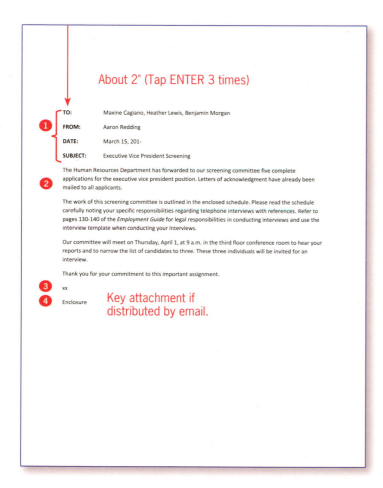

### Heading: 1

- Begin the memo about 2" from the top of the page.
- Format the memo heading in bold and uppercase.
- Tap TAB once or twice after each heading to align the text that follows each item. You may also set a left tab at 1" and tap TAB once.
- Tap the ENTER key once after each line of the heading.

### Body: 2

- Use the 1.08" default line spacing. Tap ENTER once after each paragraph.

### Notations:

- Reference initials 3: Tap ENTER once after the body.
- Enclosure or attachment notation 4: Key one line below the reference initials. Use *Enclosure* when items are enclosed in an envelope and *Attachment* if items are attached with the memo to an email.
- Key the copy notation one line below the enclosure notation or one line below the reference initials if no enclosure notation is needed.

### Distribution lists:

When memos are sent to more than one person, key the names after the word TO and separate them with commas, or key them in a list. Generally, names should be in alphabetical order by last name or listed in order of rank.

TO: Maxine Cagiano, Heather Lewis, Benjamin Morgan     or     TO:     Maxine Cagiano
Heather Lewis
Benjamin Morgan

# Lesson 60 Hess Office Park

## Skill Building

### 60b Timed Writing

1. Key a 1' timing on each paragraph; work to increase speed.
2. Key a 3' timing on all paragraphs.

If you wish to advance in your career, you must learn how to make good decisions. You can develop decision-making skills by learning to follow six basic steps. The first three steps help you to see the problem. They are identifying the problem, analyzing the problem to find causes and consequences, and making sure you define the goals that your solution must meet.

Now you are ready to solve the problem using the last three steps. They include finding alternative solutions to the problem, analyzing each of the alternatives carefully to locate the best solution, and putting the best solution into action. Once you have implemented a plan of action, check to make sure that it meets all of your objectives. If it does not, then determine if the problem is with the solution or with the way it is being implemented. Always keep all options open.

## Project Setting

 **NOTE**

Hess Property Enterprises prefers to use periods rather than hyphens to separate units in telephone numbers. Parentheses are not used for the area code.

Using periods and no parentheses is the current trend in industry today.

### HESS OFFICE PARK

At the end of each module in this book, you will work as an assistant to Patrick J. Hess, manager of Hess Office Park, a 500-acre office park managed by Hess Property Enterprises. You will apply the keying, formatting, and word processing skills that you have developed in the module.

You will learn to apply **standard operating procedures** (SOPs). These procedures enable you to work independently without extensive directions. Pay particular attention to the SOPs and the documents you prepare in this lesson because they will provide you with information that you will use each time you work with Hess Office Park. The logo and contact information are shown below.

**Hess Office Park**
100 Hess Boulevard, Austin, TX 78712-2149
Phone 512.555.0157 | Fax 512.555.0158
www.hesspropertyenterprises.com

 **TIP**

Read the letter prepared in *60-d2* to learn about Hess Office Park. Read the standard operating procedures for the project carefully. You will not be reminded to do these steps. Refer to them as needed during the project.

### Standard operating procedures for the project:

1. Use block letter style with open punctuation and the Hess Office Park letterhead from the data files. Include an appropriate salutation and use Sincerely as the complimentary closing. Begin the data at approximately 2". Use **Patrick J. Hess | Manager** as the writer's name and title.

2. Prepare all documents using Retrospect document theme.

3. Create envelopes for letters only when directed, as many letters are attached to an email.

4. The data files also contain a Hess Office Park memo form. Use an appropriate subject line if a subject line is not provided.

5. Add your reference initials and other notations as appropriate.

About 2" (Tap ENTER 3 times)

**TO:**        Maxine Cagiano, Heather Lewis, Benjamin Morgan ↓ 1

**FROM:**     Aaron Redding ↓ 1

**DATE:**     March 15, 201- ↓ 1

**SUBJECT:**  Executive Vice President Screening ↓ 1

The Human Resources Department has forwarded to our screening committee five complete applications for the executive vice president position. Letters of acknowledgment have already been mailed to all applicants. ↓ 1

The work of this screening committee is outlined in the enclosed schedule. Please read the schedule carefully noting your specific responsibilities regarding telephone interviews with references. Refer to pages 130-140 of the *Employment Guide* for legal responsibilities in conducting interviews and use the interview template when conducting your interviews.

Our committee will meet on Thursday, April 1, at 9 a.m. in the third floor conference room to hear your reports and to narrow the list of candidates to three. These three individuals will be invited for an interview.

Thank you for your commitment to this important assignment. ↓ 1

Typist's first and last initials

xx ↓ 1

Enclosure

Key **Enclosure** if item distributed with memo is in an envelope; key **Attachment** when memo and items are distributed by email.

Memo

### 59-d1

**Two-Page Letter**

brown-mayfield ltrhd
testing

1. In the open document, key just through the first paragraph of the two-page letter shown on pages 279–280.
2. Insert the data file *testing* below the first paragraph (Insert/Text/Object/Text from File), which is the remaining text of the two-page letter. **Note:** Be sure to position the insertion point where you want the text to appear before inserting the file.
3. Create a header to include the three required items of a multiple-page header.
4. Tap ENTER once after the date to leave one blank line between the header and the letter. Suppress the header on the first page.
5. Add a copy notation to **Susan Wyman**.
6. Proofread and check; click Next Activity. (*59-d1*)

### 59-d2

**Two-Page Letter**

application

**REVIEW**

**Date**

Insert/Text/Date & Time

1. In the open document, position the date at about 2" and format as a modified block document with mixed punctuation.
2. Add the mailing notation **Confidential**.
3. Add the reference line **Re: Position #1839**.
4. Create a header to include the three required items of a multiple-page header. Insert the Date command and choose to update automatically.
5. Tap ENTER once after the date to leave one blank line between the header and the letter. Suppress the header on the first page.
6. Delete the reference initials since this is a personal business letter prepared by the sender.
7. Create an envelope and add to the document; key the mailing notation **Confidential** below the return address at about 1".
8. Proofread and check; click Log out to exit *KPDO*. (*59-d2*)

Spanic/iStockphoto.com

## ! WORKPLACE SUCCESS

Letters should be carefully planned. List all the points that need to be covered and make sure they relate to the main purpose of the letter. Letters need to be accurate and written in a timely manner. Business letters often have financial implications, so check to make sure that all stated facts are accurate.

Letters are a more formal means of communicating than are emails, text messages, or memos. Letters should be formal and factual, and at the same time be reader friendly. If the letter is part of a package, limit the cover letter to one page and relegate technical details to enclosed documents. Avoid language that is specific to gender, race, or religion in all business correspondence. For example, use words such as workforce rather than manpower and chairperson rather than chairman.

**56-d1**    **Memo**

1. Key the memo on page 264.
2. Proofread and check, click Next Activity. (*56-d1*)

---

**56-d2**

**Create Quick Part**

 memo letterhead

1. In the open document, select the entire document by pressing CTRL + A. Create a Quick Part named **sanchez memo letterhead**.
2. Key the description **sanchez memo letterhead**. Click OK.
3. Proofread; click Next Activity. You will use the Quick Part in the next document.

---

**56-d3**

**Use Memo Quick Part**

1. In a new document, insert the Quick Part *sanchez memo letterhead* created in *56-d2*. Key the memo shown below.
2. Key your reference initials and the attachment notation.
3. Proofread and check; click Next Activity. (*56-d3*)

---

To: New Sales Representatives | Date: Current date | Subject: Focus on Recycling and Reusing

As you talk with potential clients, please remember to emphasize recycling and reusing. Before meeting with clients, review their business operations and have specific recommendations for both recycling and reusing. Here are a few examples you might share.

1. Recycling: Purchase products that can be recycled and that have minimal packaging. Set up special recycle boxes that are easy and convenient for everyone to use.

2. Reusing: Make double-side copies, reuse office supplies (such as file folders and hanging files), use the back of used paper for scratch paper, reuse interoffice envelopes, save to a hard drive or server to avoid printing, and use ceramic mugs instead of disposable cups.

Please refer to the attached newsletter that highlights unique and effective ways that our current clients are cutting costs while sustaining our world.

---

**56-d4**

**New Template from Existing Template**

1. *KPDO* Users: Start with step 2. *Word* Users: In a new document, download the Fax cover sheet (featuring eFax App for Word 2013) template.
2. In the open document (*vanhuss fax*), key **VanHuss & VanHuss, Inc.** in the company Name Box. Key the contact information: **120 East Main Street | Ada, OK 74820-5602 | Phone: 580.555.0188 | Fax: 580.555.0143 | www.vanhuss&vanhuss.com** and **FROM: Susie VanHuss**
3. (*Word* users only; not for *KPDO*.) Save as a *Word* template named **vanhuss fax**. The template will be saved to Custom Office Templates unless your instructor directs you otherwise. Close the template.
4. Proofread; click Exit *Word*. (*56-d4*) Click Log out to exit *KPDO*.

Mr. Dylan Franz
Page 2
Current date

The enclosed packet of materials provides you with detailed information about the testing system, training, and costs for a site license.

Sincerely

Vikram Yadama
Sales Manager

xx

Enclosure

c       Susan Wyman

**Two-Page Letter, Page 2**

# Lesson 57 Letter Review

## Skill Building

### 57b Textbook Keying

Key each line once, concentrating on using good keying techniques.

adjacent reaches

1 Sand castles are fun to build but are poor shelter in a downpour.
2 The Hoosiers scored three points in the fourth to avoid an upset.
3 Her articles are going to be reported in an edition of the paper.
4 Fewer people attend West Point to play polo than to join a choir.
5 A dazed beggar scattered after a red car swerved on a wet street.

one hand

6 Mimi feasts on milky eggs at noon after I feed Kipp plum dessert.
7 Mo started ragweed tests in a vacated garage after greeting Dave.
8 You debate Phil after I defeat John; rest up, you brave braggart!
9 Handiwork is busy work, but it's also a memento of a rich entity.

balanced hand

10 The hairy ape bit the fish, but the apricot and corn lay dormant.
11 Henry may dismantle an authentic antique auto for Zoe's sorority.
12 An Irish auditor quit work at the city and ambled to the fields.

## Communication

### 57c

References/Communication Skills/Commas

1. Complete the Comma exercise in *KPDO*.
2. For each group of sentences, select the sentence that has applied the use of commas correctly. Key the sentence number and then key the letter that corresponds to the correct sentence, e.g., (1a).
2. Proofread and check; click Next Activity. (57c)

**1a.** The legislators voted on Policy #2083 on May 23, 2010, at 5 p.m.
**1b.** The legislators voted on Policy #2,083 on May 23, 2010 at 5 p.m.

**2a.** To view Michelle's entire social networking site I need her permission.
**2b.** To view Michelle's entire social networking site, I need her permission.

**3a.** The parents volunteered to bring coffee, juice, milk, and pastries.
**3b.** The parents volunteered to bring coffee juice milk and pastries.

**4a.** Several club members designed an attractive logo, and the fundraising committee created an online store for selling merchandise.
**4b.** Several club members designed an attractive logo and the fundraising committee created an online store for selling merchandise.

**5a.** Mr. Rankin explained "Monday is the deadline for our class blog."
**5b.** Mr. Rankin explained, "Monday is the deadline for our class blog."

**6a.** The independent film festival will be held in Baton Rouge, Louisiana, on May 11-15.
**6b.** The independent film festival will be held in Baton Rouge Louisiana on May 11-15.

**7a.** Chef Nate I appreciate your answering my questions about organic gardening on your blog.
**7b.** Chef Nate, I appreciate your answering my questions about organic gardening on your blog.

**Brown-Mayfield Corporate Development**

203 East Ridge Road, Bangor, ME 04401
Telephone: 207.555.0132    Fax: 207.555.0133

Current date

Mr. Dylan Franz
Human Resources Department
Covin Industries
23891 Magnolia Street
Birmingham, AL 35244-9730

Dear Mr. Franz

Automated Test Development and Generation System    <span style="color:red">Subject line</span>

Recently, we decided to upgrade our system and market it as a system rather than as a complete testing service provided by our staff. The system automates all phases of assessment: generating tests, taking tests, and scoring tests. It enables an organization such as yours to incorporate quality testing in the selecting and training of employees.

Users have identified numerous advantages of our automated test development and generation system. The test generation component enables you to maintain a large database of all standard types of test items, including the following:

True/False	Modified true/false
Multiple choice	Multiple answer
Fill in the blank	Matching
Numeric response	Short answer
Essay	Problem
Case	Bimodal
Yes/no	Ordering

Validated items enable you to generate a test automatically that meets high standards. These items are stored with complex competency identifiers, answer keys, critiques of answers, and a variety of item statistics.

The test administration component enables your employees to take the test in an online testing setting. At the conclusion of the tests, the results with feedback can be viewed by the employee.

The scoring component enables you to produce score reports and itemize analysis statistics. These statistics can then be added to the item database to be used in future test generation purposes. In addition to individual score reports, reports for groups and a variety of subgroups can be prepared automatically.

**Two-Page Letter, Page 1**

# BUSINESS LETTER REVIEW

References/Documents Formats/Block Letter and Modified Block Letter

The block letter style and modified block letter style are the typical business letter formats used. The two punctuation styles include open and mixed punctuation.

**Block letter style:** All letter parts are keyed at the left margin.

**Modified block style:** Date, complimentary closing, writer's name and title are keyed at the center of the page.

**Open punctuation:** Does not include punctuation after the salutation or after the complimentary closing.

**Mixed punctuation:** Includes a colon after the salutation and comma after complimentary closing.

Compare the illustrations below to understand each letter style and punctuation style. Full-page models are shown on pages 269–270.

**Block Letter Style with Open Punctuation**

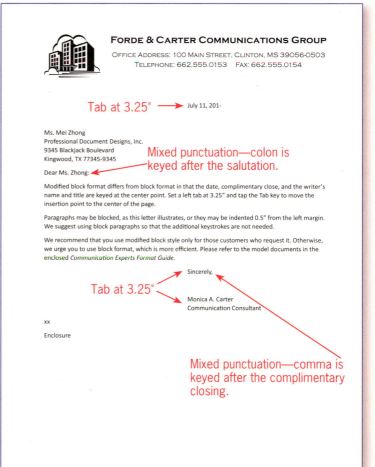

**Modified Block Letter Style with Mixed Punctuation**

**Insert/Header & Footer/Header**

1. In the open document, create a header for the second page of the memo. Include the recipient's name, page number, and date.

2. Tap ENTER once after keying the date. Do not print the header on the first page.

3. Proofread and check; click Next Activity. *(59-drill1)*

## Document Design ⟩ TWO-PAGE LETTERS AND MEMOS

Letters and memos that are more than one page in length require special layout considerations. For letters, use letterhead paper for the first page only, and for additional pages, use plain paper that matches the letterhead in quality and color. Be sure that there are at least two lines of text from the final paragraph of the body on the last page with the closing lines. Study the full-page model on pages 279–280.

### To format multipage letters and memos:

1. Position the date on the first page approximately 2" from the top of the page. Be sure the date begins 0.5" below the letterhead.

2. Begin the text on the second and succeeding pages at 1".

3. Create a header ❶ that includes the recipient's name, page number, and date on separate lines, and suppress the header on the first page.

**Page 1**                    **Page 2**

## LETTER PARTS

**Letterhead:** Preprinted stationery that includes the company name, logo, address, and other optional information, such as a telephone number, email address, or web address.

**Dateline:** Date the letter is prepared. Position at about 2" (tap ENTER three times); begin at least 0.5" below the letterhead.

**Block Letter with Open Punctuation**

**Letter address:** Complete address of letter recipient. Tap ENTER two times after the date. Generally includes receiver's name, company name, street address, city, state (one space after the state), and ZIP Code. Include personal title (Mr., Ms., Dr.). Capitalize the first letter of each word. Remove the added space between the lines of the letter address.

**Salutation (or greeting):** Tap ENTER one time after the letter address. Include a courtesy title with the name, e.g., Dear Mr. Nibert. Use *Ladies and Gentlemen* when addressing a company.

**Body:** Message of the letter. Tap ENTER one time after the salutation. Use the 1.08" default line spacing; tap ENTER once between paragraphs.

**Complimentary closing:** Formal good-bye. Tap ENTER one time after the body. Capitalize only the first letter of the first word of the closing.

**Writer's name and title:** Tap ENTER two times after the complimentary closing. Include a personal title (Mr., Ms.) only if it is not apparent to the reader if the person is male or female (Jan, Pat, Chris). Key the name and title on either one or two lines, whichever gives better balance. Use a comma to separate name and title if on one line. If two lines are used, remove the added space between the two lines.

**Reference initials:** Tap ENTER one time after the writer's name and title. Replace *xx* with your initials. Include no spaces or periods.

**Enclosure notation:** Tap ENTER one time after the reference initials. If multiple enclosures are listed, set a tab at 1" and remove added space between lines.

**Copy notation:** Tap ENTER one time after the reference initials or enclosure notation if an enclosure notation is included. If multiple copies are listed, set a tab at 0.5" to align and remove added space between lines.

**New Commands**      • Header

**New Commands**

**59b**

## HEADER

A header contains text that is keyed in the top margin of the page. Generally the header is suppressed on the first page. In this module you will prepare a header for a two-page memo and letter.

To insert a header for a multiple-page letter or memo:
Insert/Header & Footer/Header

1. Display the Built-in gallery of Header styles. Click the Blank style.

2. Key the name of the recipient and tap ENTER.

3. Key **Page** followed by a space.

4. From the Header & Footer group, click the Page Number drop-list arrow and choose Current Position. Choose the Plain Number style. Tap ENTER.

5. In the Insert group, click Date & Time. Select the month, day, and year format (October 10, 201-). Tap ENTER to leave a blank space between the header and the first line of the text.

6. In the Options group, select Different First Page to suppress the header on the first page.

📄	Top of Page	▶
📄	Bottom of Page	▶
📄	Page Margins	▶
📄	Current Position	▶
📄	Format Page Numbers...	
📄	Remove Page Numbers	

☑ Different First Page
☐ Different Odd & Even Pages
☑ Show Document Text

Options

To edit a header:
Insert/Header & Footer/Header

To edit a header, click Edit Header. An alternate method is to double-click in the header section of the document. To move to the text of the document, double-click in the document—not the header.

To remove a header, click Remove Header.

Mr. Scott Collins
Page 2
Current date
— Tap ENTER once after date to leave blank line.

The enclosed packet of materials provides you with detailed information about the testing software and costs for a site license. Our sales representative, Susan Wyman, will call you next week to answer questions you might have about the software.

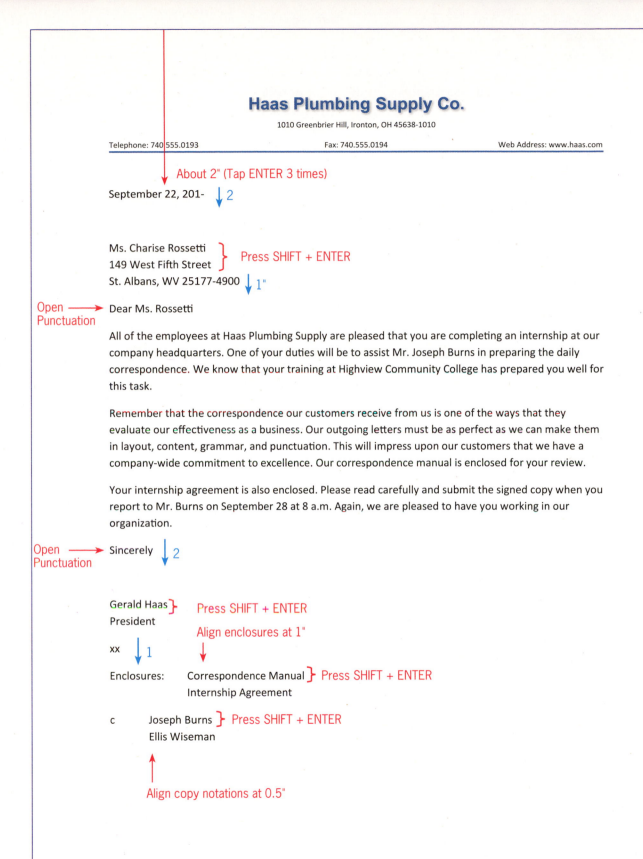

## Haas Plumbing Supply Co.

1010 Greenbrier Hill, Ironton, OH 45638-1010

Telephone: 740 555.0193          Fax: 740.555.0194          Web Address: www.haas.com

About 2" (Tap ENTER 3 times)

September 22, 201-  ↓ 2

Ms. Charise Rossetti  } Press SHIFT + ENTER
149 West Fifth Street
St. Albans, WV 25177-4900  ↓ 1"

Open → Dear Ms. Rossetti
Punctuation

All of the employees at Haas Plumbing Supply are pleased that you are completing an internship at our company headquarters. One of your duties will be to assist Mr. Joseph Burns in preparing the daily correspondence. We know that your training at Highview Community College has prepared you well for this task.

Remember that the correspondence our customers receive from us is one of the ways that they evaluate our effectiveness as a business. Our outgoing letters must be as perfect as we can make them in layout, content, grammar, and punctuation. This will impress upon our customers that we have a company-wide commitment to excellence. Our correspondence manual is enclosed for your review.

Your internship agreement is also enclosed. Please read carefully and submit the signed copy when you report to Mr. Burns on September 28 at 8 a.m. Again, we are pleased to have you working in our organization.

Open → Sincerely  ↓ 2
Punctuation

Gerald Haas } Press SHIFT + ENTER
President

Align enclosures at 1"

xx  ↓ 1

Enclosures:      Correspondence Manual } Press SHIFT + ENTER
                 Internship Agreement

c        Joseph Burns } Press SHIFT + ENTER
         Ellis Wiseman

Align copy notations at 0.5"

**Block Letter with Open Punctuation**

**58-d1**

**Block Letter**

hill univ letterhead

1. In the open document, key the letter with special letter parts on page 275.
   **Note:** Most letters do not include this many special letter parts.
2. Proofread and check; click Next Activity. (*58-d1*)

---

**58-d2**

**Envelope**

1. Create an envelope for John Conner, one of the recipients of a blind copy in *58-d1*. The address is **Mr. John Conner, 209 Sweet Acre Drive, Decatur, AL 35601-4892**.
2. At about 1", key the mailing notation **CONFIDENTIAL**. At about 1.2", right-aligned, key the mailing notation **SPECIAL DELIVERY**.
3. Proofread and check; click Next Activity. (*58-d2*)

---

**58-d3**

**Modified Block Letter**

fair

1. In the open document, format the letter as a modified block letter with mixed punctuation.
2. In the correct position, key the attention line **Attention Order Department**.
3. In the correct position, key the subject line **Annual Craft Fair Booth**.
4. Proofread and check; click Next Activity. (*58-d3*)

---

**58-d4**

**Compose Letter**

**TIP**

Do not key reference initials since you are the writer of this letter.

1. Compose a letter of appreciation to a person who has recently done something for you. Examples may include served as a job reference, directed you to a resource, introduced you to a potential employer, or spoke to your class.
2. Key all the letter parts for a block letter with open punctuation. Be sure to check for accurate mailing information for the letter address.
3. Key **Thank You** as the subject of the letter.
4. In the body of the letter, first thank the person for the specific action or gift that was given to you. Next explain specific reasons why you are grateful and how you have benefited from this kindness (e.g., after the introduction to Mr. Jones you now have an interview scheduled next week).
5. Send a blind copy to your instructor.
6. Proofread; close the document. (*58-d4*)
7. Click Exit *Word*.
8. Click Log out to exit *KPDO*.

## FORDE & CARTER COMMUNICATIONS GROUP

OFFICE ADDRESS: 100 MAIN STREET, CLINTON, MS 39056-0503
TELEPHONE: 662.555.0153    FAX: 662.555.0154

*About 2" (Tap ENTER 3 times)*

*Tab 3.25"* → July 11, 201-

Ms. Mei Zhong
Professional Document Designs, Inc.
9345 Blackjack Boulevard
Kingwood, TX 77345-9345

Dear Ms. Zhong:    *Mixed Punctuation*

Modified block format differs from block format in that the date, complimentary close, and the writer's name and title are keyed at the center point. Set a left tab at 3.25" and tap the Tab key to move the insertion point to the center of the page.

Paragraphs may be blocked, as this letter illustrates, or they may be indented 0.5" from the left margin. We suggest using block paragraphs so that the additional keystrokes are not needed.

We recommend that you use modified block style only for those customers who request it. Otherwise, we urge you to use block format, which is more efficient. Please refer to the model documents in the enclosed *Communication Experts Format Guide*.

Sincerely,    *Mixed Punctuation*

*Tab 3.25"*

Monica A. Carter
Communication Consultant

xx

Enclosure

**Modified Block Letter with Mixed Punctuation**

About 2" (Tap ENTER 3 times)
May adjust date higher if special parts
move too far down on page.

# Hill University

Cultural Center                                             Erin   Bland, Coordinator

Box 910

Charleston, WV 25301-0910 | 304.555.0167 | www.hillculturalcenter.edu

May 25, 201-

SPECIAL DELIVERY          Mailing notation

Attention Order Department
Redmon Publishers
5280 Circle Point
Long Beach, CA 90840-0792

Re: Purchase Order W1029 ⟵          Reference line

Ladies and Gentlemen

Summer Workshop ⟵          Subject line

The Cultural Center at Hill University is hosting a summer workshop entitled "Women of the Mountains." Elizabeth is our keynote speaker, and we know our attendees will be clamoring for her exciting book, *The Legacy of Mountain Women*.

A purchase order with shipping instructions for 100 copies of Ms. Gainwright's book is enclosed. These books must be delivered to the Massey Convention Center during the first week in June where they will be stored until the seminar on June 15.

If you have questions regarding this order, please call me at 10 a.m. or 2 p.m. on either Thursday or Friday. We appreciate your assisting us with this order and special delivery.

Sincerely

Erin Bland, Coordinator

xx

Enclosure

bc        John Connor          Blind copy notation (Not printed on the addressee's copy)
          Angela Ward

**Special Letter Parts**

**57-d1**

**Create Quick Part**

 closing

1. In the open document, select the closing lines used by Gerald Haas (complimentary closing through reference initials) and create a Quick Part named **Gerald Closing Lines**.
2. Key the description **Gerald Closing lines**.
3. Proofread; click Next Activity. You will use the Quick Part in the next document.

**57-d2**

**Block Letter**

 haas letterhead

1. In the open document, key the block letter on page 269 with open punctuation. Begin the date at about 2".
2. Insert the Quick Part *Gerald Closing lines*, created in *57-d1* above.
3. Align the enclosure notations at the default tab set at 1".
4. Send a copy to **Joseph Burns** and **Ellis Wiseman**; align the names at the default 0.5" tab.
5. Press SHIFT + ENTER to remove the added space between the letter address, writer's name and title, enclosures, and individuals receiving copies of this letter.
6. Add an envelope to the letter. (Mailings/Create/Envelope)
7. Proofread and check; click Next Activity. (*57-d2*)

**57-d3**

**Modified Block Letter**

 f & c letterhead

1. In the open document, key the modified block letter on page 270 with mixed punctuation.
2. Set a left tab at 3.25" for keying the date, complimentary close, writer's name, and title. *Hint:* To set a left tab, check the tab selector to be sure the left tab is selected. Then, click the Horizontal Ruler where you want to set the left tab.

3. Add an envelope to the letter.
4. Proofread and check; click Next Activity. (*57-d3*)

**57-d4**

**Block Letter**

 puppies

1. In the open document, add the letter parts that are missing and format the letter as a block letter with open punctuation. Here is information you will need.

   Date: **Use current date**

   Letter recipient: **Ms. Sarah Atkinson, 1234 Elm Lane, Bronx, NY 10466-1234**

   Sender of letter: **Andrew Rogers | Kennel Manager**

   Salutation: **Dear Ms. Atkinson**

   Complimentary closing: **Sincerely**

   Copy: **Daniel Foster**

   Attachment notation is needed as letter and picture are being attached to email.
2. Add an envelope to the letter.
3. Proofread and check; click Exit *Word*. (*57-d4*)
4. Click Log out to exit *KPDO*.

A **blind copy notation** (bc) indicates that others are receiving a copy of the letter without the addressee's knowledge. Tap ENTER one time after the reference initials, enclosure notation, or copy notation (if any). The blind copy notation appears on copies but not on the original. Align multiple recipients at the 0.5" tab. **Note:** Email messages containing attached letters may be addressed with blind copy recipients.

John Mastrangelo, President
xx
Enclosure
bc      Norman Elswick
Sheila Solari

A **mailing notation** such as FACSIMILE, OVERNIGHT, SPECIAL DELIVERY, or REGISTERED provides a record of how the letter was sent. Other notations such as CONFIDENTIAL or PERSONAL indicate how the recipient should treat the letter.

Key special notations in UPPERCASE at the left margin one line below the date. On the envelope, key notations that affect postage right-aligned below the stamp (about line 1.2"). Key envelope notations that pertain to the recipient below the return address (about line 1").

December 14, 201-
CONFIDENTIAL
Mr. Joshua Clinard
Clinard Security Services
207 Hollyhill Avenue
Downers Grove, IL 60515-0935
Dear Mr. Clinard

To add notations to an envelope:

1. Click the Add to Document button.
2. Position the insertion point one line space below the return address or about 1". Key the recipient's notation, e.g., CONFIDENTIAL, at the left margin.
3. Position the insertion point on about 1.2". Click the Align Right button. Key the mailing notation, e.g., SPECIAL DELIVERY.

# Lesson 58 Special Letter Parts

## Skill Building

### 58b  Timed Writing

1. Key a 1' timing on each paragraph; work to increase speed.
2. Key a 3' timing on all paragraphs.

You may be familiar with the expression that we live in an information age now. People interpret this expression in a host of diverse ways, but most people agree on two key things. The first thing is that a huge amount of information exists today; some even think we suffer from information overload. The second thing is that technology has changed the way we access these large pools of data.

Some people are quick to point out that a large difference exists between the quantity and the quality of information. It is very critical to recognize that anyone who has access can simply post information on the Internet. No test exists to screen for junk before something is posted. Some of the data may be helpful and accurate. However, much of it must be analyzed quite carefully to judge if it is valid.

Just how do you ascertain if the data accessed is valid? Some of the similar techniques that can be used with print media can be applied with electronic media. An effective way to assess material is to examine its source carefully. What do you know about the people who provided this information? If you cannot unearth the answer to this question, you should be wary of trusting it.

## Communicating Today ▶

### TRENDS IN SPECIAL LETTER PARTS

Only when special circumstances demand it, a letter will include one or more of several special letter parts used commonly in business today. These special letter parts include mailing notations, reference line, attention line, subject line, enclosure/attachment notations, and copy notations.

Although technology has changed the manner in which we distribute letters, mailing notations are very important as they provide special directions on how a letter is treated by the writer and how it will be treated upon arrival by the recipient. This mailing notation keyed on the letter serves as an official record of the exact treatment specified and received.

A change to note is the use of blind copies. As many letters are now attached to emails, businesses are using the bc section of their email systems to send blind copies of the letter to those recipients that are not to be known by the recipient.

Another change we find is the increased use of the attachment notation. This change is evident as more letters are being attached to an email rather than mailed. The letter is attached along with the attachments mentioned in the letter.

# Document Design

## SPECIAL LETTER PARTS

**58c**

References/Document
Formats/Letter with Special Parts

Special letter parts may often be added to a business letter. When adding special letter parts causes the letter to move too far down on the page, adjust the date higher than the standard 2". Always preview letters to determine the most attractive appearance. Be sure the date begins 0.5" below the letterhead. Special letter parts are explained below and illustrated on a full-page model on page 275.

An **attention line** is used to direct a letter to a position or department within an organization. It is keyed as the first line of the letter address. Whenever an attention line is used to direct a letter to a department, division, or company, the correct salutation is *Ladies and Gentlemen*. If it is used for a specific position title, then the salutation would be Dear (position title), such as *Dear Office Manager*.

> Attention Accounting Department
> Chou and Chou Furniture Company
> 189 First Avenue
> Olympia, WA 99504-6480
>
> Ladies and Gentlemen:

A **reference line** is used to direct the reader to source documents or to files. Tap ENTER one time after the letter address.

> Ms. Allison Raymond
> P.O. Box 3100
> Natchez, MS 39120-2030
>
> Re: Order No. R1084
>
> Dear Ms. Raymond:

A **subject line** provides the reader with a short description of the purpose of the letter. Tap ENTER one time after the salutation. Key the subject line using initial caps; do not key the word *Subject*.

> Dear Mr. Jones:
>
> Projected Sales Figures
>
> The sales figures for the first quarter have been released.

# Appendices

# Appendix A Numeric Keypad

## Skill Building

**Keypad Lessons**

Keypad instruction is available from the Keypad tab in KPDO. The NUMLOCK key must be on for you to use the software. The Summary Report shows the exercise you have completed and the scores achieved. Complete each lesson before keying the related practice on the next few pages.

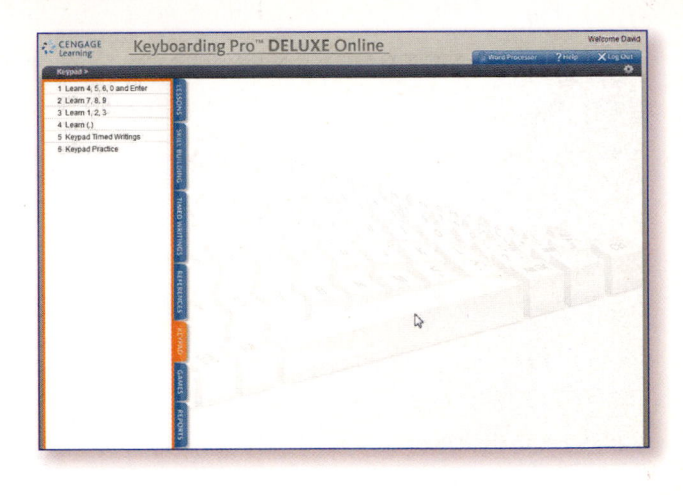

**Keypad Timed Writings**

Select Keypad Analysis on the Keypad lesson menu for additional keypad practice. Nine activities are available, each of which emphasizes a certain row or number type.

**Keypad Practice**

Select the Keypad Practice button to practice the exercises on the next few pages. Tap ENTER on the keypad after each number. Tap ENTER twice to sum the amounts keyed. Click the Print button to print the figures.

## DRILL 1

### 4, 5, 6, 0

Complete Lesson 1 before keying Drill 1.

1. Turn on NUMLOCK. Click the Keypad Practice button.
2. Tap ENTER after each number.
3. To obtain a total, tap ENTER twice after the last number in a group.
4. Key each problem until the same answer is obtained twice; you can then be reasonably sure that you have the correct answer.

Follow these directions for each lesson.

© Cengage Learning

a	b	c	d	e	f
46	55	56	46	55	56
45	64	45	45	64	45
66	56	64	66	56	64
56	44	65	56	44	65
54	65	45	54	65	45
65	54	44	65	54	44
466	445	546	654	465	665
564	654	465	545	446	645
456	464	546	545	564	456
556	544	644	466	644	646
644	455	464	654	464	554
454	546	565	554	456	656
400	404	505	606	500	600
404	505	606	500	600	400
500	600	400	404	505	606
650	506	404	550	440	550
506	460	605	460	604	640
406	500	640	504	460	560
504	640	550	440	660	406
560	450	650	450	505	550
640	504	440	640	450	660
400	600	500	500	600	400
650	505	404	606	540	560
504	404	640	404	406	606

## DRILL 2

### 7, 8, 9

Complete Lesson 2 before keying Drill 2.

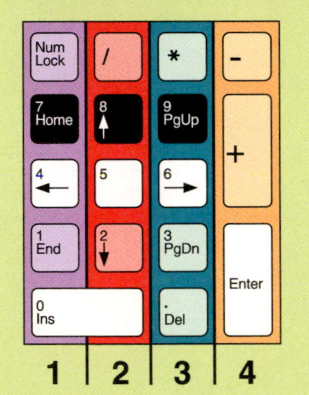

© Cengage Learning

**1   2   3   4**

a	b	c	d	e	f
74	85	96	70	80	90
47	58	96	87	78	98
90	70	80	90	90	70
89	98	78	89	77	87
86	67	57	48	68	57
59	47	48	67	58	69
470	580	690	770	707	407
999	969	888	858	474	777
777	474	888	585	999	696
858	969	747	770	880	990
757	858	959	857	747	678
579	849	879	697	854	796
857	967	864	749	864	795
609	507	607	889	990	448
597	847	449	457	684	599
85	74	96	98	78	88
957	478	857	994	677	579
657	947	479	76	94	795
887	965	789	577	649	849
90	80	70	806	709	407
407	567	494	97	80	70
50	790	807	90	75	968
408	97	66	480	857	57
87	479	567	947	808	970
690	85	798	587	907	89
94	754	879	67	594	847
489	880	97	907	69	579

**1, 2, 3**

Complete Lesson 3 before keying Drill 3.

★ **TECHNIQUE TIP**

Keep fingers curved and upright over home keys. Keep right thumb tucked under palm.

© Cengage Learning

a	b	c	d	e	f
11	22	33	14	15	16
41	52	63	36	34	35
24	26	25	22	42	62
27	18	39	30	20	10
30	30	10	19	61	43
32	31	21	53	83	71
414	141	525	252	636	363
141	111	252	222	363	333
111	414	222	525	333	636
111	141	222	252	366	336
152	342	624	141	243	121
330	502	331	302	110	432
913	823	721	633	523	511
702	612	513	712	802	823
213	293	821	813	422	722
24	36	15	12	32	34
115	334	226	254	346	246
20	140	300	240	105	304
187	278	347	159	357	158
852	741	963	654	321	987
303	505	819	37	92	10
28	91	37	22	13	23
524	631	423	821	922	733
15	221	209	371	300	25
823	421	24	31	19	107
652	813	211	354	231	187
50	31	352	16	210	30

## DRILL 4

### Decimal

Follow the directions given. The decimal (.) key is usually located at the bottom right of the keypad. Use the third finger to reach down to tap the decimal key.

⭐ **TECHNIQUE TIP**

Tap each key with a quick, sharp stroke. Release the key quickly. Keep the fingers curved and upright, the wrist low and relaxed.

a	b	c	d	e	f
.28	.19	.37	.42	.81	.96
.51	.67	.81	.27	.55	.80
.64	.50	.60	.50	.62	.43
7.10	8.91	5.64	3.12	6.04	5.01
5.32	4.27	9.21	6.47	5.28	3.24
8.94	3.06	7.38	5.89	1.37	6.78
3.62	36.94	86.73	.60	8.21	4.02
8.06	10.31	537.34	5.21	100.89	6.51
321.04	10.55	687.52	164.84	.85	207.65
.75	.26	10.85	627.98	2.57	46.51
687.46	357.95	159.46	85.21	654.32	753.15
20.46	220.48	6.10	3.04	123.54	315.47
761.64	2.82	627.25	196.25	82.99	4.02
285.46	34.60	.29	89.24	512.69	99.80
33.99	739.45	290.23	563.21	701.21	546.78
60.41	52.79	105.87	951.32	357.02	123.94
108.97	211.00	46.24	82.47	61.28	75.61
3.54	5.79	5.41	1.32	8.54	.27
.05	1.19	77.54	112.96	33.68	2.75
112.54	561.34	114.85	.24	647.21	432.89
35.67	22.01	67.90	41.08	71.28	11.00
579.21	105.24	731.98	258.96	741.21	546.21
.34	1.68	.24	.87	.63	.54
21.87	54.89	2.34	5.89	4.68	10.72

**1 | 2 | 3 | 4**

## DRILL 5

### Review

Keep fingers curved and upright over home keys. Keep right thumb tucked under palm.

1 | 2 | 3 | 4

a	b	c	d	e	f
349	854	961	789	631	80
64	97	164	64	972	167
108	326	207	207	803	549
25	40	83	153	54	23
51	467	825	347	901	208
873	54	258	540	467	375
106	208	504	45	95	34
24	13	13	126	238	160
94	648	21	52	178	341
157	72	341	412	57	89
687	645	32	87	461	541
21	58	647	281	38	1,923
2,753	1,002	549	105	20	567
3,054	25	4,008	2,194	3,079	2,089
369	4,770	158	3,066	657	478
1,004	123	2,560	38	2,098	3,257
71.64	2.72	27.59	89.24	4.02	.57
285.36	118.50	438.96	102.46	55.71	6.37
3.79	24.73	4.71	527.90	.64	1.27
42.08	63.87	91.47	159.34	28.47	1.25
31.07	128.46	1.50	.28	374.95	116.00
365.87	.24	163.48	22.84	24.96	514.38
.25	394.28	452.87	349.51	852.43	234.94
147.25	32.54	821.47	164.87	.08	3.54
183.12	20.80	.60	5.07	121.07	.97

# Appendix B Windows 8

## START WINDOWS 8

*Windows 8* is an operating system software released by Microsoft. The operating system software controls the operations of the computer and works with the application software. *Windows 8* works with *Word* in opening, printing, deleting, and saving files. It also allows you to work with photos, play music and videos, and access the Internet.

When you turn on your computer, the *Windows 8* Lock screen displays. Press any key to display the *Windows 8* Sign-in screen. Key your password and press ENTER to display the *Windows 8* Start Screen.

**Windows 8 Lock screen**

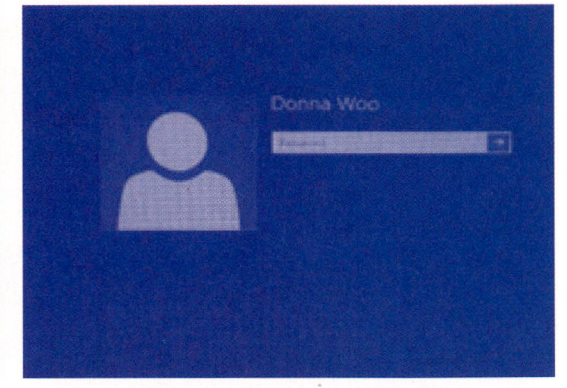

**Windows 8 Sign-in screen**

## WINDOWS 8 START SCREEN

The *Windows 8* Start screen contains tiles that represent an application or a *Windows 8* feature; click the tile to start the application. Some tiles are live in that they show updated information, such as the Weather, News, and Finance tiles. If you do not see the tile for the application that you wish to launch, scroll to the right to view more apps, or right-click an empty spot on the Start screen and click the **All apps** button in the lower-right. The Desktop tile, in the lower-left, provides access to the *Windows 8* desktop.

To display the Start screen from any location, tap the Windows key (⊞) or move the mouse to the lower-left corner of the screen to display the Start icon and click on it.

Desktop Tile ⟶

**WINDOWS 8 DESKTOP**

The *Windows 8* desktop displays when you click the Desktop tile on the *Windows 8* Start screen. To display the desktop from any location, press ⊞ + D. Refer to the illustration below to familiarize yourself with the basic screen elements.

- ■ *Taskbar* ❶. The taskbar displays across the bottom of the window. Use the mouse to point to each item in the taskbar. Look for the ScreenTip that displays identifying each element.

  - • *Program and file buttons*. Buttons display for the programs that are open or pinned to the taskbar and allow you to switch between them easily. The *Internet Explorer* ❷ icon is displayed to provide quick access to the Internet. The *File Explorer* ❸ icon provides quick access to your files.

  - • *Notification area* ❹. The notification area provides helpful information, such as the date and time and the status of the computer. When you plug in a USB drive, *Windows* displays an icon in the notification area letting you know that the hardware is connected.

- ■ *Icons and Shortcuts* ❺. Icons, small pictures representing certain items, may be displayed on the desktop. The Recycle Bin, shown as a wastepaper basket, displays when *Windows* is installed. Other icons and shortcuts may be added.

- ■ *Desktop* ❻. This is the work area where you will be working on your documents and programs.

**SHUT DOWN COMPUTER**

*Microsoft* has made it easy for you to interface with the *Windows 8* features by using either keyboard shortcuts or by moving the mouse to the "hot corners" of the computer screen. Many of the keyboard shortcuts utilize the Windows key (Winkey) and another key. For example, pressing Winkey + D displays the *Windows* desktop, and Winkey + E opens *File Explorer*. The Windows key (⊞) is located to the left of the space bar.

Charms are icons that provide quick access to *Windows 8* launch areas. The five Charms are Search, Share, Start, Devices, and Settings. Point to the lower-right corner of the screen to display the Charms bar. You can also display the Charms bar by pressing Winkey + C.

**Charms bar**

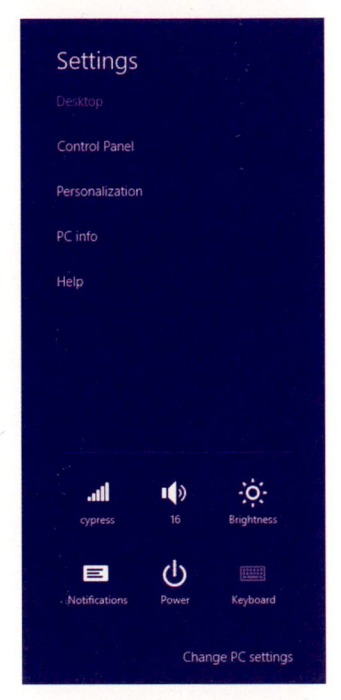

**Settings options**

To shut down the computer:

1. Display the Charms bar, Winkey + C.
2. Click the Settings charm to display the Settings options.
3. Click Power to display the Power options menu.
4. Click Shut down.

**Power options**

---

DRILL 1	START WINDOWS

1. Sign in to *Windows 8*.

2. Display the *Windows 8* Start screen.

3. Click the Weather tile; the Weather app displays full screen.

4. Click the Winkey to display the Start screen.

5. Click the Finance tile to display the Finance app. Click the right arrow in the lower-right corner of the screen to scroll through the Finance app.

6. Move the mouse to the lower-left corner of the screen; click the Start screen icon.

7. Right-click on any empty spot on the Start screen and click the All apps button.

8. Press Winkey + C to display the Charms bar.

9. Click the Settings charm.

10. Click Power, then Shut down.

## WINDOWS 8 HELP

The *Windows 8 Help and Support* feature contains documentation on how to use *Windows 8*; this feature is stored on your computer. Additional links are provided that will take you to the Microsoft site for more information, if you are connected to the Internet.

The easiest way to display Windows Help and Support is to press F1 from the Desktop. The Help feature can also be access from Settings options (Charms bar/Settings/Help). To search for help, key your topic in the Search box, then click the Search button. A list of topics will display; click the link to display the information.

| DRILL 2 | USING WINDOWS HELP |

1. Sign in to *Windows 8*. From the *Windows 8* desktop, press F1.

2. The *Windows 8* Help and Support screen displays.

3. Click Get started.

4. Click the Get to know Windows link.

5. Key **keyboard shortcuts** in the Search box.

6. Click the Search button.

7. Click the link–Mouse and Keyboard: What's new.

8. Read the information that displays. Click the Print button in the upper-right of the screen.

9. Click the exit button in the upper-right of the pane to close the Windows Help and Support screen.

# Appendix C File Management

## FILE EXPLORER

Data is stored in files on the computer. To use the files, you need to know the name of the file and the location in which the file is saved. *Windows 8* stores related files in folders. Folders can also be stored within folders, called subfolders. *File Explorer* provides the interface for you to manage the file system. Click the File Explorer icon on the Taskbar to display the *File Explorer* window.

The left pane is the Navigation pane, which shows the drives on the computer and the files stored on each drive. If an expand icon ▷ displays to the left of the folder or drive, that means that the folder or drive contains subfolders. You can expand the list to view the subfolders by clicking the ▷ icon. Once the list is expanded, the expand icon changes to a collapse icon; clicking the collapse icon ◢ will hide the subfolders.

The Contents pane lists the contents of the folders. Click on a folder in the Navigation pane to display the contents of the folder in the Contents pane. If you want to get a preview of what a file looks like, click the View tab, then in the Panes group click Preview pane to display an additional pane that shows a preview of your file.

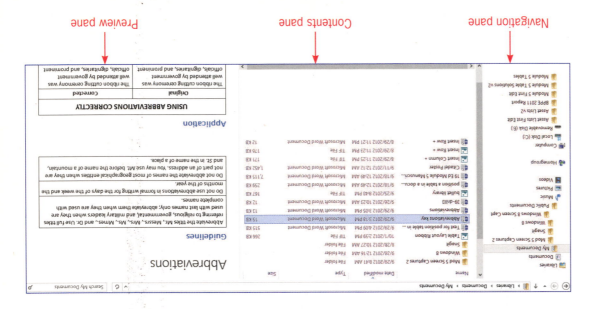

Navigation pane     Contents pane     Preview pane

When you open *File Explorer*, it displays four default libraries—Documents, Music, Pictures, and Videos. The libraries display similar types of files regardless of the drive they are stored on. The Pictures Library will list all the pictures stored on the C: drive as well as any that you may have on a USB drive or other external drives that are plugged into the computer. The Documents Library lists all the documents (*Word, Excel, PowerPoint*, etc.) that are stored on drives connected to the computer. This differs from the way the Navigation pane displays the folders, in that the Navigation pane displays according to the contents of each drive.

Documents, by default, save in the My Documents folder. To view the My Documents folder, move the mouse over Documents in the left pane; then click the expand icon. Click the expand icon to the left of the My Documents folder to display its contents.

Files can be stored in various locations or drives on the computer. To view the drives on your computer, click Computer in the Navigation pane. The drives on your computer display in the right pane. The drives are labeled with letters followed by a colon (C:, D:, E:). The hard drive, which stores the software, is usually labeled as drive (C:). If you are using a USB drive to save your files, the USB drive is often designated as drive E: or F:.

## FILE ADDRESSES

The address bar, located above the Navigation and Contents pane, shows the location or address of the file. Each level of the file hierarchy is separated with a ▶ symbol; the highest level display at the left of the address bar. The ▶ symbol indicates the next lower level. The illustration below shows that the selected file, Windows 8 Manuscript, is located in the Windows 8 subfolder ❶, which is located in the My Documents folder ❷, in the Documents Library ❸.

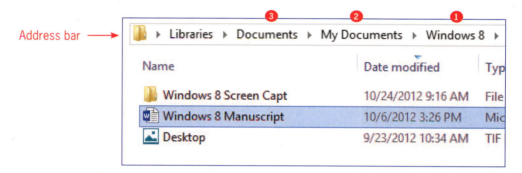

You can move up the hierarchy by clicking on the higher level in the address bar or by clicking on a higher level in the Navigation pane. You can also display the contents of the folder by clicking on the folder name in the address bar.

## WORK WITH FILES AND FOLDERS

Folders are extremely important in organizing files. You will create and manage folders and the files within them so that you can easily locate them. A folder can store files; or a folder may contain subfolders, which store files. The use of folders and subfolders helps to reduce clutter so that you can find, navigate, and manage your files, folders, and disks with greater speed.

### NAMING FILES

Good file organization begins with giving your folders and files names that are logical and easy to understand. A filename should be meaningful and reflect the contents of the file. Filenames can be up to 255 characters long (but in practice you won't use filenames that long). In addition, the following symbols cannot be used in a filename: \ / : * ? " , . The descriptive name is followed by a period (.), which is used to separate the descriptive name from the file extension. The file extension is three or four letters that follow the period. When renaming a file, do not delete or change file extensions as this may cause problems opening the file.

# FILE EXPLORER HOME RIBBON

Commands that are commonly used are located on the Home tab. The ribbon is divided into groups, similar to that of other *Microsoft Office* products. The commands to create new folders, rename files and folders, and copy, move and delete files are all located on the Home tab.

To create a file folder:
Home/New/New Folder

1. In the left pane of *File Explorer*, click the drive or folder that is to contain the new folder.
2. Follow the path to create a new folder. A yellow folder icon displays at the top of the right pane with the words *New folder* highlighted.
3. Key the new folder name and tap ENTER.

To rename a file or folder:
Home/Organize/Rename

1. Access *File Explorer* and display the contents of your removable storage drive (or the location where you have been instructed to save your document files or folders).
2. Click the file or folder icon to be renamed.
3. Click Rename on the ribbon.
4. Key the new name and tap ENTER.

## COPY, MOVE, OR DELETE FILES OR FOLDERS

To move a file or folder to a new location, select the file and click the *Move to* command. Select a location from the drop list or click *Choose location* to display the *Move items* dialog box. Select the location the file or folder is to be moved to, then click the *Move* button.

*Copy* a file to leave it in its current location and make a duplicate of it in another location. To place a copy of a file or folder in a new location, select the file and click the *Copy to* command. Select a location from the drop list or click *Choose location* to display the *Copy items* dialog box. Select the location the file or folder is to be copied to, then click the *Copy* button.

To delete a file or folder, highlight the file or folder icon in the *Explorer* window and click Delete in the ribbon. When you delete a file or folder from the hard drive, it is not removed from the storage immediately. It moves to the Recycle Bin and remains there until the Recycle Bin is emptied. This gives you the opportunity to restore the file to its original location if you discover that it should not have been deleted.

 TIP
The names of the files need to be selected from the Contents pane in order to use the Home commands in the Home ribbon.

## SKYDRIVE APP

*Microsoft* made the SkyDrive an integral part of the *Windows 8* operating system by placing the SkyDrive app on the Start screen. The SkyDrive is a service that allows you to store documents, photos, videos, and audio files on the *Microsoft* servers. A benefit of storing files on the SkyDrive is the ability to access the files from any computer or *Windows* phone. The files can be shared with family and friends. Co-workers can collaboratively work on *Microsoft Office* documents. You need to have a *Microsoft* account to access the SkyDrive.

### To access the SkyDrive: *(Internet connection needed with a Microsoft account.)*

1. From the *Windows 8* Start screen, click the SkyDrive app icon.
2. Your SkyDrive Home location displays. Folders display the folder name and the number of files in the folder. Files display the file name and an icon identifying the file type. Picture files contain a preview of the picture file.
3. Click the file or folder to open it.

### To upload a file to SkyDrive:

1. From the *Windows 8* Start screen, click the SkyDrive app icon.
2. Right-click any blank area to display a toolbar at the bottom of the screen.
3. Click New Folder. Key the folder name in the Create Folder dialog box.
4. Click the new folder to open it.
5. Right-click in the new folder and choose Upload.
6. Browse to select the file(s) to upload. A ✓ displays in the upper-right of each file that is selected. After all files are selected, click the *Add to SkyDrive* button.
7. The status of the upload displays in the upper-right corner of the SkyDrive screen. "Done" displays when the upload is complete.

### To download a file to your computer:

1. Select the file(s) to be downloaded.
2. Click the Download button.
3. Choose the location to place the file.
4. Click the *Choose this folder* button in the lower-right; then click OK.

**TIP**

Updates are continually made to the SkyDrive. Read your screen carefully as appearance and steps may vary over time.

---

**DRILL 3** | **UPLOADING A FILE TO SKYDRIVE** | genevieve

1. Click the SkyDrive app on the Start screen.
2. On your SkyDrive home page, right-click and choose New Folder.
3. Name the folder **SkyDrive Assignments**.
4. Click the folder to open it. Right-click in the folder and choose Upload.
5. Find and select the data file called **genevieve**.

6. Click the Add to SkyDrive button.
7. Click the down arrow to the right of SkyDrive Assignments; choose your SkyDrive from the list that displays.
8. Press the Winkey to return to the Start screen.
9. Log off or shut down the computer.

---

# Appendix D Reference Guide

## Capitalization

### Capitalize:

1. First word of a sentence and of a direct quotation.

We were tolerating instead of managing diversity.
The speaker said, "We must value diversity, not merely recognize it."

2. Names of proper nouns—specific persons, places, or things.

*Common nouns:* continent, river, car, street
*Proper nouns:* Asia, Mississippi, Buick, State St.

3. Derivatives of proper nouns and geographical names.

American history     English accent
German food     Ohio Valley
Tampa, Florida     Mount Rushmore

4. A personal or professional title when it precedes the name or a title of high distinction without a name.

Lieutenant Kahn     Mayor Walsh
Doctor Welby     Mr. Ty Brooks
Dr. Frank Collins     Miss Tate
the President of the United States

5. Days of the week, months of the year, holidays, periods of history, and historic events.

Monday, June 8     Labor Day     Renaissance

6. Specific parts of the country but not compass points that show direction.

Midwest     the South     northwest of town

7. Family relationships when used with a person's name.

Aunt Helen     my dad     Uncle John

8. Noun preceding a figure except for common nouns such as line, page, and sentence.

Unit 1    Section 2    page 2    verse 7    line 2

9. First and main words of side headings, titles of books, and works of art. Do not capitalize words of four or fewer letters that are conjunctions, prepositions, or articles.

Computers in the News     Raiders of the Lost Ark

10. Names of organizations and specific departments within the writer's organization.

Girl Scouts     our Sales Department

## Number Expression

### General guidelines

1. Use **words** for numbers one through *ten* unless the numbers are in a category with related larger numbers that are expressed as figures.

He bought three acres of land. She took two acres.
She wrote 12 stories and 2 plays in 13 years.

2. Use **words** for approximate numbers or large round numbers that can be expressed as one or two words. Use **numbers** for round numbers in millions or higher with their word modifier.

We sent out about three hundred invitations.
She contributed $3 million dollars.

3. Use **words** for numbers that begin a sentence.

Six players were cut from the ten-member team.

4. Use **figures** for the larger of two adjacent numbers.

We shipped six 24-ton engines.

### Times and dates

5. Use **words** for numbers that precede o'clock (stated or implied).

We shall meet from two until five o'clock.

6. Use **figures** for times with a.m. or p.m. and days when they follow the month.

Her appointment is for 2:15 p.m. on July 26, 2011.

7. Use **ordinals** for the day when it precedes the month.

The 10th of October is my anniversary.

### Money, percentages, and fractions

8. Use **figures** for money amounts and percentages. Spell out cents and *percent* except in statistical copy.

A 16 percent sale saved me $141; Joe, 91 cents.

9. Use **words** for fractions unless the fractions appear in combination with whole numbers.

one-half of her lesson     5 1/2     18 3/4

### Addresses

10. Use **words** for street names First through Tenth and **figures** or ordinals for streets above Tenth. Use **figures** for house numbers other than **one**. (If street name is a number, separate it from house number with a dash.)

One Lytle Place     Second Ave.     142--53rd St.

## Use an apostrophe

1. To make most singular nouns and indefinite pronouns possessive (add **apostrophe** and **s**).

   computer + 's = computer's   Jess + 's = Jess's
   anyone's          one's          somebody's

2. To make a plural noun that does not end in s possessive (add **apostrophe** and **s**).

   women + 's = women's   men + 's = men's
   deer + 's = deer's        children + 's = children's

3. To make a plural noun that ends in s possessive. Add only the **apostrophe**.

   boys + ' = boys'        managers + ' = managers'

4. To make a compound noun possessive or to show joint possession. Add **apostrophe** and **s** to the last part of the hyphenated noun.

   son-in-law's          Rob and Gen's game

5. To form the plural of numbers and letters, add **apostrophe** and **s**. To show omission of letters or figures, add an **apostrophe** in place of the missing items.

   7's          A's          It's          add'l

## Use a colon

1. To introduce a listing.

   The candidate's strengths were obvious: experience, community involvement, and forthrightness.

2. To introduce an explanatory statement.

   Then I knew we were in trouble: The item had not been scheduled.

## Use a comma

1. After an introductory phrase or dependent clause.

   After much deliberation, the jury reached its decision. If you have good skills, you will find a job.

2. After words or phrases in a series.

   Mike is taking Greek, Latin III, and Chemistry II.

3. To set off nonessential or interrupting elements.

   Troy, the new man in MIS, will install the hard drive. He cannot get to the job, however, until next Friday.

4. To set off the date from the year and the city from the state.

   John, will you please reserve the center in Billings, Montana, for January 10, 2011.

5. To separate two or more parallel adjectives (adjectives could be separated by *and* instead of a comma).

   The loud, whining guitar could be heard above the rest.

6. Before the conjunction in a compound sentence. The comma may be omitted in a very short sentence.

   You must leave immediately, or you will miss your flight. We tested the software and they loved it.

7. Set off appositives and words of direct address.

   Karen, our team leader, represented us at the conference.
   Paul, have you ordered the DVD-ROM drive?

## Use a hyphen

1. To show end-of-line word division.
2. In many compound words—check a dictionary if unsure.
   • Two-word adjectives before a noun:
     two-car family
   • Compound numbers between twenty-one and ninety-nine.
   • Fractions and some proper nouns with prefixes/suffixes.
     two-thirds        ex-Governor        all-American

## Use italic or underline

1. With titles of complete literary works.
   *College Keyboarding*        *Hunt for Red October*
2. To emphasize special words or phrases.
   What does *professional* mean?

## Use a semicolon

1. To separate independent clauses in a compound sentence when the conjunction is omitted.

   Please review the information; give me a report by Tuesday.

2. To separate independent clauses when they are joined by conjunctive adverbs (*however, nevertheless, consequently,* etc.).

   The traffic was heavy; consequently, I was late.

3. To separate a series of elements that contain commas.

   The new officers are: Fran Pena, president; Harry Wong, treasurer; and Muriel Williams, secretary.

## Use a dash

1. To show an abrupt change of thought.
   Invoice 76A—which is 10 days overdue—is for $670.
2. After a series to indicate a summarizing statement.
   Noisy fuel pump, worn rods, and failing brakes—for all these reasons I'm trading the car.

## Use an exclamation point

After emphatic interjections or exclamatory sentences.
Terrific!   Hold it!   You bet!   What a great surprise!

## Proofreading Procedures

Proofread documents so that they are free of errors. Error-free documents send the message that you are detail-oriented and a person capable of doing business. Apply these procedures after you key a document.

1. Use Spelling & Grammar to check the document.
2. Proofread the document on screen to be sure that it makes sense. Check for these types of errors:
   - Words, headings, and/or amounts omitted.
   - Extra words or lines not deleted during the editing stage.
   - Incorrect sequence of numbers in a list.
3. Preview the document on screen using the Print Preview feature. Check the vertical placement, presence of headers or footers, page numbers, and overall appearance.
4. Save the document again and print.
5. Check the printed document by comparing it to the source copy (textbook). Check all figures, names, and addresses against the source copy. Check that the document style has been applied consistently throughout.
6. If errors exist on the printed copy, revise the document, save, and print.
7. Verify the corrections and placement of the second printed copy.

## Proofreaders' Marks

Mark	Meaning	Mark	Meaning		
#	Add horizontal space	/ or lc	Lowercase		
			Align		space
~~	Bold	Cap or ≡	Capitalize		
⌐	Move left	◡	Close up		
⌐		Move right	ϑ	Delete	
⌐	Move up	∧	Insert		
⌐	Move down	∨ ∨	Insert quotation marks		
¶	Paragraph		marks		
sp	Spell out	___	Underline or italic		
~ or tr	Transpose	... or stet	Let it stand; ignore correction		

## Addressing Procedures

The Envelope feature inserts the delivery address automatically if a letter is displayed. Title case, used in the letter address, is acceptable in the envelope address. An alternative style for envelopes is uppercase with no punctuation.

Business letters are usually mailed in envelopes that have the return address preprinted; return addresses are printed only for personal letters or when letterhead is not available. The default size of Word is a size 10 envelope (4⅛" by 9½"); other sizes are available using the Options feature.

An address must contain at least three lines; addresses of more than six lines should be avoided. The last line of an address must contain three items of information: (1) the city, (2) the state, and (3) the ZIP Code, preferably a 9-digit code.

Place mailing notations that affect postage (e.g., REGISTERED, CERTIFIED) below the stamp position (about line 1.2"); place other special notations (e.g., CONFIDENTIAL, PERSONAL) below the return address about line 1".

IMAGE MAKERS
5131 Moss Springs Road
Columbia, SC 29209-4768

REGISTERED

Ms. Amy Vreede
Communications Limited
57 Santa Ynez Street
Santa Ana, CA 92708-1537

## Folding and Inserting Procedures

### Large envelopes (No. 10, 9, 7¾)

**Step 1**    **Step 2**    **Step 3**

© Cengage Learning

**Step 1:** With document face up, fold slightly less than 1/3 of sheet up toward top.
**Step 2:** Fold down top of sheet to within 1/2" of bottom fold.
**Step 3:** Insert document into envelope with last crease toward bottom of envelope.

## Formatting Decisions

Decisions regarding document formats require consideration of four elements: (1) attractiveness of the format, (2) readability of the format, (3) effective use of space on the page, and (4) efficiency in producing the format. Please note several formatting decisions made in this text regarding defaults in *Word 2013*.

### Styles

*Word 2013* offers a quick gallery of styles on the Home tab. Using these styles results in efficient production of attractive report headings, page number, and table styles.

### Default Line Spacing

The default line spacing of 1.08 in *Word 2013* provides readers with an open and readable copy.

### Space after the Paragraph

The default space after a paragraph in *Word 2013* is 8 point after the paragraph. This automatic spacing saves time and creates an attractive document.

### Remove Space after the Paragraph

While enjoying the benefits of efficiency, it is also necessary to consider the amount of space that is being consumed. For example, extra spacing between the lines of the letter address requires too much space and is not an attractive layout. Note the formats in this book when the extra spacing is removed by simply tapping SHIFT+ENTER after those short lines. Other examples include removing the extra space between the writer's name and title in the closing lines of a letter.

### Margins

The default margins for *Word 2013* are 1" top, bottom, left side, and right side. With the side margin default of 1", additional space is needed for the binding of leftbound reports.

### Fonts and Document Themes

Microsoft provides TrueType fonts in *Office 2013* and a number of new document themes that incorporate color and a variety of fonts depending on the theme selected. Many documents presented in the text are based on the default document theme *Office*, and use the default heading font, Calibri Light, and the default body text font, Calibri 11 point. For most reports in the report module, the *Word 2013* style set is applied to the document theme. See the illustration below of the default headings and fonts, using the Office theme and *Word 2013* style set.

---

# Title (28 pt. Calibri Light, Automatic—Black)

Subtitle (11 pt. Calibri, Black, Text 1, Lighter 35%)

## Heading 1 (16 pt. Calibri Light, Blue, Accent 1, Darker 25%)

### Heading 2 (13 pt. Calibri Light, Blue, Accent 1, Darker 25%)

Heading 3 (12 pt. Calibri Light, Blue, Accent 1, Darker 50%)

*Heading 4 (11 pt. Calibri Light, Italic, Blue, Accent 1, Darker 25%)*

The default body text is Calibri, 11 pt. Color Automatic (Black).

Default Document Theme: Office  (with 18 document formatting style sets that can be applied)

**Letterhead.** Company name and address. May include other data.

**Date.** Date letter is mailed. Usually in month, day, year order. Military style is an option (day/month/year).

**Letter address.** Address of the person who will receive the letter. Include personal title (Mr., Ms., Dr.), name, professional title, company, and address. Remove the extra spacing in the letter address.

**Salutation.** Greeting. Corresponds to the first line of the letter address. Usually includes name and courtesy title; use *Ladies and Gentlemen* if letter is addressed to a company name.

**Body.** Message. Key in default line spacing; tap ENTER once between paragraphs.

**Complimentary close.** Farewell, such as *Sincerely.*

**Writer.** Name and professional title. If the name and title are keyed on two lines, remove the extra spacing between the lines.

**Initials.** Identifies person who keyed the document (for example, tr). May include identification of writer (ARB:tr).

**Enclosure.** Copy is enclosed with the document. May specify contents. If more than one line is used, align at 1" and remove the extra spacing between the lines.

**Copy notation.** Indicates that a copy of the letter is being sent to person name. If more than one line is used, align at 0.5" and remove the extra spacing between the lines.

**Note:** To remove extra spacing between lines, press SHIFT + ENTER.

## Block Letter (Open Punctuation)

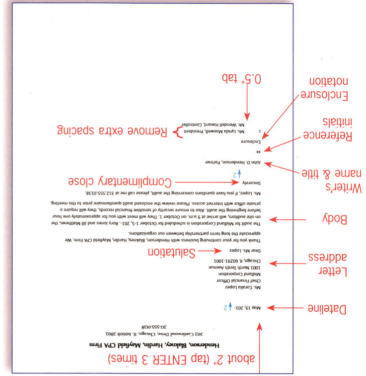

Henderson, Blakney, Hardin, Mayfield CPA Firm
203 Castlewood Drive, Chicago, IL 60606-3893
312.555.0138

May 19, 201-

Ms. Corala Lopez
Chief Financial Officer
Midland Corporation
1001 North Tenth Avenue
Chicago, IL 60291-1001

Dear Ms. Lopez

Thank you for your continuing business with Henderson, Blakney, Hardin, Mayfield CPA Firm. We appreciate the long-term partnership between our organizations.

The audit for Midland Corporation is scheduled for October 1-5, 201-. Rory Jones and Jill Matthews, the on-site auditors, will arrive at 9 a.m. on October 1. They will meet with you approximately one hour before beginning the audit. Also to ensure security of sensitive financial records, they will require a private office with Internet access. Please review the enclosed audit questionnaire prior to this meeting.

Ms. Lopez, if you have questions concerning the audit, please call me at 312.555.0138.

Sincerely

John D. Henderson, Partner

xx

Enclosure

c  Ms. Lynda Maxwell, President
   Mr. Wendell Havard, Controller

## Modified Block Letter (Mixed Punctuation)

IMAGE MAKERS
5131 Moss Springs Road
Columbia, SC 29209-4768
803-555-0177

January 14, 201-

Ms. Kathryn Vanderford
Professional Document Designs, Inc.
P.O. Box 3891
Weatherford, TX 76086-3891

Dear Ms. Vanderford:

Your inquiry concerning a comparison of the modified block letter format and the block letter format is one often answered by our document designers. The modified block format differs from block format in that the date, complimentary close, and the writer's name and title are keyed at the center point. For production efficiency, we recommend block paragraphs.

Although modified block format is an accepted letter style, we do recommend the block letter style. The block letter style is more efficient for a standard letter style, requires no additional settings by the user, and is attractive.

For additional formats, please refer to the enclosed report related to formatting with the latest version of Word and the Model Documents Reference Guide. Our designers are available at 666.555.0197 to assist you with your design needs.

Sincerely,

Jeremy Gillespie
Communication Consultant

xx

Enclosures

## Envelope

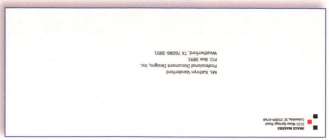

IMAGE MAKERS
5131 Moss Springs Road
Columbia, SC 29209-4768

Ms. Kathryn Vanderford
Professional Document Designs, Inc.
P.O. Box 3891
Weatherford, TX 76086-3891

## Letters with Special Parts

Letters and memos longer than one page require a header on the second and subsequent pages. Appropriate placement of the following special letter parts are illustrated below: mailing notation, attention line, subject line, copy notation, blind copy notation, and reference line.

Subject line

Two-page header

Copy notation

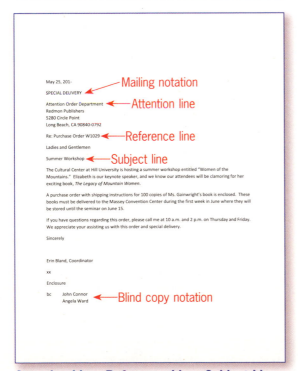

Mailing notation

Attention line

Reference line

Subject line

Blind copy notation

**Attention Line, Reference Line, Subject Line, and Blind Copy Notation**

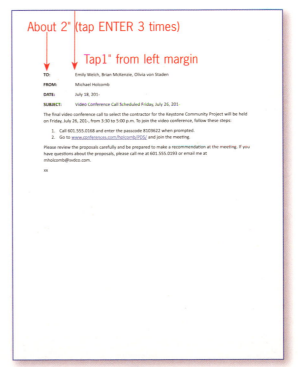

About 2" (tap ENTER 3 times)

Tap 1" from left margin

**Memo**

# Academic Reports in MLA Style

**Font:** 12-point Times New Roman.

**Margins:** Side margins 1".

**Report heading:** Key at 1". Include writer's name, instructor's name, assignment name, and date in DDMMYY order (Ex. 10 April 2014).

**Spacing:** DS paragraphs and indent 0.5".

**Report title:** Center one line after the report heading; capitalize all main words.

**Headings:** Key Level 1 headings in this report at the left margin.

**Numbers:** Number pages at top right; include the writer's last name and the page number (LName 1).

**Internal citations:** References cited are indicated within the text in parenthesis. Indent quotes of 40 or more words 1" from left margin.

**Works cited:** Lists all references in alphabetical order by authors' last names. Format as hanging indent.

MLA Works Cited page

MLA Report, Page 1

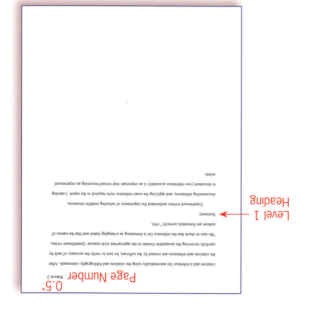

MLA Report, Page 2

## Academic Reports in APA Style

**Font:** 12-point Times New Roman.

**Margins:** Side margins 1".

**Spacing:** DS paragraphs and indent 0.5".

**Report title:** Center one line after the report heading; capitalize all main words.

**Headings:** Key Level 1 headings in this report at the left margin.

**Page numbers:** Key a running head that includes the title of the paper (limited to 50 characters) at the left margin and the page number aligned at the right.

**Internal citations:** References cited are indicated within the text in parenthesis. Indent quotes of 40 or more words 0.5" from left margin.

**Bibliography:** Lists all references in alphabetical order by authors' last names. Format as hanging indent.

Running head at 0.5"

Long quotation

Level 1 headings

**APA Report, Page 1**

Running head

**APA Report, Page 2**

Running head at 0.5"

**APA Bibliography page**

**Margins:** Tap ENTER three times to begin first page of report at 2"; default 1" top margin for succeeding pages; default 1" for bottom margin.

Unbound report: Side margins 1"

Leftbound report: Side margins 1.5"

**Titles:** Title style. Main words capitalized.

**Spacing:** Default line spacing; paragraphs blocked. Tap ENTER once between paragraphs.

**Page numbers:** Second and subsequent pages are numbered at top right of the page. One blank line follows the page number.

**Side headings:** Heading 1 style. Main words capitalized.

## Unbound Report, Page 1

About 2" (tap ENTER 3 times)

Title Report Writing and Technology — Title style

**Heading 1 Style**

Bulleted list

## Unbound Report, Page 2 (Plain Number 3 Style)

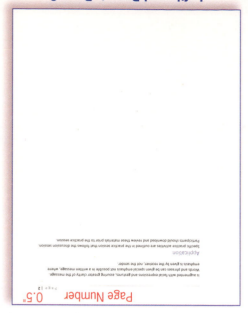

Page Number 0.5"

## Leftbound Report with Footnote, Page 1

About 2" (tap ENTER 3 times)

Title — Title style

Training 1—Introduction to Communication

1.5"

Heading 1 style — Written Communication

Bulleted list

Explanatory Footnote

## Leftbound Report, Page 2 (Page Number Style)

Page Number 0.5"

## Cover Page

Hess Office Park Fourth Quarter Activity Report

OCTOBER – DECEMBER 201-

Patrick J. Hess
HESS OFFICE PARK | 100 HESS BOULEVARD, AUSTIN, TX 78712-2149

**Cover Page**

## Table of Contents

ii

**Table of Contents**

## Hess Office Park Fourth Quarter Activity Report

Quarter Ended December 31, 201-

The Hess Office Park Fourth Quarter Activity report is prepared for the Owners and Tenants Association and is presented at the January meeting of the Association. The staff of Hess Office Park is pleased to report the following activities during the fourth quarter, ending December 31, 201-. Activities include work accomplished in the community as well as achievements in the office park.

### New Owners and Tenants

One new owner and four new tenants have joined Hess Office Park in the fourth quarter. One tenant vacated space as of December 1. The table below outlines the changes in detail.

Space Changes in Fourth Quarter				
Type of Lease				
	Owner	Tenant	Change	Suites Assigned
1		Ayesha Liem	Add	311
2		Ethan Madison	Add	323-325
3	Riley Grant		Add	410-412
4		Jackson Price	Add	422-423
5		Paula Bowen	Terminate	521-525

These changes represent an increase of 5 percent over last year's fourth quarter and a gain of 20 percent this year. This past year Patrick Hess, manager of Hess Office Park, has added the following recruitment activities:

- Joined the Chamber of Commerce and five civic organizations.
- Accepted office of vice president for one civic organization.
- Accepted leadership role in securing funding for college scholarships for area students.

These networks are producing excellent connections and resulted in one added owner and two additional tenants to Hess Office Park.

### 5K Scholarship Fun Run

Hess Office Park is the site for the 5K Scholarship Fun Run sponsored by the East Central Education Foundation (ECEF) to be held on April 10, 201-. Scholarship monies are awarded to freshmen students entering college in the fall semester.

PATRICK J. HESS 1

**Leftbound Report with Footer, Page 1**

FOURTH QUARTER ACTIVITY REPORT

Mr. Robert Kaczynski, president of ECEF, is the contact person and has signed the official agreement with our office. Hess Office Park will designate spaces in the south parking lot on Friday afternoon and all day on Saturday. Tables and chairs will be set up along the race route for volunteers to distribute drinks and snacks to the runners/walkers. Security and police assistance will be provided at the main intersection of Hess Boulevard and Elm Street. Space will also be provided for vendors near the entrance of the office park.

### Staff Updates

We are pleased to welcome Dan Rivera, who joined our staff on October 1 as an accountant. Dan holds a master's degree in accounting and has worked as an auditor for seven years and three years as a forensic accountant. Dan and his wife, Marilyn, recently moved to Austin from San Antonio. They have two sons. Danny is 3 and Sam is 1. We look forward to Dan's contributions to our office.

### Holiday Closings

Holiday closings are approved annually by the Board of Directors. The table below lists the six approved closings.

Hess Office Park	
201-Holiday Closings	
New Year's Day	January 1
Memorial Day	May 26
Independence Day	July 4
Labor Day	September 4
Thanksgiving	November 23-24
Christmas	December 24-26

In case of emergency, tenants and owners are to contact Colton Blake at 512.555.0100.

### Summary

The fourth quarter has shown positive growth and preliminary data indicates additional growth for the first quarter of next year. Additional information is available on our website at www.hesspropertyenterprises.com.

PATRICK J. HESS 2

**Page 2 with Header and Footer**

# Resume

## Maria J. Rex
2104 Adger Road, Columbia, SC 29204-3253
803.555.0194 | Maria.Rex@wcc.edu | http://www.linkedin.com/in/rex

### Qualifications Profile for Office Manager
Highly effective, results-oriented, administrative office professional with AS degree and two years of relevant part-time work experience, including demonstrated effective supervisory, customer service, records management, time management, and project management skills. Create professional documents that enhance company image and productivity using Word, Excel, and PowerPoint. Strong written, oral, and electronic communication skills. Excellent interpersonal skills. Honest, ethical, and possess strong work ethic.

### Education
AS degree in Business Administration with majors in Office Administration and Office Management from Wexford Community College, Columbia, SC, May 2012, 3.65 GPA.
High school diploma with career emphasis in English and business, Maxwell High School, Charleston, SC, August, 2010, 3.85 GPA.

### Experience
Wexford Community College, President's Office, Columbia, SC, internship, summer 2012.
- Prepared correspondence, reports, and presentations for senior administrators.
- Scheduled and coordinated special events with high-level constituents.
- Received outstanding evaluation, commending my professionalism, social skills, creativity, reliability, problem-solving skills, and the excellent quality of all work.

Pat's Fitness and Wellness Center, supervisor and promoted to office manager for the 3:30 to 7:30 shift (20-25 hours per week) from June 2010 through May 2012.
- Managed two teams of trainers and one team of nutrition counselors; resolved conflicts for clients. Responsible for correspondence with referring physicians, vendors, and clients.
- Managed facility, records, billing, equipment, and supplies; developed procedures.
- Increased client participation and revenue from my shift over 20 percent while reducing expenses by 12 percent.

### Honors and Activities
Named a Dean's Scholar; received the Outstanding Business Student Award. Member of Student Advisory Council, president of the Wexford Honor Society, and president of the Office Management Club.

---

# Personal Business Letter

## Maria J. Rex
2104 Adger Road, Columbia, SC 29204-3253
803.555.0194 | Maria.Rex@wcc.edu | http://www.linkedin.com/in/rex

*The return address may be keyed immediately above the date, or you may create a personal letterhead as shown here.*

Current date

Mr. Eric Todd, President and CEO
CunCo Consulting Alliance
416 West Bay Street
Savannah, GA 31401-1115

Dear Mr. Todd

Ben Sullivan, your manager of business development, sent me a copy of the job description posted for the office manager position open at CunCo and suggested that I contact you. My qualifications match the requirements for the office manager you are seeking. Please consider me as an applicant for that position.

My education and my two years of experience managing the four-hour evening shift of two teams of trainers and one of nutrition counselors enabled me to develop the team management and the operational management skills that you require. Our teamwork resulted in a significant revenue increase and expense reduction.

My internship in the President's Office at Wexford Community College enabled me to refine my organizational, problem-solving, and soft skills. Both my experience at Pat's Fitness and Wellness Center and in the President's office required extensive Word, Excel, and PowerPoint use and excellent communication skills. I delivered high-quality products and met very tight deadlines consistently. I understand how those skills can be of value to CunCo.

After you have had an opportunity to review the enclosed resume as well as my LinkedIn Profile, I look forward to meeting with you to discuss how my qualifications and my office management career aspirations can be applied to your position at CunCo Consulting Alliance.

Sincerely

Maria J. Rex

Enclosure

---

# Table (formatted with Table Style)

### REGENTS MEMORIAL MEDICAL CENTER
**February Seminars**

Seminar Title	Description	Registration
Surgical Weight Loss	Methods of losing weight, including healthy diet, exercise and medication, will be discussed in detail. Surgical weight loss is an option for those who are motivated and willing to commit to lifestyle changes.	Classes will be held at the Outpatient Surgery Center 75 Pacific Crest Laguna Niguel, CA 92677-5773. Call 949.555.0111 to register.
Life in Motion with Osteoarthritis	Osteoarthritis no longer means that you need to live with a painful disability. Modern medicine, diet, exercise, and surgery can help you enjoy life more fully. Intricate surgical procedures including joint replacement and spinal fusion will be covered.	Register online at www.regents.org/calendar, Materials fee $10.00.
Expert's Cancer Updates	The cancer experts at Regents Medical Center will unveil the latest results of the latest cancer studies. New breakthrough treatments will be discussed. They will explain what you should know about cancer screenings. Tips on preventing various types of cancers will be provided.	Call 949.555.0100 or register online at www.regents.org/calendar.

---

# Newsletter

## Hess Pet Center News and Views

Hess Pet Center now provides full-service luxury pet care to dog owners. Recently, we have been inundated with requests from current clients and from employees in Hess Office Park to expand our services to cat owners. Providing services to cat owners has always been part of our long-range business plan; therefore we decided to survey all of our clients and Hess Office Park employees.

### Survey Results
First, we asked our current clients if they had any objections to adding cats to the facilities. None of our current clients objected to having cats in the facility. More than 20 percent of our current clients have both dogs and cats. Approximately 25 percent of Hess Office Park employees indicated that they needed services for cats.

### Action Plan
We will begin with a pilot project immediately that will include three types of services for cats:
- Total professional care provided by board-certified veterinarians and highly trained technicians.
- Luxury boarding.
- Boutique that provides one-stop shopping to meet your cat's needs and desires.

The architects and construction team met and agreed that we could finish an expansion area of the new addition and have a nice area to meet the demand for accommodations for cats. This expansion will not impact the construction completion dates. Space in the veterinary clinic and the boutique is already available.

Some of our clients even sent pictures of their dogs with cats that belonged to their friends who want to use our services. Andy VanHuis is pictured below with his friend, Choo Turnquist.

What was even more surprising were responses from clients who only have dogs, but who indicated many of their friends would like to use our services for their cats. Several cats. They all sent pictures of their friends' cats. They all indicated we could publish their names and pictures in our newsletter. Sadie Skinlik, shown above, is one that would likely be a frequent boarder at Hess Pet Center.

**Sun Property and Casualty Insurance Company**

1592 S. Plaza Way | Flagstaff, AZ 86011-7155

Phone: 928.555.0174 | Solana.Rodriquez@apic.com | Fax: 928.555.0136

**NEWS RELEASE**                                   Contact Person: Solana Rodriquez

Current date

For Release: Immediately

**SUN NAMES NEW PRESIDENT AND CHIEF EXECUTIVE OFFICER**

FLAGSTAFF, AZ—The Sun Property and Casualty Insurance Company announced today that its Board of Director unanimously approved Amy T. Ledbetter as its new chief executive officer. Ledbetter replaces Mark Daff, who served as the chief executive officer for the past eight years.

Ledbetter had served as senior vice president and chief financial officer for the past five years. Her first experience with Sun came as an intern when she was an accounting student at Meadowfield University. After she completed her accounting degree, she worked two years as a public accountant and earned her Certified Public Accountant (CPA) license. After completing her MBA degree at Eastwell International Graduate School of Business, she joined Sun as an accountant in the Corporate Finance Department.

Ledbetter is married to Kirk T. Parham, a nationally known pediatrician. They have two teenage children—a son, Joseph, and a daughter, Caitlyn.

###

**News Release**

---

Itinerary for Laurie Hammer July 14 – 16, 201-	
**Wednesday, July 14**	**Columbia to Cincinnati**
4:40 p.m.	Leave Columbia on non-stop Cincola Flight 5173 and arrive in Cincinnati at 5:55 p.m.; Metro Rental Car (Confirmation #67540912); Riverside Hotel (Confirmation #34898732)
8:15 p.m.	Picked up at hotel by Dave Calhoun and Jack Shaut; dinner at Royal Mason
**Thursday, July 15**	**Cincinnati**
8:00 a.m.	Leave for Natorp Publishing Center; 6319 Natorp Boulevard, Mason, Ohio
9:00 a.m.	Meet with President and Editor-in-chief; President's office—Suite 600
9:45 a.m.	Meet with the Editorial Team, Fifth Floor Conference Room
11:45 a.m.	Break
12:00 noon	Working lunch, Fifth Floor Conference Room
2:00 p.m.	Meet with book designers, Fifth Floor Conference Room
2:30 p.m.	Break
3:00 p.m.	Meet with the Production Team, Fifth Floor Conference Room
5:30 p.m.	Return to hotel
7:30 p.m.	Meet Project Team for dinner; Chez Ruby; 644 Walnut Street; map in Travel folder.
**Friday, July 16**	**Cincinnati to Columbia**
7:45 a.m.	Return rental car: Cincola Flight 6754 departs at 9:20 a.m. and arrives in Columbia at 10:40 a.m.

**Itinerary**

---

# Minutes

Nursing Partnership Board
Hospital Atrium
January 15, 201-, 10:30 a.m.

Board members present were Lester Caldwell, chair and university representative; Mary Freeman, meeting facilitator; Jane Metze, technical college representative; Wanda Stewart, project coordinator; Bentley Burns, project assistant; and Tyler Walker, hospital representative.

**Proposal**
Mary Freeman presented the original agreement with the markup showing all of the changes in it. She pointed out that these changes were recommended at the last meeting. The Board agreed that the revised version accurately reflected the discussion of the previous meeting. Mary Freeman was asked to revise the final agreement with the changes noted.

**Terms**
Bentley Burns presented the changes reflecting the additional $1,000,000 committed by the fifth area hospital. The hospital also committed to the $50,000 annual contribution for the next five years. The Board discussed several alternatives for distributing the additional funds and then agreed that the best approach was to use the same distribution formula as it previously agreed to use for the funds contributed by the other four hospitals. Mary Freeman was asked to revise the final agreement to reflect the additional funds and the distribution formula. She agreed to finalize all documents within one week.

**Hospital Perspective**
Tyler Walker presented the attached funding plan submitted by the five hospitals. The Board reviewed and approved the plan.

**Technical College Perspective**
Jane Metze presented the attached fund usage plan submitted by the technical college. The Board reviewed and approved the plan.

**University perspective**
Lester Caldwell presented the attached fund usage plan submitted by the university. The Board reviewed and approved the plan.

**Project Approval**
Lester Caldwell thanked the members of the Board for all the hard work and the effective collaboration that resulted in approval of the plans presented by the hospitals, the technical college, and the university. He indicated that the next big hurdle is to ensure that the plans are implemented effectively. After considerable discussion of how plans would be implemented, the Board approved the entire project.

**Minutes (Page 1)**

---

Minutes—Nursing Partnership Board            2            January 15, 201-

**Next meeting**
The chair reminded the group that the next Nursing Partnership Board meeting is scheduled for February 8 at 10:30 in the Hospital Atrium.

**Adjournment**
The meeting adjourned at 12:05 p.m.

**Minutes (Page 2)**

The numbered parts are found on most computers. The location of some parts will vary.

1. **CPU (Central Processing Unit):** Internal operating unit or "brain" of computer.
2. **CD-ROM drive:** Reads data from and writes data to a CD or DVD.
3. **Monitor:** Displays text and graphics on a screen.
4. **Mouse:** Used to input commands.
5. **Keyboard:** An arrangement of letter, figure, symbol, control, function, and editing keys and a numeric keypad.

## KEYBOARD ARRANGEMENT

1. **Alphanumeric keys:** Letters, numbers, and symbols.
2. **Numeric keypad:** Keys at the right side of the keyboard used to enter numeric copy and perform calculations.
3. **Function (F) keys:** Used to execute commands, sometimes with other keys. Commands vary with software.
4. **Arrow keys:** Move insertion point up, down, left, or right.
5. **ESC (Escape):** Closes a software menu or dialog box.
6. **TAB:** Moves the insertion point to a preset position.
7. **CAPS LOCK:** Used to make all capital letters.
8. **SHIFT:** Makes capital letters and symbols shown at tops of number keys.
9. **CTRL (Control):** With other key(s), executes commands. Commands may vary with software.
10. **ALT (Alternate):** With other key(s), executes commands. Commands may vary with software.
11. **Space Bar:** Inserts a space in text.
12. **ENTER (return):** Moves insertion point to margin and down to next line. Also used to execute commands.
13. **DELETE:** Removes text to the right of insertion point.
14. **NUM LOCK:** Activates/deactivates numeric keypad.
15. **INSERT:** Activates insert or typeover.
16. **BACKSPACE:** Deletes text to the left of insertion point.

Align Text	Home/Paragraph/Align Left, Center, Align Text Right, or Justify	
Blank Page Page Break	Inert/Pages/Blank Page Insert/Pages/Page Break	Blank Page / Page Break
Bookmark	Insert/Links/Bookmark	Bookmark
Breaks	Page Layout/Page Setup/Breaks	Breaks
Bullets or Numbering	Home/Paragraph/Bullets or Numbering	
Captions	References/Captions/Insert Caption	Insert Caption
Center Page	Page Layout/Page Setup/Dialog Box Launcher/Layout tab/Vertical alignment/Center	Page — Vertical alignment: Center
Change User Name	File/Options/General	User name: Susie H. VanHuss / Initials: shvh / ☑ Always use these values regardless of sign in to Office.
Close Document	File/Close or Close button at top right of screen	Close ✕
Co-authoring— co-author joining, paragraph locked, two co-authors	SkyDrive/Share/Open	Connie Forde is editing this document. / 2 / The initial work involved i: baseboards in the closet a be added to the area whe new flooring.

Columns—Create Columns—Unequal Width	Page Layout/Page Setup/Columns Page Layout/Page Setup/Columns/ More Columns	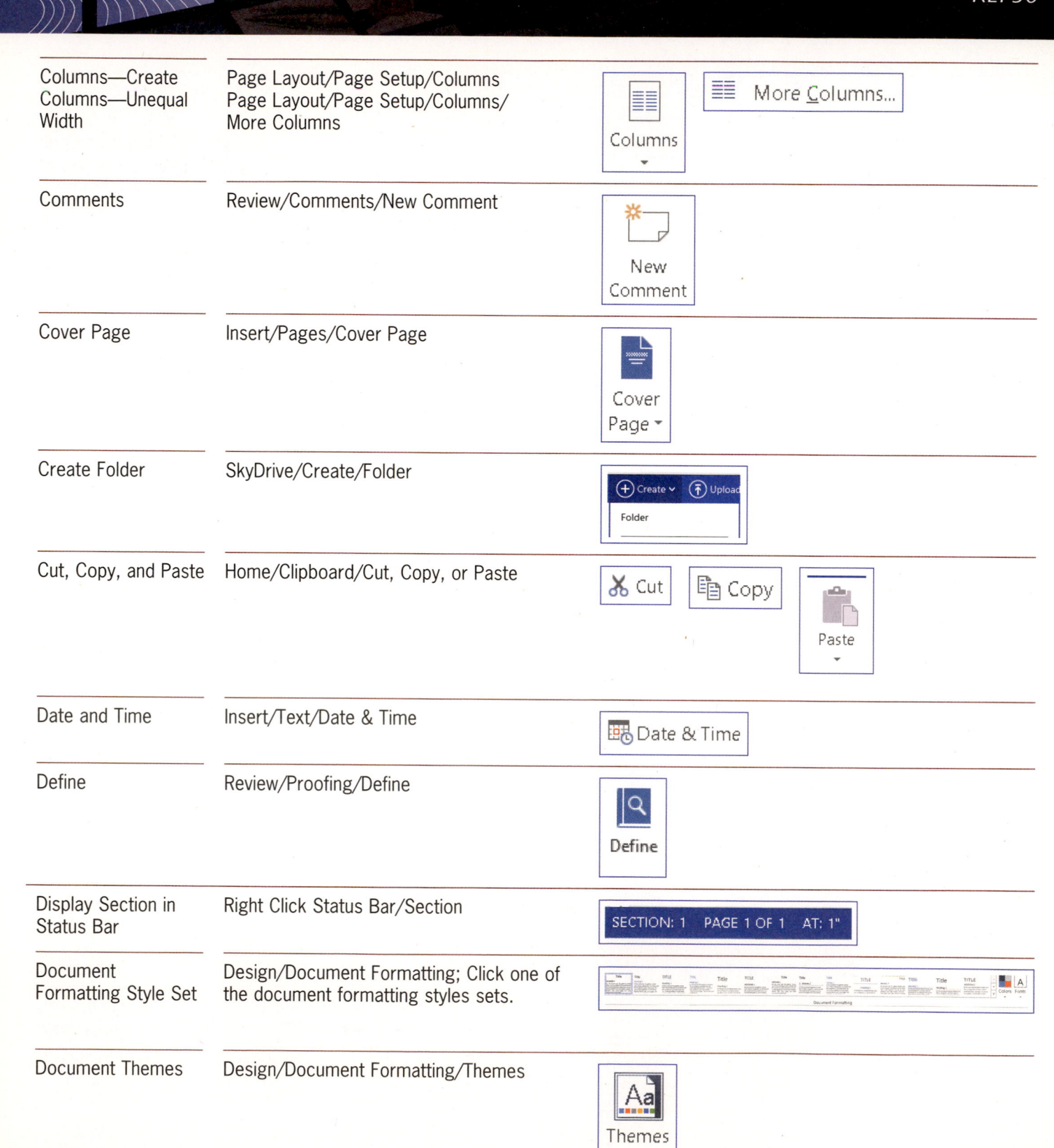
Comments	Review/Comments/New Comment	
Cover Page	Insert/Pages/Cover Page	
Create Folder	SkyDrive/Create/Folder	
Cut, Copy, and Paste	Home/Clipboard/Cut, Copy, or Paste	
Date and Time	Insert/Text/Date & Time	
Define	Review/Proofing/Define	
Display Section in Status Bar	Right Click Status Bar/Section	
Document Formatting Style Set	Design/Document Formatting; Click one of the document formatting styles sets.	
Document Themes	Design/Document Formatting/Themes	

Drop Cap	Insert/Text/Drop Cap	
Edit in Word Web App and Edit in Word	SkyDrive/Open File/Edit Document	
Envelopes and Labels	Mailings/Create/Envelopes or Labels	
Find, Replace, and Select	Home/Editing/Find, Replace, or Select	
Find, Share, or Comment	SkyDrive/Open Document/Find, Share, or Comment	
Footnote	References/Footnotes/Insert Footnote	
Format Painter	Home/Clipboard/Format Painter	
Formulas in Table	Table Tools/Layout/Data/Formula	
GoTo	Home/Editing; Click the drop-list arrow on the Find command; then click Go To.	
Hanging indent	Ruler/Indent Markers	

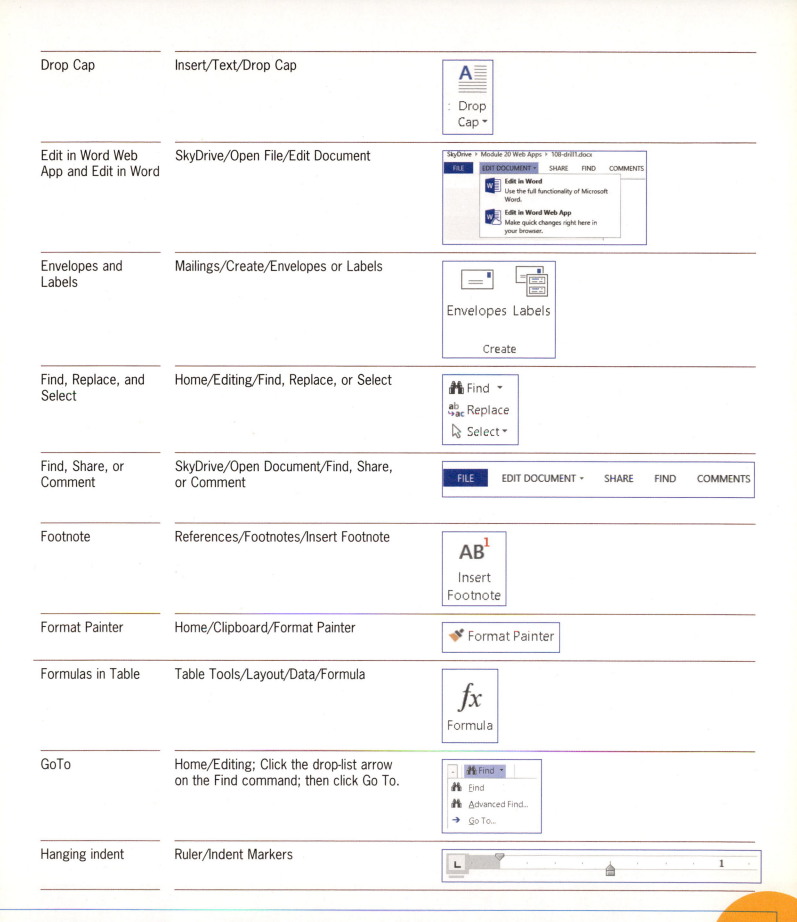

Header and Footer	Insert/Header & Footer/Header or Footer	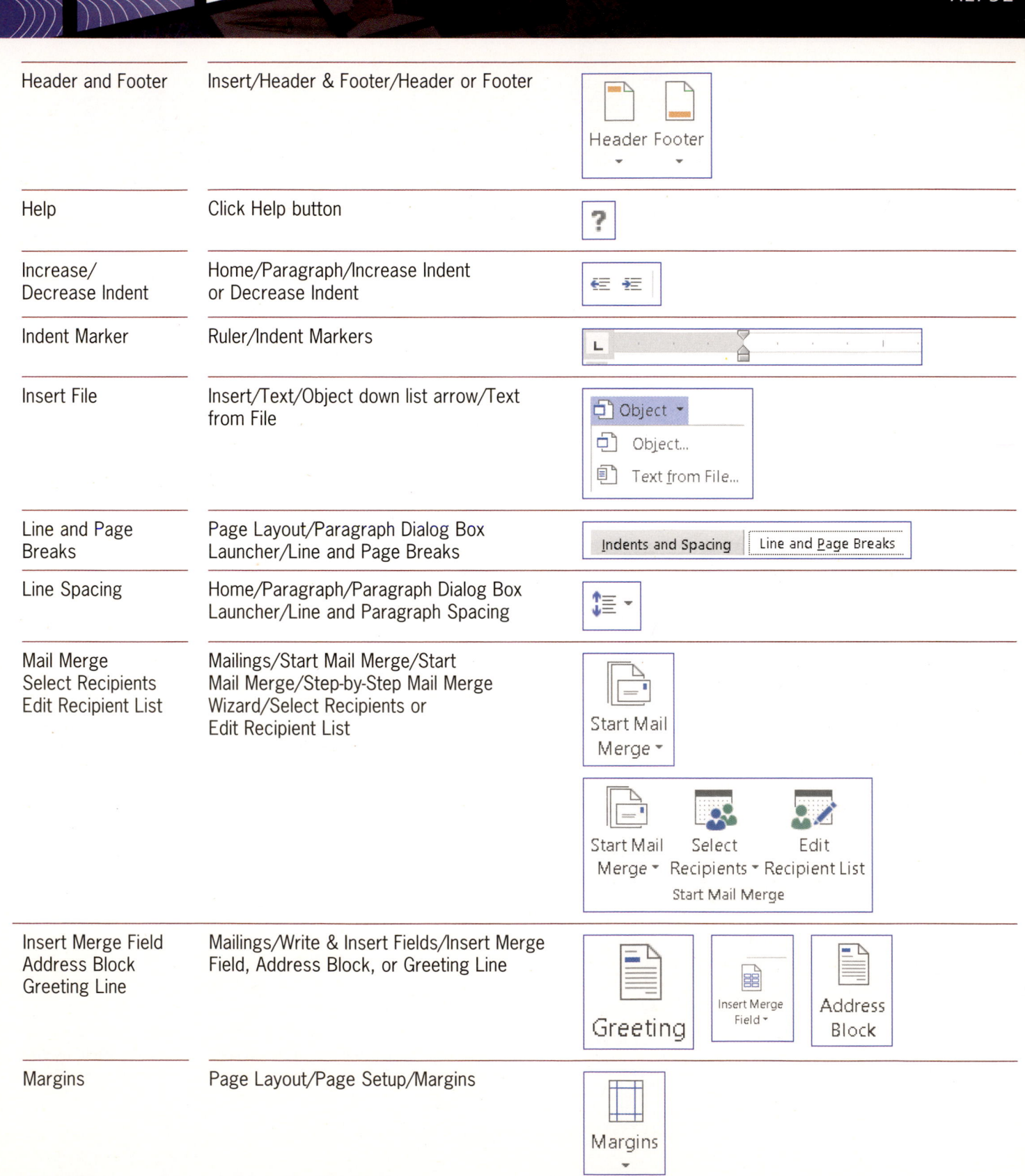
Help	Click Help button	
Increase/ Decrease Indent	Home/Paragraph/Increase Indent or Decrease Indent	
Indent Marker	Ruler/Indent Markers	
Insert File	Insert/Text/Object down list arrow/Text from File	
Line and Page Breaks	Page Layout/Paragraph Dialog Box Launcher/Line and Page Breaks	
Line Spacing	Home/Paragraph/Paragraph Dialog Box Launcher/Line and Paragraph Spacing	
Mail Merge Select Recipients Edit Recipient List	Mailings/Start Mail Merge/Start Mail Merge/Step-by-Step Mail Merge Wizard/Select Recipients or Edit Recipient List	
Insert Merge Field Address Block Greeting Line	Mailings/Write & Insert Fields/Insert Merge Field, Address Block, or Greeting Line	
Margins	Page Layout/Page Setup/Margins	

Mini toolbar	Appears when text is selected	
Multilevel list	Home/Paragraph/Multilevel List	
Navigation Pane	View/Show/Navigation Pane	
Open New/Existing Document	File/New or Open; then locate the file	
Page Borders Page Color	Design/Page Background/Page Borders	
Page Break	CTRL + ENTER or Insert Pages/Page Break	
Page Numbers— Insert	Insert/Header & Footer/Page Number	
Page Orientation	Page Layout/Page Setup/Orientation	
Paragraph Borders and Shading	Design/Page Background/Page Borders	
Paste Options button	Home/Clipboard/Paste/Click a Paste Option	

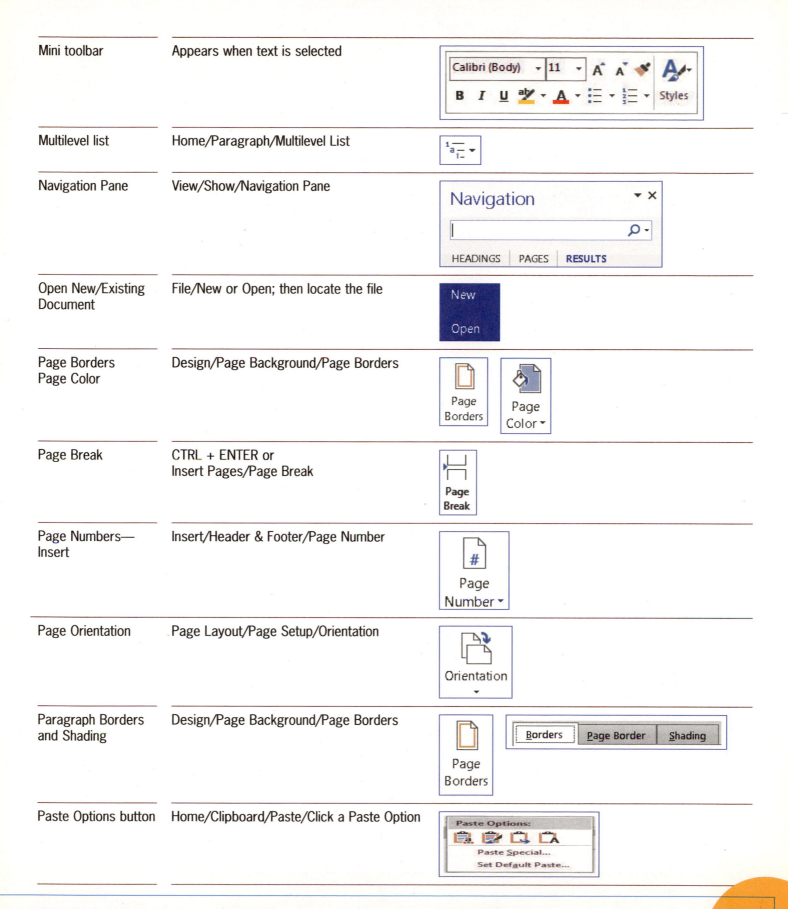

Save and Save As	File/Save As/SkyDrive or File/Save As Computer	
(to SkyDrive or Computer)		
Ruler—View	To display: Click View/Show/Ruler	
Remove Space After Paragraph	SHIFT + ENTER or Home/Paragraph/Line and Paragraph Spacing	
Quick Parts	Insert/Text/Quick Parts	
Quick Access Toolbar	Upper-left corner of screen/Use down arrow customize	
Print	File/Print	
Pictures or Online Pictures—Insert	Insert/Illustrations/Pictures or Online Pictures/Locate and select picture/Insert	
Picture—Styles	Picture Tools/Styles	
Pictures—Size	Picture Tools/Format/Size/Height or Width Arrows	
Picture—Format	Picture Tools/Format	
Pictures—Crop	Picture Tools Format/Size/Crop	

Save in New Folder	File/Save or Save As; Click New Folder and key name	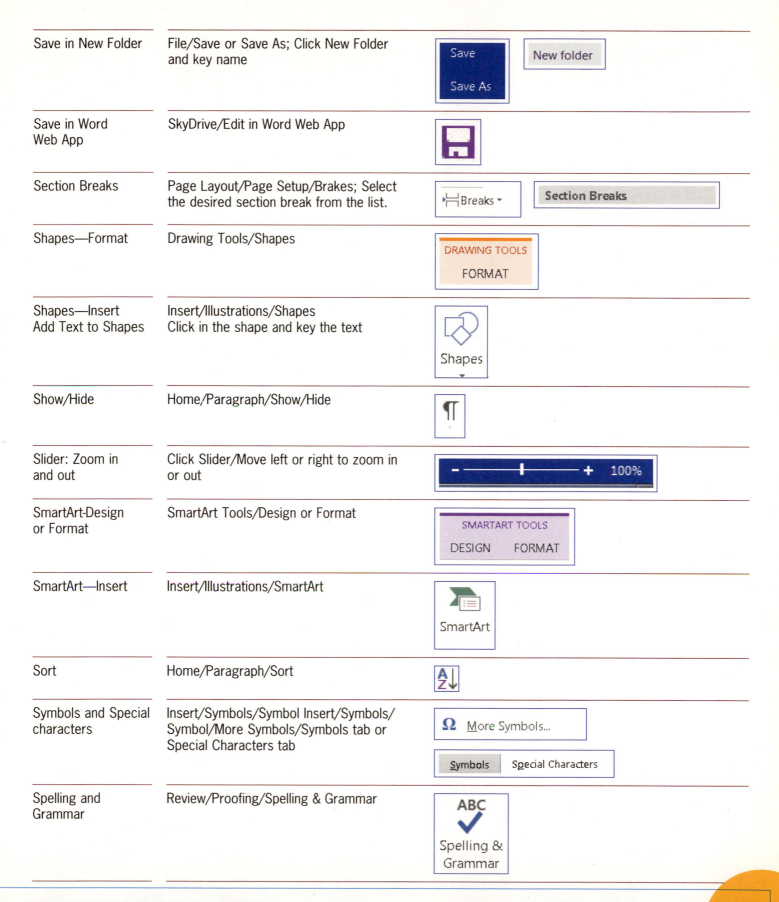
Save in Word Web App	SkyDrive/Edit in Word Web App	
Section Breaks	Page Layout/Page Setup/Brakes; Select the desired section break from the list.	
Shapes—Format	Drawing Tools/Shapes	
Shapes—Insert Add Text to Shapes	Insert/Illustrations/Shapes Click in the shape and key the text	
Show/Hide	Home/Paragraph/Show/Hide	
Slider: Zoom in and out	Click Slider/Move left or right to zoom in or out	
SmartArt-Design or Format	SmartArt Tools/Design or Format	
SmartArt—Insert	Insert/Illustrations/SmartArt	
Sort	Home/Paragraph/Sort	
Symbols and Special characters	Insert/Symbols/Symbol Insert/Symbols/ Symbol/More Symbols/Symbols tab or Special Characters tab	
Spelling and Grammar	Review/Proofing/Spelling & Grammar	

Split pane	View/Window/Split	
Status line	Right-click on the status line located at the bottom of the screen.	
Styles—Insert	Home/Styles/Quick Styles	
Table of Contents	References/Table of Contents/Table of Contents	
Table of Contents—Update	References/Table of Contents/Update Table of Contents	
Table of Figures	References/Captions/Insert Table of Figures	
Tables	Insert/Tables/Table	
Tables—Adjust Column Width using the Ruler	Ruler/Column Marker/Drag to appropriate position	
Tables—Design or Layout	Table Tools/Design or Layout	
Tables—Cell Alignment	Table Tools/Layout/Alignment	
Tables—Cell Height and Width	Table Tools/Layout/Cell Size	

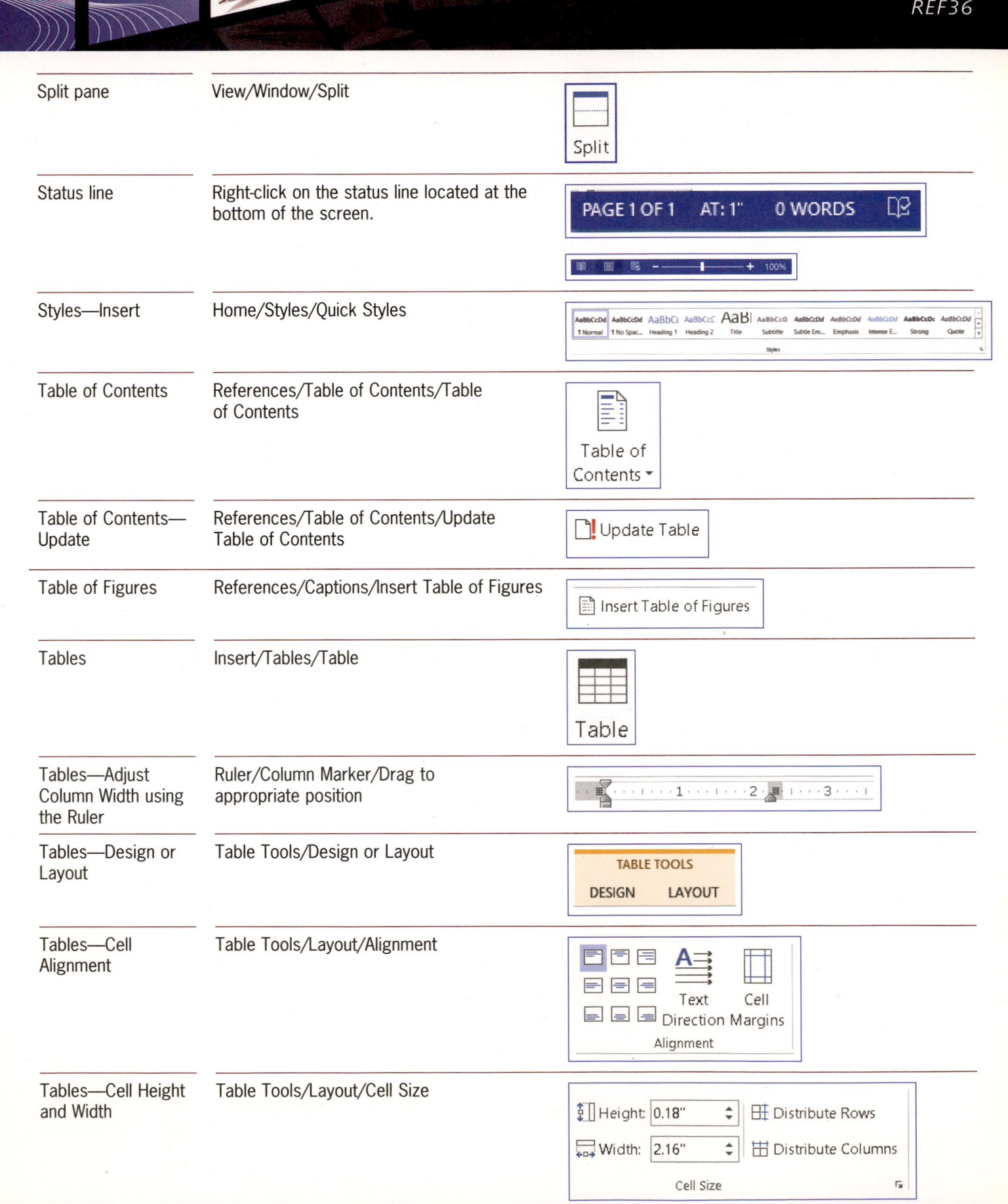

Tables—Decimal Tab in Table	Select Column/Click Tab Selector button/Select decimal tab/Click appropriate position on Ruler	
Tables—Insert and Delete Rows and Columns	Table Tools/Layout; Click appropriate command to insert and delete rows and columns.	
Tables—Insert using the Table grid	Insert/Tables/Table/Drag to select number of rows and columns	
Tables—Merge or Split Cells	Table Tools/Layout; Click appropriate command to merge or split cells.	
Tables—Properties	Table Tools/Layout/Table/Properties	
Tables—Repeat Header Rows	Table Tools Layout/Data/Repeat Header Rows	
Tables—Styles and Shading	Table Tools/Design/Table Styles	
Tabs—Bar, Left, Center, Right, and Decimal	View Ruler/Tab Alignment Button/click on Horizontal Ruler	
Tabs—Modify Tabs using Horizontal Ruler	Select desired tab; Click and drag the tab to the desired location on the ruler.	
Tabs—Modify Tabs using the Tabs dialog box	Home/Paragraph/Paragraph Dialog Box Launcher/Tabs	

Templates	File/New	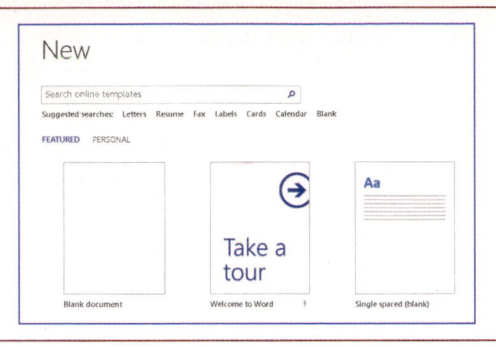
Text Box	Insert/Text/Text Box	
Text Formats	Home/font/Click desired text format command (Font, Font Size, Grow Font, Shrink Font, Change Case, Clear Formatting, Bold, Italic, Underline, Strikethrough, Subscript, Superscript, Text effects, Text Highlight Color, Font Color)	
Thesaurus	Review/Proofing/Thesaurus	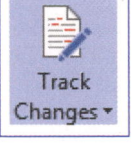
Track Changes	Review/Tracking/Track Changes	
Track Change Options	Review/Tracking/Change Tracking Options Dialog Box Launcher	
Track Changes—Review Changes	Review/Changes/Accept, Reject, Previous, or Next	
Upload File	SkyDrive/Upload	

Vertical Page Position	To turn on: Right-click status bar/Click Vertical Page Position	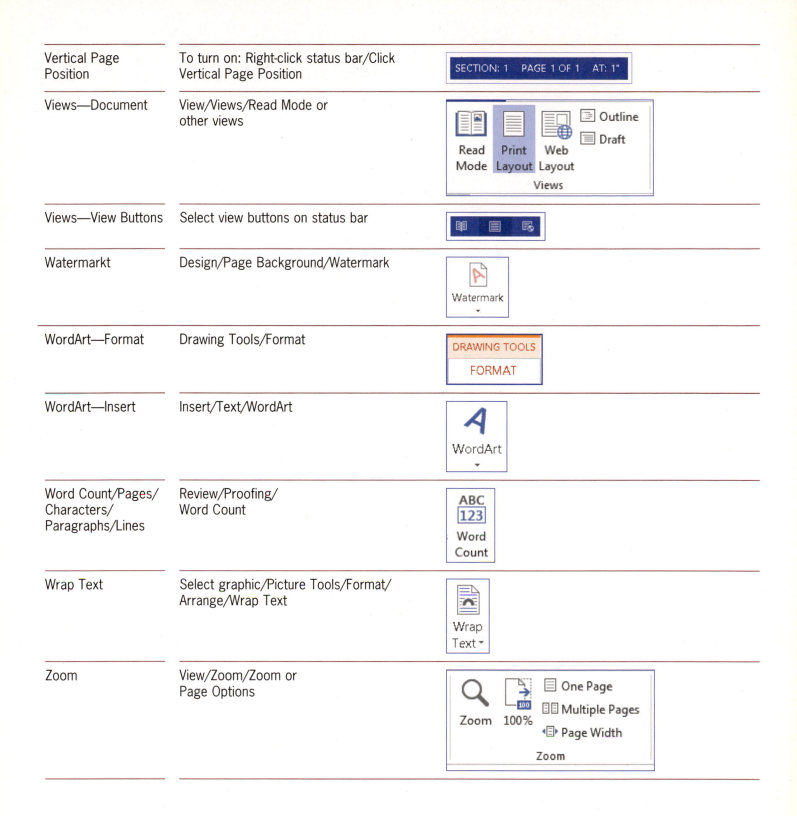
Views—Document	View/Views/Read Mode or other views	
Views—View Buttons	Select view buttons on status bar	
Watermarkt	Design/Page Background/Watermark	
WordArt—Format	Drawing Tools/Format	
WordArt—Insert	Insert/Text/WordArt	
Word Count/Pages/ Characters/ Paragraphs/Lines	Review/Proofing/ Word Count	
Wrap Text	Select graphic/Picture Tools/Format/ Arrange/Wrap Text	
Zoom	View/Zoom/Zoom or Page Options	

# Index

Leadership, 518; effective, 518
Leadership skills, 518
Lease agreements, 492. *See also* Rental
    agreements; preparing, 492–495
Lease form, 494
Left pane, 82
Left Shift, 13, 15
Leftbound reports, 178–184, 332, 389;
    margins, 179
Legal documents, 479–504; corporate,
    479–483; document design, 480;
    guidelines for designing, 480;
    preparing, 488–491; using bookmarks,
    488–491
Legal pleadings, 484–487; templates, 484
Lesson Report screen, 4
Letter address, 127, 268
Letter parts, 268. *See also specific types*;
    special, 272–276
Letter Review, 266–271
Letterhead, 127, 268
Letters. *See also specific types*:
    application, 444, 445; employment, 443;
    job acceptance/refusal, 444, 447; mail
    merge, 367; personalizing form, 380
Line breaks, 186
Line spacing, 96, 98–99, 125
Lists: bullet, 96; formatting, 96; multilevel,
    96; numbered, 96

## M

M control of, 26, 28, 33, 36
Mail merge, 367. *See also* Mailings tab;
    editing document, 372
Mail merge wizard, 368–372
Mailing notation, 274
Mailings tab, 370, 371, 376
Main document, 367
Main pane, 82
Margins, 179
Markup, 410
Maximize button, 83
Medical correspondence, 455;
    confidentiality of, 458
Medical report forms, 470; body of, 470;
    conclusion of, 470; heading of, 470

Memos, 121–124, 263–264; templates,
    259–260; two-page letters and, 278–280
Merge. *See* Mail merge
Merge fields, 367
Microsoft Live, 531, 533
Microsoft Live account, 243
Mini toolbar, 94
Minimize button, 83
Minus sign (-), control of, 63
Minutes, 414
Mixed punctuation, 136, 267, 268, 270
MLA styles: internal citations in, 196;
    reports, 195; works cited page in,
    196–198
Modified block letter, 267, 268, 270
Mouse, scrolling with, 104
Multicultural literacy, 377
Multilevel lists, 96, 331, 337
Multi-page reports, 185–191

## N

N control of, 9–12, 36
Names, of letter writer, 127
Navigation, 104
Negotiation skills, 518
New button, 87
New Document screen, 82
New Folder, creating, 84–85
New Folder button, 85
New Folder Name box, 85
New keys, procedure for learning, 5
News release, 423
Newsletters, 315, 321
Nine (9), control of, 48
Normal style, 172
Number expression, 52, 56, REF16
Number sign (#), control of, 55
Numeric Keypad, REF2-REF7
Numbered lists, 96
Numbering, 103

## O

O control of, 17–18, 33, 36
*Office 2013 Apps*, 81

Omit box, 132
One (1), control of, 42, 43
Online pictures, 216
Open punctuation, 267, 268, 269
Organizational skills, 130, 158

## P

P control of, 20–22, 33
Page borders, 217, 308
Page breaks, 186, 199
Page color background, 314
Page formats: centering, 114; tabs, 135
Page numbers, 188; changing format,
    349; inserting, 185; preliminary pages,
    349; removing from first page, 185
Page orientation, 293–294
Palmetto Event Solutions, Inc., 116–118,
    139–141, 166–169, 206–209,
    232–235, 236–242, 250; e-mail,
    composing, 141; Kansas city office,
    237–242; letter preparation, 140,
    141; memo preparation, 140; wealth
    protection strategies seminar, 166–169
Panes, splitting, 358–359
Paragraph borders, 308
Paragraph styles, 172
Paragraphs: alignment, 97; formatting, 96,
    101; removing space after, 125
Parentheses (), control of, 59
Paste command, 111–112
Paste Options button, 112
Percent sign (%): control of, 57; spacing
    with, 57
Period (.), control of, 14–15
Picture(s), 302; compressing, 215;
    cropping, 214; formatting, 213–215,
    303–304; inserting, 213, 302; moving,
    215; online, 216; sizing, 214; styles,
    309–310; text wrap, 215
Pin icon, 92
Plus sign (+), control of, 63
Positioning: graphics, 318–319; image,
    319
Pound symbol (#), control of, 55
Preliminary pages, 347–352
Printing, document, 87